Read, **Reason**, Write

AN ARGUMENT TEXT AND READER

Read, **Reason**, Write

AN ARGUMENT TEXT AND READER

TWELFTH EDITION

Dorothy U. Seyler
Allen Brizee

Mc
Graw
Hill
Education

READ, REASON, WRITE: AN ARGUMENT TEXT AND READER, TWELFTH EDITION

Published by McGraw-Hill Education, 2 Penn Plaza, New York, NY 10121. Copyright © 2019 by McGraw-Hill Education. All rights reserved. Printed in the United States of America. Previous editions © 2015, 2012, and 2010. No part of this publication may be reproduced or distributed in any form or by any means, or stored in a database or retrieval system, without the prior written consent of McGraw-Hill Education, including, but not limited to, in any network or other electronic storage or transmission, or broadcast for distance learning.

Some ancillaries, including electronic and print components, may not be available to customers outside the United States.

This book is printed on acid-free paper.

1 2 3 4 5 6 7 8 9 LCR 21 20 19 18

ISBN: 978-1-259-91627-4
MHID: 1-259-91627-8

Brand Manager: *Penina Braffman Greenfield*
Product Developer: *Elizabeth Murphy*
Marketing Manager: *Marisa Cavanaugh*
Content Project Manager: *Lisa Bruflodt*
Buyer: *Sandy Ludovissy*
Designer: *Jessica Cuevas*
Content Licensing Specialist: *DeAnna Dausener*
Cover Image: © *Piriya Photography/Moment/Getty Images*
Compositor: *Lumina Datamatics, Inc.*

All credits appearing on page or at the end of the book are considered to be an extension of the copyright page.

Library of Congress Cataloging-in-Publication Data
Names: Seyler, Dorothy U., author. | Brizee, Allen, author.
Title: Read, reason, write : an argument text and reader / Dorothy U. Seyler,
    Allen Brizee.
Description: Twelfth edition. | New York, NY : McGraw-Hill Education, 2019.
Identifiers: LCCN 2017045184 (print) | LCCN 2017046594 (ebook) | ISBN
    9781260195088 (Online) | ISBN 9781259916274 (softbound) | ISBN
    9781260195064 (looseleaf)
Subjects: LCSH: English language—Rhetoric. | Persuasion (Rhetoric) | College
    readers. | Report writing.
Classification: LCC PE1408 (ebook) | LCC PE1408 .S464 2019 (print) | DDC
    808/.0427—dc23
LC record available at https://lccn.loc.gov/2017045184

The Internet addresses listed in the text were accurate at the time of publication. The inclusion of a Web site does not indicate an endorsement by the authors or McGraw-Hill Education, and McGraw-Hill Education does not guarantee the accuracy of the information presented at these sites.

mheducation.com/highered

Brief Contents

Contents

New to the Twelfth Edition

This new edition continues the key features of previous editions while adding new material that will make it even more helpful to both students and instructors. Significant changes include the following:

- **New readings.** This edition features a rich collection of eighty readings, both timely and classic, that provide examples of the varied uses of language and strategies for argument. Forty-six of these readings are entirely new to this edition and include high-quality examples of argument written by author and activist Kaye Wise Whitehead, philosopher and novelist Kwame Anthony Appiah, Pulitzer Prize-winning foreign policy journalist Anne Applebaum, noted author and professor of psychology Steven Pinker, political columnist and CNN host Fareed Zakaria, astrophysicist Neil deGrasse Tyson, and engineer and U.S. Army Reserve soldier Lisa Jaster—to name only a few.

- **New coverage.** An entirely new section in Chapter 5 introduces students to the concepts of visual rhetoric and visual literacy, including Gestalt principles and the C.A.R.P. design model. Chapter 6 includes additional in-depth coverage of deductive reasoning in written argument, and Chapter 13 is updated to address changes in technology for drafting, revising, editing, and proofreading a paper, as well as submitting it to an instructor.

- **New visuals.** Almost all of the readings in this edition feature compelling visuals that illustrate the topics discussed therein. At the outset of each chapter, students are presented with a visual prompt tied to critical thinking questions that engage them with key concepts covered throughout that chapter.

- **Updated documentation coverage.** MLA coverage is updated throughout to align with the eighth edition of the *MLA Handbook*. Chapter 14 includes instruction around these new guidelines, including ten new example MLA citation models. This chapter also covers the latest APA guidelines for using and citing secondary sources.

- **Focus on current issues that are relevant to students.** Of the seven chapters in the anthology section, all have new readings and several take on a new and timely focus. For example, Chapter 17 on marriage focuses on the issue of marriage equality, Chapter 18 on education concentrates on the topics of school choice and tuition, and Chapter 20 on laws and rights examines guns on campus and the "Dream Act."

Features of *Read, Reason, Write*

Read, Reason, Write supports and aligns with the WPA Outcomes Statement for First-Year Composition (NCTE, 2014). This text's content and presentation are guided by decades of classroom experience and by research and theory in composition and rhetoric. This combination has made *Read, Reason, Write* a best-selling text for now twelve editions.

- **Teaches critical thinking, reading, and composing through a step-by-step approach to inquiry, analysis, and writing.** This text introduces students to various genres and guides them in analyzing style, rhetorical construction, and effectiveness. It provides exercises for individual and group work to practice critical reading and analysis. Questions are included to guide students in responding to, analyzing, evaluating, and researching and writing about content.

- **Provides instruction for beginning, drafting, completing, and then revising summaries, analyses, and arguments.** Guided by convention expectations, the text provides instruction in overall organization, paragraph structure, and sentence-level issues such as tone, mechanics, and attribution tailored to various genres. The text also contains instruction in analyzing and using graphics, images, and document design, helping students to think critically about—and also produce—visually enhanced communication.

- **Provides instruction in both classical and contemporary rhetorical theory.** The text presents rhetorical theories in an accessible way to help instructors teach and students learn these concepts. But, *Read, Reason, Write* also presents argument as contextual: written (or spoken) to a specific audience with the expectation of counterarguments.

- **Includes guidelines and revision boxes throughout.** These tools provide an easy reference for students.

- **Offers thorough and easy-to-reference coverage of both MLA and APA documentation requirements.**

- **Features nine student essays.** These illustrate the kinds of writing students will be asked to prepare in the course—summaries, analyses, arguments, and formally documented papers.

- **Presents a rich collection of readings.** Readings are both timely and classic, providing examples of the varied uses of language and strategies for argument.

- **Offers a brief but comprehensive introduction to reading and analyzing literature.** Found in the appendix, this section also contains a student essay of literary analysis.

Let Connect Composition Help Your Students Achieve their Goals

Connect is a highly reliable, easy-to-use homework and learning management solution that embeds learning science and award-winning adaptive tools to improve student results. Connect Composition addresses the specific needs of the writing course and various redesign models of instruction. In addition to the innovative content, revolutionary learning technology drives skills for the Argument course through a selection of corresponding toolsets.

Power of Process

One overarching goal is at the heart of *Power of Process*: for students to become self-regulating, strategic readers and writers. *Power of Process* facilitates engaged reading and writing processes using research-based best practices suggested by major professional reading and writing organizations.

    Power of Process promotes close, strategic reading and critical thinking, leading to richer, more insightful academic reading and writing in the Argument course and beyond.

Connect Composition eReader

The Connect Composition eReader provides approximately seventy compelling readings that instructors can incorporate into their syllabi. Readings are available across a wide variety of genres, including arguments and literary selections. Instructors can filter the readings by theme, discipline, genre, rhetorical mode, reading level, and word count.

LearnSmart Achieve

LearnSmart Achieve offers students an adaptive, individualized learning experience designed to ensure the efficient mastery of reading and writing skills in tandem. By

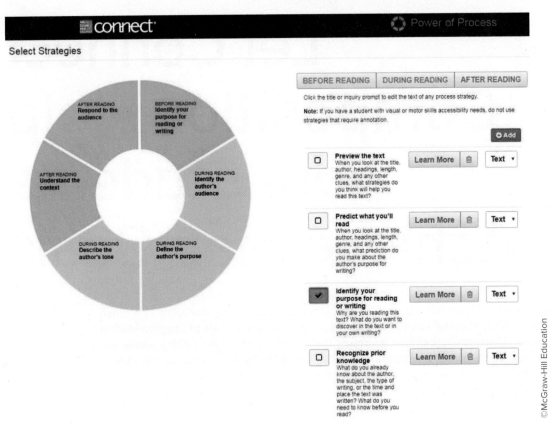

Power of Process

targeting students' particular strengths and weaknesses, *LearnSmart Achieve* customizes its lessons and facilitates high-impact learning at an accelerated pace.

LearnSmart Achieve provides instruction and practice for your students in the following areas.

UNIT	TOPIC	
THE WRITING PROCESS	The Writing Process Generating Ideas Planning and Organizing	Writing a Rough Draft Revising Proofreading, Formatting, and Producing Texts

CRITICAL READING	Reading to Understand
	  Literal Meaning
	Evaluating Truth and
	  Accuracy in a Text
		Evaluating the Effectiveness and
		  Appropriateness of a Text

THE RESEARCH PROCESS	Developing and
	  Implementing a
	  Research Plan
	Evaluating Information and
	  Sources
		Integrating Source Material into
		  a Text
		Using Information Ethically and
		  Legally

REASONING AND ARGUMENT	Developing an Effective Thesis or Claim Using Evidence and Reasoning to Support a Thesis or Claim	Using Ethos (Ethics) to Persuade Readers Using Pathos (Emotion) to Persuade Readers Using Logos (Logic) to Persuade Readers
GRAMMAR AND COMMON SENTENCE PROBLEMS	Parts of Speech Phrases and Clauses Sentence Types Fused (Run-on) Sentences Comma Splices Sentence Fragments Pronouns	Pronoun-Antecedent Agreement Pronoun Reference Subject-Verb Agreement Verbs and Verbals Adjectives and Adverbs Dangling and Misplaced Modifiers Mixed Constructions Verb Tense and Voice Shifts
PUNCTUATION AND MECHANICS	Commas Semicolons Colons End Punctuation Apostrophes Quotation Marks Dashes	Parentheses Hyphens Abbreviations Capitalization Italics Numbers Spelling
STYLE AND WORD CHOICE	Wordiness Eliminating Redundancies Sentence Variety Coordination and Subordination	Faulty Comparisons Word Choice Clichés, Slang, and Jargon Parallelism
MULTILINGUAL WRITERS	Helping Verbs, Gerunds and Infinitives, and Phrasal Verbs Nouns, Verbs, and Objects Articles	Count and Noncount Nouns Sentence Structure and Word Order Subject-Verb Agreement Participles and Adverb Placement

LearnSmart Achieve can be assigned by units and/or topics.

Book-Specific Resources for Instructors

The following teaching resources are available in Connect. Please contact your local McGraw-Hill representative for the username and password to access these resources.

Gradeable Assessments tied to Readings

Instructors can assign gradeable assessments tied to more than sixty of the reading selections in the twelfth edition of *Read, Reason, Write*. More than 700 new assessments are now available through Connect.

The *Read, Reason, Write* Master Course

In the *Read, Reason, Write* Master Course, which you can copy to your own Connect account and adapt as you wish, you will find various Connect Composition assignment types to accelerate learning, including *LearnSmart Achieve* topics, pre- and post-tests,

Power of Process assignments, Writing Assignments, and Discussion Board prompts for every chapter of the text. Contact your local McGraw-Hill representative to copy the course to your Connect account.

Instructor's Manual

The Instructor's Manual is written with the diverse needs of composition instructors in mind. Faculty new to teaching reading will appreciate the brief presentations of theory that accompany the reading pedagogy in the textbook, as well as the suggestions for how to teach some of the more difficult argument writing skills. Faculty new to teaching writing will find help with ways to organize chapters into teachable sections and suggestions for selecting among the easier and more challenging readings.

Flexible Content for Your Argument Course: Customize *Read, Reason, Write* with Create™

As an alternative to the traditional text, instructors may use McGraw-Hill Create™ to arrange chapters to align with their syllabus, eliminate those they do not wish to assign, and add any of the *Read, Reason, Write* content available only in Create™ to build one or multiple print or e-book texts, including Connect Composition access codes. McGraw-Hill Create is a self-service Web site that allows instructors and departments to create customized course materials using McGraw-Hill's comprehensive, cross-disciplinary content and digital products. Through Create™, instructors may also add their own material, such as a course syllabus, a course rubric, course standards, and any specific instruction for students.

From the Authors

I have written in previous prefaces to *Read, Reason, Write* that being asked to prepare a new edition is much like being asked back to a friend's home: You count on it and yet are still delighted when the invitation comes. But an invitation to a 12th edition?! I am amazed and humbled. I am also delighted to introduce you to my new coauthor Allen and to share with you our story. Allen is actually a former student of mine from NVCC. He was kind enough to let me know when he completed his PhD and took a position at Loyola University Maryland in Baltimore—and thus made it easy for me to find him when the time came to bring in a new member of the team.

We can assert that while Allen has brought some fresh ideas to this edition, the essential character of this text remains the same: to help students become better writers of the kinds of papers they are most often required to write both in college and the workplace, that is, summaries, analyses, reports, arguments, and documented essays. *Read, Reason, Write* remains committed to showing students how reading, analytic, argumentative, and research skills are interrelated and how these skills combine to develop critical thinking.

It continues to be true that no book of value is written alone. Over its more than thirty years of life, a chorus of voices have enriched this text, too many now to list them all. Two editors should be given a special thanks, though: Steve Pensinger, who led the team through four early editions, and Lisa Moore, who brought new ideas to the 6th and 7th editions. Other sponsoring editors, developmental editors, and production editors have enriched my journey through eleven editions and aided us in preparing this 12th edition. May you all live long and prosper!

With Allen's support I will once more close by dedicating *Read, Reason, Write* to my daughter Ruth, who, in spite of her own career and interests, continues to give generously of her time, reading possible essays and listening patiently to my endless debates about changes. And for all of the new students who will use this edition: May you understand that it is the liberal education that makes continued growth of the human spirit both possible and pleasurable.

Dorothy U. Seyler, Professor Emerita,
Northern Virginia Community College

Allen Brizee, Associate Professor,
Loyola University Maryland

About the Authors

DOROTHY SEYLER is professor emerita of English at Northern Virginia Community College. A Phi Beta Kappa graduate of the College of William & Mary, Dr. Seyler holds advanced degrees from Columbia University and the State University of New York at Albany. She taught at Ohio State University, the University of Kentucky, and Nassau Community College before moving with her family to Northern Virginia.

In addition to articles published in both scholarly journals and popular magazines, Dr. Seyler is the author of ten college textbooks, including *Introduction to Literature, Doing Research, Steps to College Reading,* and *Patterns of Reflection. Read, Reason, Write* was first published in 1984. In 2007, she was elected to membership in the Cosmos Club in Washington, D.C., for "excellence in education."

Professor Seyler is also the author of *The Obelisk and the Englishman: The Pioneering Discoveries of Egyptologist William Bankes* (2015), a "fascinating story," according to *Kirkus Reviews,* "of a figure who deserves to be much better known." She enjoys tennis, golf, and travel—and writing about both sports and travel.

ALLEN BRIZEE is associate professor of writing at Loyola University Maryland. At Loyola, Professor Brizee teaches courses in first-year writing, rhetoric, technical writing, and writing for the Web. He also coordinates the writing internship program. Allen began his educational journey as a student of Dorothy's at Northern Virginia Community College (NVCC). After graduating, he transferred to Virginia Tech, where he earned a BA in English (Phi Beta Kappa) and a master's in English.

Professor Brizee taught part time at NVCC, The George Washington University, and the University of Maryland while working as a technical writer. He then completed his PhD at Purdue and, while there, also worked on the widely used Purdue Online Writing Lab (OWL).

Dr. Brizee's research interests include writing pedagogy and civic engagement, and he has published articles in a number of academic journals. He coauthored *Partners in Literacy: A Writing Center Model for Civic Engagement* and coedited *Commitment to Justice in Jesuit Higher Education*, 3rd edition. He enjoys collaborating with community groups in Baltimore and participating in medieval martial arts.

Critical Reading and Analysis

Writers and Their Sources

READ: What is the situation in the photo? Who are the two figures, where are they, and how do they differ?

REASON: What ideas are suggested by the photo?

REFLECT/WRITE: Why might this visual have been chosen for Chapter 1?

"Are you happy with your new car?" Oscar asks.

"Oh, yes, I love my new car," Rachel responds.

"Why?" queries Oscar.

"Oh, it's just great—and Dad paid for most of it," Rachel exclaims.

"So you like it because it was cheap," Oscar says. "But wasn't your father going to pay for whatever car you chose?"

"Well, yes—within reason."

"Then why did you choose the Corolla? Why is it so great?"

Rachel ponders a moment and then replies: "It's small enough for me to feel comfortable driving it, but not so small that I would be frightened by trucks. It gets good mileage, and Toyota cars have a good reputation."

"Hmm. Maybe I should think about a Corolla. Then again, I wouldn't part with my Miata!" Oscar proclaims.

A simple conversation, right? In fact, this dialogue represents an *argument*. You may not recognize it as a "typical" argument. After all, there is no real dispute between Oscar and Rachel—no yelling, no hurt feelings. But in its most basic form, an argument is a *claim* (Rachel's car is great) supported by *reasons* (the car's size, mileage, and brand). Similar arguments could be made in favor of this car in other contexts. For instance, Rachel might have seen (and been persuaded by) a television or online Toyota advertisement, or she might have read an article making similar claims in a magazine such as *Consumer Reports*. In turn, she might decide to develop her argument into an essay or speech for one of her courses.

READING, WRITING, AND THE CONTEXTS OF ARGUMENT

Arguments, it seems, are everywhere. Well, what about this textbook, you counter. Its purpose is to inform, not to present an argument. True—to a degree. But textbook authors also make choices about what is important to include and how students should learn the material. Even writing primarily designed to inform says to readers: Do it my way! Well, what about novels, you "argue." Surely they are not arguments. A good point—to a degree. The ideas about human life and experience we find in novels are more subtle, more indirect, than the points we meet head-on in many arguments. Still, expressive writing presents ideas, ways of seeing the world. It seems that arguments can be simple or profound, clearly stated or implied. And we can find them in many—if not most—of our uses of language.

You can accept this larger scope of argument and still expect that in your course on argument and critical thinking you probably will not be asked to write a textbook or a novel. You might, though, be asked to write a summary or a style analysis, so you should think about how those tasks might connect to the world of argument. Count on this: You will be asked to write! Why work on your writing skills? Here are good answers to this question:

- Communication is the single most important skill sought by employers.
- The better writer you become, the better reader you will be.

- The more confident a writer you become, the more efficiently you will handle written assignments in all your courses.
- The more you write, the more you learn about who you are and what really matters to you.

You are about to face a variety of writing assignments. Always think about what role each assignment asks of you. Are you a student demonstrating knowledge? A citizen arguing for tougher drunk-driving laws? A scholar presenting the results of research? A friend having a conversation about a new car? Any writer—including you—will take on different roles, writing for different audiences, using different strategies to reach each audience. There are many kinds of argument and many ways to be successful—or unsuccessful—in preparing them. Your argument course will be challenging. This text will help you meet that challenge.

RESPONDING TO SOURCES

If this is a text about *writing* arguments, why does it contain so many readings? (You noticed!) There are good reasons for the readings you find here:

- College and the workplace demand that you learn complex information through reading. This text will give you lots of practice.
- You need to read to develop your critical thinking skills.
- Your reading will often serve as a basis for writing. In a course on argument, the focus of attention shifts from you to your subject, a subject others have debated before you. You will need to understand the issue, think carefully about the views of others, and only then join in the conversation.

To understand how critical thinkers may respond to sources, let's examine "The Gettysburg Address," Abraham Lincoln's famous speech dedicating the Gettysburg Civil War battlefield. We can use this document to see the various ways writers respond—in writing—to the writing of others.

THE GETTYSBURG ADDRESS | ABRAHAM LINCOLN

Fourscore and seven years ago our fathers brought forth on this continent a new nation, conceived in liberty and dedicated to the proposition that all men are created equal. Now we are engaged in a great civil war, testing whether that nation, or any nation so conceived and so dedicated, can long endure. We are met on a great battlefield of that war. We have come to dedicate a portion of that field as a final resting place for those who here gave their lives that that nation might live. It is altogether fitting and proper that we should do this. But, in a larger sense, we cannot dedicate—we cannot consecrate—we cannot hallow—this ground. The brave men, living and dead, who struggled here have consecrated it far above our poor power to add or to detract. The world will little note nor long remember what we say here, but it can never forget what they did here. It is for us, the living, rather to be dedicated here to the unfinished work which they who fought here have thus far so nobly advanced. It is rather for us to be here dedicated to the great task remaining before us—that from these honored dead we take increased devotion to that cause for which they gave the last full measure of devotion; that we here highly resolve that these dead shall not have died in vain; that this nation, under God, shall have a new birth of freedom; and that government of the people, by the people, for the people shall not perish from the earth.

Abraham Lincoln, "The Gettysburg Address," (1863).

What Does It Say?

THE RESPONSE TO CONTENT

Instructors often ask students to *summarize* their reading of a complex chapter, a supplementary text, or a series of journal articles on library reserve. Frequently, book report assignments specify that summary and evaluation be combined. Your purpose in writing a summary is to show your understanding of the work's main ideas and of the relationships among those ideas. If you can put what you have read into your own words and focus on the text's chief points, then you have command of that material. Here is a sample restatement of Lincoln's "Address":

> Our nation was initially built on a belief in liberty and equality, but its future is now being tested by civil war. It is appropriate for us to dedicate this battlefield, but those who fought here have dedicated it better than we. We should dedicate ourselves to continue the fight to maintain this nation and its principles of government.

Sometimes it is easier to recite or quote famous or difficult works than to state, more simply and in your own words, what has been written. The ability to summarize reflects strong writing skills. For more coverage of writing summaries, see pp. 10–12. (For coverage of paraphrasing, a task similar to summary, see pp. 15–19.)

How Is It Written?
How Does It Compare
with Another Work?

THE ANALYTIC RESPONSE

Summary requirements are often combined with analysis or evaluation, as in a book report. Most of the time you will be expected to *do something* with what you have read, and to summarize will be insufficient. Frequently you will be asked to analyze a work—that is, to explain the writer's choice of style (or the work's larger rhetorical context). This means examining sentence patterns, organization, metaphors, and other techniques selected by the writer to convey attitude and give force to ideas. Developing your skills in analysis will make you both a better reader and a better writer.

   Many writers have examined Lincoln's word choice, sentence structure, and choice of metaphors to make clear the sources of power in this speech.* Analyzing Lincoln's style, you might examine, among other elements, his effective use of *tricolon:* the threefold repetition of a grammatical structure, with the three points placed in ascending order of significance.

---

* See, for example, Gilbert Highet's essay, "The Gettysburg Address," in *The Clerk of Oxenford: Essays on Literature and Life* (New York: Oxford UP, 1954), to which I am indebted in the following analysis.

Lincoln uses two effective tricolons in his brief address. The first focuses on the occasion for his speech, the dedication of the battlefield: "we cannot dedicate—we cannot consecrate—we cannot hallow. . . ." The best that the living can do is formally dedicate; only those who died there for the principle of liberty are capable of making the battlefield "hallow." The second tricolon presents Lincoln's concept of democratic government, a government "of the people, by the people, for the people." The purpose of government—"for the people"—resides in the position of greatest significance.

A second type of analysis, a comparison of styles of two writers, is a frequent variation of the analytic assignment. By focusing on similarities and differences in writing styles, you can see more clearly the role of choice in writing and may also examine the issue of the degree to which differences in purpose affect style. One student, for example, produced a thoughtful and interesting study of Lincoln's style in contrast to that of Martin Luther King, Jr.:

> Although Lincoln's sentence structure is tighter than King's, and King likes the rhythms created by repetition, both men reflect their familiarity with the King James Bible in their use of its cadences and expressions. Instead of saying eighty-seven years ago, Lincoln, seeking solemnity, selects the biblical expression "Fourscore and seven years ago." Similarly, King borrows from the Bible and echoes Lincoln when he writes "Five score years ago."

Is It Logical?
Is It Adequately Developed?
Does It Achieve Its Purpose?   THE EVALUATION RESPONSE

Even when the stated purpose of an essay is "pure" analysis, the analysis implies a judgment. We analyze Lincoln's style because we recognize that "The Gettysburg Address" is a great piece of writing and we want to see how it achieves its power. On other occasions, evaluation is the stated purpose for close reading and analysis. The columnist who challenges a previously published editorial has analyzed the editorial and found it flawed. The columnist may fault the editor's logic or lack of adequate or relevant support for the editorial's main idea. In each case the columnist makes a negative evaluation of the editorial, but that judgment is an informed one based on the columnist's knowledge of language and the principles of good argument.

Part of the ability to judge wisely lies in recognizing each writer's (or speaker's) purpose, audience, and occasion. It would be inappropriate to assert that Lincoln's address is weakened by its lack of facts about the battle. The historian's purpose is to record the number killed or to analyze the generals' military tactics. Lincoln's purpose was different.

> As Lincoln reflected upon this young country's being torn apart by civil strife, he saw the dedication of the Gettysburg battlefield as an opportunity to challenge the country to fight for its survival and the principles upon which it was founded. The result was a brief but moving speech that appropriately examines the connection between the life and death of soldiers and the birth and survival of a nation.

These sentences begin an analysis of Lincoln's train of thought and use of metaphors. The writer shows an understanding of Lincoln's purpose and the context in which he spoke.

How Does It Help Me to Understand
Other Works, Ideas, Events?   THE RESEARCH RESPONSE

Frequently you will read not to analyze or evaluate but rather to use the source as part of learning about a particular subject. Lincoln's address is significant for the Civil War historian both as an event of that war and as an influence on our thinking about that war. "The Gettysburg Address" is also vital to the biographer's study of Lincoln's life or to the literary critic's study either of famous speeches or of the Bible's influence on English writing styles. Thus Lincoln's brief speech is a valuable source for students in a variety of disciplines. It becomes part of their research process. Able researchers study it carefully, analyze it thoroughly, place it in its proper historical, literary, and personal contexts, and use it to develop their own arguments.

To practice reading and responding to sources, study the following article by Deborah Tannen. The exercises that follow will check your reading skills and your understanding of the various responses to reading just discussed. Use the prereading questions to become engaged with Tannen's essay.

WHO DOES THE TALKING HERE? | DEBORAH TANNEN

Professor of linguistics at Georgetown University, Deborah Tannen writes popular books on the uses of language by "ordinary" people. Among her many books are *Talking from 9 to 5* (1994) and *I Only Say This Because I Love You* (2004). Here she responds to the debate over who talks more, men or women.

PREREADING QUESTIONS What is the occasion for Tannen's article—what is she responding to? Who does most of the talking in your family—and are you okay with the answer?

It's no surprise that a one-page article published this month in the journal *Science* inspired innumerable newspaper columns and articles. The study, by Matthias Mehl and four colleagues, claims to lay to rest, once and for all, the stereotype that women talk more than men, by proving—scientifically—that women and men talk equally.   1

The notion that women talk more was reinforced last year when Louann Brizendine's "The Female Brain" cited the finding that women utter, on average, 20,000 words a day, men 7,000. (Brizendine later disavowed the statistic, as there was no study to back it up.) Mehl and his colleagues outfitted 396 college students with devices that recorded their speech. The female subjects spoke an average of 16,215 words a day, the men 15,669. The difference is insignificant. Case closed.   2

Or is it? Can we learn who talks more by counting words? No, according to a forthcoming article surveying 70 studies of gender differences in talkativeness. (Imagine—70 studies published in scientific journals, and we're still asking the question.) In their survey, Campbell Leaper and Melanie Ayres found that counting words yielded no consistent differences, though number of words per speaking turn did. (Men, on average, used more.)   3

4   This doesn't surprise me. In my own research on gender and language, I quickly surmised that to understand who talks more, you have to ask: What's the situation? What are the speakers using words for?

5   The following experience conveys the importance of situation. I was addressing a small group in a suburban Virginia living room. One man stood out because he talked a lot, while his wife, who was sitting beside him, said nothing at all. I described to the group a complaint common among women about men they live with: At the end of a day she tells him what happened, what she thought and how she felt about it. Then she asks, "How was your day?"—and is disappointed when he replies, "Fine," "Nothing much" or "Same old rat race."

©Corbis/VCG/Getty Images RF

Who is the most passive figure in this group?

6   The loquacious man spoke up. "You're right," he said. Pointing to his wife, he added, "She's the talker in our family." Everyone laughed. But he explained, "It's true. When we come home, she does all the talking. If she didn't, we'd spend the evening in silence."

7   The "how was your day?" conversation typifies the kind of talk women tend to do more of: spoken to intimates and focusing on personal experience, your own or others'. I call this "rapport-talk." It contrasts with "report-talk"—giving or exchanging information about impersonal topics, which men tend to do more.

8   Studies that find men talking more are usually carried out in formal experiments or public contexts such as meetings. For example, Marjorie Swacker observed an academic conference where women presented 40 percent of the papers and were 42 percent of the audience but asked only 27 percent of the questions; their questions were, on average, also shorter by half than the men's questions. And David and Myra Sadker showed that boys talk more in mixed-sex classrooms—a context common among college students, a factor skewing the results of Mehl's new study.

9   Many men's comfort with "public talking" explains why a man who tells his wife he has nothing to report about his day might later find a funny story to tell at dinner with two other couples (leaving his wife wondering, "Why didn't he tell me first?").

In addition to situation, you have to consider what speakers are doing with 10 words. Campbell and Ayres note that many studies find women doing more "affiliative speech" such as showing support, agreeing or acknowledging others' comments. Drawing on studies of children at play as well as my own research of adults talking, I often put it this way: For women and girls, talk is the glue that holds a relationship together. Their best friend is the one they tell everything to. Spending an evening at home with a spouse is when this kind of talk comes into its own. Since this situation is uncommon among college students, it's another factor skewing the new study's results.

Women's rapport-talk probably explains why many people think women talk 11 more. A man wants to read the paper, his wife wants to talk; his girlfriend or sister spends hours on the phone with her friend or her mother. He concludes: Women talk more.

Yet Leaper and Ayres observed an overall pattern of men speaking more. 12 That's a conclusion women often come to when men hold forth at meetings, in social groups or when delivering one-on-one lectures. All of us—women and men—tend to notice others talking more in situations where we talk less.

Counting may be a start—or a stop along the way—to understanding gender 13 differences. But it's understanding when we tend to talk and what we're doing with words that yields insights we can count on.

Deborah Tannen, "Who Does the Talking Here?" *The Washington Post,* 15 Jul. 2007. Copyright ©2007 Deborah Tannen. Reprinted by permission.

QUESTIONS FOR READING AND REASONING

1. What was the conclusion of the researchers who presented their study in *Science*?
2. Why are their results not telling the whole story, according to Tannen? Instead of counting words, what should we study?
3. What two kinds of talk does Tannen label? Which gender does the most of each type of talking?
4. What is Tannen's main idea or thesis?

QUESTIONS FOR REFLECTION AND WRITING

5. How do the details—and the style—in the opening and concluding paragraphs contribute to the author's point? Write a paragraph answer to this question. Then consider: Which one of the different responses to reading does your paragraph illustrate?
6. Do you agree with Tannen that understanding how words are used must be part of any study of men and women talking? If so, why? If not, how would you respond to her argument?
7. "The Gettysburg Address" is a valuable document for several kinds of research projects. For what kinds of research would Tannen's essay be useful? List several possibilities and be prepared to discuss your list with classmates.

WRITING SUMMARIES

Preparing a good summary is not easy. *A summary briefly restates, in your own words, the main points of a work in a way that does not misrepresent or distort the original.* A good summary shows your grasp of main ideas and your ability to express them clearly. You need to condense the original while giving all key ideas appropriate attention. As a student you may be assigned a summary to

- show that you have read and understood assigned works;
- complete a test question;
- have a record of what you have read for future study or to prepare for class discussion; or
- explain the main ideas in a work that you will also examine in some other way, such as in a book review.

When assigned a summary, pay careful attention to word choice. Avoid judgment words, such as "Brown then proceeds to develop the *silly* idea that. . . ." Follow these guidelines for writing good summaries.

GUIDELINES for Writing Summaries

1. **Write in a direct, objective style, using your own words.** Use few, if any, direct quotations, probably none in a one-paragraph summary.
2. **Begin with a reference to the writer (full name) and the title of the work, and then state the writer's thesis.** (You may also want to include where and when the work was published.)
3. **Complete the summary by providing other key ideas.** Show the reader how the main ideas connect and relate to one another.
4. **For short summaries, do not include specific examples, illustrations, or background sections. For longer summaries of a complex work, use specific examples sparingly.** Instead, paraphrase information from the original piece (see pp. 16–18 for more information on paraphrasing).
5. **Combine main ideas into fewer sentences than were used in the original.**
6. **Keep the parts of your summary in the same balance as you find in the original.** If the author devotes about 30 percent of the essay to one idea, that idea should get about 30 percent of the space in your summary.
7. **Select precise, accurate verbs to show the author's relationship to ideas.** Write Jones *argues*, Jones *asserts*, Jones *believes*. Do not use vague verbs that provide only a list of disconnected ideas. Do *not* write Jones *talks about*, Jones *goes on to say.*
8. **Do not make any judgments about the writer's style or ideas.** Do *not* include your personal reaction to the work.

EXERCISE: Summary

With these guidelines in mind, read the following two summaries of Deborah Tannen's "Who Does the Talking Here?" (see pp. 7–9). Then answer the question: What is flawed or weak about each summary? To aid your analysis, (1) underline or highlight all words or phrases that are inappropriate in each summary, and (2) put the number of the guideline next to any passage that does not adhere to that guideline.

SUMMARY 1

I really thought that Deborah Tannen's essay contained some interesting ideas about how men and women talk. Tannen mentioned a study in which men and women used almost the same number of words. She goes on to talk about a man who talked a lot at a meeting in Virginia. Tannen also says that women talk more to make others feel good. I'm a man, and I don't like to make small talk.

SUMMARY 2

In Deborah Tannen's "Who Does the Talking Here?" (published July 15, 2007), she talks about studies to test who talks more—men or women. Some people think the case is closed—they both talk about the same number of words. Tannen goes on to say that she thinks people use words differently. Men talk a lot at events; they use "report-talk." Women use "rapport-talk" to strengthen relationships; their language is a glue to maintain relationships. So just counting words does not work. You have to know why someone is speaking.

Although we can agree that the writers of these summaries have read Tannen's essay, we can also find weaknesses in each summary. Certainly the second summary is more helpful than the first, but it can be strengthened by eliminating some details, combining some ideas, and putting more focus on Tannen's main idea. Here is a much-improved version:

REVISED SUMMARY

In Deborah Tannen's essay "Who Does the Talking Here?" (published July 15, 2007), Tannen asserts that recent studies to determine if men or women do the most talking are not helpful in answering that question. These studies focus on just counting the words that men and women use. Tannen argues that the only useful study of this issue is one that examines how each gender uses words and in which situations each gender does the most talking. She explains that men tend to use "report-talk" whereas women tend to use "rapport-talk." That is, men will do much of the talking in meetings when they have something to report. Women, on the other hand, will do more of the talking when they are seeking to connect in a relationship, to make people feel good. So, if we want to really understand the differences, we need to stop counting words and listen to what each gender is actually doing with the words that are spoken.

At times you may need to write a summary of a page or two rather than one paragraph. Frequently, long reports are preceded by a one-page summary. A longer summary may become part of an article-length review of an important book. Or instructors may want a longer summary of a lengthy or complicated article or text chapter. The following is an example of a summary of a lengthy article on cardiovascular health.

SAMPLE LONGER SUMMARY

In her article "The Good Heart," Anne Underwood (*Newsweek,* October 3, 2005) explores recent studies regarding heart disease that, in various ways, reveal the important role that one's attitudes have on physical health, especially the health of the heart. She begins with the results of a study published in *The New England Journal of Medicine* that examined the dramatic increase in cardiovascular deaths after an earthquake in Los Angeles in 1994. People who were not hurt by the quake died as a result of the fear and stress brought on by the event. As Underwood explains in detail, however, studies continue to show that psychological and social factors affect coronaries even more than sudden shocks such as earthquakes. For example, according to Dr. Michael Frenneaux, depression "at least doubles an otherwise healthy person's heart-attack risk." A Duke University study showed that high levels of hostility also raised the risk of death by heart disease. Another study showed that childhood traumas can increase heart disease risks by 30 to 70 percent. Adults currently living under work and family stress also increase their risks significantly.

How do attitudes make a difference? A number of studies demonstrate that negative attitudes, anger, and hostile feelings directly affect the chemistry of the body in ways that damage blood vessels. They also can raise blood pressure. Less directly, people with these attitudes and under stress often eat more, exercise less, and are more likely to smoke. These behaviors add to one's risk. Some physicians are seeking to use this information to increase the longevity of heart patients. They are advising weight loss and exercise, yoga and therapy, recognizing, as Underwood concludes, that "the heart does not beat in isolation, nor does the mind brood alone."

Observe the differences between the longer summary of Anne Underwood's article and the paragraph summary of Deborah Tannen's essay:

- Some key ideas or terms may be presented in direct quotation.
- Results of studies may be given in some detail.
- Appropriate transitional and connecting words are used to show how the parts of the summary connect.
- The author's name is often repeated to keep the reader's attention on the article summarized, not on the author of the summary.

ACTIVE READING: USE YOUR MIND!

Reading is not about looking at black marks on a page—or turning the pages as quickly as we can. Reading means constructing meaning, getting a message. We read with our brains, not our eyes and hands! This concept is often underscored by the term *active reading*. To help you always achieve active reading, not passive page turning, follow these guidelines.

GUIDELINES for Active Reading

1. **Understand your purpose in reading.** Do not just start turning pages to complete an assignment. Think first about your purpose. Are you reading for knowledge on which you will be tested? Focus on your purpose as you read, asking yourself, "What do I need to learn from this work?"

2. **Reflect on the title before reading further.** Titles are the first words writers give us. Take time to look for clues in a title that may reveal the work's subject and perhaps the writer's approach or attitude as well. Henry Fairlie's title "The Idiocy of Urban Life," for example, tells you both Fairlie's subject (urban or city living) and his position (urban living is idiotic).

3. **Become part of the writer's audience.** Not all writers have you and me in mind when they write. As an active reader, you need to "join" a writer's audience by learning about the writer, about the time in which the piece was written, and about the writer's expected audience. For readings in this text you are aided by introductory notes; study them.

4. **Predict what is coming.** Look for a writer's main idea or purpose statement. Study the work's organization. Then use this information to anticipate what is coming. When you read "There are three good reasons for requiring a dress code in schools," you know the writer will list *three* reasons.

5. **Concentrate.** Slow down and give your full attention to reading. Watch for transition and connecting words that show you how the parts of a text connect. Read an entire article or chapter at one time—or you will need to start over to make sense of the piece.

6. **Annotate as you read.** The more senses you use, the more active your involvement. That means marking the text as you read (or taking notes if the material is not yours). Underline key sentences, such as the writer's thesis. Then, in the margin, indicate that it is the thesis. With a series of examples (or reasons), label them and number them. When you look up a word's definition, write the definition in the margin next to the word. Draw diagrams to illustrate concepts; draw arrows to connect example to idea. Studies have shown that students who annotate their texts get higher grades. Do what successful students do.

7. **Keep a reading journal.** In addition to annotating what you read, you may want to develop the habit of writing regularly in a journal. A reading journal gives you a place to note impressions and reflections on your reading, your initial reactions to assignments, and ideas you may use in your next writing.

EXERCISE: Active Reading

Read the following essay, studying the annotations that are started for you. As you read, add your own notes. Then test your active reading by responding to the questions that follow the essay.

ACTUALLY, LET'S NOT BE IN THE MOMENT | RUTH WHIPPMAN

Formerly a producer and director of BBC documentaries, Ruth Whippman now lives in California with her family and devotes her professional life to writing. She is the author of *The Pursuit of Happiness* and *America the Anxious* as well as essays that appear frequently in newspapers and magazines. The following article, drawn from her second book, was published November 27, 2016.

Topic?

1   I'm at the kitchen sink, after a long day of work and kids and chores and the emotional exhaustion of a toxic election season, attempting to mindfully focus on congealed SpaghettiOs. My brain flits to the Netflix queue. I manhandle my thoughts back to the leaky orange glob in front of me. My brain flits to the president-elect.

Not dishwashing — idea of mindfulness

2   I'm making a failed attempt at "mindful dishwashing," the subject of a how-to article an acquaintance recently shared on Facebook. According to the practice's thought leaders, in order to maximize our happiness, we should refuse to succumb to domestic autopilot and instead be fully "in" the present moment, engaging completely with every clump of oatmeal and decomposing particle of scrambled egg. Mindfulness is supposed to be a defense against the pressures of modern life, but it's starting to feel suspiciously like it's actually adding to them. It's a special circle of self-improvement hell, striving not just for a Pinterest-worthy home, but a Pinterest-worthy mind.

3   Perhaps the single philosophical consensus of our time is that the key to contentment lies in living fully mentally in the present. The idea that we should be constantly policing our thoughts away from the past, the future, the imagination or the abstract and back to whatever is happening *right now* has gained traction with spiritual leaders and investment bankers, armchair philosophers and government bureaucrats and human resources departments. Corporate America offers its employees mindfulness training to "streamline their productivity," and the United States military offers it to the Marine Corps. Americans now spend an

©Photodisc/Alamy Stock Photo RF

Wash with your hands; contemplate more important issues with your mind!

estimated $4 billion each year on "mindfulness products." "Living in the Moment" has monetized its folksy charm into a multibillion-dollar spiritual industrial complex.

So does the moment really deserve its many accolades? It is a philosophy 4 likely to be more rewarding for those whose lives contain more privileged moments than grinding, humiliating or exhausting ones. Those for whom a given moment is more likely to be "sun-dappled yoga pose" than "hour 11 manning the deep-fat fryer."

On the face of it, our lives are often much more fulfilling lived outside the 5 present than in it. As anyone who has ever maintained that they will one day lose 10 pounds or learn Spanish or find the matching lids for the Tupperware will know, we often anticipate our futures with more blind optimism than the reality is likely to warrant.

Surely one of the most magnificent feats of the human brain is its ability to 6 hold past, present, future and their imagined alternatives in constant parallel, to offset the tedium of washing dishes with the chance to be simultaneously mentally in Bangkok, or in Don Draper's bed, or finally telling your elderly relative that despite her belief that "no one born in the 1970s died," using a car seat isn't spoiling your child. It's hard to see why greater happiness would be achieved by reining in that magical sense of scope and possibility to outstare a SpaghettiO.

What differentiates humans from animals is exactly this ability to step men- 7 tally outside of whatever is happening to us right now, and to assign it context and significance. Our happiness does not come so much from our experiences themselves, but from the stories we tell ourselves that make them matter.

But still, the advice to be more mindful often contains a hefty scoop of mor- 8 alizing smugness, a kind of "moment-shaming" for the distractible, like a stern teacher scolding us for failing to concentrate in class. The implication is that by neglecting to live in the moment we are ungrateful and unspontaneous, we are wasting our lives, and therefore if we are unhappy, we really have only ourselves to blame.

This judgmental tone is part of a long history of self-help-based cultural 9 thought policing. At its worst, the positive-thinking movement deftly rebranded actual problems as "problematic thoughts." Now mindfulness has taken its place as the focus of our appetite for inner self-improvement. Where once problems ranging from bad marriages and work stress to poverty and race discrimination were routinely dismissed as a failure to "think positive," now our preferred solution to life's complex and entrenched problems is to instruct the distressed to be more mindful.

This is a kind of neo-liberalism of the emotions, in which happiness is seen 10 not as a response to our circumstances but as a result of our own individual mental effort, a reward for the deserving. The problem is not your sky-high rent or meager paycheck, your cheating spouse or unfair boss or teetering pile of dirty dishes. The problem is you.

It is, of course, easier and cheaper to blame the individual for thinking the 11 wrong thoughts than it is to tackle the thorny causes of his unhappiness. So we give inner-city schoolchildren mindfulness classes rather than engage with education inequality, and instruct exhausted office workers in mindful breathing rather than giving them paid vacation or better health care benefits.

12   In reality, despite many grand claims, the scientific evidence in favor of the Moment's being the key to contentment is surprisingly weak. When the United States Agency for Healthcare Research and Quality conducted an enormous meta-analysis of over 18,000 separate studies on meditation and mindfulness techniques, the results were underwhelming at best.

13   Although some of the studies did show that mindfulness meditation or other similar exercises might bring some small benefits to people in comparison with doing nothing, when they are compared with pretty much any general relaxation technique at all, including exercise, muscle relaxation, "listening to spiritual audiotapes" or indeed any control condition that gives equal time and attention to the person, they perform no better, and in many cases, worse.

14   So perhaps, rather than expending our energy struggling to stay in the Moment, we should simply be grateful that our brains allow us to be elsewhere.

Ruth Whippman, "Actually, Let's Not Be in the Moment," *The New York Times,* 27 Nov. 2016. Copyright ©2016 by Ruth Whippman. Used with permission of the author.

QUESTIONS FOR READING AND REASONING

1. What is the meaning of *mindfulness*? How do we practice it?
2. What are the presumed advantages of the practice of mindfulness?
3. What is the author's view of this new concept? State her view as a thesis—the claim of her essay.
4. How does Whippman support her claim? List specific details of her support.

QUESTIONS FOR REFLECTION AND WRITING

5. In paragraph 3, Whippman demonstrates the current popularity of mindfulness; what is clever about her discussion in this paragraph?
6. What is the most interesting piece of information or concept, for you, in Whippman's essay? Why? Write a journal entry—four or five sentences at least—in response to this question.

USING PARAPHRASE

Paraphrasing's goal is the same as summary's: an accurate presentation of the information and ideas of someone else. Unlike summary, we paraphrase an entire short work. This can be a poem (see pp. 528–29 for a paraphrase of a poem) or a complex section of prose that needs a simpler (but often longer than the original) restatement so that we are clear about its meaning. We paraphrase short but complex pieces; we summarize an entire essay or chapter or book.

Writers also use paraphrasing to restate *some* of the information or ideas from a source as part of developing their own work. They do this extensively in a researched essay, but they may also paraphrase parts of a source to add support to their discussion—or to be clear about another writer's ideas that they will evaluate or challenge in some way.

Think, for a moment, about the writing process. Writers use many kinds of experiences to develop their work. Formal researched essays contain precise documentation and may use summary, paraphrase, and direct quotations, but they rarely include personal references. Today, however, writers may blend styles and strategies—in personal essays and researched essays, for example—rather than keeping them distinct. And some scholars today also write books for nonspecialists. In these books—or articles—documentation is placed only at the back, a more informal style is used, and personal experiences may be included to engage readers. Journalists, too, often blend personal experience and informal styles while drawing on one or more sources to develop and support their ideas. Among the readings in this text you will find a few personal essays and scholarly essays as well as works demonstrating a blending of styles and strategies. This blending can be confusing for college students. Make sure that you always understand what kind of work you are expected to produce in each class, for every assignment.

Now, to illustrate paraphrase, suppose you don't want to summarize Lincoln's entire speech, but you do want to use his opening point as a lead-in to commenting on our own times. You might write:

> Lincoln's famous speech at the dedication of the Gettysburg battlefield begins with the observation that our nation was initially built on a belief in liberty and equality, but the country's future had come to a point of being tested. We are not actually facing a civil war today, but we are facing a culture war, a war of opposing values and beliefs, that seems to be tearing our country apart.

Paraphrasing—putting Lincoln's idea into your own words—is a much more effective opening than quoting Lincoln's first two sentences. It's his idea that you want to use, not his language.

NOTE: Observe three key points:

1. The idea is Lincoln's but the word choice is entirely different. Resist the urge to borrow any of Lincoln's phrases—that would be quoting and would require quotation marks—and that does not serve your purpose.
2. You still give credit to Lincoln for the idea.
3. Summary, paraphrasing, and quoting all share this one characteristic: You let readers know that you are using someone else's information or ideas.

EXERCISE: Paraphrase

1. Find several examples of paraphrasing in Whippman's essay.

2. Assume that you are writing an essay on the disadvantages of mindfulness. Paraphrase the ideas in Whippman's paragraphs 9 and 10 to use in your assumed essay.

3. For an essay on the problems with the concept of mindfulness, evaluate the following two paragraphs that use some material from Whippman's essay.

PARAPHRASE 1

The currently popular concept of mindfulness actually comes with problems. This concept seems to suggest that it's our fault if we are unhappy; we have failed to live each moment with positive thoughts. Mindfulness also shifts the focus from trying to address real problems in education and the workplace to teaching students and workers deep breathing exercises, as Ruth Whippman observes.

PARAPHRASE 2

The currently popular concept of mindfulness actually comes with problems. In her essay "Actually, Let's Not Be in the Moment," Ruth Whippman worries that mindfulness seems to blame unhappy people for failing to live each moment with positive thoughts. As Whippman observes, mindfulness also shifts the focus from trying to address real problems in education and the workplace to teaching student and workers deep breathing exercises.

ACKNOWLEDGING SOURCES INFORMALLY

As you have seen in the summaries and paraphrases above, even when you are not writing a formally documented paper, you must identify each source by author. What follows are some of the conventions of writing to use when writing about sources.

Referring to People and Sources

Readers in academic, professional, and business contexts expect writers to follow specific conventions of style when referring to authors and to various kinds of sources. Study the following guidelines and examples, and then mark the next few pages for easy reference—perhaps by turning down a corner of the first and last pages.

References to People

- In a first reference, give the person's full name (both the given name and the surname): *Ellen Goodman, Robert J. Samuelson.* In second and subsequent references, use only the last name (surname): *Goodman, Samuelson.*
- Do not use Mr., Mrs., or Ms. Special titles such as President, Chief Justice, or Doctor may be used in the first reference with the person's full name.

- Never refer to an author by her or his first name. Write *Tannen,* not *Deborah; Lincoln,* not *Abraham.*

References to Titles of Works

Titles of works must *always* be written as titles. Titles are indicated by capitalization and by either quotation marks or italics. The examples provided below show when to use quotation marks and when to use italics.

Guidelines for Capitalizing Titles

- The first and last words are capitalized.
- The first word of a subtitle is capitalized.
- All other words in titles are capitalized except
  - Articles (*a, an, the*).
  - Coordinating conjunctions (*and, or, but, for, nor, yet, so*).
  - Prepositions (*in, for, about*).

Titles Requiring Quotation Marks

Titles of works published within other works—within a book, magazine, or newspaper—are indicated by quotation marks.

ESSAYS	"Who Does the Talking Here?"
SHORT STORIES	"The Story of an Hour"
POEMS	"To Daffodils"
ARTICLES	"Choose Your Utopia"
CHAPTERS	"Writers and Their Sources"
LECTURES	"Crazy Mixed-Up Families"
TV EPISODES	"Pride and Prejudice" (one drama on the television show *Masterpiece Theatre*)

Titles Requiring Italics

Titles of works that are separate publications and, by extension, titles of items such as works of art and websites are in italics.

PLAYS	*A Raisin in the Sun*
NOVELS	*War and Peace*
NONFICTION BOOKS	*Read, Reason, Write: An Argument Text and Reader*
BOOK-LENGTH POEMS	*The Odyssey*
MAGAZINES AND JOURNALS	*Wired*
NEWSPAPERS	*The Wall Street Journal*
FILMS	*The Wizard of Oz*

PAINTINGS	*The Birth of Venus*
TELEVISION PROGRAMS	*Star Trek*
WEBSITES	*www.worldwildlife.org*
DATABASES	*ProQuest*

Read the following article and respond by answering the questions that follow. Observe, as you read, how the author refers to the various sources he uses to develop his article and how he presents material from those sources. We will use this article as a guide to handling quotations.

THE FUTURE IS NOW: IT'S HEADING RIGHT AT US, BUT WE NEVER SEE IT COMING | JOEL ACHENBACH

A former humor columnist and currently a staff writer for *The Washington Post,* Joel Achenbach also has a regular blog *www.washingtonpost.com.* His books include anthologies of his columns and *Captured by Aliens: The Search for Life and Truth in a Very Large Universe* (2003). The following article was published April 13, 2008.

PREREADING QUESTIONS What is nanotechnology? What do you think will be the next big change—and what field will it come from?

1   The most important things happening in the world today won't make tomorrow's front page. They won't get mentioned by presidential candidates or Chris Matthews[1] or Bill O'Reilly[2] or any of the other folks yammering and snorting on cable television.

2   They'll be happening in laboratories—out of sight, inscrutable and unhyped until the very moment when they change life as we know it.

3   Science and technology form a two-headed, unstoppable change agent. Problem is, most of us are mystified and intimidated by such things as biotechnology, or nanotechnology, or the various other -ologies that seem to be threatening to merge into a single unspeakable and incomprehensible thing called biotechnonanogenomicology. We vaguely understand that this stuff is changing our lives, but we feel as though it's all out of our control. We're just hanging on tight, like Kirk and Spock when the Enterprise starts vibrating at Warp 8.

4   What's unnerving is the velocity at which the future sometimes arrives. Consider the Internet. This powerful but highly disruptive technology crept out of the lab (a Pentagon think tank, actually) and all but devoured modern civilization—with almost no advance warning. The first use of the word "internet" to refer to a computer network seems to have appeared in this newspaper on Sept. 26, 1988, in the Financial section, on page F30—about as deep into the paper as you can go without hitting the bedrock of the classified ads.

---

[1] Political talk-show host on MSNBC.—Ed.
[2] Former radio and television talk-show host on the FOX News Channel.—Ed.

The entire reference: "SMS Data Products Group Inc. in McLean won a 5
$1,005,048 contract from the Air Force to supply a defense data network internet
protocol router." Perhaps the unmellifluous compound noun "data network
internet protocol router" is one reason more of us didn't pay attention. A couple
of months later, "Internet"—still lacking the "the" before its name—finally elbowed
its way to the front page when a virus shut down thousands of computers. The
story referred to "a research network called Internet," which "links as many as
50,000 computers, allowing users to send a variety of information to each other."
The scientists knew that computer networks could be powerful. But how many
knew that this Internet thing would change the way we communicate, publish,
sell, shop, conduct research, find old friends, do homework, plan trips and on
and on?

Joe Lykken, a theoretical physicist at the Fermilab research center in Illinois, 6
tells a story about something that happened in 1990. A Fermilab visitor, an
English fellow by the name of Tim Berners-Lee, had a new trick he wanted to
demonstrate to the physicists. He typed some code into a little blank box on the
computer screen. Up popped a page of data.

Lykken's reaction: *Eh.*   7

He could already see someone else's data on a computer. He could have 8
the colleague e-mail it to him and open it as a document. Why view it on a separate page on some computer network?

But of course, this unimpressive piece of software was the precursor to what 9
is known today as the World Wide Web. "We had no idea that we were seeing
not only a revolution, but a trillion-dollar idea," Lykken says.

Now let us pause to reflect upon the fact that Joe Lykken is a very smart 10
guy—you don't get to be a theoretical physicist unless you have the kind of brain
that can practically bend silverware at a distance—and even he, with that giant
cerebral cortex and the billions of neurons flashing and winking, saw the
proto-Web and harrumphed. It's not just us mortals, even scientists don't always
grasp the significance of innovations. Tomorrow's revolutionary technology may
be in plain sight, but everyone's eyes, clouded by conventional thinking, just
can't detect it. "Even smart people are really pretty incapable of envisioning a
situation that's substantially different from what they're in," says Christine
Peterson, vice president of Foresight Nanotech Institute in Menlo Park, Calif.

So where does that leave the rest of us?   11

In technological Palookaville.   12

Science is becoming ever more specialized; technology is increasingly a se- 13
ries of black boxes, impenetrable to but a few. Americans' poor science literacy
means that science and technology exist in a walled garden, a geek ghetto. We
are a technocracy in which most of us don't really understand what's happening
around us. We stagger through a world of technological and medical miracles.
We're zombified by progress.

Peterson has one recommendation: Read science fiction, especially "hard 14
science fiction" that sticks rigorously to the scientifically possible. "If you look out
into the long-term future and what you see looks like science fiction, it might be
wrong," she says. "But if it doesn't look like science fiction, it's definitely wrong."

15   That's exciting—and a little scary. We want the blessings of science (say, cheaper energy sources) but not the terrors (monsters spawned by atomic radiation that destroy entire cities with their fiery breath).

16   Eric Horvitz, one of the sharpest minds at Microsoft, spends a lot of time thinking about the Next Big Thing. Among his other duties, he's president of the Association for the Advancement of Artificial Intelligence. He thinks that, sometime in the decades ahead, artificial systems will be modeled on living things. In the Horvitz view, life is marked by robustness, flexibility, adaptability. That's where computers need to go. Life, he says, shows scientists "what we can do as engineers—better, potentially."

17   Our ability to monkey around with life itself is a reminder that ethics, religion and old-fashioned common sense will be needed in abundance in decades to come. . . . How smart and flexible and rambunctious do we want our computers to be? Let's not mess around with that Matrix business.

18   Every forward-thinking person almost ritually brings up the mortality issue. What'll happen to society if one day people can stop the aging process? Or if only rich people can stop getting old?

19   It's interesting that politicians rarely address such matters. The future in general is something of a suspect topic . . . a little goofy. Right now we're all focused on the next primary, the summer conventions, the Olympics and their political implications, the fall election. The political cycle enforces an emphasis on the immediate rather than the important.

20   And in fact, any prediction of what the world will be like more than, say, a year from now is a matter of hubris. The professional visionaries don't even talk about predictions or forecasts but prefer the word "scenarios." When Sen. John McCain, for example, declares that radical Islam is the transcendent challenge of the 21st century, he's being sincere, but he's also being a bit of a soothsayer. Environmental problems and resource scarcity could easily be the dominant global dilemma. Or a virus with which we've yet to make our acquaintance. Or some other "wild card."

21   Says Lykken, "Our ability to predict is incredibly poor. What we all thought when I was a kid was that by now we'd all be flying around in anti-gravity cars on Mars."

22   Futurists didn't completely miss on space travel—it's just that the things flying around Mars are robotic and take neat pictures and sometimes land and sniff the soil.

23   Some predictions are bang-on, such as sci-fi writer Arthur C. Clarke's declaration in 1945 that there would someday be communications satellites orbiting the Earth. But Clarke's satellites had to be occupied by repairmen who would maintain the huge computers required for space communications. Even in the late 1960s, when Clarke collaborated with Stanley Kubrick on the screenplay to *2001: A Space Odyssey*, he assumed that computers would, over time, get bigger. "The HAL 9000 computer fills half the spaceship," Lykken notes.

24   Says science-fiction writer Ben Bova, "We have built into us an idea that tomorrow is going to be pretty much like today, which is very wrong."

The future is often viewed as an endless resource of innovation that will make problems go away—even though, if the past is any judge, innovations create their own set of new problems. Climate change is at least in part a consequence of the invention of the steam engine in the early 1700s and all the industrial advances that followed. 25

Look again at the Internet. It's a fantastic tool, but it also threatens to disperse information we'd rather keep under wraps, such as our personal medical data, or even the instructions for making a fission bomb. 26

We need to keep our eyes open. The future is going to be here sooner than we think. It'll surprise us. We'll try to figure out why we missed so many clues. And we'll go back and search the archives, and see that thing we should have noticed on page F30. 27

QUESTIONS FOR READING AND REASONING

1. What is Achenbach's subject? What is his thesis? Where does he state it?

2. What two agents together are likely to produce the next big change?

3. Summarize the evidence Achenbach provides to support the idea that we don't recognize the next big change until it is here.

4. If we want to try to anticipate the next big change, what should we do?

5. What prediction did Arthur C. Clarke get right? In what way was his imagination incorrect? What can readers infer from this example?

6. Are big changes always good? Explain.

7. How does Achenbach identify most of his sources? He does not identify Chris Matthews or Bill O'Reilly in paragraph 1. What does this tell you about his expected audience?

PRESENTING DIRECT QUOTATIONS: A GUIDE TO FORM AND STYLE

Although most of your papers will be written in your own words and style, you will sometimes use direct quotations. Just as there is a correct form for references to people and to works, there is a correct form for presenting borrowed material in direct quotations. Study the guidelines and examples and then mark these pages, as you did the others, for easy reference.

Reasons for Using Quotation Marks

We use quotation marks in four ways:

- To indicate dialogue in works of fiction and drama
- To indicate the titles of some kinds of works
- To indicate the words that others have spoken or written
- To separate ourselves from or call into question particular uses of words

The following guidelines apply to all four uses of quotation marks, but the focus will be on the third use.

A Brief Guide to Quoting

1. *Quote accurately.* Do not misrepresent what someone else has written. Take time to compare what you have written with the original.

2. *Put all words taken from a source within quotation marks.* (To take words from a source without using quotation marks is to plagiarize, a form of stealing punished in academic and professional communities.)

3. *Never change any of the words within your quotation marks.* Indicate any deleted words with ellipses [spaced periods (. . .)]. If you need to add words to make the meaning clear, place the added words in [square brackets], not (parentheses).

4. *Always make the source of the quoted words clear.* If you do not provide the author of the quoted material, readers will have to assume that you are calling those words into question—the fourth reason for quoting. Observe that Achenbach introduces Joe Lykken in paragraph 6 and then uses his last name or "he" through the next three paragraphs so that readers always know to whom he is referring and quoting.

5. *When quoting an author who is quoted by the author of the source you are using, you must make clear that you are getting that author's words from your source, not directly from that author.*
    For example:

ORIGINAL:	"We had no idea that we were seeing not only a revolution, but a trillion-dollar idea."
INCORRECT:	Referring to his first experience with the World Wide Web, Lykken observed: "We had no idea that we were seeing . . . a revolution."
CORRECT:	To make his point about our failure to recognize big changes when they first appear, Achenbach quotes theoretical physicist Joe Lykken's response to first seeing the World Wide Web: "We had no idea that we were seeing . . . a revolution."

6. *Place commas and periods inside the closing quotation mark—even when only one word is quoted:* Unable to anticipate big changes coming from modern science, we are, Achenbach observes, in "technological Palookaville."

7. ***Place colons and semicolons outside the closing quotation mark:*** Achenbach jokingly explains our reaction to the complexities of modern technologies in his essay "The Future Is Now": "We're zombified by progress."

8. ***Do not quote unnecessary punctuation.*** When you place quoted material at the end of a sentence you have written, use only the punctuation needed to complete your sentence.

   ORIGINAL: The next big change will be "happening in laboratories—out of sight, inscrutable, and unhyped."

   INCORRECT: Achenbach explains that we will be surprised by the next big change because it will, initially, be hidden, "happening in laboratories—."

   CORRECT: Achenbach explains that we will be surprised by the next big change because it will, initially, be hidden, "happening in laboratories."

9. ***When the words you quote are only a part of your sentence, do not capitalize the first quoted word, even if it was capitalized in the source.*** **Exception:** You introduce the quoted material with a colon.

   INCORRECT: Achenbach observes that "The future is often viewed as an endless resource of innovation."

   CORRECT: Achenbach observes that "the future is often viewed as an endless resource of innovation."

   ALSO CORRECT: Achenbach argues that we count too much on modern science to solve problems: "The future is often viewed as an endless resource of innovation."

10. ***Use single quotation marks (the apostrophe key on your keyboard) to identify quoted material within quoted material:*** Achenbach explains that futurists "prefer the word 'scenarios.'"

11. ***Depending on the structure of your sentence, use a colon, a comma, or no punctuation before a quoted passage.*** A colon provides a formal introduction to a quoted passage. (See the example in item 9.) Use a comma only when your sentence requires it. Quoted words presented in a "that" clause are not preceded by a comma.

   ORIGINAL: "What's unnerving is the velocity at which the future sometimes arrives."

   CORRECT: "What's unnerving," Achenbach notes, "is the velocity at which the future sometimes arrives."

   ALSO CORRECT: Achenbach observes that we are often unnerved by "the velocity at which the future sometimes arrives."

12. ***To keep quotations brief, omit irrelevant portions. Indicate missing words with ellipses.*** For example: Achenbach explains that "we want the blessings of science . . . but not the terrors." Some instructors want the ellipses placed in square brackets— [. . .]—to show that you have added them to the original. Modern Language Association

(MLA) style does not require the square brackets unless you are quoting a passage that already has ellipses as part of that passage. The better choice would be not to quote that passage.

13. ***Consider the poor reader.***
   - Always give enough context to make the quoted material clear.
   - Do not put so many bits and pieces of quoted passages into one sentence that your reader struggles to follow the ideas.
   - Make sure that your sentences are complete and correctly constructed. Quoting is never an excuse for a sentence fragment or distorted construction.

> **NOTE:** All examples of quoting given above are in the present tense. We write that "Achenbach notes," "Achenbach believes," "Achenbach asserts." Even though his article was written in the past, we use the present tense to describe his ongoing ideas. (APA style differs somewhat; if you are going to document in APA style, check guidelines for using present or past tense when writing about the ideas of others.)

FOR READING AND ANALYSIS

As you read the following article, practice active reading, including annotating each essay. Concentrate first on what the author has to say, but also observe the organization of the essay and the author's use of quotations and references to other authors and works.

FIVE LEADERSHIP LESSONS FROM JAMES T. KIRK | ALEX KNAPP

Currently social media editor at *Forbes* magazine and popular blogger, Alex Knapp has been a freelance writer and editor for many years. He holds a law degree from the University of Kansas and focuses, in his writing, on the future of technology and culture.

PREREADING QUESTIONS What lessons might Captain Kirk have to offer to businesspeople who read *Forbes* magazine? How might these lessons have value to you as a college student?

1   Captain James T. Kirk is one of the most famous Captains in the history of Starfleet. There's a good reason for that. He saved the planet Earth several times, stopped the Doomsday Machine, helped negotiate peace with the Klingon Empire, kept the balance of power between the Federation and the Romulan Empire, and even managed to fight Nazis. On his five-year mission commanding the U.S.S. *Enterprise*, as well as subsequent commands, James T. Kirk was a quintessential leader, who led his crew into the unknown and continued to succeed time and time again.

©NBC/Photofest

Kirk's success was no 2 fluke, either. His style of command demonstrates a keen understanding of leadership and how to maintain a team that succeeds time and time again, regardless of the dangers faced. Here are five of the key leadership lessons that you can take away from Captain Kirk as you pilot your own organization into unknown futures.

1. NEVER STOP LEARNING

"You know the greatest danger facing us is ourselves, an irrational fear of 3 *the unknown. But there's no such thing as the unknown—only things temporarily hidden, temporarily not understood."*

Captain Kirk may have a reputation as a suave ladies man, but don't let that 4 exterior cool fool you. Kirk's reputation at the Academy was that of a "walking stack of books," in the words of his former first officer, Gary Mitchell. And a passion for learning helped him through several missions. Perhaps the best demonstration of this is in the episode "Arena," where Kirk is forced to fight a Gorn Captain in single combat by advanced beings. Using his own knowledge and materials at hand, Kirk is able to build a rudimentary shotgun, which he uses to defeat the Gorn.

If you think about it, there's no need for a 23rd Century Starship Captain to 5 know how to mix and prepare gunpowder if the occasion called for it. After all, Starfleet officers fight with phasers and photon torpedoes. To them, gunpowder is obsolete. But the same drive for knowledge that drove Kirk to the stars also caused him to learn that bit of information, and it paid off several years later.

In the same way, no matter what your organization does, it helps to never 6 stop learning. The more knowledge you have, the more creative you can be. The more you're able to do, the more solutions you have for problems at your disposal. Sure, you might never have to face down a reptilian alien on a desert planet, but you never know what the future holds. Knowledge is your best key to overcoming whatever obstacles are in your way.

2. HAVE ADVISORS WITH DIFFERENT WORLDVIEWS

"One of the advantages of being a captain, Doctor, is being able to ask for 7 *advice without necessarily having to take it."*

Kirk's closest two advisors are Commander Spock, a Vulcan committed to a 8 philosophy of logic, and Dr. Leonard McCoy, a human driven by compassion and scientific curiosity. Both Spock and McCoy are frequently at odds with each other, recommend different courses of action and bringing very different types of arguments to bear in defense of those points of view. Kirk sometimes goes with one, or the other, or sometimes takes their advice as a springboard to developing an entirely different course of action.

9   However, the very fact that Kirk has advisors who have a different worldview not only from each other, but also from himself, is a clear demonstration of Kirk's confidence in himself as a leader. Weak leaders surround themselves with yes men who are afraid to argue with them. That fosters an organizational culture that stifles creativity and innovation, and leaves members of the organization afraid to speak up. That can leave the organization unable to solve problems or change course. Historically, this has led to some serious disasters, such as *Star Wars Episode I: The Phantom Menace.*

10   Organizations that allow for differences of opinion are better at developing innovation, better at solving problems, and better at avoiding groupthink. We all need a McCoy and a Spock in our lives and organizations.

3. BE PART OF THE AWAY TEAM

11   *"Risk is our business. That's what this starship is all about. That's why we're aboard her."*

12   Whenever an interesting or challenging mission came up, Kirk was always willing to put himself in harm's way by joining the Away Team. With his boots on the ground, he was always able to make quick assessments of the situation, leading to superior results. At least, superior for everyone with a name and not wearing a red shirt. Kirk was very much a hands-on leader, leading the vanguard of his crew as they explored interesting and dangerous situations.

13   When you're in a leadership role, it's sometimes easy to let yourself get away from leading Away Team missions. After all, with leadership comes perks, right? You get the nice office on the higher floor. You finally get an assistant to help you with day to day activities, and your days are filled with meetings and decisions to be made, and many of these things are absolutely necessary. But it's sometimes easy to trap yourself in the corner office and forget what life is like on the front lines. When you lose that perspective, it's that much harder to understand what your team is doing, and the best way to get out of the problem. What's more, when you're not involved with your team, it's easy to lose their trust and have them gripe about how you don't understand what the job is like.

14   This is a lesson that was actually imprinted on me in one of my first jobs, making pizzas for a franchise that doesn't exist anymore. Our general manager spent a lot of time in his office, focused on the paperwork and making sure that we could stay afloat on the razor-thin margins we were running. But one thing he made sure to do, every day, was to come out during peak times and help make pizza. He didn't have to do that, but he did. The fact that he did so made me like him a lot more. It also meant that I trusted his decisions a lot more. In much the same way, I'm sure, as Kirk's crew trusted his decisions, because he knew the risks of command personally.

4. PLAY POKER, NOT CHESS

"Not chess, Mr. Spock. Poker. Do you know the game?"   15

In one of my all-time favorite *Star Trek* episodes, Kirk and his crew face down   16
an unknown vessel from a group calling themselves the "First Federation."
Threats from the vessel escalate until it seems that the destruction of the
Enterprise is imminent. Kirk asks Spock for options, who replies that the
Enterprise has been playing a game of chess, and now there are no winning
moves left. Kirk counters that they shouldn't play chess—they should play poker.
He then bluffs the ship by telling them that the *Enterprise* has a substance in its
hull called "corbomite" which will reflect the energy of any weapon back against
an attacker. This begins a series of actions that enables the *Enterprise* crew to
establish peaceful relations with the First Federation.

I love chess as much as the next geek, but chess is often taken too seriously   17
as a metaphor for leadership strategy. For all of its intricacies, chess is a game of
defined rules that can be mathematically determined. It's ultimately a game of
boxes and limitations. A far better analogy to strategy is poker, not chess. Life is
a game of probabilities, not defined rules. And often understanding your opponents is a much greater advantage than the cards you have in your hand. It was
knowledge of his opponent that allowed Kirk to defeat Khan in *Star Trek II* by
exploiting Khan's two-dimensional thinking. Bluffs, tells, and bets are all a big
part of real-life strategy. Playing that strategy with an eye to the psychology of
our competitors, not just the rules and circumstances of the game, can often lead
to better outcomes than following the rigid lines of chess.

5. BLOW UP THE ENTERPRISE

"All I ask is a tall ship and a star to steer her by.' You could feel the wind at   18
your back in those days. The sounds of the sea beneath you, and even if you
take away the wind and the water it's still the same. The ship is yours. You can
feel her. And the stars are still there, Bones."

One recurring theme in the original *Star Trek* series is that Kirk's first love is the   19
Enterprise. That love kept him from succumbing to the mind-controlling spores in
"This Side of Paradise," and it's hinted that his love for the ship kept him from
forming any real relationships or starting a family. Despite that love, though, there
came a point in *Star Trek III: The Search For Spock* where Captain Kirk made a
decision that must have pained him enormously—in order to defeat the Klingons
attacking him and save his crew, James Kirk destroyed the *Enterprise*. The
occasion, in the film, was treated with the solemnity of a funeral, which no doubt
matched Kirk's mood. The film ends with the crew returning to Vulcan on a stolen
Klingon vessel, rather than the *Enterprise*. But they returned victorious.

We are often, in our roles as leaders, driven by a passion. It might be a product   20
or service, it might be a way of doing things. But no matter how much that passion
burns within us, the reality is that times change. Different products are created.
Different ways of doing things are developed. And there will come times in your
life when that passion isn't viable anymore. A time when it no longer makes sense
to pursue your passion. When that happens, no matter how painful it is, you need
to blow up the *Enterprise*. That is, change what isn't working and embark on a new
path, even if that means having to live in a Klingon ship for awhile.

FINAL TAKEAWAY:

21   In his many years of service to the Federation, James Kirk embodied several leadership lessons that we can use in our own lives. We need to keep exploring and learning. We need to ensure that we encourage creativity and innovation by listening to the advice of people with vastly different opinions. We need to occasionally get down in the trenches with the members of our teams so we understand their needs and earn their trust and loyalty. We need to understand the psychology of our competitors and also learn to radically change course when circumstances dictate. By following these lessons, we can lead our organizations into places where none have gone before.

QUESTIONS FOR READING

1. What is Knapp's subject?
2. What does the first point—never stop learning—reveal about Kirk's academy behavior?
3. What does having advisors with differing views reveal about a leader?
4. Explain what the author means by destroying the *Enterprise* as a leadership strategy.

QUESTIONS FOR REASONING AND ANALYSIS

5. Knapp appears to use just a simple list as his structure. What other structure does the author use?
6. Knapp clearly loved the *Star Trek* TV series. How does he guide readers who may not have grown up watching Captain Kirk?
7. The author argues that leaders should play poker, not chess. Explain his view of life and the point of his game analogy.

QUESTIONS FOR REFLECTION AND WRITING

8. The *Star Trek* series has been one of the most popular and long running. If you have not watched this series, has Knapp's essay piqued your interest in Captain Kirk and encouraged you to seek out the reruns? Why or why not?
9. Which of the five lessons seems most easily applied to college students? Why? Explain your choice.
10. Which of the five lessons seems least applicable to college students? Why? Now, you are one of Captain Kirk's advisors. What good advice can you find in the lesson that has been put at the bottom of the list?

1. Write a one-paragraph summary of Alex Knapp's essay. Be sure that your summary clearly states the author's main idea, the claim of his argument. Take your time and polish your word choice.

2. Read actively and then prepare a one-and-a-half-page summary of Geoffrey Stone's speech "Free Speech on Campus" (pp. 86–92). Your readers want an accurate and focused but much shorter version of the original because they will not be reading the original piece. Explain not only what the writer's main ideas are but also how the writer develops his speech. Pay close attention to your word choice.

3. A number of years ago, before the first Kindle, Bill Gates argued that e-books will replace paper books. What are the advantages of e-books? What are the advantages of paper books? Are there any disadvantages to either type of book? Which do you prefer? How would you argue for your preference?

4. Select one futuristic idea that interests you—robots in the home, driverless cars, a moon colony, or whatever captures your imagination—and see what you can learn about it. Be prepared to share your information in a class discussion, or consider exploring your topic in an essay.

CHAPTER 2

Responding Critically to Sources

©Spencer Platt/Getty Images

READ: What are the marchers protesting?

REASON: What information in the picture helps you determine the purpose of the protest march?

REFLECT/WRITE: What is the significance of the word "Nasty" in this protest sign?

In some contexts, the word *critical* carries the idea of harsh judgment: "The manager was critical of her secretary's long phone conversations." In other contexts, the term means to evaluate carefully. When we speak of the critical reader or critical thinker, we have in mind someone who reads actively, who thinks about issues, and who makes informed judgments. Here is a profile of the critical reader or thinker:

TRAITS OF THE CRITICAL READER/THINKER

- **Focused on the facts.**
  Give me the facts and show me that they are relevant to the issue.
- **Analytic.**
  What strategies has the writer/speaker used to develop the argument?
- **Open-minded.**
  Prepared to listen to different points of view, to learn from others.
- **Questioning/skeptical.**
  What other conclusions could be supported by the evidence presented?
  How thorough has the writer/speaker been?
  What persuasive strategies are used?
- **Creative.**
  What are some entirely different ways of looking at the issue or problem?
- **Intellectually active, not passive.**
  Willing to analyze logic and evidence.
  Willing to consider many possibilities.
  Willing, after careful evaluation, to reach a judgment, to take a stand on issues.

EXAMINING THE RHETORICAL CONTEXT OF A SOURCE

Reading critically requires preparation. Instead of "jumping into reading," begin by asking questions about the work's rhetorical context. Rhetoric is about the *art of writing* (or *speaking*). Someone has chosen to shape a text in a particular way at this time for an imagined audience to accomplish a specific goal. The better you understand all of the decisions shaping a particular text, the better you will understand that work. And, then, the better you will be able to judge the significance of that work. So, try to answer the following five questions before reading. Then complete your answers while you read— or by doing research and thinking critically after you finish reading.

Who Is the Author?

Key questions to answer include:

- *Does the author have a reputation for honesty, thoroughness, and fairness?* Read the biographical note, if there is one. Ask your instructor about the author, or learn about the author in a biographical dictionary or online. Try *Book Review Digest* (in your library or online) for reviews of the author's books.

- *Is the author writing within his or her area of expertise?* People can voice opinions on any subject, but they cannot transfer expertise from one subject area to another. A football player endorsing a political candidate is a citizen with an opinion, not an expert on politics.

- *Is the author identified with a particular group or set of beliefs? Does the biography place the writer or speaker in a particular institution or organization?* For example, a member of a Republican administration may be expected to favor a Republican president's policies. A Roman Catholic priest may be expected to take a stand against abortion. These kinds of details provide hints, but you should not decide, absolutely, what a writer's position is until you have read the work with care. Be alert to reasonable expectations but avoid stereotyping.

What Type—or Genre—of Source Is It?

Are you reading a researched and documented essay by a specialist—or the text of a speech delivered the previous week to a specific audience? Is the work an editorial—or a letter to the editor? Does the columnist (such as Adam Grant, who appears later in this chapter) write business columns? Is the cartoon a comic strip or a political cartoon from the editorial page of a newspaper? (You will see both kinds of cartoons in this text.) Know what kind of text you are reading before you start. That's the only way to give yourself the context you need to be a good critical reader.

What Kind of Audience Does the Author Anticipate?

Understanding the intended audience helps you answer questions about the depth and sophistication of the work and a possible bias or slant.

- *Does the author expect a popular audience, a general but educated audience, or a specialist audience of shared expertise? Does the author anticipate an audience that shares cultural, political, or religious values?* Often you can judge the expected audience by noting the kind of publication in which the article appears, the publisher of the book, or the venue for the speech. For example, *Reader's Digest* is written for a mass audience, and *Psychology Today* for a general but more knowledgeable reader. By contrast, articles in *The Journal of the American Medical Association* (*JAMA*) are written by physicians and research scientists for a specialized reader. (It would be inappropriate, then, for a general reader to complain that an article in *JAMA* is not well written because it is too difficult.)

- *Does the author expect an audience favorable to his or her views? Or with a "wait and see" attitude? Or even hostile?* Some newspapers and television news organizations are consistently liberal, whereas others are noticeably conservative. (Do you know the political leanings of your local paper? Of the TV news that you watch? Of the blogs or websites you choose?) Remember: All arguments are "slanted" or "biased"—that is, they take a stand. That's as it should be. Just be sure to read or listen with an awareness of the author's particular background, interests, and possible stands on issues.

What Is the Author's Primary Purpose?

Is the work primarily informative or persuasive in intent? Designed to entertain or be inspiring? Think about the title. Read a book's preface to learn of the author's goals. Pay attention to tone as you read.

What Are the Author's Sources of Information?

Much of our judgment of an author and a work is based on the quality of the author's choice of sources. So always ask yourself: Where was the information obtained? Are sources clearly identified? Be suspicious of those who want us to believe that their unnamed "sources" are "reliable." Pay close attention to dates. A biography of King George III published in 1940 may still be the best source. An article urging more development based on county population statistics from the 1990s is no longer reliable.

NOTE: None of the readings in this textbook were written for publication in this textbook. They have all come from some other context. To read them with understanding you must identify the original context and think about how that should guide your reading.

EXERCISES: Examining the Context

1. For each of the following works, comment on what you might expect to find. Consider author, occasion, audience, and reliability.
   a. An article on the Republican administration, written by a former campaign worker for a Democratic presidential candidate.
   b. A discussion, published in *The Boston Globe,* of the New England Patriots' hope for the next Super Bowl.
   c. A letter to the editor about conservation, written by a member of the Sierra Club. (What is the Sierra Club? Check out its website.)
   d. A column in *Newsweek* on economics. (Look at the business section of this magazine. Your library has it or has access to it through a database.)
   e. A 1988 article in *Nutrition Today* on the best diets.
   f. A biography of Benjamin Franklin published by Oxford University Press.

    g. A *Family Circle* article about a special vegetarian diet written by a physician. (Who is the audience for this magazine? Where is it sold?)

    h. An editorial in *The New York Times* written after the Supreme Court's striking down of Washington, D.C.'s handgun restrictions.

    i. A speech on new handgun technology delivered at a convention of the National Rifle Association.

    j. An editorial in your local newspaper titled "Stop the Highway Killing."

2. Analyze an issue of your favorite magazine. Look first at the editorial pages and the articles written by staff, then at articles contributed by other writers. Answer these questions for both staff writers and contributors:

    a. Who is the audience?

    b. What is the purpose of the articles and of the entire magazine?

    c. What type of article dominates the issue?

3. Select one environmental website and study what is offered. The EnviroLink Network (www.envirolink.org) will lead you to many sites. Write down the name of the site you chose and its address (URL). Then answer these questions:

    a. Who is the intended audience?

    b. What seems to be the primary purpose or goal of the site?

    c. What type of material dominates the site?

    d. For what kinds of writing assignments might you use material from the site?

ANALYZING THE STYLE OF A SOURCE

Critical readers read for implication and are alert to tone or nuance. When you read, think not only about *what* is said but also about *how* it is said. Consider the following passage:

> The fact that there are now over forty college football "bowl" games is a joke and shows that the NCAA and participating schools have sold their souls to corporate sponsors and just want to make a quick buck at the expense of student athletes.

This passage observes that the number of bowl games is large, that big money in college sports, especially football, can have negative repercussions, while student athletes are often exploited for their labor and sacrifices. But it actually says more than that, doesn't it? Note the writer's attitude toward the NCAA and colleges who belong to that organization, as well as the corporate partners who sponsor these games.

How can we rewrite this passage to make it more favorable? Here is one version produced by students in a group exercise:

> The large number of college football bowl games, now over forty, may indicate that the NCAA and participating schools have lost focus on the purpose of athletics in American higher education by developing cozy relationships with corporate partners and their lucrative sponsorship deals.

The writers have not changed their critical view of the large number of college football bowl games and the risks of nonprofit educational institutions making a lot of money with big companies. But in this version the number of bowl games, the NCAA, and the colleges are not ridiculed. What are the differences in the two passages? The only differences are the word choice and the order in which those words appear in the sentence.

Denotative and Connotative Word Choice

The students' ability to rewrite the passage on college football bowl games to give it a positive attitude tells us that although some words may have similar meanings, they cannot always be substituted for one another without changing the message. Words with similar meanings have similar *denotations.* Often, though, words with similar denotations do not have the same connotations. A word's *connotation* is what the word suggests, what we associate the word with. The words *house* and *home,* for example, both refer to a building in which people live, but the word *home* suggests ideas—and feelings—of family and security. Thus the word *home* has a strong positive connotation. *House* by contrast brings to mind a picture of a physical structure only because the word doesn't carry any "emotional baggage."

We learn the connotations of words the same way we learn their denotations—in context. Most of us, living in the same culture, share the same connotative associations of words. At times, the context in which a word is used will affect the word's connotation. For example, the word *buddy* usually has positive connotations. We may think of an old or trusted friend. But when an unfriendly person who thinks a man may have pushed in front of him says, "Better watch it, *buddy,*" the word has a negative connotation. Social, physical, and language contexts control the connotative significance of words. Become more alert to the connotative power of words by asking what words the writers could have used instead.

NOTE: Writers make choices; their choices reflect and convey their attitudes. *Studying the context in which a writer uses emotionally charged words is the only way to be sure that we understand the writer's attitude.*

EXERCISES: Connotation

1. For each of the following words or phrases, list at least two synonyms that have a more negative connotation than the given word.
    a. child
    b. persistent
    c. thin
    d. a large group
    e. scholarly
    f. trusting
    g. underachiever
    h. quiet

2. For each of the following words, list at least two synonyms that have a more positive connotation than the given word.
    a. notorious
    b. fat
    c. politician
    d. old (people)
    e. fanatic
    f. reckless
    g. drunkard
    h. cheap

3. Read the following paragraph and decide how the writer feels about the activity described. Note the choice of details and the connotative language that make you aware of the writer's attitude.

Needing to complete a missed assignment for my physical education class, I dragged myself down to the tennis courts on a gloomy afternoon. My task was to serve five balls in a row into the service box. Although I thought I had learned the correct service movements, I couldn't seem to translate that knowledge into a decent serve. I tossed up the first ball, jerked back my racket, swung up on the ball—clunk—I hit the ball on the frame. I threw up the second ball, brought back my racket, swung up on the ball—ping—I made contact with the strings, but the ball dribbled down on my side of the net. I trudged around the court, collecting my tennis balls; I had only two of them.

4. Write a paragraph describing an activity that you liked or disliked without saying how you felt. From your choice of details and use of connotative language, convey your attitude toward the activity. (The paragraph in exercise 3 is your model.)
5. Select one of the words listed below and explain, in a paragraph, what the word connotes to you personally. Be precise; illustrate your thoughts with details and examples.

   a. nature
   b. mother
   c. romantic
   d. geek
   e. playboy
   f. artist

COLLABORATIVE EXERCISES: On Connotation

1. List all of the words you know for *human female* and for *human male*. Then classify them by connotation (positive, negative, neutral) and by level of usage (formal, informal, slang). Is there any connection between type of connotation and level of usage? Why are some words more appropriate in some social contexts than in others? Can you easily list more negative words used for one sex than for the other? Why?
2. Some words can be given a different connotation in different contexts. First, for each of the following words, label its connotation as positive, negative, or neutral. Then for each word with a positive connotation, write a sentence in which the word would convey a more negative connotation. For each word with a negative connotation, write a sentence in which the word would suggest a more positive connotation.

   a. natural
   b. old
   c. committed
   d. free
   e. chemical
   f. lazy

3. Each of the following groups of words might appear together in a thesaurus, but the words actually vary in connotation. After looking up any words whose connotation you are unsure of, write a sentence in which each word is used correctly. Briefly explain why one of the other words in the group should not be substituted.

   a. brittle, hard, fragile
   b. quiet, withdrawn, glum
   c. shrewd, clever, cunning
   d. strange, remarkable, bizarre
   e. thrifty, miserly, economical

Tone

We can describe a writer's attitude toward the subject as positive, negative, or (rarely) neutral. Attitude is the writer's position on, or feelings about, his or her subject. The way that attitude is expressed—the voice we hear and the feelings conveyed through that voice—is the writer's *tone*. Writers can choose to express attitude through a wide variety of tones. We may reinforce a negative attitude through an angry, somber, sad, mocking, peevish, sarcastic, or scornful tone. A positive attitude may be revealed through an enthusiastic, serious, sympathetic, jovial, light, or admiring tone. We cannot be sure that just because a writer selects a light tone, for example, the attitude must be positive. Humor columnists often choose a light tone to examine serious social and political issues. Given their subjects, we recognize that the light and amusing tone actually conveys a negative attitude toward the topic.

COLLABORATIVE EXERCISES: On Tone

With your class partner or in small groups, examine the following three paragraphs, which are different responses to the same event. First, decide on each writer's attitude. Then describe, as precisely as possible, the tone of each paragraph.

1. It is tragically inexcusable that this young athlete was not examined fully before he was allowed to join the varsity team. The physical examinations given were unbelievably sloppy. What were the coach and trainer thinking of not to insist that each youngster be examined while undergoing physical stress? Apparently they were not thinking about our boys at all. We can no longer trust our sons and our daughters to this inhuman system so bent on victory that it ignores the health—indeed the very lives—of our children.

2. It was learned last night, following the death of varsity fullback Jim Bresnick, that none of the players was given a stress test as part of his physical examination. The oversight was attributed to laxness by the coach and trainer, who are described today as being "distraught." It is the judgment of many that the entire physical education program must be reexamined with an eye to the safety and health of all students.

3. How can I express the loss I feel over the death of my son? I want to blame someone, but who is to blame? The coaches, for not administering more rigorous physical checkups? Why should they have done more than other coaches have done before or than other coaches are doing at other schools? My son, for not telling me that he felt funny after practice? His teammates, for not telling the coaches that my son said he did not feel well? Myself, for not knowing that something was wrong with my only child? Who is to blame? All of us and none of us. But placing blame will not return my son to me; I can only pray that other parents will not have to suffer so. Jimmy, we loved you.

Level of Diction

In addition to responding to a writer's choice of connotative language, observe the *level of diction* used. Are the writer's words primarily typical of conversational language or of a more formal style? Does the writer use slang words or technical words? Is the word choice concrete and vivid or abstract and intellectual? These differences help to shape tone and affect our response to what we read. Lincoln's word choice in "The Gettysburg Address" (see pp. 4–5) is formal and abstract. Lincoln writes "on this continent" rather than "in this land," "we take increased devotion" rather than "we become more committed." Another style, the technical, will be found in some articles in this text. The social scientist may write that "the child . . . is subjected to extremely punitive discipline," whereas a nonspecialist, more informally, might write that "the child is controlled by beatings or other forms of punishment."

One way to create an informal style is to choose simple words: *land* instead of *continent*. To create greater informality, a writer can use contractions: *we'll* for *we will*. There are no contractions in "The Gettysburg Address."

NOTE: In your academic and professional writing, you should aim for a style informal enough to be inviting to readers but one that, in most cases, avoids contractions or slang words.

Sentence Structure

Attitude is conveyed and tone created primarily through word choice, but sentence structure and other rhetorical strategies are also important. Studying a writer's sentence patterns will reveal how they affect style and tone. When analyzing these features, consider the following questions:

1. *Are the sentences generally long or short, or varied in length?*
Are the structures primarily:

- *Simple* (one independent clause)
  In 1900, empires dotted the world.
- *Compound* (two or more independent clauses)
  Women make up only 37 percent of television characters, yet women make up more than half of the population.
- *Complex* (at least one independent and one dependent clause)
  As nations grew wealthier, traditional freedom wasn't enough.

Sentences that are both long and complex create a more formal style. Compound sentences joined by *and* do not increase formality much because such sentences are really only two or more short, simple patterns hooked together. On the other hand, a long "simple" sentence with many modifiers will create a more formal style. The following example, from an essay on leadership by Michael Korda, is more complicated than the sample compound sentence above:

- *Expanded simple sentence*
  [A] leader is like a mirror, reflecting back to us our own sense of purpose, putting into words our own dreams and hopes, transforming our needs and fears into coherent policies and programs.[1]

In "The Gettysburg Address" three sentences range from 10 to 16 words, six sentences from 21 to 29 words, and the final sentence is an incredible 82 words. All but two of Lincoln's sentences are either complex or compound-complex sentences. By contrast, in "The Future Is Now," Joel Achenbach includes a paragraph with five sentences. These sentences are composed of 7, 11, 3, 11, and 19 words each. All five are simple sentences.

2.   *Does the writer use sentence fragments (incomplete sentences)?*

Although many instructors struggle to rid student writing of fragments, professional writers know that the occasional fragment can be used effectively for emphasis. Science fiction writer Bruce Sterling, thinking about the "melancholic beauty" of a gadget no longer serving any purpose, writes:

- Like Duchamp's bottle-rack, it becomes a found objet d'art. A metallic fossil of some lost human desire. A kind of involuntary poem.

The second and third sentences are, technically, fragments, but because they build on the structure of the first sentence, readers can add the missing words *It becomes* to complete each sentence. The brevity, repetition of structure, and involvement of the reader to "complete" the fragments all contribute to a strong conclusion to Sterling's paragraph.

3.   *Does the writer seem to be using an overly simplistic style? If so, why?*

Overly simplistic sentence patterns, just like an overly simplistic choice of words, can be used to show that the writer thinks the subject is silly or childish or insulting. In one of her columns, Ellen Goodman objects to society's oversimplifying of addictions and its need to believe in quick and lasting cures. She makes her point with reference to two well-known examples—but notice her technique:

- Hi, my name is Jane and I was once bulimic but now I am an exercise guru. . . .
- Hi, my name is Oprah and I was a food addict but now I am a size 10.

4.   *Does the writer use parallelism (coordination) or antithesis (contrast)?*

When two phrases or clauses are parallel in structure, the message is that they are equally important. Look back at Korda's expanded simple sentence. He coordinates three phrases, asserting that a leader is like a mirror in these three ways:

- Reflects back our purpose
- Puts into words our dreams
- Transforms our needs and fears

Antithesis creates tension. A sentence using this structure says "not this" but "that." Lincoln uses both parallelism and antithesis in one striking sentence:

- The world will little note nor long remember
    <u>wha</u>t we say here,
  but it [the world] can never forget
    <u>wha</u>t they did here.

Metaphors

When Korda writes that a leader is like a mirror, he is using a *simile.* When Lincoln writes that the world will not remember, he is using a *metaphor*—actually *personification.* Metaphors, whatever their form, all make a comparison between two items that are not really alike. The writer is making a *figurative comparison,* not a literal one. The writer wants us to think about some ways in which the items are similar. Metaphors state directly or imply the comparison; similes express the comparison using a connecting word; personification always compares a nonhuman item to humans. The exact label for a metaphor is not as important as

- recognizing the use of a figure of speech,
- identifying the two items being compared,
- understanding the point of the comparison, and
- grasping the emotional impact of the figurative comparison.

> **REMEMBER:** Pay attention to each writer's choice of metaphors. Metaphors reveal much about feelings and perceptions of life. And, like connotative words, they affect us emotionally even if we are not aware of their use. Become aware. Be able to "open up"—explain—metaphors you find in your reading.

EXERCISE: Opening Up Metaphors

During World War II, E. B. White, the essayist and writer of children's books, defined the word *democracy* in one of his *New Yorker* columns. His definition contains a series of metaphors. One is: Democracy "is the hole in the stuffed shirt through which the sawdust slowly trickles." We can open up or explain the metaphor this way:

> Just as one can punch a hole in a scarecrow's shirt and discover that there is only sawdust inside, nothing to be impressed by, so the idea of equality in a democracy "punches" a hole in the notion of an aristocratic ruling class and reveals that aristocrats, underneath, are ordinary people, just like you and me.[2]

Here are two more of White's metaphors on democracy. Open up each one in a few sentences.

> Democracy is "the dent in the high hat."
> Democracy is "the score at the beginning of the ninth."

Organization and Examples

Two other elements of writing, organization and choice of examples, also reveal attitude and help to shape the reader's response. When you study a work's organization, ask yourself questions about both placement and volume. Where are these ideas placed? At the beginning or end—the places of greatest emphasis—or in the middle, suggesting that they are less important? With regard to volume, ask yourself, "What parts of the discussion are developed at length? What points are treated only briefly?" *Note:* Sometimes simply counting the number of paragraphs devoted to the different parts of the writer's subject will give you a good understanding of the writer's main idea and purpose in writing.

Repetition

Well-written, unified essays will contain some repetition of key words and phrases. Some writers go beyond this basic strategy and use repetition to produce an effective cadence, like a drum beating in the background, keeping time to the speaker's fist pounding the lectern. In his repetition of the now-famous phrase "I have a dream," Martin Luther King, Jr., gives emphasis to his vision of an ideal America. In the following paragraph, a student tried her hand at repetition to give emphasis to her definition of liberty:

> Liberty is having the right to vote and not having other laws which restrict that right; it is having the right to apply to the university of your choice without being rejected because of race. Liberty exists when a gay man has the right to a teaching position and is not released from the position when the news of his orientation is disclosed. Liberty exists when a woman who has been offered a job does not have to decline for lack of access to day care for her children, or when a 16-year-old boy from the inner city can get an education and is not instead compelled to go to work to support his family.

These examples suggest that repetition generally gives weight and seriousness to writing and thus is appropriate when serious issues are being discussed in a forceful style.

Hyperbole, Understatement, and Irony

These three strategies create some form of tension to gain emphasis. Hyperbole overstates:

- "I will love you through all eternity!"

Understatement says less than is meant:

- Coming in soaking wet, you say, "It's a bit damp outside."

Irony creates tension by stating the opposite of what is meant:

- To a teen dressed in torn jeans and a baggy sweatshirt, the parent says, "Dressed for dinner, I see."

Quotation Marks, Italics, and Capital Letters

Several visual techniques can also be used to give special attention to certain words. A writer can place a word or phrase within quotation marks to question its validity or meaning in that context. Ellen Goodman writes, for example:

- I wonder about this when I hear the word "family" added to some politician's speech.[3]

Goodman does not agree with the politician's meaning of the word *family*. The expression *so-called* has the same effect:

- There have been restrictions on the Tibetans' so-called liberty.

Italicizing a key word or phrase or using all caps also gives additional emphasis. Dave Barry, in an essay satirizing "smart" technology, uses all caps for emphasis:

- Do you want appliances that are smarter than you? Of course not. Your appliances should be DUMBER than you, just like your furniture, your pets and your representatives in Congress.[4]

Capitalizing words not normally capitalized has the same effect of giving emphasis. As with exclamation points, writers need to use these strategies sparingly, or the emphasis sought will be lost.

EXERCISES: Recognizing Elements of Style

1. Name the technique or techniques used in each of the following passages. Then briefly explain the idea of each passage.
   a. We are becoming the tools of our tools. (Henry David Thoreau)[5]
   b. The bias and therefore the business of television is to *move* information, not collect it. (Neil Postman)[6]
   c. If guns are outlawed, only the government will have guns. Only the police, the secret police, the military. The hired servants of our rulers. Only the government—and a few outlaws. (Edward Abbey)[7]
   d. Having read all the advice on how to live 900 years, what I think is that eating a tasty meal once again will surely doom me long before I reach 900 while not eating that same meal could very well kill me. It's enough to make you reach for a cigarette! (Russell Baker)[8]
   e. If you are desperate for a quick fix, either legalize drugs or repress the user. If you want a civilized approach, mount a propaganda campaign against drugs. (Charles Krauthammer)[9]
   f. Oddly enough, the greatest scoffers at the traditions of American etiquette, who scorn the rituals of their own society as stupid and stultifying, voice respect for the customs and folklore of Native Americans, less industrialized people, and other societies they find more "authentic" than their own. (Judith Martin)[10]
   g. Text is story. Text is event, performance, special effect. Subtext is ideas. It's motive, suggestions, visual implications, subtle comparisons. (Stephen Hunter)[11]
   h. This flashy vehicle [the school bus] was as punctual as death: seeing us waiting at the cold curb, it would sweep to a halt, open its mouth, suck the boy in, and spring away with an angry growl. (E. B. White)[12]

2. Read the following essay by Alexandra Petri. Use the questions that precede and follow the essay to help you determine Petri's attitude toward her subject and to characterize her style.

■ ■

NASTY WOMEN HAVE MUCH WORK TO DO | ALEXANDRA PETRI

A graduate of Harvard College, Alexandra Petri is the author of *A Field Guide to Awkward Silences* (2015) and humor columnist for *The Washington Post*, writing the *ComPost* blog and weekly columns. Her columns are usually humorous but never frivolous. The following column was published October 22, 2016—close to Halloween.

PREREADING QUESTIONS What is Petri's purpose in writing? What does she want to accomplish—besides being funny?

"Such a nasty woman."
—Donald Trump

The nasty women gather on the heath just after midnight. It is Nasty Women's   1
Sabbath, Election Eve, and they must make haste.

Their sturdy he-goats and their broomsticks are parked with the valet.   2
Beyond the circle, their familiar owls and toads and pussycats strut back and forth, boasting of being grabbed or not grabbed.

A will-o'-the-wisp zigzags back and forth over the assemblage (it is bad with   3
directions, like a nasty woman).

They have much to do and the hour is late.   4

They must sabotage the career of an upwardly mobile young general named   5
Macbeth.

They must lure an old wizard into a cave and lock him there so that Camelot   6
may fall.

They must finish Ron and Harry's homework for them (again).   7

No, wait, I am suggesting that.   8

They must turn some people into newts and let some of them get better and   9
let others run for office and go on prime-time cable.

They must transform all of Odysseus's sailors into swine and then back   10
again, get Sabrina through high school, freeze Narnia permanently, complete all sorts of housework for Samantha Stevens.

They have a good many apples to poison and drug and mermaid voices to   11
steal and little dogs to get, too.

And then they have an election to rig.   12

They must make haste. The vagenda is quite full.   13

They gather around the bubbling cauldron as the squirrels scurry off into   14
hiding and the bats fly in.

One particularly nasty woman who has been juggling a lot at home and at   15
work lately flies in late on her Swiffer and apologizes; she has not even had time to put a wart on her nose or a bat into her hair. Nasty women know that it only *looks* easy.

The nasty women gather around the cauldron and lean in.   16

What great plans are these women cooking up together?

17   They lean in with the ingredients that they have been gathering for days, for years, to make the potion potent.

18   Eye of newt. Wool of bat. Woman cards, both tarot and credit. Binders. Lemons. Lemonade. Letters to the editor saying that a woman could not govern at that time of month—when in fact she would be at the height of her power and capable of unleashing the maximum number of moon-sicknesses against our enemies, but the nasty women do not stoop to correct this.

19   They toss in pieces of meat and legs with nothing else attached and dolls and sweethearts and sugars and all the other *things* they were told to be, and like it.

20   They drop in paradoxes: powerful rings that give you everything and keep you from getting the job, heels that only move forward by moving backward, skirts that are too long and too short at the same time, comic-book drawings whose anatomy defies gravity, suits that become pantsuits when a woman slips them on, enchanted shirts and skirts and sweaters that can ask for it, whatever it is, on their own. They take the essence of a million locker rooms wrung out of towels and drop it in, one drip at a time. Then stir.

21   They sprinkle it with the brains of the people who did not recognize that they were doctors, pepper it with ground-up essays by respected men asking why women aren't funny, whip in six pounds of pressure and demands for perfection. They drizzle it with the laughter of women in commercials holding salads and the rueful smiles of women in commercials peddling digestive yogurts. They toss in

some armpit hair and a wizened old bat, just to be safe. And wine. Plenty of wine. And cold bathwater. Then they leave it to simmer.

And they whisper incantations into it, too. They whisper to it years of shame 22 and blame and what-were-you-wearing and boys-will-be-boys. They tell the formless mass in the cauldron tales of the too many times that they were told they were too much. Too loud. Too emotional. Too bossy. Insufficiently smiling. The words shouted at them as they walked down the streets. The words typed at them when their minds traveled through the Internet. Every concession they were told to make so that they took up less space. Every time they were too mean or too nice or shaped wrong. Every time they were told they were different, other, objects, the princess at the end of the quest, the grab-bag prize for the end of the party.

They pour them all into a terrible and bitter brew and stir to taste.   23

It tastes nasty. It is the taste of why we cannot have nice things, and they are 24 used to that.

Perhaps if the potion works, they will not have to be.   25

The nasty women have a great deal to do before the moon sinks back 26 beneath the horizon.

But that is all right. They know how to get things done.   27

QUESTIONS FOR READING AND REASONING

1. Humor is a strategy, perhaps a purpose, but it is not a subject. Is Petri's subject the three witches of *Macbeth*? Halloween witches? Consider her title and think about how best to state her subject.

2. Remembering that humor pieces also have a point to make, how would you state the author's claim?

3. Where does the expression "nasty women" come from?

4. Examine the list of things that the gathered women have to do in paragraphs 5–11. How does Petri create humor in this list? What in the list seems more serious? Why?

5. Reread the list of what goes into the cauldron. What do many of the details have in common?

QUESTIONS FOR REFLECTION AND WRITING

6. What specific strategies are used by Petri to create tone and convey attitude?

7. What specific passages or recurring element do you find the most amusing? Why?

WRITING ABOUT STYLE

What does it mean to "do a style analysis"? A style analysis answers the question "How is it written?" Let's think through the steps in preparing a study of a writer's choice and arrangement of language.

Understanding Purpose and Audience

A style analysis is not the place for challenging the ideas of the writer. A style analysis requires the discipline to see how a work has been put together *even if you disagree with the writer's views.* You do not have to agree with a writer to appreciate his or her skill in writing.

If you think about audience in the context of your purpose, you should conclude that a summary of content does not belong in a style analysis. Why? Because we write style analyses for people who have already read the work. Remember, though, that your reader may not know the work in detail, so give examples to illustrate the points of your analysis.

Planning the Essay

First, organize your analysis according to elements of style, not according to the organization of the work. Scrap any thoughts of "hacking" your way through the essay, commenting on the work paragraph by paragraph. This approach invites summary and means that you have not selected an organization that supports your purpose in writing. Think of an essay as like the pie in Figure 2.1. We could divide the pie according to key ideas—if we were summarizing. But we can also carve the pie according to elements of style, the techniques we have discussed in this chapter. This is the general plan you want to follow for your essay.

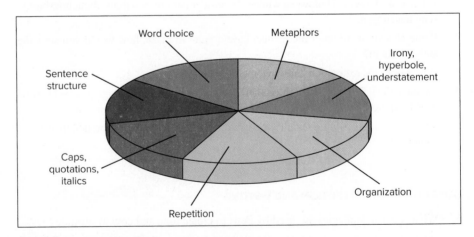

FIGURE 2.1 **Analyzing Style**

Choose those techniques you think are most important in creating the writer's attitude, and discuss them one at a time. Do not try to include the entire pie; instead, select three or four elements to examine in detail. If you were asked to write an analysis of the Alexandra Petri article, for example, you might select her use of sentence structure, hyperbole, and irony. These are three techniques that stand out in Petri's writing.

Drafting the Style Analysis

If you were to select three elements of style, as in the Alexandra Petri example above, your essay might look something like this:

Paragraph 1: Introduction

> 1. Attention-getter
> 2. Author, title, publication information of article/book
> 3. Brief explanation of author's subject
> 4. Your thesis—that you will be analyzing style

Paragraph 2: First body paragraph

> Analysis of sentence structure. (See below for more details on body paragraphs.)

Paragraph 3: Second body paragraph

> 1. Topic sentence that introduces analysis of hyperbole
> 2. Three or more examples of hyperbole
> 3. Explanation of how each example connects to the author's thesis—that is, how the example of hyperbole works to convey attitude. This is your analysis; don't forget it!

Paragraph 4: Third body paragraph

> Analysis of irony—with same three parts as listed above.

Paragraph 5: Conclusion

> Restate your thesis: We can understand Petri's point through a study of these three elements of her style.

A CHECKLIST FOR REVISION

When revising and polishing your draft, use these questions to complete your essay.

☐ Have I handled all titles correctly?

☐ Have I correctly referred to the author?

☐ Have I used quotation marks correctly when presenting examples of style? (Use the guidelines in Chapter 1 for these first three questions.)

☐ Do I have an accurate, clear presentation of the author's subject and thesis?

☐ Do I have enough examples of each element of style to show my readers that these elements are important?

☐ Have I connected examples to the author's thesis? That is, have I shown my readers how these techniques work to develop the author's attitude?

To reinforce your understanding of style analysis, read the following essay by Ellen Goodman, answer the questions that follow, and then study the student essay that analyzes Goodman's style.

IN PRAISE OF A SNAIL'S PACE | ELLEN GOODMAN

Author of *Close to Home* (1979), *At Large* (1981), and *Keeping In Touch* (1985), collections of her essays, Ellen Goodman began as a feature writer for *The Boston Globe* in 1967 and was a syndicated columnist from 1976 until her retirement in 2009. The following column was published August 13, 2005.

PREREADING QUESTIONS Why might someone write in praise of snail mail? What does Goodman mean by "hyperactive technology"?

1   CASCO BAY, Maine—I arrive at the island post office carrying an artifact from another age. It's a square envelope, handwritten, with a return address that can be found on a map. Inside is a condolence note, a few words of memory and sympathy to a wife who has become a widow. I could have sent these words far more efficiently through e-mail than through this "snail mail." But I am among those who still believe that sympathy is diluted by two-thirds when it arrives over the Internet transom.

2   I would no more send an e-condolence than an e-thank you or an e-wedding invitation. There are rituals you cannot speed up without destroying them. It would be like serving Thanksgiving dinner at a fast-food restaurant.

3   My note goes into the old blue mailbox and I walk home wondering if slowness isn't the only way we pay attention now in a world of hyperactive technology.

4   Weeks ago, a friend lamented the trouble she had communicating with her grown son. It wasn't that her son was out of touch. Hardly. They were connected across miles through e-mail and cell phone, instant-messaging and text-messaging. But she had something serious to say and feared that an e-mail would elicit a reply that said: I M GR8. Was there no way to get undivided attention in the full in-box of his life? She finally chose a letter, a pen on paper, a stamp on envelope.

5   How do you describe the times we live in, so connected and yet fractured? Linda Stone, a former Microsoft techie, characterizes ours as an era of "continuous partial attention." At the extreme end are teenagers instant-messaging while they are talking on the cell phone, downloading music and doing homework. But adults too live with all systems go, interrupted and distracted, scanning everything, multi-technological-tasking everywhere.

Are we having fun yet?

We suffer from the illusion, Stone says, that we can expand our personal   6
bandwidth, connecting to more and more. Instead, we end up overstimulated,
overwhelmed and, she adds, unfulfilled. Continuous partial attention inevitably
feels like a lack of full attention.

But there are signs of people searching for ways to slow down and listen up.   7
We are told that experienced e-mail users are taking longer to answer, freeing
themselves from the tyranny of the reply button. Caller ID is used to find out who
we don't have to talk to. And the next "killer ap," they say, will be e-mail software
that can triage the important from the trivial.

Meanwhile, at companies where technology interrupts creativity and online   8
contact prevents face-to-face contact, there are no e-mail-free Fridays. At others,
there are bosses who require that you check your BlackBerry at the meeting
door.

If a ringing cell phone once signaled your importance to a client, now that   9
client is impressed when you turn off the cell phone. People who stayed connected 10 ways, 24-7, now pride themselves on "going dark."

"People hunger for more attention," says Stone, whose message has been   10
welcomed even at a conference of bloggers. "Full attention will be the aphrodi-
siac of the future."

Indeed, at the height of our romance with e-mail, "You've Got Mail" was the   11
cinematic love story. Now e-mail brings less thrill—"who will be there?" And more

dread—"how many are out there?" Today's romantics are couples who leave their laptops behind on the honeymoon.

12   As for text-message flirtation, a young woman ended hers with a man who wrote, "C U L8R." He didn't have enough time to spell out Y-O-U?

13   Slowness guru Carl Honore began "In Praise of Slowness" after he found himself seduced by a book of condensed classic fairy tales to read to his son. One-minute bedtime stories? We are relearning that paying attention briefly is as impossible as painting a landscape from a speeding car.

14   It is not just my trip to the mailbox that has brought this to mind. I come here each summer to stop hurrying. My island is no Brigadoon: WiFi is on the way, and some people roam the island with their cell phones, looking for a hot spot. But I exchange the Internet for the country road.

15   Georgia O'Keeffe once said that it takes a long time to see a flower. No technology can rush the growth of the leeks in the garden. All the speed in the Internet cannot hurry the healing of a friend's loss. Paying attention is the coin of this realm.

16   Sometimes, a letter becomes the icon of an old-fashioned new fashion. And sometimes, in this technological whirlwind, it takes a piece of snail mail to carry the stamp of authenticity.

QUESTIONS FOR READING AND REASONING

1.   What has Goodman just done? How does this action serve the author as a lead-in to her subject?

2.   What is Goodman's main idea or thesis?

3.   What examples illustrate the problem the author sees in our times? What evidence does she present to suggest that people want to change the times?

4.   What general solutions does Goodman suggest?

QUESTIONS FOR REFLECTION AND WRITING

5.   How do the details at the beginning and end of the essay contribute to Goodman's point? Write a paragraph answer to this question. Then consider: Which one of the different responses to reading does your paragraph illustrate?

6.   The author describes our time as one of "continuous partial attention." Does this phrase sum up our era? Why or why not? If you agree, do you think this is a problem? Why or why not?

7.   For what kinds of research projects would this essay be useful? List several possibilities to discuss with classmates.

STUDENT ESSAY

A CONVINCING STYLE

James Goode

Ellen Goodman's essay, "In Praise of a Snail's Pace," is not, of course, about snails. It is about a way of communicating that our society has largely lost or ignored: the capability to pay full attention in communications and relationships. Her prime example of this is the "snail mail" letter, used for cards, invitations, and condolences. Anything really worth saying, she argues, must be written fully and sent by mail to make us pay attention. Goodman's easy, winning style of word choice and metaphor persuades us to agree with her point, a point also backed up by the logic of her examples.

"In Praise of a Snail's Pace" starts innocently. The author is merely taking a walk to the post office with a letter, surely nothing unusual. But as Goodman describes her letter, she reveals her belief that "snail mail" is a much more authentic way of sharing serious tidings than a message that "arrives over the Internet transom." The letter, with its "square" envelope and "handwritten" address, immediately sounds more personal than the ultramodern electronic message. The words have guided the reader's thinking. Goodman also describes our times as "connected yet fractured" and us as living in a world of "continuous partial attention." "Being connected" becomes synonymous by the end of the essay with "not paying attention." Word choice is crucial here. The author creates in the reader's mind a dichotomy: be fast and false, or slow down and mean it.

Goodman's metaphors make a point, too. "A picture is worth a thousand words" and the pictures created by the words here further the fast/slow debate. The idea that sending an e-condolence would be "like serving Thanksgiving dinner at a fast-food restaurant" gives an instant image of the worthlessness of an e-mail condolence note. The mother trying to get attention in the "full in-box" of her son's life shows us that a divided and distracted brain answering five hundred e-mails cannot be expected to concentrate on any of them. Again, trying to pay attention briefly is just as impossible as "painting a landscape from a speeding car." The "tyranny" of the reply button must be overcome by our "going dark." Getting away from our electronic world, Goodman reasons, helps us restore meaning to what we do.

But while the reader listens to clever words and paints memorable mind pictures, any resistance is worn away with a steady stream of examples. From the author mailing an envelope to Georgia O'Keeffe's remark that it takes a long time to see a flower, example after example supports her view. The mother wishing for the total attention of her son and the office workers' turning off cell phones and computers have already been mentioned. Linda Stone, a former Microsoft techie and a credible authority on modern communications and their effects on users, is quoted several times. Goodman notes with excellent effect that Stone's message has been received even at a conference of bloggers—if the most connected group out there supports this, why shouldn't everyone else? The author herself comes to an island every year to escape the mad hurry of the business world by wandering country roads. These examples build until the reader is convinced that snail mail is the mark of authenticity and connectedness.

"In Praise of a Snail's Pace" is a thoughtful essay that takes aim at the notion that one person can do it all and still find meaning. The "connected" person is in so much of a hurry that he or she must not be really interested in much of anything. By showing "interrupted and distracted" readers that "no technology can rush the growth of the leeks in the garden," the author makes a convincing case for the real effectiveness of written mail. Whether through word choice, metaphor, or example, Ellen Goodman's message comes through: Slow down and send some "snail mail" and be really connected for once.

Courtesy of James Goode.

ANALYZING TWO OR MORE SOURCES

Scientists examining the same set of facts do not always draw the same conclusions; neither do historians and biographers agree on the significance of the same documents. How do we recognize and cope with these disparities? As critical readers we analyze what we read, pose questions, and refuse to believe everything we find in print or online. To develop these skills in recognizing differences, instructors frequently ask students to contrast the views of two or more writers. In psychology class, for example, you may be asked to contrast the views of Sigmund Freud and John B. Watson on child development. In a communications course, you may be asked to contrast the moderator styles of two talk-show hosts. We can examine differences in content or presentation, or both. Here are guidelines for preparing a contrast of sources.

GUIDELINES for Preparing a Contrast Essay

- **Work with sources that have something in common.** Think about the context for each, that is, each source's subject and purpose. (There is little sense in contrasting a textbook chapter, for example, with a TV talk show because their contexts are so different.)
- **Read actively to understand the content of the two sources.** Record or save films, radio, or TV shows so that you can listen/view them several times, just as you would read a written source more than once.
- **Analyze for differences, focusing on your purpose in contrasting.** If you are contrasting the ideas of two writers, for example, then your analysis will focus on ideas, not on writing style. To explore differences in two news accounts, you may want to consider all of the following: the impact of placement in the newspaper/magazine, accompanying photographs or graphics, length of each article, what is covered in each article, and writing styles. Prepare a list of specific differences.
- **Organize your contrast.** It is usually best to organize by points of difference. If you write first about one source and then about the other, the ways that the sources differ may not be clear for readers. Take the time

to plan an organization that clearly reveals your contrast purpose in writing. To illustrate, a paper contrasting the writing styles of two authors can be organized according to the following pattern:

Introduction: Introduce your topic and establish your purpose to contrast styles of writer A and writer B.

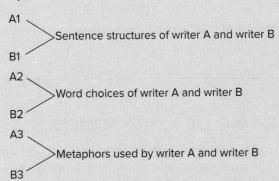

A1
B1 — Sentence structures of writer A and writer B

A2
B2 — Word choices of writer A and writer B

A3
B3 — Metaphors used by writer A and writer B

Conclusion: Explain the effect of the differences in style of the writers.

- **Illustrate and discuss each of the points of difference for each of the sources.** Provide examples and explain the impact of the differences.
- **Always write for an audience who may be familiar with your general topic but not with the specific sources you are discussing.** Be sure to provide adequate context (names, titles of works, etc.).

SYNTHESIZING TWO OR MORE SOURCES

Sometimes we have the writing goal of synthesizing sources rather than contrasting them. because the goal is to show the sources basically agree. You can still use the contrast structure even though your purpose is to demonstrate similarities rather than differences. If the sources contain some differences, you might want to begin by noting those, but then proceed to organize by points of similarity.

Remember that summarizing first one source and then the other does not produce a synthesis. Instead, you are actually leaving your reader with the task of finding the similarities. But when you group points of similarity, you are then doing the analysis for the reader, fulfilling your purpose in writing.

EXERCISE: Analyzing Two Sources

In chapter 1, Ruth Whippman has written to question the popular current view that we need to develop "mindfulness." You will find that many have written about the topic of mindfulness. Locate a second article on this subject, and read to see if the author agrees with Whippman or supports the concept of mindfulness. If there is agreement, prepare a synthesis of the two articles. If there is disagreement, prepare a contrast of the two articles. You may be asked to prepare just an outline, rather than completing an essay.

You may be asked to prepare the outline on your own or with a classmate who has the same second article as you do.

■ ■

WHY I TAUGHT MYSELF TO PROCRASTINATE | ADAM GRANT

Adam Grant, a Phi Beta Kappa graduate from Harvard with a PhD in organizational psychology from the University of Michigan, is The Wharton School's top-rated professor. He is the author of two books, *Originals* (how individuals champion new ideas) and *Give and Take*, named one of the best books of 2013. He has been widely recognized for his work in business innovation as well as for his guidelines in developing both creative and moral children.

PREREADING QUESTIONS Why would anyone recommend procrastinating? What might be Grant's twist on this topic?

Normally, I would have finished this column weeks ago. But I kept putting it off because my New Year's resolution is to procrastinate more.   1

I guess I owe you an explanation. Sooner or later.   2

We think of procrastination as a curse. Over 80 percent of college students are plagued by procrastination, requiring epic all-nighters to finish papers and prepare for tests. Roughly 20 percent of adults report being chronic procrastinators. We can only guess how much higher the estimate would be if more of them got around to filling out the survey.   3

But while procrastination is a vice for productivity, I've learned—against my natural inclinations—that it's a virtue for creativity.   4

Intent on her work, but has she paused to "pro-crastinate"?

©Gastuner/Shutterstock.com RF

For years, I believed that anything worth doing was worth doing early. In graduate school I submitted my dissertation two years in advance. In college,   5

I wrote my papers weeks early and finished my thesis four months before the due date. My roommates joked that I had a productive form of obsessive-compulsive disorder. Psychologists have coined a term for my condition: pre-crastination.

6   Pre-crastination is the urge to start a task immediately and finish it as soon as possible. If you're a serious pre-crastinator, progress is like oxygen and postponement is agony. When a flurry of emails land in your inbox and you don't answer them instantly, you feel as if your life is spinning out of control. When you have a speech to give next month, each day you don't work on it brings a creeping sense of emptiness, like a dementor is sucking the joy from the air around you (look it up—now!).

7   In college, my idea of a productive day was to start writing at 7 a.m. and not leave my chair until dinnertime. I was chasing "flow," the mental state described by the psychologist Mihaly Csikszentmihalyi in which you are so completely absorbed in a task that you lose a sense of time and place. I fell so deeply into that zone of concentration that my roommates once gave a party while I was writing and I didn't even notice.

8   But procrastinators, as the writer Tim Urban describes it on the blog Wait But Why, are at the mercy of an Instant Gratification Monkey who inhabits their brains, constantly asking questions like "Why would we ever use a computer for work when the Internet is sitting right there waiting to be played with?"

9   If you're a procrastinator, overcoming that monkey can require herculean amounts of willpower. But a pre-crastinator may need equal willpower to *not* work.

10   A few years ago, though, one of my most creative students, Jihae Shin, questioned my expeditious habits. She told me her most original ideas came to her after she procrastinated. I challenged her to prove it. She got access to a couple of companies, surveyed people on how often they procrastinated, and asked their supervisors to rate their creativity. Procrastinators earned significantly higher creativity scores than pre-crastinators like me.

11   I wasn't convinced. So Jihae, now a professor at the University of Wisconsin, designed some experiments. She asked people to come up with new business ideas. Some were randomly assigned to start right away. Others were given five minutes to first play Minesweeper or Solitaire. Everyone submitted their ideas, and independent raters rated how original they were. The procrastinators' ideas were 28 percent more creative.

12   Minesweeper is awesome, but it wasn't the driver of the effect. When people played games before being told about the task, there was no increase in creativity. It was only when they first learned about the task and then put it off that they considered more novel ideas. It turned out that procrastination encouraged divergent thinking.

13   Our first ideas, after all, are usually our most conventional. My senior thesis in college ended up replicating a bunch of existing ideas instead of introducing new ones. When you procrastinate, you're more likely to let your mind wander. That gives you a better chance of stumbling onto the unusual and spotting unexpected patterns. Nearly a century ago, the psychologist Bluma Zeigarnik found

that people had a better memory for incomplete tasks than for complete ones. When we finish a project, we file it away. But when it's in limbo, it stays active in our minds.

Begrudgingly, I acknowledged that procrastination might help with everyday 14 creativity. But monumental achievements are a different story, right?

Wrong. Steve Jobs procrastinated constantly, several of his collaborators 15 have told me. Bill Clinton has been described as a "chronic procrastinator" who waits until the last minute to revise his speeches. Frank Lloyd Wright spent almost a year procrastinating on a commission, to the point that his patron drove out and insisted that he produce a drawing on the spot. It became Fallingwater, his masterpiece. Aaron Sorkin, the screenwriter behind *Steve Jobs* and *The West Wing*, is known to put off writing until the last minute. When Katie Couric asked him about it, he replied, "You call it procrastination, I call it thinking."

So what if creativity happens not in spite of procrastination, but because of 16 it? I decided to give it a try. The good news is that I am no stranger to self-discipline. So I woke up one morning and wrote a to-do list for procrastinating more. Then I set out to achieve the goal of not making progress toward my goals. It didn't go excellently.

My first step was to delay creative tasks, starting with this article. I resisted 17 the temptation to sit down and start typing, and instead waited. While procrasti-nating (i.e., thinking), I remembered an article I had read months earlier on pre-crastination. It dawned on me that I could use my own experiences as a pre-crastinator to set the stage for readers.

Next, I drew some inspiration from George Costanza on *Seinfeld*, who made 18 it a habit to quit on a high note. When I started writing a sentence that felt good, I stopped in the middle of it and walked away. When I returned to writing later that day, I was able to pick up where I had left the trail of thought. Mitch Albom, author of *Tuesdays With Morrie*, uses the same trick. "If you quit in the middle of a sentence, that's just great," he told me. "You can't wait to get back to it the next morning."

Once I did finish a draft, I put it away for three weeks. When I came back to 19 it, I had enough distance to wonder, "What kind of idiot wrote this garbage?" and rewrote most of it. To my surprise, I had some fresh material at my disposal: During those three weeks, for example, a colleague had mentioned the fact that Mr. Sorkin was an avid procrastinator.

What I discovered was that in every creative project, there are moments that 20 require thinking more laterally and, yes, more slowly. My natural need to finish early was a way of shutting down complicating thoughts that sent me whirling in new directions. I was avoiding the pain of divergent thinking—but I was also missing out on its rewards.

Of course, procrastination can go too far. Jihae randomly assigned a third 21 group of people to wait until the last minute to begin their project. They weren't as creative either. They had to rush to implement the easiest idea instead of working out a novel one.

To curb that kind of destructive procrastination, science offers some useful 22 guidance. First, imagine yourself failing spectacularly, and the ensuing frenzy of anxiety may jump-start your engine. Second, lower your standards for what counts as progress, and you will be less paralyzed by perfectionism. Carving out small windows of time can help, too: The psychologist Robert Boice helped graduate students overcome writer's block by teaching them to write for 15 minutes a day. My favorite step is pre-commitment: If you're passionate about gun control, go to the app stickK and fork over some cash in advance. If you don't meet your deadline, your money will be donated to the National Rifle Association. The fear of supporting a cause you despise can be a powerful motivator.

23   But if you're a procrastinator, next time you're wallowing in the dark playground of guilt and self-hatred over your failure to start a task, remember that the right kind of procrastination might make you more creative. And if you're a pre-crastinator like me, it may be worth mastering the discipline of forcing yourself to procrastinate. You can't be afraid of leaving your work un

Adam Grant, "Why I Taught Myself to Procrastinate," *The New York Times*, 16 Jan. 2016. Copyright ©2016 by Adam Grant. Used with permission of the author.

QUESTIONS FOR READING

1. What does a good procrastinator allow for?
2. What does *pre-crastination* mean? Which term best describes the author?
3. Who are some of the most famous procrastinators? What happened when Grant chose to procrastinate while writing this essay?

QUESTIONS FOR READING AND ANALYSIS

4. What is Grant's thesis—the claim of his argument? Try to state it with precision.
5. Although the author can be said to have a serious topic, how does he avoid preaching? Find several examples of style elements that add a light touch to his essay.

QUESTIONS FOR REFLECTION AND WRITING

6. Have you experienced an "in the flow" level of concentration that would have let you work in the midst of a party? If so, how did you do it? If not, why not?
7. Are you a pro- or a pre-crastinator? A good or a bad procrastinator? Are you likely to try Grant's advice for becoming a good procrastinator? Why or why not?

1. Analyze the style of one of the essays from section 5 of this text. Do not comment on every element of style; select several elements that seem to characterize the writer's style and examine them in detail. Remember that style analyses are written for an audience familiar with the work, so summary is not necessary.

2. Many of the authors included in this text have written books that you will find in your library. Select one that interests you, read it, and prepare a review of it that synthesizes summary, analysis, and evaluation. Prepare a review of about 300 words; assume that the book has just been published.

3. Choose two newspaper and/or magazine articles that differ in their discussion of the same person, event, or product. You may select two different articles on a person in the news, two different accounts of a news event, an advertisement and a *Consumer Reports* analysis of the same product, or two reviews of a book or movie. Analyze differences in both content and presentation, and then consider why the two accounts differ. Organize by points of difference, and write to an audience not necessarily familiar with the articles.

4. Choose a recently scheduled public event (the Super Bowl, the Olympics, a presidential election, the Academy Award presentations, the premiere of a new television series), and find several articles written before and several after the event. First compare articles written after the event to see if they agree factually. If not, decide which article appears to be more accurate and why. Then examine the earlier material and decide which was the most and which the least accurate. Write an essay in which you explain the differences in speculation before the event and why you think these differences exist. Your audience will be aware of the event, but not necessarily aware of the articles you are studying.

CREDITS

1. Michael Korda. "How to Be a Leader." *Newsweek*, 5 Jan. 1981.
2. E. B. White. "The Meaning of Democracy." *The New Yorker*, 3 July 1943.
3. Ellen Goodman. "Family Ties Pulled Tight at Holiday Dinners." *The Washington Post*, 24 Nov. 1989.
4. Dave Barry. "Remote Control." *The Washington Post*, 5 Mar. 2000.
5. Henry David Thoreau. *Walden* (1854).
6. Neil Postman. *The Disappearance of Childhood*. Vintage Books, 1994, p. 82.
7. Edward Abbey. *Abbey's Road*. Dutton, 1979.
8. Russell Baker. "Sunday Observer: Eat What You Are." *The New York Times Magazine*, 10 Oct. 1982.
9. Charles Krauthammer. "Legalize? No. Deglamorize." *The Washington Post*, 20 May 1988.
10. Judith Martin. "The Roles of Manners." *The Responsive Community*, Spring 1996.
11. Stephen Hunter. "Look Out Below: At the Movies, Subtext Plays a Summer Role." *The Washington Post*, 18 Aug. 2002, p. G01.
12. E. B. White. "Education" in *One Man's Meat*. Harper & Row, 1944.

The World of Argument

©AP Images/Bill Clark

CHAPTER 3

Understanding the Basics of Argument

CUL DE SAC

BY RICHARD THOMPSON

READ: What is the situation? What is the reaction of the younger children? What does the older boy try to do?

REASON: Why is the older boy frustrated?

REFLECT/WRITE: What can happen to those who lack scientific knowledge?

In this section we will explore the processes of thinking logically and analyzing issues to reach informed judgments. Remember: Mature people do not need to agree on all issues to respect one another's good sense, but they do have little patience with uninformed or illogical statements masquerading as argument.

CHARACTERISTICS OF ARGUMENT

Argument Is Conversation with a Goal

When you enter into an argument (as speaker, writer, or reader), you become a participant in an ongoing debate about an issue. Since you are probably not the first to address the issue, you need to be aware of the ways that the issue has been debated by others and then seek to advance the conversation, just as you would if you were having a more casual conversation with friends. If the time of the movie is set, the discussion now turns to whose car to take or where to meet. If you were to just repeat the time of the movie, you would add nothing useful to the conversation. Also, if you were to change the subject to a movie you saw last week, you would annoy your friends by not offering useful information or showing that you valued the current conversation. Just as with your conversation about the movie, you want your argument to stay focused on the issue, to respect what others have already contributed, and to make a useful addition to our understanding of the topic.

Argument Takes a Stand on an Arguable Issue

A meaningful argument focuses on a debatable issue. We usually do not argue about facts. "Professor Jones's American literature class meets at 10:00 on Mondays" is not arguable. It is either true or false. We can check the schedule of classes to find out. (Sometimes the facts change; new facts replace old ones.) We also do not debate personal preferences for the simple reason that they are just that—personal. If the debate is about the appropriateness of boxing as a sport, for you to declare that you would rather play tennis is to fail to advance the conversation. You have expressed a personal preference, interesting perhaps, but not relevant to the debate.

Argument Uses Reasons and Evidence

Some arguments merely "look right." That is, conclusions are drawn from facts, but the facts are not those that actually support the assertion, or the conclusion is not the only or the best explanation of those facts. To shape convincing arguments, we need more than an array of facts. We need to think critically, analyze the issue, see relationships, weigh evidence. We need to avoid the temptation to "argue" from emotion only, or to believe that just stating our opinion is the same thing as building a sound argument.

Argument Incorporates Values

Arguments are based not just on reason and evidence but also on the beliefs and values we hold and think that our audience may hold as well. In a reasoned debate, you want to make clear the values that you consider relevant to the argument. In an editorial defending the sport of boxing, one editor wrote that boxing "is a sport because the world has not yet become a place in which the qualities that go into excellence in boxing [endurance, agility, courage] have no value" (*The Washington Post,* February 5, 1983). But James J. Kilpatrick also appeals to values when he argues, in an editorial critical of boxing, that we should not want to live in a society "in which deliberate brutality is legally authorized and publicly applauded" (*The Washington Post,* December 7, 1982). Observe, however, the high level of seriousness in the appeal to values. Neither writer settles for a simplistic personal preference: "Boxing is exciting" or "Boxing is too violent."

Argument Recognizes the Topic's Complexity

Much false reasoning (the logical fallacies discussed in Chapter 6) results from a writer's oversimplifying an issue. A sound argument begins with an understanding that most issues are terribly complicated. The wise person approaches such ethical concerns as abortion or euthanasia or such public policy issues as tax cuts or trade agreements with the understanding that there are many philosophical, moral, and political issues that complicate discussions of these topics. Recognizing an argument's complexity may also lead us to an understanding that there can be more than one "right" position. The thoughtful arguer respects the views of others, seeks common ground when possible, and often chooses a conciliatory approach.

THE SHAPE OF ARGUMENT: WHAT WE CAN LEARN FROM ARISTOTLE

Still one of the best ways to understand the basics of argument is to reflect on what the Greek philosopher Aristotle describes as the three "players" in any argument: the *writer* (or *speaker*), the *argument itself,* and the *reader* (or *audience*). Aristotle also reminds us that a writer's credibility (*ethos*) and appeals to the reader's logic (*logos*) and emotions (*pathos*) are important in understanding and evaluating an argument. Moreover, he notes that the occasion or "situation" (*kairos*) should be considered. Let's examine each part of this model of argument.

Ethos (about the Writer/Speaker)

It seems logical to begin with *ethos* because without this player we have no argument. We could, though, end with the writer because Aristotle asserts that this player in any argument is the most important. No argument, no matter how logical, no matter how appealing to one's audience, can succeed if the audience rejects the arguer's credibility, his or her *ethical* qualities.

Think how often in political contests those running attack their opponent's character rather than the candidate's programs. Remember the smear campaign against Obama—he is (or was) a Muslim and therefore unfit to be president, the first point an error of fact, the second point an emotional appeal to voters' fears. Candidates try these smear tactics, even without evidence, because they understand that every voter they can convince of an opponent's failure of *ethos* is a citizen who will vote for them.

Many American voters want to be assured that a candidate is patriotic, religious (but of course not fanatic!), a loyal spouse, and a loving parent. At times, we even lose sight of important differences in positions as we focus on the person instead. But this tells us how much an audience values their sense of the arguer's credibility. During his campaign for reelection, after the Watergate break-in, Nixon was attacked with the line "Would you buy a used car from this guy?" (In defense of used-car salespeople, not all are untrustworthy!)

Logos (about the Logic of the Argument)

Logos refers to the argument itself—to the assertion and the support for it. Aristotle maintains that part of an arguer's appeal to his or her audience lies in the logic of the argument and the quality of the support provided. Even the most credible of writers will not move thoughtful audiences with inadequate evidence or sloppy reasoning. Yes, "arguments" that appeal to emotions, to our needs and fantasies, will work for some audiences—look at the success of advertising, for example. But if you want to present a serious claim to critical readers, then you must pay attention to your argument. Paying attention means not only having good reasons but also organizing them clearly. Your audience needs to see *how* your evidence supports your point. Consider the following argument in opposition to the war on Iraq.

> War can be justified only as a form of self-defense. To initiate a war, we need to be able to show that our first strike was necessary as a form of self-defense. The Bush administration argued that Iraq had weapons of mass destruction and intended to use them against us. Responding to someone's "intent" to do harm is always a difficult judgment call. But in this case, there were no weapons of mass destruction, so there could not have been any intent to harm the United States, or at least none that was obvious and immediate. Thus we must conclude that this war was not the right course of action for the United States.

You may disagree (many will) with this argument's assertion, but you can respect the writer's logic, the clear connecting of one reason to the next. One good way to strengthen your credibility is to get respect for clear reasoning.

Pathos (about Appeals to the Audience)

Argument implies an audience, those whose views we want to influence in some way. Aristotle labels this player *pathos,* the Greek word for both passion and suffering (hence *pathology,* the study of disease). Arguers need to be aware of their audience's feelings on the issue, the attitudes and values that will affect their response to the argument.

There are really two questions arguers must answer: "How can I engage my audience's interest?" and "How can I engage their sympathy for my position?"

Some educators and health experts believe that childhood obesity is a major problem in the United States. Other Americans are much more focused on the economy—or their own careers. Al Gore is passionately concerned about the harmful effects of global warming; others, though increasingly fewer, think he lacks sufficient evidence of environmental degradation. How does a physician raise reader interest in childhood obesity? How does Gore convince doubters that we need to reduce carbon emissions? To prepare an effective argument, we need always to plan our approach with a clear vision of how best to connect to a specific audience—one that may or may not agree with our interests or our position.

Kairos (about the Occasion or Situation)

While *ethos, logos,* and *pathos* create the traditional three-part communication model, Aristotle adds another term to enhance our understanding of any argument "moment." The term *kairos* refers to the occasion for the argument, the situation that we are in. What does this moment call for from us? Is the lunch table the appropriate time and place for an argument with your coworker over her failure to meet a deadline that is part of a joint project? You have just received a 65 on your history test; is this the best time to e-mail your professor to protest the grade? Would the professor's office be the better place for your discussion than an e-mail sent just a few minutes after you have left class?

Personal confrontation at a business meeting: Not cool.

©George Doyle/Getty Images RF

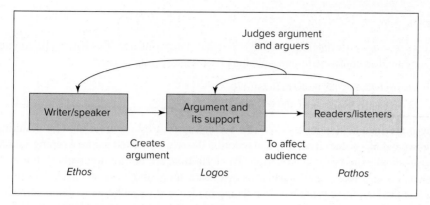

FIGURE 3.1 **Aristotelian Structure of Argument**

The concept of *kairos* asks us to consider what is most appropriate for the occasion, to think through the best time, place, and genre (type of argument) to make a successful argument. This concept has special meaning for students in a writing class who sometimes have difficulty thinking about audience at all. When practicing writing for the academic community, you may need to modify the language or tone that you use in other situations.

We argue in a specific context of three interrelated parts, as illustrated in Figure 3.1.

We present support for an assertion to a specific audience whose expectations and character we have given thought to when shaping our argument. And we present ourselves as informed, competent, and reliable so that our audience will give us their attention.

THE LANGUAGE OF ARGUMENT

We could title this section the *languages* of argument because arguments come in visual language as well as in words. But visual arguments—images, cartoons, photos, ads—are almost always accompanied by some words: figures speaking in bubbles, a caption, a slogan (Nike's "Just Do It!"). So we need to think about the kinds of statements that make up arguments, whether those arguments are legal briefs or cartoons, casual conversations or scholarly essays. To build an argument we need some statements that support other statements that present the main idea or claim of the argument.

- Claims: usually either inferences or judgments, for these are debatable assertions.
- Support: facts, opinions based on facts (inferences), or opinions based on values, beliefs, or ideas (judgments) or some combination of the three.

Let's consider what kinds of statements each of these terms describes.

Facts

Facts are statements that are verifiable. Factual statements refer to what can be counted or measured or confirmed by reasonable observers or trusted experts.

> There are twenty-six desks in Room 110.
>
> In the United States about 400,000 people die each year as a result of smoking.

These are factual statements. We can verify the first by observation—by counting. The second fact comes from medical records. We rely on trusted record-keeping sources and medical experts for verification. By definition, we do not argue about the facts. Usually. Sometimes "facts" change, as we learn more about our world. For example, only in the last thirty years has convincing evidence been gathered to demonstrate the relationship between smoking and various illnesses of the heart and lungs. And sometimes "facts" are false facts. These are statements that sound like facts but are incorrect. For example: Nadel has won more Wimbledon titles than Federer. Not so.

Inferences

Inferences are opinions based on facts. Inferences are the conclusions we draw from an analysis of facts.

> There will not be enough desks in Room 110 for upcoming fall-semester classes.
>
> Smoking is a serious health hazard.

Predictions of an increase in student enrollment for the coming fall semester lead to the inference that most English classes scheduled in Room 110 will run with several more students per class than last year. The dean should order new desks. Similarly, we infer from the number of deaths that smoking is a health problem; statistics show more people dying from tobacco than from AIDS, or murder, or car accidents, causes of death that get media coverage but do not produce nearly as many deaths.

Inferences vary in their closeness to the facts supporting them. That the sun will "rise" tomorrow is an inference, but we count on its happening, acting as if it is a fact. However, the first inference stated above is based not just on the fact of twenty-six desks but on another inference—a projected increase in student enrollment—and two assumptions. The argument looks like this:

FACT:	There are twenty-six desks in Room 110.
INFERENCE:	There will be more first-year students next year.
ASSUMPTIONS:	1. English will remain a required course.
	2. No additional classrooms are available for English classes.
CLAIM:	There will not be enough desks in Room 110 for upcoming fall-semester classes.

This inference could be challenged by a different analysis of the facts supporting enrollment projections. Or, if additional rooms can be found, the dean will not need to order new desks. Inferences can be part of the support of an argument, or they can be the claim of an argument.

Judgments

Judgments are opinions based on values, beliefs, or philosophical concepts. (Judgments also include opinions based on personal preferences, but we have already excluded these from argument.) Judgments concern right and wrong, good and bad, better or worse, should and should not:

> No more than twenty-six students should be enrolled in any English class.
>
> Cigarette advertising should be eliminated, and the federal government should develop an antismoking campaign.

> **NOTE:** Placing such qualifiers as "I believe," "I think," or "I feel" in an assertion does not free you from the need to support that claim. The statement "I believe that President Obama was a great president" calls for an argument based on evidence and reasons.

To support the first judgment, we need to explain what constitutes overcrowding, or what constitutes the best class size for effective teaching. If we can support our views on effective teaching, we may be able to convince the college president that ordering more desks for Room 110 is not the best solution to an increasing enrollment in English classes. The second judgment also offers a solution to a problem, in this case a national health problem. To reduce the number of deaths, we need to reduce the number of smokers, either by encouraging smokers to quit or nonsmokers not to start. The underlying assumption: Advertising does affect behavior.

EXERCISE: Facts, Inferences, and Judgments

Compile a list of three statements of fact, three inferences, and three judgments. Try to organize them into three related sets, as illustrated here:

- Smoking is prohibited in some restaurants.
- Secondhand smoke is a health hazard.
- Smoking should be prohibited in all restaurants.

We can classify judgments to see better what kind of assertion we are making and, therefore, what kind of support we need to argue effectively.

FUNCTIONAL JUDGMENTS (guidelines for judging how something or someone works or could work)

Tiger Woods is the best golfer to play the game.

Antismoking advertising will reduce the number of smokers.

AESTHETIC JUDGMENTS (guidelines for judging art, literature, music, or natural scenes)

The sunrise was beautiful.

The Great Gatsby's structure, characters, and symbols are perfectly wedded to create the
novel's vision of the American dream.

ETHICAL JUDGMENTS (guidelines for group or social behavior)

Lawyers should not advertise.

It is discourteous to talk during a film or lecture.

MORAL JUDGMENTS (guidelines of right and wrong for judging individuals and for establishing legal principles)

Taking another person's life is wrong.

Equal rights under the law should not be denied on the basis of race or gender.

Functional and aesthetic judgments generally require defining key terms and establishing
criteria for the judging or ranking made by the assertion. How, for example, do we
compare golfers? On the amount of money won? The number of tournaments won? Or
the consistency of winning throughout one's career? What about the golfer's quality and
range of shots? Ethical and moral judgments may be more difficult to support because
they depend not just on how terms are defined and criteria established but on values and
beliefs as well. If taking another person's life is wrong, why isn't it wrong in war? Or is
it? These are difficult questions that require thoughtful debate.

EXERCISES: Understanding Assumptions, Facts, False Facts, Inferences, and Judgments

1.   Categorize the judgments you wrote for the previous exercise (p. 71) as aesthetic,
     moral, ethical, or functional. Alternatively, compile a list of three judgments that
     you then categorize.

2.   For each judgment listed for exercise 1, generate one statement of support, either a
     fact or an inference or another judgment. Then state any underlying assumptions
     that are part of each argument.

3.   Read the following article and then complete the exercise that follows. This exer-
     cise tests both careful reading and your understanding of the differences among
     facts, inferences, and judgments.

YOUR BRAIN LIES TO YOU | SAM WANG and SANDRA AAMODT

Dr. Samuel S. H. Wang is a professor of molecular biology and neuroscience at
Princeton, where he manages a research lab. Dr. Sandra Aamodt, former editor of
Nature Neuroscience, is a freelance science writer. Drs. Wang and Aamodt are the
authors of *Welcome to Your Brain: Why You Lose Your Car Keys but Never Forget How
to Drive and Other Puzzles of Everyday Life* (2008). They also manage a blog—"Welcome
to Your Brain."

False beliefs are everywhere. Eighteen percent of Americans think the sun   1
revolves around the earth, one poll has found. Thus it seems slightly less egre-
gious that, according to another poll, 10 percent of us think that Senator Barack
Obama, a Christian, is instead a Muslim. The Obama campaign has created a
Web site to dispel misinformation. But this effort may be more difficult than it
seems, thanks to the quirky way in which our brains store memories—and
mislead us along the way.

The brain does not simply gather and stockpile information as a computer's   2
hard drive does. Current research suggests that facts may be stored first in the
hippocampus, a structure deep in the brain about the size and shape of a fat
man's curled pinkie finger. But the information does not rest there. Every time we
recall it, our brain writes it down again, and during this re-storage, it is also repro-
cessed. In time, the fact is gradually transferred to the cerebral cortex and is
separated from the context in which it was originally learned. For example, you
know that the capital of California is Sacramento, but you probably don't remember how you learned it.

This phenomenon, known as source amnesia, can also lead people to forget   3
whether a statement is true. Even when a lie is presented with a disclaimer,
people often later remember it as true.

With time, this misremembering only gets worse. A false statement from a   4
non-credible source that is at first not believed can gain credibility during the
months it takes to reprocess memories from short-term hippocampal storage to
longer-term cortical storage. As the source is forgotten, the message and its
implications gain strength. This could explain why, during the 2004 presidential
campaign, it took some weeks for the Swift Boat Veterans for Truth campaign
against Senator John Kerry to have an effect on his standing in the polls.

Even if they do not understand the neuroscience behind source amnesia,   5
campaign strategists can exploit it to spread misinformation. They know that if
their message is initially memorable, its impression will persist long after it is
debunked. In repeating a falsehood, someone may back it up with an opening
line like "I think I read somewhere" or even with a reference to a specific
source.

In one study, a group of Stanford students was exposed repeatedly to an   6
unsubstantiated claim taken from a Web site that Coca-Cola is an effective paint
thinner. Students who read the statement five times were nearly one-third more
likely than those who read it only twice to attribute it to *Consumer Reports* (rather
than *The National Enquirer,* their other choice), giving it a gloss of credibility.

Adding to this innate tendency to mold information we recall is the way our   7
brains fit facts into established mental frameworks. We tend to remember news
that accords with our worldview, and discount statements that contradict it.

In another Stanford study, 48 students, half of whom said they favored   8
capital punishment and half of whom said they opposed it, were presented with
two pieces of evidence, one supporting and one contradicting the claim that
capital punishment deters crime. Both groups were more convinced by the
evidence that supported their initial position.

9   Psychologists have suggested that legends propagate by striking an emotional chord. In the same way, ideas can spread by emotional selection, rather than by their factual merits, encouraging the persistence of falsehoods about Coke—or about a presidential candidate.

10   Journalists and campaign workers may think they are acting to counter misinformation by pointing out that it is not true. But by repeating a false rumor, they may inadvertently make it stronger. In its concerted effort to "stop the smears," the Obama campaign may want to keep this in mind. Rather than emphasize that Mr. Obama is not a Muslim, for instance, it may be more effective to stress that he embraced Christianity as a young man.

11   Consumers of news, for their part, are prone to selectively accept and remember statements that reinforce beliefs they already hold. In a replication of the study of students' impressions of evidence about the death penalty, researchers found that even when subjects were given a specific instruction to be objective, they were still inclined to reject evidence that disagreed with their beliefs.

12   In the same study, however, when subjects were asked to imagine their reaction if the evidence had pointed to the opposite conclusion, they were more open-minded to information that contradicted their beliefs. Apparently, it pays for consumers of controversial news to take a moment and consider that the opposite interpretation may be true.

13   In 1919, Justice Oliver Wendell Holmes of the Supreme Court wrote that "the best test of truth is the power of the thought to get itself accepted in the competition of the market." Holmes erroneously assumed that ideas are more likely to spread if they are honest. Our brains do not naturally obey this admirable dictum, but by better understanding the mechanisms of memory perhaps we can move closer to Holmes's ideal.

Sam Wang and Sandra Aamodt, "Your Brain Lies to You," *The New York Times*, 27 June 2008. Reprinted by permission of the authors.

Label each of the following sentences as F (fact), FF (false fact), I (inference), or J (judgment).

_____ 1. Campaigns have trouble getting rid of misinformation about their candidate.

_____ 2. When we reprocess information we may get the information wrong, but we always remember the source.

_____ 3. The Obama campaign should have stressed that he became a Christian as a young man.

_____ 4. Most of us remember information that matches our view of the world.

_____ 5. When students were told to be objective in evaluating evidence, they continued to reject evidence they disagreed with.

_____ 6. Coke is an effective paint thinner.

_____ 7. True statements should be accepted and false statements rejected.

_____ 8. Justice Holmes was wrong about the power of truth to spread more widely than falsehood.

_____ 9. The more we understand about the way the world works, the better our chances of separating truth from falsehood.

_____ 10. Americans do not seem to understand basic science.

■ ■

THE SHAPE OF ARGUMENT: WHAT WE CAN LEARN FROM TOULMIN

British philosopher Stephen Toulmin adds to what we have learned from Aristotle by focusing our attention on the basics of the argument itself. First, consider this definition of argument: *An argument consists of evidence and/or reasons presented in support of an assertion or claim that is either stated or implied.* For example:

CLAIM:	We should not go skiing today
GROUNDS:	because it is too cold.
GROUNDS:	Because some laws are unjust,
CLAIM:	civil disobedience is sometimes justified.
GROUNDS:	It's only fair and right for academic institutions to
CLAIM:	accept students only on academic merit.

The parts of an argument, Toulmin asserts, are actually a bit more complex than these examples suggest. Each argument has a third part that is not stated in the preceding examples. This third part is the "glue" that connects the support—the evidence and reasons—to the argument's claim and thus fulfills the logic of the argument. Toulmin calls this glue an argument's *warrants.* These are the principles or assumptions that allow us to assert that our evidence or reasons—what Toulmin calls the *grounds*—do indeed support our claim. Figure 3.2 illustrates these basics of the Toulmin model of argument.

CLAIM:	Academic institutions should accept students only on academic merit.
GROUNDS:	It is only fair and right.
WARRANT:	(1) Fair and right are important values. (2) Academic institutions are only about academics.

FIGURE 3.2 **The Toulmin Structure of Argument**

Look again at the sample arguments to see what warrants must be accepted to make each argument work:

CLAIM:	We should not go skiing today.
GROUNDS:	It is too cold.
WARRANTS:	When it is too cold, skiing is not fun; the activity is not sufficient to keep one from becoming uncomfortable. AND: Too cold is what is too cold for me.

CLAIM:	Civil disobedience is sometimes justified.
EVIDENCE:	Some laws are unjust.
WARRANTS:	To get unjust laws changed, people need to be made aware of the injustice. Acts of civil disobedience will get people's attention and make them aware that the laws need changing.

Warrants play an important role in any argument, so we need to be sure to understand what they are. Note, for instance, the second warrant operating in the first argument: The temperature considered uncomfortable for the speaker will also be uncomfortable for her companions—an uncertain assumption. In the second argument, the warrant is less debatable, for acts of civil disobedience usually get media coverage and thus dramatize the issue. The underlying assumptions in the third example stress the need to know one's warrants. Both warrants will need to be defended in the debate over selection by academic merit only.

COLLABORATIVE EXERCISE: Building Arguments

With your class partner or in small groups, examine each of the following claims. Select two, think of one statement that could serve as evidence for each claim, and then think of the underlying assumption(s) that complete each of the arguments.

1. Professor X is not a good instructor.
2. Americans need to reduce the fat in their diets.
3. Tiger Woods is a great golfer.
4. Military women should be allowed to serve in combat zones.
5. College newspapers should be free of supervision by faculty or administrators.

Toulmin was particularly interested in the great range or strength or probability of various arguments. Some kinds of arguments are stronger than others because of the language or logic they use. Other arguments must, necessarily, be heavily qualified for the claim to be supportable. Toulmin developed his language to provide a strategy for analyzing the degree of probability in a given argument and to remind us of the need to qualify some kinds of claims. You have already seen how the idea of warrants, or assumptions, helps us think about the "glue" that presumably makes a given argument work. Taken together, Toulmin terms and concepts help us analyze the arguments of others and prepare more convincing arguments of our own.

Claims

A claim is what the argument asserts or seeks to prove. It answers the question "What is your point?" In an argumentative speech or essay, the claim is the speaker's or writer's main idea or thesis. Although an argument's claim "follows" from reasons and evidence, we often present an argument—whether written or spoken—with the claim stated near the beginning of the presentation. We can better understand an argument's claim by recognizing that we can have claims of fact, claims of value, and claims of policy.

Claims of Fact

Although facts usually support claims, we do argue over some facts. Historians and biographers may argue over what happened in the past, although they are more likely to argue over the significance of what happened. Scientists also argue over the facts, over how to classify an unearthed fossil, or whether the fossil indicates that the animal had feathers. For example:

CLAIM: The small, predatory dinosaur *Deinonychus* hunted its prey in packs.

This claim is supported by the discovery of several fossils of *Deinonychus* close together and with the fossil bones of a much larger dinosaur. Their teeth have also been found in or near the bones of dinosaurs that have died in a struggle.

Assertions about what will happen are sometimes classified as claims of fact, but they can also be labeled as inferences supported by facts. Predictions about a future event may be classified as claims of fact:

CLAIM: The United States will win the most gold medals at the 2016 Olympics.

CLAIM: I will get an A on tomorrow's psychology test.

What evidence would you use to support each of these claims? (And, did the first one turn out to be correct?)

Claims of Value

These include moral, ethical, and aesthetic judgments. Assertions that use such words as *good* or *bad, better* or *worse,* and *right* or *wrong* will be claims of value. The following are all claims of value:

CLAIM: Roger Federer is a better tennis player than Andy Roddick.

CLAIM: *Adventures of Huckleberry Finn* is one of the most significant American novels.

CLAIM: Cheating hurts others and the cheater too.

CLAIM: Abortion is wrong.

Arguments in support of judgments demand relevant evidence, careful reasoning, and an awareness of the assumptions one is making. Support for claims of value often include other value statements. For example, to support the claim that censorship is bad, arguers often assert that the free exchange of ideas is good and necessary in a democracy. The support is itself a value statement.

Claims of Policy

Finally, claims of policy are assertions about what should or should not happen, what the government ought or ought not to do, how to best solve social problems. Claims of policy debate, for example, college rules, state gun laws, or federal aid to Africans suffering from AIDS. The following are claims of policy:

CLAIM:	College newspapers should not be controlled in any way by college authorities.
CLAIM:	States should not have laws allowing people to carry concealed weapons.
CLAIM:	The United States must provide more aid to African countries where 25 percent or more of the citizens have tested positive for HIV.

Claims of policy are often closely tied to judgments of morality or political philosophy, but they also need to be grounded in feasibility. That is, your claim needs to be doable, to be based on a thoughtful consideration of the real world and the complexities of public policy issues.

Grounds (or Data or Evidence)

The term *grounds* refers to the reasons and evidence provided in support of a claim. Although the words *data* and *evidence* can also be used, note that *grounds* is the most general term because it includes reasons or logic as well as examples or statistics. We determine the grounds of an argument by asking the question "Why do you think that?" or "How do you know that?" When writing your own arguments, you can ask yourself these questions and answer by using a *because* clause:

CLAIM:	Smoking should be banned in restaurants because
GROUNDS:	secondhand smoke is a serious health hazard.
CLAIM:	Federer is a better tennis player than Roddick because
GROUNDS:	1. he was ranked number one longer,
	2. he won more tournaments than Roddick, and
	3. he won more major tournaments than Roddick.

Warrants

Why should we believe that your grounds do indeed support your claim? Your argument's warrants answer this question. They explain why your evidence really is evidence. Sometimes warrants reside in language itself, in the meanings of the words we are using. If I am *younger* than my brother, then my brother must be *older* than I am. In a court case attempting to prove that Jones murdered Smith, the relation of evidence to claim is less assured. If the police investigation has been properly managed and the physical evidence is substantial, then Smith may be Jones's murderer. The prosecution has—presumably beyond a reasonable doubt—established motive, means, and opportunity for Smith to commit the murder. In many arguments based on statistical data, the argument's warrant rests on complex analyses of the statistics—and on the conviction that the statistics have been developed without error.

Still, without taking courses in statistics and logic, you can develop an alertness to the "good sense" of some arguments and the "dubious sense" of others. You know, for example, that good SAT scores are a predictor of success in college. Can you argue that you will do well in college because you have good SATs? No. We can determine only a statistical probability. We cannot turn probabilities about a group of people into a warrant about one person in the group. (In addition, SAT scores are only one predictor. Another key variable is motivation.)

What is the warrant for the Federer claim?

CLAIM:	Federer is a better tennis player than Roddick.
GROUNDS:	The three facts listed above.
WARRANT:	It is appropriate to judge and rank tennis players on these kinds of statistics. That is, the better player is one who has held the number-one ranking for the longest time, has won the most tournaments, and also has won the most major tournaments.

Backing

Standing behind an argument's warrant may be additional *backing*. Backing answers the question "How do we know that your evidence is good evidence?" You may answer this question by providing authoritative sources for the data used (for example, the Census Bureau or the U.S. Tennis Association). Or, you may explain in detail the methodology of the experiments performed or the surveys taken. When scientists and social scientists present the results of their research, they anticipate the question of backing and automatically provide a detailed explanation of the process by which they acquired their evidence. In criminal trials, defense attorneys challenge the backing of the prosecution's argument. They question the handling of blood samples sent to labs for DNA testing, for instance. The defense attorneys want jury members to doubt the *quality* of the evidence.

This discussion of backing returns us to the point that one part of any argument is the audience. To create an effective argument, ask yourself: Will my warrants and backing be accepted? Is my audience likely to share my values, religious beliefs, or scientific approach? If you are speaking to a group at your church, then backing based on the religious beliefs of that church may be effective. If you are preparing an argument for a general audience, then using specific religious assertions as warrants or backing probably will not result in an effective argument.

Qualifiers

Some arguments are absolute; they can be stated without qualification. *If I am younger than my brother, then he must be older than I am.* Most arguments need some qualification; many need precise limitations. If, when playing bridge, I am dealt eight spades, then my opponents and partner together must have five spade cards—because there are thirteen cards of each suit in a deck. My partner *probably* has one spade but *could* be void of spades. My partner *possibly* has two or more spades, but I would be foolish to count on it. When bidding my hand, I must be controlled by the laws of probability. Look again at the smoking-ban claim. Observe the absolute nature of both the claim and its support. If second-hand smoke is indeed a health hazard, it will be that in *all* restaurants, not just in some. With each argument ask what qualification is needed for a successful argument.

Sweeping generalizations often come to us in the heat of a debate or when we first start to think about an issue. For example: *Gun control is wrong because it restricts individual rights.* But on reflection surely you would not want to argue against all forms of gun control. (Remember: An unqualified assertion is understood by your audience to be absolute.) Would you sell guns to felons in jail or to children on the way to school? Obviously not. So, let's try the claim again, this time with two important qualifiers:

QUALIFIED CLAIM:	Adults without a criminal record should not be restricted in the purchase of guns.

Others may want this claim further qualified to eliminate particular types of guns or to control the number purchased or the process for purchasing. The gun-control debate is not about absolutes; it is all about which qualified claim is best.

Rebuttals

Arguments can be challenged. Smart debaters assume that there are people who will disagree with them. They anticipate the ways that opponents can challenge their arguments. When you are planning an argument, you need to think about how you can counter or rebut the challenges you anticipate. Think of yourself as an attorney in a court case preparing your argument *and* a defense of the other attorney's challenges to your argument. If you ignore the important role of rebuttals, you may not win the jury to your side.

USING TOULMIN'S TERMS TO ANALYZE ARGUMENTS

Terms are never an end in themselves; we learn them when we recognize that they help us to organize our thinking about a subject. Toulmin's terms can aid your reading of the arguments of others. You can "see what's going on" in an argument if you analyze it, applying Toulmin's language to its parts. Not all terms will be useful for every analysis because, for example, some arguments will not have qualifiers or rebuttals. But to recognize that an argument is *without qualifiers* is to learn something important about that argument.

First, here is a simple argument broken down into its parts using Toulmin's terms:

GROUNDS:	Because Dr. Bradshaw has an attendance policy,
CLAIM:	students who miss more than seven classes will
QUALIFIER:	most likely (last year, Dr. Bradshaw did allow one student, in unusual circumstances, to continue in the class) be dropped from the course.
WARRANT:	Dr. Bradshaw's syllabus explains her attendance policy, a
BACKING:	policy consistent with the concept of a discussion class that depends on student participation and consistent with the attendance policies of most of her colleagues.
REBUTTAL:	Although some students complain about an attendance policy of any kind, Dr. Bradshaw does explain her policy and her reasons for it the first day of class. She then reminds students that the syllabus is a contract between them; if they choose to stay, they agree to abide by the guidelines explained on the syllabus.

This argument is brief and fairly simple. Let's see how Toulmin's terms can help us analyze a longer, more complex argument. Read actively and annotate the following essay while noting the existing annotations using Toulmin's terms. Then answer the questions that follow the article.

THE SECRET TO EFFICIENT TEAMWORK IS RIDICULOUSLY SIMPLE | ERIN BRODWIN

Erin Brodwin is the science editor for *Business Insider* and has published in other magazines, such as *Scientific American*, *Popular Science*, *Newsweek*, and *Psychology Today*. She received a bachelor's from the University of California, San Diego, and a master's degree from the City University of New York's Graduate School of Journalism. This article was published in *Business Insider* on January 23, 2015.

PREREADING QUESTIONS Why do you think women are paid less than men? Why do you think women do not advance as far as men in the workplace?

Want to avoid another boring, unproductive meeting? **1**   *Introduction*

Invite more women. **2**   *Primary claim*

Two new studies from scientists at MIT, Carnegie Mellon, and Union College **3**   *Grounds*
suggest the most efficient groups—the ones who are the best at collaborating, analyzing problems, and solving them the fastest and most effectively—weren't comprised simply of the smartest people.

Instead, they had just three things in common, one of which was simply that **4**
they had more women.

You might be thinking to yourself, well of course the more *diverse* teams did **5**   *Anticipated challenge*
better; the greater the range of opinions and ideas, the better, right?

Not quite. The groups in the study didn't get smarter when they simply **6**   *Rebuttal*
included an even number of women and men. It was even more specific than   *Secondary claim*
that: **The more women a team had, the better they performed.**

This result makes a little more sense in light of another part of the study **7**   *Backing*
which looked at how well the members of a team could read the emotions of their fellow teammates. Women did consistently better on this test, which involved looking at images of people's faces in which only their eye regions were showing and identifying what complex emotion they were feeling, from shame to curiosity.

Here's a female example from the emotion-reading test: The word choices **8**
were reflective, aghast, irritated, and impatient. Which emotion do you think she's feeling?

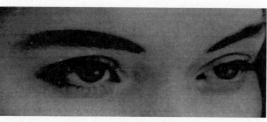

©Courtesy of Simon Baron-Cohen

"Reading the Mind in the Eyes" Test Revised Version.

9   Reflective was the correct choice.

10   In this test and others designed to measure how well a person can read and interpret others' feelings, women consistently score higher than men—a concept known as "emotional intelligence" and first coined by psychologist Daniel Goleman in 1995.

11   In another large study from this year of more than 4,600 people, for example, women scored higher in almost all aspects of emotional intelligence (labeled EIQ in this chart for shorthand), including understanding, facilitating, and managing emotions, than their male counterparts.

	MALES	FEMALES
Perception	7.40 (1.8)	8.03 (1.7)
Understanding	6.78 (1.6)	7.43 (1.6)
Facilitation	6.55 (1.6)	7.02 (1.5)
Management	5.88 (1.4)	6.57 (1.4)
TIE Total	26.62 (5.2)	29.06 (5.0)

Women outperformed men in every subscale of the TIE, and consequently in the total score.
"TIE: An Ability Test of Emotional Intelligence," PLOS One.

12   These results held steady even when teams weren't physically together but instead worked exclusively online. Even without being able to see their fellow team-members' faces, women performed consistently better than men at gauging other people's emotions.

13   How do they do this? It's called *reading between the lines.*

14   Oh yeah. Recent research has suggested that when it comes to picking out the emotional undercurrents of emails and texts, the vast majority of us are usually way off base (Does an extra exclamation mark mean she's being sarcastic, or extra enthusiastic?!).

Warrant

15   But those of us who can accurately detect the hidden emotions in the written word are also, perhaps, the ones who are better at working together in groups. And more often than not, those people tend to be female.

Warrant continued

Primary claim restated through implied terms

16   This finding squares with other research on women in professional leadership roles. One recent report found, for example, that companies with women on their boards had far higher average returns on equity than those without women on their boards; another concluded that companies led by female CEOs outperform companies led by male CEOs by nearly 50%.

Erin Brodwin, "The Secret to Efficient Teamwork Is Ridiculously Simple," *Business Insider,* 23 Jan. 2015. Copyright ©2015 Business Insider. Used with permission.

QUESTIONS FOR READING

1. What is Brodwin's subject? (Women in the workplace is not sufficiently precise as an answer.)

2. What does new research show about women and their impact on teams and efficiency in the workplace?

3. According to psychologists, what are the reasons behind the differences between women and men who work in teams?

QUESTIONS FOR REASONING AND ANALYSIS

4. What is Brodwin's claim?

5. What is her primary support? (Add a "because" clause to her claim to find her grounds.)

6. Review the author's comments about women in the workplace. What, in Brodwin's view, is their reason for performing differently than men? Does the author provide evidence for this warrant? Is support needed?

QUESTIONS FOR REFLECTION AND WRITING

7. Reflect on the author's position regarding women in the workplace. Do you believe Brodwin's claim? Do you agree with her conclusion?

8. Brodwin asserts that women simply *read between the lines* more effectively than do men. If this is the case, how might businesses and non-profit organizations apply this skill to increase efficiency? And how might these organizations "train up" men who may be lagging in emotional IQ, or EIQ?

9. How can professional organizations increase their number of female employees?

Toulmin's terms can help you to see what writers are actually "doing" in their arguments. Just remember that writers do not usually follow the terms in precise order. Indeed, you can find both grounds and backing in the same sentence, or claim and qualifiers in the same paragraph, and so on. Still, the terms can help you to sort out your thinking about a claim you want to support. Now use your knowledge of argument as you read and analyze the following arguments.

FOR ANALYSIS AND DEBATE

A SAFE PLACE FOR FREEDOM OF EXPRESSION | CHRISTINA PAXSON

The 19th president of Brown University since 2012, Christina Paxson holds a PhD in economics from Columbia University. She taught at Princeton and was Dean of the Wilson School there before moving to Brown. In this essay, published in 2016, she presents her views on a college's search for balance between free speech and protecting students.

PREREADING QUESTIONS Consider Paxson's title. What view of campus speech do you think she will develop?

New students are entering colleges and universities at a time of fierce 1 debate about whether institutions of higher education are becoming places that stifle speech in the interest of protecting students from ideas and perspectives they don't want to hear. In the clash over freedom of expression and the supposed coddling of American college students, safe spaces and trigger warnings are held up as the poster children of overprotective universities.

2   In the setting of private institutions, this is not a First Amendment issue. Private colleges and universities could restrict the expression of ideas and beliefs within their campuses, if they chose to do so. But most private colleges and universities wisely do *not* make this choice. Instead, colleges and universities protect the rights of members of their communities to express a full range of ideas, however controversial.

3   That is because freedom of expression is an essential component of academic freedom, which protects the ability of universities to fulfill their core mission of advancing knowledge. Suppressing ideas at a university is akin to turning off the power at a factory. As scholars and students, our responsibility is to subject old truths to scrutiny and put forward new ideas to improve them.

4   At universities, we also advance understanding about issues of justice and fairness, and these discussions can be equally, if not more, difficult. From the earliest days of this country, college campuses have been the sites of fierce debates about slavery, war, women's rights and racial justice. These discussions create rocky moments, and they should.

5   If we don't have these debates—if we limit the flow of ideas—then in 50 years we will be no better than we are today.

6   I don't share the view that American college students want to be protected from ideas that make them uncomfortable. Just the opposite. Over the past few years, our students have addressed topics that make many people very uncomfortable indeed—racism, sexual assault, religious persecution. These are some of the toughest problems facing society today, and we do not shy away from them.

7   As for "safe spaces"—the term is used in so many different ways that it is impossible to discuss it without being precise about its meaning. The term emerged from the women's movement nearly 50 years ago to refer to forums where women's rights issues were discussed. Then it was extended to denote spaces where violence and harassment against the lesbian, gay, bisexual, transgender and queer community would not be tolerated, and then extended yet again to mean places where students from marginalized groups can come together to feel comfortable discussing their experiences and just being themselves.

8   If this is what a safe space means, then, yes, Brown has them. Proudly. And even the campuses that decry these spaces have them also. I'm not talking about rooms with Play-Doh and coloring books like one set up by Brown campus organizers specifically as a resource to support survivors of sexual assault in one instance some years ago. There have been many unfortunate mischaracterizations in the media of the intent of that support space as a so-called shield from ideas.

9   Rather, we see safe spaces in the choices our students make every day. Students find many opportunities through clubs and organizations to meet those who share similar backgrounds and interests—religious, political and otherwise.

10   In her memoir *My Beloved World*, Supreme Court Justice Sonia Sotomayor talks about Acción Puertorriqueña, a Princeton group for students of Puerto Rican heritage. Although she made it a point to develop relationships with people

from different backgrounds, that group gave her a much-needed anchor in an unfamiliar environment. Maybe this isn't what the critics mean when they deride "safe spaces," but these spaces deserve to exist at colleges across the country.

I would say the same for trigger warnings, which are meant to alert students 11 who have been subjected to trauma, such as sexual assault and combat, that some material in class may be disturbing. Faculty should be free to use them at their discretion.

My final point—often missed in the media debates—is this: Universities are 12 doing something difficult and important. We are grappling with how to create peaceful, just and prosperous societies, even as we live in a society that often feels more divided and rancorous than ever, fractured along lines of race, ethnicity, income and ideology.

With the right of academic freedom comes the moral responsibility to think 13 carefully about how that right is exercised in the service of society to confront these divides.

At Brown, as at many institutions of higher education, we are not coddling 14 our students—or limiting freedom of expression. Instead, we are teaching them, encouraging them and giving them the space to have the discussions that will make them better scholars and prepare them to best serve society.

Christina Paxson, "Brown University President: A Safe Space for Freedom of Expression," *The Washington Post,* 5 Sept. 2016. Reprinted by permission of Dr. Christina Paxson, President, Brown University

QUESTIONS FOR READING

1. What, in Paxson's view, is the purpose of a university?
2. Why is freedom of expression essential to fulfill that purpose?
3. What did safe spaces mean initially? What has the term evolved to mean?
4. What is the purpose of trigger warnings?

QUESTIONS FOR REASONING AND ANALYSIS

5. What is the author's claim? What are her reasons and evidence in support of this claim?
6. Who does the author blame for distorting, in her view, the value of safe spaces and trigger warnings? How does this advance her argument?
7. Examine Paxson's opening paragraphs. What does she seek to gain with her lengthy introduction?

QUESTIONS FOR REFLECTION AND WRITING

8. Are you aware of the view that American colleges have become overly protective of students? Do you think this view is accurate? Why or why not?
9. Paxson asserts that her university fosters debate and free expression while also providing safe spaces and trigger warnings. Is it possible to have both? If you agree, how can you add to the author's argument? If you disagree, how would you refute Paxson?

FREE SPEECH ON CAMPUS | GEOFFREY R. STONE

A noted American law and First Amendment scholar, Geoffrey Stone holds an endowed chair at The University of Chicago Law School. Stone's most recently published book is *Sex and the Constitution: Sex, Religion, and Law from America's Origins to the Twenty-First Century* (2017). What follows is a speech he gave to the American Law Institute on May 17, 2016.

PREREADING QUESTIONS Given his recent book and his opening paragraph below, what approach to Stone's discussion of free speech might you expect? What might be gained by this approach?

1   Academic freedom is *not* a law of nature. It is not something to be taken for granted. It is, rather, a hard-bought acquisition in a lengthy struggle for academic integrity.

2   Indeed, until well into the 19th century, real freedom of thought was neither practiced nor professed in American universities. To the contrary, any real freedom of inquiry or expression in American colleges in this era was smothered by the prevailing theory of "doctrinal moralism," which assumed that the worth of an idea must be judged by what the institution's leaders thought its moral value to be. Thus, through the first half of the nineteenth century, American higher education squelched any notion of free discussion or intellectual curiosity. Indeed, as the nation moved towards Civil War, any professor or student in the North who defended slavery, or any professor or student in the South who challenged slavery, could readily be dismissed, disciplined, or expelled.

3   Between 1870 and 1900, though, there was a genuine revolution in American higher education. With the battle over Darwinism, new academic goals came to be embraced. For the first time, to criticize, as well as to preserve, traditional moral values and understandings became an accepted function of higher education. By 1892, William Rainey Harper, the first president of The University of Chicago, could boldly assert: "When for any reason the administration of a university attempts to dislodge a professor or punish a student because of his political or religious sentiments, at that moment the institution has ceased to be a university."

4   But, despite such sentiments, the battle for academic freedom has been a contentious and a continuing one. In the closing years of the 19th century, for example, businessmen who had accumulated vast industrial wealth began to support universities on an unprecedented scale. But that support was not without strings, and during this era professors who offended wealthy trustees by criticizing the ethics of their business practices were dismissed from such leading universities as Cornell and Stanford.

5   Then, during World War I, when patriotic zealots persecuted and even prosecuted those who questioned the wisdom or the morality of the war, universities collapsed almost completely in their defense of academic freedom. Students and professors were systematically expelled or fired at such institutions as Columbia and Virginia merely for "encouraging a spirit of indifference towards the war."

6   Similar issues arose again, with a vengeance, during the age of McCarthy. In the late 1940s and 1950s, most universities excluded those even suspected of

Students protest against a speaker on the Texas A&M campus.

entertaining Communist sympathies from university life. Yale President Charles Seymour went so far as to boast that "there will be no witch hunts at Yale, because there will be no witches. We will neither admit nor hire anyone with Communist sympathies."

We now face a similar set of challenges. We live today in an era of political correctness in which students themselves demand censorship, and colleges and universities, afraid to offend their students, too often surrender academic freedom to charges of offense.   7

To give just a few examples, several colleges and universities, including Brown, Johns Hopkins, and Williams, have recently withdrawn speaker invitations because of student objections to the views of the invited speakers, Northwestern University recently subjected a professor to a sustained sexual harassment investigation for publishing an essay in the *Chronicle of Higher Education* criticizing Northwestern's sexual harassment investigations, Colorado College suspended a student for making a joke that mocked feminism, William & Mary, DePaul University, and the University of Colorado all disciplined students for criticizing their affirmative action programs, and the University of Kansas disciplined a professor for condemning the National Rifle Association.   8

At Wesleyan University, after the school newspaper published a student op-ed criticizing the Black Lives Matter movement, other students demanded that the university defund the school paper; at Amherst College, students demanded that the administration remove posters stating that "All Lives Matter;" at Emory University, students demanded that the university punish other students who had chalked "Trump in 2016" on the university's sidewalks because, in their words, a university is "supposed to be a safe place and this made us feel unsafe;" and at Harvard, African-   9

American students demanded that a professor be taken to the woodshed for saying in class that he would be "lynched" if he gave a closed book examination.

10   The latter is an example of so-called micro-aggressions—words or phrases that may make students uncomfortable or may make them feel "unsafe." Saying "off the reservation" has been deemed a micro-aggression to Native Americans, saying "America is a melting pot" has been deemed a micro-aggression to new immigrants, and saying "As a woman, I know what you must go through as a racial minority" has been deemed a micro-aggression to racial minorities. Such micro-aggressions, whether used by faculty or students, have been deemed punishable by colleges and universities across the nation. A recent survey revealed that 72% of current college students support disciplinary action against any student or faculty member who expresses views that they deem "racist, sexist, homophobic or otherwise offensive."

11   Another recent invention is the trigger warning. A trigger warning is a requirement that before professors assign readings or hold classes that might make some students feel uncomfortable, they must warn students in advance that the readings or the class will deal with such sensitive topics as rape, affirmative action, abortion, murder, slavery, the Holocaust, religion, homosexuality, or immigration. The idea is that students who would be upset can then avoid having to deal with such emotionally fraught material.

12   So, where did all this come from? It was not too long ago when college students were demanding the right to free speech. Now, they demand the right to be free from speech that they find to be offensive, upsetting, or emotionally disturbing. The current phenomenon is based on the assumption that students should not be made to feel uncomfortable or unsafe.

13   One often-expressed theory is that this has happened because students of this generation, unlike their predecessors, are weak, fragile, and emotionally unstable. The explanation is that this generation of young adults has been raised by so-called helicopter parents, who have protected, rewarded, and celebrated them in every way from the time they were infants. They have therefore never learned to deal with challenge, defeat, uncertainty, anxiety, stress, insult, or fear.

14   On this view, this generation of college students is, in fact, emotionally incapable of dealing with challenge. But if this is so, the proper role of a university is not to protect and pamper them, but to prepare them for the challenges of the real world. The goal should not be to shield them from discomfort, insult, and insecurity, but to enable them to be effective citizens of the world. On this view, if their parents have, indeed, failed them, then their colleges and universities should save them from themselves.

15   There is, however, another possibility. It is that students, or at least some students, have always felt this way, but until now they were too intimidated, too shy, too deferential to speak up. On this view of the matter, this generation of college students deserves credit, because instead of remaining silent and oppressed, they have the courage to demand respect, equality, and safety.

16   My own view, for what it's worth, is that there is an element of truth in both of these perspectives, but I am inclined to think that the former view explains more of the current reality than the latter.

Faced with the ongoing challenge to academic freedom at American univer- [17] sities, The University of Chicago President Robert Zimmer charged a faculty committee last year with the task of drafting a formal statement for The University of Chicago on Freedom of Expression. The goal of that committee, which I chaired, was to stake out The University of Chicago's position on these issues. The Committee consisted of seven very distinguished faculty members from across the University. After broad consultation, we produced a brief, three-page report. At the risk of being self-indulgent, I want to read you some excerpts from that report:

> Because the University is committed to free and open inquiry in all [18] matters, it guarantees all members of the University community the broadest possible latitude to speak, write, listen, challenge, and learn. Of course, the ideas of different members of the University community will often and quite naturally conflict. But it is not the proper role of the University to attempt to shield individuals from ideas and opinions they find unwelcome, disagreeable, or even deeply offensive.

> Although the University greatly values civility, and although all members [19] of the University community share in the responsibility for maintaining a climate of mutual respect, concerns about civility and mutual respect can never be used as a justification for closing off discussion of ideas, however offensive or disagreeable those ideas may be to some members of our community.

> The freedom to debate and discuss the merits of competing ideas does [20] not, of course, mean that individuals may say whatever they wish, wherever they wish. The University may restrict expression that violates the law, that falsely defames a specific individual, that constitutes a genuine threat or harassment, that unjustifiably invades substantial privacy or confidentiality interests, or that is otherwise directly incompatible with the core functioning of the University. But these are narrow exceptions to the general principle of freedom of expression, and it is vitally important that these exceptions never be used in a manner that is inconsistent with the University's commitment to a completely free and open discussion of ideas.

> In a word, the University's fundamental commitment is to the principle [21] that robust debate and deliberation may not be suppressed because the ideas put forth are thought by some or even by most members of the University community to be offensive, unwise, immoral, or wrong-headed. It is for the individual members of the community, not for the University as an institution, to make those judgments for themselves, and to act on those judgments not by seeking to suppress speech, but by openly and vigorously contesting the ideas that they oppose. Indeed, fostering the ability of members of the University community to engage in such debate and deliberation in an effective and responsible manner is an essential part of the University's educational mission.

> As a corollary to the University's commitment to protect and promote [22] free expression, members of the University community must also act in conformity with the principle of free expression. Although members of the University are free to criticize and contest the views expressed on campus, and to criticize and contest speakers who are invited to express their views

on campus, they may not obstruct or otherwise interfere with the freedom of others to express views they reject or even loathe. To this end, the University has a solemn responsibility not only to promote a lively and fearless freedom of debate and deliberation, but also to protect that freedom when others attempt to restrict it. As University of Chicago President William Rainey Harper observed 125 years ago, without a vibrant commitment to free and open inquiry, a university ceases to be a university.

23   Interestingly, when we wrote this report, we were thinking only about The University of Chicago. To our surprise, the report has had a national and even international impact. Indeed, I'm pleased to say that our report has since been adopted by a range of other universities, including such diverse institutions as Princeton, Purdue, Johns Hopkins, American University, the University of Wisconsin, and Louisiana State University.

24   But now that I've finished congratulating myself, let me elaborate a bit. Why should a university take the position that members of the university community should be free to advance any and all ideas, however offensive, obnoxious, and wrong-headed they might be? For lawyers, the reasons are familiar.

25   First, one thing we have learned from bitter experience is that even the ideas we hold to be most certain might in fact turn out to be wrong. As confident as we might be in our own wisdom, experience teaches that certainty is different from truth.

26   Second, history teaches that suppression of speech breeds suppression of speech. If today I am permitted to silence those whose views I find distasteful, I have then opened the door to allow others down the road to silence me. The neutral principle of no suppression of ideas protects us all.

27   Third, a central precept of free expression is the concern with chilling effect. That problem is especially acute today because of the effects of social media. It used to be the case that students and faculty members were generally willing to take controversial positions because the risks were relatively modest. After all, one could say something provocative, and the statement soon disappeared from view. But in a world of social media, where every comment you make can be circulated to the world and can be called up by prospective employers or graduate schools or neighbors with the click of a button, the potential costs of speaking courageously—of taking controversial positions, of taking risks—is greater than ever before in history. Indeed, according to a recent survey, 65% of all college students now say that it is unsafe for them to express unpopular views, and this clearly has an effect on faculty as well. In this setting, it is especially important for universities to stand up for free expression.

28   So, how should this work in practice? Should students be allowed to express whatever views they want—however offensive they might be to others? Yes. Absolutely. Should those who disagree and who are offended by the views and speech of others be allowed to condemn that speech and those speakers in the most vehement terms? Yes. Absolutely. Should those who are offended and who disagree be allowed to demand that the university punish those who have offended them? Yes. Absolutely. Should the university punish those whose speech annoys, offends, and insults others? Absolutely not. That is the core meaning of academic freedom.

But what should a university do? A university should educate its students 29 about the importance of civility and mutual respect. These are core values for students, for professors, for citizens, and even for lawyers. But these are values that should be reinforced by education and example, not by censorship. Moreover, a university should encourage disagreement, argument, and debate. It should instill in its students and faculty the importance of winning the day by facts, by ideas, and by persuasion, rather than by force, obstruction, or censorship.

The bottom line is this: For a university to fulfill its most fundamental mission, 30 it must be a SAFE SPACE for even the most loathsome, odious, offensive, disloyal arguments. Students should be encouraged to be tough, fearless, rigorous and effective advocates and critics.

At the same time, though, a university has to recognize that, our society 31 being flawed as it is, the costs of free speech will often fall most heavily on those groups and individuals who feel the most marginalized, unwelcome, and disrespected.

All of us feel that way sometimes, but in our often unjust society the individ- 32 uals who most often bear the brunt of free speech—at least of certain types of free speech—tend to be racial minorities; religious minorities; women; gays, lesbians and transsexuals; immigrants; and so on. Universities must be sensitive to this reality. Even if they cannot "solve" this problem by censorship, this does not mean that they can't take other steps to address the special challenges faced by groups and individuals who are most often made to feel unwelcome and unvalued by others.

Universities should take this challenge seriously. They should support 33 students who feel vulnerable, marginalized, silenced, and demeaned. They should help those students learn how to speak up, how to respond effectively, how to challenge those whose attitudes, whose words, and whose beliefs offend, appall, and outrage them. This is a core responsibility of universities, for the world is not a safe space, and it is our job to enable our graduates to win the battles they will need to fight in the years and decades to come. This is not a challenge that universities can or should ignore.

Having said all of this, I don't mean to suggest that there aren't hard cases. 34 As you well know, as simple as it may be to state a principle, it is always much more difficult to apply to concrete situations. So, as a law professor, let me leave you with a few hypothetical situations for you to mull over on your own.

First, suppose a sociology professor gives a talk on campus condemning 35 homosexuality as immoral and calling on "normal" students to steer clear of fags, perverts, and sexual degenerates. What, if anything, should the chair of the sociology department do?

Second, suppose a student hangs a Confederate flag, a swastika, an image 36 of an aborted fetus, or a vote for Trump sign on the door to his dorm room? What, if anything, should the resident head do?

Third, suppose the dean of a university's law school goes on Fox News and 37 says "Abortion is murder. We should fire any woman faculty member and expel any woman student who has had an abortion." the president of the university is then inundated with complaints from alumni saying, in effect, "I'll never give another nickel to your damn school as long as she remains dean of the law school." What, if anything, should the president of the university do?

38   As these hypotheticals suggest, there are, in fact, interesting cases. But we should not let the marginal cases obscure the clarity of our core commitment to academic freedom. That commitment is now seriously and dangerously under attack. It will be interesting to see whether our universities today have the courage, the integrity, and the fortitude to be true universities. It does remain to be seen.

39   Thank you.

Geoffrey R. Stone, "Free Speech on Campus," speech delivered at the American Law Institute's 93rd annual meeting, 17 May 2016. Used with permission of the author.

QUESTIONS FOR READING

1. What point does Stone establish in his six-paragraph introduction?
2. What is the challenge to free speech that colleges face today? Who on campus is bringing this challenge?
3. What are "micro-aggressions" and "trigger warnings"?
4. What are two ways of explaining the current campus situation? What is Stone's opinion of the explanations?
5. What, in essence, is The University of Chicago's position on free expression?

QUESTIONS FOR REASONING AND ANALYSIS

6. In his speech, Stone is defending his college's position on free expression. What is his claim?
7. What three basic reasons are presented in support of his claim?
8. To make free expression work, what must universities do? What is their responsibility to students, in Stone's view?
9. Has the author successfully supported his claim? If so, how? If not, how would you refute his argument?
10. What does Stone accomplish at the end of his speech with his three examples of "hard cases"?

QUESTIONS FOR REFLECTION AND WRITING

11. Stone asserts that a commitment to academic freedom is under attack. Do you agree? Why or why not?
12. Examine the arguments of Paxson and Stone: What attitudes do they share? How do their positions differ?
13. Which author comes closest to representing your views? After reading the argument of the other author, has your position changed in any way? If so, why? If not, why?
14. Take one of Stone's "hard cases" and explain how you think the case should be handled. Support your position.

1. Compare the style and tone of Paxson's and Stone's essays. Has each one written in a way that works for the author's approach to this issue? Be prepared to explain your views or develop them into a comparative analysis of style.

2. Reread and study the essay "Your Brain Lies to You" (pp. 72–74) and then analyze the argument's parts, using Toulmin's terms.

3. Student drinking—including binge and underage drinking—remains an issue on college campuses. Should colleges actively seek to control binge and underage drinking on campus? Draw on your own experience as well as what statistics and discussions of this problem that you may find online to develop a claim that you can support.

Writing Effective Arguments

READ: Who are the figures in the painting? What are they doing?

REASON: What details in the painting help to date the scene?

REFLECT/WRITE: What is significant about the moment captured in this painting?

The basics of good writing remain much the same for works as seemingly different as the personal essay, the argument, and the researched essay. Good writing is focused, organized, and concrete. Effective essays are written in a style and tone that are suited to both the audience and the writer's purpose. These are sound principles, all well known to you. But how, exactly, do you achieve them when writing argument? This chapter will help you answer that question.

KNOW YOUR AUDIENCE

Too often, students plunge into writing without thinking much about audience, for, after all, their "audience" is only the instructor who has given the assignment, and their purpose is to complete the assignment and get a grade. These views of audience and purpose are likely to lead to badly written arguments. First, if you are not thinking about readers who may disagree with you, you may not develop the best defense of your claim. Second, you may ignore your essay's needed introductory material on the assumption that the instructor, knowing the assignment, has a context for understanding your writing. To avoid these pitfalls, use the following questions to sharpen your understanding of audience.

Who Is My Audience?

If you are writing an essay for the student newspaper, your audience consists—primarily—of students, but do not forget that faculty and administrators also read the student newspaper. If you are preparing a letter-to-the-editor refutation of a recent column in your town's newspaper, your audience will be the readers of that newspaper—that is, adults in your town. Some instructors give assignments that create an audience such as those just described so that you will practice writing with a specific audience in mind.

If you are not assigned a specific audience, imagine your classmates, as well as your instructor, as part of your audience. In other words, you are writing to readers in the academic community. These readers are intelligent and thoughtful, expecting sound reasoning and convincing evidence. From diverse cultures and experiences, these readers also represent varied values and beliefs. Do not confuse the shared expectations of writing conventions with shared beliefs.

What Will My Audience Know about My Topic?

What can you expect a diverse group of readers to know? Whether you are writing on a current issue or a centuries-old debate, you must expect most readers to have some knowledge of the issues. Their knowledge does not free you from the responsibility of developing your support fully, though. In fact, their knowledge creates further demands. For example, most readers know the main arguments on both sides of the abortion issue. For you to write as if they do not—and thus to ignore the arguments of the opposition—is to produce an argument that probably adds little to the debate on the subject.

On the other hand, what some readers "know" may be little more than an overview of the issues from TV news—or the emotional outbursts of a family member. Some readers may be misinformed or prejudiced, but they embrace their views enthusiastically nonetheless. So, as you think about the ways to develop and support your argument, you will have to assess your readers' knowledge and sophistication. This assessment will help you decide how much background information to provide or what false facts need to be revealed and dismissed.

Where Does My Audience Stand on the Issue?

Expect readers to hold a range of views, even if you are writing to students on your campus or to an organization of which you are a member. It is not true, for instance, that all students want coed dorms or pass/fail grading. And if everyone already agrees with you, you have no reason to write. An argument needs to be about a topic that is open to debate. So:

- Assume that some of your audience will probably never agree with you but may offer you grudging respect if you compose an effective argument.
- Assume that some readers do not hold strong views on your topic and may be open to convincing if you present a good case.
- Assume that those who share your views will still be looking for a strong argument in support of their position.
- Assume that if you hold an unpopular position your best strategy will be a conciliatory approach. (See p. 99 for a discussion of the conciliatory argument.)

How Should I Speak to My Audience?

Your audience will form an opinion of you based on how you write and how you reason. The image of argument—and the arguer—that we have been creating in this text's discussion is of thoughtful claims defended with logic and evidence. However, the heated debate at yesterday's lunch does not resemble this image of argument. Sometimes the word *persuasion* is used to separate the emotionally charged debate from the calm, intellectual tone of the academic argument. Unfortunately, this neat division between argument and persuasion does not describe the real world of debate. The thoughtful arguer also wants to be persuasive, and highly emotional presentations can contain relevant facts in support of a sound idea. Instead of thinking of two separate categories—argument and persuasion—think instead of a continuum from the most rigorous logic to extreme flights of fantasy. Figure 4.1 suggests this continuum with some kinds of arguments placed along it.

Where should you place yourself along this continuum of language? You will have to answer this question with each specific writing context. Much of the time you will choose "thoughtful, restrained language," as expected by the academic community, but there may be times that you will use various persuasive strategies. Probably you will not

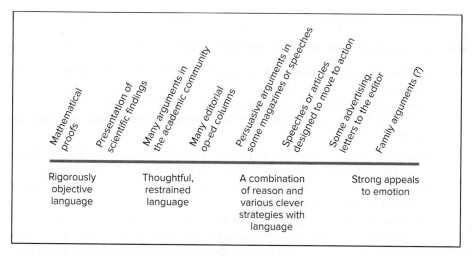

FIGURE 4.1 **A Continuum of Argumentative Language**

select "strong appeals to emotion" for your college or workplace writing. Remember that you have different roles in your life, and you use different *voices* as appropriate to each role. Most of the time, you will want to use the serious voice you normally select for serious conversations with other adults. This is the voice that will help you establish your credibility, your *ethos.*

As you learned in Chapter 2, irony is a useful rhetorical strategy for giving one's words greater emphasis by actually writing the opposite of what you mean. Many writers use irony effectively. Irony catches our attention, makes us think, and engages us with the text. Sarcasm is not quite the same as irony. Irony can cleverly focus on life's complexities. Sarcasm is more often vicious than insightful, relying on harsh, negative word choice. Probably in most of your academic work, you will want to avoid sarcasm and think carefully about using any strongly worded appeal to your readers' emotions. Better to persuade your audience with the force of your reasons and evidence than to lose them because of the static of nasty language. But the key, always, is to know your audience and understand how best to present a convincing argument to that specific group.

UNDERSTAND YOUR WRITING PURPOSE

There are many types or genres of argument and different reasons for writing—beyond wanting to write convincingly in defense of your views. Different types of arguments require different approaches, or different kinds of evidence. It helps to be able to recognize the kind of argument you are contemplating.

What Type (Genre) of Argument Am I Preparing?

Here are some useful ways to classify arguments and think about their support.

- **Investigative paper similar to those in the social sciences.** If you are asked to collect evidence in an organized way to support a claim about advertising strategies or violence in children's TV programming, then you will be writing an investigative essay. You will present evidence that you have gathered and analyzed to support your claim.

- **Evaluation.** If your assignment is to explain why others should read a particular book or take a particular professor's class, then you will be preparing an evaluation argument. Be sure to think about your criteria: What makes a book or a professor good? Why do you dislike Lady Gaga? Is it her music—or her lifestyle?

- **Definition.** If you are asked to explain the meaning of a general or controversial term, you will be writing a definition argument. What do we mean by *wisdom*? What are the characteristics of *cool*? A definition argument usually requires both specific details to illustrate the term and general ideas to express its meaning.

- **Claim of values.** If you are given the assignment to argue for your position on euthanasia, trying juveniles as adults, or the use of national identification cards, recognize that your assignment calls for a position paper, a claim based heavily on values. Pay close attention to your warrants or assumptions in any philosophical debate.

- **Claim of policy.** If you are given a broad topic: "What should we do about _____?" and you have to fill in the blank, your task is to offer solutions to a current problem. What should we do about childhood obesity? About home foreclosures? These kinds of questions are less philosophical and more practical. Your solutions must be workable.

- **Refutation or rebuttal.** If you are given the assignment to find a letter to the editor, a newspaper editorial, or an essay in this text with which you disagree, your job is to write a refutation essay, a specific challenge to a specific argument. You know, then, that you will refer repeatedly to the work you are rebutting, so you will need to know it thoroughly.

What Is My Goal?

It is also helpful to consider your goal in writing. Does your topic call for a strong statement of views (i.e., "These are the steps we must take to reduce childhood obesity")? Or is your goal an exploratory one, a thinking through of possible answers to a more philosophical question ("Why is it often difficult to separate performance from personality when we evaluate a star?")? Thinking about your goal as well as the argument's genre will help to decide on the kinds of evidence needed and on the approach to take and tone to select.

Will the Rogerian or Conciliatory Approach Work for Me?

Psychologist Carl Rogers asserts that the most successful arguments take a conciliatory approach. The characteristics of this approach include

- showing respect for the opposition in the language and tone of the argument,
- seeking common ground by indicating specific facts and values that both sides share, and
- qualifying the claim to bring opposing sides more closely together.

In their essay "Euthanasia—A Critique," authors Peter A. Singer and Mark Siegler provide a good example of a conciliatory approach. They begin their essay by explaining and then rebutting the two main arguments in favor of euthanasia. After stating the two arguments in clear and neutral language, they write this in response to the first argument:

> We agree that the relief of pain and suffering is a crucial goal of medicine. We question, however, whether the care of dying patients cannot be improved without resorting to the drastic measure of euthanasia. Most physical pain can be relieved with the appropriate use of analgesic agents. Unfortunately, despite widespread agreement that dying patients must be provided with necessary analgesia, physicians continue to underuse analgesia in the care of dying patients because of the concern about depressing respiratory drive or creating addiction. Such situations demand better management of pain, not euthanasia.[1]

In this paragraph the authors accept the value of pain management for dying patients. They go even further and offer a solution to the problem of suffering among the terminally ill—better pain management by doctors. They remain thoughtful in their approach and tone throughout, while sticking to their position that legalizing euthanasia is not the solution.

Consider how you can use the conciliatory approach to write more effective arguments. It will help you avoid "overheated" language and maintain your focus on what is doable in a world of differing points of view. There is the expression that "you can catch more flies with honey than with vinegar." Using "honey" instead of "vinegar" might also make you feel better about yourself.

MOVE FROM TOPIC TO CLAIM TO POSSIBLE SUPPORT

When you write a letter to the editor of a newspaper, you have chosen to respond to someone else's argument that has bothered you. In this writing context, you already know your topic and, probably, your claim as well. You also know that your purpose will be to refute the article you have read. In composition classes, the context is not always so clearly established, but you will usually be given some guidelines with which to get started.

Selecting a Topic

Suppose that you are asked to write an argument that is in some way connected to First Amendment rights. Your instructor has limited and focused your topic choice and purpose. Start thinking about possible topics that relate to freedom of speech and censorship issues. To aid your topic search and selection, use one or more invention strategies:

- Brainstorm (make a list).
- Freewrite (write without stopping for ten minutes).
- Map or cluster (connect ideas to the general topic in various spokes, a kind of visual brainstorming).
- Read through this text for ideas.

Your invention strategies lead, let us suppose, to the following list of possible topics:

> Administrative restrictions on the college newspaper
> Hate speech restrictions or codes
> Deleting certain books from high school reading lists
> Controls and limits on alcohol and cigarette advertising
> Restrictions on violent TV programming
> Dress codes/uniforms

Looking over your list, you realize that the last item, dress codes/uniforms, may be about freedom but not freedom of speech, so you drop it from consideration. All of the other topics have promise. Which one do you select? Two considerations should guide you: interest and knowledge. First, your argument is likely to be more thoughtful and lively if you choose an issue that matters to you. But unless you have time for study, you are wise to choose a topic about which you already have some information and ideas. Suppose that you decide to write about television violence because you are concerned about violence in American society and have given this issue some thought. It is time to phrase your topic as a tentative thesis or claim.

Drafting a Claim

Good claim statements will keep you focused in your writing—in addition to establishing your main idea for readers. Give thought both to your position on the issue and to the wording of your claim. *Claim statements to avoid:*

- Claims using vague words such as *good* or *bad*.

  VAGUE: TV violence is bad for us.
  BETTER: We need more restrictions on violent TV programming.

- Claims in loosely worded "two-part" sentences.

  UNFOCUSED: Campus sexual assault is a serious problem, and we need to do something about it.
  BETTER: College administrators and students need to work together to reduce both the number of campus sexual assaults and the fear of sexual assault.

- Claims that are not appropriately qualified.

  OVERSTATED: Violence on television is making us a violent society.

  BETTER: TV violence is contributing to viewers' increased fear of violence and insensitivity to violence.

- Claims that do not help you focus on your purpose in writing.

  UNCLEAR PURPOSE: Not everyone agrees on what is meant by violent TV programming.

  (Perhaps this is true, but more important, this claim suggests that you will define violent programming. Such an approach would not keep you focused on a First Amendment issue.)

  BETTER: Restrictions on violent TV programs can be justified.

  (Now your claim directs you to the debate over restrictions of content.)

Listing Possible Grounds

As you learned in Chapter 3, you can generate grounds to support a claim by adding a "because" clause after a claim statement. We can start a list of grounds for the topic on violent TV programming in this way:

We need more restrictions on violent television programming *because*

- Many people, including children and teens, watch many hours of TV (get stats).
- People are affected by the dominant activities/experiences in their lives.
- There is a connection between violent programming and desensitizing and fear of violence and possibly more aggressive behavior in heavy viewers (get detail of studies).
- Society needs to protect young people.

You have four good points to work on, a combination of reasons and inferences drawn from evidence.

Listing Grounds for the Other Side or Another Perspective

Remember that arguments generate counterarguments. Continue your exploration of this topic by considering possible rebuttals to your proposed grounds. How might someone who does not want to see restrictions placed on television programming respond to each of your points? Let's think about them one at a time:

We need more restrictions on violent television programming because

1. *Many people, including children and teens, watch many hours of TV.*

Your opposition cannot really challenge your first point on the facts, only its relevance to restricting programming. The opposition might argue that if parents think their children are watching too much TV, they should turn it off. The restriction needs to be a family decision.

2.   *People are affected by the dominant activities/experiences in their lives.*

It seems common sense to expect people to be influenced by dominant forces in their lives. Your opposition might argue, though, that many people have the TV on for many hours but often are not watching it intently for all of that time. The more dominant forces in our lives are parents and teachers and peers, not the TV. The opposition might also argue that people seem to be influenced to such different degrees by television that it is not fair or logical to restrict everyone when perhaps only a few are truly influenced by their TV viewing to a harmful degree.

3.   *There is a connection between violent programming and desensitizing and fear of violence and possibly more aggressive behavior in heavy viewers.*

Some people are entirely convinced by studies showing these negative effects of violent TV programming, but others point to the less convincing studies or make the argument that if violence on TV were really so powerful an influence, most people would be violent or fearful or desensitized.

4.   *Society needs to protect young people.*

Your opposition might choose to agree with you in theory on this point—and then turn again to the argument that parents should be doing the protecting. Government controls on programming restrict adults as well as children, whereas it may only be some children who should watch fewer hours of TV and not watch adult "cop" shows at all.

Working through this process of considering opposing views can help you see

- where you may want to do some research for facts to provide backing for your grounds,
- how you can best develop your reasons to take account of typical counterarguments, and
- if you should qualify your claim in some ways.

Planning Your Approach

Now that you have thought about arguments on the other side, you decide that you want to argue for a qualified claim that is also more precise:

> To protect young viewers, we need restrictions on violence in children's programs and ratings for prime-time adult shows that clearly establish the degree of violence in those shows.

This qualified claim responds to two points of the rebuttals. Our student hasn't given in to the other side but has chosen to narrow the argument to emphasize the protection of children, an area of common ground.

Next, it's time to check some of the articles in this text or go online to get some data to develop points 1 and 3. You need to know that 99 percent of homes have at least one TV; you need to know that by the time young people graduate from high school, they have spent more time in front of the TV than in the classroom. Also, you can find the average number of violent acts by hour of TV in children's programs. Then, too, there are the various studies of fearfulness and aggressive behavior that will give you some statistics to use to develop the third point. Be sure to select reliable sources and then cite the sources you use. *Citing sources is not only required and right; it is also part of the process of establishing your credibility and thus strengthening your argument.*

Finally, how are you going to answer the point about parents controlling their children? You might counter that in theory this is the way it should be—but in fact not all parents are at home watching what their children are watching, and not all parents care enough to pay attention. However, all of us suffer from the consequences of those children who are influenced by their TV watching to become more aggressive or fearful or desensitized. These children grow up to become the adults the rest of us have to inter-act with, so the problem becomes one for the society as a whole to solve. If you had not disciplined yourself to go through the process of listing possible rebuttals, you may not have thought through this part of the debate.

DRAFT YOUR ARGUMENT

Many of us can benefit from a step-by-step process of invention—such as we have been exploring in the last few pages. In addition, the more notes you have from working through the Toulmin structure, the easier it will be to get started on your draft. Students report that they can control their writing anxiety when they generate detailed notes. A page of notes that also suggests an organizational strategy can remove that awful feeling of staring at a blank computer screen.

In the following chapters on argument, you will find specific suggestions for orga-nizing the various kinds of arguments. But you can always rely on one of these two basic organizations, regardless of the specific genre:

PLAN 1: ORGANIZING AN ARGUMENT

Attention-getting opening (why the issue is important, or current, etc.)

Claim statement

Reasons and evidence in order from least important to most important

Challenge to potential rebuttals or counterarguments

Conclusion that reemphasizes claim

PLAN 2: ORGANIZING AN ARGUMENT

Attention-getting opening

Claim statement (or possibly leave to the conclusion)

Order by arguments of opposing position, with your challenge to each

Conclusion that reemphasizes (or states for the first time) your claim

GUIDELINES for Drafting

- **Try to get a complete draft in one sitting so that you can read the whole piece.**
- **If you can't think of a clever opening, state your claim and move on to the body of your essay.** After you draft your reasons and evidence, a good opening may occur to you.
- **If you find that you need something more in some parts of your essay, leave space there as a reminder that you will need to return to that paragraph later.**
- **Try to avoid using either a dictionary or thesaurus while drafting.** Your goal is to get the ideas down. You will polish later.
- **Learn to draft at your computer.** Revising is so much easier that you will be more willing to make significant changes if you work at your PC. If you are handwriting your draft, leave plenty of margin space for additions or for directions to shift parts around.

REVISE YOUR DRAFT

If you have drafted at the computer, begin revising by printing a copy of your draft. Most of us cannot do an adequate job of revision by looking at a computer screen. Then remind yourself that revision is a three-step process: rewriting, editing, and proofreading.

Rewriting

You are not ready to polish the writing until you are satisfied with the argument. Look first at the total piece. Do you have all the necessary parts: a claim, support, some response to possible counterarguments? Examine the order of your reasons and evidence. Do some of your points belong, logically, in a different place? Does the order make the most powerful defense of your claim? Be willing to move whole paragraphs around to test the best organization. Also reflect on the argument itself. Have you avoided logical fallacies? Have you qualified statements when appropriate? Do you have enough support? The best support?

Consider development: Is your essay long enough to meet assignment requirements? Are points fully developed to satisfy the demands of readers? One key to development is the length of your paragraphs. If most of your paragraphs are only two or three sentences, you have not developed the point of each paragraph satisfactorily. It is possible that some paragraphs need to be combined because they are really on the same topic. More typically, short paragraphs need further explanation of ideas or examples to illustrate ideas. Compare the following paragraphs for effectiveness:

First Draft of a Paragraph from an Essay on Gun Control

One popular argument used against the regulation of gun ownership is the need of citizens, especially in urban areas where the crime rate is higher, to possess a handgun for personal protection, either carried or kept in the home. Some citizens may not be aware of the dangers to themselves or their families when they purchase a gun. Others, more aware, may embrace the myth that "bad things only happen to other people."

Revised Version of the Paragraph with Statistics Added

One popular argument used against the regulation of gun ownership is the need of citizens, especially in urban areas where the crime rate is higher, to possess a handgun for personal protection, whether it is carried or kept in the home. Although some citizens may not be aware of the dangers to themselves or their families when they purchase a gun, they should be. According to the Center to Prevent Handgun Violence, from their Web page "Firearm Facts," "guns that are kept in the home for self-protection are 22 times more likely to kill a family member or friend than to kill in self-defense." The Center also reports that guns in the home make homicide three times more likely and suicide five times more likely. We are not thinking straight if we believe that these dangers apply only to others.

A quick trip to the Web has provided this student with some facts to support his argument. Observe how he has referred informally but fully to the source of his information. (If your instructor requires formal MLA documentation in all essays, then you will need to add a Works Cited page and give a full reference to the website. See Chapter 14.)

Editing

Make your changes, print another copy, and begin the second phase of revision: editing. As you read through this time, pay close attention to unity and coherence, sentence patterns, and word choice. Read each paragraph as a separate unit to be certain that everything is on the same subtopic. Then look at your use of transition and connecting words, both within and between paragraphs. Ask yourself: Have you guided the reader through the argument using appropriate connectors such as *therefore, in addition, as a consequence, also,* and so forth?

Read again, focusing on each sentence, checking to see that you have varied sentence patterns and length. Read sentences aloud to let your ear help you find awkward constructions or unfinished thoughts. Strive as well for word choice that is concrete and specific, avoiding wordiness, clichés, trite expressions, or incorrect use of specialized terms. Observe how Samantha edited one paragraph in her essay "Balancing Work and Family":

Draft Version of Paragraph

Women have come a long way in equalizing themselves, but inequality within marriages do exist. One reason for this can be found in the media. Just last week America turned on thier televisions to watch a grotesque dramatization of skewed priorities. On *Who Wants to Marry a Millionaire*, a panel of women

Vague reference.
Wordy.

Short sentences.

Vague reference.

vied for the affections of a millionaire who would choose one of them to be his wife. This show said that women can be purchased. Also that men must provide and that money is worth the sacrifice of one's individuality. The show also suggests that physical attraction is more important than the building of a complete relationship. Finally, the show says that women's true value lies in thier appearance. This is a dangerous message to send to both men women viewers.

Edited Version of Paragraph

Although women have come a long way toward equality in the workplace, inequality within marriages can still be found. The media may be partly to blame for this continued inequality. Just last week Americans watched a grotesque dramatization of skewed priorities. On *Who Wants to Marry a Millionaire,* a panel of women vied for the affections of a millionaire who would choose one of them to be his wife. Such displays teach us that women can be purchased, that men must be the providers, that the desire for money is worth the sacrifice of one's individuality, that physical attraction is more important than a complete relationship, and that women's true value lies in their appearance. These messages discourage marriages based on equality and mutual support.

Samantha's editing has eliminated wordiness and vague references and has combined ideas into one forceful sentence. Support your good argument by taking the time to polish your writing.

A Few Words about Word Choice and Tone

You have just been advised to check your word choice to eliminate wordiness, vagueness, clichés, and so on. Here is a checklist of problems often found in student papers with some ways to fix the problems:

- *Eliminate clichés.* Do not write about "the fast-paced world we live in today" or the "rat race." First, do you know for sure that the pace of life for someone who has a demanding job is any faster than it was in the past? Using time effectively has always mattered. Also, clichés suggest that you are too lazy to find your own words.

- *Avoid jargon.* In the negative sense of this word, *jargon* refers to nonspecialists who fill their writing with "heavy-sounding terms" to give the appearance of significance. Watch for any overuse of "scientific" terms such as *factor* or *aspect,* or other vague, awkward language.

- *Avoid language that is too informal for most of your writing contexts.* What do you mean when you write: "*Kids* today watch too much TV"? Alternatives include *children, teens, adolescents.* These words are less slangy and more precise.

- *Avoid nasty attacks on the opposition.* Change "those jerks who are foolish enough to believe that TV violence has no impact on children" to language that explains your counterargument without attacking those who may disagree with you. After all, you want to change the thinking of your audience, not make them resent you for name-calling.

- *Avoid all discriminatory language.* In the academic community and the adult workplace, most people are bothered by language that belittles any one group. This includes language that is racist or sexist or reflects negatively on older or differently abled persons or those who do not share your sexual orientation or religious beliefs. Just don't do it!

Proofreading

You also do not want to lose the respect of readers because you submit a paper filled with "little" errors—errors in punctuation, mechanics, and incorrect word choice. Most readers will forgive one or two little errors but will become annoyed if they begin to pile up. So, after you are finished rewriting and editing, print a copy of your paper and read it slowly, looking specifically at punctuation, at the handling of quotations and references to writers and to titles, and at those pesky words that come in two or more "versions": *to, too,* and *two; here* and *hear; their, there,* and *they're;* and so forth. If instructors have found any of these kinds of errors in your papers over the years, then focus your attention on the kinds of errors you have been known to make.

Refer to Chapter 1 for handling references to authors and titles and for handling direct quotations. Use a glossary of usage for homonyms (words that sound alike but have different meanings), and check a handbook for punctuation rules. Take pride in your work and present a paper that will be treated with respect. What follows is a checklist of the key points for writing good arguments that we have just examined.

A CHECKLIST FOR REVISION

- ☐ Have I selected an issue and purpose consistent with assignment guidelines?
- ☐ Have I stated a claim that is focused, appropriately qualified, and precise?
- ☐ Have I developed sound reasons and evidence in support of my claim?
- ☐ Have I used Toulmin's terms to help me study the parts of my argument, including rebuttals to counterarguments?
- ☐ Have I taken advantage of a conciliatory approach and emphasized common ground with opponents?
- ☐ Have I found a clear and effective organization for presenting my argument?
- ☐ Have I edited my draft thoughtfully, concentrating on producing unified and coherent paragraphs and polished sentences?
- ☐ Have I eliminated wordiness, clichés, jargon?
- ☐ Have I selected an appropriate tone for my purpose and audience?
- ☐ Have I used my word processor's spell-check and proofread a printed copy with great care?

FOR ANALYSIS AND DEBATE

FIVE MYTHS ABOUT TORTURE AND TRUTH | DARIUS REJALI

A professor of political science at Reed College, Iranian-born Darius Rejali is a recognized expert on the causes and meaning of violence, especially on torture, in our world. His books *Torture and Democracy* (2007) and *Spirituality and the Ethics of Torture* (2009) have won acclaim and resulted in frequent interviews for Rejali. The following essay appeared on December 16, 2007, in *The Washington Post*.

PREREADING QUESTIONS Can you think of five myths about torture? What do you expect rejali to cover in this essay?

1   *So the CIA did indeed torture Abu Zubaida, the first al-Qaeda terrorist suspect to have been waterboarded. So says John Kiriakou, the first former CIA employee directly involved in the questioning of "high-value" al-Qaeda detainees to speak out publicly. He minced no words last week in calling the CIA's "enhanced interrogation techniques" what they are.*

2   *But did they work? Torture's defenders, including the wannabe tough guys who write Fox's "24," insist that the rough stuff gets results. "It was like flipping a switch," said Kiriakou about Abu Zubaida's response to being waterboarded. But the al-Qaeda operative's confessions—descriptions of fantastic plots from a man who intelligence analysts were convinced was mentally ill—probably didn't give the CIA any actionable intelligence. Of course, we may never know the whole truth, since the CIA destroyed the videotapes of Abu Zubaida's interrogation. But here are some other myths that are bound to come up as the debate over torture rages on.*

3   **1. Torture worked for the Gestapo.** Actually, no. Even Hitler's notorious secret police got most of their information from public tips, informers and interagency cooperation. That was still more than enough to let the Gestapo decimate anti-Nazi resistance in Austria, Czechoslovakia, Poland, Denmark, Norway, France, Russia and the concentration camps.

4   Yes, the Gestapo did torture people for intelligence, especially in later years. But this reflected not torture's efficacy but the loss of many seasoned professionals to World War II, increasingly desperate competition for intelligence among Gestapo units and an influx of less disciplined younger members. (Why do serious, tedious police work when you have a uniform and a whip?) It's surprising how unsuccessful the Gestapo's brutal efforts were. They failed to break senior leaders of the French, Danish, Polish and German resistance. I've spent more than a decade collecting all the cases of Gestapo torture "successes" in multiple languages; the number is small and the results pathetic, especially compared with the devastating effects of public cooperation and informers.

5   **2. Everyone talks sooner or later under torture.** Truth is, it's surprisingly hard to get anything under torture, true or false. For example, between 1500 and 1750, French prosecutors tried to torture confessions out of 785 individuals. Torture was legal back then, and the records document such practices as the bone-crushing use of splints, pumping stomachs with water until they swelled and pouring boiling oil on the feet. But the number of prisoners who said anything was low, from 3 percent in Paris to 14 percent in Toulouse (an exceptional high). Most of the time, the torturers were unable to get any statement whatsoever.

And such examples could be multiplied. The Japanese fascists, no strangers 6
to torture, said it best in their field manual, which was found in Burma during
World War II: They described torture as the clumsiest possible method of gathering intelligence. Like most sensible torturers, they preferred to use torture for
intimidation, not information.

   3. People will say anything under torture. Well, no, although this is a favorite 7
chestnut of torture's foes. Think about it: Sure, someone would lie under torture,
but wouldn't they also lie if they were being interrogated without coercion?

   In fact, the problem of torture does not stem from the prisoner who *has* infor- 8
mation; it stems from the prisoner who doesn't. Such a person is also likely to lie,
to say anything, often convincingly. The torture of the informed may generate no
more lies than normal interrogation, but the torture of the ignorant and innocent
overwhelms investigators with misleading information. In these cases, nothing is
indeed preferable to anything. Anything needs to be verified, and the CIA's own
1963 interrogation manual explains that "a time-consuming delay results"—hardly
useful when every moment matters.

   Intelligence gathering is especially vulnerable to this problem. When police offi- 9
cers torture, they know what the crime is, and all they want is the confession. When
intelligence officers torture, they must gather information about what they don't know.

   4. Most people can tell when someone is lying under torture. Not so—and 10
we know quite a bit about this. For about 40 years, psychologists have been
testing police officers as well as normal people to see whether they can spot
lies, and the results aren't encouraging. Ordinary folk have an accuracy rate of
about 57 percent, which is pretty poor considering that 50 percent is the flip of a
coin. Likewise, the cops' accuracy rates fall between 45 percent and
65 percent—that is, sometimes less accurate than a coin toss.

   Why does this matter? Because even if torturers break a person, they have to 11
recognize it, and most of the time they can't. Torturers assume too much and reject
what doesn't fit their assumptions. For instance, Sheila Cassidy, a British physician,
cracked under electric-shock torture by the Chilean secret service in the 1970s and
identified priests who had helped the country's socialist opposition. But her devout
interrogators couldn't believe that priests would ever help the socialists, so they
tortured her for another week until they finally became convinced. By that time,
she was so damaged that she couldn't remember the location of the safe house.

   In fact, most torturers are nowhere near as well trained for interrogation as 12
police are. Torturers are usually chosen because they've endured hardship and
pain, fought with courage, kept secrets, held the right beliefs and earned a
reputation as trustworthy and loyal. They often rely on folklore about what lying
behavior looks like—shifty eyes, sweaty palms and so on. And, not surprisingly,
they make a lot of mistakes.

   5. You can train people to resist torture. Supposedly, this is why we can't 13
know what the CIA's "enhanced interrogation techniques" are: If Washington
admits that it waterboards suspected terrorists, al-Qaeda will set up
"waterboarding-resistance camps" across the world. Be that as it may, the truth
is that no training will help the bad guys.

   Simply put, nothing predicts the outcome of one's resistance to pain better 14
than one's own personality. Against some personalities, nothing works; against
others, practically anything does. Studies of hundreds of detainees who broke

under Soviet and Chinese torture, including Army-funded studies of U.S. prisoners of war, conclude that during, before and after torture, each prisoner displayed strengths and weaknesses dependent on his or her own character. The CIA's own "Human Resources Exploitation Manual" from 1983 and its so-called Kubark manual from 1963 agree. In all matters relating to pain, says Kubark, the "individual remains the determinant."

15   The thing that's most clear from torture-victim studies is that you can't train for the ordeal. There is no secret knowledge out there about how to resist torture. Yes, there are manuals, such as the IRA's "Green Book," the anti-Soviet "Manual for Psychiatry for Dissidents" and "Torture and the Interrogation Experience," an Iranian guerrilla manual from the 1970s. But none of these volumes contains specific techniques of resistance, just general encouragement to hang tough. Even al-Qaeda's vaunted terrorist-training manual offers no tips on how to resist torture, and al-Qaeda was no stranger to the brutal methods of the Saudi police.

16   And yet these myths persist. "The larger problem here, I think," one active CIA officer observed in 2005, "is that this kind of stuff just makes people feel better, even if it doesn't work."

Darius Rejali, "Five Myths About Torture and Truth," *The Washington Post,* 17 Dec. 2007. Reprinted by permission of the author.

QUESTIONS FOR READING

1. What context for his discussion does the author provide in the opening two paragraphs?
2. What worked better than torture for the Gestapo? What led to an increase in torture in the Gestapo?
3. What do the data show about getting people to speak by torturing them?
4. Who are the people most likely to lie under torture?
5. Why are interrogators not very good at recognizing when the tortured are lying?

QUESTIONS FOR REASONING AND ANALYSIS

6. What structure does the author use? What kind of argument is this?
7. What is Rejali's position on torture, the claim of his argument?
8. What grounds does he present in support of his claim?
9. Describe Rejali's style; how does his style of writing help his argument?

QUESTIONS FOR REFLECTION AND WRITING

10. Which of the five discussions has surprised you the most? Why?
11. Has the author convinced you that all five myths lack substance? Why or why not? If you disagree, how would you refute Rejali?
12. Why do intelligence and military personnel continue to use harsh interrogation strategies even though the evidence suggests that what, if anything, they learn will not be useful? Ponder this question.

TORURE IS WRONG—BUT IT MIGHT WORK | M. GREGG BLOCHE

A law professor at Georgetown University, Gregg Bloche is also a physician. His MD and JD degrees are both from Yale University. Bloche specializes in medical ethics, health care law, and human rights law. Widely published, he is the author of *The Hippocratic Myth* (2011). His essay on torture appeared on May 29, 2011.

PREREADING QUESTIONS **Has Bloche intrigued you with his title? What do you expect his position to be?**

Torture, liberals like me often insist, isn't just immoral, it's ineffective. We like this proposition because it portrays us as protectors of the nation, not wusses willing to risk American lives to protect terrorists. And we love to quote seasoned interrogators' assurances that building rapport with the bad guys will get them to talk. 1

But the killing of Osama bin Laden four weeks ago has revived the old debate about whether torture works. Could it be that "enhanced interrogation techniques" employed during the George W. Bush administration helped find bin Laden's now-famous courier and track him to the terrorist in chief's now-infamous lair? 2

Sen. John McCain (R-Ariz.) and current administration officials say no. Former attorney general Michael Mukasey and former vice president Dick Cheney say yes. 3

The idea that waterboarding and other abuses may have been effective in getting information from detainees is repellant to many, including me. It's contrary to the meme many have embraced: that torture doesn't work because people being abused to the breaking point will say anything to get the brutality to stop— anything they think their accusers want to hear. 4

What is water-boarding?

Water-boarding is a harsh interrogation method that simulates drowning and near death; origins traced to the Spanish Inquisition.

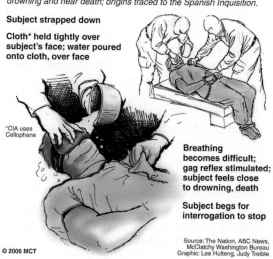

Subject strapped down

Cloth* held tightly over subject's face; water poured onto cloth, over face

*CIA uses Cellophane

Breathing becomes difficult; gag reflex stimulated; subject feels close to drowning, death

Subject begs for interrogation to stop

Source: The Nation, ABC News, McClatchy Washington Bureau
Graphic: Lee Hulteng, Judy Treible

© 2006 MCT

©Hulteng/MCT/Newscom

But this position is at odds with some behavioral science, I've learned. The architects of enhanced interrogation are doctors who built on a still-classified, research-based model that suggests how abuse can indeed work. 5

I've examined the science, studied the available paper trail and interviewed key actors, including several who helped develop the enhanced interrogation program and who haven't spoken publicly before. This inquiry has made it possible to piece together the model that under-girds enhanced interrogation. 6

7   This model holds that harsh methods can't, by themselves, force terrorists to tell the truth. Brute force, it suggests, stiffens resistance. Rather, the role of abuse is to induce hopelessness and despair. That's what sleep deprivation, stress positions and prolonged isolation were designed to do. Small gestures of contempt—facial slaps and frequent insults—drive home the message of futility. Even the rough stuff, such as "walling" and waterboarding, is meant to dispirit, not to coerce.

8   Once a sense of hopelessness is instilled, the model holds, interrogators can shape behavior through small rewards. Bathroom breaks, reprieves from foul-tasting food and even the occasional kind word can coax broken men to comply with their abusers' expectations.

9   Certainly, interrogators using this approach have obtained false confessions. Chinese interrogators did so intentionally, for propaganda purposes, with American prisoners during the Korean War. McCain and other critics of "torture-lite" cite this precedent to argue that it can't yield reliable information. But the same psychological sequence—induction of hopelessness, followed by rewards to shape compliance—can be used to get terrorism suspects to tell the truth, or so the architects of enhanced interrogation hypothesize.

10   Critical to this model is the ability to assess suspects' truthfulness in real time. To this end, CIA interrogators stressed speedy integration of intelligence from all sources. The idea was to frame questions to detect falsehoods; interrogators could then reward honesty and punish deceit.

11   It's been widely reported that the program was conceived by a former Air Force psychologist, James Mitchell, who had helped oversee the Pentagon's program for training soldiers and airmen to resist torture if captured. That Mitchell became the CIA's maestro of enhanced interrogation and personally waterboarded several prisoners was confirmed in 2009 through the release of previously classified documents. But how Mitchell got involved and why the agency embraced his methods remained a mystery.

12   The key player was a clinical psychologist turned CIA official, Kirk Hubbard, I learned through interviews with him and others. On the day 19 hijackers bent on mass murder made their place in history, Hubbard's responsibilities at the agency included tracking developments in the behavioral sciences with an eye toward their tactical use. He and Mitchell knew each other through the network of psychologists who do national security work. Just retired from the Air Force, Mitchell figured he could translate what he knew about teaching resistance into a methodology for breaking it. He convinced Hubbard, who introduced him to CIA leaders and coached him through the agency's bureaucratic rivalries.

13   Journalistic accounts have cast Mitchell as a rogue who won a CIA contract by dint of charisma. What's gone unappreciated is his reliance on a research base. He had studied the medical and psychological literature on how Chinese interrogators extracted false confessions. And he was an admirer of Martin Seligman, the University of Pennsylvania psychologist who had developed the concept of "learned helplessness" and invoked it to explain depression.

Mitchell, it appears, saw connections and seized upon them. The despair 14 that Chinese interrogators tried to instill was akin to learned helplessness. Seligman's induction of learned helplessness in laboratory animals, therefore, could point the way to prison regimens capable of inducing it in people. And—this was Mitchell's biggest conceptual jump—the Chinese way of shaping behavior in prisoners who were reduced to learned helplessness held a broader lesson.

To motivate a captive to comply, a Chinese interrogator established an 15 aura of omnipotence. For weeks or months, the interrogator was his prisoner's sole human connection, with monopoly power to praise, punish and reward. Rapport with the interrogator offered the only escape from despair. This opened possibilities for the sculpting of behavior and belief. For propaganda purposes, the Chinese sought sham confessions. But Mitchell saw that behavioral shaping could be used to pursue other goals, including the extraction of truth.

Did the methods Mitchell devised help end the hunt for bin Laden? Have 16 they prevented terrorist attacks? We'll never know. Not only are counterterrorism operations shrouded in secrecy, but it's impossible to prove or disprove claims that enhanced interrogation works better than other methods when prisoners are intent on saying nothing.

Scientific study of this question would require random sorting of suspects 17 into groups that receive either torture-lite or conventional forms of interrogation. To frame this inquiry is to show why it can't be carried out: It would violate international law and research ethics. The CIA, Hubbard told me, conducted no such study for this reason.

So we're left with the unsavory possibility that torture-lite works—and that it 18 may have helped find bin Laden. It does no good to point out, as some human rights advocates have, that the detainees who yielded information about his courier did so after the abuse stopped. The model on which enhanced interrogation is based can account for this. The detainees' cooperation could have ensued from hopelessness and despair, followed by interrogators' adroit use of their power to punish and reward.

This possibility poses the question of torture in a more unsettling fashion, 19 by denying us the easy out that torture is both ineffective and wrong. We must choose between its repugnance to our values and its potential efficacy. To me, the choice is almost always obvious: Contempt for the law of nations would put us on a path toward a more brutish world. Conservatives are fond of saying, on behalf of martial sacrifice, that freedom isn't free. Neither is basic decency.

M. Gregg Bloche, "Torture Is Wrong—But It Might Work," *The Washington Post,* 29 May 2011. Used with permission of the author.

QUESTIONS FOR READING

1. What argument is embraced by those who are opposed to the use of torture?

2. What did Bloche learn about the purpose of "enhanced interrogation"? How is it used as part of a process for getting information?

3. The debate over the use of enhanced interrogation techniques and of hidden sites continues. Bloche mentions several studies in his discussion. See what more you can learn about this debate. Ponder this question: Why do some continue these strategies when studies fail to confirm that they work?

4. What must interrogators assess for this model to work? How do they try to do this?

5. Why can we not know for certain if torture works?

QUESTIONS FOR REASONING AND ANALYSIS

6. What is Bloche's claim? (Be careful; it is not a simple statement.)

7. What grounds does he present in support of his claim?

8. Study the author's introduction. What does he gain by announcing his position on torture in his opening paragraph?

9. Study Bloche's conclusion: Why is deciding on one's position more difficult now? What does Bloche mean by his final sentence?

QUESTIONS FOR REFLECTION AND WRITING

10. Has Bloche convinced you that the issue of using enhanced interrogation has become more complex? Why or why not? If you disagree with the author, how would you refute him?

11. Both Bloche and Rejali discuss the issue of interrogators needing to assess what, if any, good information they may be getting from interrogation. What does this tell you about the task of intelligence gathering? Ponder this issue for class discussion or writing.

1. Do Rejali and Bloche hold opposing viewpoints on the use of torture—or are their differences more that of approach and focus? Read each author again and then write an analysis of their differences in style, approach to the issue, and position on the issue.

2. Reflect on what you have learned about torture from Rejali and Bloche and then consider: What may be the greatest "unknown" part of the equation in the use of interrogation as a strategy for finding people who have broken the law? Or, put another way, what do you see as the biggest problem to ensuring success from questioning people under pressure to get intelligence from them?

3. The debate over the use of enhanced interrogation techniques and of hidden sites continues. Bloche mentions several studies in his discussion. Go online and see what more you can learn about this debate. Ponder this question: Why do some continue these strategies when studies fail to confirm that they work?

4. Should the debate over enhanced interrogation procedures be about effectiveness or ethics? And if it should be about effectiveness, then how much evidence is needed to defend torture on the grounds that it works? Ponder these questions.

CREDIT

1. Peter A. Singer and Mark Siegler. "Euthanasia—A Critique." *New England Journal of Medicine*, 28 June 1990, vol. 322, pp. 1881-1888.

Reading, Analyzing, and Using Visuals and Statistics in Argument

READ: This is a photo of President John F. Kennedy; where was it taken?

REASON: What is your initial reaction to the photo? How does it make you feel? What does it make you think about?

REFLECT/WRITE: There are many images of President Kennedy; why would we select this one for your consideration? What comment does it make that extends beyond one particular president?

We live in a visual age. Many of us go to movies to appreciate and judge the film's visual effects. The Web is awash in pictures, colorful icons, animated GIFs, and videos. Perhaps the best print symbol of our visual age in print is *USA Today,* a paper filled with color photos and many tables and other graphics as a primary way of presenting information. *USA Today* has forced the more traditional papers to add color to compete. We also live in a numerical age. We refer to the events of September 11, 2001, as 9/11—without any disrespect. This chapter brings together these markers of our times as they are used in argument—and as argument. Finding statistics and visuals used as part of argument, we also need to remember that cartoons and advertisements are arguments in and of themselves.

RESPONDING TO VISUAL ARGUMENTS

Many arguments bombard us today in visual forms. These include photos, political cartoons, and advertising. Most major newspapers have a political cartoonist whose drawings appear regularly on the editorial page. Some comic strips are also political in nature, at least some of the time. These cartoons are designed to make a political point in a visually clever and amusing way. (That is why they are both "cartoons" and "political" at the same time.) Their uses of irony and caricatures of known politicians make them among the most emotionally powerful, indeed stinging, of arguments.

Photographs accompany many newspaper and magazine articles, and they often tell a story. Indeed, some photographers are famous for their ability to capture a personality or a newsworthy moment. So accustomed to these visuals today, we sometimes forget to study photographs. Be sure to examine each photo, remembering that authors and editors have selected each one for a reason.

Advertisements are among the most creative and powerful forms of argument today. Remember that ads are designed to take your time (for shopping) and your money. Their messages need to be powerful to motivate you to action. With some products (what most of us consider necessities), ads are designed to influence product choice, to get us to buy brand A instead of brand B. With other products, ones we really do not need or that may actually be harmful to us, ads need to be especially clever. Some ads do provide information (car X gets better gas mileage than car Y). Other ads (perfume ads, for example) take us into a fantasy land so that we will spend $50 on a small but pretty bottle. Another type of ad is the "image advertisement," an ad that assures us that a particular company is top-notch. If we admire the company, we will buy its goods or services. Understanding a few basic design principles, outlined below, will help you read, analyze, and even create these types of visual arguments.

Visual Rhetoric and Visual Literacy

Because visual argument, also known as visual rhetoric, is such a common and powerful form of communication, you will be expected to read, analyze, and even create communication that mixes text with images—this is known as visual literacy. More than merely making something "pretty," visual literacy is based in cognitive psychology, as well as cultural and rhetorical theory. The basic concepts below—Gestalt principles, reading patterns, focal points, and colors—provide an introduction to visual rhetoric and visual literacy.

Gestalt Principles and the C.A.R.P. Design Model

The Gestalt principles of design evolved from Gestalt theory, a psychological approach to analyzing human perceptions and human behavior first theorized by the Berlin School of Experimental Psychology. When applied to visuals, Gestalt principles hold that certain designs and graphic forms have a greater impact on people when used in specific combinations with one another. For example, the first element of the C.A.R.P. model, contrast, refers to the visual and cognitive impact something like black text can have when placed on a white background. When the contrast decreases, for example if gray text is used on a white background, the visual and cognitive impact decreases: Decrease contrast and you decrease impact. Take a look at the design of this book; notice that the text, text boxes, and images contrast with their backgrounds to ensure impact and readability. The elements of the C.A.R.P. model are explained below:

The C.A.R.P. Design Model

- **Contrast:** Design elements, such as text, have more impact and are more readable when placed over backgrounds that are a different color or shade. For example, the guidelines boxes below create contrast with the text within them but also with the white page behind them.
- **Alignment:** Design elements are carefully placed in some way to create a notable pattern and establish a connection with one another. Note the guidelines boxes again: Even though the boxes are separate, the red line on the left continues in each box, creating alignment between them.
- **Repetition:** Design elements, such as logos, icons, or colors, help readers understand that they are still within the larger piece of work. For example, the pages of the MLA section of *Read, Reason, Write* are edged in blue to help you find them within the text and to help you understand that you are still in the MLA section.
- **Proximity:** Design elements are placed near one another if they share similar concepts or ideas. For example, navigation links on a website are not randomly placed around a page. Rather, navigation links are placed near one another, usually in navigation bars at the top or on the edges of a Web page. Because navigation links share the similar purpose of helping users move around the website, they are placed in proximity to one another.

Reading Patterns

In cultures that read from left to right, readers looking at a print document usually begin in the top left corner, move right and then down the page in a Z pattern. Similarly, online readers usually move down a Web page in an F pattern, which is influenced by the location of navigation bars and headings. Of course, reading patterns also depend on the location of design elements, such as focal points and colors, so remember that the design of the work will have an impact on the reading pattern of the audience.

Focal Points

Focal points are design elements that immediately catch readers' attention and draw their eyes to them. For example, human faces or the faces of animals, especially cute ones like puppies and kittens, are strong focal points. Circles and spheres, whether complete or just partially visible, are also strong focal points. But a document's focal point does not have to be a face or a sphere; white space may also form a focal point, especially if it is placed near a dense collection of text.

Colors

Colors are some of the most powerful design features used in visual rhetoric. They can form focal points (see the text in red below), influence reading patterns, and serve as essential elements of the C.A.R.P. design principles. But colors are also culturally dependent; that is, the meaning of colors sometimes depends on the cultural context. For example, in Western cultures, red means **ALARM**, but in some Asian cultures, red means good luck and good fortune. In Western cultures, white means purity, but in some Asian cultures, it means death. So, why do you think wedding dresses in China are red, while wedding dresses in America are white? Exactly. Note that when creating images using colors, you also need to remember that some segment of your audience, especially males, may have some sort of color vision deficiency. The most common color vision deficiency is red-green color blindness.

Below are general guidelines for reading visuals and guidelines for reading arguments presented in photographs, political cartoons, and advertisements. You can practice these steps with the exercises that follow.

GUIDELINES for Reading Visuals

- **What is the context and purpose of the visual and who is the audience?**
- **Does the visual follow the C.A.R.P. model?** If not, why not?
- **How is the visual designed?** Does the visual follow the Z reading pattern or the F reading pattern?
- **What is the focal point?**
- **Are colors used, or is the image grayscale or black and white?**

GUIDELINES for Reading Photographs

- **Is a scene or situation depicted?** If so, study the details to identify the situation.
- **Identify each figure in the photo.**
- **What details of scene or person(s) carry significance?**
- **How does the photograph make you feel?**

GUIDELINES for Reading Political Cartoons

- **What scene is depicted?** Identify the situation.
- **Identify each of the figures in the cartoon.** Are they current politicians, figures from history or literature, the "person in the street," or symbolic representations?
- **Who speaks the lines in the cartoon?**
- **What is the cartoon's general subject?** What is the point of the cartoon, the claim of the cartoonist?

GUIDELINES for Reading Advertisements

- **What product or service is being advertised?**
- **Who seems to be the targeted audience?**
- **What is the ad's primary strategy?** To provide information? To reinforce the product's or company's image? To appeal to particular needs or desires? For example, if an ad shows a group of young people having fun and drinking a particular beer, to what needs/desires is the ad appealing?
- **Does the ad use specific rhetorical strategies such as humor, understatement, or irony?**
- **What is the relation between the visual part of the ad (photo, drawing, typeface, etc.) and the print part (the text, or copy)?** Does the ad use a slogan or catchy phrase? Is there a company logo? Is the slogan or logo clever? Is it well known as a marker of the company? What may be the effect of these strategies on readers?
- **What is the ad's overall visual impression?** Consider both images and colors used.

EXERCISES: Analyzing Photos, Cartoons, and Ads

1. Analyze the photo on p. 116, using the guidelines previously listed.
2. Review the photos that open Chapters 1, 4, 5, 8, 19, and 21. Select the one you find most effective. Analyze it in detail to show why you think it is the best.
3. Review the cartoons that open Chapters 3, 6, 7, 11, 16, and 20. Select the one you find most effective. Analyze it in detail to show why you think it is the cleverest.
4. Analyze the ads on pp. 121–123, again using the guidelines listed above. After answering the guideline questions, consider these as well: Will each ad appeal effectively to its intended audience? If so, why? If not, why not?

the river of life

Retracing a historic journey to help fight malaria.

In 1858, Scottish missionary David Livingstone embarked on a historic journey along the Zambezi River in southern Africa. On that trip, malaria claimed the life of Livingstone's wife, Mary Livingstone himself also later died from the disease.

Today, 150 years later, malaria remains a threat. Over one million people, mostly children and pregnant women, die from malaria each year. About 40 percent of the global population is vulnerable to the disease.

But an unprecedented global action—by governments and corporations, NGOs and health organizations—has been mobilized against malaria. And this combined effort is yielding results:

• Across Africa, people are receiving anti-malarial medications, as well as bed nets and insecticides that protect against the mosquitoes that transmit the disease.

Photo by Helge Bendl

• In Rwanda, malaria cases are down by 64 percent, and deaths by 66 percent. Similar results are seen in Ethiopia and Zambia. And in Mozambique, where 9 out of 10 children had been infected, that number is now 2 in 10.

• Scientists are expanding the pipeline of affordable, effective anti-malarial medicines, while also making progress on discovering a vaccine.

April 25 is World Malaria Day. As part of that event, a team of medical experts will retrace Livingstone's journey along the Zambezi, the "River of Life." As part of the Roll Back Malaria Zambezi Expedition, they will travel 1,500 miles in inflatable boats through Angola, Namibia, Botswana, Zambia, Zimbabwe and Mozambique.

By exposing the difficulties of delivering supplies to remote areas, the expedition will demonstrate that only a coordinated, cross-border action can beat back the disease, and turn the lifeline of southern Africa into a "River of Life" for those threatened by malaria.

ExxonMobil is the largest non-pharmaceutical private-sector contributor to the fight against malaria. But our support is more than financial. We are actively partnering with governments and agencies in affected countries, enabling them to combat malaria with the same disciplined, results-based business practices that ExxonMobil employs in its global operations.

Livingstone once said, "I am prepared to go anywhere, provided it be forward." The communities burdened by this disease cannot move forward until malaria is controlled and, someday, eradicated. We urge everyone to join in this global effort.

For more information, visit www.zambezi-expedition.org and www.rollbackmalaria.org.

ExxonMobil
Taking on the world's toughest energy challenges.

Courtesy Exxon-Mobil Corporation.

Courtesy of Peace Corps.

Your business side. Your creative side.
Inspire both. Intr oducing Avid's new editing lineup.

Quality, performance and value. A new way of thinking. A new way of doing business.
Take a closer look at **Avid.com/NewThinkingScript.**

Artist: Richard Borge, www.richardborge.com; Creative Director: Dan Greenwald;
Design Studio: White Rhino; Client: AVID. ©2008 Avid Technology Inc.

READING GRAPHICS

Graphics—photographs, diagrams, tables, charts, and graphs—present a good bit of information in a condensed but also visually engaging format. Graphics are everywhere: in textbooks, magazines, newspapers, and the Web. It's a rare training session or board meeting that is conducted without the use of graphics to display information. So, you want to be able to read graphics and create them, when appropriate, in your own writing. First, study the chart below that illustrates the different uses of various visuals. General guidelines for reading graphics follow. The guidelines will use Figure 5.1 to illustrate points. Study the figure repeatedly as you read through the guidelines.

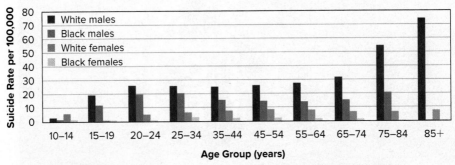

FIGURE 5.1 Differences in Suicide Rate According to Race, Gender, and Age
Data from the U.S. Bureau of the Census, 1994.

Understanding How Graphics Differ

Each type of visual serves specific purposes. You can't use a pie chart, for example, to explain a process; you need a diagram or a flowchart. So, when reading graphics, understand what each type can show you. When preparing your own visuals, select the graphic that will most clearly and effectively present the particular information you want to display.

TYPE	PURPOSE	EXAMPLE
Diagram	show details, demonstrate process	drawing of knee tendons, photosynthesis
Table	list numerical information	income of U.S. households
Bar chart	comparative amounts of related numbers	differences in suicide rates by age and race
Pie chart	relative portions of a whole	percentages of Americans by educational level
Flowchart	steps in a process	purification of water
Graph	relationship of two items	income increases over time
Map	information relative to a geographical area	locations of world's rain forests

GUIDELINES for Reading Graphics

1. **Locate the particular graphic referred to in the text and study it at that point in your reading.** Graphics may not always be placed on the same page as the text reference. Stop your reading to find and study the graphic; that's what the writer wants you to do. Find Figure 5.1 on the previous page.

2. **Read the title or heading of the graphic.** Every graphic is given a title. What is the subject of the graphic? What kind of information is provided? Figure 5.1 shows differences in suicide rates by race, gender, and age.

3. **Read any notes, description, and the source information at the bottom of the graphic.** Figure 5.1 came from the U.S. Bureau of the Census for 1994. Critical questions: What is this figure showing me? Is the information coming from a reliable source? Is it current enough to still be meaningful?

4. **Study the labels—and other words—that appear as part of the graphic.** You cannot draw useful conclusions unless you understand exactly what is being shown. Observe in Figure 5.1, that the four bars for each age group (shown along the horizontal axis) represent white males, black males, white females, and black females, in that order, for each age category.

5. **Study the information, making certain that you understand what the numbers represent.** Are the numerals whole numbers, numbers in hundreds or thousands, or percentages? In Figure 5.1, we are looking at suicide *rates per 100,000 people* for four identified groups of people at different ages. So, to know exactly how many white males between 15 and 19 commit suicide, we need to know how many white males between 15 and 19 there are (or were in 1994) in the United States population. The chart does not give us this information. It gives us *comparative rates* per 100,000 people in each category and tells us that almost 20 in every 100,000 white males between 15 and 19 commit suicide.

6. **Draw conclusions.** Think about the information in different ways. Critical questions: What does the author want to accomplish by including these figures? How are they significant? What conclusions can you draw from Figure 5.1? Answer these questions to guide your thinking:

   a. Which of the four compared groups faces the greatest risk from suicide over his or her lifetime? Would you have guessed this group? Why or why not? What might be some of the causes for the greatest risk to this group?

   b. What is the greatest risk factor for increased suicide rate—race, gender, age, or a combination? Does this surprise you? Would you have guessed a different factor? Why?

   c. Which group, as young teens, is at greatest risk? Are you surprised? Why or why not? What might be some of the causes for this?

Graphics provide information, raise questions, explain processes, engage us emotionally, make us think. Study the various graphics in the exercises that follow to become more expert in reading and responding critically to visuals.

EXERCISES: Reading and Analyzing Graphics

1. Study the pie charts in Figure 5.2 and then answer the following questions.

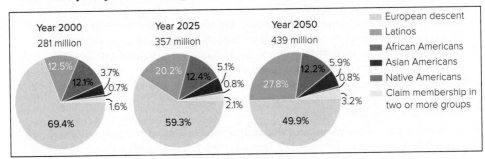

FIGURE 5.2 **The Shifting of U.S. Racial-Ethnic Mix**

   a. What is the subject of the charts?
   b. In addition to the information within the pie charts, what other information is provided?
   c. Which group increases by the greatest relative amount? How would you account for that increase?
   d. Which figure surprises you the most? Why?
2. Study the line graph in Figure 5.3 and then answer the following questions.

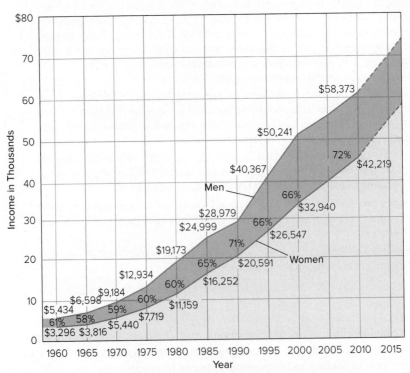

FIGURE 5.3 **The Gender Gap Over Time: What Percentage of Men's Income Do Women Earn?**

a. What two subjects are treated by the graph?
b. In 2000, what percentage of men's income did women earn?
c. During which five-year period did men's incomes increase by the greatest amount?
d. Does the author's prediction for the year 2005 suggest that income equality for women will have taken place?
e. Are you bothered by the facts on this graph? Why or why not?

3. Study the table in Figure 5.4 and then answer the following questions.

	1970		2000		2009	
	MEN	**WOMEN**	**MEN**	**WOMEN**	**MEN**	**WOMEN**
Life expectancy	67.1	74.1	74.24	79.9	75.6	80.8
% of BAs awarded	57	43	45	55	38	62
% of MSs awarded	60	40	45	55	37.4	62.6
% of PhDs awarded	87	13	45	55	37.4	62.6
% in legal profession	95	5	70	30	n/a	n/a
Median earnings	$26,760	$14,232	$33,345	$25,862	$62,455	$44,857

FIGURE 5.4 **Men and Women in a Changing Society.**

for 1970: 1966 *Statistical Abstract,* U.S. Dept of Commerce, Economics and Statistics Administration, Bureau of the Census. For 2009: U.S. Bureau of the Census and National Center for Educational Statistics.

a. What is being presented and compared in this table?
b. What, exactly, do the numerals in the second line represent? What, exactly, do the numerals in the third line represent? (Be sure that you understand what these numbers mean.)
c. For the information given in lines 2, 3, 4, and 5, in which category have women made the greatest gains on men?
d. Which figure surprises you the most? Why?

4. Maps can be used to show all kinds of information, not just the locations of cities, rivers, or mountains. Study the map in Figure 5.5 and then answer the questions that follow.

a. What, exactly, does the map show? Why does it not "look right"?
b. How many electoral votes did each candidate win?
c. How are the winning states for each candidate clustered? What conclusions can you draw from observing this clustering?
d. What advice would you give to each party to ensure that party's presidential win in 2020?
e. How would the map look if it were drawn to show population by state?

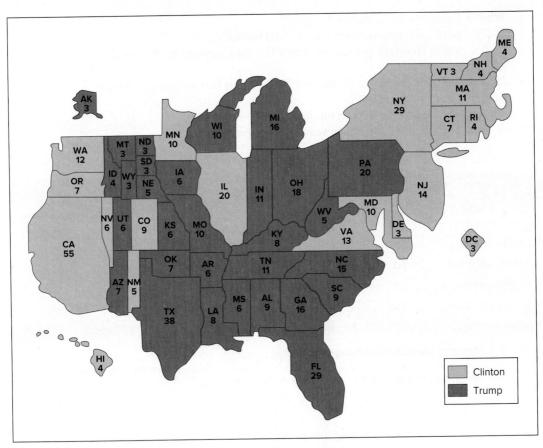

FIGURE 5.5 Electoral Votes per State for the 2016 Presidential Election

Reprinted by permission of Sam Wang.

THE USES OF AUTHORITY AND STATISTICS

Most of the visuals you have just studied provide a way of presenting statistics—data that many today consider essential to defending a claim. One reason you check the source information accompanying graphics is that you need to know—and evaluate—the authority of that source. When a graphic's numbers have come from the Census Bureau, you know you have a reliable source. When an author writes that "studies have shown . . . ," you should be suspicious of the authority of the data. All elements of the arguments we read—and write—affect a writer's credibility.

Judging Authorities

We know that movie stars and sports figures are not authorities on soft drinks and watches. But what about *real* authorities? When writers present the opinions or research findings of authorities as support for a claim, they are saying to readers that the authority is trustworthy and the opinions valuable. But what they are asserting is actually an assumption or warrant, part of the glue connecting evidence to claim. Remember: Warrants can be challenged. If the "authority" can be shown to lack authority, then the logic of the argument is destroyed. Use this checklist of questions to evaluate authorities:

☐ *Is the authority actually an authority on the topic under discussion?* When a famous scientist supports a candidate for office, he or she speaks as a citizen, not as an authority.

☐ *Is the work of the authority still current?* Times change; expertise does not always endure. Galileo would be lost in the universe of today's astrophysicists. Be particularly alert to the dates of information in the sciences in general, in genetics and the entire biomedical field, in health and nutrition. It is almost impossible to keep up with the latest findings in these areas of research.

☐ *Does the authority actually have legitimate credentials?* Are the person's publications in respected journals? Is he or she respected by others in the same field? *Just because it's in print or online does not mean it's a reliable source!*

☐ *Do experts in the field generally agree on the issue?* If there is widespread disagreement, then referring to one authority does not do much to support a claim. This is why you need to understand the many sides of a controversial topic before you write on it, and you need to bring knowledge of controversies and critical thinking skills to your reading of argument. This is also why writers often provide a source's credentials, not just a name, unless the authority is quite famous.

☐ *Is the authority's evidence reliable, so far as you can judge, but the interpretation of that evidence seems odd, or seems to be used to support strongly held beliefs?* Does the evidence actually connect to the claim? A respected authority's work can be stretched or manipulated in an attempt to defend a claim that the authority's work simply does not support.

EXERCISES: Judging Authorities

1. Jane Goodall has received worldwide fame for her studies of chimpanzees in Gombe and for her books on those field studies. Goodall is a vegetarian. Should she be used as an authority in support of a claim for a vegetarian diet? Why or why not? Consider:
   a. Why might Goodall have chosen to become a vegetarian?
   b. For what arguments might Goodall be used as an authority?
   c. For what arguments might she be used effectively for emotional appeal?
2. Suppose a respected zoologist prepares a five-year study of U.S. zoos, compiling a complete list of all animals at each zoo. He then updates the list for each of the five years, adding births and deaths. When he examines his data, he finds that deaths are one and one-half times the number of births. He considers this loss alarming and writes a paper arguing for the abolishing of zoos on the grounds that too many ani-

mals are dying. Because of his reputation, his article is published in a popular science magazine. How would you evaluate his authority and his study?

a.   Should you trust the data? Why or why not?

b.   Should you accept his conclusions? Why or why not?

c.   Consider: What might be possible explanations for the birth/death ratio?

Understanding and Evaluating Statistics

There are two useful clichés to keep in mind: "Statistics don't lie, but people lie with statistics" and "There are lies, damned lies, and statistics." The second cliché is perhaps a bit cynical. We don't want to be naïve in our faith in numbers, but neither do we want to become so cynical that we refuse to believe any statistical evidence. What we do need to keep in mind is that when statistics are presented in an argument, they are being used by someone interested in winning that argument.

Some writers use numbers without being aware that the numbers are incomplete or not representative. Some present only part of the relevant information. Some may not mean to distort, but they do choose to present the information in language that helps their cause. There are many ways, some more innocent than others, to distort reality with statistics. Use the following guidelines to evaluate the presentation of statistical information.

GUIDELINES for Evaluating Statistics

- **Is the information current and therefore still relevant?** Crime rates in your city based on 2000 census data probably are no longer relevant, certainly not current enough to support an argument for increased (or decreased) police department spending.

- **If a sample was used, was it randomly selected and large enough to be significant?** Sometimes in medical research, the results of a small study are publicized to guide researchers to important new areas of study. When these results are reported in the press or on TV, however, the small size of the study is not always made clear. Thus one week we learn that coffee is bad for us, the next week that it is okay.

- **What information, exactly, has been provided?** When you read "Two out of three chose the Merit cigarette combination of low tar and good taste," you must ask yourself "Two-thirds of how many altogether?"

- **How have the numbers been presented?** And what is the effect of that presentation? Numbers can be presented as fractions, whole numbers, or percentages. Writers who want to emphasize budget increases will use whole numbers—billions of dollars. Writers who want to de-emphasize those increases select percentages. Writers who want their readers to respond to the numbers in a specific way add words to direct their thinking: "a *mere* 3 percent increase" or "the *enormous* $5 billion increase."

EXERCISES: Reading Tables and Charts and Using Statistics

1. Figure 5.6 (p. 132), a table from the Census Bureau, shows U.S. family income data from 1980 to 2009. Percentages and median income are given for all families and then, in turn, for white, black, Asian, and Hispanic families. Study the data and then complete the exercises that follow.

   a. In a paper assessing the advantages of a growing economy, you want to include a paragraph on family income growth to show that a booming economy helps everyone, that "a rising tide lifts all boats." Select data from the table that best support your claim. Write a paragraph beginning with a topic sentence and including your data as support. Think about how to present the numbers in the most persuasive form.

   b. Write a second paragraph with the topic sentence "Not all Americans have benefited from the boom years" or "A rising tide does not lift all boats." Select data from the table that best support this topic sentence and present the numbers in the most persuasive form.

   c. Exchange paragraphs with a classmate and evaluate each other's selection and presentation of evidence.

2. Go back to Figure 5.1 (p. 124) and reflect again on the information that it depicts. Then consider what conclusions can be drawn from the evidence and what the implications of those conclusions are. Working in small groups or with a class partner, decide how you want to use the data to support a point.

3. Figure 5.7 (p. 133), another table from the Census Bureau, presents mean earnings by highest degree earned. First, be sure that you know the difference between mean and median (which is the number used in Figure 5.6). Study the data and reflect on the conclusions you can draw from the statistics. Consider: Of the various groups represented, which group most benefits from obtaining a college degree—as opposed to having only a high school diploma?

WRITING THE INVESTIGATIVE ARGUMENT

The first step in writing an investigative argument is to select a topic to study. Composition students can write successful investigative essays on the media, on campus issues, and on various local concerns. Although you begin with a topic—not a claim—since you have to gather evidence before you can see what it means, you should select a topic that holds your interest and that you may have given some thought to before choosing to write. For example, you may have noticed some clever ads for jeans or beer, or perhaps you are bothered by plans for another shopping area along a major street near your home. Either one of these topics can lead to an effective investigative, or inductive, argument.

Gathering and Analyzing Evidence

Let's reflect on strategies for gathering evidence for a study of magazine ads for a particular kind of product (the topic of the sample student paper that follows).

- Select a time frame and a number of representative magazines.
- Have enough magazines to render at least twenty-five ads on the product you are studying.

Year	Number of families (1,000)	Percent distribution							Median income (dollars)
		Under $15,000	$15,000 to $24,999	$25,000 to $34,999	$35,000 to $49,999	$50,000 to $74,999	$75,000 to $99,999	$100,000 and over	
ALL FAMILIES [1]									
1990	66,322	8.7	9.4	10.3	15.6	22.5	14.6	19.1	54,369
2000 [2]	73,778	7.0	8.6	9.3	14.3	19.8	15.1	26.2	61,063
2008	78,874	8.4	9.2	9.9	13.7	19.3	14.2	26.0	61,521
2009 [3]	76,867	8.7	9.1	10.0	13.8	19.4	13.5	25.6	60,088
WHITE									
1990	56,803	6.6	8.7	10.0	15.8	23.3	15.4	20.4	56,771
2000 [2]	61,330	5.7	7.9	9.0	14.2	20.1	15.8	27.7	63,849
2008 [4, 5]	64,183	6.9	8.5	9.5	13.4	19.8	15.0	27.5	65,000
2009 [3, 4, 5]	64,145	7.2	8.4	9.5	13.8	19.9	14.1	27.0	62,545
BLACK									
1990	7,471	23.9	14.7	12.5	14.4	17.5	8.8	8.2	32,946
2000 [2]	8,731	15.7	14.0	12.8	15.8	16.7	10.3	13.0	40,547
2008 [4, 5]	9,359	18.2	14.4	12.8	15.3	16.6	9.8	13.4	39,879
2009 [3, 4, 5]	9,367	18.0	14.5	13.3	15.2	16.4	10.6	12.1	38,409
ASIAN AND PACIFIC ISLANDER									
1990	1,536	8.1	7.8	8.2	11.6	21.2	15.0	28.5	64,969
2000 [2]	2,962	6.2	6.4	6.4	11.7	17.3	15.5	37.0	75,393
2008 [4, 7]	3,494	7.7	7.2	7.6	12.8	16.0	13.0	36.6	73,578
2009 [3, 4, 7]	3,592	6.9	7.0	7.9	10.4	17.7	12.3	37.7	75,027
HISPANIC ORIGIN [8]									
1990	4,961	17.0	16.3	13.6	17.3	19.1	8.5	8.2	36,034
2000 [2]	8,017	12.8	14.6	13.0	18.1	19.4	10.5	12.0	41,469
2008	10,503	15.5	14.6	14.1	16.8	17.2	9.6	12.5	40,466
2009 [3]	10,422	15.2	14.7	14.3	16.0	17.9	9.5	12.4	39,730

[Constant dollars based on CPI-U-RS deflator. Families as of March of following year, (66,322 represents 66,322,000). Based on Current Population Survey, Annual Social and Economic Supplement (ASEC); see text, this section, Section 1, and Appendix III. For data collection changes over time, see <http://www.census.gov/hhes/www/income/data/historical/history.html>. For definition of median, see Guide to Tabular Presentation]

[1] Includes other races not shown separately.   [2] Data reflect implementation of Census 2000-based population controls and a 28,000 household sample expansion to 78,000 households.   [3] Median income is calculated using $2,500 income intervals. Beginning with 2009 income data, the Census Bureau expanded the upper income intervals used to calculate medians to $250,000 or more. Medians falling in the upper open-ended interval are plugged with "$250,000." Before 2009, the upper open-ended interval was $100,000 and a plug of "$100,000" was used.   [4] Beginning with the 2003 Current Population Survey (CPS), the questionnaire allowed respondents to choose more than one race. For 2002 and later, data represent persons who selected this race group only and excludes persons reporting more than one race. The CPS in prior years allowed respondents to report only one race group. See also comments on race in the text for Section 1.   [5] Data represent White alone, which refers to people who reported White and did not report any other race category.   [6] Data represent Black alone, which refers to people who reported Black and did not report any other race category.   [7] Data represent Asian alone, which refers to people who reported Asian and did not report any other race category. [8] People of Hispanic origin may be any race.

FIGURE 5.6 **Money Income of Families—Percent Distribution by Income Level in Constant (2009) Dollars: 1980 to 2009.**

U.S. Census *Bureau, Income, Poverty and Health Insurance Coverage in the United States, 2009* Current Population Reports, P60-238 and historical Tables - Table F-23, September 2010

- Once you decide on the magazines and issues to be used, pull *all* ads for your product. Your task is to draw useful conclusions based on adequate data objectively collected. You can't leave some ads out and have a valid study.
- Study the ads, reflecting on the inferences they allow you to draw. The inferences become the claim of your argument. You may want to take the approach of classifying the ads, that is, grouping them into categories by the various appeals used to sell the product.

Characteristic	Total persons	Mean earnings by level of highest degree (dol.)							
		Not a high school graduate	High school graduate only	Some college, no degree	Associate's	Bachelor's	Master's	Professional	Doctorate
All persons [1] . . .	**42,469**	**20,241**	**30,627**	**32,295**	**39,771**	**58,665**	**73,738**	**127,803**	**103,054**
Age:									
25 to 34 years old. . . .	35,595	19,415	30,627	31,392	35,544	45,662	58,997	86,440	74,628
35 to 44 years old. . . .	49,356	24,728	27,511	39,606	42,489	66,346	80,583	136,366	108,147
45 to 54 years old. . . .	51,956	23,725	36,090	44,135	45,145	69,548	86,532	146,808	112,134
55 to 64 years old. . . .	50,372	24,537	34,583	42,547	42,344	59,670	75,372	149,184	110,895
65 years old and over .	37,544	19,395	28,469	29,602	33,541	44,147	45,138	95,440	95,585
Sex:									
Male.	50,180	23,036	35,468	39,204	47,572	69,479	90,954	150,310	114,347
Female	33,797	15,514	24,304	23,340	33,432	43,689	58,534	89,897	83,706
White [2].	43,337	20,457	31,429	33,119	40,632	57,762	73,771	127,942	104,533
Male.	51,287	23,353	36,416	40,352	48,521	71,286	81,776	149,149	115,497
Female	34,040	15,187	24,615	25,537	33,996	43,309	58,036	89,526	85,682
Black [2].	33,362	18,938	25,970	29,129	33,734	47,799	60,067	102,328	82,510
Male.	37,553	21,829	30,723	33,969	41,142	55,655	68,890	(B)	(B)
Female	29,831	15,644	22,954	25,433	29,464	42,567	54,523	(B)	(B)
Hispanic [3].	29,565	19,816	25,998	29,836	33,783	49,017	71,322	79,220	88,435
Male.	32,279	21,588	28,908	35,089	38,768	58,570	80,737	(B)	89,968
Female	25,713	16,170	21,473	24,281	29,785	39,568	61,843	(B)	(B)

[In dollars. For persons 18 years old and over with earnings. Persons as of March 2010. Based on Current Population Survey; see text, Section 1 and Appendix III. For definition of mean, see Guide to Tabular Presentation]

B Base figure too small to meet statistical standards for reliability of a derived figure.   [1] Includes other races not shown separately.   [2] For persons who selected this race group only. [3] Persons of Hispanic origin may be any race.

FIGURE 5.7 Mean Earnings by Highest Degree Earned: 2009
U.S. Census Bureau, Current population survey, unpublished data.

More briefly, consider your hunch that your area does not need another shopping mall. What evidence can you gather to support a claim to that effect? You could locate all existing strip or enclosed malls within a ten-mile radius of the proposed new mall site, visit each one, and count the number and types of stores already available. You may discover that there are plenty of malls but that the area really needs a grocery store or a bookstore. So instead of reading to find evidence to support a claim, you are creating the statistics and doing the analysis to guide you to a claim. Just remember to devise objective procedures for collecting evidence so that you do not bias your results.

Planning and Drafting the Essay

You've done your research and studied the data you've collected; how do you put this kind of argument together? Here are some guidelines to help you draft your essay.

Analyzing Evidence: The Key to an Effective Argument

This is the thinking part of the process. Anyone can count stores or collect ads. What is your point? How does the evidence you have collected actually support your claim? You must guide readers through the evidence. Consider this example:

GUIDELINES for Writing an Investigative Argument

- **Begin with an opening paragraph that introduces your topic in an interesting way.** Possibilities include beginning with a startling statistic or explaining what impact the essay's facts will have on readers.

- **Devote space early in your paper to explaining your methods or procedures, probably in your second or third paragraph.** For example, if you have obtained information through questionnaires or interviews, recount the process: the questions asked, the number of people involved, the basis for selecting the people, and so on.

- **Classify the evidence that you present.** Finding a meaningful organization is part of the originality of your study and will make your argument more forceful. It is the way you see the topic and want readers to see it. If you are studying existing malls, you might begin by listing all of the malls and their locations. But then do not go store by store through each mall. Rather, group the stores by type and provide totals.

- **Consider presenting evidence in several ways, including in charts and tables as well as within paragraphs.** Readers are used to visuals, especially in essays containing statistics.

- **Analyze evidence to build your argument.** Do not ask your reader to do the thinking. No data dumps! Explain how your evidence *is* evidence by discussing the connection between facts and the inferences they support.

In a study of selling techniques used in computer ads in business magazines, a student, Brian, found four major selling techniques, one of which he classifies as "corporate emphasis." Brian begins his paragraph on corporate emphasis thus:

> In the technique of corporate emphasis, the advertiser discusses the whole range of products and services that the corporation offers, instead of specific elements. This method relies on the public's positive perception of the company, the company's accomplishments, and its reputation.

Brian then provides several examples of ads in this category, including an IBM ad:

> In one of its eight ads in the study, IBM points to the scientists on its staff who have recently won the Nobel Prize in physics.

But Brian does not stop there. He explains the point of this ad, connecting it to the assertion that this technique emphasizes the company's accomplishments:

> The inference we are to draw is that IBM scientists are hard at work right now in their laboratories developing tomorrow's technology to make the world a better place in which to live.

Preparing Graphics for Your Essay

Tables, bar charts, and pie charts are particularly helpful ways to present statistical evidence you have collected for an inductive argument. One possibility is to create a pie chart showing your classification of ads (or stores or questions on a questionnaire) and the relative amount of each item. For example, suppose you find four selling strategies. You can show in a pie chart the percentage of ads using each of the four strategies.

Computers help even the technically unsophisticated prepare simple charts. You can also do a simple table. When preparing graphics, keep these points in mind:

- Every graphic must be introduced and referred to in the text at the appropriate place—where you are discussing the information in the visual. Graphics are not disconnected attachments to an argument. They give a complete set of data in an easy-to-digest form, but some of that data must be discussed in the essay.
- Every graphic (except photographs) needs a label. Use Figure 1, Figure 2, and so forth. Then, in the text refer to each graphic by its label.
- Every graphic needs a title. Always place a title after Figure 1 (and so forth), on the same line, at the top or bottom of your visual.
- In a technically sophisticated world, hand-drawn graphics are not acceptable. Underline the graphic's title line, or place the visual within a box. (Check the toolbar at the top of your screen.) Type elements within tables. Use a ruler or compass to prepare graphics, or learn to use the graphics programs in your computer.

A CHECKLIST FOR REVISION

- ☐ Have I stated a claim that is precise and appropriate to the data I have collected?
- ☐ Have I fully explained the methodology I used in collecting my data?
- ☐ Have I selected a clear and useful organization?
- ☐ Have I presented and discussed enough specifics to show readers how my data support my conclusions?
- ☐ Have I used graphics to present the data in an effective visual display?
- ☐ Have I revised, edited, and proofread my paper?

STUDENT ESSAY

BUYING TIME

Garrett Berger

Chances are you own at least one wristwatch. Watches allow us immediate access to the correct time. They are indispensable items in our modern world, where, as the saying is, time is money. Today the primary function of a wristwatch does not necessarily guide its design; like clothes, houses, and cars, watches have become fashion statements and a way to flaunt one's wealth.

Introduction connects to reader.

To learn how watches are being sold, I surveyed all of the full-page ads from the November issues of four magazines. The first two, *GQ* and *Vogue,* are well-known fashion magazines. *The Robb Report* is a rather new magazine that caters to the overclass. *Forbes* is of course a well-known financial magazine. I was rather surprised at the number of advertisements I found. After surveying 86 ads, marketing 59 brands, I have concluded that today watches are being sold through five main strategies: DESIGN/BRAND appeal, CRAFTSMANSHIP, ASSOCIATION, FASHION appeal, and EMOTIONAL appeal. The percentage of ads using each of these strategies is shown in Figure 1.

In most DESIGN/BRAND appeal ads, only a picture and the brand name are used. A subset of this category uses the same basic strategy with a slogan or phrases to emphasize something about the brand or product. A Mont Blanc ad shows a watch profile with a contorted metal link band, asking the question "Is that you?" The reputation of the name and the appeal of the design sell the watch. Rolex, perhaps the best-known name in high-end watches, advertises, in *Vogue,* its "Oyster Perpetual Lady-Datejust Pearlmaster." A close-up of the watch face showcases the white, mother-of-pearl dial, sapphire bezel, and diamond-set band. A smaller, more complete picture crouches underneath, showing the watch on its side. The model name is

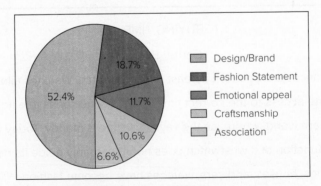

FIGURE 1 **Percentage of Total Ads Using Each Strategy**

displayed along a gray band that runs near the bottom. The Rolex crest anchors the bottom of the page. Forty-five ads marketing 29 brands use the DESIGN/BRAND strategy. A large picture of the product centered on a solid background is the norm.

CRAFTSMANSHIP, the second strategy, focuses on the maker, the horologer, and the technical sides of form and function. Brand heritage and a unique, hand-crafted design are major selling points. All of these ads are targeted at men, appearing in every magazine except *Vogue.* Collector pieces and limited editions were commonly sold using this strategy. The focus is on accuracy and technical excellence. Pictures of the inner works and cutaways, technical information, and explanations of movements and features are popular. Quality and exclusivity are all-important.

A Cronoswiss ad from *The Robb Report* is a good example. The top third pictures a horologer, identified as "Gerd-R Lange, master watchmaker and founder of Cronoswiss in Munich," directly below. The middle third of the ad shows a watch, white-faced with a black leather band. The logo and slogan appear next to the watch. The bottom third contains copy beginning with the words "My watches are a hundred years behind the times." The rest explains what that statement means. Mr. Lange apparently believes that technical perfection in horology has already been attained. He also offers his book, *The Fascination of Mechanics,* free of charge along with the "sole distributor for North America" at the bottom. A "Daniel Roth" ad from the same magazine displays the name across the top of a white page; toward the top, left-hand corner a gold buckle and black band lead your eye to the center, where a gold watch with a transparent face displays its inner works exquisitely. Above and to the right, copy explains the exclusive and unique design accomplished by inverting the movement, allowing it to be viewed from above.

Discussion of second category.

Detailed examples to illustrate second category.

Discussion of third
category.

The third strategy is to sell the watch by establishing an ASSOCIATION with an object, experience, or person, implying that its value and quality are beyond question. In the six ads I found using this approach, watches are associated with violins, pilots, astronauts, hot air balloons, and a hero of the free world. This is similar to the first strategy, but relies on a reputation other than that of the maker. The watch is presented as being desirable for the connections created in the ad.

Parmigiani ran an ad in *The Robb Report* featuring a gold watch with a black face and band illuminated by some unseen source. A blue-tinted violin rises in the background; the rest of the page is black. The brief copy reads: "For those who think a Stradivarius is only a violin. The Parmigiani Toric Chronograph is only a wristwatch." "The Moon Watch" proclaims an Omega ad from *GQ*. Inset on a white background is a picture of an astronaut on the moon saluting the American flag. The silver watch with a black face lies across the lower part of the page. Omega's logo appears at the top (Figure 2).

FIGURE 2 **Example of Association Advertising**

The fourth strategy is to present the watch simply as a FASHION statement. In this line of attack, the ads appeal to our need to be current, accepted, to fit in and be like everyone else, or to make a statement, setting us apart from others as hip and cool. The product is presented as a necessary part of our wardrobes. The watch is fashionable and will send the "right" message. Design and style are the foremost concerns; "the look" sells the watch.

Techno Marine has an ad in *GQ* which shows a large close-up of a watch running down the entire length of the left side of the page. Two alternate color schemes are pictured on the right, separating small bits of copy. At the bottom on the right are the name and logo. The first words at the top read: "Keeping time—you keep your closet up to the minute, why not your wrist? The latest addition to your watch wardrobe should be the AlphaSport." Longines uses a similar strategy in *Vogue.* Its ad is divided in half lengthwise. On the left is a black-and-white picture of Audrey Hepburn. The right side is white with the Longines' logo at the top and two ladies' watches in the center. Near the bottom is the phrase "Elegance is an Attitude." Retailers appear at the bottom. The same ad ran in *GQ,* but with a man's watch and a picture of Humphrey Bogart. A kind of association is made, but quality and value aren't the overriding concerns. The point is to have an elegant attitude like these fashionable stars did, one that these watches can provide and enhance.

The fifth and final strategy is that of EMOTIONAL appeal. The ads using this approach strive to influence our emotional responses and allege to influence the emotions of others towards us. Their power and appeal are exerted through the feelings they evoke in us. Nine out of ten ads rely on a picture as the main device to trigger an emotional link between the product and the viewer. Copy is scant; words are used mainly to guide the viewer to the advertiser's desired conclusions.

Discussion of fourth category.

Discussion of fifth category.

A Frederique Constant ad pictures a man, wearing a watch, mulling over a chess game. Above his head are the words "Inner Passion." The man's gaze is odd; he is looking at something on the right side of the page, but a large picture of a watch superimposed over the picture hides whatever it is that he is looking at. So we are led to the watch. The bottom third is white and contains the maker's logo and the slogan "Live your Passion." An ad in *GQ* shows a man holding a woman. He leans against a rock; she reclines in his arms. Their eyes are closed, and both have peaceful, smiling expressions. He is wearing a Tommy Hilfiger watch. The ad spans two pages; a close-up of the watch is presented on the right half of the second page. The only words are the ones in the logo. This is perhaps one of those pictures that are worth a thousand words. The message is he got the girl because he's got the watch.

Strong conclusion; the effect of watch ads.

Even more than selling a particular watch, all of these ads focus on building the brand's image. I found many of the ads extremely effective at conveying their messages. Many of the better-known brands favor the comparatively simple DESIGN/BRAND appeal strategy, to reach a broader audience. Lesser-known, high-end makers contribute many of the more specialized strategies. We all count and mark the passing hours and minutes. And society places great importance on time, valuing punctuality. But these ads strive to convince us that having "the right time" means so much more than "the time."

Courtesy of Garrett Berger

FOR READING AND ANALYSIS

EVERY BODY'S TALKING | JOE NAVARRO

Joe Navarro spent more than twenty-five years in the FBI, specializing in counterintelligence and profiling. He is recognized as an authority on nonverbal messages, especially given off by those who are lying, and he continues to consult to government and industry. He has also turned his expertise to poker and has published, with Marvin

Karlines, *Read, Em and Reap* (2006) and, on his own, *What Every Body Is Saying* (2008). The following essay appeared in *The Washington Post* on June 24, 2008.

PREREADING QUESTIONS What does the term "counterintelligence" mean? How much attention do you give to body language messages from others?

Picture this: I was sailing the Caribbean for three days with a group of friends 1
and their spouses, and everything seemed perfect. The weather was beautiful, the ocean diaphanous blue, the food exquisite; our evenings together were full of laughter and good conversation.

Things were going so well that one friend said to the group, "Let's do this 2
again next year." I happened to be across from him and his wife as he spoke those words. In the cacophony of resounding replies of "Yes!" and "Absolutely!" I noticed that my friend's wife made a fist under her chin as she grasped her necklace. This behavior stood out to me as powerfully as if someone had shouted, "Danger!"

I watched the words and gestures of the other couples at the table, and 3
everyone seemed ecstatic—everyone but one, that is. She continued to smile, but her smile was tense.

Her husband has treated me as a brother for more than 15 years, and 4
I consider him the dearest of friends. At that moment I knew that things between him and his wife were turning for the worse. I did not pat myself on the back for making these observations. I was saddened.

For 25 years I worked as a paid observer. I was a special agent for the FBI 5
specializing in counterintelligence—specifically, catching spies. For me, observing human behavior is like having software running in the background, doing its job—no conscious effort needed. And so on that wonderful cruise, I made a "thin-slice assessment" (that's what we call it) based on just a few significant behaviors. Unfortunately, it turned out to be right: Within six months of our return, my friend's wife filed for divorce, and her husband discovered painfully that she had been seeing someone else for quite a while.

When I am asked what is the most reliable means of determining the health 6
of a relationship, I always say that words don't matter. It's all in the language of the body. The nonverbal behaviors we all transmit tell others, in real time, what we think, what we feel, what we yearn for or what we intend.

Now I am embarking on another cruise, wondering what insights I will have 7
about my travel companions and their relationships. No matter what, this promises to be a fascinating trip, a journey for the mind and the soul. I am with a handful of dear friends and 3,800 strangers, all headed for Alaska; for an observer it does not get any better than this.

While lining up to board on our first day, I notice just ahead of me a couple 8
who appear to be in their early 30s. They are obviously Americans (voice, weight and demeanor).

Not so obvious is their dysfunctional relationship. He is standing stoically, 9
shoulders wide, looking straight ahead. She keeps whispering loudly to him, but she is not facing forward. She violates his space as she leans into him. Her face is tense and her lips are narrow slivers each time she engages him with what

clearly appears to be a diatribe. He occasionally nods his head but avoids contact with her. He won't let his hips near her as they start to walk side by side. He reminds me of Bill and Hillary Clinton walking toward the Marine One helicopter immediately after the Monica Lewinsky affair: looking straight ahead, as much distance between them as possible.

Illustrations in Joe Navarro, "Every Body's Talking," *The Washington Post*, June 24, 2008. Illustrations by Peter Arkle. Reprinted by permission.

10   I think everyone can decipher this one from afar because we have all seen situations like this. What most people will miss is something I have seen this young man do twice now, which portends poorly for both of them. Every time

she looks away, he "disses" her. He smirks and rolls his eyes, even as she stands beside him. He performs his duties, pulling their luggage along; I suspect he likes to have her luggage nearby as a barrier between them. I won't witness the dissolution of their marriage, but I know it will happen, for the research behind this is fairly robust. When two people in a relationship have contempt for each other, the marriage will not last.

When it comes to relationships and courtship behaviors, the list of useful 11 cues is long. Most of these behaviors we learned early when interacting with our mothers. When we look at loving eyes, our own eyes get larger, our pupils dilate, our facial muscles relax, our lips become full and warm, our skin becomes more pliable, our heads tilt. These behaviors stay with us all of our lives.

I watched two lovers this morning in the dining room. Two young people, 12 perhaps in their late 20s, mirror each other, staring intently into each other's eyes, chin on hand, head slightly tilted, nose flaring with each breath. They are trying to absorb each other visually and tactilely as they hold hands across the table.

Over time, those who remain truly in love will show even more indicators of 13 mirroring. They may dress the same or even begin to look alike as they adopt each other's nonverbal expressions as a sign of synchrony and empathy. They will touch each other with kind hands that touch fully, not with the fingertips of the less caring.

They will mirror each other in ways that are almost imperceptible; they will 14 have similar blink rates and breathing rates, and they will sit almost identically. They will look at the same scenery and not speak, merely look at each other and take a deep breath to reset their breathing synchrony. They don't have to talk. They are in harmony physically, mentally and emotionally, just as a baby is in exquisite synchrony with its mother who is tracing his every expression and smile.

As I walk through the ship on the first night, I can see the nonverbals of 15 courtship. There is a beautiful woman, tall, slender, smoking a cigarette outside. Two men are talking to her, both muscular, handsome, interested. She has crossed her legs as she talks to them, an expression of her comfort. As she holds her cigarette, the inside of her wrist turns toward her newfound friends. Her interest and comfort with them resounds, but she is favoring one of them. As he speaks to her, she preens herself by playing with her hair. I am not sure he is getting the message that she prefers him; in the end, I am sure it will all get sorted out.

At the upscale lounge, a man is sitting at the bar talking animatedly to the 16 woman next to him and looking at everyone who walks by. The woman has begun the process of ignoring him, but he does not get it. After he speaks to her a few times, she gathers her purse and places it on her lap. She has turned slightly away from him and now avoids eye contact. He has no clue; he thinks he is cool by commenting on the women who pass by. She is verbally and non-verbally indifferent.

17   The next night it is more of the same. This time, I see two people who just met talking gingerly. Gradually they lean more and more into each other. She is now dangling her sandal from her toes. I am not sure he knows it. Perhaps he sees it all in her face, because she is smiling, laughing and relaxed. Communication is fluid, and neither wants the conversation to end. She is extremely interested.

18   All of these individuals are carrying on a dialogue in nonverbals. The socially adept will learn to read and interpret the signs accurately. Others will make false steps or pay a high price for not being observant. They may end up like my friend on the Caribbean cruise, who missed the clues of deceit and indifference.

19   This brings me back to my friend and his new wife, who are on this wonderful voyage. They have been on board for four days, and they are a delight individually and together. He lovingly looks at her; she stares at him with love and admiration. When she holds his hand at dinner, she massages it ever so gently. Theirs is a strong marriage. They don't have to tell me. I can sense it and observe it. I am happy for them and for myself. I can see cues of happiness, and they are unmistakable. You can't ask for more.

Joe Navarro, "Every Body's Talking," *The Washington Post,* 24 June 2008. Used with permission of the author.

QUESTIONS FOR READING

1. What is Navarro's subject? (Do not answer "taking cruises"!)
2. What clues are offered to support the conclusion that the two cruise couples' relationships are about to dissolve?
3. What are the nonverbal messages that reveal loving relationships?
4. What nonverbal messages should the man in the lounge be observing?

QUESTIONS FOR REASONING AND ANALYSIS

5. What is Navarro's claim?
6. What kind of evidence does he provide?
7. How do the illustrations contribute to the argument? What is effective about the author's opening?

QUESTIONS FOR REFLECTION AND WRITING

8. Has the author convinced you that nonverbal language reveals our thoughts and feelings? Why or why not?
9. Can you "read" the nonverbal language of your instructors? Take some time to analyze each of your instructors. What have you learned? (You might also reflect on what messages you may be sending in class.)

For all investigative essays—inductive arguments—follow the guidelines in this chapter and use the student essay as your model. Remember that you will need to explain your methods for collecting data, to classify evidence and present it in several formats, and also to explain its significance for readers. Just collecting data does not create an argument. Here are some possible topics to explore:

1. Study print or online ads for one type of product (e.g., cars, cosmetics, cigarettes) to draw inferences about the dominant techniques used to sell that product. Remember that the more ads you study, the more support you have for your inferences. You should study at least twenty-five ads.

2. Study print or online ads for one type of product as advertised in different types of magazines or on different types of websites clearly directed to different audiences to see how (or if) selling techniques change with a change in audience. (Remember: To demonstrate no change in techniques can be just as interesting a conclusion as finding changes.) Study at least twenty-five ads, in a balanced number from the different magazines or websites.

3. Select a major figure currently in the news and conduct a study of bias in one of the newsmagazines (e.g., *Time, U.S. News & World Report,* or *Newsweek*) or a newspaper. Use at least eight issues of the magazine or newspaper from the last six months and study all articles on your figure in each of those issues. To determine bias, look at the amount of coverage, the location (front pages or back pages), the use of photos (flattering or unflattering), and the language of the articles.

4. Conduct a study of amounts of violence on TV by analyzing, for one week, all prime-time programs that may contain violence. (That is, eliminate sitcoms and decide whether you want to include or exclude news programs.) Devise some classification system for types of violence based on your prior TV viewing experience before beginning your study—but be prepared to alter or add to your categories based on your viewing of shows. Note the number of times each violent act occurs. You may want to consider the total length of time (per program, per night, per type of violent act) of violence during the week you study. Give credit to any authors in this text or other publications for any ideas you borrow from their articles.

5. As an alternative to topic 4, study the number and types of violent acts in children's programs on Saturday mornings. (This and topic 4 are best handled if you can record and then replay the programs several times.)

6. Conduct a survey and analyze the results on some campus issue or current public policy issue. Prepare questions that are without bias and include questions to get information about the participants so that you can correlate answers with the demographics of your participants (e.g., age, gender, race, religion, proposed major in college, political affiliation, or whatever else you think is important to the topic studied). Decide whether you want to survey students only or both students and faculty. Plan how you are going to reach each group.

CHAPTER 6

Learning More about Argument: Induction, Deduction, Analogy, and Logical Fallacies

PEARLS BEFORE SWINE   *BY STEPHAN PASTIS*

READ: What is the situation? What are Pig's reactions to what he is told?

REASON: Who are the only creatures who can never lie? What is Pig's solution to what he has been told? Are we invited to accept Pig's solution?

REFLECT/WRITE: What makes the cartoon amusing? What is its more serious message?

You can build on your knowledge of the basics of argument, examined in Chapter 3, by understanding some traditional forms of argument: induction, deduction, and analogy. It is also important to recognize arguments that do not meet the standards of good logic.

INDUCTION

Induction is the process by which we reach inferences—opinions based on facts, or on a combination of facts and less debatable inferences. The inductive process moves from particular to general, from support to assertion. We base our inferences on the facts we have gathered and studied. In general, the more evidence, the more convincing the argument. No one wants to debate tomorrow's sunrise; the evidence for counting on it is too convincing. Most inferences, though, are drawn from less evidence, so we need to examine these arguments closely to judge their reasonableness.

The pattern of induction looks like this:

EVIDENCE: There is the dead body of Smith. Smith was shot in his bedroom between the hours of 11:00 a.m. and 2:00 a.m., according to the coroner. Smith was shot by a .32-caliber pistol. The pistol left in the bedroom contains Jones's fingerprints. Jones was seen, by a neighbor, entering the Smith home at around 11:00 the night of Smith's death. A coworker heard Smith and Jones arguing in Smith's office the morning of the day Smith died.

CLAIM: Jones killed Smith.

The facts are presented. The jury infers that Jones is a murderer. Unless there is a confession or a trustworthy eyewitness, the conclusion is an inference, not a fact. This is the most logical explanation. The conclusion meets the standards of simplicity and frequency while accounting for all of the known evidence.

The following paragraph illustrates the process of induction. In their book *Discovering Dinosaurs,* authors Mark Norell, Eugene Gaffney, and Lowell Dingus answer the question "Did dinosaurs really rule the world?"

For almost 170 million years, from the Late Triassic to the end of the Cretaceous, there existed dinosaurs of almost every body form imaginable: small carnivores, such as *Compsognathus* and *Ornitholestes,* ecologically equivalent to today's foxes and coyotes; medium-sized carnivores, such as *Velociraptor* and the troödontids, analogous to lions and tigers; and the monstrous carnivores with no living analogs, such as *Tyrannosaurus* and *Allosaurus.* Included among the ornithischians and the elephantine sauropods are terrestrial herbivores of diverse body form. By the end of the Jurassic, dinosaurs had even taken to the skies. The only habitats that dinosaurs did not dominate during the Mesozoic were aquatic. Yet, there were marine representatives, such as the primitive toothed bird *Hesperornis.* Like penguins, these birds were flightless, specialized for diving, and probably had to return to land to reproduce. In light of this broad morphologic diversity [number of body forms], dinosaurs did "rule the planet" as the dominant life form on Earth during most of the

Mesozoic [era that includes the Triassic, Jurassic, and Cretaceous periods, 248 to 65 million years ago].[1]

Observe that the writers organize evidence by type of dinosaur to demonstrate the range and diversity of these animals. A good inductive argument is based on a sufficient volume of *relevant* evidence. The basic shape of this inductive argument is illustrated in Figure 6.1.

CLAIM:	Dinosaurs were the dominant life form during the Mesozoic era.
GROUNDS:	The facts presented in the paragraph.
ASSUMPTION (WARRANT):	The facts are representative, revealing dinosaur diversity.

FIGURE 6.1 **The Shape of an Inductive Argument**

COLLABORATIVE EXERCISE: Induction

With your class partner or in small groups, make a list of facts that could be used to support each of the following inferences:

1. Fido must have escaped under the fence during the night.
2. Sue must be planning to go away for the weekend.
3. Students who do not hand in all essay assignments fail Dr. Bradshaw's English class.
4. The price of Florida oranges will go up in grocery stores next year.
5. Yogurt is a better breakfast food than bread.

DEDUCTION

Although induction can be described as an argument that moves from particular to general, from facts to inference, deduction cannot accurately be described as the reverse. Deductive arguments are more complex. *Deduction is the reasoning process that draws a conclusion from the logical relationship of two assertions, usually one broad judgment or definition and one more specific assertion, often an inference.* Suppose, on the way out of American history class, you say, "Abraham Lincoln certainly was a great leader." Someone responds with the expected question: "Why do you think so?" You explain: "He was great because he performed with courage and a clear purpose in a time of crisis." Your explanation contains a conclusion and an assertion about Lincoln (an inference) in support. But behind your explanation rests an idea about leadership, in the terms of deduction, *a premise.* The argument's basic shape is illustrated in Figure 6.2.

CLAIM:	Lincoln was a great leader.
GROUNDS:	1. People who perform with courage and clear purpose in a crisis are great leaders.
	2. Lincoln was a person who performed with courage and a clear purpose in a crisis.
ASSUMPTION (WARRANT):	The relationship of the two reasons leads, logically, to the conclusion.

FIGURE 6.2 **The Shape of a Deductive Argument**

Traditionally, the deductive argument is arranged somewhat differently from these sentences about Lincoln. The two reasons are called *premises;* the broader one, called the *major premise*, is written first and the more specific one, the *minor premise*, comes next. The premises and conclusion are expressed to make clear that assertions are being made about categories or classes. When all three steps are used, the structure is called a *syllogism. Syllogisms* may also include more than one *minor premise*, but for now, we will just focus on the three-step deductive process. To illustrate:

MAJOR PREMISE: All people who perform with courage and a clear purpose in a crisis are great leaders.

MINOR PREMISE: Lincoln was a person who performed with courage and a clear purpose in a crisis.

CONCLUSION: Lincoln was a great leader.

If these two premises are correctly, that is, logically, constructed, then the conclusion follows logically, and the deductive argument is *valid*. This does not mean that the conclusion is necessarily *true*. It does mean that if you accept the truth of the premises, then you must accept the truth of the conclusion, because in a valid argument the conclusion follows logically, necessarily. How do we know that the conclusion must follow if the argument is logically constructed? Let's think about what each premise is saying and then diagram each one to represent each assertion visually. The first premise says that all people who act a particular way are people who fit into the category called "great leaders":

The second premise says that Lincoln, a category of one, belongs in the category of people who act in the same particular way that the first premise describes:

If we put the two diagrams together, we have the following set of circles, demonstrating that the conclusion follows from the premises:

We can also make negative and qualified assertions in a deductive argument. For example:

PREMISE: No cowards can be great leaders.

PREMISE: Falstaff was a coward.

CONCLUSION: Falstaff was not a great leader.

Or, to reword the conclusion to make the deductive pattern clearer: No Falstaff (no member of this class) is a great leader. Diagramming to test for validity, we find that the first premise says no A's are B's:

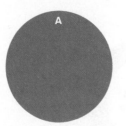   

The second premise asserts all C's are A's:

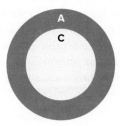

Put together, we see that the conclusion follows necessarily from the premises: No C's can possibly be members of class B.

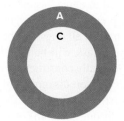 

Some deductive arguments merely look right, but the two premises do not lead logically to the conclusion that is asserted. We must read each argument carefully or diagram each one to make certain that the conclusion follows from the premises. Consider the following argument: *Unions must be communistic because they want to control wages.* The sentence contains a conclusion and one reason, or premise. From these two parts of a deductive argument we can also determine the unstated premise, just as we could with the Lincoln argument: *Communists want to control wages.* If we use circles to represent the three categories of people in the argument and diagram the argument, we see a different result from the previous diagrams:

Diagramming the argument reveals that it is invalid; that is, it is not logically constructed because the statements do not require that the union circle be placed inside the communist circle. We cannot draw the conclusion we want from any two premises, only from those that provide a logical basis from which a conclusion can be reached.

We must first make certain that deductive arguments are properly constructed or valid. But suppose the logic works and yet you do not agree with the claim? Your complaint, then, must be with one of the premises, a judgment or inference that you do not accept as true. Consider the following argument:

MAJOR PREMISE:	(All) dogs make good pets.
MINOR PREMISE:	Fido is a dog.
CONCLUSION:	Fido will make a good pet.

This argument is valid. (Diagram it; your circles will fit into one another just as with the Lincoln argument.) However, you are not prepared to agree, necessarily, that Fido will make a good pet. The problem is with the major premise. For the argument to work, the assertion must be about *all* dogs, but we know that not all dogs will be good pets.

When composing a deductive argument, your task will be to defend the truth of your premises. Then, if your argument is valid (logically constructed), readers will have no alternative but to agree with your conclusion. If you disagree with someone else's logically constructed argument, then you must show why one of the premises is not true. Your counterargument will seek to discredit one (or both) of the premises. The Fido argument can be discredited by your producing examples of dogs that have not made good pets.

Sometimes, a deductive argument, or *syllogism*, does not include a premise. When a premise is missing from the deductive process, the syllogism becomes an *enthymeme*. Enthymemes are syllogisms that are missing a premise. A missing premise does not necessarily make a syllogism invalid or incorrect. In fact, omitting or skipping a *premise* is fairly common in everyday discourse. For instance, the syllogism above involving dogs makes sense—if you agree with the existing premises—even if one of the premises is omitted:

MINOR PREMISE:	Fido is a dog.
CONCLUSION:	Fido will make a good pet.
MISSING PREMISE (MAJOR PREMISE):	(All) dogs make good pets.

Or

MAJOR PREMISE:	(All) dogs make good pets.
CONCLUSION:	Fido will make a good pet.
MISSING PREMISE (MINOR PREMISE):	Fido is a dog.

As we have seen, this argument, with or without all three parts, fails on its logic. But upon first reading or hearing the enthymeme above, someone who is not paying attention might be misled.

Enthymemes are one of the most common ways people argue in conversations, and especially online, so it is important that you pay attention to information that may be missing. This process is known as critical thinking. If you do not use critical thinking, you may be manipulated into agreeing with an argument that you do not really support.

A deductive argument can serve as the core of an essay, an essay that supports the argument's claim by developing support for each of the premises. Since the major premise is either a broad judgment or a definition, it will need to be defended on the basis of an appeal to values or beliefs that the writer expects readers to share. The minor premise, usually an inference about a particular situation (or person), would be supported by relevant evidence, as with any inductive argument. You can see this process at work in the Declaration of Independence. Questions follow the Declaration to guide your analysis of this famous example of the deductive process.

THE DECLARATION OF INDEPENDENCE

In Congress, July 4, 1776
The unanimous declaration of the thirteen
United States of America

When in the course of human events, it becomes necessary for one people to dissolve the political bands which have connected them with another, and to assume among the powers of the earth, the separate and equal station to which the Laws of Nature and of Nature's God entitle them, a decent respect to the opinions of mankind requires that they should declare the causes which impel them to the separation. 1

We hold these truths to be self-evident, that all men are created equal, that they are endowed by their Creator with certain unalienable rights, that among these are life, liberty and the pursuit of happiness. That to secure these rights, governments are instituted among men, deriving their just powers from the consent of the governed. That whenever any form of government becomes destructive of these ends, it is the right of the people to alter or to abolish it, and to institute new government, laying its foundation on such principles and organizing its powers in such form, as to them shall seem most likely to effect their safety and happiness. Prudence, indeed, will dictate that governments long established should not be changed for light and transient causes; and accordingly all experience hath shown, that mankind are more disposed to suffer, while evils are sufferable, than to right themselves by abolishing the forms to which they are accustomed. But when a long train of abuses and usurpations, pursuing invariably the same object evinces a design to reduce them under absolute despotism, it is their right, it is their duty, to throw off such government, and to provide new guards for their future security. Such has been the patient sufferance of these Colonies; and such is now the necessity which constrains them to alter their 2 former systems of government. The history of the present King of Great Britain is a history of repeated injuries and usurpations, all having in direct object the establishment of an absolute tyranny over these States. To prove this, let facts be submitted to a candid world.

3   He has refused his assent to laws, the most wholesome and necessary for the public good.

4   He has forbidden his Governors to pass laws of immediate and pressing importance, unless suspended in their operation till his assent should be obtained; and when so suspended, he has utterly neglected to attend to them.

5   He has refused to pass other laws for the accommodation of large districts of people, unless those people would relinquish the right of representation in the Legislature, a right inestimable to them and formidable to tyrants only.

6   He has called together legislative bodies at places unusual, uncomfortable, and distant from the depository of their public records, for the sole purpose of fatiguing them into compliance with his measures.

7   He has dissolved representative houses repeatedly, for opposing with manly firmness his invasions on the rights of the people.

8   He has refused for a long time, after such dissolutions, to cause others to be elected; whereby the legislative powers, incapable of annihilation, have returned to the people at large for their exercise; the State remaining in the meantime exposed to all the dangers of invasion from without and convulsions within.

9   He has endeavoured to prevent the population of these States; for that purpose obstructing the laws of naturalization of foreigners; refusing to pass others to encourage their migration hither, and raising the conditions of new appropriations of lands.

10   He has obstructed the administration of justice, by refusing his assent to laws for establishing judiciary powers.

11   He has made judges dependent on his will alone, for the tenure of their offices, and the amount and payment of their salaries.

12   He has erected a multitude of new offices, and sent hither swarms of officers to harass our people, and eat out their substance.

13   He has kept among us, in times of peace, standing armies without the consent of our legislatures.

14   He has affected to render the military independent of and superior to the civil power.

15   He has combined with others to subject us to a jurisdiction foreign to our constitution, and unacknowledged by our laws; giving his assent to their acts of pretended legislation:

16   For quartering large bodies of armed troops among us:

17   For protecting them, by a mock trial, from punishment for any murders which they should commit on the inhabitants of these States:

18   For cutting off our trade with all parts of the world:

19   For imposing taxes on us without our consent:

20   For depriving us, in many cases, of the benefits of trial by jury:

21   For transporting us beyond seas to be tried for pretended offences:

For abolishing the free system of English laws in a neighbouring Province, 22 establishing therein an arbitrary government, and enlarging its boundaries so as to render it at once an example and fit instrument for introducing the same absolute rule into these Colonies:

For taking away our Charters, abolishing our most valuable laws, and altering 23 fundamentally the forms of our governments:

For suspending our own Legislatures, and declaring themselves invested 24 with power to legislate for us in all cases whatsoever.

He has abdicated government here, by declaring us out of his protection 25 and waging war against us.

He has plundered our seas, ravaged our coasts, burnt our towns, and 26 destroyed the lives of our people.

He is at this time transporting large armies of foreign mercenaries to com- 27 plete the works of death, desolation and tyranny, already begun with circumstances of cruelty and perfidy scarcely paralleled in the most barbarous ages, and totally unworthy the head of a civilized nation.

He has constrained our fellow citizens taken captive on the high seas to 28 bear arms against their country, to become the executioners of their friends and brethren, or to fall themselves by their hands.

He has excited domestic insurrections amongst us, and has endeavoured to 29 bring on the inhabitants of our frontiers, the merciless Indian savages, whose known rule of warfare, is an undistinguished destruction of all ages, sexes, and conditions.

In every stage of these oppressions we have petitioned for redress in the 30 most humble terms; our repeated petitions have been answered only by repeated injury. A prince whose character is thus marked by every act which may define a tyrant is unfit to be the ruler of a free people.

Nor have we been wanting in attention to our British brethren. We have 31 warned them from time to time of attempts by their legislature to extend an unwarrantable jurisdiction over us. We have reminded them of the circumstances of our emigration and settlement here. We have appealed to their native justice and magnanimity, and we have conjured them by the ties of our common kindred to disavow these usurpations, which would inevitably interrupt our connections and correspondence. They too have been deaf to the voice of justice and of consanguinity. We must, therefore, acquiesce in the necessity, which denounces our separation, and hold them, as we hold the rest of mankind, enemies in war, in peace friends.

We, therefore, the Representatives of the United States of America, in 32 General Congress assembled, appealing to the Supreme Judge of the world for the rectitude of our intentions, do, in the name, and by the authority of the good people of these Colonies, solemnly publish and declare, That these United Colonies are, and of right ought to be Free and Independent States; that they are absolved from all allegiance to the British Crown, and that all political connection between them and the State of Great Britain, is and ought to be totally dissolved; and that as Free and Independent States, they have full power to levy war, conclude peace, contract alliances, establish commerce, and to do all other acts and things which Independent States may of right do. And for the support of this declaration, with a firm reliance on the protection of Divine Providence, we mutually pledge to each other our lives, our fortunes, and our sacred honor.

QUESTIONS FOR ANALYSIS

1.   What is the Declaration's central deductive argument? State the argument in the shape illustrated above: major premise, minor premise, conclusion. Construct a valid argument. If necessary, draw circles representing each of the three terms in the argument to check for validity. (*Hint:* Start with the claim "George III's government should be overthrown.")

2.   Which paragraphs are devoted to supporting the major premise? What kind of support has been given?

3.   Which paragraphs are devoted to supporting the minor premise? What kind of support has been given?

4.   Why has more support been given for one premise than the other?

EXERCISES: Completing and Evaluating Deductive Arguments

Turn each of the following statements into valid deductive arguments. (You have the conclusion and one premise, so you will have to determine the missing premise that would complete the argument. Draw circles if necessary to test for validity.) Then decide which arguments have premises that could be supported. Note the kind of support that might be provided. Explain why you think some arguments have insupportable premises. Here is an example:

PREMISE:	All Jesuits are priests.
PREMISE:	No women are priests.
CONCLUSION:	No women are Jesuits.

Since the circle for women must be placed outside the circle for priests, it must also be outside the circle for Jesuits. Hence the argument is valid. The first premise is true by definition; the term *Jesuit* refers to an order of Roman Catholic priests. The second premise is true for the Roman Catholic Church, so if the term *priest* is used only to refer to ordained people in the Roman Catholic Church, then the second premise is also true by definition.

1.   Ms. Ferguson is a good teacher because she can explain the subject matter clearly.
2.   Segregated schools are unconstitutional because they are unequal.
3.   Michael must be a good driver because he drives fast.
4.   The media clearly have a liberal bias because they make fun of religious fundamentalists.

ANALOGY

The argument from analogy is an argument based on comparison. Analogies assert that since A and B are alike in several ways, they must be alike in another way as well. The argument from analogy concludes with an inference, an assertion of a significant similarity in the two items being compared. The other similarities serve as evidence in support of the inference. The shape of an argument by analogy is illustrated in Figure 6.3.

GROUNDS:	A has characteristics 1, 2, 3, and 4.
	B has characteristics 1, 2, and 3.
CLAIM:	B has characteristic 4 (as well).
ASSUMPTION	If B has three characteristics in common with A, it must have
(WARRANT):	the key fourth characteristic as well.

FIGURE 6.3 **The Shape of an Argument by Analogy**

Although analogy is sometimes an effective approach to an issue because clever and imaginative comparisons are often moving, analogy is not as rigorously logical as either induction or deduction. Frequently, an analogy is based on only two or three points of comparison, whereas a sound inductive argument presents many examples to support its conclusion. Further, to be convincing, the points of comparison must be fundamental to the two items being compared. An argument for a county leash law for cats developed by analogy with dogs may cite the following similarities:

- Cats are pets, just like dogs.
- Cats live in residential communities, just like dogs.
- Cats can mess up other people's yards, just like dogs.
- Cats, if allowed to run free, can disturb the peace (fighting, making noise at night), just like dogs.

Does it follow that cats should be required to walk on a leash, just like dogs? If such a county ordinance were passed, would it be enforceable? Have you ever tried to walk a cat on a leash? In spite of legitimate similarities brought out by the analogy, the conclusion does not logically follow because the arguer is overlooking a fundamental difference in the two animals' personalities. Dogs can be trained to a leash; most cats (Siamese are one exception) cannot be so trained. Such thinking will produce sulking cats and scratched owners. But the analogy, delivered passionately to the right audience, could lead community activists to lobby for a new law.

Observe that the problem with the cat-leash-law analogy is not in the similarities asserted about the items being compared but rather in the underlying assumption that the similarities logically support the argument's conclusion. A good analogy asserts many points of comparison and finds likenesses that are essential parts of the nature or purpose of the two items being compared. The best way to challenge another's analogy is to point out a fundamental difference in the nature or purpose of the compared items. For all of their similarities, when it comes to walking on a leash, cats are *not* like dogs.

EXERCISES: Analogy

Analyze the following analogies. List the stated and/or implied points of comparison and the conclusion in the pattern illustrated in Figure 6.3. Then judge each argument's logic and effectiveness as a persuasive technique. If the argument is not logical, state the fundamental difference in the two compared items. If the argument could be persuasive, describe the kind of audience that might be moved by it.

1. College newspapers should not be under the supervision or control of a faculty sponsor. Fortunately, no governmental sponsor controls *The New York Times*, or we would no longer have a free press in this country. We need a free college press, too, one that can criticize college policies when they are wrong.

2. Let's recognize that college athletes are really professional and start paying them properly. College athletes get a free education, and spending money from boosters. They are required to attend practices and games, and—if they play football or basketball—they bring in huge revenues for their "organization." College coaches are also paid enormous salaries, just like professional coaches, and often college coaches are tapped to coach professional teams. The only difference: The poor college athletes don't get those big salaries and huge signing bonuses.

3. Just like any business, the federal government must be made to balance its budget. No company could continue to operate in the red as the government does and expect to be successful. A constitutional amendment requiring a balanced federal budget is long overdue.

LOGICAL FALLACIES

A thorough study of argument needs to include a study of logical fallacies because so many "arguments" fail to meet standards of sound logic and good sense. Why do people offer arguments that aren't sensible?

Causes of Illogic

Ignorance

One frequent cause for illogical debate is a lack of knowledge of the subject. Some people have more information than others. The younger you are, the less you can be expected to know about complex issues. On the other hand, if you want to debate a complex or technical issue, then you cannot use ignorance as an excuse. Instead, read as much as you can, listen carefully to discussions, ask questions, and select topics about which you have knowledge or will research before writing.

Egos

Ego problems are another cause of weak arguments. Those with low self-esteem often have difficulty in debates because they attach themselves to their ideas and then feel personally attacked when someone disagrees with them. Remember: Self-esteem is enhanced when others applaud our knowledge and thoughtfulness, not our irrationality.

Prejudices

The prejudices and biases that we carry around, having absorbed them "ages ago" from family and community, are also sources of irrationality. Prejudices range from the worst ethnic, religious, or sexist stereotypes to political views we have adopted uncritically (Democrats are all bleeding hearts; Republicans are all rich snobs) to perhaps less serious but equally insupportable notions (if it's in print, it must be right). People who see the world through distorted lenses cannot possibly assess facts intelligently and reason logically from them.

A Need for Answers

Finally, many bad arguments stem from a human need for answers—any answers—to the questions that deeply concern us. We want to control our world because that makes us feel secure, and having answers makes us feel in control. This need can lead to illogic from oversimplifying issues.

Based on these causes of illogic, we can usefully divide fallacies into (1) oversimplifying the issue and (2) ignoring the issue by substituting emotion for reason.

Fallacies That Result from Oversimplifying

Errors in Generalizing

Errors in generalizing include overstatement and hasty or faulty generalization. All have in common an error in the inductive pattern of argument. The inference drawn from the evidence is unwarranted, either because too broad a generalization is made or because the generalization is drawn from incomplete or incorrect evidence.

Overstatement occurs when the argument's assertion is unqualified—referring to all members of a category. Overstatements often result from stereotyping, giving the same traits to everyone in a group. Overstatements are frequently signaled by words such as *all*, *every*, *always*, *never*, and *none*. But remember that assertions such as "children love clowns" are understood to refer to "all children," even though the word *all* does not appear in the sentence. It is the writer's task to qualify statements appropriately, using words such as *some*, *many*, or *frequently*, as appropriate.

Overstatements are discredited by finding only one exception to disprove the assertion. One frightened child who starts to cry when the clown approaches will destroy the argument. Here is another example:

- Lawyers are only interested in making money.

  (What about lawyers who work to protect consumers, or public defenders who represent those unable to pay for a lawyer?)

Hasty or faulty generalizations may be qualified assertions, but they still oversimplify by arguing from insufficient evidence or by ignoring some relevant evidence. For example:

- Political life must lead many to excessive drinking. In the last six months the paper has written about five members of Congress who either have confessed to alcoholism or have been arrested on DUI charges.

  (Five is not a large enough sample from which to generalize about *many* politicians. Also, the five in the newspaper are not a representative sample; they have made the news because of their drinking.)

Forced Hypothesis

The *forced hypothesis* is also an error in inductive reasoning. The explanation (hypothesis) offered is "forced," or illogical, because either (1) sufficient evidence does not exist to draw any conclusion or (2) the evidence can be explained more simply or more sensibly by a different hypothesis. This fallacy often results from not considering other possible explanations. You discredit a forced hypothesis by providing alternative conclusions that are more sensible than or just as sensible as the one offered. Consider this example:

- Professor Redding's students received either A's or B's last semester. He must be an excellent teacher.

  (The grades alone cannot support this conclusion. Professor Redding could be an excellent teacher; he could have started with excellent students; he could be an easy grader.)

Non Sequitur

The term *non sequitur*, meaning literally "it does not follow," could apply to all illogical arguments, but the term is usually reserved for those in which the conclusions are not logically connected to the reasons. In a hasty generalization, for example, there is a connection between support (five politicians in the news) and conclusion (many politicians with drinking problems), just not a convincing connection. With the *non sequitur* there is no recognizable connection, either because (1) whatever connection the arguer sees is not made clear to others or because (2) the evidence or reasons offered are irrelevant to the conclusion. For example:

- Donna will surely get a good grade in physics; she earned an A in her biology class.

  (Doing well in one course, even one science course, does not support the conclusion that the student will get a good grade in another course. If Donna is not good at math, she definitely will not do well in physics.)

Slippery Slope

The *slippery slope* argument asserts that we should not proceed with or permit A because if we do, the terrible consequences X, Y, and Z will occur. This type of argument oversimplifies by assuming, without evidence and usually by ignoring historical examples, existing laws, or any reasonableness in people that X, Y, and Z will follow inevitably from A. This kind of argument rests on the belief that most people will not want the final, awful Z to occur. The belief, however accurate, does not provide a sufficiently good reason for avoiding A. One of the best-known examples of slippery slope reasoning can be found in the gun-control debate:

- If we allow the government to register handguns, next it will register hunting rifles; then it will prohibit all citizen ownership of guns, thereby creating a police state or a world in which only outlaws have guns.

  (Surely no one wants the final dire consequences predicted in this argument. However, handgun registration does not mean that these consequences will follow. The United States has never been a police state, and its system of free elections guards against such a future. Also, citizens have registered cars, boats, and planes for years without any threat of their confiscation.)

False Dilemma

The *false dilemma* oversimplifies by asserting only two alternatives when there are more than two. The either–or thinking of this kind of argument can be an effective tactic if undetected. If the arguer gives us only two choices and one of those is clearly unacceptable, then the arguer can push us toward the preferred choice. For example:

- The Federal Reserve System must lower interest rates, or we will never pull out of the recession.

  (Clearly, staying in a recession is not much of a choice, but the alternative may not be the only or the best course to achieve a healthy economy. If interest rates go too low, inflation can result. Other options include the government's creating new jobs and patiently letting market forces play themselves out.)

False Analogy

When examining the shape of analogy, we also considered the problems with this type of argument. (See pp. 160–61.) Remember that you challenge a false analogy by noting many differences in the two items being compared or by noting a significant difference that has been ignored.

Post Hoc Fallacy

The term *post hoc,* from the Latin *post hoc, ergo propter hoc* (literally, "after this, therefore because of it"), refers to a common error in arguments about cause. One oversimplifies by confusing a time relationship with cause. Reveal the illogic of *post hoc* arguments by pointing to other possible causes:

- We should throw out the entire city council. Since the members were elected, the city has gone into deficit spending.

  (Assuming that deficit spending in this situation is bad, was it caused by the current city council? Or did the current council inherit debts? Or is the entire region suffering from a recession?)

EXERCISES: Fallacies That Result from Oversimplifying

1. Here is a list of the fallacies we have examined so far. Make up or collect from your reading at least one example of each fallacy.
   a. Overstatement
   b. Stereotyping
   c. Hasty generalization
   d. Forced hypothesis
   e. *Non sequitur*
   f. Slippery slope
   g. False dilemma
   h. False analogy
   i. *Post hoc* fallacy

2. Explain what is illogical about each of the following arguments. Then name the fallacy represented. (Sometimes an argument will fit into more than one category. In that case name all appropriate terms.)
   a. Everybody agrees that we need stronger drunk-driving laws.
   b. The upsurge in crime on Sundays is the result of the reduced rate of church attendance in recent years.

   c. The government must create new jobs. A factory in Illinois has laid off half its workers.

   d. Steve has joined the country club. Golf must be one of his favorite sports.

   e. Blondes have more fun.

   f. You'll enjoy your Volvo; foreign cars never break down.

   g. Gary loves jokes. He would make a great comedian.

   h. The economy is in bad shape because of the Federal Reserve Board. Ever since it expanded the money supply, the stock market has been declining.

   i. Either we improve the city's street lighting, or we will fail to reduce crime.

   j. DNA research today is just like the study of nuclear fission. It seems important, but it's just another bomb that will one day explode on us. When will we learn that government must control research?

   k. To prohibit prayer in public schools is to limit religious practice solely to internal belief. The result is that an American is religiously "free" only in his or her own mind.

   l. Professor Johnson teaches in the political science department. I'll bet she's another socialist.

   m. Coming to the aid of any country engaged in civil war is a bad idea. Next we'll be sending American troops, and soon we'll be involved in another Vietnam.

   n. We must reject affirmative action in hiring or we'll have to settle for incompetent employees.

Fallacies That Result from Avoiding the Real Issue

There are many ways to divert attention from the issue under debate. Of the six discussed here, the first three try to divert attention by introducing a separate issue or "sliding by" the actual issue. The following three divert by appealing to the audience's emotions or prejudices. In the first three the arguer tries to give the impression of good logic. In the last three the arguer charges forward on emotional manipulation alone.

Begging the Question

To assume that part of your argument is true without supporting it is to *beg the question.* Arguments seeking to pass off as proof statements that must themselves be supported are often introduced with such phrases as "the fact is" (to introduce opinion), "obviously," and "as we can see." For example:

- Clearly, lowering grading standards would be bad for students, so a pass/fail system should not be adopted.

  (Does a pass/fail system lower standards? No evidence has been given. If so, is that necessarily bad for students?)

Red Herring

The *red herring* is a foul-smelling argument indeed. The debater introduces a side issue, some point that is not relevant to the debate:

- The senator is an honest woman; she loves her children and gives to charities.

  (The children and charities are side issues; they do not demonstrate honesty.)

Straw Man

The *straw man* argument attributes to opponents incorrect and usually ridiculous views that they do not hold so that their position can be easily attacked. We can challenge this illogic by demonstrating that the arguer's opponents do not hold those views or by demanding that the arguer provide some evidence that they do:

- Those who favor gun control just want to take all guns away from responsible citizens and put them in the hands of criminals.

  (The position attributed to proponents of gun control is not only inaccurate but actually the opposite of what is sought by gun-control proponents.)

Ad Hominem

One of the most frequent of all appeals to emotion masquerading as argument is the *ad hominem* argument (literally, argument "to the man"). When someone says that "those crazy liberals at the ACLU just want all criminals to go free," or a pro-choice demonstrator screams at those "self-righteous fascists" on the other side, the best retort may be silence, or the calm assertion that such statements do not contribute to meaningful debate.

Common Practice or Bandwagon

To argue that an action should be taken or a position accepted because "everyone is doing it" is illogical. The majority is not always right. Frequently, when someone is defending an action as ethical on the ground that everyone does it, the action isn't ethical and the defender knows it isn't. For example:

- There's nothing wrong with fudging a bit on your income taxes. After all, the superrich don't pay any taxes, and the government expects everyone to cheat a little.

  (First, not everyone cheats on taxes; many pay to have their taxes done correctly. And if it is wrong, it is wrong regardless of the number who do it.)

Ad Populum

Another technique for arousing an audience's emotions and ignoring the issue is to appeal *ad populum,* "to the people," to the audience's presumed shared values and beliefs. Every Fourth of July, politicians employ this tactic, appealing to God, mother, apple pie, and "traditional family values." Simply reject the argument as illogical.

- Good, law-abiding Americans must be sick of the violent crimes occurring in our once godly society. But we won't tolerate it anymore; put the criminals in jail and throw away the key.

  (This does not contribute to a thoughtful debate on criminal justice issues.)

EXERCISES: Fallacies That Result from Ignoring the Issue

1. Here is a list of fallacies that result from ignoring the issue. Make up or collect from your reading at least one example of each fallacy.
   a. Begging the question
   b. Red herring

    c. Straw man

    d. *Ad hominem*

    e. Common practice or bandwagon

    f. *Ad populum*

2. Explain what is illogical about each of the following arguments. Then name the fallacy represented.

    a. Gold's book doesn't deserve a Pulitzer Prize. She had been married four times.

    b. I wouldn't vote for him; many of his programs are basically socialist.

    c. Eight out of ten headache sufferers use Bayer to relieve headache pain. It will work for you, too.

    d. We shouldn't listen to Colman McCarthy's argument against liquor ads in college newspapers because he obviously thinks young people are ignorant and need guidance in everything.

    e. My roommate Joe does the craziest things; he must be neurotic.

    f. Since so many people obviously cheat the welfare system, it should be abolished.

    g. She isn't pretty enough to win the contest, and besides she had her nose "fixed" two years ago.

    h. Professors should chill out; everybody cheats on exams from time to time.

    i. The fact is that bilingual education is a mistake because it encourages students to use only their native language and that gives them an advantage over other students.

    j. Don't join those crazy liberals in support of the American Civil Liberties Union. They want all criminals to go free.

    k. Real Americans understand that free-trade agreements are evil. Let your representatives know that we want American goods protected.

EXERCISE: Analyzing Arguments

Option 1: The Online Post. Posting online poses one of the most serious challenges to our communication and to our logic today. Yet, much of the information we use comes from online sources. It is vital, therefore, that you think critically about what you post and what you read online. Examine the following online post from a popular social media application. If you find logical fallacies, identify and explain them.

> To My Online Friends
>
> 1   To my online friends: Over the past few weeks, I've been reading your posts about the benefits of the "environmental" regulations the EPA passed a few years ago. YOU PEOPLE ARE IDIOTS AND YOU DON'T KNOW WHAT YOU'RE TALKING ABOUT! Because of these

regulations, I no longer have a job. Due to some over-educated scientists coming in here and finding some leaks from our plant into the river, the power-hungry bureaucrats at the EPA in Washington, D.C., fined us. Because of these fines, I was furloughed. Well, I got word today that this "furlough" is now permanent. I've been laid off. So now, Midville Steel is probably going to reduce production, hundreds of people are going to lose their jobs, and the town itself is going to crumble. It's all the EPA's fault, and you liberals out there don't even know it!

2   I've tried to be patient with all of your posts, but now I have to explain the truth. Midville Steel has been a wonderful employer. They have refurbished *every* park in town, and they built our new baseball and softball fields. Every year, they sponsor our Fall Festival, and they contributed to our downtown revitalization project. The company and its employees don't deserve the punishment that the EPA is forcing on us. But most importantly, Midville Steel employs 2,700 people, and hundreds of them are going to lose their jobs because of unfair EPA regulations. The EPA just wants to impose strict regulations on American industry to help companies in other countries.

3   So I hope that all of you EPA-loving tree huggers out there are happy. And if you don't agree with my opinions, then just unfriend me now. Because if you don't like my opinion, then you don't like *me*. Good Americans recognize government overreach when they see it, and really, we only have two options here: shut down the EPA or shut down American industry.

Option 2: The Online Conversation. Online conversations can be a wonderful way to keep in touch with friends and family and to share information with people around the world. But as you probably already know, text messages, email, and other forms of digital media are imperfect mediums of communication. Conversations can quickly spiral out of control, and all involved can find themselves using insults and faulty logic to "win" an argument, especially about contentious issues. Examine the following social media conversation. If you find logical fallacies, identify and explain them.

Online Conversation

1   **Kim**: I just saw #algore 's movie An Inconvenient Truth for the first time in my composition class. I'm shocked. I really had no idea things were so bad. If we don't do something about pollution now, the air we breathe is going to give us cancer, the seas are going to rise and flood the coastlines, and our storms are just going to get worse. Maria, have you seen the movie?

2   **Maria**: OMG that movie is so old. I can't believe you think that stuff is true. My cousin works for the power company, and he says that the coal they burn isn't that bad. It's clean burning coal. Please don't turn into a tree hugging #hippie. They smell like #patchouli, get arrested protesting my cousin's plant, and are losers.

3   **Kim**: Wow. Chill out. Just because your cousin works at the plant doesn't mean he's an expert on #climatechange. That's probably why he drives that huge old #gasguzzler. And just because I care about the environment doesn't mean I'm a tree hugging hippie. How about you actually check your facts before getting so judgmental? We need to reduce pollution, or we're all going to get cancer. Don't you care about that?

4   **Maria**: Are you insulting my cousin? I'm unfriending you. #liberalloser !

5   **Kim**: Wtvs. Seeya. #planethater

6   **Maria**: #stinkyhippie

FOR READING AND ANALYSIS

DECLARATION OF SENTIMENTS | ELIZABETH CADY STANTON

Elizabeth Cady Stanton (1815–1902) was one of the most important leaders of the women's rights movement. Educated at the Emma Willard Seminary in Troy, New York, Stanton studied law with her father before her marriage. At the Seneca Falls Convention in 1848 (the first women's rights convention), Stanton gave the opening speech and read her "Declaration of Sentiments." She founded and became president of the National Women's Suffrage Association in 1869.

PREREADING QUESTION As you read, think about the similarities and differences between this document and the Declaration of Independence. What significant differences in wording and content do you find?

When, in the course of human events, it becomes necessary for one portion of the family of man to assume among the people of the earth a position different from that which they have hitherto occupied, but one to which the laws of nature and of nature's God entitle them, a decent respect to the opinions of mankind requires that they should declare the causes that impel them to such a course.

We hold these truths to be self-evident: that all men and women are created equal; that they are endowed by their Creator with certain inalienable rights; that among these are life, liberty, and the pursuit of happiness; that to secure these rights governments are instituted, deriving their just powers from the consent of the governed. Whenever any form of government becomes destructive of these ends, it is the right of those who suffer from it to refuse allegiance to it, and to insist upon the institution of a new government, laying its foundation on such principles, and organizing its powers in such form, as to them shall seem most likely to effect their safety and happiness. Prudence, indeed, will dictate that governments long established should not be changed for light and transient causes; and accordingly all experience hath shown that mankind are more disposed to suffer, while evils are sufferable, than to right themselves by abolishing the forms to which they were accustomed. But when a long train of abuses and usurpations, pursuing invariably the same object evinces a design to reduce them under absolute despotism, it is their duty to throw off such government, and to provide new guards for their future security. Such has been the patient sufferance of the women under this government, and such is now the necessity which constrains them to demand the equal station to which they are entitled.

Library of Congress, Prints & Photographs Division [LC-USZ62-48965]

Elizabeth Cady Stanton and her daughter, Harriot. from a daguerreotype 1856.

3   The history of mankind is a history of repeated injuries and usurpations on the part of man toward woman, having in direct object the establishment of an absolute tyranny over her. To prove this, let facts be submitted to a candid world.

4   He has never permitted her to exercise her inalienable right to the elective franchise.

5   He has compelled her to submit to laws, in the formation of which she had no voice.

6   He has withheld from her rights which are given to the most ignorant and degraded men—both natives and foreigners.

7   Having deprived her of this first right of a citizen, the elective franchise, thereby leaving her without representation in the halls of legislation, he has oppressed her on all sides.

8   He has made her, if married, in the eye of the law, civilly dead.

9   He has taken from her all right in property, even to the wages she earns.

10   He has made her, morally, an irresponsible being, as she can commit many crimes with impunity, provided they be done in the presence of her husband. In the covenant of marriage, she is compelled to promise obedience to her husband, he becoming, to all intents and purposes, her master—the law giving him power to deprive her of her liberty, and to administer chastisement.

11   He has so framed the laws of divorce, as to what shall be the proper causes, and in case of separation, to whom the guardianship of the children shall be given, as to be wholly regardless of the happiness of women—the law, in all cases, going upon a false supposition of the supremacy of man, and giving all power into his hands.

       After depriving her of all rights as a married woman, if single, and the owner of property, he has taxed her to support a government which recognizes her only
12   when her property can be made profitable to it.

13   He has monopolized nearly all the profitable employments, and from those she is permitted to follow, she receives but a scanty remuneration. He closes against her all the avenues to wealth and distinction which he considers most honorable to himself. As a teacher of theology, medicine, or law, she is not known.

14   He has denied her the facilities for obtaining a thorough education, all colleges being closed against her.

15   He allows her in Church, as well as State, but a subordinate position, claiming Apostolic authority for her exclusion from the ministry, and, with some exceptions, from any public participation in the affairs of the Church.

16   He has created a false public sentiment by giving to the world a different code of morals for men and women, by which moral delinquencies which exclude women from society, are not only tolerated, but deemed of little account in man.

17   He has usurped the prerogative of Jehovah himself, claiming it as his right to assign for her a sphere of action, when that belongs to her conscience and to her God.

He has endeavored, in every way that he could, to destroy her confidence in 18 her own powers, to lessen her self-respect, and to make her willing to lead a dependent and abject life.

Now in view of this entire disfranchisement of one-half the people of this 19 country, their social and religious degradation—in view of the unjust laws above mentioned, and because women do feel themselves aggrieved, oppressed, and fraudulently deprived of their most sacred rights, we insist that they have imme-diate admission to all the rights and privileges which belong to them as citizens of the United States.

In entering upon the great work before us, we anticipate no small amount of 20 misconception, misrepresentation, and ridicule; but we shall use every instru-mentality within our power to effect our object. We shall employ agents, circulate tracts, petition the State and National legislatures, and endeavor to enlist the pulpit and the press in our behalf. We hope this Convention will be followed by a series of Conventions embracing every part of the country.

QUESTIONS FOR READING

1. Summarize the ideas of paragraphs 1 and 2. Be sure to use your own words.
2. What are the first three facts given by Stanton? Why are they presented first?
3. How have women been restricted by law if married or owning property? How have they been restricted in education and work? How have they been restricted psychologically?
4. What, according to Stanton, do women demand? How will they seek their goals?

QUESTIONS FOR REASONING AND ANALYSIS

5. What is Stanton's claim? With what does she charge men?
6. Most—but not all—of Stanton's charges have been redressed, however slowly. Which continue to be legitimate complaints, in whole or in part?

QUESTIONS FOR REFLECTION AND WRITING

7. Do we need a new declaration of sentiments for women? If so, what specific charges would you list? If not, why not?
8. Do we need a declaration of sentiments for other groups—children, minorities, the elderly, animals? If so, what specific charges should be listed? Select one group (that concerns you) and prepare a declaration of sentiments for that group. If you do not think any group needs a declaration, explain why.

IN DEFENSE OF POLITICS, NOW MORE THAN EVER BEFORE | PETER WEHNER

A senior fellow at the Ethics and Public Policy Center, Peter Wehner has served in the last three Republican administrations. Wehner is the author, with Michael Gerson, of *City of Man: Religion and Politics in a New Era* (2010). His articles have been published in many newspapers and magazines, and he appears frequently on radio and TV talk shows. This article first appeared in *The New York Times* in 2016.

PREREADING QUESTIONS Do you think it's possible to defend politics? If your answer is "Not at all," do you recognize a fallacy in your thinking?

Members of Congress for 2015 standing on the Capitol steps.

1   One of John F. Kennedy's favorite books was John Buchan's 1940 memoir, *Pilgrim's Way*. Buchan, who served as a member of Parliament for the combined Scottish universities, wrote, "Public life is regarded as the crown of a career, and to young men it is the worthiest ambition." Politics, he added, "is still the greatest and most honorable adventure."

2   These days it would be hard to find a handful of people in America who agree with Buchan's sentiment. According to a 2015 Pew Research Center survey, trust in government is at one of the lowest levels in a half-century. Almost three-quarters of Americans believe elected officials put their own interests ahead of the country's interest. Much of the public has utter contempt for the political class.

3   Some of this is justified. Politicians aren't putting forward solutions to the problems facing many Americans. There's also their hypocrisy and corruption, as

well as the triviality and rhetorical wasteland that characterizes much of public discourse. But that is hardly the whole of it. There are very good people who are quietly doing their jobs well and with integrity. I would hasten to point out, too, that voters are complicit in this problem, because they choose the people who represent them. The people who plant the flowers have some responsibility for the condition of the garden.

Repairing our politics begins with understanding the nature of the enter- 4 prise. Alleviating the public's bitter mistrust of politics requires coming to terms with its mundane realities and limits.

If the 20th-century American theologian Reinhold Niebuhr were to comment 5 on the current state of affairs, he would warn us against cynicism and idealism, writes Wilfred M. McClay, a historian at the University of Oklahoma. Our disappointments arise from our excessive expectations. "We assume we are better people than we seem to be," according to Professor McClay, "and we assume that our politics should therefore be an endlessly uplifting pursuit, full of joy and inspiration and self-actualization rather than endless wrangling, head-butting, and petty self-interest."

Politics is less than perfect because we are less than perfect. We therefore 6 need to approach it with some modesty. Politics is not like mathematics, where clear premises and deductive reasoning can lead to exact answers. We would all do better if we took to heart the words of the political scientist Harry Clor, author of "On Moderation." "There are truths to be discovered," he wrote, but they are "complex and many-sided; the best way to get to them is by engaging contrary ideas in a manner approximating dialogue."

In the throes of partisan disagreements, it can be tempting to think of 7 American politics as a Manichaean struggle of good versus evil. As someone who has been involved in his share of intense political debates, and has been a senior White House aide, I'm keenly aware of how easy it is to adopt this parochial mind-set, to feel that one is part of a tribal community.

Instead, we need the self-confidence to admit that at best we possess only a 8 partial understanding of the truth, which can be enlarged by refining our views in light of new arguments, new circumstances and new insights. But this requires us to listen to others, to weigh their arguments with care, and maybe even to learn from them.

"You used to not be able to talk about politics at a polite dinner party because 9 you would probably have a fight," Lilliana Mason, who teaches political science at the University of Maryland, recently told *The Washington Post*, in a revealing article about how most Trump voters in Virginia, where I live, don't know any Clinton voters and vice versa. "Increasingly, you can talk about politics at a dinner party because most of the people at the dinner party probably agree with you."

In creating a world that continually reinforces what we believe, it gets harder 10 to comprehend the attitudes animating others. The more distant our opponents are, the more likely we are to dismiss and dehumanize them. There's no common ground, no acknowledgment that those who hold different views from us might have a legitimate point, an understandable grievance, a reasonable concern. This is when politics becomes blood sport.

11   We are living through an especially partisan time now, but factionalism has always been a problem, under every type of political system. One possible answer comes from Montaigne, who pretty much invented the essay as we know it: "I embark upon discussion and argument with great ease and liberty," he writes in "On the Art of Conversation." "Since opinions do not find in me a ready soil to thrust and spread their roots into, no premise shocks me, no belief hurts me, no matter how opposite to my own they may be."

12   "Whenever we meet opposition, we do not look to see if it is just, but how we can get out of it, rightly or wrongly," he wrote a little later in the same essay. "Instead of welcoming arms we stretch out our claws." Calmly, as always, he proposes a solution: "When I am contradicted it arouses my attention, not my wrath. I move toward the man who contradicts me: he is instructing me. The cause of truth ought to be common to both of us."

13   Our low regard for politics is leading us to undervalue the craft of governing, to lose sight of the idea that there is anything at all that "ought to be common to both of us," never mind truth. We are attracted to political novices and so-called outsiders, which leaves open the possibility of the rise of demagogic figures. Such a person might say, as the Republican nominee for president has: "I'll give you everything. I will give you what you've been looking for for 50 years. I'm the only one."

14   Our democratic belief that anyone can be a political leader paradoxically feeds into the anti-democratic belief that we should look to one person to quickly and easily save us. No one, alone, can fix it, and in our system of government, this authoritarian approach is a prescription for catastrophe. Our confusion about and contempt for politics is also blinding us to the possibility that it can advance the human good. There are those moments in American history when great issues of justice have been at stake, from ending slavery and segregation to opposing Communism and fascism to protecting the physically disabled and the unborn.

15   More often, though, politics is about making institutions work somewhat better, helping people's lives at the margins, giving men and women the room to make the most of their talents and skills. It's about making our schools better and our communities safer. The people who give up on politics and who reflexively denigrate those who are practitioners of it are doing a disservice to our country. Skepticism is fine; caustic cynicism is not.

16   "Political activity is a type of moral activity," the British political theorist Bernard Crick wrote in "In Defense of Politics." "It does not claim to settle every problem or to make every sad heart glad," he added, "but it can help some way in nearly everything and, where it is strong, it can prevent the vast cruelties and deceits of ideological rule."

17   Thinking about politics as a moral activity may seem unimaginable during this malicious and degrading political year. But doing so, in a realistic and sober way, is the first step toward repairing America's shattered political culture and restoring politics to the pride of place it deserves in our national life.

Peter Wehner, "In Defense of Politics, Now More than Ever," *The New York Times,* 29 Oct. 2016. Used with permission of the author.

QUESTIONS FOR READING

1. What is the widely held view of politicians in America today? What are some legitimate reasons for this view? Who besides the politicians are also responsible for this problem?
2. What is a key reason that our politics often fail to meet expectations?
3. How do we need to change our thinking about who owns the "truth"? What was Montaigne's attitude toward those who contradicted him?
4. What can politics accomplish?
5. What are the dangers in believing that one leader can fix everything?

QUESTIONS FOR REASONING AND ANALYSIS

6. What set of views does the author seek to refute? How does he view political activity? What, then, is his central point, the claim of his argument?
7. What does Wehner accomplish in his three-paragraph opening?
8. How does the author develop and support his claim?

QUESTIONS FOR REFLECTION AND WRITING

9. Has anyone ever suggested to you that participation in public life should be viewed as "the crown of a career"? Why do you think our times have lost awareness of this concept?
10. What elected officials, serving currently or having recently served, do you admire? (Take time to reflect on this question; there are good people deeply involved in public service.) What do you admire about those on your list?
11. Do you agree with Wehner that truth is complex and many political problems lack easy solutions? If so, why? If not, how would you refute him?
12. How close do you come to meeting Montaigne's standard of openness to others with opposing views? What are the challenges to engaging in meaningful debate with others? Should we make the effort? Reflect on these issues that Wehner has raised.

CREDIT

1. Mark Norell, Eugene Gaffney, and Lowell Dingus. *Discovering Dinosaurs: In the American Museum of Natural History*. Alfred A. Knopf, 1995.

Studying Some Arguments by Genre

Definition Arguments

READ: How does the cat respond to the big dog's questions?

REASON: Does the big dog expect the responses he gets to his questions? How do you know?

REFLECT/WRITE: What is a rhetorical question? What is the risk of using one?

"Define your terms!" someone yells in the middle of a heated debate. Although yelling may not be the best strategy, the advice is sound for writers of argument. People do disagree over the meaning of words. Although we cannot let words mean whatever we want and still communicate, we do recognize that many words have more than one meaning. In addition, some words carry strong connotations, the emotional associations we attach to them. For this reason, realtors never sell *houses;* they always sell *homes.* They want you to believe that the house they are showing will become the home in which you will feel happy and secure.

Many important arguments turn on the definition of key terms. If you can convince others that you have the correct definition, then you are well on your way to winning your argument. The civil rights movement, for example, really turned on a definition of terms. Leaders argued that some laws are unjust, that because it is the law does not necessarily mean it is right. Laws requiring separate schools and separate drinking fountains and seats at the back of the bus for blacks were, in the view of civil rights activists, unjust laws, unjust because they are immoral and as such diminish us as humans. If obeying unjust laws is immoral, then it follows that we should not obey such laws. And when we recognize that obeying such laws hurts us, we have an obligation to act to remove unjust laws. Civil disobedience—illegal behavior to some—becomes, by definition, the best moral behavior.

Attorney Andrew Vachss has argued that there are no child prostitutes, only prostituted children. Yes, there are children who engage in sex for money. But, Vachss argues, that is not the complete definition of a prostitute. A prostitute chooses to exchange sex for money. Children do not choose; they are exploited by adults, beaten and in other ways abused if they do not work for the adult controlling them. If we agree with his definition, Vachss expects that we will also agree that the adults must be punished for their abuse of those prostituted children.

DEFINING AS PART OF AN ARGUMENT

There are two occasions for defining words as a part of your argument:

- You need to define any technical terms that may not be familiar to readers—or that readers may not understand as fully as they think they do. David Norman, early in his book on dinosaurs, writes:

  Nearly everyone knows what some dinosaurs look like, such as *Tyrannosaurus,* *Triceratops,* and *Stegosaurus.* But they may be much more vague about the lesser known ones, and may have difficulty in distinguishing between dinosaurs and other types of prehistoric creatures. It is not at all unusual to overhear an adult, taking a group of children around a museum display, being reprimanded sharply by the youngsters for failing to realize that a woolly mammoth was not a dinosaur, or—more forgivably—that a giant flying reptile such as *Pteranodon,* which lived at the time of the dinosaurs, was not a dinosaur either.[1]

  So what exactly is a dinosaur? And how do paleontologists decide on the groups they belong to?

Norman answers his questions by explaining the four characteristics that all dinosaurs have. He provides what is often referred to as a *formal definition.* He places the dinosaur in a class, established by four criteria, and then distinguishes this animal from other animals that lived a long time ago. His definition is not open to debate. He is presenting the definition and classification system that paleontologists, the specialists, have established.

● You need to define any word you are using in a special way. If you were to write: "We need to teach discrimination at an early age," you should add: "by *discrimination* I do not mean prejudice. I mean discernment, the ability to see differences." (*Sesame Street* has been teaching children this good kind of discrimination for many years.) The word *discrimination* used to have only a positive connotation; it referred to an important critical thinking skill. Today, however, the word has been linked to prejudice; to discriminate is to act on one's prejudice against some group. Writing today, you need to clarify when you are using the word in its original, positive meaning.

WHEN DEFINING *IS* THE ARGUMENT

We also turn to definition because we believe that a word is being used incorrectly or is not fully understood. Columnist George Will once argued that we should forget *values* and use instead the word *virtues*—that we should seek and admire virtues, not values. His point was that the term *values,* given to us by today's social scientists, is associated with situational ethics, or with an "if it feels good, do it" approach to action. He wants people to return to the more old-fashioned word *virtues* so that we are reminded that some behavior is right and some is wrong, and that neither the situation nor how we might "feel" about it alters those truths. In discussions such as Will's the purpose shifts. Instead of using definition as one step in an argument, definition becomes the central purpose of the argument. Will rejects the idea that *values* means the same thing as *virtues* and asserts that it is virtue—as he defines it—that must guide our behavior. An extended definition *is* the argument.

STRATEGIES FOR DEVELOPING AN EXTENDED DEFINITION

Arguing for your meaning of a word provides your purpose in writing. But it may not immediately suggest ways to develop such an argument. Let's think in terms of what definitions essentially do: They establish criteria for a class or category and then exclude other items from that category. (A pen is a writing instrument that uses ink.) Do you see your definition as drawing a line or as setting up two entirely separate categories? For example:

When does interrogation	become	torture?

One might argue that some strategies for making the person questioned uncomfortable are appropriate to interrogation (reduced sleep or comforts, loud noise). But at some point (stretching on a rack or waterboarding) one crosses a line to torture. To define torture, you have to explain where that line is—and how the actions on one side of the line are different from those on the other side.

What are the characteristics of wisdom as opposed to knowledge?

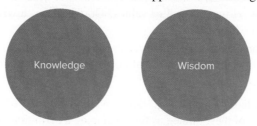

Do we cross a line from knowledge to become wise? Many would argue that wisdom requires traits or skills that are not found simply by increasing one's knowledge. The categories are separate. Others might argue that, while the categories are distinct, one does need knowledge to also be wise.

Envisioning these two approaches supports the abstract thinking that defining requires. Then what? Use some of the basic strategies of good writing:

- *Descriptive details.* Illustrate with specifics. List the traits of a leader or a courageous person. Explain the behaviors that we find in a wise person, or the behaviors that should be called torture. Describe the situations in which liberty can flourish, or the situations that result from unjust laws. Remember to use negative traits as well as positive ones. That is, show what is *not* covered by the word you are defining.

- *Examples.* Develop your definition with actual or hypothetical examples. Churchill, Lincoln, and FDR can all be used as examples of leaders. The biblical Solomon is generally acknowledged as a good example of a wise person. You can also create a hypothetical wise or courteous person, or a person whose behavior you would consider virtuous.

- *Comparison and/or contrast.* Clarify and limit your definition by contrasting it with words of similar—but not exactly the same—meanings. For example, what are the differences between knowledge and wisdom or interrogation and torture? The goal of your essay is to establish subtle but important differences so that your readers understand precisely what you want a given word to mean. In an essay at the end of this chapter, Robin Givhan distinguishes among *glamour, charisma,* and *cool* as a way to develop her definition of *glamour.*

- *History of usage or word origin.* The word's original meanings can be instructive. If the word has changed meaning over time, explore these changes as clues to how the word can (or should) be used. If you want readers to reclaim *discrimination* as a positive trait, then show them how that was part of the word's original meaning before the word became tied to prejudice. Word origin—etymology—can also give us insight into a word's meaning. Many words in English come from another language, or they are a combination of two words. The words *liberty* and *freedom* can usefully be discussed by examining etymology. Most dictionaries provide some word origin information, but the best source is—always—the *Oxford English Dictionary.*

- *Use or function.* A frequent strategy for defining is explaining an item's use or function: A pencil is a writing instrument. A similar approach can give insight into more general or abstract words as well. For example, what do we have—or gain— by emphasizing virtues instead of values? Or, what does a wise person *do* that a non-wise person does not do?

- *Metaphors.* Consider using figurative comparisons. When fresh, not clichés, they add vividness to your writing while offering insight into your understanding of the word.

In an essay titled "Why I Blog," Andrew Sullivan, one of the Web's earliest bloggers, uses many of these strategies for developing a definition of the term *blog:*

- *Word origin.* "The word *blog* is a conflation of two words: *web* and *log.* . . . In the monosyllabic vernacular of the Internet, *web log* soon became the word *blog.*"

- *One-sentence definition.* "It contains in its four letters a concise and accurate self-description: it is a log of thoughts and writing posted publicly on the World Wide Web."

- *Descriptive details.* "This form of instant and global self-publishing . . . allows for no retroactive editing. . . . [I]ts truth [is] inherently transitory."

- *Contrast.* "The wise panic that can paralyze a writer . . . is not available to a blog-ger. You can't have blogger's block."

- *Metaphors.* "A blog . . . bobs on the surface of the ocean but has its anchorage in waters deeper than those print media is technologically able to exploit."[2]

These snippets from Sullivan's lengthy essay give us a good look at defining strategies in action.

GUIDELINES for Evaluating Definition Arguments

When reading definition arguments, what should you look for? The basics of good argument apply to all arguments: a clear statement of claim, qualified if appropriate, a clear explanation of reasons and evidence, and enough relevant evidence to support the claim. How do we recognize these qualities in a definition argument? Use the following points as guides to evaluating:

- **Why is the word being defined?** Has the writer convinced you of the need to understand the word's meaning or change the way the word is commonly used?

- **How is the word defined?** Has the writer established his or her definition, clearly distinguishing it from what the writer perceives to be objectionable definitions? It is hard to judge the usefulness of the writer's position if the differences in meaning remain fuzzy. If George Will is going to argue for using *virtues* instead of *values,* he needs to be sure that readers understand the differences he sees in the two words.

- **What strategies are used to develop the definition?** Can you recognize the different types of evidence presented and see what the writer is doing in his or her argument? This kind of analysis can aid your evaluation of a definition argument.

- **What are the implications of accepting the author's definition?** Why does George Will want readers to embrace *virtues* rather than *values*? Will's argument is not just about subtle points of language. His argument is also about attitudes that affect public policy issues. Part of any evaluation of a definition argument must include our assessment of the author's definition.

- **Is the definition argument convincing?** Do the reasons and evidence lead you to agree with the author, to accept the idea of the definition and its implications as well?

PREPARING A DEFINITION ARGUMENT

In addition to the guidelines for writing arguments presented in Chapter 4, you can use the following advice specific to writing definition arguments.

Planning

1. *Think:* Why do you want to define your term? To add to our understanding of a complex term? To challenge the use of the word by others? If you don't have a good reason to write, find a different word to examine.

2. *Think:* How are you defining the word? What are the elements/parts/steps in your definition? Some brainstorming notes are probably helpful to keep your definition concrete and focused.

3. *Think:* What strategies will you use to develop and support your definition? Consider using several of these possible strategies for development:

   - *Word origin or history of usage*
   - *Descriptive details*
   - *Comparison and/or contrast*
   - *Examples*
   - *Function or use*
   - *Metaphors*

Drafting

1. Begin with an opening paragraph or two that introduces your subject in an interesting way. Possibilities include the occasion that has led to your writing—explain, for instance, a misunderstanding about your term's meaning that you want to correct.

2. Do *not* begin by quoting or paraphrasing a dictionary definition of the term. "According to Webster …" is a tired approach lacking reader interest. If the dictionary definition were sufficient, you would have no reason to write an entire essay to define the term.

3. State your claim—your definition of the term—early in your essay, if you can do so in a sentence or two. If you do not state a brief claim, then establish your purpose in writing early in your essay. (You may find that there are too many parts to your definition to combine into one or two sentences.)

4. Use several specific strategies for developing your definition. Select strategies from the list above and organize your approach around these strategies. That is, you can develop one paragraph of descriptive details, another of examples, another of contrast with words that are not exactly the same in meaning.

5. Consider specifically refuting the error in word use that led to your decision to write your own definition. If you are motivated to write based on what you have read, then make a rebuttal part of your definition argument.

6. Consider discussing the implications of your definition. You can give weight and value to your argument by explaining the larger significance of your definition.

A CHECKLIST FOR REVISION

☐ Do I have a good understanding of my purpose? Have I made this clear to readers?

☐ Have I clearly stated my definition? Or clearly established the various parts of the definition that I discuss in separate paragraphs?

☐ Have I organized my argument, building the parts of my definition into a logical, coherent structure?

☐ Have I used specifics to clarify and support my definition?

☐ Have I used the basic checklist for revision in Chapter 4 (see p. 107)?

STUDENT ESSAY

PARAGON OR PARASITE?

Laura Mullins

Attention-getting introduction.

Do you recognize this creature? He is low maintenance and often unnoticeable, a favorite companion of many. Requiring no special attention, he grows from the soil of pride and rejection, feeding regularly on a diet of ignorance and insecurity, scavenging for hurt feelings and defensiveness, gobbling up dainty morsels of lust and scandal. Like a cult leader clothed in a gay veneer, disguising himself as blameless, he wields power. Bewitching unsuspecting but devoted groupies, distracting them from honest self-examination, deceiving them into believing illusions of grandeur or, on the other extreme, unredeemable worthlessness, he breeds jealousy, hate, and fear; thus, he thrives. He is Gossip.

Clever extended metaphor.

One of my dearest friends is a gossip. She is an educated, honorable, compassionate, loving woman whose character and judgment I deeply admire and respect. After sacrificially raising six children, she went on to study medicine and become a doctor who graciously volunteers her expertise. How, you may be wondering, could a gossip deserve such praise? Then you do not understand the word. My friend is my daughter's godmother; she is my gossip, or *godsib,* meaning sister-in-god. Derived from Middle English words *god,* meaning spiritual, and *sip/sib/syp,* meaning kinsman, this term was used to refer to a familiar acquaintance, close family friend, or intimate relation, according to the *Oxford English Dictionary.* As a male, he would have joined in fellowship and celebration with the father of the newly born; if a female, she would have been a trusted friend, a birth-attendant or midwife to the mother of the baby. The term grew to include references to the type of easy, unrestrained conversation shared by these folks.

Subject introduced.

Etymology of gossip and early meanings.

As is often the case with words, the term's meaning has certainly evolved, maybe eroded from its original idea. Is it harmless, idle chat, innocuous sharing of others' personal news, or back-biting, rumor-spreading, and manipulation? Is it a beneficial activity worthy of pursuit, or a deplorable danger to be avoided?

Current meanings.

In her article "Evolution, Alienation, and Gossip" (for the Social Issues Research Centre in Oxford, England), Kate Fox writes that

Good use of sources to develop definition.

"gossip is not a trivial pastime; it is essential to human social, psychological, and even physical well-being." Many echo her view that gossip is a worthy activity, claiming that engaging in gossip produces endorphins, reduces stress, and aids in building intimate relationships. Gossip, seen at worst as a harmless outlet, is encouraged in the workplace. Since much of its content is not inherently critical or malicious, it is viewed as a positive activity. However, this view does nothing to encourage those speaking or listening to evaluate or examine motive or purpose; instead, it seems to reflect the "anything goes" thinking so prevalent today.

Conversely, writer and high school English and geography teacher Lennox V. Farrell of Toronto, Canada, in his essay titled "Gossip: An Urban Form of Sorcery," presents gossip as a kind of "witchcraft . . . based on using unsubstantiated accusations by those who make them, and on uncritically accepting these by those enticed into listening." Farrell uses gossip in its more widely understood definition, encompassing the breaking of confidences, inappropriate sharing of indiscretions, destructive tale-bearing, and malicious slander.

What, then, is gossip? We no longer use the term to refer to our children's godparents. Its current definition usually comes with derogatory implications. Imagine a backyard garden: You see a variety of greenery, recognizing at a glance that you are looking at different kinds of plants. Taking a closer look, you will find the gossip vine; inconspicuously blending in, it doesn't appear threatening, but ultimately it destroys. If left in the garden it will choke and then suck out life from its host. Zoom in on the garden scene and follow the creeping vine up trees and along a fence where two neighbors visit. You can overhear one woman saying to the other, "I know I should be

Good use of metaphor to depict gossip as negative.

the last to tell you, but your husband is being unfaithful to me."
(Caption from a cartoon by Alan De la Nougerede.)

The current popular movement to legitimize gossip seems an excuse to condone the human tendency to puff-up oneself. Compared in legal terms, gossip is to conversation as hearsay is to eyewitness testimony; it's not credible. Various religious doctrines abhor the idea and practice of gossip. An old Turkish proverb says, "He who gossips to you will gossip of you." From the Babylonian Talmud, which calls gossip the three-pronged tongue, destroying the one talking, the one listening, and the one being spoken of, to the Upanishads, to the Bible, we can conclude that no good fruit is born from gossip. Let's tend our gardens and check our motives when we have the urge to gossip. Surely we can find more noble pursuits than the self-aggrandizement we have come to know as gossip.

Conclusion states view that gossip is to be avoided—the writer's thesis.

Courtesy of Laura Mullins.

FOR ANALYSIS AND DEBATE

GLAMOUR, THAT CERTAIN SOMETHING | ROBIN GIVHAN

Robin Givhan is a graduate of Princeton and holds a master's degree in journalism from the University of Michigan. When she was fashion editor at *The Washington Post*, she won a Pulitzer Prize (2006) for criticism, the first time the prize was awarded to a fashion writer. In 2010 she moved to *The Daily Beast* and *Newsweek*, but was laid off by these publications in December 2012, when *Newsweek* gave up print journalism. Givhan's coverage of the world of fashion frequently becomes a study of culture, as we see in the following column, published February 17, 2008, shortly before the 2008 Academy Awards show.

PREREADING QUESTIONS What is the difference between glamour and good looks? What famous people do you consider glamorous?

Glamour isn't a cultural necessity, but its usefulness can't be denied.   1

It makes us feel good about ourselves by making us believe that life can   2
sparkle. Glamorous people make difficult tasks seem effortless. They appear to cruise through life shaking off defeat with a wry comment. No matter how hard they work for what they have, the exertion never seems to show. Yet the cool confidence they project doesn't ever drift into lassitude.

3   Hollywood attracts people of glamour—as well as the misguided souls who confuse it with mere good looks—because that is where it is richly rewarded. And the Academy Awards are the epicenter of it all. We'll watch the Oscars next Sunday to delight in the stars who glide down the red carpet like graceful swans or who swagger onto the stage looking dashing.

4   Of course, we'll watch for other reasons, too. There's always the possibility of a supremely absurd fashion moment or an acceptance speech during which the winner becomes righteously indignant—Michael Moore–style—or practically hyperventilates like Halle Berry. While Moore, a nominee, is not glamorous, he is compelling for the sheer possibility of an impolitic eruption. Berry isn't glamorous either, mostly because nothing ever looks effortless with her. (She has even expressed anguish over her beauty.) Mostly, though, we will watch in search of "old Hollywood" glamour. But really, is there any other kind?

5   Among the actors who consistently manage to evoke memories of Cary Grant or Grace Kelly are George Clooney and Cate Blanchett. There's something about the way they present themselves that speaks to discretion, sex appeal and glossy perfection. As an audience, we think we know these actors but we really don't. We know their image, the carefully crafted personality they display to the public. If they have been to rehab, they went quietly and without a crowd of paparazzi.

6   Their lives appear to be an endless stream of lovely adventures, minor mishaps that turn into cocktail party banter, charming romances and just enough gravitas to keep them from floating away on a cloud of frivolity.

7   These actors take pretty pictures because they seem supremely comfortable with themselves. It's not simply their beauty we're seeing; it's also an unapologetic pleasure in being who they are.

Oscar nominee Tilda Swinton has the kind of striking, handsome looks of   8
Anjelica Huston or Lauren Bacall. But Swinton doesn't register as glamorous as
much as cool. She looks a bit androgynous and favors the eccentric Dutch
design team of Viktor & Rolf, which once populated an entire runway show with
Swinton doppelgangers. Coolness suggests that the person knows something or
understands something that average folks haven't yet figured out. Cool people
are a step ahead. Glamour is firmly situated in the now.

There's nothing particularly intimate about glamour, which is why it plays   9
so well on the big screen and why film actors who embody it can sometimes be
disappointing in real life. Glamour isn't like charisma, which is typically described
as the ability to make others feel important or special.

Neither quality has much to do with a person's inner life. Glamour is no mea-   10
sure of soulfulness or integrity. It isn't about truth, but perception. *Redbook*
traffics in truth. *Vogue* promotes glamour.

Although Hollywood is the natural habitat for the glitterati, they exist   11
everywhere: politics, government, sports, business. Tiger Woods brought
glamour to golf with his easy confidence and his ability to make the professional
game look as simple as putt-putt. Donald Trump aspires to glamour with his
flashy properties and their gold-drenched decor. But his efforts are apparent, his
yearning obvious. The designer Tom Ford is glamorous. The man never rumples.

In the political world, Barack Obama has glamour. Bill Clinton has charisma.   12
And Hillary Clinton has an admirable work ethic. Bill Clinton could convince
voters that he felt their pain. Hillary Clinton reminds them detail by detail of how
she would alleviate it. Glamour has a way of temporarily making you forget about
the pain and just think the world is a beautiful place of endless possibilities.

Ronald Reagan evoked glamour. His white-tie inaugural balls and morning-   13
coat swearing-in were purposefully organized to bring a twinkle back to the
American psyche. George W. Bush has charisma, a.k.a. the likability factor,
although it does not appear to be helping his approval rating now. Still, he
remains a back-slapper and bestower of nicknames.

Charisma is personal. Glamour taps into a universal fairy tale. It's   14
unconcerned with the nitty-gritty. Instead, it celebrates the surface gloss. And
sometimes, a little shimmer can be hard to resist.

QUESTIONS FOR READING

1. How does glamour make us feel?
2. Where do we usually find glamour? Why?
3. Which celebrities today best capture Hollywood's glamour of the past?
4. What traits do the glamorous have?
5. Explain the differences among glamour, charisma, and cool.

QUESTIONS FOR REASONING AND ANALYSIS

6. Examine the opening three sentences in paragraph 12. What makes them effective?

7. What are the specific strategies Givhan uses to develop her definition?

8. What is Givhan's claim?

QUESTIONS FOR REFLECTION AND WRITING

9. Givhan asserts that glamour is in the present but "cool people are a step ahead." Does this contrast make sense to you? Why or why not?

10. Do we ever really know the glamorous, charismatic, and cool celebrities? Explain.

11. Givhan provides specific examples of people with glamour. Are there others you would add to her list? If so, explain why, based on Givhan's definition.

12. Some young people aspire to be cool. How would you advise them? What should one do, how should one behave, to be cool? Is "cool" a trait that we can "put on" if we wish? Why or why not?

CROSSING THE AEGEAN IS 'TRAUMATIC.' YOUR BAD HAIR DAY ISN'T.   NICHOLAS HASLAM

Professor and head of the School of Psychological Sciences at the University of Melbourne, Nick Haslam received his PhD in clinical and social psychology from the University of Pennsylvania and taught in the United States for several years before returning to Australia. Haslam has written in his academic areas of interest, but also frequently contributes to newspapers in several countries. His essay on trauma is one of those op-ed articles.

PREREADING QUESTIONS How do you use the word *trauma*? Based on his expertise and the title above, do you think Haslam is likely to agree with your use of the word?

1   These days, "trauma" seems epidemic.

2   A group of Columbia Law School students felt the "traumatic effects" of the Michael Brown grand jury decision so keenly, they argued, that they needed their finals postponed. A handful of Emory University students were "traumatized" by finding "Trump 2016" chalked on campus sidewalks. A young professor chronicled his traumatizing graduate training, which included discrimination and job anxiety. And in an interview, a "trauma-sensitive yoga" instructor talked through her "hair trauma": "I grew up with really curly, frizzy hair in Miami, Florida. When you're 13, a bad hair day is overwhelming," she said. "Even though I would never compare that to someone who was abused, it's an experience that shaped my identity and, at the time, was intolerable."

3   These aren't isolated incidents. Trauma is being used to describe an increasingly wide array of events. By today's standards, it can be caused by a microaggression, reading something offensive without a trigger warning or even watching upsetting news unfold on television. As one blogger wrote, "Trauma now seems to be pretty much anything that bothers anyone, in any way, ever."

4   This is not a mere terminological fad. It reflects a steady expansion of the word's meaning by psychiatrists and the culture at large. And its promiscuous

use has worrying implications. When we describe misfortune, sadness or even pain as trauma, we redefine our experience. Using the word "trauma" turns every event into a catastrophe, leaving us helpless, broken and unable to move on.

Like democracy, alarm clocks and the Olympics, we owe "trauma" to the 5 ancient Greeks. For them, trauma was severe physical injury; the word shares its linguistic root with terms for breaking apart and bruising. Of course, doctors still use "trauma" to describe physical harm. But more and more, we understand the term in a second way—as an emotional injury rather than a physical wound.

This shift started in the late 19th century, when neurologists such as 6 Jean-Martin Charcot and Sigmund Freud posited that some neuroses were caused by deeply distressing experiences. The idea was revolutionary—a dawning recognition that shattered minds could be explained psychologically as well as biologically.

Refugees crossing the Aegean to the island of Lesbos, seeking a new life.

Ideas about psychological trauma continued to take shape in the 20th 7 century, but the physical sense still dominated. In 1952, the first edition of *The Diagnostic and Statistical Manual of Mental Disorders*, which catalogues psychological illnesses, mentioned the term only in relation to brain injuries caused by force or electric shock.

By 1980, that had changed. The DSM's third edition recognized post- 8 traumatic stress disorder for the first time, though the definition of a "traumatic event" was relatively focused—it had to be "outside the range of usual human experience" and severe enough to "evoke significant symptoms of distress in almost everyone." The DSM-III's authors argued that common experiences such as chronic illness, marital conflict and bereavement did not meet the definition.

Later editions of psychiatry's "bible"—really more like a field guide to the 9 species of human misery—loosened the definition further, expanding it to incorporate indirect experiences such as violent assaults of family members and friends, along with "developmentally inappropriate sexual experiences" and occasions when people witness serious injury or death. One study found that 19 events qualified as traumatic in the DSM-IV; just 14 would have qualified in the revised edition of the DSM-III.

10   This broadening of the definition was justified in part by the finding that people who were indirectly exposed to stressful events could develop PTSD symptoms. Even so, researchers became concerned that elastic concepts of trauma "risk trivializing the suffering of those exposed to catastrophic life events." As psychologist Stephen Joseph explained in a 2011 interview, "The DSM over-medicalizes human experience. Things which are relatively common, relatively normal, are turned into psychiatric disorders."

11   An Army National Guard medic argued in *Scientific American* that "clinicians aren't separating the few who really have PTSD from those who are experiencing things like depression or anxiety or social and reintegration problems, or who are just taking some time getting over it." This, he worried, would lead to people being "pulled into a treatment and disability regime that will mire them in a self-fulfilling vision of a brain rewired, a psyche permanently haunted."

12   That hasn't stopped definition expansion. The federal Substance Abuse and Mental Health Services Administration, for example, now says trauma can involve ongoing circumstances rather than a distinct event—no serious threat to life or limb necessary. Trauma, by the agency's definition, doesn't even have to be outside normal experience. No wonder clinicians increasingly identify such common experiences as uncomplicated childbirth, marital infidelity, wisdom-tooth extraction and hearing offensive jokes as possible causes of PTSD.

13   This thinking has seeped into our culture as well. The word "trauma" itself has exploded in popularity in recent decades. A search of the 500 billion words that make up the Google Books database reveals that "trauma" appeared at four times the rate in 2005 as in 1965. According to Google Trends, interest in the word has grown by a third in the past five years.

14   How to explain this change? For one thing, the broadening of "trauma" coincides with other psychological shifts, such as a sense that our life outcomes are out of our control. According to one study, young people increasingly believe that their destinies are determined by luck, fate or powerful people besides themselves. People who hold these beliefs are more likely to feel helpless and unable to manage stress. Trauma is a way to explain life's problems as someone else's fault.

15   A second explanation can be found in my work on "concept creep." In recent decades, several psychological concepts have undergone semantic inflation. The definitions of abuse, addiction, bullying, mental disorder and prejudice have all expanded to include a broad range of phenomena. This reflects a growing sensitivity to harm in Western societies. By broadening the reach of these concepts—recognizing emotional manipulation as abuse, the spreading of rumors as bullying and increasingly mild conditions as psychiatric problems—we identify more people as victims of harm. We express a well-intentioned unwillingness to accept things that were previously tolerated, but we also risk over-sensitivity: defining relatively innocuous phenomena as serious problems that require outside intervention. The expansion of the concept of trauma runs the same risk.

All of this is problematic. The way we interpret an experience affects how we 16 respond to it. Interpreting adversity as trauma makes it seem calamitous and likely to have lasting effects. When an affliction is seen as traumatic, it becomes something overwhelming—something that breaks us, that is likely to produce post-traumatic symptoms and that requires professional intervention. Research shows that people who tend to interpret negative events as catastrophic and long-lasting are more susceptible to post-traumatic reactions. Perceiving challenging life experiences as traumas may therefore increase our vulnerability to them.

Our choice of language matters. A famous study by cognitive psychologist 17 Elizabeth Loftus illustrates why. Loftus showed people films of traffic accidents and asked them to judge the speed of the cars involved, using subtly varying instructions. Different study participants were asked how fast the cars were going when they "smashed," "collided," "bumped," "hit" or "contacted" each other. Despite watching the very same collisions, people judged the cars to be traveling 28 percent faster when they were described as "smashing" rather than "contacting."

To define all adversities as traumas is akin to seeing all collisions as smashes. 18 People collide with misfortune all the time: Sometimes it smashes them, but often they merely make contact.

Another fine invention of the ancient Greeks was stoicism. Contrary to 19 popular opinion, the stoics did not think we should simply endure or brush off adversity. Rather, they believed that we should confront suffering with composure and rational judgment. We should all cultivate stoic wisdom to judge the difference between traumas that can break us apart and normal adversities that we can overcome.

Nick Haslam, "Crossing the Aegean is 'Traumatic.' Your Bad Hair Day Isn't," *The Washington Post*, 14 Aug. 2016. Used with permission of the author.

QUESTIONS FOR READING

1. What was the original meaning of the word *trauma*? What second meaning developed over time? When was trauma officially accepted as a psychological disorder?

2. How has the term expanded subsequent to the 4th edition of the DSM?

3. What kinds of human experience are now described as traumatic by the Substance Abuse and Mental Health Services Administration?

4. What causes does Haslam offer to account for the expanding meaning of trauma—and other concepts—in our culture?

5. Why does the author find these changing views distressing? What can happen when we see adversities as traumas?

QUESTIONS FOR REASONING AND ANALYSIS

6. What point does the author want to make about the changing definition of trauma? That is, what is Haslam's claim?

7. What specific strategies for defining are used by Haslam?

8. What does the author seek to accomplish in paragraph 15? How does this discussion of language advance his argument?

9. What is clever about Haslam's discussion of the Greek philosophy of Stoicism in the final paragraph?

QUESTIONS FOR REFLECTION AND WRITING

10. Which defining strategies are most effectively used by Haslam? Defend your selection.

11. Do you agree with Haslam that not only has the meaning of trauma been greatly expanded but also that this is a problem? If you disagree, how would you refute his argument? (*Note:* There is good evidence that our choice of language matters.)

12. Does your experience confirm Haslam's analysis that we tend today, as a culture, to label many kinds of unpleasant experiences as cause for trauma? If so, what examples can you add to this discussion?

SUGGESTIONS FOR DISCUSSION AND WRITING

1. In the student essay, Laura Mullins defines the term *gossip*. Select one of the following words to define and prepare your own extended definition argument, using at least three of the strategies for defining described in this chapter. For each word in the list, you see a companion word in parentheses. Use that companion word as a word that you contrast with the word you are defining. (For example, how does gossip differ from conversation?) The idea of an extended definition argument is to make fine distinctions among words similar in meaning.

   courtesy (manners)   hero (star)
   wisdom (knowledge)   community (subdivision)
   patriotism (chauvinism)   freedom (liberty)

2. Select a word you believe is currently misused. It can be misused because it has taken on a negative (or positive) connotation that it did not originally have, or because it has changed meaning and lost something in the process. A few suggestions include *awful, awesome, fabulous, exceptional* (in education), *propaganda*.

3. Define a term that is currently used to label people with particular traits or values. Possibilities include *nerd, yuppie, freak, jock, redneck, bimbo, wimp*. Reflect, before selecting this topic, on why you want to explain the meaning of the word you have chosen. One purpose might be to explain the word to someone from another culture. Another might be to defend people who are labeled negatively by a term; that is, you want to show why the term should not have a negative connotation.

CREDITS

1. David Norman. *Dinosaur!* John Wiley & Sons, 1991.
2. Andrew Sullivan. "Why I Blog." *The Atlantic,* Nov. 2008.

Evaluation Arguments

READ: What is the situation? Where are we?

REASON: Look at the faces; what do you infer to be the attitude of the participants?

REASON/WRITE: What is the photo's message?

"I really love Ben's Camaro; it's so much more fun to go out with him than to go with Gregory in his Volvo wagon," you confide to a friend. "On the other hand, Ben always wants to see the latest horror movie—and boy are they horrid! I'd much rather watch one of our teams play—whatever the season; sports events are so much more fun than horror movies!"

"Well, at least you and Ben agree not to listen to Amy Winehouse CDs. Her life was so messed up; why would anyone admire her music?" your friend responds.

CHARACTERISTICS OF EVALUATION ARGUMENTS

Evaluations. How easy they are to make. We do it all the time. So, surely an evaluation argument should be easy to prepare. Not so fast. Remember at the beginning of the discussion of argument in Chapter 3, we observed that we do not argue about personal preferences because there is no basis for building an argument. If you don't like horror movies, then don't go to them—even with Ben! However, once you assert that sporting events are more fun than horror movies, you have shifted from personal preference to the world of argument, the world in which others will judge the effectiveness of your logic and evidence. On what basis can you argue that one activity is more fun than the other? And, always more fun? And, more fun for everyone? You probably need to qualify this claim and then you will need to establish the criteria by which you have made your evaluation. Although you might find it easier to defend your preference for a car for dates, you, at least in theory, can build a convincing argument for a qualified claim in support of sporting events. Your friend, though, will have great difficulty justifying her evaluation of Winehouse based on Winehouse's lifestyle. An evaluation of her music needs to be defended based on criteria about music—unless she wants to argue that any music made by people with unconventional or immoral lifestyles will be bad music, a tough claim to defend.

In a column for *Time* Magazine, Charles Krauthammer argues that Tiger Woods is the greatest golfer ever to play the game. He writes:

> How do we know? You could try Method 1: Compare him directly with the former greatest golfer, Jack Nicklaus. ... But that is not the right way to compare. You cannot compare greatness directly across the ages. There are so many intervening variables: changes in technology, training, terrain, equipment, often rules and customs.
>
> How then do we determine who is greatest? Method 2: The Gap. Situate each among his contemporaries. Who towers? ... Nicklaus was great, but he ran with peers: Palmer, Player, Watson. Tiger has none.[1]

Krauthammer continues with statistics to demonstrate that there is no one playing now with Tiger who comes close in number of tournaments won, number of majors won, and number of strokes better in these events than the next player. He then applies the Gap Method to Babe Ruth in baseball, Wayne Gretzky in hockey, and Bobby Fischer in chess to demonstrate that it works to reveal true greatness in competition among the world's best.

Krauthammer clearly explains his Gap Method, his basic criterion for judging greatness. Then he provides the data to support his conclusions about who are or were the greatest in various fields. His is a convincing evaluation argument.

These examples suggest some key points about evaluation arguments:

- **Evaluation arguments are arguments, not statements of personal preferences.** As such, they need a precise, qualified claim and reasons and evidence for support, just like any argument.

- **Evaluation arguments are about "good" and "bad," "best" and "worst."** These arguments are not about what we should or should not do or why a situation is the way it is. The debate is not whether one should select a boyfriend based on the kind of car he drives or why horror movies have so much appeal for many viewers. The argument is that sports events are great entertainment, or better entertainment than horror movies.

- **Evaluation arguments need to be developed based on a clear statement of the criteria for evaluating.** Winehouse won Grammys for her music—why? By what standards of excellence do we judge a singer? A voice with great musicality and nuance? The selection of songs with meaningful lyrics? The ability to engage listeners—the way the singer can "sell" a song? The number of recordings sold and awards won? All of these criteria? Something else?

- **Evaluation arguments, to be successful, may need to defend the criteria, not just to list them and show that the subject of the argument meets those criteria.** Suppose you want to argue that sporting events are great entertainment because it is exciting to cheer with others, you get to see thrilling action, and it is good, clean fun. Are sports always "good, clean fun"? Some of the fighting in hockey matches is quite vicious. Some football players get away with dirty hits. Krauthammer argues that his Gap Method provides the better criterion for judging greatness and then shows why it is the better method. Do not underestimate the challenge of writing an effective evaluation argument.

TYPES OF EVALUATION ARGUMENTS

The examples we have examined above are about people or items or experiences in our lives. Tiger Woods is the greatest golfer ever, based on the Gap Method strategy. Sports events are more fun to attend than horror movies. We can (and do!) evaluate just about everything we know or do or buy. This is one type of evaluation argument. In this category we would place the review—of a book, movie, concert, or something similar.

A second type of evaluation is a response to another person's argument. We are not explaining why the car or college, sitcom or singer, is good or great or the best. Instead, we are responding to one specific argument we have read (or listened to) that we think is flawed—flawed in many ways or in one significant way that essentially destroys the argument. This type of evaluation argument is called a rebuttal or refutation argument.

Sometimes our response to what we consider a really bad argument is to go beyond the rebuttal and write a counterargument. Rather than writing about the limitations and flaws in our friend's evaluation of Winehouse as a singer not to be listened to, we decide to write our own argument evaluating Winehouse's strengths as a contemporary singer. This counterargument is best described as an evaluation argument, not a refutation. Similarly, we can disagree with someone's argument defending restrictions placed by colleges on student file sharing. But if we decide to write a counterargument defending students' rights to share music files, we have moved from rebuttal to our own position paper, our own argument based on values. Counterarguments are best seen as belonging to one of the other genres of argument discussed in this section of the text.

GUIDELINES for Analyzing an Evaluation Argument

The basics of good argument apply to all arguments: a clear statement of claim, qualified as appropriate, a clear explanation of reasons and evidence, and enough relevant evidence to support the claim. When reading evaluation arguments, use the following points as additional guides:

- **What is the writer's claim?** Is it clear, qualified if necessary, and focused on the task of evaluating?

- **Has the writer considered audience as a basis for both claim and criteria?** Your college may be a good choice for you, given your criteria for choosing, but is it a good choice for others? Qualifications need to be based on audience: College A is a great school for young people in need of B and with X amount of funds. Or: *The Da Vinci Code* is an entertaining read for those with some understanding of art history and knowledge of the Roman Catholic Church.

- **What criteria are presented as the basis for evaluation?** Are they clearly stated? Do they seem reasonable for the topic of evaluation? Are they defended if necessary?

- **What evidence and/or reasons are presented to show that the item under evaluation meets the criteria?** Specifics are important in any evaluation argument.

- **What are the implications of the claim?** If we accept the Gap Method for determining greatness, does that mean that we can never compare stars from different generations? If we agree with the rebuttal argument, does that mean that there are no good arguments for the claim in the essay being refuted?

- **Is the argument convincing?** Does the evidence lead you to agree with the author? Do you want to buy that car, listen to that music, read that book, see that film as a result of reading the argument?

PREPARING AN EVALUATION ARGUMENT

In addition to the guidelines for writing arguments presented in Chapter 4, you can use the following advice specific to writing evaluation arguments.

Planning

1. **Think:** Why do you want to write this evaluation? Does it matter, or are you just sharing your personal preferences? Select a topic that requires you to think deeply about how we judge that item (college, book, album, etc.).

2. **Think about audience:** Try to imagine writing your evaluation for your class-mates, not just your instructor. Instead of thinking about an assignment to be graded, think about why we turn to reviews, for example. What do readers want to learn? They want to know if they should see that film. Your job is to help them make that decision.

3. **Think:** What are my criteria for evaluation? And, how will I measure my topic against them to show that my evaluation is justified? You really must know how you would determine a great singer or a great tennis player before you write, or you risk writing only about personal preferences.

4. **Establish a general plan:** If you are writing a review, be sure to study the work carefully. Can you write a complete and accurate summary? (It is easier to review an album than a live concert because you can replay the album to get all the details straight.) You will need to balance summary, analysis, and evaluation in a review— and be sure that you do not mostly write summary or reveal the ending of a novel or film! If you are evaluating a college or a car, think about how to order your cri-teria. Do you want to list all criteria first and then show how your item connects to them, point by point? Or, do you want the criteria to unfold as you make specific points about your item?

   To analyze a film, consider the plot, the characters, the actors who play the lead characters, any special effects used, and the author's (and director's) "take" on the story. If the "idea" of the film is insignificant, then it is hard to argue that it is a great film. Analysis of style in a book needs to be connected to that book's intended audience. Style and presentation will vary depending on the knowledge and sophis-tication of the intended reader. If, for example, you have difficulty understanding a book aimed at a general audience, then it is fair to say that the author has not suc-cessfully reached his or her audience. But if you are reviewing a book intended for specialists, then your difficulties in reading are not relevant to a fair evaluation of that book. You can point out, though, that the book is tough going for a nonspecialist— just as you could point out that a movie sequel is hard to follow for those who did not see the original film.

Drafting

1. Begin with an opening paragraph or two that engages your reader while introducing your subject and purpose in writing. Is there a specific occasion that has led to your writing? And what, exactly, are you evaluating?

2. Either introduce your criteria next and then show how your item for evaluation meets the criteria, point by point, through the rest of the essay; or, decide on an order for introducing your criteria and use that order as your structure. Put the most important criterion either first or last. It can be effective to put the most controver-sial point last.

3. If you are writing a review, then the basic criteria are already established. You will need some combination of summary, analysis, and evaluation. Begin with an attention-getter that includes a broad statement of the work's subject or subject category: This is a *biography* of Benjamin Franklin; this is a *female*

action-hero film. An evaluation in general terms can complete the opening paragraph. For example:

> Dr. Cynthia Pemberton's new book, *More Than a Game: One Woman's Fight for Gender Equity in Sport,* is destined to become a classic in sport sociology, sport history, and women's studies.

4. The rest of the review will then combine summary details, analysis of presentation, and a final assessment of the work in the concluding paragraph. From the same review, after learning specifics of content, we read:

> The target audience for this book includes educators, coaches, athletes, and administrators at any level. Additionally, anyone interested in studying women's sports or pursuing a Title IX case will love this book.

5. Consider discussing the implications of your evaluation. Why is this important? Obviously for a book or film or art show, for example, we want to know if this is a "must read" or "must see." For other evaluation arguments, let us know why we should care about your subject and your perspective. Charles Krauthammer does not just argue that Tiger Woods is the greatest golfer ever; he also argues that his Gap Method is the best strategy for evaluation. That's why he shows that it works not just to put Woods ahead of Nicklaus but also to put other greats in their exalted place in other sports.

A CHECKLIST FOR REVISION

☐ Do I have a good understanding of my purpose? Have I made my evaluation purpose clear to readers?

☐ Have I clearly stated my claim?

☐ Have I clearly stated my criteria for evaluation—or selected the appropriate elements of content, style, presentation, and theme for a review?

☐ Have I organized my argument into a coherent structure by some pattern that readers can recognize and follow?

☐ Have I provided good evidence and logic to support my evaluation?

☐ Have I used the basic checklist for revision in Chapter 4? (See p. 107.)

STUDENT REVIEW

WINCHESTER'S ALCHEMY: TWO MEN AND A BOOK

Ian Habel

One can hardly imagine a tale promising less excitement for a general audience than that of the making of the *Oxford English Dictionary (OED).* The sensationalism of murder and insanity would have to labor intensely against the burden of lexicography in crafting a genuine page-turner on the subject. Much to my surprise, Simon Winchester, in writing *The Professor and the Madman: A Tale of Murder, Insanity, and the Making of the Oxford English Dictionary,* has succeeded in producing so compelling a story that I was forced to devour it completely in a single afternoon, an unprecedented personal feat.

The Professor and the Madman is the story of the lives of two apparently very different men and the work that brought them together. Winchester begins by recounting the circumstances that led to the incarceration of Dr. W. C. Minor, a well-born, well-educated, and quite insane American ex-Army surgeon. Minor, in a fit of delusion, had murdered a man whom he believed to have crept into his Lambeth hotel room to torment him in his sleep. The doctor is tried and whisked off to the Asylum for the Criminally Insane, Broadmoor.

The author then introduces readers to the other two main characters: the *OED* itself and its editor James Murray, a lowborn, self-educated Scottish philologist. The shift in narrative focus is used to dramatic effect. The natural assumption on the part of the reader that these two seemingly unrelated plots must eventually meet urges us to read on in anticipation of that connection. As each chapter switches focus from one man to the other, it is introduced by a citation from the *OED,* reminding us that the story is ultimately about the dictionary. The citations also serve to foreshadow and provide a theme for the chapter. For example, the *OED* definition of *murder* heads the first chapter, relating to the details of Minor's crime.

Winchester acquaints us with the shortcomings of seventeenth- and eighteenth-century attempts at compiling a comprehensive dictionary of the English language. He takes us inside the meetings of the Philological Society, whose members proposed the compilation of the dictionary to end all dictionaries. The *OED* was to include examples of usage illustrating every shade of meaning for every word in the English language. Such a mammoth feat would require enlisting thousands of volunteer readers to comb the corpus of English literature in search of illustrative quotations to be submitted on myriad slips of paper. These slips of paper on each word would in turn be studied by a small army of editors preparing the definitions.

It is not surprising that our Dr. Minor, comfortably tucked away at Broadmoor, possessing both a large library and seemingly infinite free time, should become one of those volunteer readers. After all, we are still rightfully assuming some connection of the book's two plot lines. Yet what sets Dr. Minor apart from his fellow volunteers (aside from the details of his incarceration) is the remarkable efficiency with which he approached his task. Not content merely to fill out slips of paper for submission, Minor methodically indexed every possibly useful mention of any word appearing in his personal library. He then asked to be kept informed of the progress of the work, submitting quotations that would be immediately useful to editors. In this way he managed to "escape" his cell and plunge himself into the work of contemporaries, to become a part of a major event of his time.

Minor's work proved invaluable to the *OED's* staff of editors, led by James Murray. With the two plot lines now intertwined, readers face such questions as "Will they find out that Minor is insane?" "Will Minor and Murray ever meet?" and "How long will they take to complete the dictionary?" The author builds suspense regarding a meeting of Minor and Murray by providing a false account of their first encounter, as reported by the American press, only to shatter us with the fact that this romantic version did not happen. I'll let Winchester give you the answers to these questions, while working his magic on you, drawing you into this fascinating tale of the making of the world's most famous dictionary.

Courtesy of Ian Habel.

EVALUATING AN ARGUMENT: THE REBUTTAL OR REFUTATION ESSAY

When your primary purpose in writing is to challenge someone's argument rather than to present your own argument, you are writing a *rebuttal* or *refutation*. A good refutation demonstrates, in an orderly and logical way, the weaknesses of logic or evidence in the argument. Study the following guidelines to prepare a good refutation essay and then study the sample refutation that follows. It has been annotated to show you how the author has structured his rebuttal.

GUIDELINES for Preparing a Refutation or Rebuttal Argument

1. **Read accurately.** Make certain that you have understood your opponent's argument. If you assume views not expressed by the writer and accuse the writer of holding those illogical views, you are guilty of the straw man fallacy, of attributing and then attacking a position that the person does not hold. Look up terms and references you do not know and examine the logic and evidence thoroughly.

2. **Pinpoint the weaknesses in the original argument.** Analyze the argument to determine, specifically, what flaws the argument contains. If the argument contains logical fallacies, make a list of the ones you plan to discredit. Examine the evidence presented. Is it insufficient, unreliable, or irrelevant? Decide, before drafting your refutation, exactly what elements of the argument you intend to challenge.

3. **Write your claim.** After analyzing the argument and deciding on the weaknesses to be challenged, write a claim that establishes that your disagreement is with the writer's logic, assumptions, or evidence, or a combination of these.

4. **Draft your essay, using the following three-part organization:**

   a. *The opponent's argument.* Usually you should not assume that your reader has read or remembered the argument you are refuting. Thus at the beginning of your essay, you need to state, accurately and fairly, the main points of the argument to be refuted.

   b. *Your claim.* Next make clear the nature of your disagreement with the argument you are rebutting.

   c. *Your refutation.* The specifics of your rebuttal will depend on the nature of your disagreement. If you are challenging the writer's evidence, then you must present the evidence that will show why the evidence used is unreliable or misleading. If you are challenging assumptions, then you must explain why they do not hold up. If your claim is that the piece is filled with logical fallacies, then you must present and explain each fallacy.

GLOBALIZATION SHOULDN'T BE A DIRTY WORD | DOUGLAS HOLTZ-EAKIN

Recognized as a scholar of applied economic policy, Douglas Holtz-Eakin served, between 2001 and 2008, in a number of government positions, including director of the Congressional Budget Office. He is currently president of the American Action Forum. His essay on globalization appeared in 2016.

PREREADING QUESTIONS Given the article's title and opening paragraph, what purpose do you expect the author to have? What does the term *globalization* mean to you?

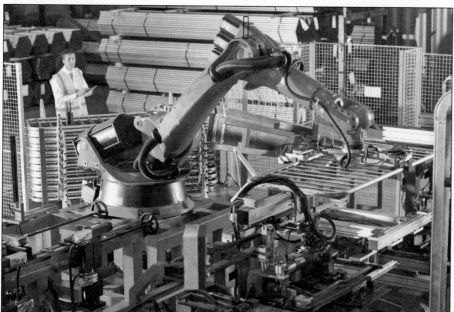

©Echo/Juice Images/Getty Images RF

Robots reduce factory jobs—but someone designed the robot and some company now makes them!

"Globalization"—broadly defined as market-driven, cross-national flows of goods, services and investments—has become a dirty word. It is derided by U.S. presidential candidates, feared and rejected by the public, and evidently headed to the dustbin of policy ideals. This, despite its contributions in the past two decades to dramatically reducing poverty in developing countries and improving productivity and standards of living in the developed world. What can get globalization back on track?

1 Attention-getting opening.

First, tell the truth about the successes and failures of globalization. The North American Free Trade Agreement was a success, both economically and strategically. In purely economic terms, it benefited Canada, Mexico and (modestly) the United States. It also solidified a democratic neighbor on the southern border. It was a success and should not be mischaracterized for cheap political gain.

2 1st point of refutation: Globalization has been mischaracterized.

3   The entry of China and India into the world trading system was also an enormously successful global anti-poverty program. But it is also true that its effect on global wage scales was far greater than anticipated, and Western policy responses were inadequate to deal with the fallout. Globalization is neither a resounding success nor an unmitigated disaster; the truth lies in between.

2nd point: Isolationism will hurt the U.S. economically.

4   Second, stop further deterioration. The toughest moment for globalization—the entrance of China and India—is in the rear-view mirror and won't be repeated. The greatest danger of *this* moment is not that additional steps on the path to globalization—the TPP or the Transatlantic Trade and Investment Partnership—will not go forward. Rather, the greatest danger is self-inflicted wounds—actively protectionist tariffs; retaliation and trade wars; and resulting global economic downdrafts. Preventing these will be the biggest test of near-term political leadership.

3rd point: Clearly state the steps needed to make globalization a success.

5   Third, improve the macro environment in which any future globalization discussion takes place. Everyday Americans recognize the post-World War II gains that accrued from aggregate growth north of 3 percent. They will similarly be acutely aware of the slow pace of economic advance that comes with our current 2 percent economic growth. Any notion that this "new normal" is somehow acceptable should be immediately discarded. Structural reforms to entitlements, the tax code, the regulatory state and education systems are necessary complements to trade agreements and globalization. Trade economics is *not* a zero-sum game, but the faster the economic growth, the more the general public will believe this.

4th point: Be honest about the effects of globalization.

6   Fourth, we must address the aftereffects. Shifts in the patterns of trade are accompanied by shifts in the pattern of employment, which may require more robust transition assistance in the form of income support or training. But this is just as true of shifts in domestic trade as it is international trade. Broadly supporting workers through job transitions will ease the fears of globalization.

5th point: Stress the relationship between trade agreements and U.S. strategic goals.

7   Finally, we must broaden the discussion. Any discussion of future trade agreements should openly feature their strategic importance. Just as the General Agreement on Tariffs and Trade knitted together the Western alliance and NAFTA strengthened North American democracy, agreements such as the TPP are just as important in terms of the U.S.-China strategic rivalry as they are for dollars and cents.

Douglas Holtz-Eakin, "'Globalization' Shouldn't Be a Dirty Word," *The Washington Post*, 20 Oct. 2016. Used with permission of the author.

QUESTIONS FOR READING

1. What does *globalization* mean?
2. What successes has this economic activity produced in the last two decades? What problem has it caused?
3. What can be done to stop further problems from globalization in the U.S.?

4. What will improve the macroeconomic environment? What do shifts in trade policies produce?

5. In what larger context should global trade agreements be discussed?

QUESTIONS FOR REASONING AND ANALYSIS

6. What is the author's claim? (Don't repeat the title; it is clever but not precise.)

7. Economic issues can be complex; how does Holtz-Eakin help readers follow his analysis?

8. What does the author mean when he writes that trade economics is *"not* a zero-sum game"?

QUESTIONS FOR REFLECTION AND WRITING

9. The author connects negative attitudes toward globalization with a lackluster economy. If we saw an increase in gross domestic production to 3 percent, would that help Americans see the advantages of globalization? Could you now explain to friends with this negative attitude why 3 percent growth should make them change their views?

10. Have you objected to globalization as producing nothing but trouble? If so, has Holtz-Eakin changed your thinking? If so, why? If not, why not?

FOR ANALYSIS AND DEBATE

CHRISTMAS-TREE TOTALITARIANS | THOMAS SOWELL

A former professor of economics with a PhD from the University of Chicago, Thomas Sowell is currently a senior fellow at the Hoover Institution at Stanford University. He is the author of numerous books and articles, including *Intellectuals and Society* (2009). The following column was published on December 25, 2012, in the *National Review Online*.

PREREADING QUESTIONS Does the title give you any clue as to the subject of Sowell's essay—beyond connecting it to its publication date? What might be his general subject or approach?

When I was growing up, an older member of the family used to say, "What you don't know would make a big book." Now that I am an older member of the family, I would say to anyone, "What you don't know would fill more books than the *Encyclopaedia Britannica*." At least half of society's trouble come from know-it-alls, in a world where nobody knows even 10 percent of it all.

Some people seem to think that, if life is not fair, then the answer is to turn more of the nation's resources over to politicians—who will, of course, then spend these resources in ways that increase the politicians' chance of getting reelected.

3   The annual outbursts of intolerance toward any display of traditional Christmas scenes, or even daring to call a Christmas tree by its name, show that today's liberals are by no means liberal. Behind the mist of their lofty words, the totalitarian mindset shows through.

Thomas Sowell.

©Chuck Kennedy KRT/Newscom

4   If you don't want to have a gun in your home or in your school, that's your choice. But don't be such a damn fool as to advertise to the whole world that you are in "a gun-free environment" where you are a helpless target for any homicidal fiend who is armed. Is it worth a human life to be a politically correct moral exhibitionist?

5   The more I study the history of intellectuals, the more they seem like a wrecking crew, dismantling civilization bit by bit—replacing what works with what sounds good.

6   Some people are wondering what takes so long for the negotiations about the "fiscal cliff." Maybe both sides are waiting for supplies. Democrats may be waiting for more cans to kick down the road. Republicans may be waiting for more white flags to hold up in surrender.

7   If I were rich, I would have a plaque made up, and sent to every judge in America, bearing a statement made by Adam Smith more than two-and-a-half centuries ago: "Mercy to the guilty is cruelty to the innocent."

8   If someone wrote a novel about a man who was raised from childhood to resent the successful and despise the basic values of America—and who then went on to become president of the United States—that novel would be considered too unbelievable, even for a work of fiction. Yet that is what has happened in real life.

9   Many people say, "War should be a last resort." Of course it should be a last resort. So should heart surgery, divorce, and many other things. But that does not mean that we should just continue to hope against hope indefinitely that things will work out, somehow, until catastrophe suddenly overtakes us.

10   Everybody is talking about how we are going to pay for the huge national debt, but nobody seems to be talking about the runaway spending that created that record-breaking debt. In other words, the big spenders get political benefits from handing out goodies, while those who resist giving them more money to spend will be blamed for sending the country off the "fiscal cliff."

11   When Barack Obama refused to agree to a requested meeting with Israeli prime minister Benjamin Netanyahu—the leader of a country publically and repeatedly threatened with annihilation by Iran's leaders, as the Iranians move toward creating nuclear bombs—I thought of a line from the old movie classic *Citizen Kane*: "Charlie wasn't cruel. He just did cruel things."

12   There must be something liberating about ignorance. Back when most members of Congress had served in the military, there was a reluctance of

politicians to try to tell military leaders how to run the military services. But, now that few members of Congress have ever served in the military, they are ready to impose all sorts of fashionable notions on the military.

After watching a documentary about the tragic story of Jonestown, I was struck by the utterly unthinking way that so many people put themselves completely at the mercy of a glib and warped man, who led them to degradation and destruction. And I could not help thinking of the parallel with the way we put a glib and warped man in the White House.

There are people calling for the banning of assault weapons who could not define an "assault weapon" if their lives depended on it. Yet the ignorant expect others to take them seriously.

Thomas Sowell, "Christmas-Tree Totalitarians," *National Review Online*, 25 Dec. 2012. Reprinted by permission of Thomas Sowell and Creators Syndicate, Inc. © 2012 Creators Syndicate, Inc.

QUESTIONS FOR READING

1. Who, in Sowell's view, are totalitarians?
2. Who are "politically correct moral exhibitionist[s]"?
3. What action leads the author to write that Obama does "cruel things"? What else does Sowell call Obama?

QUESTIONS FOR REASONING AND ANALYSIS

4. Sowell writes about Christmas trees, the fiscal cliff, Obama, guns, and the national debt; how do these topics connect to give Sowell his general subject?
5. What, then, is the author's claim? Do you see a general theme that unites the many issues Sowell includes?
6. How does the author develop and support his claim?
7. Examine Sowell's style and tone. How would you characterize his tone? Is his approach likely to be effective for his primary audience? Explain.

QUESTIONS FOR REFLECTION AND WRITING

8. Do you find any logical fallacies in Sowell's argument? If so, how would you challenge them?
9. Has Sowell supported his general claim and specific generalizations to your satisfaction? Why or why not?

1. Think about sports stars you know. Write an argument defending one player as the best in his or her field of play. Think about whether you want to use Krauthammer's "Method 1" or "Method 2" or your own method for your criteria. (Remember that you can qualify your argument; you could write about the best college football player this year, for example.)

2. If you like music, think about what you might evaluate from this field. Who is the best rock band? Hip-hop artist? Country-western singer? And so forth. Be sure to make your criteria for evaluation clear.

3. You have had many instructors—and much instruction—in the last twelve-plus years. Is there one teacher who is/was the best? If so, why? Is there a teaching method that stands out in your memory for the excellence of its approach? Find an evaluation topic from your educational experiences.

4. Select an editorial, op-ed column, letter to the editor, or one of the essays in this text as an argument with which you disagree. Prepare a refutation of the work's logic or evidence or both. Follow the guidelines for writing a refutation or rebuttal in this chapter.

5. What is your favorite book? Movie? Television show? Why is it your favorite? Does it warrant an argument that it is really good, maybe even the best, in some way or in some category (sitcoms, for example)? Write a review, following the guidelines for this type of evaluation argument given in this chapter.

CREDIT

1. Charles, Krauthammer, "The Greatness Gap," *Time* magazine, 1 July 2002.

CHAPTER 9

The Position Paper: Claims of Values

Congress of the United States
begun and held at the City of New-York, on
Wednesday the Fourth of March, one thousand seven hundred and eighty nine

THE ...

RESOLVED ...

ARTICLES ...

Article the first ...
Article the second ...
Article the third ...
Article the fourth ...
Article the fifth ...
Article the sixth ...
Article the seventh ...
Article the eighth ...
Article the ninth ...
Article the tenth ...
Article the eleventh ...
Article the twelfth ...

ATTEST,

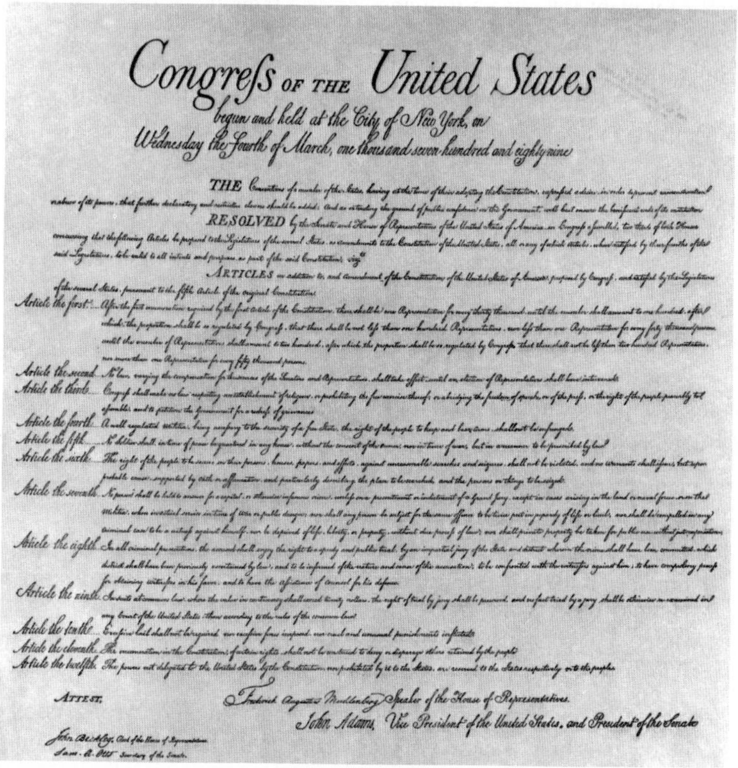

READ: The Bill of Rights, pictured above, was written to amend a very important document in U.S. history. What document does the Bill of Rights amend? Why was the Bill of Rights written?

REASON: What does the Bill of Rights establish for U.S. citizens? Why do you think the Bill of Rights is included as the picture representing this chapter?

REFLECT/WRITE: The original fourteen copies of the Bill of Rights were handwritten for distribution. What are the advantages of distributing a document like the Bill of Rights through today's mass media technology? What are the disadvantages?

As we established in Chapter 4, all arguments involve values. Evaluation arguments require judgment—thoughtful judgment, one hopes, based on criteria—but judgment nonetheless. If you believe that no one should spend more than $25,000 for a car, then you will not appreciate the qualities that attract some people to Mercedes. When one argues that government tax rates should go up as income goes up, it is because one believes that it is *right* for government to redistribute income to some degree: The rich pay more in taxes, the poor get more in services. When countries ban the importing of ivory, they do so because they believe it is *wrong* to destroy the magnificent elephant just so humans can use their ivory tusks for decorative items. (Observe that the word *magnificent* expresses a value.)

Some arguments, though, are less about judging what is good or best, or less about how to solve specific problems, than they are about stating a position on an issue. An argument that defends a general position (segregated schools are wrong) may imply action that should result (schools should be integrated), but the focus of the argument is first to state and defend the position. It is helpful to view these arguments, based heavily on values and a logical sequencing of ideas with less emphasis on specifics, as a separate type—genre—of argument. These claims of values are often called position papers.

CHARACTERISTICS OF THE POSITION PAPER

The position paper, or claim of values, may be the most difficult of arguments simply because it is often perceived to be the easiest. Let's think about this kind of argument:

- A claim based on values and argued more with logic than specifics is usually more general or abstract or philosophical than other types of argument. Greenpeace objects to commercial fishing that uses large nets that ensnare dolphins along with commercial fish such as tuna. Why? Because we ought not to destroy such beautiful and highly developed animals. Because we ought not to destroy more than we need, to waste part of nature because we are careless or in a hurry. For Greenpeace, the issue is about values—though it may be about money for the commercial fishermen.

- The position paper makes a claim about what is right or wrong, good or bad, for us as individuals or as a society. Topics can range from capital punishment to pornography to reducing the amount of trash we toss.

- Although a claim based on values is often developed in large part by a logical sequencing of reasons, support of principles also depends on relevant facts. Remember the long list of specific abuses listed in the Declaration of Independence (see pp. 153–156). If Greenpeace can show that commercial fisheries can be successful using a different kind of net or staying away from areas heavily populated by dolphins, it can probably get more support for its general principles.

- A successful position paper requires more than a forceful statement of personal beliefs. If we can reason logically from principles widely shared by our audience, we are more likely to be successful. If we are going to challenge their beliefs or values, then we need to consider the conciliatory approach as a strategy for getting them to at least listen to our argument.

GUIDELINES for Analyzing a Claim of Value

When reading position papers, what should you look for? Again, the basics of good argument apply here as well as with definition arguments. To analyze claims of values specifically, use these questions as guides:

- **What is the writer's claim?** Is it clear?
- **Is the claim qualified if necessary?** Some claims of value are broad philosophical assertions ("Capital punishment is immoral and bad public policy"). Others are qualified ("Capital punishment is acceptable only in crimes of treason").
- **What facts are presented?** Are they credible? Are they relevant to the claim's support?
- **What reasons are given in support of the claim?** What assumptions are necessary to tie reasons to claim? Make a list of reasons and assumptions and analyze the writer's logic. Do you find any fallacies?
- **What are the implications of the claim?** For example, if you argue for the legalization of all recreational drugs, you eliminate all "drug problems" by definition. But what new problems may be created by this approach? Consider more car accidents and reduced productivity for openers.
- **Is the argument convincing?** Does the evidence provide strong support for the claim? Are you prepared to agree with the writer, in whole or in part?

PREPARING A POSITION PAPER

In addition to the guidelines for writing arguments presented in Chapter 4, you can use the following advice specific to writing position papers or claims of value.

Planning

1. **Think:** What claim, exactly, do you want to support? Should you qualify your first attempt at a claim statement?
2. **Think:** What grounds (evidence) do you have to support your claim? You may want to make a list of the reasons and facts you would consider using to defend your claim.
3. **Think:** Study your list of possible grounds and identify the assumptions (warrants) and backing for your grounds.
4. **Think:** Now make a list of the grounds most often used by those holding views that oppose your claim. This second list will help you prepare counterarguments to

possible rebuttals, but first it will help you test your commitment to your position. If you find the opposition's arguments persuasive and cannot think how you would rebut them, you may need to rethink your position. Ideally, your two lists will confirm your views but also increase your respect for opposing views.

5. **Consider:** How can I use a conciliatory approach? With an emotion-laden or highly controversial issue, the conciliatory approach can be an effective strategy. Conciliatory arguments include

    - the use of nonthreatening language,
    - the fair expression of opposing views, and
    - a statement of the common ground shared by opposing sides.

You may want to use a conciliatory approach when (1) you know your views will be unpopular with at least some members of your audience; (2) the issue is highly emotional and has sides that are "entrenched" so that you are seeking some accommodations rather than dramatic changes of position; (3) you need to interact with members of your audience and want to keep a respectful relationship going. The sample student essay on gun control (at the end of this chapter) illustrates a conciliatory approach.

Drafting

1. Begin with an opening paragraph or two that introduces your topic in an interesting way. Possibilities include a statement of the issue's seriousness or reasons why the issue is currently being debated—or why we should go back to reexamine it. Some writers are spurred by a recent event that receives media coverage; recounting such an event can produce an effective opening. You can also briefly summarize points of the opposition that you will challenge in supporting your claim. Many counter-arguments are position papers.

2. Decide where to place your claim statement. Your best choices are either early in your essay or at the end of your essay, after you have made your case. The second approach can be an effective alternative to the more common pattern of stating one's claim early.

3. Organize evidence in an effective way. One plan is to move from the least import-ant to the most important reasons, followed by rebuttals to potential counterargu-ments. Another possibility is to organize by the arguments of the opposition, explaining why each of their reasons fails to hold up. A third approach is to orga-nize logically. That is, if some reasons build on the accepting of other reasons, you want to begin with the necessary underpinnings and then move forward from those.

4. Maintain an appropriate level of seriousness for an argument of principle. Of course, word choice must be appropriate to a serious discussion, but in addition be sure to present reasons that are also appropriately serious. For example, if you are defending the claim that music albums should not be subject to content labeling because such censorship is inconsistent with First Amendment rights, do not trivi-alize your argument by including the point that young people are tired of adults controlling their lives. (This is another issue for another paper.)

5. Provide a logical defense of or specifics in support of each reason. You have not finished your task by simply asserting several reasons for your claim. You also need to present facts or examples for or a logical explanation of each reason. For example, you have not defended your views on capital punishment by asserting that it is right or just to take the life of a murderer. Why is it right or just? Executing the murderer will not bring the victim back to life. Do two wrongs make a right? These are some of the thoughts your skeptical reader may have unless you explain and justify your reasoning. *Remember:* Quoting another writer's opinion on your topic does not provide proof for your reasons. It merely shows that someone else agrees with you.

A CHECKLIST FOR REVISION

- ☐ Do I have a clear statement of my claim? Is it qualified, if appropriate?
- ☐ Have I organized my argument, building the parts of my support into a clear and logical structure that readers can follow?
- ☐ Have I avoided logical fallacies?
- ☐ Have I found relevant facts and examples to support and develop my reasons?
- ☐ Have I paid attention to appropriate word choice, including using a conciliatory approach if that is a wise strategy?
- ☐ Have I used the basic checklist for revision in Chapter 4 (see p. 107)?

STUDENT ESSAY

EXAMINING THE ISSUE OF GUN CONTROL

Chris Brown

The United States has a long history of compromise. Issues such as representation in government have been resolved because of compromise, forming some of the bases of American life. Americans, however, like to feel that they are uncompromising, never willing to surrender an argument. This attitude has led to a number of issues in modern America that are unresolved, including the issue of gun control. Bickering over the issue has slowed progress toward legislation that will solve the serious problem of gun violence in America, while keeping recreational use of firearms available to responsible people. To resolve the conflict over guns, the arguments of

Introduction connects ambivalence in American character to conflict over gun control.

both sides must be examined, with an eye to finding the flaws in both. Then perhaps we can reach some meaningful compromises.

Student organizes by arguments for no gun control.

Gun advocates have used many arguments for the continued availability of firearms to the public. The strongest of these defenses points to the many legitimate uses for guns. One use is protection against violence, a concern of some people in today's society. There are many problems with the use of guns for protection, however, and these problems make the continued use of firearms for protection dangerous. One such problem is that gun owners are not always able to use guns responsibly. When placed in a situation in which personal

1. Guns for protection.

injury or loss is imminent, people often do not think intelligently. Adrenaline surges through the body, and fear takes over much of the thinking process. This causes gun owners to use their weapons, firing at whatever threatens them. Injuries and deaths of innocent people, including family members of the gun owner, result. Removing guns from the house may be the best solution to these sad consequences.

Responding to this argument, gun advocates ask how they are to defend themselves without guns. But guns are needed for protection from other guns. If there are no guns, people need only to protect themselves from criminals using knives, baseball bats, and other weapons. Obviously the odds of surviving a knife attack are greater than the odds of surviving a gun attack. One reason is that a gun is an impersonal weapon. Firing at someone from fifty feet away requires much less commitment than charging someone with a knife and stabbing repeatedly. Also, bullet wounds are, generally, more severe than knife wounds. Guns are also more likely to be misused when a dark figure is in one's house. To kill with the gun requires only to point and shoot; no recognition of the figure is needed. To kill with a knife, by contrast, requires getting within arm's reach of the figure, and knowing, for sure, the identity of your presumed opponent.

There are other uses of guns, including recreation. Hunting and target shooting are valid, responsible uses of guns. How do we keep guns available for recreation? The answer is in the form of gun clubs and hunting clubs. Many are already established; more can be constructed. These clubs can provide recreational use of guns for responsible people while keeping guns off the streets and out of the house.

2. Recreational uses.

The last argument widely used by gun advocates is the constitutional right to bear arms. The fallacies in this argument are that the Constitution was written in a vastly different time. This different time had different uses for guns, and a different type of gun. Firearms were defended in the Constitution because of their many valid uses and fewer problems. Guns were mostly muskets, guns that were not very accurate beyond close range. Also, guns took more than thirty seconds to load in the eighteenth century and could fire only one shot before reloading. These differences with today's guns affect the relative safety of guns then and now. In addition, those who did not live in the city at the time used hunting for food as well as for recreation; hunting was a necessary component of life. That is not true today. Another use of guns in the eighteenth century was as protection from animals. Wild animals such as bears and cougars were much more common. Settlers, explorers, and hunters needed protection from these animals in ways not comparable with modern life.

3. Second Amendment rights.

Finally, Revolutionary America had no standing army. Defense of the nation and of one's home from other nations relied on local militia. The right to bear arms granted in the Constitution was inspired by the need for national protection as well as by the other outdated needs previously discussed. Today America has a standing army with enough weaponry to adequately defend itself from outside aggressors. There is no need for every citizen to carry a musket, or an AK-47, for the protection of the nation. It would seem, then, that the Second Amendment does not fully apply to modern society. While it justifies gun ownership, it is open to restrictions and controls based on the realities of today's world.

Student establishes a compromise position.

To reach a compromise, we also have to examine the other side of the issue. Some gun-control advocates argue that all guns are unnecessary and should be outlawed. The problem with this argument is that guns will still be available to those who do not mind breaking the law. Until an economically sound and feasible way of controlling illegal guns in America is found, guns cannot be totally removed, no matter how much legislation is passed. This means that if guns are to be outlawed for other than recreational uses, a way must be found to combat the illegal gun trade that will evolve. Tough criminal laws and a large security force are all that can be offered to stop illegal uses of guns until better technology is available. This means that, perhaps, a good resolution would involve gradual restrictions on guns, until eventually guns were restricted only to recreational uses in a controlled setting for citizens not in the police or military.

Conclusion restates student's claim.

Both sides on this issue have valid points. Any middle ground needs to offer something to each side. It must address the reasons people feel they need guns for protection and allow for valid recreational use, but keep military-style guns off the street, except when in the hands of properly trained police officers. Time and money will be needed to move toward the removal of America's huge gun arsenal. But sooner or later a compromise on the issue of gun control must be made to make America a safer, better place to live.

Courtesy of Chris Brown.

ENDING INTOLERANCE TOWARD MINORITY COMMUNITIES: HATE ATTACKS ON SIKH AMERICANS

ZAINAB CHAUDRY

Born in Pakistan, fluent in five languages, Zainab Chaudry is the Maryland outreach manager for CAIR, the Council on American-Islamic Relations. At night she writes, using her blog *The Memorist*, to reflect on life and politics. The article below was written for CAIR August 11, 2014.

PREREADING QUESTIONS Who or what is a Sikh? (If you do not know, look it up before reading the essay.) What are some examples of hate attacks?

Two years after the senseless shooting at a Sikh temple in Oak Creek, Wisconsin that claimed six innocent lives, the challenges facing the Sikh American community have only been compounded. 1

Members of this religious minority continue to be subjected to hate and bias attacks from racists due to their physical appearance and traditional attire. 2

Last Thursday, a Sikh man walking with his mother was approached by three teenagers who yelled racial and ethnic slurs at his mom before calling him "Osama bin Laden" and physically assaulting him. 3

Only a few days before that, a 29-year-old father of two, Sandeep Singh, was also victimized in a brutal hate crime. As he walked home with friends, a man in a truck began shouting racial slurs and abuse at Singh, who wears a turban. When Singh confronted him, the man reportedly mowed him down with his truck. Singh is now hospitalized, struggling to recover from the extensive injuries he sustained. 4

©Scott Olson/Getty Images

5   Physically, both of these victims are expected to recuperate; however, the mental and emotional trauma they have endured will take much longer to heal.

6   This most recent wave of attacks has heightened tensions in an already marginalized community that has suffered tremendous backlash in post-9/11 America.

7   These incidents fueled by bigotry and hatred must stop.

8   It is unconscionable, unjustifiable, and un-American to verbally or physically assault anyone based on their race, religion, ethnicity, gender, or sexual orientation.

9   Hate is divisive and robs us of compassion and understanding. Intolerance blinds us to the vast diversity that strengthens and beautifies our nation.

10   The Sikh community is compassionate, and proud. Many Sikhs in America have shared heartbreaking stories of their struggle to reconcile their religious beliefs with their American identity.

11   It is unacceptable that they—or members of any ethnic or religious group—feel fearful of practicing their religion.

12   As a civil rights activist committed to advancing justice for all people, I strongly believe that if we are not a part of the solution, then we are part of the problem.

13   Martin Luther King, Jr., rightfully said: "Injustice anywhere is a threat to justice everywhere." We cannot afford to idly sit back and ignore the threat bigotry and racism pose in our society; we must unequivocally condemn it.

14   Groups in both public and private sectors must work together to combat these issues that overshadow the discourse in marginalized communities across the nation.

15   Faith in our justice system must be restored. Law enforcement officials must take appropriate steps to discourage repeat attacks; they must conduct thorough, fair investigations and they must be held accountable in making sure justice is served.

16   And, perhaps most importantly, victims like Sandeep Singh and their families must be made to feel safe again in an environment that appears increasingly hostile towards all they represent.

17   Only when we unite as Americans to send a strong, clear message that racism and bigotry are unacceptable, can we effectively work to cure the intolerance that infects our society.

Zainab Chaudry, "Ending Intolerance Toward Minority Communities: Hate Attacks on Sikh Americans," altmuslimah.com, 11 Aug. 2014, www.altmuslimah.com Used with permission of the author.

QUESTIONS FOR READING

1.   What examples are provided of hate attacks on Sikhs? What does the author tell readers about Sikhs?

2.   What reasons does Chaudry offer to develop her subject?

3.   What solutions to the problem of hate attacks are offered by the author?

QUESTIONS FOR REASONING AND ANALYSIS

4. Although Chaudry appears to be writing about hate attacks on Sikh Americans, what is her broader subject? What, then, is her main point, her claim?

5. Examine the author's reasons, her value statements; which are most effective in your view? Why?

6. Chaudry lists our justice system as one solution to reducing hate attacks; what other solutions does she present?

QUESTIONS FOR REFLECTION AND WRITING

7. Why is "injustice anywhere" a "threat to justice everywhere"? Explain why this should be so.

8. Chaudry argues that not only is hate divisive but it also "robs us of compassion and understanding." Does this assertion about human psychology make sense to you? If you disagree with the assertion, how would you refute it?

9. Have you thought about trying to be part of the solution to bigotry and hate? If so, what would you recommend that we do to address this problem in American society? If you don't think we should try to be part of the solution, how would you defend that position?

A NEVER ENDING WAR | KAYE WISE WHITEHEAD

Karsonya (Kaye) Wise Whitehead is an associate professor of communication and African and African American Studies in the Department of Communication at Loyola University Maryland. A former Baltimore City middle school teacher, she is the founding executive director of the Black Feminist Writer's Project. She is also the author of four books, the most recent of which is *RaceBrave: New and Selected Works*. Her commentary below was published in *The Baltimore Sun* in 2014.

PREREADING QUESTIONS Knowing that the author is an associate professor of communication who studies race, class, and gender, what do you expect Whitehead's subject to be? What makes Whitehead's title catchy and compelling?

In the days leading up to the end of the Michael Dunn "loud music" case—in   1
which a white Florida man shot and killed a 17-year-old black teen after getting into an argument over the boy's so-called "thug" music—I was overwhelmed with feelings of restlessness, worry, frustration and fear.

They were the same feelings I had at the end of the George Zimmerman trial.   2
The same ones I have when I think about the day when my sons will be old enough to drive or walk to the store by themselves. I worry so much about what could happen to them simply because they are black and male. I feel like my husband and I are in the midst of this never-ending war, the same war that my parents and my grandparents fought. It is the same war that black people have been fighting in this country since American slavery was first legalized. This war is simply to keep our boys safe in a society that devalues them, suspects them, fears them and often dismisses them. It is a war that I now fear I am losing.

3   When my sons were first born, we held them in our arms and promised them that we would love and protect them. When they learned how to crawl, we ran around the house moving things out of their way. When they learned how to toddle, we walked behind them, always ready to catch them right before they fell. When they started school, we used to check in with their teachers every day to make sure that they were comfortable and safe and happy. We taught them how to say please and thank you, how to raise their hands in school before they spoke and how to wait their turn. We taught them to be respectful and polite. We spent hours reading to and with them, taking them to the library, to the museums and to see Shakespeare in the Park. We saved our money, moved into a safe neighborhood and sacrificed so that they could attend the best schools, take piano and play sports. We took them to church and made sure that they learned their scriptures and prayed before they ate their food. We really believed that we were doing everything that we could do to keep them safe, to beat the odds and to win this war. There was a moment when Barack Obama was first elected president that I thought that the war had finally ended and that we had won. We celebrated because we believed that the work that had been done to create a fair and just society. We believed that America was finally colorblind and post racial. We have come to realize that we were wrong.

4   We are still living in a country where our sons will be judged by the color of their skin and not the content of their character. I believe that it does not matter how much education they have or how polite they are or how much money we make or that they can play the piano and fence and swim. In this country, no matter where they are or what they are doing, they will still be seen as threats and thugs and criminals. They will be seen as disposable.

Karsonya Wise Whitehead, "A Never Ending War," *The Baltimore Sun*, 18 Feb. 2014. Used with permission of the author.

QUESTIONS FOR READING

1.   What caused the author to feel restless, worried, frustrated, and fearful?

2.   What steps has the author taken to try to keep her sons safe?

3.   What war is the author referring to?

QUESTIONS FOR REASONING AND ANALYSIS

4.   What leads the author to think that America was "finally colorblind"?

5.   What is the ethical issue the author is trying to understand and deal with in her op-ed?

6.   What position does she reach on the issue? Does she offer a specific claim statement or imply one?

7. What kind of evidence does Whitehead use to support her claims? Do you think her evidence is legitimate? Do you think her claims are effective? Why or why not? Explain.

8. Do you think that people of color, especially males, are at greater risk when they wear a hoodie or listen to loud music in their cars? Be prepared to defend your view.

9. Many states have "stand-your-ground" laws that allow people to use deadly force in self-defense if they feel their lives are threatened. Are stand-your-ground laws necessary and moral? Are they effective in reducing crime? How might these laws be manipulated in cases where self-defense is not clear? Be prepared to discuss or write about this issue.

ON ASSISTED SUICIDE, GOING BEYOND "DO NO HARM"   HAIDER JAVED WARRAICH

Haider Javed Warraich is a graduate of Aga Khan University Medical College in Pakistan and took his residency at Harvard Medical School. He is now a fellow in cardiovascular medicine at the Duke University Medical Center and the author of *Modern Death: How Medicine Changed the End of Life*. This op-ed essay was published in 2016 in *The New York Times*.

PREREADING QUESTIONS How does one go beyond doing no harm? What do you expect the author's focus to be?

1   Durham, N.C.—Out of nowhere, a patient I recently met in my clinic told me, "If my heart stops, doctor, just let me go."

2   "Why?" I asked him.

3   Without hesitating, he replied, "Because there are worse states than death."

4   Advances in medical therapies, in addition to their immense benefits, have changed death to *dying*—from an instantaneous event to a long, drawn-out process. Death is preceded by years of disability, countless procedures and powerful medications. Only one in five patients is able to die at home. These days many patients fear what it takes to live more than death itself.

5   That may explain why this year, behind the noise of the presidential campaign, the right-to-die movement has made several big legislative advances. In June, California became the fifth and largest state to put an assisted suicide law into effect; this week the District of Columbia Council passed a similar law. And on Tuesday voters in Colorado will decide whether to allow physician-assisted suicide in their state as well.

6   Yet even as assisted suicide has generated broader support, the group most vehemently opposed to it hasn't budged: doctors.

7   That resistance is traditionally couched in doctors' adherence to our understanding of the Hippocratic oath. But it's becoming harder for us to know what is meant by "do no harm." With the amount of respirators and other apparatus at

our disposal, it is almost impossible for most patients to die unless doctors' or patients' families end life support. The withdrawal of treatment, therefore, is now perhaps the most common way critically ill patients die in the hospital.

8   While "withdrawal" implies a passive act, terminating artificial support feels decidedly active. Unlike assisted suicide, which requires patients to be screened for depression, patients can ask for treatment withdrawal even if they have major depression or are suicidal. Furthermore, withdrawal decisions are usually made for patients who are so sick that they frequently have no voice in the matter.

9   Some doctors skirt the question of assisted suicide through opiate prescriptions, which are almost universally prescribed for patients nearing death. Even though these medications can slow down breathing to the point of stoppage, doctors and nurses are very comfortable giving them, knowing that they might hasten a "natural" death.

10   In extreme cases, when even morphine isn't enough, patients are given anesthesia to ease their deaths. The last time I administered what is called terminal sedation, another accepted strategy, was in the case of a patient with abdominal cancer whose intestines were perforated and for whom surgery was not an option. The patient, who had been writhing uncontrollably in pain, was finally comfortable. Yet terminal sedation, necessary as it was, felt closer to active euthanasia than assisted suicide would have.

11   While the way people die has changed, the arguments made against assisted suicide have not. We are warned of a slippery slope, implying that legalization of assisted suicide would eventually lead to eugenic sterilization reminiscent of Nazi Germany. But no such drift has been observed in any of the countries where it has been legalized.

12   We are cautioned that legalization would put vulnerable populations like the uninsured and the disabled at risk; however, years of data from Oregon demonstrate that the vast majority of patients who opt for it are white, affluent and highly educated.

13   We are also told that assisted suicide laws will allow doctors and nurses to avoid providing high-quality palliative care to patients, but the data suggests the opposite: A strong argument for legalization is that it sensitizes doctors about ensuring the comfort of patients with terminal illnesses; if suicide is an option, they'll do what they can to preclude it.

14   And, again, we are counseled that physicians should do no harm. But medical harm is already one of the leading causes of death—and in any case, isn't preventing patients from dying on their terms its own form of medical harm?

15   With the right safeguards in place, assisted suicide can help give terminally ill patients a semblance of control over their lives as disease, disability and the medical machine tries to wrest it away from them. In Oregon, of the exceedingly few patients who have requested a lethal prescription—1,545 in 18 years— about 35 percent never uses it; for them, it is merely a means to self-affirmation, a reassuring option.

Instead of using our energies to obfuscate and obstruct how patients might 16
want to end their lives when faced with life-limiting disease, we physicians need
to reassess how we can help patients achieve their goals when the end is near.
We need to be able to offer an option for those who desire assisted suicide, so
that they can openly take control of their death.

Instead of seeking guidance from ancient edicts, we need to re-evaluate just 17
what patients face in modern times. Even if it is a course we personally wouldn't
recommend, we should consider allowing it for patients suffering from debilitating disease. How we die has changed tremendously over the past few
decades—and so must we.

Haider Warrach, "On Assisted Suicide, Going Beyond 'Do No Harm,'" *The New York Times*, 4 Nov. 2016.
Used with permission of the author.

QUESTIONS FOR READING

1. How has "death" changed today?
2. How do many critically ill patients now die in the hospital?
3. What are the usual arguments against assisted suicide?
4. In Warraich's view, what does assisted suicide give to dying patients?

QUESTIONS FOR REASONING AND ANALYSIS

5. What is Warraich's position on assisted suicide?
6. Who appears to be the author's primary audience for this argument? Why, then, does he
    publish his argument in a general newspaper? What other audience does he wish to
    reach and convince?
7. What does the author gain by including the standard arguments against his position?
8. Evaluate Warraich's introduction.

QUESTIONS FOR REFLECTION AND WRITING

9. Which of the arguments against assisted suicide do you think are the most powerful?
    Why?
10. Which of the author's arguments for assisted suicide are the most effective? Why?
11. Has Warraich changed your thinking on this subject in any way? Why or why not?

1. Chris Brown, in the student essay, writes a conciliatory argument seeking common ground on the volatile issue of gun control. Write your own conciliatory argument on this issue, offering a different approach than Brown, but citing Brown for any ideas you borrow from his essay. Alternatively, write a counterargument of his essay.

2. There are other "hot issues," issues that leave people entrenched on one side or the other, giving expression to the same arguments again and again without budging many, if any, readers. Do not try to write on any one of these about which you get strongly emotional. Select one that you can be calm enough over to write a conciliatory argument, seeking to find common ground. Some of these issues include same-sex marriage, legalizing recreational drugs, capital punishment, mainstreaming students with disabilities, the use of torture to interrogate terrorists. Exclude abortion rights from the list—it is too controversial for most writers to handle successfully.

3. Other issues that call for positions based on values stem from First Amendment rights. Consider a possible topic from this general area. Possibilities include:

   Hate speech should (or should not) be a crime.

   Obscenity and pornography on the Web should (or should not) be restricted.

   Hollywood films should (or should not) show characters smoking.

4. Consider issues related to college life. Should all colleges have an honor code—or should existing codes be eliminated? Should students be automatically expelled for plagiarism or cheating? Should college administrators have any control over what is published in the college newspaper?

CHAPTER 10

Arguments about Cause

©John Lamparski/WireImage/Getty Images

READ: What can you conclude about the occupation of the figure in the ad?

REASON: What argument does the ad make? What visual strategies are used? What assumption about the audience is made?

REFLECT/WRITE: Is the ad effective? Why or why not?

Because we want to know *why* things happen, arguments about cause are both numerous and important to us. We begin asking why at a young age, pestering adults with questions such as "Why is the sky blue?" and "Why is the grass green?" And, to make sense of our world, we try our hand at explanations as youngsters, deciding that the first-grade bully is "a bad boy." The bully's teacher, however, will seek a more complex explanation because an understanding of the causes is the place to start to guide the bully to more socially acceptable behavior.

As adults we continue the search for answers. We want to understand past events: Why was President Kennedy assassinated? We want to explain current situations: Why do so many college students binge drink? And of course we also want to predict the future: Will the economy improve if there is a tax cut? All three questions seek a causal explanation, including the last one. If you answer the last question with a yes, you are claiming that a tax cut is a cause of economic improvement.

CHARACTERISTICS OF CAUSAL ARGUMENTS

Causal arguments vary not only in subject matter but in structure. Here are the four most typical patterns:

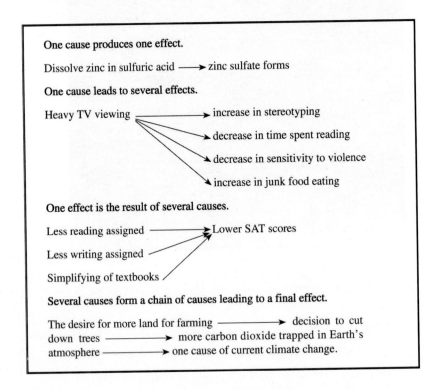

One cause produces one effect.

Dissolve zinc in sulfuric acid ⟶ zinc sulfate forms

One cause leads to several effects.

Heavy TV viewing ⟶ increase in stereotyping
decrease in time spent reading
decrease in sensitivity to violence
increase in junk food eating

One effect is the result of several causes.

Less reading assigned
Less writing assigned ⟶ Lower SAT scores
Simplifying of textbooks

Several causes form a chain of causes leading to a final effect.

The desire for more land for farming ⟶ decision to cut down trees ⟶ more carbon dioxide trapped in Earth's atmosphere ⟶ one cause of current climate change.

These models lead to several key points about causal arguments:

- **Most causal arguments are highly complex.** Except for some simple chemical reactions, most arguments about cause are difficult, can involve many steps, and are often open to challenge. Even arguments based in science lead to shrill exchanges. Think, then, how much more open to debate are arguments about economic fluctuations around the world or arguments about human behavior. Many people think that "it's obvious" that violent TV and video games lead to more aggressive behavior. And yet, psychologists, in study after study, have not demonstrated conclusively that there is a clear causal connection. One way to challenge this causal argument is to point to the majority of people who do not perform violent acts even though they have watched television and played video games while growing up.

- **Because of the multiple and intertwined patterns of causation in many complex situations, the best causal arguments keep focused on their purpose.** For example, you are concerned with global warming. Cows contribute to global warming. Are we going to stop cattle farming? Not likely. Factories contribute to global warming. Are we going to tear down factories? Not likely—but we can demand that smokestacks have filters to reduce harmful emissions. Focus your argument on the causes that readers are most likely to accept because they are most likely to accept the action that the causes imply.

- **Learn and use the specific terms and concepts that provide useful guides to thinking about cause.** First, when looking for the cause of an event, we look for an *agent*—a person, situation, another event that led to the effect. For example, a lit cigarette dropped in a bed caused the house fire—the lit cigarette is the agent. But why, we ask, did someone drop a lit cigarette on a bed? The person, old and ill, took a sleeping pill and dropped the cigarette when he fell asleep. Where do we stop in the chain of causes?

  Second, most events do not occur in a vacuum with a single cause. There are *conditions* surrounding the event. The man's age and health were conditions. Third, we can also look for *influences.* The sleeping pill certainly influenced the man to drop the cigarette. Some conditions and influences may qualify as *remote causes. Proximate causes* are more immediate, usually closer in time to the event or situation. The man's dozing off is a proximate cause of the fire. Finally, we come to the *precipitating cause,* the triggering event—in our example, the cigarette's igniting the combustible mattress fabric. Sometimes we are interested primarily in the precipitating cause; in other situations, we need to go further back to find the remote causes or conditions that are responsible for what has occurred.

- **Be alert to the difference between cause and correlation.** First, be certain that you can defend your pattern of cause and effect as genuine causation, not as correlation only. Married people are better off financially, are healthier, and report happier sex lives than singles or cohabiting couples. Is this a correlation only? Or does marriage itself produce these effects? Linda Waite is one sociologist who argues that marriage is the cause. Another example: Girls who participate in after-school activities are much less likely to get pregnant. Are the activities a cause?

Probably not. But there are surely conditions and influences that have led to both the decision to participate in activities and the decision not to become pregnant.

An Example of Causal Complexity: Lincoln's Election and the Start of the Civil War

If Stephen Douglas had won the 1860 presidential election instead of Abraham Lincoln, would the Civil War have been avoided? An interesting question posed to various American history professors and others, including Waite Rawls, president of the Museum of the Confederacy. Their responses were part of an article that appeared in *The Washington Post* on November 7, 2010.

Obviously, this is a question that cannot be answered, but it led Rawls to discuss the sequence of causes leading to the breakout of the war. Rawls organizes his brief causal analysis around a great metaphor: the building and filling and then lighting of a keg of powder. Let's look at his analysis.

Existing Conditions
"The wood for the keg was shaped by the inability of the founding fathers to solve the two big problems of state sovereignty and slavery in the shaping of the Constitution."

More Recent Influences
1. "[T]he economics of taxes and the politics of control of the westward expansion were added to those two original issues as the keg was filled with powder."
2. "By the time of the creation of the Republican Party in 1856, the powder keg was almost full and waiting for a fuse. And the election of any candidate from the Republican Party—a purely sectional party—put the fuse in the powder keg, and the Deep South states seceded. But there was still no war."

Proximate Causes
"Two simultaneous mistakes in judgment brought the matches out of the pocket—the Deep South mistakenly thought that Lincoln, now elected, would not enforce the Union, and Lincoln mistakenly thought that the general population of the South would not follow the leadership" of the Deep South states.

Precipitating Causes
1. "Lincoln struck the match when he called the bluff of the South Carolinians and attempted to reinforce Fort Sumter, but that match could have gone out without an explosion."
2. "Lincoln struck a second, more fateful match, when he called for troops to put down the 'insurrection.' That forced the Upper South and Border States into a conflict that they had vainly attempted to avoid." (Blog from *The Washington Post*, November 7, 2010. Reprinted by permission of Waite Rawls.)

Rawls concludes that the election of Lincoln did not start the war; it was only one step in a complex series of causes that led to America's bloodiest war. His analysis helps us see the complexity of cause/effect analysis.

Mill's Methods for Investigating Causes

John Stuart Mill, a 19th-century British philosopher, explained in detail some important ways of investigating and demonstrating causal relationships: commonality, difference, and process of elimination. We can benefit in our study of cause by understanding and using his methods.

1. **Commonality.** One way to isolate cause is to demonstrate that one agent is *common* to similar outcomes. For instance, twenty-five employees attend a company luncheon. Late in the day, ten report to area hospitals, and another four complain the next day of having experienced vomiting the night before. Public health officials will soon want to know what these people ate for lunch. Different people during the same twelve-hour period had similar physical symptoms of food poisoning. The common factor may well have been the tuna salad they ate for lunch.

2. **Difference.** Another way to isolate cause is to recognize one key *difference*. If two situations are alike in every way but one, and the situations result in different outcomes, then the one way they differ must have caused the different outcome.

   Studies in the social sciences are often based on the single-difference method. To test for the best teaching methods for math, an educator could set up an experiment with two classrooms similar in every way except that one class devotes fifteen minutes three days a week to instruction by drill. If the class receiving the drill scores much higher on a standard test given to both groups of students, the educator could argue that math drills make a measurable difference in learning math. But the educator should be prepared for skeptics to challenge the assertion of only one difference between the two classes. Could the teacher's attitude toward the drills also make a difference in student learning? If the differences in student scores are significant, the educator probably has a good argument.

3. **Process of elimination.** We can develop a causal argument around a technique we all use for problem solving: *the process of elimination*. When something happens, we examine all possible causes and eliminate them, one by one, until we are satisfied that we have isolated the actual cause (or causes).

   When the Federal Aviation Administration has to investigate a plane crash, it uses this process, exploring possible causes such as mechanical failure, weather, human error, or terrorism. Sometimes the process isolates more than one cause or points to a likely cause without providing absolute proof.

EXERCISE: Understanding Causal Patterns

From the following events or situations, select the one you know best and list as many conditions, influences, and causes—remote, proximate, precipitating—as you can think of. You may want to do this exercise with your class partner or in small groups. Be prepared to explain your causal pattern to the class.

1. Decrease in marriage rates in the United States
2. Arctic ice melt
3. Increase in the numbers of women elected to public office
4. High salaries of professional athletes
5. Increased interest in soccer in the United States
6. Comparatively low scores by U.S. students on international tests in math and science

■ ■

GUIDELINES for Analyzing Causal Arguments

When analyzing causal arguments, what should you look for? The basics of good argument apply to all arguments: a clear statement of claim, qualified if appropriate; a clear explanation of reasons and evidence; and enough relevant evidence to support the claim. How do we recognize these qualities in a causal argument? Use these points as guides to analyzing:

- **Does the writer carefully distinguish among types of causes?** Word choice is crucial. Is the argument that A and A alone caused B or that A was one of several contributing causes?

- **Does the writer recognize the complexity of causation and not rush to assert only one cause for a complex event or situation?** The credibility of an argument about cause is quickly lost if readers find the argument oversimplified.

- **Is the argument's claim clearly stated, with qualifications as appropriate?** If the writer wants to argue for one cause, not the only cause, of an event or situation, then the claim's wording must make this limited goal clear to readers. For example, one can perhaps build the case for heavy television viewing as one cause of stereotyping, loss of sensitivity to violence, and increased fearfulness. But we know that the home environment and neighborhood and school environments also do much to shape attitudes.

- **What reasons and evidence are given to support the argument?** Can you see the writer's pattern of development? Does the reasoning seem logical? Are the data relevant? This kind of analysis of the argument will help you evaluate it.

- **Does the argument demonstrate causality, not just a time relationship or correlation?** A causal argument needs to prove *agency:* A is the cause of B, not just something that happened before B or something that is present when B is present. March precedes April, but March does not cause April to arrive.

- **Does the writer present believable causal agents, agents consistent with our knowledge of human behavior and scientific laws?** Most educated people do not believe that personalities are shaped by astrological signs or that scientific laws are suspended in the Bermuda Triangle, allowing planes and ships to vanish or enter a fourth dimension.

- **What are the implications for accepting the causal argument?** If A and B clearly are the causes of C, and we don't want C to occur, then we presumably must do something about A and B—or at least we must do something about either A or B and see if reducing or eliminating one of the causes significantly reduces the incidence of C.
- **Is the argument convincing?** After analyzing the argument and answering the questions given in the previous points, you need to decide if, finally, the argument works.

PREPARING A CAUSAL ARGUMENT

In addition to the guidelines for writing arguments presented in Chapter 4, you can use the following advice specific to writing causal arguments.

Planning

1. **Think:** What are the focus and limits of your causal argument? Do you want to argue for one cause of an event or situation? Do you want to argue for several causes leading to an event or situation? Do you want to argue for a cause that others have overlooked? Do you want to show how one cause is common to several situations or events? Diagramming the relationship of cause to effect may help you see what you want to focus on.

2. **Think:** What reasons and evidence do you have to support your tentative claim? Consider what you already know that has led to your choice of topic. A brainstorming list may be helpful.

3. **Think:** How, then, do you want to word your claim? As we have discussed, wording is crucial in causal arguments. Review the discussion of characteristics of causal arguments if necessary.

4. **Reality check:** Do you have a claim worth defending in a paper? Will readers care?

5. **Think:** What, if any, additional evidence do you need to develop a convincing argument? You may need to do some reading or online searching to obtain data to strengthen your argument. Readers expect relevant, reliable, current statistics in most arguments about cause. Assess what you need and then think about what sources will provide the needed information.

6. **Think:** What assumptions (warrants) are you making in your causal reasoning? Are these assumptions logical? Will readers be likely to agree with your assumptions, or will you need to defend them as part of your argument? For example: One reason to defend the effects of heavy TV watching on viewers is the commonsense argument that what humans devote considerable time to will have a significant effect on their lives. Will your readers be prepared to accept this commonsense reasoning, or will they remain skeptical, looking for stronger evidence of a cause/effect relationship?

Drafting

1. Begin with an opening paragraph or two that introduces your topic in an interesting way. Lester Thurow in "Why Women Are Paid Less Than Men" writes:

    > In the 40 years from 1939 to 1979 white women who work full time have with monotonous regularity made slightly less than 60 percent as much as white men.
    > Why?

    This opening establishes the topic and Thurow's purpose in examining causes. The statistics get the reader's attention.

2. Do not begin by announcing your subject. Avoid openers such as: In this essay I will explain the causes of teen vandalism.

3. Decide where to place your claim statement. You can conclude your opening paragraph with it, or you can place it in your conclusion, after you have shown readers how best to understand the causes of the issue you are examining.

4. Present reasons and evidence in an organized way. If you are examining a series of causes, beginning with background conditions and early influences, then your basic plan will be time sequence. Readers need to see the chain of causes unfolding. Use appropriate terms and transitional words to guide readers through each stage in the causal pattern. If you are arguing for an overlooked cause, begin with the causes that have been put forward and show what is flawed in each one. Then present and defend your explanation of cause. This process of elimination structure works well when readers are likely to know what other causes have been offered in the past. You can also use one of Mill's other two approaches, if one of them is relevant to your topic.

5. Address the issue of correlation rather than cause, if appropriate. After presenting the results of a study of marriage that reveals many benefits (emotional, physical, financial) of marriage, Linda Waite examines the question that she knows skeptical readers may have: Does marriage actually *cause* the benefits, or is the relationship one of *correlation* only—that is, the benefits of marriage just happen to come with being married; they are not caused by being married.

6. Conclude by discussing the implications of the causal pattern you have argued for, if appropriate. Lester Thurow ends by asserting that if he is right about the cause of the gender pay gap, then there are two approaches society can take to remove the pay gap. If, in explaining the causes of teen vandalism, you see one cause as "group behavior," a gang looking for something to do, it then follows that you can advise young readers to stay out of gangs. Often with arguments about cause, there are personal or public policy implications in accepting the causal explanation.

A CHECKLIST FOR REVISION

☐ Do I have a clear statement of my claim? Is it appropriately qualified and focused? Is it about an issue that matters?

☐ Have I organized my argument so that readers can see my pattern for examining cause?

☐ Have I used the language for discussing causes correctly, distinguishing among conditions and influences and remote and proximate causes? Have I selected the correct word—either *affect* or *effect*—as needed?

☐ Have I avoided the *post hoc* fallacy and the confusing of correlation and cause?

☐ Have I carefully examined my assumptions and convinced myself that they are reasonable and can be defended? Have I defended them when necessary to clarify and thus strengthen my argument?

☐ Have I found relevant facts and examples to support and develop my argument?

☐ Have I used the basic checklist for revision in Chapter 4 (see p. 107)?

FOR ANALYSIS AND DEBATE

"DARING TO DISCUSS WOMEN IN SCIENCE": A RESPONSE TO JOHN TIERNEY | CAROLINE SIMARD

Caroline Simard is a board member of the Ada Initiative and research consultant to the Anita Borg Institute for Women and Technology, at the Stanford University School of Medicine. She holds a PhD in communication and social science and works to find ways to increase the number of women and underrepresented minorities in science, technology, engineering, and mathematics (STEM), and business fields. Simard's essay, a response to an article by John Tierney, was posted to the *Huffington Post* on June 9, 2010.

PREREADING QUESTIONS What type of argument do you anticipate, given the title and headnote information? What other type of argument should you anticipate, given the essay's location in this text?

On Monday [June 2010], John Tierney of *The New York Times* published a 1 provocative article, "Daring to Discuss Women in Science," in which he argues that biology may be a factor to explain why women are not reaching high-level positions. He suggests that boys are innately more gifted at math and science and that the dearth of women in science may point to simple biological differences. If this is the case, why would we waste our time trying to get more women in science?

Mr. Tierney, let's indeed discuss women in science. 2

First, let me start by saying that I applaud the discussion—all potential 3 explanations for a complex issue and all evidence need to be considered, even the ones that are not popular in the media or not "politically correct." I also believe that Larry Summers's now infamous comments about the possibility that biological differences account for the dearth of women scientists and technologists was, similarly, in the spirit of intellectual debate.

4   The problem with the biology argument that "boys are just more likely to be born good at math and science" isn't that it's not "politically correct"—it's that it assumes that we can take away the power of societal influences, which have much more solid evidence than the biology hypothesis. Tierney makes the point himself in his article—in order to provide evidence for biological differences, he cites a longitudinal Duke [University] study which shows that the highest achievers in SAT math tests (above 750), which counted 13 boys for every girl in the early 80s, became a ratio of 4 boys to 1 girl in 1991, "presumably because of sociocultural factors." Hmm, isn't this actual evidence that biology is not what is at play here? If it is possible to reduce the gender achievement gap in math by 3 thanks to "sociocultural factors," I rest my case. Sociocultural factors are indeed extremely powerful.

5   The Duke study also notes that the 4/1 achievement gap at the highest score hasn't changed in the last 20 years despite ongoing programs to encourage girls in math and science, whereas the highest achievers in writing ability (SAT above 700) shows a ratio of 1.2 girls for every boy, slightly favoring girls. However, if the premise is that boys are inherently "better" at math, and girls are inherently better at writing, why would the achievement gap be so large in math and negligible in writing? The stagnant 4 to 1 ratio is not evidence that there is an innate biological difference in math aptitude, but rather confirmation that persistent sociocultural barriers remain—that is, science and math are still thought of as male domains.

6   Research shows that math and science are indeed thought of as stereotypically male domains. Project Implicit at Harvard University studied half a million participants in 34 countries and found that 70 percent of respondents worldwide have implicit stereotypes associating science with male more than with female. Years of research by Claude Steele and Joshua Aronson and their colleagues show that implicit stereotypes affect girls' performance in math—a phenomenon called "stereotype threat." When girls receive cues that "boys are better at math," their scores in math suffer. One study in a classroom setting showed that the difference in performance between boys and girls in math SAT scores was eliminated by simply having a mentor telling them that math is learned over time rather than "innate."

©Nick Rowe/Getty Images RF

7   The problem is, girls are routinely getting the message that they don't belong in math and science, further undermining their performance (and Mr. Tierney's article isn't exactly helping in changing the stereotype for the general public). The result of this implicit (unconscious) stereotype is that parents, teachers, and school counselors are less likely to encourage girls to pursue math and science than they are boys. These girls are then less likely to seek advanced math classes and would be unlikely, without those opportunities, to make it to the above 700 SAT math score regardless of ability.

Anecdotally, I had this experience with my daughter a couple of years ago. 8 At age 10, she had somehow decided that she wasn't good at math (despite being raised in a household with 2 PhDs). With her self-confidence plummeting, math homework became very painful in our household. When I dug deeper, I found that she mistakenly believed that you were either born with math ability or you weren't—that this was an innate biological ability as opposed to something you could learn, and that somehow she hadn't been "born with it." Once I actively dispelled that notion and provided her with additional mentoring, her math performance significantly improved. I never hear her say that she isn't good at math anymore, and her math homework is flawless.

The Duke article, and Tierney, raises an important question about preference, 9 however, that research suggests that boys are more interested in "things" and girls are more interested in "people" and thus gravitate towards fields reflecting that interest. In this research too, there is debate about what in this difference is "nature" versus "nurture"—there are powerful socialization forces at play. Regardless, we have to dispel the notion that science is only about "things" and not about people or somehow disconnected from all social relevance. Indeed, some of the most successful interventions to increase girls' interest in math and science have been to reframe the curriculum to provide examples and projects that are grounded in the interests of a diverse population of students. The EPICS program at Purdue University is a great example of grounding engineering disciplines in socially relevant contexts and has been shown to engage a diversity of students.

What we need, to put this debate to rest, is to replicate these findings in a 10 country where science and math are not viewed as stereotypically male. The most recent cross-national comparison study, published in 2010 in *Psychological Bulletin* by Nicole Else-Quest and her colleagues and comparing 43 countries, shows that the achievement difference in math between girls and boys varies broadly across countries.

Their research shows that country-by-country variation is correlated with 11 gender differences in self-confidence in math, which is compounded by stereotype threat. One of the strongest predictors of the gender gap in math achievement is a given country's level of gender equity in science jobs, consistent with socialization arguments: "if girls' mothers, aunts, and sisters do not have STEM careers, they will perceive that STEM is a male domain and thus feel anxious about math, lack the confidence to take challenging math courses, and underachieve on math tests."

Until girls stop getting the signal that math is for boys, the 4 to 1 gender gap 12 in highest achievement categories of math and science will persist. This has nothing to do with innate ability.

Mr. Tierney, I look forward to your subsequent articles on this issue. Let's 13 indeed dare to discuss women in science and continue to bring to bear the most relevant research on this issue.

Caroline Simard, "'Daring to Discuss Women in Science': A Response to John Tierney," HuffPostTech, 9 June 2010. www.huffingtonpost.com/caroline-simard/daring-to-discuss-women-i_b_605303.html Used with permission of the author.

QUESTIONS FOR READING

1. What is the occasion for Simard's posting? What is her topic?

2. What is Tierney's position on the issue?

3. What sociocultural factors are the causes of the gender gap in math and science, in Simard's view?

QUESTIONS FOR REASONING AND ANALYSIS

4. What is Simard's claim? (Try to state it with precision.)

5. What *kinds* of grounds does Simard present? What point about Tierney's warrant does the author want to make with the evidence she includes?

6. Examine Simard's style and tone; how do they help her argument?

QUESTIONS FOR REFLECTION AND WRITING

7. In the debate over women in science, there are two related assumptions: (1) Math ability is inborn and (2) Boys are innately better at math than girls. Have you heard either one—or both—of these views? Has Simard convinced you that the evidence challenges these ideas? Why or why not?

8. Why can stereotypes be a "threat"? How can ideas "threaten" us? Explain and illustrate to answer these questions.

A NEW WAVE OF EQUALITY | DAVID A. STRAUSS

David Strauss is professor of law and faculty director of the Jenner and Block Supreme Court and Appellate Clinic at the University of Chicago Law School. He is a graduate of Harvard College, Oxford University, and Harvard Law School. Prior to joining academia, Strauss worked at the Justice Department. He has argued eighteen cases before the U.S. Supreme Court and is the author of *The Living Constitution* (2010). His specialty in constitutional law shows through in his essay here, first published in 2015.

PREREADING QUESTIONS Does the title intrigue you? Any idea what wave of equality Strauss is referring to?

1   Both sides seem to want to strike a pose of wounded innocence in the dispute about laws passed by Indiana and Arkansas to exempt religious believers from legal requirements that conflict with their beliefs. Supporters of the laws insist that they have nothing to do with same-sex marriage or the rights of gay people. The laws, we're supposed to believe, are simply about religious freedom, which everyone likes, or big government, which no one does.

2   But the opponents of those laws, while not as disingenuous, are faking it, too. They are scrambling to find differences between what Indiana and Arkansas have passed and the similar federal and state laws that have been on the books for years. That way the opponents can avoid saying what they actually believe: When it comes to same-sex marriage, the law should sometimes forbid people from acting even on their sincere religious beliefs.

The Supreme Court Building, Washington, D.C.

That's what this controversy is really about. It's not a misunderstanding that   3
can be "clarified" by some technical amendment, as Indiana attempted to do. It
is a big and illuminating moment in history—a conflict between the demands of
religion and the demands of society. Such conflicts can sometimes be a terrible
thing, but they can also be a source of great moral progress.

In this kind of conflict, religion is not always the bad guy, but it is also not always   4
the good guy, and it does not always lose or always win. Religion and society mold
each other. Sometimes religion forces itself on society and on the state in ways that
we should all be thankful for. Religious groups played a crucial role in the abolition
of slavery, and they were hugely important in the struggle for civil rights in the
mid-20th century. Religious groups have often been the most important advocates
of doing more for the poor and for society's outcasts. In all those ways and many
others, religious groups have made a recalcitrant society conform to a vision rooted
in religious belief, and we are immeasurably better off for it.

On the other hand, for centuries, freedom to act on one's conscientious   5
religious beliefs would have meant, for many, the freedom to kill heretics and
infidels. Pressure from the state and society forced religious adherents to behave
better, and over time—this is the important part—the religions themselves
changed their doctrines and belief systems to conform to society's demands.
Religions that not so long ago preached intolerance now condemn persecution
and embrace the diversity of religious belief. More recently, we have seen
religious believers abandon white supremacy as a creed and, more recently still
(and, in many cases, not completely), accept that women should have the same
freedom as men to choose their own destiny. The religious doctrines changed for
many reasons, but change they did, and that was partly because the larger society
insisted that discriminatory behavior change. The change in belief followed.

6   The defenders of laws such as Indiana's don't like to talk about this. They act as if no one's conscientious religious beliefs ever dictated discrimination. The defenders of these laws don't want to acknowledge—what is surely true—that even today there are employers who do not want to hire women because their sincere religious belief is that women should keep the home and raise the children. The government does not allow those people to act on their religious beliefs. There is a sense in which that kind of coercion is tragic, but it is also progress. You can, legalistically, insist that the government's interest in preventing race and sex discrimination is, in the language of those laws, a "compelling" interest that overcomes the religious obligation, but when did it become so compelling? Beliefs such as those, about women, would have seemed thoroughly mainstream just a few decades ago. They are not mainstream anymore, because they changed under pressure from society and the law.

7   That is what we are seeing now: one of those moments in history when pressure from the larger society pushes against religious belief and insists that believers, at least when doing business with the public, not act even on sincere objections to same-sex marriage. Already we have seen those religious objections diminish as religions accommodate themselves to the principle that gay people should not be discriminated against. But the process is incomplete. Of course there is room for debate about the pace of change, and there is always an imperative to act respectfully toward those with whom one disagrees. But this is a difficult, challenging conflict, the birth pangs of a new wave of equality. We should not expect it to be easy, and we should recognize it for the momentous event that it is.

David Strauss, "A New Wave of Equality," *The Washington Post,* 11 Apr. 2015. Used with permission of the author.

QUESTIONS FOR READING

1. Who are the "two sides"?
2. What is each side pretending the conflict is about? What is it actually about, in the author's view?
3. In what way was religion a cause for social change?
4. What previous religious beliefs did society change?
5. What more recent changes have society and the law produced in spite of religious opposition?

QUESTIONS FOR REASONING AND ANALYSIS

6. What is Strauss's claim?
7. Does your sentence reveal that this is a causal argument? If not, reword and/or expand your claim statement to clarify the essay's causal nature.
8. Strauss is examining sensitive issues. Examine his style and tone. List specific ways in which he seeks to conciliate readers with varying views.

9. Strauss acknowledges that laws opposing discrimination against women and gays have come rather quickly, leading to conflicts within our society. What might help to explain the current pace of social change?

QUESTIONS FOR REFLECTION AND WRITING

10. The author accepts that current legal conflicts can be "terrible," even "tragic," but he still asks readers to see this new wave of equality as a great moment. Do you agree with the author? If so, why? If not, how would you seek to refute Strauss's argument?

11. Some people devote their lives to creating the changes that surprise—and at times distress—others. How do you account for such different responses to change?

1. Think about your educational experiences as a basis for generating a topic for a causal argument. For example: What are the causes of writer's block? Why do some apparently good students (based on class work, grades, etc.) do poorly on standardized tests? How does pass/fail grading affect student performance? What are the causes of high tuition and fees? What might be some of the effects of higher college costs? What are the causes of binge drinking among college students? What are the effects of binge drinking?

2. *Star Trek,* in its many manifestations, continues to play on television and in movies—why? What makes it so popular? Why are horror movies popular? What are the causes for the great success of the Harry Potter books? If you are familiar with one of these works, or another work that has been amazingly popular, examine the causes for that popularity.

3. The gender pay gap (see Figure 5.3 in Chapter 5) reflects earnings differences between all working men and all working women. It is not a comparison of earnings by job. What might be some of the causes for women continuing to earn less than men—in spite of the fact that more women than men now earn BA degrees? Consider what you know about women in the workforce who work full time. (The pay gap is also not about full- versus part-time work; both men and women work part time as well as full time.) Look at other graphics in Chapter 5 and think about what you have learned from Caroline Simard regarding women in STEM fields. Be prepared to discuss some causes of the pay gap or prepare an essay on the topic. (Be sure to qualify your claim as appropriate, based on what you know.)

CREDIT

1. Lester Thurow, "Why Women Are Paid Less Than Men," *The New York Times,* 8 Mar. 1981.

CHAPTER 11

Presenting Proposals: The Problem/Solution Argument

READ: What is the subject of this cartoon?

REASON: How does the cartoon visualize the subject? What do you see between the primary sign and the "exit" sign?

REFLECT/WRITE: Toles illustrates a problem but not solutions. What have some states done to address the problem? What solutions can you suggest?

You think that there are several spots on campus that need additional lighting at night. You are concerned that the lake near your hometown is green, with algae floating on it. You believe that cyclists on the campus need to have paths and a bike lane on the main roads into the college. These are serious local issues; you should be concerned about them. And, perhaps it is time to act on your concerns—how can you do that? You can write a proposal, perhaps a letter to the editor of your college or hometown newspaper.

These three issues invite a recommendation for change. And to make that recommendation is to offer a solution to what you perceive to be a problem. Public policy arguments, whether local and specific (lampposts or bike lanes) or more general and far-reaching (e.g., the federal government must stop the flow of illegal drugs into the country), can best be understood as arguments over solutions to problems. If there are only ten students on campus who bike to class or only 200 Americans wanting to buy cocaine, then most people would not agree that we have two serious problems in need of debate over the best solutions. But when the numbers become significant, we see a problem and start seeking solutions.

Consider some of these issues stated as policy claims:

- The college needs bike lanes on campus roads and more bike paths across the campus.
- We need to spend whatever is necessary to stop the flow of drugs into this country.

Each claim offers a solution to a problem, as we can see:

- Cyclists will be safer if there are bike lanes on main roads and more bike paths across the campus.
- The way to address the drug problem in this country is to eliminate the supply of drugs.

The basic idea of policy proposals looks like this:

Somebody	**should (or should not)**	**do X—because:**
(Individual, organization, government)		*(solve this problem)*

Observe that proposal arguments recommend action. They look to the future. And they often advise the spending of someone's time and/or money.

CHARACTERISTICS OF PROBLEM/ SOLUTION ARGUMENTS

- *Proposal arguments may be about local and specific problems or about broader, more general public policy issues.* We need to "think globally" these days, but we still often need to "act locally," to address the problems we see around us in our classrooms, offices, and communities.
- *Proposal arguments usually need to define the problem.* How we define a problem has much to do with what kinds of solutions are appropriate. For example, many

people are concerned about our ability to feed a growing world population. Some will argue that the problem is not an agricultural one—how much food we can produce. The problem is a political one—how we distribute the food, at what cost, and how competent or fair some governments are in handling food distribution. If the problem is agricultural, we need to worry about available farmland, water supply, and farming technology. If the problem is political, then we need to concern ourselves with price supports, distribution strategies, and embargoes for political leverage. To develop a problem/solution argument, you first need to define the problem.

- *How we define the problem also affects what we think are the causes of the problem.* Cause is often a part of the debate, especially with far-reaching policy issues, and may need to be addressed, particularly if solutions are tied to eliminating what we consider to be the causes. Why are illegal drugs coming into the United States? Because people want those drugs. Do you solve the problems related to drug addicts by stopping the supply? Or do you address the demand for drugs in the first place?

- *Proposal arguments need to be developed with an understanding of the processes of government, from college administrations to city governments to the federal bureaucracy.* Is that dying lake near your town on city property or state land? Are there conservation groups in your area who can be called on to help with the process of presenting proposals to the appropriate people?

- *Proposal arguments need to be based on the understanding that they ask for change—and many people do not like change, period.* Probably all but the wealthiest Americans recognize that our health-care system needs fixing. That doesn't change the fact that many working people struggling to pay premiums are afraid of any changes introduced by the federal government.

- *Successful problem/solution arguments offer solutions that can realistically be accomplished.* Consider Prohibition, for example. This was a solution to problem drinking—except that it did not work, could not be enforced, because the majority of Americans would not abide by the law.

GUIDELINES for Analyzing Problem/Solution Arguments

When analyzing problem/solution arguments, what should you look for? In addition to the basics of good argument, use these points as guides to analyzing:

- **Is the writer's claim not just clear but also appropriately qualified and focused?** For example, if the school board in the writer's community is not doing a good job of communicating its goals as a basis for its funding package, the writer needs to focus just on that particular school board, not on school boards in general.

- **Does the writer show an awareness of the complexity of most public policy issues?** There are many different kinds of problems with American schools and many more causes for those problems. A simple solution—a longer school year, more money spent, vouchers—is not likely to solve the mixed bag of problems. Oversimplified arguments quickly lose credibility.

- **How does the writer define and explain the problem?** Is the way the problem is stated clear? Does it make sense to you? If the problem is being defined differently than most people have defined it, has the writer argued convincingly for looking at the problem in this new way?

- **What reasons and evidence are given to support the writer's solutions?** Can you see how the writer develops the argument? Does the reasoning seem logical? Are the data relevant? This kind of analysis will help you evaluate the proposed solutions.

- **Does the writer address the feasibility of the proposed solutions?** Does the writer make a convincing case for the realistic possibility of achieving the proposed solutions?

- **Is the argument convincing?** Will the solutions solve the problem as it has been defined? Has the problem been defined accurately? Can the solutions be achieved?

Read and study the following annotated argument. Complete your analysis by answering the questions that follow.

WANT MORE SCIENTISTS? TURN GRADE SCHOOLS INTO LABORATORIES | PRIYA NATARAJAN

A professor in both the astronomy and physics departments at Yale University, Priya Natarajan is a theoretical astrophysicist. She was educated first in Delhi and then at MIT. Natarajan's areas of investigation include black hole physics and gravitational lensing. Interested as well in enhancing general science literacy, Natarajan serves on the Advisory Board of NOVA ScienceNow, speaks at conferences, and writes newspaper articles. The following op-ed essay was published on February 5, 2012.

PREREADING QUESTIONS When you were in grade school, did you like to "discover things" in the natural world? How would you encourage early study of science?

Author states problem.

1   "What's your major?" Ask a college freshman this question, and the answer may be physics or chemistry. Ask a sophomore or a junior, however, and you're less likely to hear about plans to enter the "STEM" fields—science, technology, engineering and mathematics. America's universities are not graduating nearly enough scientists, engineers and other skilled professionals to keep our country globally competitive in the decades ahead.

And this is despite evidence such as a recent Center on Education and the 2
Workforce report that forecasts skill requirements through 2018 and clearly
shows the importance of STEM fields. The opportunities for those with just a high
school education are restricted, it says—many high-paying jobs are open only to
people with STEM college degrees.

States seriousness of problem.

These young scientists are excited by what they are learning.

Still, as many as 60 percent of students who enter college with the intention 3
of majoring in science and math change their plans. Because so many students
intend to major in a STEM subject but don't follow through, many observers have
assumed that universities are where the trouble starts. I beg to differ.

A cause author will refute.

I am a professor of astronomy and physics at Yale University, where I teach an 4
introductory class in cosmology. I see the deficiencies that first-year students
show up with. My students may have dexterity with the equations they're required
to know, but they lack the capacity to apply their knowledge to real-life problems.
This critical shortcoming appears in high school and possibly in elementary
grades—long before college. If we want more Americans to pursue careers in
STEM professions, we have to intervene much earlier than we imagined.

Author's solution.

Many efforts are underway to get younger students interested in science 5
and math. One example is the Tree of Life's online "treehouse" project, a collection of information about biodiversity compiled by hundreds of experts and
amateurs. Students can use this tool to apply what they are learning in the
classroom to the world around them. Starting early in children's education, we
need to provide these types of engaging, interactive learning environments that
link school curricula to the outside world.

Specific strategies for solving problem.

My own schooling is an example. Growing up in Delhi, India, I did puzzles, 6
explored numbers and searched for patterns in everyday settings long before

I ever saw an equation. One assignment I vividly remember asked us to find examples of hexagons. I eagerly pointed out hexagons everywhere: street tiles, leaves, flowers, signs, buildings. I was taught equations only after I learned what they meant and how to think about them. As a result, I enjoyed math, and I became good at it.

7   Not all American children have this experience, but they can. The Khan Academy, for example, has pioneered the use of technology to encourage unstructured learning outside the classroom and now provides teaching supplements in 36 schools around the country. For instance, recent reports describe a San Jose charter school using Khan's instructional videos in ninth-grade math classes to tailor lessons to each student's pace.

8   Perhaps more than English or history, STEM subjects require an enormous amount of foundational learning before students can become competent. Students usually reach graduate school before they can hope to make an original contribution. They can experiment in high school labs, but the U.S. schools' approach to math and science lacks, in large part, a creative element. We need to help students understand that math and science are cumulative disciplines, and help them enjoy learning even as they gradually build a base of knowledge.

9   One way to do this is to encourage students to engage in self-guided or collaborative research projects—something the Internet has made much more feasible. An example from my own field is Zooniverse, a collection of experimental projects in which students can classify galaxies and search for new planets or supernovae using real data collected by NASA. Taking part in such explorations early will help students understand that science and math aren't just abstract equations, but tools we use to understand our world. By the time they get to college, they will have mastered the rhythm of the scientific method—learn, apply, learn, apply—and enjoy the process.

10   Six years ago, I had a student in an introductory cosmology class for non–science majors who had entered Yale as an economics major, a choice based primarily on pressure from his parents. After one summer researching gamma-ray bursts—the most energetic explosions in the universe—he is currently finishing up a PhD in physics at Berkeley. He was hooked by the opportunity to apply what he learned in the classroom to a challenging scientific problem. He loved the thrill of figuring something out.

Author states her claim.

11   Without firsthand experience of the scientific method and its eventual payoff, students will continue to flock to other majors when their science and math courses become too demanding. If we want more scientists and engineers later, we need to teach children about the joys of hard work and discovery now.

Priya Natarajan, "Want More Scientists? Turn Grade Schools into Laboratories," *The Washington Post,* 5 Feb. 2012. Reprinted by permission of the author.

QUESTIONS FOR READING

1. What are the STEM fields? Why are these fields important?

2. What percentage of college students planning to major in math or science end up changing fields?

3. What do many college students lack that leads them to have trouble in advanced STEM courses?

QUESTIONS FOR REASONING AND ANALYSIS

4. What is the problem Natarajan examines? What has caused this problem, in the author's view? What, then, is her claim?

5. How does the author support her claim?

QUESTIONS FOR REFLECTION AND WRITING

6. Few would question the reality of the problem Natarajan addresses; the issue is how to solve it. Do you agree that at least much of the cause rests with the early teaching of math and science? If yes, why? If no, why not?

7. From your experience, can you suggest other ways to improve early education in math and science?

AFTER ARMSTRONG'S FALL, THE CASE FOR PERFORMANCE ENHANCEMENT | BRADEN ALLENBY

President's Professor and Lincoln Professor of Engineering and Ethics in the School of Sustainable Engineering at Arizona State University, Braden Allenby holds a PhD in environmental sciences from Rutgers University in addition to a law degree. He entered academia after twenty years as counsel to AT&T. He is the coauthor, with Daniel Serewitz, of *The Techno-Human Condition* (2011) and author of *Reconstructing Earth: Technology and Environment in the Age of Humans* (2005).

PREREADING QUESTIONS Is there a case for performance enhancement? How do you expect Allenby to develop his argument?

In the past month, cyclist Lance Armstrong has been stripped of his seven 1
Tour de France titles. His commercial sponsors, including Nike, have fled. He has resigned as chairman of Livestrong, the anti-cancer charity he founded. Why? Because the U.S. Anti-Doping Agency and the International Cycling Union say he artificially enhanced his performance in ways not approved by his sport and helped others on his team do the same.

This may seem like justice, but that's an illusion. Whether Armstrong cheated 2
is not the core consideration. Rather, his case shows that enhancement is here to stay. If everyone's enhancing, it's a reality that we should embrace.

Look at any sport. People are running, swimming and biking faster and 3
farther; linemen are bulkier than ever; sluggers have bigger muscles and hit more home runs. This might be due to better nutrition. Perhaps it is a result of

©Doug Pensinger/Getty Images

Lance Armstrong in a happier mood before his medals are taken from him for doping.

legally prescribed drugs. Heck, it might simply be because of better training. But illegal enhancement has never been more evident or more popular.

4   Moreover, enhancement science—pharmacology, nanotechnology, biotechnology and genetics—is more sophisticated than ever. A recent *Nature* article, for example, discusses oxygen-carrying particles that could be inserted in athletes' blood and DNA therapies that could enhance muscle performance.

5   In an earlier time, rules limiting the use of such technology may have been a brave attempt to prevent cheating. Now, they are increasingly ineffectual. Humans are becoming a design space. That athletes are on the cutting edge of this engineering domain is neither a prediction nor a threat. It is the status quo.

6   Get over it.

7   Professional athletes didn't always make big bucks, so when enhancement techniques were primitive, the payoff wasn't necessarily worth the health risks. And with less demand, there were fewer nerds in fewer laboratories creating enhancement technologies. Anabolic steroids, for example, weren't developed until the 1930s. Can you imagine Babe Ruth using a low-oxygen chamber that simulated a high-altitude environment to increase his red-blood-cell count and improve his respiration system's efficiency? That's just one new way a player can get an edge.

Today, the gap between superstar athletes and almost-stars is rapidly 8 growing. The benefits of being at the top of your game—money, sponsors, cars, houses, movie careers, book deals and groupies—have never been clearer. After all, how many lucrative marketing contracts go to bronze medalists?

To perform consistently, 21st-century athletes enhance legally with better 9 gear, specialized diets, physical trainers, vitamin B, and energy drinks and gels. Why not add drugs and other technologies to the list of legal enhancements, especially when most of us are enhancing our workplace concentration with a morning coffee or energy shot?

In my engineering and sustainability classes, I ask my students how many 10 have played sports in high school or college. Usually, at least half raise their hands. Then I ask how many know people who enhanced illegally. The hands stay up, even if I limit the question to high school athletes. Enhancement—legal or illegal, according to confused, arbitrary and contradictory criteria—is pervasive. Indeed, surveys show that significant numbers of non-athletes, especially in high school and college, use steroids to try to improve their appearance rather than to augment their play on the field. This should not be surprising, given the popularity of other cosmetic-enhancement techniques such as discretionary plastic surgery, even among young people.

Armstrong's alleged doping in the Tour de France is just more evidence that 11 human excellence is increasingly a product of enhancement.

Mischaracterizing a fundamental change in sports as merely individual viola- 12 tions of the rules has serious consequences. For example, this thinking has led to inadequate research on the risks of enhancement technologies, especially new ones. Why research something that can't be used? My anecdotal class surveys show that students have significant skepticism about the reported side effects of such treatments and drugs, as well as perceptions of bias among regulators against enhancement. As a result of such attitudes, there's a tendency to play down the risks of some technologies. Call it the "Reefer Madness" response—ignoring real risks because you think the danger is exaggerated. This is ignorance born of prohibition.

What should be done? Past a certain age, athletes should be allowed to use 13 whatever enhancements they think appropriate based on objective data. Providing reliable information about the full range of technologies should become the new mission of a (renamed) Anti-Doping Agency, one not driven by an anti-enhancement agenda. It wouldn't have to be a free-for-all: Age limits and other appropriate regulations could limit dangerous enhancements for non-professionals; those that are too risky could be restricted or, yes, banned.

How? Perhaps the Food and Drug Administration could take over these 14 duties from the Anti-Doping Agency, using its own calculus. Is the proposed enhancement technology effective? Does it hurt more than it helps? It's doubtful that a genetic enhancement, for example, would be allowed. The field is too new. However, some supplements such as creatine, alphalipoic acid and at least some currently banned steroids would probably be acceptable.

In professional sports, normal people do not compete normally. We watch 15 athletes who are enhanced—through top-notch training, equipment and sometimes illegal substances—compete for our amusement. And, despite our sanctimonious claims that this is wrong, we like it that way. So we do athletes a deep disservice by clinging to our whimsical illusion of reality at the cost of their livelihood. If we allow football players to take violent hits and suffer concussions so that we might be entertained, why not allow them to use substances that might cause them health problems? It's their decision.

16   If you yearn to watch "purer" athletes, check out a Division III football game. Visit the minor league ballpark near you. Set up an amateur league. Better yet, train for a marathon sans enhancement.

17   But don't force the Tour de France to cling to outdated ideas of how athletes pedaling for their professional lives should behave. Cyclists have enhanced, are enhancing now and will continue to enhance. In his stubborn refusal to admit guilt in the face of the evidence, maybe this is what Armstrong is trying to tell us.

Braden Allenby, "After Armstrong's Fall, the Case for Performance Enhancement," *The Washington Post,* 28 Oct., 2012. Reprinted by permission of the author.

QUESTIONS FOR READING

1. What are some of the ways that athletes are enhancing their performance?
2. How has enhancement science changed?
3. Why has enhancement become so appealing to athletes?
4. What is a consequence of continuing to try to stop illegal doping?
5. How are our expectations of professional athletes different from that of amateurs?

QUESTIONS FOR REASONING AND ANALYSIS

6. What is Allenby's claim? How does he defend and support it?
7. In two paragraphs, the author discusses some specifics of managing sports with enhancement rules lifted. First, how does this discussion aid his argument? Second, do his suggestions seem sensible and feasible? Why or why not?

QUESTIONS FOR REFLECTION AND WRITING

8. Allenby suggests that since everybody is doing it, we should "get over it" and accept the reality of enhancement. This is a pragmatic approach to the problem; are you content with a pragmatic approach to doping in sports? Why or why not?
9. To what extent are we, the spectators, to blame for illegal doping?
10. Why do we play (and watch) competitive sports? Be prepared to discuss or write about questions 9 and 10.

PREPARING A PROBLEM/SOLUTION ARGUMENT

In addition to the guidelines for writing arguments presented in Chapter 4, you can use the following advice specific to defending a proposal.

Planning

1. **Think:** What should be the focus and limits of your argument? There's a big difference between presenting solutions to the problem of physical abuse of women by men and presenting solutions to the problem of sexual assault on your college campus. Select a topic that you know something about, one that you can realistically handle.

2. **Think:** What reasons and evidence do you have to support your tentative claim? Think through what you already know that has led you to select your particular topic. Suppose you want to write on the issue of sexual assault. Is this choice due to a recent event on the campus? Was this event the first in many years or the last in a trend? Where and when are the assaults occurring? A brainstorming list may be helpful.

3. **Reality check:** Do you have a claim worth defending? Will readers care? Binge drinking and the polluting of the lake near your hometown are serious problems. Problems with your class schedule may not be—unless your experience reveals a college-wide problem.

4. **Think:** Is there additional evidence that you need to obtain to develop your argument? If so, where can you look for that evidence? Are there past issues of the campus paper in your library? Will the campus police grant you an interview?

5. **Think:** What about the feasibility of each solution you plan to present? Are you thinking in terms of essentially one solution with several parts to it or several separate solutions, perhaps to be implemented by different people? Will coordination be necessary to achieve success? How will this be accomplished? For the problem of campus rape, you may want to consider several solutions as a package to be coordinated by the counseling service or an administrative vice president.

Drafting

1. Begin by either reminding readers of the existing problem you will address or arguing that a current situation should be recognized as a problem. In many cases, you can count on an audience who sees the world as you do and recognizes the problem you will address. But in some cases, your first task will be to convince readers that a problem exists that should worry them. If they are not concerned, they won't be interested in your solutions.

2. Early in your essay define the problem—as you see it—for readers. Do not assume that they will necessarily accept your way of seeing the issue. You may need to defend your understanding of the problem before moving on to solutions.

3. If appropriate, explain the cause or causes of the problem. If your proposed solution is tied to removing the cause or causes of the problem, then you need to establish cause and prove it early in your argument. If cause is important, argue for it; if it is irrelevant, move to your solution.

4. Explain your solution. If you have several solutions, think about how best to order them. If several need to be developed in a sequence, then present them in that necessary sequence. If you are presenting a package of diverse actions that together will solve the problem, then consider presenting them from the simplest to the more complex. With the problem of campus sexual assault, for example, you may want to suggest better lighting on campus paths at night plus a safety escort service for women who are afraid to walk home alone, and sensitivity training. Adding more lampposts may be easier than coordinating campus-wide harassment training.

5. Explain the process for achieving your solution. If you have not thought through the political or legal steps necessary to implement your solution, then this step cannot be part of your purpose in writing. However, anticipating a skeptical audience that says "How are we going to do that?" you would be wise to have precise steps to offer your reader. You may have obtained an estimate of costs for new lighting on your campus and want to suggest specific paths that need the lights. You may have investigated safety escort services at other colleges and can spell out how such a service can be implemented on your campus. Showing readers that you have thought ahead to the next steps in the process can be an effective method of persuasion.

6. Support the feasibility of your solution. Be able to estimate costs. Show that you know who would be responsible for implementation. Specific information strengthens your argument.

7. Show how your solution is better than others. Anticipate challenges by including reasons for adopting your program rather than another program. Explain how your solution will be more easily adopted or more effective when implemented than other possibilities. Of course, a less practical but still viable defense is that your solution is the right thing to do. Values also belong in public policy debates, not just issues of cost and acceptability.

A CHECKLIST FOR REVISION

☐ Do I have a clear statement of my policy claim? Is it appropriately qualified and focused?

☐ Have I clearly explained how I see the problem to be solved? If necessary, have I argued for seeing the problem my way?

☐ Have I presented my solutions—and argued for them—in a clear and logical structure? Have I explained how these solutions can be implemented and why they are better than other solutions that have been suggested?

☐ Have I used data that are relevant and current?

☐ Have I used the basic checklist for revision in Chapter 4? (See p. 107.)

FOR ANALYSIS AND DEBATE

MY FIGHT AGAINST SEXUAL HARASSMENT | GRETCHEN CARLSON

A graduate of Stanford University and a child prodigy on the violin, Gretchen Carlson was the first Miss America to win as a classical violinist. Her career as a news anchor, primarily on Fox News, is well known. Carlson has also been an advocate for workplace equality and is now, as a result of her experience with harassment at Fox News, "the face" in the battle for safe work environments for women. She is the author of a candid memoir, *Getting Real* (2015). Her essay below appeared in 2016.

PREREADING QUESTIONS How widespread do you think sexual harassment is? How serious is this problem?

I've never been a good sleeper, but now more than ever, after having lost my job   1
as a news anchor this past summer, I find myself lying awake at night thinking about my daughter—and your daughters, too. I've been asking myself this simple question: Will our girls finally be the ones to have workplaces free from sexual harassment? This question became even more compelling during the presidential race, where offensive comments about women were dismissed as "locker room talk."

I want to do everything I can to end sexual harassment in the workplace.   2
I didn't expect to be cast in this role. But as a result of the news reports concerning my departure from Fox News, letters, emails and texts from victims of harassment have poured in to me, and I can't turn away.

Just a few weeks ago, the   3
comedian Heather McDonald, inspired by my story, publicly spoke about the time her boss just came out and asked if he could hold her breasts, as if that were a normal part of a working relationship. A former flight attendant wrote to tell me that her boss routinely harassed her sexually, and when she complained to human resources, they told her that she was the one who needed sexual harassment training. A tenured teacher at a religious school told me she had to quit her job. An Iraq war veteran, who endured repeated sexual harassment in the Army, returned to civilian life only to find even greater abuse on Wall Street.

©Noam Galai/Getty Images

Gretchen Carlson.

4   Since my story went public, I've been cast as a victim—another role I never thought I'd have to play. My parents raised me with a never-give-up attitude, telling me I could be anything I wanted to be. I was a serious violinist and a valedictorian of my high school class. I knew all about hard work.

5   But within months of my first job in television, I found myself alone in the news van with a cameraman I barely knew, and our conversation went from normal chitchat to something much more sinister. He wanted to know how I felt when he put the microphone under my shirt and touched my breasts.

6   That wasn't the first time I'd been sexually harassed. After being crowned Miss America in 1989, I experienced sexual harassment twice. On one occasion, a well-known television executive stuck his tongue down my throat in the back seat of a car we were sharing. And just a few weeks later, a famous publicist in Los Angeles shoved my head into his crotch so forcefully I couldn't breathe.

7   But at that first job, I was in the workplace, so the cameraman's actions filled me with a terrible dread that my career could be in jeopardy. Even though I knew what he did wasn't right, I didn't want to tell a soul. I was afraid that his actions would reflect badly on me.

8   According to the National Women's Law Center, almost half of all women have been sexually harassed at work. And those are the ones who have been brave enough to reveal it. Why don't women tell?

9   That is the question we hear all the time. If it was so bad, why didn't they just find another job? That's what President-elect Donald J. Trump suggested when asked what his daughter should do if she encountered sexual harassment.

10   Here's why women don't come forward. We don't want to be labeled troublemakers. We don't want to put our careers at risk. And in the end, one of our greatest fears is that we won't be believed. "He said, she said" is still a convenient phrase that equates victims with harassers. It trivializes workplace harassment and has become synonymous with "Don't take that risk; they won't believe you anyway."

11   So how do we fix this? It's not going to happen because we're talking about it more. I'm hopeful that more women will now feel able to come forward to say, "this is not O.K.," but they need our support.

12   First, companies should not be allowed to force employees to sign contracts that include arbitration clauses under which all discrimination disputes, including sexual harassment claims, can be resolved only in a secret proceeding. Women who are unaware that other women have come forward are less likely to speak up themselves. Secrecy silences women and leaves harassers free from accountability.

13   Also, arbitration rarely favors the accuser. Victims of harassment deserve access to public courts, access to information as provided by the rules of evidence and civil procedure (which do not apply to arbitration), and the right of appeal if legal errors are made (there is no appeal from unjust results in arbitration). I plan to testify before Congress to help fight forced arbitration.

14   We also need to revisit the issue of whether human resources departments are the right places for victims to go to lodge a complaint. Can women feel safe

telling their stories to H.R. employees who are hired by the same company executives who may be implicated in the harassment?

Next, we should reassess sexual harassment training at companies across 15 the country. Certainly, some programs are positive forums for raising awareness. But others may be corporate facades designed to create the illusion of compliance with anti-harassment laws and policies. At the very least there should be a standard by which the effectiveness of these programs can be measured.

Finally, I believe a fundamental factor is the way we choose to raise our kids. 16 Let's teach our girls and boys how to show the same respect to their colleagues in the workplace they show their moms and sisters at home.

The most important part of this, in my mind, is men and women working 17 together. This is not only a women's issue. It's a societal issue.

Men need to hire more women and put them in higher positions of power 18 within organizations. Despite his earlier comments, Mr. Trump has said that he, more than anyone, respects women. It's my hope that he will now place well-qualified women in positions of real authority in his new administration.

Men also need to stop enabling harassers by egging them on or covering up 19 or excusing their bad behavior. Women shouldn't be expected to solve this issue alone. We need men to be onboard, too.

Gretchen Carlson, "My Fight Against Sexual Harassment," *The New York Times,* 12 Nov. 2016. Used with permission.

QUESTIONS FOR READING

1. Who is Gretchen Carlson? What are her accomplishments?
2. Why is she "famous" now?
3. Why don't many women report harassment at work?
4. What needs to happen to fix this problem?

QUESTIONS FOR REASONING AND ANALYSIS

5. Write a statement of Carlson's claim that reveals her essay as a problem/solution type of argument.
6. What kind of essay do the opening paragraphs seem to suggest? What does the author gain by her choice of opening?
7. Carlson's essay is clearly organized. What does she do first, second, and third?
8. The author recommends several specific solutions: what are they? Evaluate them for feasibility and effectiveness.

QUESTIONS FOR REFLECTION AND WRITING

9. Have you been involved in sexual harassment at school or work? If so, how did you respond? Do you have any regrets? Any advice for others?
10. Look again at Carlson's recommended solutions. Which action is the most important, in your view? Why?

A MODEST PROPOSAL | JONATHAN SWIFT

For Preventing the Children of Poor People in Ireland from Being a Burden to Their Parents or Country, and for Making Them Beneficial to the Public

Born in Dublin, Jonathan Swift (1667–1745) was ordained in the Anglican Church and spent many years as dean of St. Patrick's in Dublin. Swift was also involved in the political and social life of London for some years, and throughout his life he kept busy writing. His most famous imaginative work is *Gulliver's Travels* (1726). Almost as well known is the essay that follows, published in 1729. Here you will find Swift's usual biting satire but also his concern to improve humanity.

PREREADING QUESTIONS Swift was a minister, but he writes this essay as if he were in a different job. What "voice" or persona do you hear? Does Swift agree with the views of this persona?

Jonathan Swift

1   It is a melancholy object to those who walk through this great town[1] or travel in the country, where they see the streets, the roads, and cabin doors crowded with beggars of the female sex, followed by three, four, or six children, all in rags, and importuning every passenger for an alms. These mothers, instead of being able to work for their honest livelihood, are forced to employ all their time in strolling to beg sustenance for their helpless infants, who, as they grow up, either turn thieves for want of work, or leave their dear native country to fight for the pretender[2] in Spain or sell themselves to the Barbados.

2   I think it is agreed by all parties that this prodigious number of children in the arms, or on the backs, or at the heels of their mothers, and frequently of their fathers, is in the present deplorable state of the kingdom a very great additional grievance; and therefore, whoever could find out a fair, cheap, and easy method of making these children sound and useful members of the commonwealth would deserve so well of the public as to have his statue set up for a preserver of the nation.

3   But my intention is very far from being confined to provide only for the children of professed beggars; it is of a much greater extent, and shall take in the

---

[1] Dublin.—Ed.

[2] James Stuart, claimant to the British throne lost by his father, James II, in 1688.—Ed.

whole number of infants at a certain age who are born of parents in effect as little able to support them as those who demand our charity in the streets.

As to my own part, having turned my thoughts for many years upon this important subject, and maturely weighed the several schemes of other projectors,[3] I have always found them grossly mistaken in the computation. It is true a child just dropped from its dam may be supported by her milk for a solar year with little other nourishment; at most not above the value of two shillings, which the mother may certainly get, or the value in scraps, by her lawful occupation of begging; and, it is exactly at one year that I propose to provide for them in such a manner as instead of being a charge upon their parents or the parish, or wanting food and raiment for the rest of their lives, they shall on the contrary contribute to the feeding, and partly to the clothing, of many thousands. 4

There is likewise another great advantage in my scheme, that it will prevent those voluntary abortions, and that horrid practice of women murdering their bastard children, alas, too frequent among us, sacrificing the poor innocent babes, I doubt, more to avoid the expense than the shame, which would move tears and pity in the most savage and inhuman breast. 5

The number of souls in this kingdom being usually reckoned one million and a half, of these I calculate there may be about two hundred thousand couples whose wives are breeders; from which number I subtract thirty thousand couples who are able to maintain their own children, although I apprehend there cannot be so many, under the present distress of the kingdom; but this being granted, there will remain a hundred and seventy thousand breeders. I again subtract fifty thousand for those women who miscarry, or whose children die by accident or disease within the year. There only remain a hundred and twenty thousand children of poor parents annually born. The question therefore is, how this number shall be reared and provided for, which, as I have already said, under the present situation of affairs, is utterly impossible by all the methods hereto proposed. For we can neither employ them in handicraft or agriculture; we neither build houses (I mean in the country) nor cultivate land. They can very seldom pick up a livelihood by stealing until they arrive at six years old, except where they are of towardly parts[4]; although I confess they learn the rudiments much earlier, during which time they can, however, be properly looked upon only as probationers, as I have been informed by a principal gentleman in the country of Cavan, who protested to me that he never knew above one or two instances under the age of six, even in the part of the kingdom renowned for the quickest proficiency in that art. 6

I am assured by our merchants that a boy or girl before twelve years old is no saleable commodity; and even when they come to this age they will not yield above three pounds, or three pounds and a half a crown at most, on the exchange; which cannot turn to account either to the parents or the kingdom, the charge of nutriment and rags having been at least four times that value. 7

I shall now therefore humbly propose my own thoughts, which I hope will not be liable to the least objection. 8

---

[3] Planners.—Ed.

[4] Innate abilities.—Ed.

9   I have been assured by a very knowing American of my acquaintance in London that a young healthy child well nursed is at a year old a most delicious, nourishing, and wholesome food, whether stewed, roasted, baked, or boiled; and I make no doubt that it will equally serve in a fricassee or ragout.

10   I do therefore humbly offer it to public consideration that of the hundred and twenty-thousand children, already computed, twenty thousand may be reserved for breed, whereof only one fourth part to be males, which is more than we allow to sheep, black cattle, or swine; and my reason is that these children are seldom the fruits of marriage, a circumstance not much regarded by our savages, therefore one male will be sufficient to serve four females. That the remaining hundred thousand may at a year old be offered in sale to the persons of quality and fortune, through the kingdom, always advising the mother to let them suck plentifully in the last month, so as to render them plump and fat for the table. A child will make two dishes at an entertainment for friends; and when the family dines alone, the fore or hind quarter will make a reasonable dish, and seasoned with a little pepper or salt will be very good boiled on the fourth day, especially in winter.

11   I have reckoned upon a medium that a child just born will weigh twelve pounds, and in a solar year if tolerably nursed increaseth to twenty-eight pounds.

12   I grant this food will be somewhat dear, and therefore very proper for landlords, who, as they have already devoured most of the parents, seem to have the best title to the children.

13   Infant's flesh will be in season throughout the year, but more plentiful in March, and a little before and after. For we are told by a grave author, an eminent French physician,[5] that fish being a prolific diet, there are more children born in Roman Catholic countries about nine months after Lent than at any other season; therefore reckoning a year after Lent, the markets will be more glutted than usual, because the number of Popish infants is at least three to one in this kingdom; and therefore it will have one other collateral advantage, by lessening the number of Papists among us.

14   I have already computed the charge of nursing a beggar's child (in which list I reckon all cottagers, laborers, and four-fifths of the farmers) to be about two shillings per annum, rags included; and I believe no gentleman would repine to give ten shillings for the carcass of a good fat child, which, as I have said, will make four dishes of excellent nutritive meat, when he hath only some particular friend or his own family to dine with him. Thus the squire will learn to be a good landlord, and grow popular among his tenants; the mother will have eight shillings net profit, and be fit for work until she produces another child.

15   Those who are more thrifty (as I must confess the times require) may flay the carcass; the skin of which artificially dressed will make admirable gloves for ladies and summer boots for fine gentlemen.

16   As to our city of Dublin, shambles[6] may be appointed for this purpose, in the most convenient parts of it, and butchers we may be assured will not be wanting; although I rather recommend buying the children alive, and dressing them hot from the knife as we do roasting pigs.

---

[5] François Rabelais.—Ed.

[6] Butcher shops.—Ed.

A very worthy person, a true lover of his country, and whose virtues I highly [17] esteem, was lately pleased in discoursing on this matter to offer a refinement upon my scheme. He said that many gentlemen of this kingdom, having of late destroyed their deer, he conceived that the want of venison might be well supplied by the bodies of young lads and maidens, not exceeding fourteen years of age nor under twelve, so great a number of both sexes in every county being now ready to starve for want of work and service; and these to be disposed of by their parents, if alive, or otherwise by their nearest relations. But with due deference to so excellent a friend and so deserving a patriot, I cannot be altogether in his sentiments. For as to the males, my American acquaintance assured me from frequent experience that their flesh was generally tough and lean, like that of our school-boys, by continual exercise, and their taste disagreeable; and to fatten them would not answer the charge. Then as to the females, it would, I think with humble submission, be a loss to the public, because they soon would become breeders themselves; and besides, it is not probable that some scrupulous people might be apt to censure such a practice (although indeed very unjustly) as a little bordering upon cruelty; which, I confess, hath always been with me the strongest objection against any project, how wellsoever intended.

But in order to justify my friend, he confessed that this expedient was put [18] into his head by the famous Psalmanazar,[7] a native of the island Formosa who came from thence to London above twenty years ago, and in conversation told my friend that in his country when any young person happened to be put to death, the executioner sold the carcass to persons of quality as a prime dainty; and that in his time the body of a plump girl of fifteen, who was crucified for an attempt to poison the emperor, was sold to his Imperial Majesty's prime minister of state, and other great mandarins of the court, in joints from the gibbet, at four hundred crowns. Neither indeed can I deny that if the same use were made of several plump young girls in this town, who without one single groat to their fortunes cannot stir abroad without a chair, and appear at the playhouse and assemblies in foreign fineries which they never will pay for, the kingdom would not be the worse.

Some persons of a desponding spirit are in great concern about that vast [19] number of poor people who are aged, diseased, or maimed, and I have been desired to employ my thoughts what course may be taken to ease the nation of so grievous an incumbrance. But I am not in the least pain upon that matter, because it is very well known that they are every day dying and rotting by cold and famine, and filth and vermin, as fast as can be reasonably expected. And as to the younger laborers, they are now in almost as hopeful a condition. They cannot get work, and consequently pine away for want of nourishment to a degree that if at any time they are accidentally hired to common labor, they have not strength to perform it; and thus the country and themselves are in a fair way of being soon delivered from the evils to come.

I have too long digressed, and therefore shall return to my subject. I think [20] the advantages by the proposal which I have made are obvious and many, as well as of the highest importance.

---

[7] A known imposter who was French, not Formosan as he claimed.—Ed.

21   For, first, as I have already observed, it would greatly lessen the number of Papists, with whom we are yearly overrun, being the principal breeders of the nation as well as our most dangerous enemies; and who stay at home on purpose with a design to deliver the kingdom to the pretender, hoping to take their advantage by the absence of so many good Protestants, who have chosen rather to leave their country than stay at home and pay tithes against their conscience to an idolatrous Episcopal curate.

22   Secondly, the poorer tenants will have something valuable of their own, which by law may be made liable to distress,[8] and help their landlord's rent; their corn and cattle being already seized, and money a thing unknown.

23   Thirdly, whereas the maintenance of a hundred thousand children, from two years old upwards, cannot be computed at less than ten shillings a piece per annum, the nation's stock will be thereby increased fifty thousand pounds per annum, besides the profit of a new dish introduced to the tables of all gentlemen of fortune in the kingdom who have any refinement in taste. And the money will circulate among ourselves, the goods being entirely of our own growth and manufacture.

24   Fourthly, the constant breeders, besides the gain of eight shillings sterling per annum by the sale of their children, will be rid of the charge of maintaining them after the first year.

25   Fifthly, this food would likewise bring great custom to taverns, where the vintners will certainly be so prudent as to procure the best receipts for dressing it to perfection, and consequently have their houses frequented by all the fine gentlemen, who justly value themselves upon their knowledge in good eating; and a skillful cook, who understands how to oblige his guests, will contrive to make it as expensive as they please.

26   Sixthly, this would be a great inducement to marriage, which all wise nations have either encouraged by rewards or enforced by laws and penalties. It would increase the care and tenderness of mothers towards their children, when they were sure of a settlement for life to the poor babes, provided in some sort by the public, to their annual profit instead of expense. We should soon see an honest emulation among the married women, which of them could bring the fattest child to the market. Men would become as fond of their wives during the time of their pregnancy as they are now of their mares in foal, their cows in calf, or sows when they are ready to farrow; nor offer to beat or kick them (as is too frequent a practice) for fear of a miscarriage.

27   Many other advantages might be enumerated. For instance, the addition of some thousand carcasses in our exportation of barrelled beef, the propagation of swine's flesh, and improvement in the art of making good bacon, so much wanted among us by the great destruction of pigs, too frequent at our tables, which are no way comparable in taste or magnificence to a well-grown fat, yearling child, which roasted whole will make a considerable figure at a lord mayor's feast or any other public entertainment. But this and many others I omit, being studious of brevity.

---

[8] Can be seized by lenders.—Ed.

Supposing that one thousand families in this city would be constant 28 customers for infants' flesh, besides others who might have it at merry meetings, particularly weddings and christenings, I compute that Dublin would take off annually about twenty thousand carcasses, and the rest of the kingdom (where probably they will be sold somewhat cheaper) the remaining eighty thousand.

I can think of no one objection that will possibly be raised against this 29 proposal, unless it should be urged that the number of people will be thereby much lessened in the kingdom. This I freely own, and it was indeed one principal design in offering it to the world. I desire the reader will observe that I calculate my remedy for this one individual kingdom of Ireland and for no other that ever was, is, or I think ever can be upon earth. Therefore let no man talk to me of other expedients: of taxing our absentees at five shillings a pound: of using neither clothes nor household furniture except what is of our own growth and manufacture: of utterly rejecting the materials and instruments that promote foreign luxury: of curing the expensiveness or pride, vanity, idleness, and gaming in our women: of introducing a vein of parsimony, prudence and temperance: of learning to love our country, wherein we differ even from Laplanders and the inhabitants of Topinamboo[9]: of quitting our animosities and factions, nor act any longer like the Jews, who were murdering one another at the very moment their city was taken[10]: of being a little cautious not to sell our country and consciences for nothing: of teaching landlords to have at least one degree of mercy towards their tenants. Lastly, of putting a spirit of honesty, industry, and skill into our shopkeepers; who, if a resolution could now be taken to buy only our native goods, would immediately unite to cheat and exact upon us in the price, the measure, and the goodness, nor could ever yet be brought to make one fair proposal of just dealing, though often and earnestly invited to it.

Therefore I repeat, let no man talk to me of these and the like expedients, till 30 he hath at least a glimpse of hope that there will ever be some hearty and sincere attempt to put them in practice.

But as to myself, having been wearied out for many years with offering vain, 31 idle, visionary thoughts, and at length utterly despairing of success, I fortunately fell upon this proposal, which, as it is wholly new, so it hath something solid and real, of no expense and little trouble, full in our own power, and whereby we can incur no danger in disobliging England. For this kind of commodity will not bear exportation, the flesh being of too tender a consistence to admit a long continuance in salt, although perhaps I could name a country which would be glad to eat up our whole nation without it.

After all, I am not so violently bent upon my own opinion as to reject any offer 32 proposed by wise men, which shall be found equally innocent, cheap, easy, and effectual. But before something of that kind shall be advanced in contradiction to my scheme, and offering a better, I desire the author, or authors, will be pleased maturely to consider two points. First, as things now stand, how they will be able to find food and raiment for a hundred thousand useless mouths and backs. And secondly, there being a round million of creatures in human figure throughout this kingdom, whose whole subsistence put into a common stock would leave them in

---

[9] An area in Brazil.—Ed.

[10] Some Jews were accused of helping the Romans and were executed during the Roman siege of Jerusalem in a.d. 70—Ed.

debt two million of pounds sterling, adding those who are beggars by profession to the bulk of farmers, cottagers, and laborers, with their wives and children who are beggars, in effect; I desire those politicians who dislike my overture, and may perhaps be so bold to attempt an answer, that they will first ask the parents of these mortals whether they would not at this day think it a great happiness to have been sold for food at a year old in the manner I prescribe, and thereby have avoided such a perpetual scene of misfortunes as they have since gone through by the oppression of landlords, the impossibility of paying rent without money or trade, the want of common sustenance, with neither house nor clothes to cover them from the inclemencies of weather, and the most inevitable prospect of entailing the like or greater miseries upon their breed forever.

33   I profess, in the sincerity of my heart, that I have not the least personal interest in endeavoring to promote this necessary work, having no other motive than the public good of my country, by advancing our trade, providing for infants, relieving the poor, and giving some pleasure to the rich. I have no children by which I can propose to get a single penny, the youngest being nine years old, and my wife past childbearing.

Jonathan Swift, "A Modest Proposal," (1729).

QUESTIONS FOR READING

1. How is the argument organized? What is accomplished in paragraphs 1–7? In paragraphs 8–16? In paragraphs 17–19? In paragraphs 20–28? In paragraphs 29–33?

2. What specific advantages does the writer offer in defense of his proposal?

QUESTIONS FOR REASONING AND ANALYSIS

3. What specific passages and connotative words make us aware that this is a satirical piece using irony as its chief device?

4. After noting Swift's use of irony, what do you conclude to be his purpose in writing?

5. What can you conclude to be some of the problems in 18th-century Ireland? Where does Swift offer direct condemnation of existing conditions in Ireland and attitudes of the English toward the Irish?

6. What actual reforms would Swift like to see?

QUESTIONS FOR REFLECTION AND WRITING

7. What are some of the advantages of using irony? What does Swift gain by this approach? What are possible disadvantages in using irony? Reflect on irony as a persuasive strategy.

8. What are some current problems that might be addressed by the use of irony? Make a list. Then select one and think about what "voice" or persona you might use to bring attention to that problem. Plan your argument with irony as a strategy.

SUGGESTIONS FOR DISCUSSION AND WRITING

1. Think of a problem on your campus or in your community for which you have a workable solution. Organize your argument to include all relevant steps as described in this chapter. Although your primary concern will be to present your solution, depending on your topic you may need to begin by convincing readers of the seriousness of the problem or the causes of the problem—if your solutions involve removing those causes.

2. Think of a problem in education—K–12 or at the college level—that you have a solution for and that you are interested in. You may want to begin by brainstorming to develop a list of possible problems in education about which you could write—or look through Chapter 19 for ideas. Be sure to qualify your claim and limit your focus as necessary to work with a problem that is not so broad and general that your "solutions" become general and vague comments about "getting better teachers." (If one problem is a lack of qualified teachers, then what specific proposals do you have for solving that particular problem?) Include as many steps as are appropriate to develop and support your argument.

3. Think of a situation that you consider serious but that apparently many people do not take seriously enough. Write an argument in which you emphasize, by providing evidence, that the situation is a serious problem. You may conclude by suggesting a solution, but your chief purpose in writing will be to alert readers to a problem.

The Researched and Formally Documented Argument

CHAPTER 12

Locating, Evaluating, and Preparing to Use Sources

We do research all the time. You would not select a college or buy a car without doing research: gathering relevant information, analyzing that information, and drawing conclusions from your study. You may already have done some research in this course, using sources in this text or finding data online to strengthen an argument. Then you acknowledged your sources either informally in your essay or formally, following the documentation guidelines in this section. So, when you are assigned a more formal research essay, remember that you are not facing a brand-new assignment. You are just doing a longer paper with more sources, and you have this section to guide you to success.

SELECTING A GOOD TOPIC

To get started you need to select and limit a topic. One key to success is finding a workable topic. No matter how interesting or clever the topic, it is not workable if it does not meet the guidelines of your assignment. Included in those guidelines may be a required length, a required number of sources, and a due date. Understand and accept all of these guidelines as part of your writing context.

What Type of Paper Am I Preparing?

Study your assignment to understand the type of project. Is your purpose to write a report essay, an analytical essay, or an argumentative essay? Using these three categories, how would you classify each of the following topics?

1. Explain the chief solutions proposed for increasing the Southwest's water supply.
2. Compare the Freudian and behavioral models of mental illness.
3. Find the best solutions to a current environmental problem.
4. Consider: What twentieth-century invention has most dramatically changed our personal lives?

Did you recognize that the first topic calls for a report? The second topic requires an analysis of two schools of psychology, so you cannot report on only one, but you also cannot argue that one model is better than the other. Both topics 3 and 4 require an argumentative paper: You must select and defend a claim.

Who Is My Audience?

If you are writing in a specific discipline, imagine your instructor as a representative of that field, a reader with knowledge of the subject area. If you are in a composition course, your instructor may advise you to write to a general reader, someone who reads newspapers but may not have the exact information and perspective you have. For a general reader, specialized terms and concepts need definition.

NOTE: Consider the expectations of your readers. A research essay is not a personal essay. It is not about you; it is about a subject. Keep yourself in the background and carefully evaluate any use of the personal pronoun "I."

How Can I Select a Good Topic?

Choosing from assigned topics. At times students are unhappy with topic restriction. Looked at another way, your instructor has eliminated a difficult step in the research process and has helped you avoid the problem of selecting an unworkable topic. If topics are assigned, you will still have to choose from the list and develop your own claim and approach.

Finding a course-related topic. This guideline gives you many options and requires more thought about your choice. Working within the guidelines, try to write about what interests you. Here are examples of assignments turned into topics of interest to the student:

ASSIGNMENT	INTEREST	TOPIC
1. Trace the influence of any twentieth-century event, development, invention.	Music	The influence of the Jazz Age on modern music
2. Support an argument on some issue of pornography and censorship.	Computers	Censorship of pornography on the Web
3. Demonstrate the popularity of a current myth and then discredit it.	Science fiction	The lack of evidence for the existence of UFOs

Selecting a topic without any guidelines. When you are free to write on any topic, you may need to use some strategies for topic selection.

- Look through your text's table of contents or index for subject areas that can be narrowed or focused.
- Look over your class notes and think about subjects covered that have interested you.
- Consider college-based or local issues.
- Do a subject search in a database to see how a large topic can be narrowed—for example, type in "dinosaur" and observe such subheadings as *dinosaur behavior* and *dinosaur extinction.*
- Use one or more invention strategies to narrow and focus a topic:
  - Freewriting
  - Brainstorming
  - Asking questions about a broad subject, using the journalist's questions *who, what, where, when, why* and *how.*

What Kinds of Topics Should I Avoid?

Here are several kinds of topics that are best avoided because they usually produce disasters, no matter how well the student handles the rest of the research process:

1. *Topics that are irrelevant* to your interests or the course. If you are not interested in your topic, you will not produce a lively, informative paper. If you select a topic far removed from the course content, you may create some hostility in your instructor, who will wonder why you are unwilling to become engaged in the course.

2. *Topics that are broad subject areas.* These result in general surveys that lack appropriate detail and support.

3. *Topics that can be fully researched with only one source.* You will likely produce a summary, not a research paper.

4. *Biographical studies.* Short undergraduate papers on a person's life usually turn out to be summaries of one or two major biographies.

5. *Topics that produce a strong emotional response in you.* If there is only one "right" answer to the abortion issue and you cannot imagine counterarguments, don't choose to write on abortion. Probably most religious topics are best avoided.

6. *Topics that are too technical for you* at this point in your college work. If you do not understand the complexities of the federal tax code, then arguing for a reduction in the capital gains tax may be an unwise topic choice.

WRITING A TENTATIVE CLAIM OR RESEARCH PROPOSAL

Once you have selected and focused on a topic, write a tentative claim, research question, or research proposal. Some instructors will ask to see a statement—from a sentence to a paragraph long—to be approved before you proceed. Others may require a one-page proposal that includes a tentative claim, a basic organizational plan, and a description of types of sources to be used. Even if your instructor does not require anything in writing, you need to write something for your benefit—to direct your reading and thinking. Here are two possibilities:

1. **SUBJECT:**   Smartphones

    TOPIC: The impact of smartphones on the twenty-first century

    CLAIM: Smartphones have had the greatest impact of any technological development in the twenty-first century.

    RESEARCH PROPOSAL: I propose to show that smartphones have had the greatest impact of any technological development in the twenty-first century. I will show the influence of smartphones on the economy, on social networking, and on cultural issues to emphasize the breadth of influence. I will argue that other possibilities (such as the laptop computer) did not have the same impact as smartphones. I will check the library's book catalog and databases for sources on technological developments and on smartphones specifically. I will also interview a family friend who works for a company that makes smartphones.

This example illustrates several key ideas. First, the initial subject is both too broad and unfocused (*What* about smartphones?). Second, the claim is more focused than the topic statement because it asserts a position, a claim the student must support. Third, the research proposal is more helpful than the claim only because it includes some thoughts on developing the thesis and finding sources.

2.   Less sure of your topic? Then write a research question or a more open-ended research proposal. Take, for example, a history student studying the effects of Prohibition. She is not ready to write a thesis, but she can write a research proposal that suggests some possible approaches to the topic:

TOPIC:	The effects of Prohibition
RESEARCH QUESTION:	What were the effects of Prohibition on the United States?
RESEARCH PROPOSAL:	I will examine the effects of Prohibition on the United States in the 1920s (and possibly consider some long-term effects, depending on the amount of material on the topic). Specifically, I will look at the varying effects on urban and rural areas and on different classes in society.

PREPARING A WORKING BIBLIOGRAPHY

To begin this next stage of your research, you need to know three things:

- *Your search strategy.* If you are writing on a course-related topic, your starting place may be your textbook for relevant sections and possible sources (if the text contains a bibliography). For this course, you may find some potential sources among the readings in this text. Think about what you already know or have in hand as you plan your search strategy. As part of your research strategy, you may also want to record your tasks and how long your tasks take to complete in a log. Tracking research tasks and time will help you set short- and long-term goals and manage your project.
- *A method for recording bibliographic information.* You have two choices: the always reliable 3 × 5 index cards or a bibliography file in your personal computer.
- *The documentation format you will be using.* You may be assigned the Modern Language Association (MLA) format, or perhaps given a choice between MLA and the American Psychological Association (APA) documentation styles. Once you select the documentation style, skim the appropriate pages in Chapter 14 to get an overview of both content and style.

A list of possible sources is only a *working* bibliography because you do not yet know which sources you will use. (Your final bibliography will include only those sources you cite—actually refer to—in your paper.) A working bibliography will help you see what is available on your topic, note how to locate each source, and contain the information needed to document. Whether you are using cards or computer files, follow these guidelines:

1.   Check all reasonable catalogs and indexes for possible sources. (Use more than one reference source even if you locate enough sources there; you are looking for the best sources, not the first ones you find.)

2.   Complete a card or prepare an entry for every potentially useful source. You won't know what to reject until you start a close reading of sources.

3. Copy (or download from an online catalog) all information needed to complete a citation and to locate the source, including the DOI (digital object identifier) or URL if the source is online. (When using an index that does not give all needed information, leave a space to be filled in when you actually read the source.)

4. Put bibliographic information in the correct format for every possible source; you will save time and make fewer errors. Do not mix or blend styles. When searching for sources, have your text handy and use the appropriate models as your guide.

The following brief guide to correct form will get you started. Illustrations are for cards, but the information and order will be the same in your PC file. (Guidelines are for MLA style.)

Basic Form for Books

As Figure 12.1 shows, the basic MLA form for books includes the following information in this pattern:

1. The author's full name, last name first.
2. The title (and subtitle if there is one) of the book, in italics (underlined in handwriting).
3. The facts of publication: the city of publication (followed by a colon), the publisher (followed by a comma), and the date of publication.
4. DOI, URL, permalink, or access number.

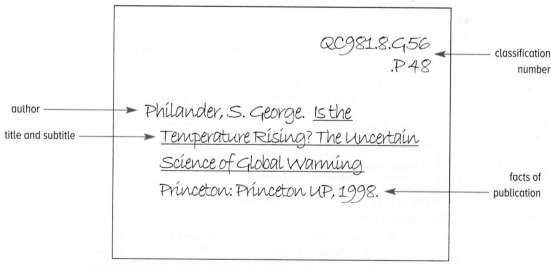

FIGURE 12.1   **Bibliography Card for a Book**

Note that periods are placed after the author's name, after the title, and at the end of the citation. Other information, when appropriate (e.g., the number of volumes), is added to this basic pattern. (See pp. 325–37 for many sample citations.) Include, in your working bibliography, the book's classification number so that you can find it in the library.

Basic Form for Articles

Figure 12.2 shows the simplest form for magazine articles. Include the following information, in this pattern:

1. The author's full name, last name first.
2. The title of the article, in quotation marks.
3. The facts of publication: the title of the periodical in italics (underlined in handwriting), the volume number (if the article is from a scholarly journal), the date (followed by a colon), and inclusive page numbers.
4. DOI, URL, permalink, or access number.

Wooten, Anne. "Bad Day at the Zoo." *Popular Science* Sept. 2007: 14–15.

FIGURE 12.2 **Bibliography Card for a Magazine Article**

You will discover that indexes rarely present information in MLA format. Here, for example, is a source on problems with zoos, found in a database:

BAD DAY AT THE ZOO.

Wooten, Anne. Popular Science, Sep 2007, Vol. 271 Issue 3, p. 14–15, 2p.

If you read the article in the magazine itself, then the correct citation, for MLA, will look like that in the sample bibliography card in Figure 12.2. (Because *Popular Science* is a magazine, not a scholarly journal, you provide month and year but not volume and issue numbers.) However, if you obtain a copy of the article from one of your library's databases, then your citation will need additional information to identify your actual source of the article:

> Wooten, Anne. "Bad Day at the Zoo." *Popular Science*, Sept. 2007, pp. 14–15. *Academic Search Complete*, Access no: 25999296, 10 Oct. 2016.

Note that the MLA now requires either a DOI, URL, or permalink. If a DOI is not available, or if the URL or permalink are too long to use, you may also use an access number (shown). The name of the database is italicized as if it were a book containing the article.

NOTE: A collection of printouts, slips of paper, and backs of envelopes is not a working bibliography! You may have to return to the library for missing information, and you risk making serious errors in documentation. Know the basics of your documentation format and follow it faithfully when collecting possible sources.

LOCATING SOURCES

All libraries contain books and periodicals and a system for accessing them. A library's *book collection* includes the general collection, the reference collection, and the reserve book collection. Electronic materials such as tapes and CDs will also be included in the general "book" collection. The *periodicals collection* consists of popular magazines, scholarly journals, and newspapers. Electronic databases with texts of articles provide alternatives to the print periodicals collection.

REMEMBER: All works, regardless of their source or the format in which you obtain them—and this includes online sources—must be fully documented in your paper.

The Book Catalog

Your chief guide to books and audiovisual materials is the library catalog, usually an electronic database accessed from computer stations in the library or, with an appropriate password, from your personal computer.

©Andrew F. Kazmierski/Shutterstock.com RF

One of the famous lions sitting in front of the New York Public Library.

In the catalog there will be at least four ways to access a specific book: the author entry, the title entry, one or more subject entries, and a keyword option. When you pull up the search screen, you will probably see that the keyword option is the default. If you know the exact title of the work you want, switch to the title option, type it in, and hit submit. If you want a list of all of the library's books on Hemingway, though, click on author and type in "Hemingway." Keep these points in mind:

- With a title search, do not type any initial article (a, an, the). To locate *The Great Gatsby,* type in "Great Gatsby."
- Use correct spelling. If you are unsure of spelling, use a keyword instead of an author or title search.
- If you are looking for a list of books on your subject, do a keyword or subject search.
- When screens for specific books are shown, either print screens of potential sources or copy all information needed for documentation—plus the call number for each book.

The Reference Collection

The research process often begins with the reference collection. You will find atlases, dictionaries, encyclopedias, general histories, critical studies, and biographies. In addition, various reference tools such as bibliographies and indexes are part of the reference collection.

Many tools in the reference collection that were once found only in print are now also online. Some are now only online. Yet online is not always the way to go. Let's consider some of the advantages of each of the formats:

Advantages of the Print Reference Collection

1. The reference tool may be only in print—use it.
2. The print form covers the period you are studying. (Most online indexes and abstracts cover only from 1980 to the present.)
3. In a book, with a little scanning of pages, you can often find what you need without getting spelling or commands exactly right.
4. If you know the best reference source to use and are looking for only a few items, the print source can be faster than the online source.

Advantages of Online Reference Materials

1. Online databases are likely to provide the most up-to-date information.
2. You can usually search all years covered at one time.
3. Full texts (with graphics) are sometimes available, as well as indexes with detailed summaries of articles. Both can be printed or emailed to your PC.
4. Through links to the Web, you have access to an amazing amount of material. (Unless you focus your keyword search, however, you may be overwhelmed.)

Before using any reference work, take a few minutes to check its date, purpose, and organization. If you are new to online searching, take a few minutes to learn about each reference tool by working through the online tutorial.

A Word about Wikipedia

Many researchers go first to a general encyclopedia, in the past in print in the reference collection, today more typically online. This is not always the best strategy. Often you can learn more about your topic from a current book or a more specialized reference source—which your reference librarian can help you find. Both may give you additional sources for your project. If—or when—you turn to a general encyclopedia, make it a good one that is available online through your library. Some colleges have told their students that *Wikipedia* is not an acceptable source for college research projects.

Databases

You will probably access databases by going to your library's home page and then clicking on the appropriate term or icon. (You may have found the book catalog by clicking on "library catalog"; you may find the databases by clicking on "library resources" or some other descriptive label.) You will need to choose a particular database and then type in your keyword for a basic search or select "advanced search" to limit that search by date or periodical or in some other way. Each library will create somewhat different screens, but the basic process of selecting among choices provided

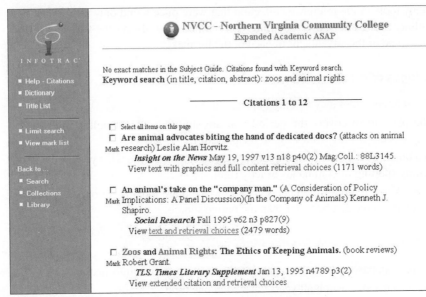

FIGURE 12.3 Partial List of Articles Found on Search Topic

and then typing in your search commands remains the same. Figure 12.3 shows a partial list of articles that resulted from a keyword search for "zoos and animal rights."

GUIDELINES for Using Online Databases

Keep these points in mind as you use online databases:

- **Although some online databases provide full texts of all articles, others provide full texts of only some of the articles indexed.** The articles not in full text will have to be located in a print collection of periodicals.

- **Articles indexed but not available in full text often come with a brief summary or abstract.** This allows you to decide whether the article looks useful for your project. *Do not treat the abstract as the article. Do not use material from it and cite the author. If you want to use the article, find it in your library's print collection or obtain it from another library.*

- **The information you need for documenting material used from an article is not in correct format for any of the standard documentation styles.** You will have to reorder the information and use the correct style for writing titles. If your instructor wants to see a list of possible sources in MLA format, do not hand in a printout of articles from an online database.

- **Because no single database covers all journals, you may want to search several databases that seem relevant to your project.** Ask your reference librarian for suggestions of various databases in the sciences, social sciences, public affairs, and education.

The Web

In addition to using electronic databases to find sources, you can search the Web directly.

Keep in mind these facts about the Web:

- The Web is both disorganized and huge, so you can waste time trying to find information that is easily obtained in a library reference book or database.
- The Web is best at providing current information, such as news and movie reviews. It is also a great source of government information.
- Because anyone can create a website and put anything on it, you will have to be especially careful in evaluating web resources. Remember that articles in magazines and journals have been selected by editors and are often peer reviewed as well, but no editor selects or rejects material on a personal website.

GUIDELINES for Searching the Web

The Web will provide useful sources for many research projects. It will be much less useful than books or online databases for others. One task of the good researcher is to think about the best places to go to get the best material for a specific project. If you think the Web will be useful for you, keep these general guidelines in mind to aid your research:

- Bookmark sites you expect to use often so that you do not have to remember a complex URL or do another Google search.
- Make your research terms as precise as possible to avoid getting overwhelmed with hits.
- If you are searching for a specific phrase, put quotation marks around the words. This will reduce the number of hits and lead to more useful sites. Example: "Rainforest depletion." Without the quotation marks, you will get a lot of information about rainforests, but not necessarily about their depletion. You will also get information on the concept of depletion that has nothing to do with rainforests.
- Complete a bibliography card or a listing in your research file on your PC—including the date you accessed the source—for each separate site from which you take material (see Chapter 14 for documentation guidelines).
- Review your online materials carefully to make sure that they are credible sources of information. Some sources are more credible than others. For instance, sites that use .edu (education institutions) and .gov (government organizations) at the end of their URLs may be more appropriate for your project than nonprofits. Lastly, URLs that end with .com are usually for-profit organizations and may or may not be credible sources for your research. (See the Evaluating Sources Guidelines later in this chapter for details.)

FIELD RESEARCH

Field research can enrich many projects. The following sections offer some suggestions.

Federal, State, and Local Government Documents

In addition to federal documents you may obtain through *PAIS* or *GPO Access,* department and agency websites, or the Library of Congress's good legislative site *Thomas* (*http://thomas.loc.gov*), consider state and county archives, maps, and other published materials. Instead of selecting a national or global topic, consider examining the debate over a controversial bill introduced in your state legislature. Use online databases to locate articles on the bill and the debate and interview legislators and journalists who participated in or covered the debates or served on committees that worked with the bill.

You can also request specific documents from appropriate state or county agencies and nonprofit organizations. One student, given the assignment of examining solutions to an ecological problem, decided to study the local problem of preserving the Chesapeake Bay. She obtained issues of the Chesapeake Bay Foundation newsletter and brochures prepared by them advising homeowners about hazardous household waste materials that end up in the bay. Added to her sources were bulletins on soil conservation and landscaping tips for improving the area's water quality. Local problems can lead to interesting research topics because they are current and relevant to you and because they involve uncovering different kinds of source materials.

Correspondence

Business and government officials are usually willing to respond to written requests for information. Make sure your correspondence is brief and well written. Either include a self-addressed, stamped envelope for the person's convenience or email your request. If you are not emailing, write as soon as you discover the need for information and be prepared to wait several weeks for a reply. It is appropriate to indicate your deadline and ask for a timely response. Three guidelines for either letters or emails to keep in mind are:

1. Explain precisely what information you need.
2. Do not request information that can be found in your library's reference collection.
3. Explain how you plan to use the information. Businesses especially are understandably concerned with their public image and will be disinclined to provide information that you intend to use as a means of attacking them.

Use reference guides to companies and government agencies or their websites to obtain addresses and the person to whom your letter or email should be sent.

Interviews

Some experts are available for personal interviews. Call or write for an appointment as soon as you recognize the value of an interview. Remember that interviews are more likely to be scheduled with state and local officials than with the president of General Motors. If you are studying a local problem, also consider leaders of the civic association with an interest in the issue. In many communities, the local historian or a librarian will be a storehouse of information about the community. Your former teachers can be interviewed for papers on education. Interviews with doctors or nurses can add a special dimension to papers on medical issues.

If an interview is appropriate for your topic, follow these guidelines:

1. Prepare specific questions in advance.
2. Arrive on time, properly dressed, and behave in a polite, professional manner.
3. Take notes, asking the interviewee to repeat key statements so that your notes are accurate.
4. Take a digital recorder or your smartphone with you and use a voice memo, but ask permission to use it before taping.
5. If you quote any statements in your paper, quote accurately, eliminating only such minor speech habits as "you know's" and "uhm's." (See Chapter 14 for proper documentation of interviews.)
6. Direct the interview with your prepared questions, but also give the interviewee the chance to approach the topic in his or her own way. You may obtain information or views that had not occurred to you.
7. Do not get into a debate with the interviewee. You are there to learn.
8. Afterward, send your interviewee a thank you email and ask if you may follow up if you have any further questions.

Lectures

Check the appropriate information sources at your school to keep informed of visiting speakers. If you are fortunate enough to attend a lecture relevant to a current project, take careful, detailed notes. Because a lecture is a source, use of information or ideas from it must be presented accurately and then documented. (See Chapter 14 for documentation format.)

Films, DVDs, Television

Your library will have audiovisual materials that provide good sources for some kinds of topics. For example, if you are studying *Death of a Salesman,* view a videotaped or digital version of the play. Also pay attention to documentaries on public television and to the many news and political talk shows on both public and commercial channels. In many cases, transcripts of shows can be obtained from the TV station. Alternatively, record the program while watching it so that you can view it several times. The documentation format for such nonprint sources is illustrated in Chapter 14.

Surveys, Questionnaires, and Original Research

Depending on your paper, you may want to conduct a simple survey or write and administer a questionnaire. Surveys can be used for many campus and local issues, for topics on behavior and attitudes of college students and/or faculty, and for topics on consumer habits. Explore www.surveymonkey.com for help administering an online survey. Simple ones are free! Remember: Surveying fifty of your Facebook friends will not produce a random sample. When writing questions, keep these guidelines in mind:

- Use simple, clear language.
- Devise a series of short questions rather than only a few that have several parts to them. (You want to separate information for better analysis.)
- Phrase questions to avoid wording that seeks to control the answer. For example, do *not* ask "Did you perform your civic duty by voting in the last election?" This is a loaded question.

In addition to surveys and questionnaires, you can incorporate some original research. As you read sources on your topic, be alert to reports of studies that you could redo and update in part or on a smaller scale. Many topics on advertising and television give opportunities for your own analysis. Local-issue topics may offer good opportunities for gathering information on your own, not just from your reading. One student, examining the controversy over a proposed new shopping mall on part of the Manassas Civil War Battlefield in Virginia, made the argument that the mall served no practical need in the community. He supported his position by describing existing malls, including the number and types of stores each contained and the number of miles each was from the proposed new mall. How did he obtain this information? He drove around the area, counting miles and stores. Sometimes a seemingly unglamorous approach to a topic turns out to be an imaginative one.

EVALUATING SOURCES, MAINTAINING CREDIBILITY

As you study your sources, keep rethinking your purpose and approach. Test your research proposal or tentative claim against what you are learning. Remember: You can always change the direction and focus of your paper as new approaches occur to you, and you can even change your position as you reflect on what you are learning.

You will work with sources more effectively if you keep in mind why you are using them. What you are looking for will vary somewhat, depending on your topic and purpose, but there are several basic approaches:

1. *Acquiring information and viewpoints firsthand.* Suppose that you are concerned about the mistreatment of animals kept in zoos. You do not want to just read what others have to say on this issue. First, visit a zoo, taking notes on what you see. Second, before you go, plan to interview at least one person on the zoo staff, preferably a veterinarian who can explain the zoo's guidelines for animal care. Only after gathering and thinking about these *primary sources* do you want to add to your knowledge by reading articles and books—*secondary sources*. Many kinds of topics require the use of both primary and secondary sources. If you want to study violence in children's TV shows, for example, you should first spend some time watching specific shows and taking notes.

2. *Acquiring new knowledge.* Suppose you are interested in breast cancer research and treatment, but you do not know much about the choices of treatment and, in general, where we are with this medical problem. You will need to turn to sources first to learn about the topic. Begin with sources that will give you an overview, perhaps a historical perspective. Begin with sources that provide an overview of how knowledge and treatment have progressed in the last thirty years. Similarly, if your topic is the effects of Prohibition in the 1920s, you will need to read first for knowledge but also with an eye to ways to focus the topic and organize your paper.

3. *Understanding the issues.* Suppose you think that you know your views on illegal immigration, so you intend to read only to obtain some useful statistical information to support your argument. Should you scan sources quickly, looking for facts you can use? This approach may be too hasty. As explained in Chapter 3, good arguments are built on a knowledge of counterarguments. You are wise to study sources presenting a variety of attitudes on your issue so that you understand—and can refute—the arguments of others. *Remember: With controversial issues often the best argument is a conciliatory one that presents a middle ground and seeks to bring people together.*

When you use facts and opinions from sources, you are saying to readers that the facts are accurate and the ideas credible. If you do not evaluate your sources before using them, you risk losing your credibility as a writer. (Remember Aristotle's idea of *ethos,* how your character is judged.) Just because they are in print does not mean that a writer's "facts" are reliable or ideas worthwhile. Judging the usefulness and reliability of potential sources is an essential part of the research process.

GUIDELINES for Evaluating Sources

Today, with access to so much material online, the need to evaluate is even more crucial. Here are some strategies for evaluating sources, with special attention to online sources:

*   **Locate the author's credentials.** Periodicals often list their writers' degrees, current position, and other publications; books, similarly, contain an "about the author" section. If you do not see this information, check various biographical dictionaries (*Biography Index, Contemporary Authors*) or look for the author's website for information. For articles on the Web, look for the author's email address or a link to a home page. *Never use a Web source that does not identify the author or the organization responsible for the material. Critical question:* Is this author qualified to write on this topic? How do I know?

*   **Judge the credibility of the work.** For books, read how reviewers evaluated the book when it was first published. For articles, judge the respectability of the magazine or journal. Study the author's use of documentation as one measure of credibility. Scholarly works cite sources. Well-researched and reliable pieces in quality popular

magazines will also make clear the sources of any statistics used or the credentials of any authority who is quoted. One good rule: Never use undocumented statistical information. Another judge of credibility is the quality of writing. Do not use sources filled with grammatical and mechanical errors. For online sources, find out what institution hosts the site. If you have not heard of the company or organization, find out more about it. *Critical question:* Why should I believe information/ideas from this source?

- **Select only those sources that are at an appropriate level for your research.** Avoid works that are either too specialized or too elementary for college research. You may not understand the former (and thus could misrepresent them in your paper), and you gain nothing from the latter. *Critical question:* Will this source provide a sophisticated discussion for educated adults?

- **Understand the writer's purpose.** Consider the writer's intended audience. Be cautious using works designed to reinforce biases already shared by the intended audience. Is the work written to persuade rather than to inform and analyze? Examine the writing for emotionally charged language. For online sources, ask yourself why this person or institution decided to have a website or contribute to a newsgroup. *Critical question:* Can I trust the information from this source, given the apparent purpose of the work?

- **In general, choose current sources.** Some studies published years ago remain classics, but many older works are outdated. In scientific and technical fields, the "information revolution" has outdated some works published only five years ago. So look at publication dates (When was the website last updated?) and pass over outdated sources in favor of current studies. *Critical question:* Is this information still accurate?

PREPARING AN ANNOTATED BIBLIOGRAPHY

An annotated bibliography is a list of sources on a topic that includes a summary of each source. As part of your research process, you may be required to prepare either a partial or a complete annotated bibliography. Instructors include this assignment to keep you moving forward in your study of sources; it is a way of checking that you have found and read useful sources in good time to complete your project. Annotating each source also demands careful reading and analysis; it provides a check against skimming a source for some information without taking time to read and understand the context in which the information is presented and the author's position on the topic. You may find that your research paper is more focused and better written if you take the time to write a brief summary statement about each source you plan to use, even if an annotated bibliography is not required.

When preparing an annotated bibliography, list sources alphabetically and in correct MLA (or APA) format (see Chapter 14). Then, immediately after each citation, place a two-to-five-sentence summary of that source. Use hanging indentation, just as you would for your list of works cited at the end of your paper. *Warning: Do not confuse an annotated bibliography with a Works Cited list.* When you complete your research essay, list all sources used *without* the summaries.

A partial annotated bibliography follows, based on the sample student research essay in Chapter 13. Use this as your model.

Tell Us What You Really Are: The Debate over

Labeling Genetically Modified Food

Selected Annotated Bibliography

David Donaldson

Brackett, Robert E. "Bioengineered Foods." Statement of Robert E. Brackett to the Senate Committee on Agriculture, Nutrition, and Forestry. U.S. Food and Drug Administration. 14 June 2005. www.fda.gov./newsevents/testimony/ucm112927.htm. Robert E. Brackett's statement to the Senate Committee on Agriculture, Nutrition, and Forestry is a lengthy, detailed review of the FDA's responsibilities in determining food safety in general and its specific procedures for approving foods developed by hybridization and bioengineering. Brackett explains that GM foods could conceivably create one of three problems: cause new allergies, cause toxicity, or produce anti-nutrients (e.g., result in a decrease in Vitamin C). The FDA has the power to screen new foods for all three potential problems and to disapprove or require labeling, as appropriate. Brackett assures the Committee that the FDA works closely with companies developing GM foods and that they carefully test for all three potential problems to maintain a safe food supply for consumers.

MacDonald, Chris, and Melissa Whellams. "Corporate Decisions about Labeling Genetically Modified Foods." *Journal of Business Ethics*, vol. 75, no. 2, 2007, pp. 181–89. JSTOR. doi:10.1007/s10551-006-9245-8. MacDonald and Whellams examine the ethical obligation of companies to label genetically modified foods. The authors explain that there is no evidence that such products pose a health risk and that the FDA sees no reason to require special labeling. The authors explain that such labeling would impose a hardship on the companies preparing GM foods. Although the authors assert that they do not necessarily oppose required labeling, they conclude that food companies are not ethically obligated to voluntarily label GM foods.

U.S. Chamber of Commerce. "Precautionary Principle." U.S. Chamber of Commerce. 2011. www.uschamber.com/precautionary-principle. The U.S. Chamber of Commerce has posted on its website a statement regarding the "precautionary principle." The Chamber asserts that it has always supported regulatory decisions based on good science and sound risk assessment. The Chamber opposes the use of the "precautionary principle"—assume the worst and regulate risks that are uncertain or unknown—as a guide for U.S. regulatory decisions.

Writing the Researched Essay

You have agonized over your topic choice, searched for good sources, read and thought about your topic, seeking a way to put together a compelling argument—while not forgetting documentation. Whew! Don't rush now. Study this chapter's writing points and apply the guidelines to the writing of a convincing essay. Here are some general guidelines for studying sources.

GUIDELINES for Studying Sources

1. **Read first; take notes later.** First, do background reading, selecting the most general sources that provide an overview of the topic.

2. **Skim what appear to be your chief sources.** Learn what other writers on the topic consider the important facts, issues, and points of debate.

3. **Annotate photocopies**—do not highlight endlessly. Instead, carefully bracket material you want to use. Then write a note in the margin indicating how and where you might use that material.

4. **Either download online sources or take careful notes on the material.** Before preparing a note on content, be sure to copy all necessary information for documenting the material—including the date you accessed the website.

5. **Initially mark key passages in books with Post-its.** Write on the Post-it how and where you might use the material. Alternatively, photocopy book pages and then annotate them. Be sure to record for yourself the source of all copied pages.

6. **As you study and annotate, create labels for source materials that will help you organize your essay.** For example, if you are writing about the problem of campus sexual assault, you might label passages as: "facts showing there is a problem," "causes of the problem," and "possible solutions to the problem."

7. **Recognize that when you are working with many sources, note taking rather than annotating copies of sources is more helpful.** Notes, whether on cards or typed on separate sheets of paper, provide an efficient method for collecting and organizing lots of information.

AVOIDING PLAGIARISM

Documenting sources accurately and fully is required of all researchers. Proper documentation distinguishes between the work of others and your ideas, shows readers the breadth of your research, and strengthens your credibility. In Western culture, copyright laws support the ethic that ideas, new information, and wording belong to their author. To borrow these without acknowledgment is against the law and has led to many celebrated lawsuits. For students who plagiarize, the consequences range from an F on the paper to suspension from college. Be certain, then, that you know what the requirements for correct documentation are; accidental plagiarism is still plagiarism and will be punished.

NOTE: MLA documentation requires precise page references for all ideas, opinions, and information taken from sources—except for common knowledge. Author and page references provided in the text are supported by complete bibliographic citations on the Works Cited page.

In sum, you are required to document the following:

- Direct quotations from sources
- Paraphrased ideas and opinions from sources
- Summaries of ideas from sources
- Factual information, except common knowledge, from sources

Understand that putting an author's ideas in your own words in a paraphrase or summary does not eliminate the requirement of documentation. To illustrate, consider the following excerpt from Thomas R. Schueler's report *Controlling Urban Runoff* (Washington Metropolitan Water Resources Planning Board, 1987: pp. 3–4) and a student paragraph based on the report.

SOURCE

The aquatic ecosystems in urban headwater streams are particularly susceptible to the impacts of urbanization. . . . Dietemann (1975), Ragan and Dietemann (1976), Klein (1979) and WMCOG (1982) have all tracked trends in fish diversity and abundance over time in local urbanizing streams. Each of the studies has shown that fish communities become less diverse and are composed of more tolerant species after the surrounding watershed is developed. Sensitive fish species either disappear or occur very rarely. In most cases, the total number of fish in urbanizing streams may also decline.

Similar trends have been noted among aquatic insects which are the major food resource for fish. . . . Higher post-development sediment and trace metals can interfere in their efforts to gather food. Changes in water temperature, oxygen levels, and substrate composition can further reduce the species diversity and abundance of the aquatic insect community.

Studies have shown that fish communities become less diverse as the amount of runoff increases. Sensitive fish species either disappear or occur very rarely, and, in most cases, the total number of fish declines. Aquatic insects, a major source of food for fish, also decline because sediment and trace metals interfere with their food-gathering efforts. Increased water temperature and lower oxygen levels can further reduce the species diversity and abundance of the aquatic insect community.

The student's opening words establish a reader's expectation that the student has taken information from a source, as indeed the student has. But where is the documentation? The student's paraphrase is a good example of plagiarism: an unacknowledged paraphrase of borrowed information that even collapses into copying the source's exact wording in two places. For MLA style, the author's name and the precise page numbers are needed throughout the paragraph. Additionally, most of the first sentence and the final phrase must be put into the student's own words or placed within quotation marks. The following revised paragraph shows an appropriate acknowledgment of the source used.

In *Controlling Urban Runoff,* Thomas Schueler explains that studies have shown "that fish communities become less diverse as the amount of runoff increases" (3). Sensitive fish species either disappear or occur very rarely, and, in most cases, the total number of fish declines. Aquatic insects, a major source of food for fish, also decline because sediment and trace metals interfere with their food-gathering efforts. Increased water temperature and lower oxygen levels, Schueler concludes, "can further reduce the species diversity and abundance of the aquatic insect community" (4).

What Is Common Knowledge?

In general, common knowledge includes

- undisputed dates,
- well-known facts, and
- generally known facts, terms, and concepts in a field of study when you are writing in that field.

So, do not cite a source for the dates of the American Revolution. If you are writing a paper for a psychology class, do not cite your text when using terms such as *ego* or *sublimation*. However, you must cite a historian who analyzes the causes of England's loss to the Colonies or a psychologist who disputes Freud's ideas. *Opinions* about well-known facts must be documented. *Discussions* of debatable dates, terms, or concepts must be documented. When in doubt, defend your integrity and document.

USING SIGNAL PHRASES TO AVOID CONFUSION

If you are an honest student, you do not want to submit a paper that is plagiarized, even though that plagiarism was unintentional on your part. What leads to unintentional plagiarism?

- A researcher takes careless notes, neglecting to include precise page numbers on the notes, but uses the information anyway, without documentation.
- A researcher works in material from sources in such a way that, even with page references, readers cannot tell what has been taken from the sources.

Good note-taking strategies will keep you from the first pitfall. Avoiding the second problem means becoming skilled in ways to include source material in your writing while still making your indebtedness to sources absolutely clear to readers. The way to do this: Give the author's name in the essay. You can also include, when appropriate, the author's credentials ("According to Dr. Hays, a geologist with the Department of Interior, ..."). These *introductory tags* or *signal phrases* give readers a context for the borrowed material, as well as serving as part of the required documentation of sources. *Make sure that each signal phrase clarifies rather than distorts an author's relationship to his or her ideas and your relationship to the source.*

> **NOTE:** Putting a parenthetical page reference at the end of a paragraph is not sufficient if you have used the source throughout the paragraph. Use introductory tags or signal phrases to guide the reader through the material.

GUIDELINES for Appropriately Using Sources

Here are three guidelines to follow to avoid misrepresenting borrowed material:

- **Pay attention to verb choice in signal phrases.** When you vary such standard wording as "Smith says" or "Jones states," be careful that you do not select verbs that misrepresent "Smith's" or "Jones's" attitude toward his or her own work. Do not write "Jones wonders" when in fact Jones has strongly asserted her views. (See pp. 299–300 for a discussion of varying word choice in signal phrases.)

- **Pay attention to the location of signal phrases.** If you mention Jones after you have presented her views, be sure that your reader can tell precisely which ideas in the passage belong to Jones. If your entire paragraph is a paraphrase of Jones's work, you are plagiarizing to conclude with "This idea is presented by Jones." Which of the several ideas in your paragraph comes from Jones? Your reader will assume that only the last idea comes from Jones.

- **Paraphrase properly.** Be sure that paraphrases are truly *in your own words*. To use Smith's words and sentence style in your writing is to plagiarize.

EXERCISES: Acknowledging Sources to Avoid Plagiarism

1. The following paragraph (from Franklin E. Zimring's "Firearms, Violence and Public Policy" [*Scientific American,* Nov. 1991]) provides material for the examples that follow of adequate and inadequate acknowledgment of sources. After reading Zimring's paragraph, study the three examples with these questions in mind: (1) Which example represents adequate acknowledgment? (2) Which examples do not represent adequate acknowledgment? (3) In exactly what ways is each plagiarized paragraph flawed?

SOURCE

Although most citizens support such measures as owner screening, public opinion is sharply divided on laws that would restrict the ownership of handguns to persons with special needs. If the U.S. does not reduce handguns and current trends continue, it faces the prospect that the number of handguns in circulation will grow from 35 million to more than 50 million within 50 years. A national program limiting the availability of handguns would cost many billions of dollars and meet much resistance from citizens. These costs would likely be greatest in the early years of the program. The benefits of supply reduction would emerge slowly because efforts to diminish the availability of handguns would probably have a cumulative impact over time. (page 54)

STUDENT PARAGRAPH 1

One approach to the problem of handgun violence in America is to severely limit handgun ownership. If we don't restrict ownership and start the costly task of removing handguns from our society, we may end up with around 50 million handguns in the country by 2040. The benefits will not be apparent right away but will eventually appear. This idea is emphasized by Franklin Zimring (54).

STUDENT PARAGRAPH 2

One approach to the problem of handgun violence in America is to restrict the ownership of handguns except in special circumstances. If we do not begin to reduce the number of handguns in this country, the number will grow from 35 million to more than 50 million within fifty years. We can agree with Franklin Zimring that a program limiting handguns will cost billions and meet resistance from citizens (54).

STUDENT PARAGRAPH 3

According to law professor Franklin Zimring, the United States needs to severely limit handgun ownership or face the possibility of seeing handgun ownership increase "from 35 million to more than 50 million within 50 years" (54). Zimring points out that Americans disagree significantly on restricting handguns and that enforcing such laws would be very expensive. He concludes that the benefits would not be seen immediately but that the restrictions "would probably have a cumulative impact over time" (54). Although Zimring paints a gloomy picture of high costs and little immediate relief from gun violence, he also presents the shocking possibility of 50 million guns by the year 2040. Can our society survive so much firepower?

Clearly, only the third student paragraph demonstrates adequate acknowledgment of the writer's indebtedness to Zimring. Notice that the placement of the last parenthetical page reference acts as a visual closure to the student's borrowing. She then turns to her response to Zimring and her own views on the problem of handguns.

2. Read the following passage and then the three plagiarized uses of it. Explain why each one is plagiarized and how it can be corrected.

Original Text: Stanley Karnow, *Vietnam, A History. The First Complete Account of Vietnam at War*. Viking Books, 1983, p. 319.

Lyndon Baines Johnson, a consummate politician, was a kaleidoscopic personality, forever changing as he sought to dominate or persuade or placate or frighten his friends and foes. A gigantic figure whose extravagant moods matched his size, he could be cruel and kind, violent and gentle, petty, generous, cunning, naïve, crude, candid, and frankly dishonest. He commanded the blind loyalty of his aides, some of whom worshipped him, and he sparked bitter derision or fierce hatred that he never quite fathomed.

   a. LBJ's vibrant and changing personality filled some people with adoration and others with bitter derision that he never quite fathomed (Karnow 319).
   b. LBJ, a supreme politician, had a personality like a kaleidoscope, continually changing as he tried to control, sway, appease, or intimidate his enemies and supporters (Karnow 319).
   c. Often, figures who have had great impact on America's history have been dynamic people with powerful personalities and vibrant physical presence. LBJ, for example, was a huge figure who polarized those who worked for and with him. "He commanded the blind loyalty of his aides, some of whom worshipped him, and he sparked bitter derision or fierce hatred" from many others (Karnow 319).

3. Read the following passage and then the four sample uses of it. Judge each of the uses for how well it avoids plagiarism and if it is documented correctly. Make corrections as needed.

Original Text: Stanley Karnow, *Vietnam, A History. The First Complete Account of Vietnam at War*. Viking Books, 1983, p. 327.

On July 27, 1965, in a last-ditch attempt to change Johnson's mind, [Senators] Mansfield and Russell were to press him again to "concentrate on finding a way out" of Vietnam—"a place where we ought not be," and where "the situation is rapidly going out of control." But the next day,

Johnson announced his decision to add forty-four American combat battalions to the relatively small U.S. contingents already there. He had not been deaf to Mansfield's pleas, nor had he simply swallowed the Pentagon's plans. He had waffled and agonized during his nineteen months in the White House, but eventually this was his final judgment. As he would later explain: "There are many, many people who can recommend and advise, and a few of them consent. But there is only one who has been chosen by the American people to decide."

a. Karnow writes that senators Mansfield and Russell continued to try to convince President Johnson to avoid further involvement in Vietnam, "a place where we ought not to be," they felt. (327).

b. Though Johnson received advice from many, in particular senators Mansfield and Russell, he believed the weight of the decision to become further engaged in Vietnam was solely his as the one " 'chosen by the American people to decide' " (Karnow 327).

c. On July 28, 1965, Johnson announced his decision to add forty-four battalions to the troops already in Vietnam, ending his waffling and agonizing of the past nineteen months of his presidency. (Karnow 357)

d. Karnow explains that LBJ took his responsibility to make decisions about Vietnam seriously (327). Although Johnson knew that many would offer suggestions, only he had " 'been chosen by the American people to decide' " (Karnow 327).

ORGANIZING THE PAPER

Armed with an understanding of writing strategies to avoid plagiarism, you are now almost ready to draft your essay. Follow these steps to get organized to write:

1. *Arrange notes (or your annotated sources) by the labels you have used and read them through.* You may discover that some notes or marked sections of sources now seem irrelevant. Set them aside, but do not throw them away yet. Some further reading and note taking may also be necessary to fill in gaps that have become apparent.

2. *Reexamine your tentative claim or research proposal.* As a result of reading and reflection, do you need to alter or modify your claim in any way? Or if you began with a research question, what now is your answer to the question? For example, is TV violence harmful to children?

3. *Decide on the claim that will direct your writing.* To write a unified essay with a "reason for being," you need a claim that meets these criteria:

   - It is a complete sentence, not a topic or statement of purpose.

     TOPIC: Sexual assault on college campuses.

     CLAIM: There are steps that both students and administrators can take to reduce incidents of campus sexual assault.

- It is limited and focused.

UNFOCUSED:	Prohibition affected the 1920s in many ways.
FOCUSED:	Prohibition was more acceptable to rural than urban areas because of differences in values, social patterns, cultural backgrounds, and the economic result of prohibiting liquor sales.

- It establishes a new or interesting approach to the topic that makes your research meaningful.

NOT INVENTIVE:	A regional shopping mall should not be built next to the Manassas Battlefield.
INVENTIVE:	Putting aside an appeal to our national heritage, one can say, simply, that there is no economic justification for the building of a shopping mall next to the Manassas Battlefield.

4. *Write down the organization that emerges from your labels and grouping of sources, and compare this with your preliminary plan.* If there are differences, justify those changes to yourself. Consider: Does the new, fuller plan provide a complete and logical development of your claim? And, will it guide you to an essay that meets your research assignment?

DRAFTING THE ESSAY

Plan Your Time

How much time will you need to draft your essay? Working with sources and taking care with documentation make research paper writing more time consuming than writing an undocumented essay. You also need to allow time between completing the draft and revising. Do not try to draft, revise, and proof an essay all in one day.

Handle In-Text Documentation as You Draft

The Modern Language Association (MLA) recommends that writers prepare their Works Cited page(s) *before* drafting their essay. With this important information prepared correctly and next to you as you draft, you will be less likely to make errors in documentation that will result in a plagiarized essay. Although you may believe that stopping to include parenthetical documentation as you write will cramp your writing, you really cannot try to insert the documentation after completing the writing. The risk of failing to document accurately is too great to chance. Parenthetical documentation is brief; listen to the experts and take the time to include it as you compose.

You saw some models of documentation in Chapter 12. In Chapter 14, you have complete guidelines and models for in-text (parenthetical) documentation and then many models for the complete citations of sources. Study the information in Chapter 14 and then draft your Works Cited page(s) as part of your preparation for writing.

Choose an Appropriate Writing Style

Specific suggestions for composing the parts of your paper follow, but first here are some general guidelines for research essay style.

Use the Proper Person

Research papers are written primarily in the third person (*she, he, it, they*) to create objectivity and to direct attention to the content of the paper. The question is over the appropriateness of the first person (*I, we*). Although you want to avoid writing "as *you* can see," do not try to avoid the use of *I* if you need to distinguish your position from the views of others. It is better to write "I" than "it is the opinion of this writer" or "the researcher learned" or "this project analyzed." On the other hand, avoid qualifiers such as "I think." Just state your ideas.

Use the Proper Tense

When you are writing about people, ideas, or events of the past, the appropriate tense is the past tense. When writing about current times, the appropriate tense is the present. Both tenses may occur in the same paragraph, as the following paragraph illustrates:

> Fifteen years ago "personal" computers were all but unheard of. Computers were regarded as unknowable, building-sized mechanized monsters that required a precise 68 degree air-conditioned environment and eggheaded technicians with thick glasses and white lab coats scurrying about to keep the temperamental and fragile egos of the electronic brains mollified. Today's generation of computers is accessible, affordable, commonplace, and much less mysterious. The astonishing progress made in computer technology in the last few years has made computers practical, attainable, and indispensable. Personal computers are here to stay.

In the above example, when the student moves from computers in the past to computers in the present, he shifts tenses accurately.

When writing about sources, the convention is to use the present tense *even* for works or authors from the past. The idea is that the source, or the author, *continues* to make the point or use the technique into the present—that is, every time there is a reader. So, write "Lincoln selects the biblical expression 'Fourscore and seven years ago' " and "King echoes Lincoln when he writes 'five score years ago.' "

Avoid Excessive Quoting

Many students use too many direct quotations. Plan to use your own words most of the time for these good reasons:

- Constantly shifting between your words and the language of your sources (not to mention all those quotation marks) makes reading your essay difficult.
- This is your paper and should sound like you.
- When you take a passage out of its larger context, you face the danger of misrepresenting the writer's views.
- When you quote endlessly, readers may begin to think either that you are lazy or that you don't really understand the issues well enough to put them in your own words. You don't want to present either image to your readers.

- You do not prove any point by quoting another person's opinion. All you indicate is that there is someone else who shares your views. Even if that person is an expert on the topic, your quoted material still represents the view of only one person. You support a claim with reasons and evidence, both of which can usually be presented in your own words.

When you must quote, keep the quotations brief, weave them carefully into your own sentences, and be sure to identify the author in a signal phrase. Study the guidelines for handling quotations on pages 23–26 for models of correct form and style.

Write Effective Beginnings

The best introduction is one that presents your subject in an interesting way to gain the reader's attention, states your claim, and gives the reader an indication of the scope and limits of your paper. In a short research essay, you may be able to combine an attention-getter, a statement of subject, and a claim in one paragraph. More typically, especially in longer papers, the introduction will expand to two or three paragraphs. In the physical and social sciences, the claim may be withheld until the conclusion, but the opening introduces the subject and presents the researcher's hypothesis, often posed as a question. Since students sometimes have trouble with research paper introductions in spite of knowing these general guidelines, several specific approaches are illustrated here:

1. In the opening to her study of car advertisements, a student, relating her topic to what readers know, reminds readers of the culture's concern with image:

   Many Americans are highly image conscious. Because the "right" look is essential to a prosperous life, no detail is too small to overlook. Clichés about first impressions remind us that "you never get a second chance to make a first impression," so we obsessively watch our weight, firm our muscles, sculpt our hair, select our friends, find the perfect houses, and buy our automobiles. Realizing the importance of image, companies compete to make the "right" products, that is, those that will complete the "right" image. Then advertisers direct specific products to targeted groups of consumers. Although targeting may be labeled as stereotyping, it has been an effective strategy in advertising.

2. Terms and concepts central to your project need defining early in your paper, especially if they are challenged or qualified in some way by your study. This opening paragraph demonstrates an effective use of definition:

   William Faulkner braids a universal theme, the theme of initiation, into the fiber of his novel *Intruder in the Dust.* From ancient times to the present, a prominent focus of literature, of life, has been rites of passage, particularly those of childhood to adulthood. Joseph

Campbell defines rites of passage as "distinguished by formal, and usually very severe, exercises of severance." A "candidate" for initiation into adult society, Campbell explains, experiences a shearing away of the "attitudes, attachments and life patterns" of childhood (9). This severe, painful stripping away of the child and installation of the adult is presented somewhat differently in several works by American writers.

3. Begin with a thought-provoking question. A student, arguing that the media both reflect and shape reality, started with these questions:

    Do the media just reflect reality, or do they also shape our perceptions of reality? The answer to this seemingly "chicken-and-egg" question is: They do both.

4. Beginning with important, perhaps startling, facts, evidence, or statistics is an effective way to introduce a topic, provided the details are relevant to the topic. Observe the following example:

    Teenagers are working again, but not on their homework. Over 40 percent of teenagers have jobs by the time they are juniors (Samuelson A22). And their jobs do not support academic learning since almost two-thirds of teenagers are employed in sales and service jobs that entail mostly carrying, cleaning, and wrapping (Greenberger and Steinberg 62–67), not reading, writing, and computing. Unfortunately, the negative effect on learning is not offset by improved opportunities for future careers.

Avoid Ineffective Openings

Follow these rules for avoiding openings that most readers find ineffective or annoying.

1. *Do not restate the title* or write as if the title were the first sentence in paragraph 1. It is a convention of writing to have the first paragraph stand independent of the title.
2. *Do not begin with "clever" visuals* such as artwork or fancy lettering.
3. *Do not begin with humor* unless it is part of your topic.
4. *Do not begin with a question that is just a gimmick, or one that a reader may answer in a way you do not intend.* Asking "What are the advantages of solar energy?" may lead a reader to answer "None that I can think of." A straightforward research question ("Is *Death of a Salesman* a tragedy?") is appropriate.
5. *Do not open with an unnecessary definition quoted from a dictionary.* "According to Webster, solar energy means …" is a tired, overworked beginning that does not engage readers.

6. *Do not start with a purpose statement:* "This paper will examine …" Although a statement of purpose is a necessary part of a report of empirical research, a report still needs an interesting introduction.

Compose Solid, Unified Paragraphs

As you compose the body of your paper, keep in mind that you want to (1) maintain unity and coherence, (2) guide readers clearly through source material, and (3) synthesize source material and your own ideas. Do not settle for paragraphs in which facts from notes are just loosely run together. Review the following discussion and study the examples to see how to craft effective body paragraphs.

Provide Unity and Coherence

You achieve paragraph unity when every sentence in a paragraph relates to and develops the paragraph's main idea. Unity, however, does not automatically produce coherence; that takes attention to wording. Coherence is achieved when readers can follow the connection between one sentence and another and between each sentence and the main idea. Strategies for achieving coherence include repetition of key words, the use of pronouns that clearly refer to those key words, and the use of transition and connecting words. Observe these strategies at work in the following paragraph:

> Perhaps the most important differences between the initiations of Robin and Biff and that experienced by Chick are the facts that Chick's epiphany does not come all at once and it does not devastate him. Chick learns about adulthood —and enters adulthood —piecemeal and with support. His first eye-opening experience occurs as he tries to pay Lucas for dinner and is rebuffed (15–16). Chick learns, after trying again to buy a clear conscience, the impropriety and affront of his actions (24). Lucas teaches Chick how he should resolve his dilemma by setting him "free" (26–27). Later, Chick feels outrage at the adults crowding into the town, presumably to see a lynching, then disgrace and shame as they eventually flee (196–97, 210).

Coherence is needed not only within paragraphs but between paragraphs as well. You need to guide readers through your paper, connecting paragraphs and showing relationships by the use of transitions. The following opening sentences of four paragraphs from a paper on solutions to sexual assault on the college campus illustrate smooth transitions:

> ¶ 3 Specialists have provided a number of reasons why people commit sexual assault.

> ¶ 4 Some of the causes of sexual assault on the college campus originate with the colleges themselves and with how they handle the problem.

¶ 5 Just as there are a number of causes for campus sexual assaults, there

are a number of ways to help solve the problem of these sexual assaults.

¶ 6 If these seem like commonsense solutions, why, then, is it so difficult

to significantly reduce the number of sexual assaults on campus?

Without awkwardly writing "Here are some of the causes" and "Here are some of the solutions," the student guides her readers through a discussion of causes for and solutions to the problem of campus sexual assault.

Guide Readers through Source Material

To understand the importance of guiding readers through source material, consider first the following paragraph from a paper on the British coal strike in the 1970s:

The social status of the coal miners was far from good. The country

blamed them for the dimmed lights and the three-day workweek. They

had been placed in the position of social outcasts and were beginning

to "consider themselves another country." Some businesses and shops

had even gone so far as to refuse service to coal miners (Jones 32).

Who has learned that the coal miners felt ostracized or that the country blamed them? As readers we cannot begin to judge the validity of these assertions without some context provided by the writer. Most readers are put off by an unattached direct quotation or some startling observation that is documented correctly but given no context within the paper. Using signal phrases that identify the author of the source and, when useful, the author's credentials helps guide readers through the source material. The following revision of the paragraph above provides not only context but also sentence variety:

The social acceptance of coal miners, according to Peter Jones, British

correspondent for *Newsweek,* was far from good. From interviews both in

London shops and in pubs near Birmingham, Jones concluded that Brit-

ishers blamed the miners for the dimmed lights and three-day workweek.

Several striking miners, in a pub on the outskirts of Birmingham, asserted

that some of their friends had been denied service by shopkeepers and

that they "consider[ed] themselves another country" (32).

Select Appropriate Signal Phrases

When you use signal phrases, try to vary both the words you use and their place in the sentence. Look, for example, at the first sentence in the sample paragraph above. The signal phrase is placed in the middle of the sentence and is set off by commas. The sentence could have been written two other ways:

The social acceptance of coal miners was far from good, according to

Peter Jones, British correspondent for *Newsweek.*

OR

According to Peter Jones, British correspondent for *Newsweek*, the
social acceptance of coal miners was far from good.

Whenever you provide a name and perhaps credentials for your source, you have these
three sentence patterns to choose from. Make a point to use all three options in your
paper. Word choice can be varied as well. Instead of writing "Peter Jones says" throughout your paper, consider some of these verb choices:

Jones *asserts*	Jones *contends*	Jones *attests to*
Jones *states*	Jones *thinks*	Jones *points out*
Jones *concludes*	Jones *stresses*	Jones *believes*
Jones *presents*	Jones *emphasizes*	Jones *agrees with*
Jones *argues*	Jones *confirms*	Jones *speculates*

> **NOTE:** Not all the words in this list are synonyms; you cannot substitute
> *confirms* for *believes*. First, select the verb that most accurately conveys the
> writer's relationship to his or her material. Then, when appropriate, vary word
> choice as well as sentence structure.

Readers need to be told how to respond to the sources used. They need to know
which sources you accept as reliable and which you disagree with, and they need you to
distinguish clearly between fact and opinion. Ideas and opinions from sources need
signal phrases and then some discussion from you.

Synthesize Source Material and Your Own Ideas

A smooth synthesis of source material is aided by signal phrases and parenthetical
documentation because they mark the beginning and ending of material taken from a
source. But a complete synthesis requires something more: your ideas about the source
and the topic. To illustrate, consider the problems in another paragraph from the British
coal strike paper:

Some critics believed that there was enough coal in Britain to
maintain enough power to keep industry at a near-normal level for
thirty-five weeks (Jones 30). Prime Minister Heath, on the other hand,
had placed the country's usable coal supply at 15.5 million tons
(Jones 30). He stated that this would have fallen to a critical 7 million tons
within a month had he not declared a three-day workweek (Jones 31).

This paragraph is a good example of random details strung together for no apparent
purpose. How much coal did exist? Whose figures were right? And what purpose do
these figures serve in the paper's development? Note that the entire paragraph is

developed with material from one source. Do sources other than Jones offer a different perspective? This paragraph is weak for several reasons: (1) It lacks a controlling idea (topic sentence) to give it purpose and direction; (2) it relies for development entirely on one source; (3) it lacks any discussion or analysis by the writer.

By contrast, the following paragraph demonstrates a successful synthesis:

> Of course, the iridium could have come from other extraterrestrial sources besides an asteroid. One theory, put forward by Dale Russell, is that the iridium was produced outside the solar system by an exploding star (500). Such an explosion, Russell states, could have blown the iridium either off the surface of the moon or directly from the star itself (500–01), while also producing a deadly blast of heat and gamma rays (Krishtalka 19). This theory seems to explain the traces of iridium in the mass extinction, but it does not explain why smaller mammals, crocodiles, and birds survived (Wilford 220). So the supernova theory took a backseat to the other extraterrestrial theories: those of asteroids and comets colliding with the Earth. The authors of the book *The Great Extinction,* Michael Allaby and James Lovelock, subtitled their work *The Solution to ... the Disappearance of the Dinosaurs.* Their theory: an asteroid or comet collided with Earth around sixty-five million years ago, killing billions of organisms, and thus altering the course of evolution (157). The fact that the theory of collision with a cosmic body warrants a book calls for some thought: Is the asteroid or comet theory merely sensationalism, or is it rooted in fact? Paleontologist Leonard Krishtalka declares that few paleontologists have accepted the asteroid theory, himself calling "some catastrophic theories ... small ideas injected with growth hormone" (22). However, other scientists, such as Allaby and Lovelock, see the cosmic catastrophic theory as a solid one based on more than guesswork (10–11).

This paragraph's synthesis is accomplished by several strategies: (1) The paragraph has a controlling idea; (2) the paragraph combines information from several sources; (3) the information is presented in a blend of paraphrase and short quotations; (4) information from the different sources is clearly indicated to readers; and (5) the student explains and discusses the information.

You might also observe the different lengths of the two sample paragraphs just presented. Although the second paragraph is long, it is not unwieldy because it achieves unity and coherence. By contrast, body paragraphs of only three sentences are probably in trouble.

Write Effective Conclusions

Sometimes ending a paper seems even more difficult than beginning one. You know you are not supposed to just stop, but every ending that comes to mind sounds more corny than clever. If you have trouble, try one of these types of endings:

1. Do not just repeat your claim exactly as it was stated in paragraph 1, but expand on the original wording and emphasize the claim's significance. Here is the conclusion of the solar energy paper:

   > The idea of using solar energy is not as far-fetched as it seemed years ago. With the continued support of government plus the enthusiasm of research groups, environmentalists, and private industry, solar energy may become a household word quite soon. With the increasing cost of fossil fuel, the time could not be better for exploring this use of the sun.

2. End with a quotation that effectively summarizes and drives home the point of your paper. Researchers are not always lucky enough to find the ideal quotation for ending a paper. If you find a good one, use it. Better yet, present the quotation and then add your comment in a sentence or two. The conclusion to a paper on the dilemma of defective newborns is a good example:

   > Dr. Joseph Fletcher is correct when he says that "every advance in medical capabilities is an increase in our moral responsibility" (48). In a world of many gray areas, one point is clear. From an ethical point of view, medicine is a victim of its own success.

3. If you have researched an issue or problem, emphasize your proposed solutions in the concluding paragraph. The student opposing a mall adjacent to the Manassas Battlefield concluded with several solutions:

   > Whether the proposed mall will be built is clearly in doubt at the moment. What are the solutions to this controversy? One approach is, of course, not to build the mall at all. To accomplish this solution, now, with the re-zoning having been approved, probably requires an act of Congress to buy the land and make it part of the national park. Another solution, one that would please the county and the developer and satisfy citizens objecting to traffic problems, is to build the needed roads before the mall is completed. A third approach is to allow the office park of the original plan to be built, but not the mall. The local preservationists had agreed to this original development proposal, but now that the issue has received national attention, they

may no longer be willing to compromise. Whatever the future of the William Center, the present plan for a new regional mall is not acceptable.

Avoid Ineffective Conclusions

Follow these rules to avoid conclusions that most readers consider ineffective and annoying.

1. *Do not introduce a new idea.* If the point belongs in your paper, you should have introduced it earlier.
2. *Do not just stop or trail off,* even if you feel as though you have run out of steam. A simple, clear restatement of the claim is better than no conclusion.
3. *Do not tell your reader what you have accomplished:* "In this paper I have explained the advantages of solar energy by examining the costs …" If you have written well, your reader knows what you have accomplished.
4. *Do not offer apologies or expressions of hope.* "Although I wasn't able to find as much on this topic as I wanted, I have tried to explain the advantages of solar energy, and I hope that you will now understand why we need to use it more" is a disastrous ending.

Choose an Effective Title

Give some thought to your paper's title since that is what your reader sees first and what your work will be known by. A good title provides information and creates interest. Make your title informative by making it specific. If you can create interest through clever wording, so much the better. But do not confuse "cutesiness" with clever wording. Review the following examples of acceptable and unacceptable titles:

VAGUE:	A Perennial Issue Unsolved
	(There are many; which one is this paper about?)
BETTER:	The Perennial Issue of Press Freedom versus Press Responsibility
TOO BROAD:	Earthquakes
	(What about earthquakes? This title is not informative.)
BETTER:	The Need for Earthquake Prediction
TOO BROAD:	*The Scarlet Letter*
	(Never use just the title of the work under discussion; you can use the work's title as a part of a longer title of your own.)
BETTER:	Color Symbolism in *The Scarlet Letter*
CUTESY:	Babes in Trouble
	(The slang "Babes" makes this title seem insensitive rather than clever.)
BETTER:	The Dilemma of Defective Newborns

REVISING THE PAPER: A CHECKLIST

After completing a first draft, catch your breath and then gear up for the next step in the writing process: revision. Revision actually involves three separate steps: *rewriting*—adding or deleting text, or moving parts of the draft around; *editing*—a rereading to correct errors from misspellings to incorrect documentation format; and then *proofreading* the typed copy. If you treat these as separate steps, you will do a more complete job of revision—and get a better grade on your paper!

Rewriting

Read your draft through and make changes as a result of answering the following questions:

Purpose and Audience

☐ Does my draft meet all of the assignment requirements and my purpose? (Double-check your writing prompt.)

☐ Are terms defined and concepts explained appropriately for my audience?

Content

☐ Do I have a clearly stated thesis—the claim of my argument?

☐ Have I presented sufficient evidence to support my claim?

☐ Are there any irrelevant sections that should be deleted?

Structure

☐ Have I ordered my paragraphs to develop my topic logically?

☐ Does the content of each paragraph help develop my claim?

☐ Is everything in each paragraph on the same subtopic to create paragraph unity?

☐ Do body paragraphs have a balance of information and analysis, of source material and my own ideas?

☐ Are there any paragraphs that should be combined? Are there any very long paragraphs that should be divided? (Check for unity.)

Editing

Make revisions in response to your application of the rewriting questions. When you are satisfied with your basic content and structure, it is time to edit. This time, pay close attention to sentences, words, and documentation format. Use the following questions to guide editing.

Document Design

☐ Have I followed MLA requirements for a 1-inch margin and 12 point Times New Roman or similar professional font?

☐ Have I double-spaced throughout, including the Works Cited pages?

Coherence

☐ Have I used connecting words and have I repeated key terms to produce paragraph coherence?

☐ Have I used transitions to show connections between paragraphs?

Sources

☐ Have I paraphrased instead of quoted whenever possible?

☐ Have I used signal phrases to create a context for source material?

☐ Have I documented all borrowed material, whether quoted or paraphrased?

☐ Are parenthetical references properly placed after borrowed material?

Style

☐ Have I varied sentence length and structure?

☐ Have I avoided long quotations?

☐ Do I have correct form for quotations? For titles?

☐ Is my language specific and descriptive?

☐ Have I avoided inappropriate shifts in tense or person?

☐ Have I removed any wordiness, deadwood, trite expressions, or clichés?

☐ Have I used specialized terms correctly?

☐ Have I avoided contractions as too informal for most research papers?

☐ Have I maintained an appropriate style and tone for academic work?

Proofreading

When your edits are complete, check that your paper format matches the guidelines described and illustrated in the research paper below. Print a copy of your paper for final proofreading and make corrections as needed. Correct all errors and keep a file of your paper before submitting a copy to your instructor.

THE COMPLETED PAPER

Your research paper should be double-spaced throughout (including the Works Cited page) with 1-inch margins on all sides. Your project will contain the following parts, in this order:

1. *A title page,* (if needed) with your title, your name, your instructor's name, the course name or number, and the date, neatly centered, if an outline follows. If there is no outline, place this information at the top left of the first page.

2. *An outline,* or statement of purpose, if required.

3. *The body or text of your paper.* Number all pages consecutively, including pages of works cited, using arabic numerals. Place numbers in the upper right-hand corner of each page. Include your last name before each page number.

4. *A list of works cited,* beginning on a separate page, follows the text. Title the first page "Works Cited." (Do not use the title "Bibliography.")

SAMPLE STUDENT ESSAY IN MLA STYLE

The following paper illustrates an argumentative essay using sources documented in MLA style.

Donaldson 1

Provide last name with page number at top right of each page.

Use heading on top left when a separate title page is not used.

Center title.

Indent paragraphs 5 spaces.

Double-space throughout.

Clear opening leads to student's thesis.

Key term defined.

David Donaldson

Professor Princiotto-Gorrell/Professor Stevens

English 203U—Research Process

7 July 2011

Tell Us What You Really Are: The Debate over

Labeling Genetically Modified Food

  The decision to eat—or not to eat—genetically modified (GM) food is a relatively new dilemma for consumers. People have been going to the grocery store for years, and up until the mid-1990s there was little question as to what they were buying. Consumers knew that when they picked up a tomato, that product was in fact a tomato, not a tomato that had been spliced, or merged, with the genes of some other organism in an attempt to get it to behave like an entirely different fruit. There were most definitely food additives, preservatives, and other questionable ingredients up until then, but before 1994, a tomato was still a tomato. Food additives, preservatives, potentially allergenic ingredients, and possibly toxic ingredients must be labeled on each product. Until GM food is proven to be safe it is essential that the federal government also require labeling to denote the presence of genetically modified organisms (GMOs). Safety is not the only factor in the GM food debate. Religious and cultural concerns, as well as the consumer's freedom of choice, must be considered when deciding whether to label GM foods.

  The genetic modification of food is defined by MacDonald and Whellams as "any change to the heritable traits of an organism achieved by intentional manipulation" (181). Or, more specifically, defined by Sarah Kirby as "the process of removing individual genes from one organism and transplanting them into another organism," it is the basis of contemporary bioengineering (352). Although there are

Donaldson 2

scientists and government officials who want to equate genetic modification with genetic hybridization, the definitions given for genetic modification do not match the definition of genetic hybridization.

It is true that plant and animal hybridization has been going on for a long time. That is how many of the flora and fauna here today were conceived. They did not just show up as they are today; rather, over time they evolved into what they are now due to progressive variations in their genes. As explained by Gudorf and Huchingson, scientists used selective breeding to achieve a desired trait, or to suppress a trait deemed undesirable (233). Kirby expands on Gudorf and Huchingson's idea by adding that selective breeding was more natural since "it was restricted to two organisms that are able to breed together" (352). In "A Defense of the U.S. Position on Labeling Genetically Modified Organisms," Sally Kirsch adds that the United States Food and Drug Administration (FDA) even cites the longevity of selective breeding to justify their stance that nothing is wrong or unsafe about GM food (25).

Bioengineering has been seen as the answer to many of the environmental issues related to climate change, to help feed growing populations in developing countries. Scientists have created "drought resistant corn and soybeans," rice with increased nutrients, and "pest resistant plants" (Kirsch 21). However, for more cosmetic reasons, they have also created the FLAVR SAVR™ tomato. This tomato would eventually become the first GM food available to consumers. The *Gale Encyclopedia of Science* article "Plant Breeding" explains that it was not until 1992 that "a tomato with delayed ripening became the first genetically modified (GM) commercial food crop" (3375). Two years

> Paragraph developed using paraphrase and direct quotations from several sources.

Donaldson 3

later, the company Calgene received approval from the FDA to sell their FLAVR SAVR™ tomatoes (Martineau 189). Kirsch notes that there was a lukewarm public greeting for Calgene's tomato, and the underwhelming sales further emphasized that the general public was apprehensive about GM food (21). However, in their article "'Does Contain' vs. 'Does Not Contain': Does it Matter Which GMO Label Is Used?" Crespi and Marette argue that "Americans are much more accepting of GMOs than the rest of the world" (328).

This is no longer a process simply by which plants are being spliced with plant genes and animals are being spliced with animal genes. Today, bioengineers can create a plant that has been spliced with animal genes (Kirby 357). The health and safety results of the GM process are still relatively unknown as this technology is still new. The uncertainty of this process is fueling the public outcry for GMO labeling in the United States. Anne MacKenzie builds on Kirby's point, arguing that because consumers have become more knowledgeable about food and health, more concerned about the safety of the food supply, have developed a greater desire to know about how their food is made, and have mounted a growing distrust of biotech companies and the government, they want more information about what is going into their food (52).

The most noted possible health hazard linked to GM foods is the potential for new or heightened food allergies. MacKenzie, Gudorf and Huchingson, and Kirby all mention new food allergies as one of the more obvious reasons to require the mandatory labeling of GM food. MacKenzie states: "Allergenicity is an important consideration for foods derived through biotechnology because of the possibility that a new protein introduced into a food could be an allergen" (51). She adds that when a food such as soy, a common allergen, is used in the

Student establishes difference between hybridization and genetic modification.

Here and below student examines possible problems with GM foods.

Donaldson 4

genetic modification process, "life-threatening" results are more likely to occur (51). Gudorf and Huchingson suggest that GM food could be held responsible for the increase in the number of people who have developed food-related allergies in the last decade (233). They also point out that, for example, people do not know specifically which peanut gene may spark their allergy (233). It could be the gene for color, the gene for oil production, or the gene that makes peanuts viable underground that contains the protein that sets off their allergy. If a scientist wants to make a strawberry that grows underground, and inserts that gene from the peanut into a strawberry's DNA, the same individuals who are allergic to peanuts could now become allergic to that particular strawberry (Gudorf and Huchingson 233).

Kirby acknowledges that GM foods may "set off" allergies, but she adds that genetic modification could also "produce dangerous toxins, increase cancer risks, produce antibiotic-resistant pathogens, and damage food quality" (359). Specifically related to allergies, Kirby explains that "people have never before been exposed to several of the foreign proteins currently being genetically spliced into foods" (360). Conversely, Robert Brackett, Director of the Center for Food Safety and Applied Nutrition, testified before the FDA that if the genetic modification process were to merge one organism with an organism that is considered a common food allergen, soy, milk, egg, etc., then that product would indeed be labeled as containing a common food allergen as is required by law (FDA). Otherwise, Brackett says, "GM food is safe and no different than its conventionally grown counterpart," which echoes the FDA spokesman quoted by MacDonald and Whellams (FDA).

Aside from health concerns, there are also religious and cultural motives that should be considered when deciding whether to label GM

Donaldson 5

food. Theologically speaking, Christianity does not necessarily reject GM food. In "Some Christian Reflections on GM Food," Donald Bruce suggests that the concern within Christianity is more a moral obligation to God's creation rather than a dietary issue (119). However, multiple interpretations are present. Genesis 1: 26–28 basically states that "Christian thinking has generally seen intervention in the natural world as ordained by God in the creation of ordinances that grant humans dominion over all the rest of creation" (Bruce 119). Conversely, there are also Christians who think that GM food is the result of humans "playing God in wrongly changing what God has created" (Bruce 121). For Christians who believe that genetically modifying food is wrong, mandatory labeling of GM food would guide them in their food choices.

For those of the Muslim or Jewish faith, GM food presents dietary concerns as well as potential moral objections. Ebrahim Moosa cites the splicing of animal genes into plants as one of the biggest worries Muslims face from GM food (135). He says that "a tomato containing a gene harvested from a flounder may not generate repugnance in an observant Muslim, since fish is permissible for adherents of this tradition, but a potato with a pig gene may well trigger visceral repugnance" (135). This is the same reason cited by Kirby (357). To emphasize his point, Moosa tells a story of Muhammad when he lived in Medina. In the story, Muhammad comes across farmers splicing different species of date-palm seedlings to increase their crop yields. Muhammad asks why they did it that way, and they reply: "That was the way they had always done it." The prophet then replies: "Well, perhaps, it would be better if you did not" (138). Kirby suggests that animal-to-plant genetic splicing is also the reason for those of the Jewish faith, or any vegetarian or vegan, to be concerned about the absence of

Donaldson 6

mandatory GM food labeling (357). Peter Sand concurs, stating that
providing consumers with information "irrespective of health concerns,"
such as labeling halal or kosher food, is essential in allowing
consumers to have genuine freedom of choice (190).

Currently, although about "80% of processed food in the United
States has a component from a genetically modified crop, a new survey
finds that only 26% of Americans think they have ever eaten such food"
(Krebs). This same United States Department of Agriculture (USDA) poll
found that 94% of respondents felt that labeling items that contained
GMOs would be a good idea (Krebs). This figure is up from a 2000
MSNBC poll that shows that "81% of people who responded were in
favor of labeling genetically engineered products" (Kirsch 21). Kirsch
follows that statement by confirming that the FDA and the biotech
industry feel the opposite (21). Kirby repeats this view, adding that the
FDA recognizes "no material difference in nutrition, composition, or
safety between genetically modified food and food that has not been
genetically modified" (qtd. in Kirby 353). Additionally, as long as the
plant or animal that DNA is taken from and the plant or animal that the
DNA is being spliced into are generally recognized as safe (GRAS), then
the product is not subject to any sort of review prior to being released to
consumers (Kirby 354). The FDA assumes that all products in the current
food supply are GRAS. However, the current system does not take into
account that the end result of tomato DNA and trout DNA is not simply a
"tomato fish," but rather an entirely new entity that could bring with it
unforeseen health risks ranging from food allergies to death.

Currently, according to Crespi and Marette, the United States has
no mandatory GMO labeling requirement (328). Sand adds that the
United States is not alone (187). He lists Canada and Argentina

**Current FDA
position on GM foods.**

Donaldson 7

specifically, because combined the three countries are responsible for approximately 80% of the world's GM crops (187). Crespi and Marette add that much of the rest of the world currently recognizes the "precautionary principle," and the potentially deleterious effects of GMOs, and those governments do not want their citizens to be exposed to what might result from the consumption of GMOs (328).

To date, there have been no documented health risks related to GM foods. Proponents of GM food, such as the FDA, use this as the basis for their argument that GM foods pose no threat to consumers, and why mandatory labeling of GM food is unnecessary. An FDA spokesman says: "We have seen no evidence that the bioengineered foods now on the market pose any human health concerns or that they are in any way less safe than crops produced through traditional breeding" (qtd. in MacDonald and Whellams 184–185). While the tone throughout their article suggests that they disagree, MacDonald and Whellams argue that there is nothing unethical about GM foods that should result in mandatory labeling (184). Anne MacKenzie, the Associate Vice-President of Science Evaluation for The Canadian Food Inspection Agency, concurs by saying that regulators have not yet noticed a "significant toxic or allergenic harm" (52). However, as stated by MacDonald and Whellams, many other countries choose to adopt the "precautionary principle" (185). This principle states that if something, like GM food, presents a potential threat to health or the environment, it is best to be cautious and to take action even if science hasn't demonstrated harmful effects (MacDonald and Whellams 185).

Because there may be serious, long-term negative implications on consumer health as a result of the continued consumption of GMOs, biotech companies, governments, and consumers should all be more

Donaldson 8

wary of GM foods (MacDonald and Whellams 185). The "precautionary principle" is law in the European Union, as they consider unknown risk sufficient to require further study before approval. The United States takes the position that if something is not demonstrated to be harmful, then there is no problem in moving forward with implementation ("Precautionary Principle"). There is strong opposition from the United States's Chamber of Commerce to the Precautionary Principle; the Chamber argues that potential but unknown risk should not stand in the way of progress ("Precautionary Principle").

The United States currently operates under a voluntary labeling program (Sand 187), including labeling of foods with GMOs and those without GMOs. However, when Marion Nestle searched for labeling of foods with GMOs, she was not surprised that her search was unsuccessful. Nestle states: "Scientifically based or not, the motivation of the biotechnology companies for opposing labeling is obvious: if the foods are labeled as GM, you might choose not to buy them" (57). The FDA's voluntary labeling program for products that do not contain GMOs can be seen at the grocery store today in products that carry a GMO-free label. The question that remains is whether "GMO-free" labels offer consumers a fully informed choice.

The lack of a mandatory labeling system in the U.S. is not because no one has tried. In 1999, Congressman Dennis Kucinich (D-OH) introduced into Congress the "Genetically Engineered Food Right to Know Act" (Kirsch 26–27). The aim of this bill was to require food that contained GM material, or was comprised of GM material, to be labeled as such (Kirsch 27). Kirby explains that this bill would have required that "food produced with GM material be labeled at each stage of the food production process," in order to mitigate cross

Attempts to get GM foods labeled.

contamination (367). This bill would have made it necessary to put a label on GM products that reads: "GENETICALLY ENGINEERED UNITED STATES GOVERNMENT NOTICE: THIS PRODUCT CONTAINS A GENETICALLY ENGINEERED MATERIAL OR WAS PRODUCED WITH A GENETICALLY ENGINEERED MATERIAL" (Kirsch 27). Heather Carr adds that Congressman Kucinich has introduced this bill into multiple sessions of Congress, including as recently as 2010, never to make it out of committee. Although support increased in the House of Representatives, it has never been enough to move the bill through.

In 2000, Senator Barbara Boxer (D-CA) introduced a similar bill that would have required a label stating: "GENETICALLY ENGINEERED. THIS PRODUCT CONTAINS A GENETICALLY ENGINEERED MATERIAL" (Kirsch 27). Like the House bill, this bill never came to fruition. The FDA maintains that GM food is safe, and because of this, biotech companies say that there is no need to liken their products to potentially dangerous products (such as cigarettes or alcohol) with what resembles a warning label.

Anne MacKenzie disagrees with the biotech companies, arguing that "consumers have a right to know" what they are eating, and how it was made (50). She suggests that mandatory consumer-friendly labeling be used, but that the labels should communicate in a way that does not mislead consumers into thinking that GM food is any different from non-GM food (50–52). She also asserts that the label "should not imply that the consumption of food derived through biotechnology has implications for public health," since currently there is no concrete evidence that GM food is either good or bad for human consumption (52). MacDonald and Whellams proffer that if this were done properly, it would be possible to label GM food while at the same time

Donaldson 10

addressing the biotech companies' concern that GM food labels would "be seen as a warning" (183).

   While MacKenzie is in favor of mandatory labeling, Lars Bracht Andersen remains apprehensive. Andersen, while supporting a consumer's right to know, also understands the biotech industry's view that "mandatory labeling, given predominantly negative consumer perceptions, is likely to effectively remove GM foods from the market" (143). He argues for voluntary labeling, stating that it would have the "least negative impact on the diversity of the market" (143). However, since voluntary labeling alone seems unlikely to protect consumers and provide adequate choice, mandatory labeling of GMO-free products and of those products that contain GMOs is essential.

Student rejects voluntary labeling and repeats his thesis that GM foods need mandatory labeling.

Works Cited

Andersen, Lars Bracht. "The EU Rules on Labeling of Genetically Modified Foods: Mission Accomplished?" *European Food & Feed Law Review,* vol. 5, no. 3, 2010, pp. 136–43. *Academic Search Complete*, eds.a.ebscohost.com.

Brackett, Robert E. "Bioengineered Foods." Statement to the Senate Committee on Agriculture, Nutrition, and Forestry. U.S. Food and Drug Administration, 14 June 2005, www.fda.gov/newsevents/ testimony/ucm/112927.htm.

Bruce, Donald. "Some Christian Reflections on GM Food." *Boundaries: Religious Traditions and Genetically Modified Foods*, edited by Conrad G. Brunk and Harold Coward. State U of New York at Albany P, 2009.

Carr, Heather. "Genetically Engineered Organism Liability Act of 2010 H.R. 5579." *Eat Drink Better,* Important Media Network, 4 Aug. 2010, eatdrinkbetter.com/2010/08/04/genetically-engineered-organism-liability-act-of-2010-h-r-5579/. Accessed 18 June 2011.

Clemmitt, Marcia. "Global Food Crisis: What's Causing the Rising Prices?" *CQ Researcher*, vol. 18, no. 24, 2008, pp. 553–76. Library.cqpress. com/cqresearcher/ document.php?id=cqresrre2008062700&typ=hitlist &num=0. Accessed 29 May 2011.

Crespi, John M., and Stephan Marette. "'Does Contain' vs. 'Does Not Contain': Does It Matter Which GMO Label Is Used?" *European Journal of Law and Economics,* vol. 16, no. 3, 2003, pp. 327–44. *SpringerLink,* Library.cqpress.com/cqresearcher/ document. php?id=cqresrre2008062700&typ=hitlist&num=0. Accessed 12 June 2011.

Davison, John. "GM Plants: Science, Politics, and EC Regulations." *Plant Science,* vol. 178, no. 2, 2010, 94–98. *ScienceDirect.*

Continue to number
pages consecutively.

Start a new page for
Works Cited.

Donaldson 12

sciencedirect.com/science?ob= ArticleListURL&_method=list&_
ArticleListID= 1063694497. Accessed 8 June 2011.

Gudorf, Christine E., and James E. Huchingson. *Boundaries: A
Casebook in Environmental Ethics.* Georgetown UP, 2010.

Kirby, Sarah. "Genetically Modified Foods: More Reasons to Label
Than Not." *Drake Journal of Agricultural Law*, vol. 6, no. 2, 2001,
pp. 351–68. *HeinOnline.* Accessed 12 June 2011.

Kirsch, Sally R. "A Defense of the U.S. Position on Labeling Genetically
Modified Organisms." *International and Comparative
Environmental Law*, vol. 1, no. 1, 2000, pp. 21–28.
HeinOnline. Accessed 9 June 2011.

Krebs, Al. "New Poll—94% of Americans Want Labels on GE Food."
Organic Consumers Association, 19 Oct. 2003, www.
organicconsumers.org/old_articles/ge/newpoll102303.php.
Accessed 9 June 2011.

MacDonald, Chris, and Melissa Whellams. "Corporate Decisions about
Labeling Genetically Modified Foods." *Journal of Business Ethics*, vol.
75, no. 2, 2007, pp. 181–89. *JSTOR.* doi:10.1007/s10551-006-9245-8.

Mackenzie, Anne A. "International Efforts to Label Food Derived
through Biotechnology," *Governing Food: Science, Safety, and
Trade,* edited by Peter W. B. Phillips and Robert Wolfe.
McGill–Queen's UP, 2001.

Martineau, Belinda. *First Fruit: The Creation of the Flavr Savr™ Tomato
and the Birth of Genetically Engineered Food.* McGraw-Hill, 2001.

Moosa, Ebrahim. "Genetically Modified Foods and Muslim Ethics."
*Boundaries: Religious Traditions and Genetically Modified
Foods,* edited by Conrad G. Brunk and Harold Coward. State U of
New York at Albany P, 2009.

Nestle, Marion. *What to Eat.* North Point Press, 2006.

Double-space throughout.

List sources alphabetically.

Use hanging indentation.

Donaldson 13

"Plant Breeding." *The Gale Encyclopedia of Science,* edited by K. Lee
Lerner and Brenda Wilmoth Lerner. 4th ed. vol. 4, pp. 3370–75.
Gale Publishing, 2008. *Gale Virtual Reference Library.* Accessed
29 May 2011.

Sand, Peter H. "Labelling Genetically Modified Food: The Right to Know."
Review of European Community & International Environmental Law,
vol. 15, no. 2, July 2006, pp. 185–92. *Wiley Online Library,* doi:
10.1111/j.1467-9388.2006.00520.x. Accessed 9 June 2011.

U.S. Chamber of Commerce. "Precautionary Principle," 4 Aug. 2010.
www.uschamber.com/precautionary-principle.

Weasel, Lisa H. *Food Fray.* AMACOM Publishing, 2009.

Courtesy of David Donaldson.

Formal Documentation: MLA Style, APA Style

In Chapter 12 you were shown, in sample bibliography cards, what information about a source you need to prepare the documentation for a researched essay. In Chapter 13 you were shown in-text documentation patterns as part of the discussion of avoiding plagiarism and writing effective paragraphs. The format shown is for MLA (Modern Language Association) style, the documentation style used in most of the humanities disciplines. APA (American Psychological Association) style is used in the social sciences. The sciences and other disciplines also have style sheets, but the most common documentation patterns used by undergraduates are MLA and APA, the two patterns explained in this chapter.

Remember that MLA recommends that writers prepare their Works Cited list—a list of all sources they have used—before drafting the essay. This list can then be used as an accurate guide to the in-text/parenthetical documentation that MLA requires along with the Works Cited list at the end of the essay. Heed this good advice. This chapter begins with guidelines for in-text documentation and then provides many models of full documentation for a Works Cited list. Never guess at documentation! Always consult this chapter to make each in-text citation and your Works Cited page(s) absolutely correct.

As you now know, MLA documentation style has two parts: in-text references to author and page number and then complete information about each source in a Works Cited list. Because parenthetical references to author and page are incomplete—readers could not find the source with such limited information—all sources referred to by author and (usually) page number in the essay require the full details of publication in a Works Cited list that concludes the essay. General guidelines for in-text citations are given below.

> **NOTE:** You need a 100 percent correspondence between the sources listed in your Works Cited and the sources you actually cite (refer to) in your essay. Do not omit from your Works Cited any sources you refer to in your essay. Do not include in your Works Cited any sources not referred to in your paper.

GUIDELINES for Using Parenthetical Documentation

- **The purpose of documentation is to make clear exactly what material in a passage has been borrowed and from what source the borrowed material has come.**
- **Parenthetical in-text documentation requires specific page references for borrowed material—unless the source is not a print one.**
- **Parenthetical documentation is required for both quoted and paraphrased material and for both print and nonprint sources.**
- **Parenthetical documentation provides as brief a citation as possible consistent with accuracy and clarity.**

THE SIMPLEST PATTERNS OF PARENTHETICAL DOCUMENTATION

The simplest in-text citation can be prepared in one of three ways:

1. Give the author's last name (full name in your first reference to the writer) in the text of your essay and put the appropriate page number(s) in parentheses following the borrowed material.

   Frederick Lewis Allen observes that, during the 1920s, urban tastes

   spread to the country (146).

2. Place the author's last name and the appropriate page number(s) in parentheses immediately following the borrowed material.

   During the 1920s, "not only the drinks were mixed, but the company as

   well" (Allen 82).

3. On the rare occasion that you cite an entire work rather than borrowing from a specific passage, give the author's name in the text and omit any page numbers.

   Leonard Sax explains, to both parents and teachers, the specific ways

   in which gender matters.

Each one of these in-text references is complete *only* when the full citation is placed in the Works Cited section of your paper:

   Allen, Frederick Lewis. *Only Yesterday: An Informal History of the*

   Nineteen-Twenties. Harper and Row, 1931.

   Sax, Leonard. *Why Gender Matters.* Random House, 2005.

The three patterns just illustrated should be used in each of the following situations:

1. The source referred to is not anonymous—the author is known.
2. The source referred to is by one author.
3. The source cited is the only work used by that author.
4. No other author in your list of sources has the same last name.
5. The source has page numbers.

PLACEMENT OF PARENTHETICAL DOCUMENTATION

The simplest placing of an in-text reference is at the end of the sentence *before* the period. When you are quoting, place the parentheses *after* the final quotation mark but still before the period that ends the sentence.

During the 1920s, "not only the drinks were mixed, but the company as well" (Allen 82).

> **NOTE:** Do not put any punctuation between the author's name and the page number.

If the borrowed material forms only a part of your sentence, place the parenthetical reference *after* the borrowed material and *before* any subsequent punctuation. This placement more accurately shows readers what is borrowed and what are your own words.

Sport, Allen observes about the 1920s, had developed into an obsession (66), another similarity between the 1920s and the 1980s.

If a quoted passage is long enough to require setting off in display form (block quotation), then place the parenthetical reference at the end of the passage, *after* the final period. Remember: Long quotations in display form *do not* have quotation marks.

It is hard to believe that when he writes about the influence of science Allen is describing the 1920s, not the 1980s:

> The prestige of science was colossal. The man in the street and the woman in the kitchen, confronted on every hand with new machines and devices which they owed to the laboratory, were ready to believe that science could accomplish almost anything. (164)

And to complete the documentation for all three examples:

Works Cited

Allen, Frederick Lewis. *Only Yesterday: An Informal History of the Nineteen-Twenties*. Harper and Row, 1931.

PARENTHETICAL CITATIONS OF COMPLEX SOURCES

Not all sources can be cited in one of the three patterns illustrated above, for not all meet the five criteria listed on p. 321. Works by two or more authors, for example, will need somewhat fuller references. Each sample form of in-text documentation given below must be completed with a full Works Cited reference, as shown above.

Two Authors, Mentioned in the Text

Richard Herrnstein and Charles Murray contend that it is "consistently . . . advantageous to be smart" (25).

Two Authors, Not Mentioned in the Text

The advantaged smart group forms a "cognitive elite" in our society (Herrnstein and Murray 26–27).

A Book in Two or More Volumes

Sewall analyzes the role of Judge Lord in Dickinson's life (2: 642–47).

OR

Judge Lord was also one of Dickinson's preceptors (Sewall 2: 642–47).

> **NOTE:** The number before the colon always signifies the volume number. The number(s) after the colon represents the page number(s).

A Book Listed by Title—Author Unknown

According to *The Concise Dictionary of American Biography,* William Jennings Bryan's 1896 campaign stressed social and sectional conflicts (117).

The New York Times' editors were not pleased with some of the changes in welfare programs ("Where" 4: 16).

Always cite the title of the article, not the title of the journal, if the author is unknown. With no opening noun or noun phrase, abbreviate the title with the first word. This is sufficient to guide readers to the correct Works Cited item.

William Jennings Bryan's 1986 campaign stressed social and sectional conflicts (*Concise Dictionary* 117).

If the title begins with a noun or noun phrase (noun plus adjective), shorten the title as shown.

A Work by a Corporate Author

A report by the Institute of Ecology's Global Ecological Problems Workshop argues that the civilization of the city can lull us into forgetting our relationship to the total ecological system on which we depend (13).

Although corporate authors may be cited with the page number within the parentheses, your writing will be more graceful if corporate authors are introduced in the sentence. Then only page numbers go in parentheses.

Two or More Works by the Same Author

During the 1920s, "not only the drinks were mixed, but the company as well" (Allen, *Only Yesterday* 82).

Frederick Lewis Allen contends that the early 1900s were a period of complacency in America (*Big Change* 4–5).

In *The Big Change*, Allen asserts that the early 1900s were a period of complacency (4–5).

If your list of sources contains two or more works by the same author, the fullest parenthetical citation includes the author's last name, followed by a comma; the work's title, shortened if possible; and the page number. If the author's name appears in the text—or the author and title both appear as in the third example above—omit these items from the parenthetical citation. When you have to include the title to distinguish among sources, it is best to put the author's name in the text.

Two or More Works in One Parenthetical Reference

Several writers about the future agree that big changes will take place in work patterns (Toffler 384–87; Naisbitt 35–36).

Separate each author with a semicolon. But if the parenthetical reference becomes disruptively long, cite the works in a "See also" note rather than in the text.

A Source without Page Numbers

It is usually a good idea to name the nonprint source within your sentence so that readers will not expect to see page numbers.

Although some still disagree, the *Oxford English Dictionary Online* defines global warming as "thought to be caused by various side-effects of modern energy consumption."

Complete Publication Information in Parenthetical Reference

At times you may want to give complete information about a source within parentheses in the text of your essay. Then a Works Cited list is not used. Use square brackets for parenthetical information within parentheses. This approach may be a good choice when you use only one source that you refer to several times. Literary analyses are one type of essay for which this approach to citation may be a good choice. For example:

> Edith Wharton establishes the bleakness of her setting, Starkfield, not
> just through description of place but also through her main character,
> Ethan, who is described as "bleak and unapproachable" (*Ethan Frome*
> [Charles Scribner's Sons, 1911, Print] 3. All subsequent references are to
> this edition). Later Wharton describes winter as "shut[ting] down on
> Starkfield" and negating life there (7).

Additional-Information Footnotes or Endnotes

At times you may need to provide additional information that is not central to your argument. These additions belong in a content note. However, use these sparingly and never as a way of advancing your thesis. Many instructors object to content notes and prefer only parenthetical citations.

"See Also" Footnotes or Endnotes

More acceptable is the note that refers to other sources of evidence for or against the point to be established. These notes are usually introduced with "See also" or "Compare," followed by the citation. For example:

> Chekhov's debt to Ibsen should be recognized, as should his debt to
> other playwrights of the 1890s who were concerned with the inner life
> of their characters.[1]

[1.] See also Eric Bentley, *In Search of Theater* (Vintage, 1959) 330; Walter Bruford, *Anton Chekhov* (Yale UP, 1957) 45.

PREPARING MLA CITATIONS FOR A WORKS CITED LIST

The partial in-text citations described and illustrated above must be completed by a full reference in a list given at the end of the essay. To prepare your Works Cited list, alphabetize, by author last name, the sources you have actually referred to in your paper and complete each citation according to the forms explained and illustrated below. (Guidelines for formatting a finished Works Cited page are found on p. 305.)

You can search the examples that follow to find the appropriate model for each of your sources, but you are less likely to make errors when you also understand the basic pieces of information—and the order of their presentation—essential to every citation.

Remember the purpose of your list: to provide the information that will let your readers locate each source you used. For example, if you used a book in a revised edition, readers must know that. Or if you used articles initially published in a magazine that you found in this textbook, then you must provide that additional information. The additional information is essential to identifying the actual source you used. MLA invites researchers to think in terms of a "container"—or a series of containers—for each source. A book has as its container the name of its publisher and the date of publication.

However, an article in this textbook would have two containers. First, the initial facts of publication for the magazine article followed by all of the details that identify *Read, Reason, Write,* namely author, title, publisher and date (this book's container) plus the page numbers on which the article appears here. Articles you find and use from an online database would also have two containers. The articles you actually used were originally published elsewhere and then reproduced in the database.

Books require the following information, in the order given, with periods after each of the four major elements:

- Author, last name first.
- Title—and subtitle if there is one—all in italics.
- The publisher's name, followed by a comma, and the date of publication, followed by a period.

Author	Title	Facts of Publication
Bellow, Saul.	*A Theft.*	Viking Books, 1989.

Forms for Books: Citing the Complete Book

A Book by a Single Author

Seyler, Dorothy U. *The Obelisk and the Englishman: The Pioneering Discoveries of Egyptologist William Bankes.* Prometheus Books, 2015.

The subtitle is included, preceded by a colon, even if there is no colon on the book's title page.

A Book by Two or Three Authors

Brizee, Allen, and Jaclyn M. Wells. *Partners in Literacy: A Writing Center Model for Civic Engagement.* Rowman & Littlefield Publishers, 2016.

Second (and third) authors' names appear in normal signature order.

A Book with Three or More Authors

Baker, Susan P., et al. *The Injury Fact Book.* Oxford UP, 1992.

Use the name of the first person listed on the title page followed by a comma and "et al." Shorten "University Press" to "UP."

Two or More Works by the Same Author

Goodall, Jane. *In the Shadow of Man.* Houghton Mifflin, 1971.

---. *Through a Window: My Thirty Years with the Chimpanzees of*

Gombe. Houghton Mifflin, 1990.

Give the author's full name with the first entry. For the second (and additional works), begin the citation with three hyphens followed by a period. Alphabetize the entries by the books' titles.

A Book Written Under a Pseudonym with Name Supplied

Wrighter, Carl P. [Paul Stevens]. *I Can Sell You Anything.* Ballantine

Books, 1972.

An Anonymous Book

Beowulf: A New Verse Translation. Translated by Seamus Heaney.

Farrar, Straus, and Giroux, 2000.

An Edited Book

Hamilton, Alexander, et al. *The Federalist Papers.* Edited by Isaac

Kramnick. Viking Books, 1987.

Lynn, Kenneth S., editor. *Huckleberry Finn: Text, Sources, and*

Critics. Harcourt Brace, 1961.

If you cite the author's work, put the author's name first and the editor's name after the title. If you cite the editor's work (an introduction or notes), then place the editor's name first, followed by a comma and "editor."

A Translation

Schulze, Hagen. *Germany: A New History.* Translated by Deborah

Lucas Schneider. Harvard UP, 1998.

Cornford, Francis MacDonald, translator. *The Republic of Plato.*

Oxford UP, 1945.

If you cite the author's work, place the author's name first and the translator's name after the title. If the translator's work is the important element, place the translator's name first. If the author's name does not appear in the title, give it after the title. For example: By Plato.

A Book in Two or More Volumes

Spielvogel, Jackson J. *Western Civilization.* West Publishers, 1991. 2 vols.

A Book in Its Second or Subsequent Edition

O'Brien, David M. *Storm Center: The Supreme Court and American Politics.* 2nd ed. W. W. Norton, 1990.

A Book in a Series

Parkinson, Richard. *The Rosetta Stone.* British Museum, 2005. British Museum Objects in Focus.

Provide the series title—and number if there is one—after publication information. Capitalize but do not italicize the series name.

A Reprint of an Earlier Work

Twain, Mark. *Adventures of Huckleberry Finn.* 1885. Centennial Facsimile Edition. Introduction by Hamlin Hill. Harper & Row, 1962.

Faulkner, William. *As I Lay Dying.* 1930. Vintage Books/Random House, 1964.

Provide the original publication date as well as the facts of publication for the reprinted version. Indicate any new material, as in the first example. The second example illustrates the paperback reprint by the original publisher.

A Book with Two or More Publishers

Green, Mark, et al. *Who Runs Congress?* Bantam Books/Grossman Publishers, 1972. Ralph Nader Congress Project.

Separate the publishers with a forward slash.

A Corporate or Governmental Author

U.S. Environmental Protection Agency. *Chesapeake Bay: Introduction to an Ecosystem.* Government Printing Office, 2012.

American Indian Education Handbook. California Department of

Education Unit, 1991.

When the author and the publisher are the same, begin with the title; do not repeat author and publisher.

Religious Texts

The Holy Bible [Usually refers to the King James Version.]

The Reader's Bible: A Narrative. Edited with introduction by Roland

Mushat Frye. Princeton UP, 1965.

Provide facts of publication for versions not well known. In the text, capitalize religious texts such as the Bible or the Koran, but do not use italics except in the Works Cited.

Forms for Books: Citing Part of a Book

A Preface, Introduction, Foreword, or Afterword

Sagan, Carl. Introduction. *A Brief History of Time: From the Big Bang*

to Black Holes. By Stephen Hawking. Bantam Books, 1988, pp. ix–x.

Use this form if you are citing the author of the introduction, preface, etc. Provide an identifying word after the author's name and give inclusive page numbers for the part of the book you are citing.

An Encyclopedia Article

Ostrom, John H. "Dinosaurs." *McGraw-Hill Encyclopedia of Science*

and Technology. 1957 edition.

"Benjamin Franklin." *Concise Dictionary of American Biography.*

Edited by Joseph E. G. Hopkins. Charles Scribner's Sons, 1964.

One or More Volumes in a Multivolume Work

James, Henry. *The Portrait of a Lady.* Vols. 3 and 4 of *The Novels and*

Tales of Henry James. Charles Scribner's Sons, 1908.

A Work in an Anthology or Collection

Hurston, Zora Neale. *The First One. Black Female Playwrights: An*

Anthology of Plays Before 1950. Edited by Kathy A. Perkins.

Indiana UP, 1989, pp. 80–88.

> Comstock, George. "The Medium and the Society: The Role of
>
> Television in American Life." *Children and Television: Images in a*
>
> *Changing Sociocultural World.* Edited by Gordon L. Berry and Joy
>
> Keiko Asamen. Sage Publications, 1993, pp. 117–31.

Give inclusive page numbers for the particular work you have used.

An Article in a Collection, Casebook, or Sourcebook

> Knapp, Alex. "Five Leadership Lesson from James T. Kirk." *Forbes.*
>
> 5 Mar. 2012. Reprinted in *Read, Reason, Write: An Argument Text and*
>
> *Reader,* 11th ed. By Dorothy U. Seyler. McGraw-Hill, 2012, pp. 28–32.

Many articles in collections have been previously published, so you must provide the original facts of publication (excluding page numbers if they are not readily available), and then the facts of publication for the collection. End with inclusive page numbers for that part of the book that you used.

Cross-References

If you are citing several articles from one collection, you can provide a citation for the entire book and then provide just the author, title, and page numbers for each specific article used. Include a cross-reference to the editor(s) of the collection with each specific article you cite.

> Head, Suzanne, and Robert Heinzman, editors. *Lessons of the*
>
> *Rainforest.* Sierra Club, 1990.
>
> Bandyopadhyay, J., and Vandana Shiva. "Asia's Forest, Asia's
>
> Cultures." Head and Heinzman, pp. 66–77.

Forms for Periodicals: Articles in Magazines, Journals, and Newspapers

Articles from the various forms of periodicals, when read in their print format, require the following information, in the order given:

- Author, last name first, followed by a period.
- Title of the article, in quotation marks, followed by a period inside the final quotation mark.
- Facts of publication, which usually include the title of the periodical in italics followed by a comma, the volume number or volume and issue number followed by a comma, the date of publication followed by a comma, inclusive page numbers for the article preceded by p. or pp., and then a period.

For articles accessed in their print format, think of the facts of publication—the details about the specific periodical—as the article's container. Articles, unlike books, are not published separately; they are "contained" within a periodical or in a book collection of articles. Articles of various kinds can also be found on a website, in which cases the website becomes the container. Identifying facts of the website must be supplied for your readers to find the work you are citing.

Article in a Journal Paged by Year

Brown, Jane D., and Carol J. Pardun. "Little in Common: Racial and

Gender Differences in Adolescents' Television Diets." *Journal of*

Broadcasting and Electronic Media, vol. 48, no. 2, 2004, pp. 266–78.

Article in a Journal Paged by Issue

Lewis, Kevin. "Superstardom and Transcendence." *Arete: The Journal*

of Sport Literature, vol. 2, no. 2, 1985, pp. 47–54.

If the journal uses both volume and issue numbers, provide both regardless of the journal's choice of paging.

Article in a Monthly Magazine

Wegner, Mary-Ann Pouls. "Gateway to the Netherworld." *Archaeology*

Jan./Feb. 2013, pp. 50–53.

Do not use volume or issue numbers with popular magazines. Cite the month(s) and year of publication and inclusive page numbers. Abbreviate all months except May, June, and July.

Article in a Weekly Magazine

Stein, Joel. "Eat This, Low Carbers." *Time*, 15 Aug. 2005, p. 78.

Provide the complete date, using the order of day, month, year.

An Anonymous Article

"Death of Perestroika." *The Economist*, 2 Feb. 1991, pp. 12–13.

The missing name indicates that the article is anonymous. Alphabetize under D.

A Published Interview

Angier, Natalie. "Ernst Mayr at 93." Interview. *Natural History Magazine*,

May 1997, pp. 8–11.

Follow the pattern for a published article, but add the descriptive label "Interview" (followed by a period) after the article's title.

A Review

> Whitehead, Barbara D. "The New Segregation." Review of *Coming*
>
> *Apart: The State of White America,* 1960–2010, by Charles Murray.
>
> *Commonweal,* 4 May 2012.

If the review is signed, begin with the author's name and then the title of the review article. Also provide the title of the work being reviewed and its author, preceded by "Review of." For reviews of art shows, videos, or computer software, provide place and date or descriptive label to make the citation clear.

Forms for Periodicals: Articles in Newspapers Accessed in Print

Article in a Newspaper

> Arguila, John. "What Deep Blue Taught Kasparov—and Us." *Christian*
>
> *Science Monitor,* 16 May 1997, p. 18.

A newspaper's title should be cited as it appears on the masthead.

Article in a Newspaper with Lettered Sections

> Taub, Amanda. "Why Some Wars Get More Attention Than Others."
>
> *The New York Times,* 2 Oct. 2016, p. A8.

Place the section letter immediately before the page number without any spacing. If the paging of the article is not consecutive, give the first page and the plus (+) sign.

An Article in a Newspaper with a Designated Edition

> Pereria, Joseph. "Women Allege Sexist Atmosphere in Offices
>
> Constitutes Harassment." *The Wall Street Journal,* eastern ed.
>
> 10 Feb. 1988, p. 23.

Cite the edition used after the title of the newspaper.

An Editorial

> "Japan's Two Nationalisms." Editorial. *The Washington Post,* 4 June
>
> 2000: B6.

Add the descriptive label "Editorial" after the article title.

A Letter to the Editor

> Wiles, Yoko A. "Thoughts of a New Citizen." Letter. *The Washington Post,* 27 Dec. 1995: A22.

A Review

> Doerr, Anthony. "Running through Time." Review of *Time Travel: A History* by James Gleick. *The New York Times Book Review*, 2 Oct. 2016, pp. 1+.

If the review is signed, begin with the author's name and then the title of the review article. Then provide the title of the work being reviewed and its author, preceded by "Review of." For reviews of art shows, videos, or computer software, provide place and date or descriptive label to make the citation clear.

Forms for Digital Sources

Remember that the purpose of a citation is to lead readers to the exact source you have used. This means that if you access an article in a digital database that was initially published in a print source, you must include this additional container, the information about the database. Researchers also use other kinds of online sources, and citations for these usually require more information than for printed sources. Include as many of the items listed below, in the order given here, as are relevant—and available—for each source. Take the time to search a website's home page to locate as much of the information as possible.

- Author (or editor, compiler, translator), last name first, ending in a period.
- Title of the work, in quotation marks if it is part of a site, in italics if it is a complete and separate work, such as an online novel, ending in a period.
- Facts of publication of the print version if the item was originally published in print, ending in a period.
- Title of the website, in italics—unless it is the same as the title of the work.
- Publisher of the site—organization or person who owns or sponsors the site.
- Date of publication.
- Digital object identifier (DOI), if any, or URL, preferably a stable URL, followed by a period.
- Your date of access only if the source is undated, likely to change, or likely to be removed.

NOTE: MLA recommends including DOIs and/or URLs, but you should omit them if your instructor prefers that you do so. Also, some articles in library databases with DOIs may not be accessible online.

Study this annotated citation as a general model:

author

title of work   title of website   sponsor of website

Yancy, George. "I Am a Dangerous Professor." *nytimes.com*. *The New York Times*. 30 Nov. 2016, www.nytimes.com/2016/11/30/opinion/i-am-a-dangerous-professor.html?ref=opinion&_r=0.

date of publication

website URL

A Published Article in an Online Database

Shin, Michael S. "Redressing Wounds: Finding a Legal Framework to Remedy Racial Disparities in Medical Care." *California Law Review*, vol. 90, no. 6, 2002, pp. 2047–2100. *JSTOR*. www.jstor.org/stable3481439.

Kumar, Sanjay. "Scientists Accuse Animal Rights Activists of Stifling Research." *British Medical Journal* 23 Nov. 2002: 1192. *EBSCOhost*, doi: 10.1136/bmj.325. 7374.1192/d.

No access date is used with databases of printed articles.

An Article in a Reference Source

"Prohibition." *Encyclopaedia Britannica Online*. 11 June 2014. www.britannica.com/topic/prohibition-alcohol-interdict.

An Online News Source

Associated Press. "Russia Voted Off UN Human Rights Council." *wtop.com* 28 Oct. 2016, hwtop.com/europe/2016/10/russia-voted-off-un-human-rights-council/. Accessed 30 Oct. 2016.

An Article in an Online Magazine

Kinsley, Michael. "Politicians Lie. Numbers Don't." *Slate*, 16 Sept. 2008. www.slate.com/articles/news_and_politics/readme/2008/09/politicians_lie_numbers_dont.html.

A Poem in a Scholarly Project

Keats, John. "Ode to a Nightingale." *Poetical Works of John Keats*. 1884. *Bartleby.com,* www.bartleby.com/126/40.html.

Information from a Government Site

"The 2008 HHS Poverty Guidelines." *ASPE*, U.S. Department of

Health and Human Services, 23 Jan. 2008, aspe.hhs.gov/

2008-hhs-poverty-guidelines.

Information from a Professional Site

"Music Instruction Aids Verbal Memory." Press Release. *American*

Psychological Association. Reported by Agnes S. Chan, 7 July 2003,

www.apa.org/news/press releases/2003/07/music-memory.aspx.

Information from a Professional Home Page or Blog

Leta, Vicky, et al. "Women Inventors Whose Contributions Still Bless

Us Today." *Mashable*, 24 Mar. 2016. mashable.com/2016/03/24/

women-inventors/?utm_cid=hp-hh-sec#yLcwQAqKgkqT.

For information from an untitled personal home page, use the label "Home page" (but not in italics or quotation marks).

Home Page for a Course or Academic Department

Loyola University Maryland Writing Department. Home page,

www.loyola.edu/academics/writing. Accessed 30 Oct. 2016.

Forms for Other Print and Nonprint Sources

The materials in this section, although often important to research projects, do not always lend themselves to documentation by the forms illustrated above. Follow the basic order of author, title, and facts of publication as much as possible. Add more information as needed to make the citation clear and useful to a reader.

An Article Published in Print and on CD or DVD

Detweiler, Richard A. "Democracy and Decency on the Internet."

Chronicle of Higher Education, 28 June 1996, p. A40. *General*

Periodicals Ondisc. UMI-ProQuest. 1997. CD.

A Work or Part of a Work on CD-ROM, DVD-ROM, Etc.

Eseiolonis, Karyn. "Giorgio de Chirico's *Mysterious Bathers.*" *A*

Passion for Art: Renoir, Cezanne, Matisse, and Dr. Barnes.

Corbis Productions, 1995. CD.

Kloss, William. "Donatello and Padua." *Great Artists of the Italian Renaissance.* The Teaching Company, 2004. DVD.

Audio (or Video) from a Website

Vachss, Andrew. "Dead and Gone." Interview by Bill Thompson. Aired on *Eye on Books,* 24 Oct. 2000. *The Zero.* Home page, www.vachss.com/index.html. Accessed 25 Sept. 2008.

A Recording

Stein, Joseph. *Fiddler on the Roof.* Jerry Bock, composer. Original-Cast Recording with Zero Mostel. Original cast recording. RCA, 1964.

The conductor and/or performers help identify a specific recording.

Plays or Concerts

Waiting for Godot by Samuel Beckett. Performers Ian McKellen and Patrick Stewart. Directed by Sean Mathias. Cort Theatre, New York City. Nov. 2013.

Principal actors, singers, musicians, and/or the director can be added as appropriate.

A Television or Radio Program

Breakthrough: Television's Journal of Science and Medicine. PBS series hosted by Ron Hendren. 10 June 1997. Television.

An Interview

Plum, Kenneth. Personal Interview, 5 Mar. 2012.

A Lecture

Bateson, Mary Catherine. "Crazy Mixed-Up Families." Northern Virginia Community College, 26 Apr. 1997.

A Personal Letter or E-mail

Usick, Patricia. "Bankes' Chapel." E-mail to the author. 3 Aug. 2015.

Maps and Charts

> *Hampshire and Dorset.* Map. Geographers' A–Z.

Cartoons and Advertisements

> Halleyscope. "Halleyscopes Are for Night Owls." Advertisement. *Natural History*, Dec. 1985, p. 15.

> United Airlines Advertisement. ESPN. 8 Aug. 2008. Television.

A Published Dissertation

> Brotton, Joyce D. *Illuminating the Present through Literary Dialogism: From the Reformation through Postmodernism.* Dissertation. George Mason U, 2002. UMI, 2002.

Government Documents

> United States. Environmental Protection Agency. *The Challenge of the Environment: A Primer on EPA's Statutory Authority.* Government Printing Office, 1972.

If the author is not given, cite the name of the government first followed by the name of the department or agency. If the author is known, give the author's name first, followed by the title, and then appropriate facts for accessing the material.

> Geller, William. *Deadly Force. U.S. Department of Justice National Institute of Justice Crime File Study Guide.* U.S. Department of Justice, www.ncjrs.gov/pdffiles1/Digitization/ 100734NCJRS.pdf. Accessed 24 Mar. 2016.

Legal Documents

> U.S. Constitution. Article 1, section 3.

The Constitution is referred to by article and section. Do not use italics. When citing a court case, give the name of the case, the volume, page of the report, and the date. Italicize the name of the case in your paper but not in the Works Cited.

> Turner v. Arkansas. 407 U.S. 366. 1972.

APA STYLE

The *APA system* identifies a source by placing the author's last name and the publication year of the source within parentheses at the point in the text where the source is cited. The in-text citations are supported by complete citations in a list of sources at the end of the paper. Most disciplines in the social sciences use APA style. The guidelines given here follow the style of the *Publication Manual of the American Psychological Association* (6th ed., 2010).

APA Style: In-Text Citations

The simplest parenthetical reference can be presented in one of three ways:

1. Place the year of publication within parentheses immediately following the author's name in the text.

   > In a typical study of preference for motherese, Fernald (1985)
   >
   > used an operant auditory preference procedure.

Within the same paragraph, additional references to the source do not need to repeat the year, if the researcher clearly establishes that the same source is being cited.

> Because the speakers were unfamiliar subjects, Fernald's work
>
> eliminates the possibility that it is the mother's voice per se that
>
> accounts for the preference.

2. If the author is not mentioned in the text, place the author's last name followed by a comma and the year of publication within parentheses after the borrowed information.

> The majority of working women are employed in jobs that are at
>
> least 75 percent female (Lawrence & Matsuda, 1997).

3. Cite a specific passage by providing the page, chapter, or figure number following the borrowed material. *Always* give specific page references for quoted material.

    - A brief quotation:

> Deuzen-Smith (1988) believes that counselors must be involved
>
> with clients and "deeply interested in piecing the puzzle of life
>
> together" (p. 29).

    - A quotation in display form:

> Bartlett (1932) explains the cyclic process of perception:
>
> > Suppose I am making a stroke in a quick game, such as tennis
> >
> > or cricket. How I make the stroke depends on the relating of
> >
> > certain new experiences, most of them visual, to other
> >
> > immediately preceding visual experiences, and to my posture,
> >
> > or balance of posture, at the moment. (p. 201)

Use this style with a quotation of forty words or more. Indent a block quotation five spaces from the left margin, do not use quotation marks, and double-space throughout. To show a new paragraph within the block quotation, indent the first line of the new paragraph an additional five spaces. Note the placing of the year after the author's name, and the page number at the end of the direct quotation.

More complicated in-text citations should be handled as follows:

Two Authors, Mentioned in the Text

> Kuhl and Meltzoff (1984) tested 4- to 5-month-olds in an experiment . . .

Two Authors, Not Mentioned in the Text

. . . but are unable to show preference in the presence of two mis-

matched modalities (e.g., a face and a voice; see Kuhl & Meltzoff, 1984).

Give both authors' last names each time you refer to the source. Connect their names with "and" in the text. Use an ampersand (&) in the parenthetical citation.

More Than Two Authors

For works coauthored by three, four, or five people, provide all last names in the first reference to the source. Thereafter, cite only the first author's name followed by "et al."

As Price-Williams, Gordon, and Ramirez have shown (1969), . . .

OR

Studies of these children have shown (Price-Williams, Gordon, &

Ramirez, 1969) . . .

THEN

Price-Williams et al. (1969) also found that . . .

If a source has six or more authors, use only the first author's last name followed by "et al." every time the source is cited.

Corporate Authors

In general, spell out the name of a corporate author each time it is used. If a corporate author has well-known initials, the name can be abbreviated after the first citation.

FIRST IN-TEXT CITATION: (National Institutes of Health [NIH], 1989)
SUBSEQUENT CITATIONS: (NIH, 1989)

Two or More Works within the Same Parentheses

When citing more than one work by the same author in a parenthetical reference, use the author's name only once and arrange the years mentioned in order; thus:

Several studies of ego identity formation (Marcia, 1966, 1983) . . .

When an author, or the same group of coauthors, has more than one work published in the same year, distinguish the works by adding the letters *a, b, c,* and so on, as needed, to the year. Give the last name only once, but repeat the year, each one with its identifying letter; thus:

Several studies (Smith, 1990a, 1990b, 1990c) . . .

When citing several works by different authors within the same parentheses, list the authors alphabetically; alphabetize by the first author when citing coauthored works. Separate authors or groups of coauthors with semicolons; thus:

Although many researchers (Archer & Waterman, 1983; Grotevant,

1983; Grotevant & Cooper, 1986; Sabatelli & Mazor, 1985) study

identity formation . . .

Personal Communication

Cite information obtained via interview, phone, letter, and e-mail communication.

According to Sandra Haun (personal interview, September 7, 2008) . . .

Because readers cannot retrieve information from these personal sources, do *not* include a citation in your list of references.

Secondary Sources

Make every effort to find, read, and cite original works. When this is not possible—the work is now out of print or the writer is quoting someone from a speech or personal communication—cite the secondary source this way:

Jennings disputes Smith's claims by recounting what she said in a

recent radio interview: "I will not be running for re-election in the

House" (as cited in Kim, 2017).

APA STYLE: PREPARING A LIST OF REFERENCES

All sources cited parenthetically in your paper—except for all types of personal communication—need a complete citation. These complete citations are placed on a separate page (or pages) after the text of the paper and before any appendices included in the paper. Sources are arranged alphabetically, and the first page is titled "References." Begin each source flush with the left margin and indent second and subsequent lines five spaces. Double-space throughout the list of references. Follow these rules for alphabetizing:

1. Organize two or more works by the same author, or the same group of coauthors, chronologically.

    Beck, A. T. (1991).

    Beck, A. T. (1993).

2. Place single-author entries before multiple-author entries when the first of the multiple authors is the same as the single author.

    Grotevant, H. D. (1983).

    Grotevant, H. D., & Cooper, C. R. (1986).

3. Organize multiple-author entries that have the same first author but different second or third authors alphabetically by the name of the second author or third and so on.

    Gerbner, G., & Gross, L.

    Gerbner, G., Gross, L., Jackson-Beeck, M., Jeffries-Fox, S., & Signorielli, N.

    Gerbner, G., Gross, L., Morgan, M., & Signorielli, N.

4. Organize two or more works by the same author(s) published in the same year alphabetically by title.

Form for Books

A book citation contains these elements in this form:

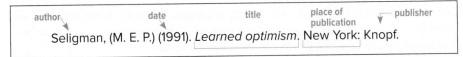

author   date   title   place of publication   publisher

Seligman, (M. E. P.) (1991). *Learned optimism.* New York: Knopf.

Authors

Give all authors' names, last name first, and initials. Separate authors with commas, use the ampersand (&) before the last author's name, and end with a period. For edited books, place the abbreviation "Ed." or "Eds." in parentheses following the last editor's name.

Date of Publication

Place the year of publication in parentheses followed by a period.

Title

Capitalize only the first word of the title and of the subtitle, if there is one, and any proper nouns. Italicize the title and end with a period. Place additional information such as number of volumes or an edition in parentheses after the title, before the period.

   Burleigh, N. (2007). *Mirage: Napoleon's scientists and the unveiling*

   of Egypt.

Publication Information

Cite the city of publication; add the state (using the Postal Service abbreviation) or country if necessary to avoid confusion; then give the publisher's name, after a colon, eliminating unnecessary terms such as *Publisher*, *Co.*, and *Inc.* End the citation with a period.

   Mitchell, J. V. (Ed.). (1985). *The ninth mental measurements yearbook.*

   Lincoln: University of Nebraska Press.

National Institute of Drug Abuse. (1993, April 13). *Annual national high*

   school senior survey. Rockville, MD: Author.

Newton, D. E. (1996). *Violence and the media.* Santa Barbara, CA:

   ABC-Clio.

Give a corporate author's name in full. When the organization is both author and publisher, place the word *Author* after the place of publication.

Form for Articles

An article citation contains these elements in this form:

author   date   title of article   title of journal

Changeaux, J.P. (1993). Chemical signaling in the brain. *Scientific American,*

volume   page

269, 58–62.

Date of Publication

Place the year of publication for articles in scholarly journals in parentheses, followed by a period. For articles in newspapers and popular magazines, give the year followed by month and day (if appropriate).

   (1997, March).

Title of Article

Capitalize only the title's first word, the first word of any subtitle, and any proper nouns. Place any necessary descriptive information in square brackets immediately after the title.

   Scott, S. S. (1984, December 12). Smokers get a raw deal [Letter to the

      Editor].

Publication Information

Cite the title of the journal in full, capitalizing according to conventions for titles. Italicize the title and follow it with a comma. Give the volume number, italicized, followed by a comma, and then inclusive page numbers followed by a period. *If a journal begins each issue with a new page 1, then also cite the issue number in parentheses immediately following the volume number. Do not use "p." or "pp." before page numbers when citing articles from scholarly journals; do use "p." or "pp." in citations to newspaper and magazine articles.

   Martin, C. L., Wood, C. H., & Little, J. K. (1990). The development of

      gender stereotype components. *Child Development, 61,* 1891–1904.

   Leakey, R. (2000, April/May). Extinctions past and present. *Time,* p. 35.

An Article or Chapter in an Edited Book

> Goodall, J. (1993). Chimpanzees—bridging the gap. In P. Cavalieri &
>
> P. Singer (Eds.), *The great ape project: Equality beyond humanity*
>
> (pp. 10–18). New York: St. Martin's.

Cite the author(s), date, and title of the article or chapter. Then cite the name(s) of the editor(s) in signature order after "In," followed by "Ed." or "Eds." in parentheses; the title of the book; the inclusive page numbers of the article or chapter, in parentheses, followed by a period. End with the city of publication and the publisher of the book.

A Report

> U.S. Merit Systems Protection Board. (1988). *Sexual harassment in the*
>
> *federal workplace: An update.* Washington, DC: U.S. Government
>
> Printing Office.

Form for Electronic Sources

As a minimum, an APA reference for any type of online source should include the following information: a document title or description, the date of publication, a way to access the document online, and, when possible, an author name.

When the online address (URL) is likely to be stable, you can cite that address. For example: www.nytimes.com. However, a good source that you find during your research may not be found later by your readers with the URL that you used. APA recommends, therefore, that such sources be documented with the item's DOI (digital object identifier) instead of its URL.

Do not place URLs within angle brackets (< >). Do not place a period at the end of the URL, even though it concludes the citation. If you have to break a URL at the end of a line, break only after a slash. Introduce the URL at the end of the citation this way: Retrieved from www.nytimes.com

DOIs are a series of numbers and letters that provide a link to a specific item, and this link does not change with time. Although DOIs are often on the first page of a document, they can, at times, be hard to locate. APA prefers that you always choose a source's DOI over its URL, if you can find it. Place the DOI at the end of the citation, and introduce the number thus: doi: [number]. Do not end the citation with a period.

Here are a few examples of citations for Web sources:

Journal Article Retrieved Online, with DOI Information

> Habermas, Jürgen. (2006). Political communication in media society.
>
> *Communication Theory 16*(4), 411–426. doi: 10.1111/j. 1468-2885
>
> .2006.00280.x

Gardiner, K., Herault, Y., Lott, I., Antonarakis, S., Reeves, R., & Dierssen, M. (2010). Down syndrome: From understanding the neurobiology to therapy. *Journal of Neuroscience 30*(45), 14943–14945. doi: 10.1523/JNEUROSCI.3728-10.2010

Electronic Daily Newspaper Article Available by Search

Schwartz, J. (2002, September 13). Air pollution con game. *Washington Times*. Retrieved from www.washtimes.com

Journal Article Available from a Periodical Database

Note that no URL is necessary; just provide the name of the database.

Dixon, B. (2001, December). Animal emotions. *Ethics & the Environment, 6*(2), 22. Retrieved from Academic Search Premier database/EBSCOhost Research Databases.

U.S. Government Report on a Government Website

U.S. General Accounting Office. (2002, March). *Identity theft: Prevalence and cost appear to be growing*. Retrieved from www.gao.gov/new.items/d02363.pdf

Cite a message posted to a newsgroup or electronic mailing list in the reference list. Cite an e-mail from one person to another *only* in the essay, not in the list of references.

SAMPLE STUDENT ESSAY IN APA STYLE

The following student essay illustrates APA style. Use 1-inch margins and double-space throughout, including any block quotations. Block quotations should be indented *five* spaces from the left margin (in contrast to the ten spaces required by MLA style). Observe the following elements: title page, running head, abstract, author/year in-text citations, subheadings within the text, and a list of references.

Note placement of running head and page number.

Running Head: DEPRESSION AND MARITAL STATUS   1

Sample title page for a paper in APA style.

The Relationship Between Depression and Marital Status

Carissa Ervine

Sociology of Mental Disorder: SOC 4714

Virginia Tech

Abstract

Many studies have examined the relationship between mental disorders, specifically depression, and marital status. From the studies, several theories have developed to explain this relationship. An examination of the studies' findings and of the theories tested demonstrates that no one theory accounts for all patterns of marital status and mental health or disorder.

Keywords: depression, marital status

Papers in APA style usually begin with an abstract.

Place keywords below the abstract.

APA Style

DEPRESSION AND MARITAL STATUS   3

Many studies have evaluated the relationship between mental disorders, more specifically depression, and marital status. These studies consistently find that people who are divorced or have never been married have more depressive symptoms than those who are married. This paper explores both the causes of and the theories that seek to explain these findings.

Definition and Description of Depression

Depression is a mood disorder in which individuals experience loss of interest or of pleasure in nearly all activities. They feel extreme sadness, despair, and hopelessness. These feelings lead to a lack of motivation to do simple, daily tasks. Many people with depression also have low self-esteem. According to the *Diagnostic and Statistical Manual of Mental Disorders* (DSM), a person must experience at least four of the symptoms listed in order to have depression: changes in appetite or weight, sleep, or psychomotor activity; decreased energy; feelings of worthlessness or guilt; difficulty concentrating or making decisions; or recurrent thoughts of death or suicide ideas or attempts.

> Subheadings are often used in papers in the social sciences.

Prevalence of Depression According to Marital Status

Throughout epidemiological research, studies have consistently shown that those who are married have fewer depressed symptoms than those who are not married (Kim & McKenry, 2005; Wade & Pevalin, 2004), and many studies have sought to find the reasons. Some think it is because marriage offers certain benefits; therefore, married people have better overall health and less depression (Kim & McKenry, 2002). When a marriage dissolves, so does that person's mental health. Marital disruption causes a significant increase in depression, even three years after a divorce (Aseltine & Kessler, 1993). It has also been found that people who are depressed before marriage have improved mental health once they are married (Lucas et al., 2003). Those who do get divorced have more depressive symptoms that may or may not disappear over time (Kim & McKenry, 2002; Lucas et al., 2003). Kim and McKenry (2002) demonstrate, though, that getting remarried after a divorce leads to a decrease in depressive symptoms.

DEPRESSION AND MARITAL STATUS 4

Studies have also evaluated whether people in marriages were happier because those who were not married, or who became divorced, got selected out of marriage due to psychological problems that make them undesirable partners. This idea is referred to as the social selection theory. Four years prior to getting divorced, people show higher rates of psychological problems than those who stayed married, although those who were widowed did not (Wade & Pevalin, 2004). People who get married and stay married have fewer depressive symptoms and better psychological well-being years before they ever got married (Lucas et al., 2003).

Some researchers assert that marriage itself is good for mental health, but that it is the quality of the marriage that matters. High marital stress causes depressive symptoms that tend to dissipate after divorce (Aseltine & Kessler, 1993; Johnson & Wu, 2002). Gove, Hughes, and Style (1983) demonstrated that marital quality and happiness are strong predictors of mental health. Actually, remaining unmarried can be more beneficial to one's psychological health than being in a continuously unhappy marriage.

Last, some studies suggest that marriage does not increase psychological well-being at all. These studies suggest that life satisfaction does change when major events ensue, and then people gradually adapt over time until their psychological health reaches their baseline (Lucas et al., 2003). Initially, people react strongly to both good and bad events, but as time passes, their emotional reactions lessen, and they return to normal (Lucas et al., 2003). Booth and Amato (1991) found that before a divorce occurs there is a rise in stress, but then stress levels return to normal two years after the divorce.

Use ampersand within parentheses; use "and" in sentences.

APA Style

DEPRESSION AND MARITAL STATUS   5

Evaluation of the Evidence

All these findings play some part in explaining why the married tend to have fewer depressive symptoms than their counterparts, but some studies were better conducted than others and used longitudinal data to explain some of the differences found. The fact that married people have better health because they get benefits from marriage seems to be the best explanation. In many instances, the social selection perspective did not hold up. For example, some studies showed that the psychological health of divorced persons improved once they remarried (Johnson & Wu, 2002). If the selection perspective held, those who remarried would not likely experience a decrease in depressive symptoms. The selection perspective would support the idea that those selected out of marriage would not even be likely to remarry. Johnson and Wu's (2002) results consistently show that marriage is better for people because of the benefits they receive from it.

Frech and Williams (2007) found that those who were depressed before marriage had a decrease in depressive symptoms once they were married, supporting the idea that marriage offers benefits. This may occur because marriage provides economic and psychosocial benefits. Those who are married may have two incomes, resulting in less stress over financial matters. Marriage also offers day-to-day companionship, decreasing social isolation (Frech & Williams, 2007). These benefits do not support the fact that marital quality matters, because they are based on marital status per se.

Some researchers who favor the social selection theory believe that high rates of distress prior to a divorce indicate psychological problems in the individual (Wade & Pevalin, 2004), although this may not necessarily be the case. Higher stress levels are common in the

DEPRESSION AND MARITAL STATUS   6

years preceding a divorce. After all, divorce is not a discrete event; many problems lead up to it. Higher levels of distress in the years before a divorce may reflect anticipation of the marital disruption (Mastekaasa, 1995). While marriage can bring many benefits, the quality of the marriage is important. High stress levels because of an unhappy marriage are likely to explain the higher stress levels leading up to divorce.

Booth and Amato (1991) also found a pre-divorce rise in stress, but then they also found that levels of stress in the individuals return to normal two years after the divorce. While this finding does appear to challenge the selection perspective, it is not consistent with many other findings that marriage is better for psychological well-being. Johnson and Wu (2002) used the same waves of people in their study; they did not find that those remaining divorced experienced a decrease in depressive symptoms over time. Nor did satisfaction levels return to the original baselines after divorce. This difference in findings is likely to be caused by a difference in the number of times the participants were studied. Booth and Amato studied their respondents only every three years, whereas Johnson and Wu studied them more often. Johnson and Wu did not find that those remaining divorced experienced a decrease in depressive symptoms over time. Lucas (2005) argues that although some adaption does occur, normally it is not complete. Many people are likely to establish new baselines of psychological well-being that are slightly lower than they were before they were divorced (Lucas et al., 2003).

While many studies find fewer depressive symptoms in married people, discrepancies in explanations still exist. The strongest evidence indicates that married people have less depression because marriage offers many benefits and social supports that the unmarried do not have. But marital quality is just as important as marital status, and this can account for why distress levels go up right before divorce occurs. A bad marriage creates stress, and distress levels increase because of this, not because of poor psychological health that an individual brings to a marriage.

Review of Theories Relating to Marital Status and Depression

As noted, several theories explain why people who are married have better mental health than those who are not. First, the social selection theory asserts that those who are married have better psychological well-being than those who do not and that the unmarried have been "selected" out of marriage. That is, those who aren't married have more mental illness, such as depression, so they are not considered to be suitable mates (Johnson & Wu, 2002). These people either never marry or get married and then divorce. Their psychological characteristics predispose them to divorce (Mastekaasa, 1992).

The crisis theory asserts that having a divorce is a life crisis that temporarily changes mental health. People encounter many stressors while going through a divorce. One of these is the adjustment to role changes. Once the transition is completed, stress levels go down and psychological well-being returns to normal (Booth & Amato, 1991). Lucas et al. (2003) also found that after the marital transition of divorce, people adapted to their new set of circumstances. Depression went down and their psychological well-being returned.

Last, role theory asserts that the stress that the divorced experience is chronic. The new social role they must take on will cause them higher levels of distress because they have less social support, more economic responsibilities, and possibly more stress associated with raising children alone (Johnson & Wu, 2002). This theory also

DEPRESSION AND MARITAL STATUS   8

asserts that these chronic stress levels will not go down as long as the divorced remain single. If a divorced person decides to remarry, then his or her stress levels begin to dissipate because there are now fewer stressful roles to fulfill. The social causation perspective also ties into this. With fewer stressful roles to take on, married people can enjoy many of the benefits that marriage offers. When a marriage dissolves, however, they no longer have these benefits.

Evaluation of Theories

Role theory gives a good explanation of why married people have better psychological well-being and fewer depressive symptoms. It is well known that stress increases the likelihood that someone will have a mental illness. It is also true that levels of depression increase when marital disruption occurs (Wade & Pevalin, 2004). The divorced are used to having a partner who can offer benefits such as greater financial security and a strong social network. With fewer resources to draw upon and more roles to take on, the divorced person is susceptible to depressive symptoms (Kim & McKerry, 2002). However, symptoms of distress and depression do decrease once a divorced person remarries and undergoes another role transition. With the new marriage, the number of required roles decreases and the increased resources of the new marriage ease depression.

In contrast, crisis theory asserts that depressive symptoms and distress decrease with time after a divorce. But crisis theory does not seem to hold up, since studies demonstrate that marriage and remarriage increase psychological well-being. The fact that remarriage increases psychological well-being also contradicts the social selection perspective. If social selection did occur, people would be selected out from remarrying at all. None of these theories, however, effectively

DEPRESSION AND MARITAL STATUS   9

examines the effect of marital quality, an issue important to understanding the relationship between depression and marital status.

The best conclusion is that no one theory is complex enough to explain the relationship between marital status and mental health. It is likely that all theories have valid points and that the reason married people experience better mental health stems from a combination of causes. Further research should focus on finding a theory that can account for more, if not all, of the forces shaping the mental health of married people.

References

Aseltine, R. H., & Kessler, R.C. (1993). Marital disruption and
depression in a community sample. *Journal of Health and
Social Behavior, 34,* 237–251.

Booth, A., & Amato, P. (1991). Divorce and psychological stress.
Journal of Health and Social Behavior, 32, 396–407.

Frech, A., & Williams, K. (2007). Depression and the psychological benefits of entering marriage. *Journal of Health and
Social Behavior, 48,* 149–163.

Gove, W. R., Hughes, M., & Style, B. S. (1983). Does marriage
have positive effects on the psychological well-being of the
individual? *Journal of Health and Social Behavior, 24,*
122–131.

Johnson, D. R., & Wu, J. (2002). An empirical test of crisis,
social selection, and role explanations of the relationship
between marital disruption and psychological distress: A
pooled time-series analysis of four wave panel data. *Journal
of Marriage and Family, 64,* 211–224.

Kim, K. H., & McKenry, P. C. (2002). The relationship between
marriage and psychological well-being. *Journal of Family
Issues, 23*(8), 885–911.

Lucas, R. E. (2005). Time does not heal all wounds: A
longitudinal study of reaction and adaption to divorce.
Psychological Science, 16(12), 945–950.

Lucas, R. E., Clark, A. E., Georgellis, Y., & Diener, E. (2003).
Reexamining adaptation and the set point model of
happiness: Reactions to changes in marital status. *Journal
of Personality and Social Psychology, 84(3),* 527–538.

Title the page
"References."

Double-space
throughout. In
each citation,
indent all lines,
after the first,
five spaces.
Note APA style
in placing dates.

APA Style

DEPRESSION AND MARITAL STATUS   11

Mastekaasa, A. (1992). Marriage and psychological well-being:

Some evidence on selection into marriage. *Journal of

Marriage and the Family, 54,* 901–911.

Mastekaasa, A. (1995). Marital dissolution and subjective

distress: Panel evidence. *European Sociological Review,

11*(20), 173–185.

Wade, T. J., & Pevalin, D. J (2004). Marital transitions and

mental health. *Journal of Health and Social Behavior, 45,*

155–170.

For two or more sources by the same author, order by the year of publication.

Courtesy of Carissa Ervine.

A Collection of Readings

This section is divided into seven chapters, each one on a current topic or set of interrelated issues open to debate. The chapters contain five or six articles to remind us that complex issues cannot be divided into simple "for" or "against" positions. This point remains true even for chapters on a specific topic. It is not sound critical thinking to be simply for or against any complicated public policy initiative. No one is "for" or "against" protecting our environment, for example. The debate begins with restrictions on the use of fossil fuels or energy use or elephant poaching. It is only when we get into policy decisions—and ways of funding those decisions or strategies for enforcing those decisions—that citizens have opposing views.

Questions follow each article to aid reading, analysis, and critical responses. In addition, each chapter opens with a visual both to enjoy and to consider seriously as a contribution to the issues discussed in the chapter. Following each opening image is a brief introduction to the chapter and several general questions to focus your thinking as you read.

The Media: Image and Reality

READ: What is the situation? Who speaks the lines?

REASON: Who, presumably, are the guys in suits sitting in front of the desk? Who, according to Wiley, must be controlling TV scheduling?

REFLECT/WRITE: What is Wiley's view of reality shows? Do you agree? Why or why not?

Although we may not agree with Marshall McLuhan that the medium itself IS the message, we still recognize that the various media influence us. They stir emotions, shape our vision of the world, and dramatically present a message designed to alter our lives. The essays in this chapter explore the effects of music and film, of advertising and television talk shows, and of course the press on the ways we "see" the world and construct our lives from those images. Note that the chapter opens with a popular medium: the cartoon. Cartoons are not just a laugh; they present a view of life and seek to shape our thinking. Be sure to take some time to study and reflect on the cartoons throughout this text.

Surely we are influenced by media messages, by the "reality" they present to us. How extensive is this influence? Most of us make purchases that have been determined at least to some extent by advertising. And we know that news sites online created for the purpose of spreading misinformation have led people to act on this fake news. Is this a problem—or an inescapable part of life? Is there anything that can—or should—be done in response to the media's desire to shape our thoughts and engage our emotions?

PREREADING QUESTIONS

1. How "real" are "reality" shows? Does it matter if they are scripted?

2. How do films reflect our world and also shape our ideas of that world?

3. What do the various forms of music (jazz, rock, rap) tell us about ourselves and our world? What does your music preference tell us about you?

4. How does advertising shape our images of the world? How realistic are these images? Do we want ads to be "realistic"? Have ads become too invasive in our lives?

5. How accurate is our press coverage? Media outlets around the world do not "see" and show the same worldview; is this a problem? What is one obvious solution for individuals who want to understand a complex world?

6. What standards of reliability, objectivity, and fairness should be set for the media? Should these differ from one medium to another?

OFF TO SEE THE WIZARD: FINDING THE VIRTUES OF HOMER, PLATO, AND JESUS IN TECHNICOLOR OZ | MARK EDMUNDSON

Mark Edmundson is a professor of English at the University of Virginia. Awarded numerous honors and awards—including NEH Distinguished Teaching Professor recognition and a Guggenheim Fellowship—Edmundson has written essays and books on a wide range of topics. In addition to *Why Read?* (2004) and *Why Teach?* (2013), he has published a biography of Freud and *Self and Soul: A Defense of Ideals* (2015). The following essay was published in *The American Scholar* in spring 2016.

PREREADING QUESTIONS Have you seen *The Wizard of Oz*? If so, think about your responses to the film. If you have not seen it, read a brief synopsis of this classic.

1 My mother wasn't prone to idealizing her childhood. She was born in 1928, the year before the great stock market crash, and she thought of herself as

a child of the Depression. Most of her early memories were sad. The one that seemed strongest was of her dear and usually stoical father in tears, the day he lost his job.

Dorothy and her friends are on their way to the Emerald City.

But there was one very bright memory that my mother brought up again and again: the day she saw *The Wizard of Oz*. She found the opening phase of the film slow enough, she told me. She did not much care for the black-and-white segment, set in dreary Kansas. 2

But when the movie went to Oz and exploded in Technicolor, my mother was thrilled. She had never seen a color film before. She, like millions of other people who've loved it, felt the greatest pleasure in being transported beyond her own world, a black-and-white world if there ever was one, into a more colorful land alive with delight and danger. 3

It's also a world alive with meaning. People in Oz have strong identities: the Wicked Witch, the Wizard, the Tin Man, the Cowardly Lion, the scatterbrained Scarecrow, and even the Munchkins, with their officers and their guilds. Then there's Dorothy, whom my mother loved most: an unformed, kindly American girl who, it happens, can sing like an angel. 4

In Oz, people want things: and if they persevere, they can get them. The Tin Man wants a heart; the Cowardly Lion wants courage (he's prone to tears); the Scarecrow could use a brain (he'd like to be "another Lincoln"); and Dorothy wants to go home. Or that's what she says. I suspect she does want to go home, but as someone different from the goodhearted, commonplace girl she is. 5

Watching her genial friends struggle in their sad and comic and touching ways for what they need, she learns about what's worth striving for in life. She sees that to have a brain, you've got to struggle to think; that to have courage you must fight for it; and that to have a heart, you've got to greet others with love 6 and hope for the best. By the end of the movie, Dorothy is smarter, kinder, and braver than she was.

7   The virtues on display in the movie have an ancient and venerable lineage. I'm not sure L. Frank Baum, who wrote the novel the movie is based on, or the hundreds of people who created this wonderful film, knew or cared about that fact, but it's true. Courage, compassion, and wisdom are the three primary ideals of the ancient world. You can learn about courage from Homer, wisdom from Plato, and compassion from Jesus of Nazareth—and also from Confucius and Buddha.

8   Homer teaches us about heroic bravery. He dramatizes the two archetypes of the warrior hero. The first is Achilles, the man-god who fears nothing and is determined to become the greatest warrior who ever lived. Achilles is always ready to die to make his name. The second is Hector, the archetype of the citizen soldier. He's not a natural warrior—he says he has had to learn to be a soldier. But he fights bravely and eventually dies defending Troy.

9   All philosophy, we hear, is a footnote to Plato, and indeed Plato is the arche-typal philosopher. Plato sought absolute knowledge: he wanted to grasp truths that would be true for all time. And in his masterwork, *The Republic,* he believes that he has.

10   Love your neighbor as yourself, says Jesus. He tells the tale of a man who is beaten and thrown in a ditch. Travelers pass him by without stopping. But a Samaritan, a man who comes from another tribe, stops and binds the injured man's wounds and takes him to an inn and sees to his care. That is what a neighbor does; that is how a man or woman of compassion behaves.

11   Ideals remind us that there is more to life than serving ourselves. They offer us the chance to do something for others. Ideals also promise unity and focus and the chance to live fully in the present.

12   Both Baum and the film's makers divine the centrality of ideals to human life, and then bring them down to earth. *The Wizard of Oz* makes ideals accessible in a form that's unintimidating and even comic. In the most light-handed way, it shows how much ideals can matter to a little American girl with some growing up to do.

13   At the climax of the movie, the Witch, having cornered the friends in her castle, says she's going to do away with them all, and Toto ("your mangy little dog"), too. Dorothy, the Witch says, will be the last one to go. She lights her broom on a torch and sets the poor Scarecrow on fire. He's about to burn to death. The Cowardly Lion and the Tin Man freeze, but Dorothy, who is a little less afraid than the rest, has the brains to pick up a bucket of water and douse her friend, whom she loves and dearly wants to save. Some guts, a little quick thinking, a lot of kindness: Dorothy summons each of the ideals when the chips are down.

14   The water from her bucket flies beyond the Scarecrow and soaks the Witch, who cries out the immortal words: "I'm melting, melting. . . . Who would have thought a good little girl like you could destroy my beautiful wickedness." What the Witch doesn't know is that after her adventures in Oz, Dorothy is more than just an everyday "good little girl." When you've acquired some guts and brains

and heart, you can make a little luck for yourself. Then all good things become possible, including the defeat of a wicked witch or any other worrisome antagonist who might cross your path.

The Wizard of Oz is a movie you can laugh with (and occasionally at), and 15 still learn from. I wager it's been an installment in the education of plenty of kids. And it was part of my mother's education, too. Child of the Depression, she needed a measure of all those ideal qualities, which she developed over time. And The Wizard of Oz helped her do it.

Mark Edmundson, "Off to See the Wizard". Reprinted from The American Scholar, vol. 85, no. 2, Spring 2016. Copyright ©2016 by Mark Edmundson.

QUESTIONS FOR READING

1. What did the author's mother like about the movie? Why could she also benefit from the film's messages?

2. What does each one of Dorothy's three friends want?

3. What are the sources of the three ideals celebrated in the film? What can we learn from Homer, Plato, and Jesus?

4. How does Dorothy demonstrate that she's learned something about these ideals?

QUESTIONS FOR REASONING AND ANALYSIS

5. Edmundson is not reviewing the film as it is released; rather he is analyzing a classic work that he expects his readers to know. What is the claim of his argument?

6. The author begins and ends with his mother. What does he gain from using this frame? How does he connect his mother's life to the message from Oz?

7. What does Edmundson accomplish by connecting the virtues he finds in Oz with their origins in the literature of the past?

8. Does Edmundson think the film is perfect? How do you know?

QUESTIONS FOR REFLECTION AND WRITING

9. The author asserts that ideals help us understand that life is not just about us, an important value Dorothy learns. Do you agree with Edmundson? If so, why? If not, why not?

10. What are the elements that shape and define a culture? (When you make a list, don't forget the visual arts.) Many would include Oz in their list of the ten most important American films. What are some of the reasons for this ranking? Has Edmundson added to the list for you? Explain.

11. Reflect on movies you have seen. Is there one that stands out as delivering some key messages about living meaningfully? Prepare an analysis of your choice for class discussion or consider developing your analysis into an essay.

Walker 1

Sienna Walker

Professor Erik Nielson

FYS 100 Rap Music

12 September 2012

Big Pun's Prophesy

Like many rap artists in the late 1990s, Big Punisher, also known as "Big Pun," documented the challenges of life in the inner city. He did so most notably in his track titled "Capital Punishment" featuring Prospect, the New York City ghetto which he describes as a place of diminishing potential. Big Punisher depicts urban life as abandoned by an unjust political system, denying its responsibility to serve the people while systematically crushing opportunities for the city's disadvantaged residents, and he calls for the minority citizens to abandon governmental constraints by representing themselves through class action. The extended metaphor of capital punishment, the image of the judge, and various stylistic techniques including delivery and rhyme scheme are the primary means by which Big Punisher expresses his criticism of the political system's failure to address the needs of the people and his encouragement of collective response from the inner city.

Big Punisher harshly criticizes the government and its policies from the start. In the third line, he claims that he has seen young citizens "led astray by the liars, death glorifiers observin' us," portraying "the Man," or any governmental authority, as dishonest and almost satanic. Additionally, from the first few lines of the first verse, the distinction between "they," presumably the establishment, and "us," the resilient minorities plagued by the struggles of street life, become apparent and will resurface throughout the track. Subsequently in the first verse, Big Pun rattles off the wrongs inflicted on his people, ranging from "purposely overtaxing" to "burning down the churches" to "million dollar bails," implying that the government is a ruthlessly oppressive and money-hungry establishment that intentionally neglects its citizens. Last, the most explicit attacks come from lines such as "God 'f' the government and its fuckin' capital punishment" and the choral refrain, "disable the Republicans." Moreover, Big Punisher uses the death sentence to further depict the metaphorical death of opportunity for inner city dwellers at the hands of the tyrannical government.

One of the principal techniques Big Punisher employs in "Capital Punishment" is the metaphor of "death by gavel" to reinforce the idea that the governing system, by its employment of the death penalty, is deliberately suffocating street life. The repetition of the song's title "Capital Punishment" blankets the track. In both the chorus and the verses, the phrase is chanted over and over, inundating the audience's consciousness much like the death sentence would hang over the head of a guilty perpetrator. Big Punisher attacks capital punishment because, even today, it represents the utmost extent to which judicial law can be exercised. This acute judicial power juxtaposed with the raw powerlessness that pervades the inner city creates distance between the two parties as expectations on both ends fail to be met. In verse three, Big Punisher raps "the Man's claws are diggin' in my back / I'm tryin' to hit him back," arguing that it is this almighty "Man," flexing his muscles in the courthouse and neglecting his supportive civic duties, who should be held responsible for a fair share of the overwhelming hardship in the streets. The image of claws in a human's back visually captures the minorities' struggles with the vicious, backstabbing authorities, represented much like a surprise attack where one opponent has an unfair advantage over another. These callous characterizations of the institution become more fully manifested through Big Punisher's use of the image of the judge.

The image of the judge adds to the theme of discriminatory punishment debilitating any urban prospects of success. Big Punisher does not limit the corruption to the streets, claiming "everybody gettin' they hustle on/judge singin' death penalty like it's his favorite fuckin' song." Instead, the way the lines are distinctly paired suggests that the "hustlin'" established on the streets seeps its way into the political system as well, corroding its responsibility to provide for its constituents. Furthermore, the judge is described with "the hammer in the palm, never shaky," also physically suggesting a rigid removal from the adversities of street life and underscoring Big Pun's previous indications of the intolerance of judicial discretion.

In addition to the content, Big Punisher's style, consisting of intricate rhyme schemes and fast-paced delivery, also contributes to the thematic prevalence of oppression which permeates the track. From the opening verse, the audience is exposed to Big Punisher's generous lyrical presentation, occasionally fitting 18 syllables in a single line. His breathless flow typifies the imaginable exhaustion of complying with the looming government, day in and day out. The institution's constant presence, "watching us close," may create the tendency to nervously rush out of view of the public eye, reminiscent of Big Punisher's fast-paced delivery. His rapid elocution can also be applied to the theme of the resiliency of the minority masses whose upbeat spirit cannot be suppressed. What is more, Big Punisher raps, "I'm stressin' the issue here/so we can cross the fiscal year/tired of gettin' fired and hired as a pistoleer" in which the end and internal rhymes illustrate the complexity and interconnectedness that characterize the government-citizen relationship. Similarly, the percussive emphasis on "fired" then "hired" within the larger end rhyme pattern beginning with "here," reflects the inner turmoil that inevitably accompanies corruption both in the streets and in the government. These stylistic sonic and literary devices serve to reinforce the underlying themes of "Capital Punishment."

However, in the midst of all the dark, oppressive policies imposed by the government, Big Punisher counters the idea of "the government tryin' to take out our sons" by declaring "we benefit the Earth with infinite worth." Although he accounts for the inevitable adversities of big city life with lines like "listen to me, shit is rough in the ghetto," his real aggression in the song is channeled not through accusing the government of its overbearing regulations and impossible standards, but through a forceful calling for change. Juxtaposed with the suicide of his cousin Juje who "lost it and turned on the oven," Big Punisher praises his sister who "just bought a home without a loan." Thus, he narrates the unbearable burdens of the deadly streets while raising up the success stories of his people, however infrequent. This praise also embraces Big Pun when he raps "we laid in the slums, made a cake out of crumbs." These examples pronounce the irrepressible ambition of the people. After considering that his people, or inner-city minorities, are entrepreneurial ("open our own labels") and charged ("my battery never die"), Big Punisher calls them to counteract.

Walker 4

Altogether, through the extended metaphor of the death penalty, the image of the unfazed judge, and various literary and sonic devices, Big Punisher describes the government as unjust and as targeted to bring about the demise of the project's masses. "Capital Punishment" renders the "Man" incapable of serving inner-city residents and thus transfers the responsibilities of the government from the authorities and into the hands of the people. Big Punisher's call to action directed to those citizens living in the margins of society may have implications beyond the ghetto and into the present, raising the question of justice here and now.

. . .

Work Cited

Big Punisher, "Capital Punishment." *Capital Punishment.* Terror Squad, Loud Records, 1998. MP3.

Courtesy of Sienna Walker.

QUESTIONS FOR READING

1. What is Walker's subject?
2. What is Big Pun's attitude toward government?
3. How are inner-city minorities depicted?
4. What does Big Pun want his listeners to do?

QUESTIONS FOR REASONING AND ANALYSIS

5. What is Walker's purpose in writing? What is her claim?
6. What strategies does she analyze?
7. How does the death penalty serve as an extended metaphor?

QUESTIONS FOR REFLECTION AND DEBATE

8. Evaluate Walker's analysis: Is it specific? Is it clear? Does it connect elements of the rap song to the song's theme?
9. Do you like rap? If so, why? If not, why not?
10. Has rap made a contribution to modern music? If yes, how? If no, why not?

COCA-COLA--TASTE THE CHANGE | STUART ELLIOTT

Stuart Elliott, a graduate of the Medill School of Journalism at Northwestern University, may be one of the most influential journalists writing about the advertising industry today. Currently, he writes for MediaVillage.com but has had a long career publishing marketing and media analysis in newspapers like *The New York Times*, *USA Today*, and *The Detroit Free Press*. He has also appeared on national television shows, been featured on cable programs, and has spoken on panels. The following article was published on January 27, 2016.

PREREADING QUESTIONS Why would a veteran journalist like Stuart Elliott write an article about Coca-Cola's new marketing campaign? What is so important about Coke ads?

After seven years of using "Open happiness" as the theme of campaigns for its flagship soft drink, the Coca-Cola Company is switching to a new slogan, "Taste the feeling," as well as broadening the ads to include all variants of the Coca-Cola trademark, such as Diet Coke, Coke Light, Coke Zero and Coke Life. Four agencies initially are working on the "Taste the feeling" campaign, the company disclosed last week, with six more to join in as the ads roll out globally this year.   1

If "Taste the feeling" sounds familiar, it may be because it echoes a previous Coca-Cola slogan, "You can't beat the feeling," from 1988. But when you've been selling sugar water for almost 130 years, you're likely to repeat a theme now and again. For instance, "taste" was used in 1957, when the pitch was "Sign of good taste," and "Life tastes good" had a brief run as a slogan in 2001. The word "real" was employed at least five times down through the decades, as in "It's the real thing" (1969) and "You can't beat the real thing" (1990).   2

"Taste the feeling" also evokes an expression in vogue among younger consumers, "the feels," as in something that elicits a wave of intense, heartfelt emotion. That's acknowledged in the introduction to a website devoted to the campaign, which begins: "Coca-Cola gives us all the feels. How does it make you feel?"   3

The bad news is that of late, Coca-Cola has been making fewer people feel as if they want to open happiness, embrace the real thing or enjoy the pause that refreshes. The Coke brand is struggling to connect with consumers who increasingly are turning away from carbonated sodas, especially colas, in favor of a multiplicity of other beverages from flavored waters to coffee to energy drinks. As a result, Coke—the most popular soft drink in the United States and most other countries—has been suffering declines in sales and market share.   4

So "Taste the feeling" will be focused more on the functional and emotional benefits of Coke the product: The uncomplicated instances of delight derived from drinking an icy cold Coca-Cola. By comparison, "Open happiness" evolved into something loftier, concentrating on the positives of Coke the brand and celebrating its role as a social facilitator and a symbol of peace, love, friendship   5 and brotherhood (shades of Don Draper's favorite spot, "I'd Like to Teach the World to Sing").

6   "We've found over time that the more we position Coke as an icon, the smaller we become," said Marcos de Quinto, the company's new chief marketing officer."The bigness of Coca-Cola resides in the fact that it's a simple pleasure—so the humbler we are, the bigger we are."

7   "We want to help remind people why they love the product as much as they love the brand," he said.

8   Or, to explain what de Quinto meant in the parlance of Norma Desmond, the larger-than-life star in the movie *Sunset Boulevard*, Coke is still big—it's the campaigns that got small.

9   That's all well and good, but I'm wondering if ads that play up what's inside the bottle will overlook the specialness of the bottle and the other unique qualities and attributes of Coca-Cola that have contributed to its status as perhaps the world's best-known (and most-liked) brand. People drink Coke, I believe, partly because it has portrayed itself as more important than Pepsi-Cola or other soft drinks—a thirst-quencher, yes, but also an intrinsic element of American popular culture and a symbol of American life.

10   To be sure, Coca-Cola's appeal stems from how it tastes and how it feels to drink one on a hot day. But Coke is also the shape of the contour bottle . . . the nostalgia invoked by a vintage ad or Coke machine . . . the "sharing is caring" message of the *Mean Joe Greene* Super Bowl commercial . . . the prominent roles the brand has played in hit songs such as "Rum and Coca-Cola" and movies like *The Coca-Cola Kid, The Gods Must Be Crazy* and *One, Two, Three* . . . and the *Coca-Cola Santa*, the version of St. Nicholas by the artist Haddon Sundblom that has appeared in Coke ads since the 1930s.

11   The first commercials in the "Taste the feeling" campaign indicate that, at least initially, the company and the agencies understand they must do more than peddle a product. For instance, in one spot, when a young guy orders a Coca-Cola, the man behind the counter lists some of its less tangible benefits: "to make you smile, to break the ice . . . to cool things down, to refresh your memory, to share, to revive a spark or to say, 'Today I'll do it' . . ."

12   The first commercials also address another need in life besides refreshment: They are liberally peppered with sex. In one, a couple meets, flirts, gets busy and argues over many bottles of Coke, with their breakup personified by a bottle shattering as it falls to the floor. In the end, a Coke helps bring them back together.

13   Coca-Cola is among the brands that plan to run commercials during Super Bowl 50 on Feb. 7 [2017]. Once again, Coke will face off against Pepsi, which is also sponsoring the halftime show.

14   Which cola will taste the feeling of victory and which the feeling of defeat? Stay tuned.

QUESTIONS FOR READING

1. What has happened that compels Elliott to write about Coca-Cola's new marketing campaign?
2. What is the difference between Coke's new marketing approach and their old one?
3. Elliott covers considerable ground in his article, discussing Coke's history, the impact of American pop culture, and even Coke's primary rival, Pepsi. What specifically is Elliott's subject if he's writing about so many different things?
4. What are some past ad campaigns from Coke that have been successful?
5. What is the problem Elliott sees in Coke's new marketing campaign?

QUESTIONS FOR REASONING AND ANALYSIS

6. Elliott's main argument is subtle, so on your first reading you may not notice it. As you reread the article, underline his thesis statement. Why do you believe that what you've identified is his thesis? Can you have an argument without a thesis statement?
7. How does Elliott go about analyzing Coke's new marketing campaign? What are his conclusions?
8. Do you agree with the author's position, analysis, and conclusions? Why or why not?

QUESTIONS FOR REFLECTION AND WRITING

9. Looking back at Super Bowl LI in 2017, who won the contest of ads between Coke and Pepsi? How do you know? Why do you think the winning brand succeeded?
10. Elliott has made a career out of analyzing marketing campaigns and media. Why is it important to think critically about marketing and media? What impact do marketing and media have on our daily lives? Our culture?
11. Do a little research on marketing and media analysis. Then pick a brand you love and write a paragraph analyzing that brand's newest marketing campaign.

MOTHER NATURE IS BROUGHT TO YOU BY... | TIM WU

Tim Wu, a native Washingtonian, is a professor at Columbia Law School. A graduate of Harvard Law School, Wu clerked for Justice Stephen Breyer. He has published widely in newspapers and magazines, including *The New Republic, Slate,* and *The New Yorker.* Wu is the author of *The Master Switch* and is best known for creating the term "net neutrality." His most recent book is *The Attention Merchants: The Epic Scramble to Get inside Our Heads* (2016), a study of the many ways that businesses seek to reach us with ads.

PREREADING QUESTIONS Based on Wu's essay title, what do you expect his subject to be? Based on what you have learned from the biographical headnote, what else might you expect the essay to explore?

This year, parks in several states including Idaho and Washington, and the   1
National Park Service, will be blazing a new trail, figuratively at least, as they begin offering opportunities to advertisers within their borders.

©Jordan Siemens/Getty Images

Jogger enjoying the beauty in Yosemite National Park.

2   King County in Washington, which manages 28,000 acres of parkland surrounding Seattle, offers a full branding menu: Naming rights or sponsorships may be had for park trails, benches and even trees. "Make our five million visitors your next customers," the county urges potential advertisers.

3   King County already partnered with Chipotle to hide 30 giant replica burritos on parkland bearing the logo of the agency and the restaurant chain. People who found the burritos won prizes from Chipotle.

4   In May, the National Park Service proposed allowing corporate branding as a matter of "donor recognition." As *The Washington Post* reported, under new rules set to go into effect at the end of the year, "an auditorium at Yosemite National Park named after Coke will now be permitted" and "visitors could tour Bryce Canyon in a bus wrapped in the Michelin Man."

5   The logic behind these efforts is, in its own way, unimpeachable. Many millions of people—that is, "green consumers"—visit parks every day, representing an unrealized marketing opportunity of great value. Yes, parks are meant to be natural, not commercial, but times are tough, or so say the backers of the new schemes.

6   The spread of advertising to natural settings is just a taste of what's coming. Over the next decade, prepare for a new wave of efforts to reach some of the last remaining bastions of peace, quiet and individual focus—like schools, libraries, churches and even our homes.

7   Some of this reflects technological change, but the real reason is the business model of what I call the "attention merchants." Unlike ordinary businesses, which sell a product, attention merchants sell people to advertisers. They do so either by finding captive audiences (like at a park or school) or by giving stuff away to gather up consumer data for resale.

Once upon a time, this was a business model largely restricted to television 8 and newspapers, where it remained within certain limits. Over the last decade, though, it has spread to nearly every new technology, and started penetrating spaces long thought inviolate.

In school districts in Minnesota and California, student lockers are sometimes 9 covered by large, banner-style advertisements, so that the school hallways are what marketers call a fully immersive experience. Other schools have allowed advertising inside gymnasiums and on report cards and permission slips. The Associated Press reported this year that a high school near South Bend, Ind., "sold the naming rights to its football field to a bank for $400,000, its baseball field to an auto dealership, its softball field to a law firm, its tennis court to a philanthropic couple and its concession stands to a tire and auto-care company and a restaurant."

Even megachurches, with their large and loyal congregations, have come to 10 see the upside of "relevant" marketing, yielding the bizarre spectacle of product placements in sermons. In one of the first such efforts, pastors in 2005 were offered a chance to win $1,000 and a trip to London if they mentioned *The Chronicles of Narnia* during services. For the 2013 release of *Superman: Man of Steel*, pastors were supplied with notes for a sermon titled *Jesus: The Original Superhero*.

Nor are our workplaces and social spheres immune. The time and energy 11 we spend socializing with friends and family has, almost incredibly, been harnessed for marketing, through the business models of Facebook, Instagram and other social media. At the office, the most successful of the productivity-killing distraction engines, BuzzFeed, brags of luring a "bored at work" network hundreds of millions strong.

Unfortunately, there is worse yet to come: The nation's most talented 12 engineers now apply themselves to making marketing platforms out of innovations—A.I. assistants like the Amazon Echo or self-driving cars. Here the intrusions will be subtle, even disguised, so as not to trip our defenses, but they will be even more powerful, going after our very decision-making processes. Consider how much we already depend on Siri or Google Maps: What happens when our most trusted tools have mixed motives?

Advertising revenue often seems like "free money," but there are enormous 13 risks for the character of any institution once it begins to rely heavily on advertising income. History and logic suggest that, once advertisers become a major funding source, they create their own priorities, and unless carefully controlled they will warp the underlying space to serve their interests.

This development raises questions beyond the mere issue of how annoying 14 ads can be. The model of individual liberty and a self-reliant citizenry was proposed by the founders and influenced by philosophers like John Stuart Mill, who envisioned sufficient time and space for self-development of character and room for making decisions that are truly ours.

Similar ideas about the prerequisite of free will are to be found in the great 15 spiritual traditions, which sanctify certain times and spaces for the sake of our spiritual development.

16   These ideals are threatened by a way of doing business that by its nature seeks to invade the most sanctified of spaces.

17   If you don't like the sound of this future, resistance is not futile—it is necessary. A commercial dystopia can be averted only by private resistance and principled decisions by the leaders of institutions.

18   The first simply requires redrawing the lines that have been eroded. Where once upon a time, tradition or religion drew those lines for us, blocking out times for family and faith, nowadays personal or family initiative are required to define parts of our lives as off limits. The default setting will always be intrusion and distraction. We need to flip the switch.

19   The second should be to reduce the attention economy by patronizing businesses or institutions with subscription models or those that keep advertising within reasonable limits.

20   Third, the leaders of schools, libraries and even the more principled technology firms should understand that there is always a hidden cost to the proposition offered by advertising. Once an institution is dependent on ad revenue, it's impossible to put the Crest 3D White Radiant Mint toothpaste back in the tube.

21   Above all, we should not simply resign ourselves to a world saturated by commercial appeals at the cost of our private and sacred spaces. As the great legal scholar Charles Black Jr. once put it, "I tremble for the sanity of a society that talks, on the level of abstract principle, of the precious integrity of the individual mind, and all the while, on the level of concrete fact, forces the individual mind to spend a good part of every day under bombardment with whatever some crowd of promoters want to throw at it."

Tim Wu, "Mother Nature Is Brought to You By . . .," *The New York Times,* 2 Dec. 2016.
Used with permission of the author.

QUESTIONS FOR READING

1. What can we expect to find in parks beginning in 2016? Why is this happening?

2. In what other new venues can we expect to find advertising?

3. Who is creating these new venues for ads?

4. What might we be losing with the increasing number of venues for ads?

5. What steps should we be taking, in the writer's view, to stop the increasing spread of advertising into so many new venues?

QUESTIONS FOR REASONING AND ANALYSIS

6. What is Wu's subject? (Restating the essay's title is not sufficient.) What is the claim of his argument?

7. Examine the essay's organization. What *type* of essay is this?

8. Wu reminds readers that originally advertising could be found mostly in newspapers and on television. Where else do we regularly find ads today? Given the spread we already live with, are you surprised to read that you may see ads in parks, schools, libraries, churches, and homes? If so, why? If not, why not?

9. Wu provides some examples of the newest ad venues, but he doesn't have to go on for pages because he knows you can add to his examples. Why is he now objecting to advertising's newest venues? What are his reasons? Is his argument convincing? Why or why not?

QUESTIONS FOR REFLECTION AND WRITING

10. Examine the author's suggestions for addressing the problem. Do these seem reasonable steps we can and should take? If so, why? If not, why not?

11. Does the branding of sports facilities (stadiums) and events (tournaments) bother you? What about at the high school level? What about billboards in state and national parks? What about all of the ads that attach themselves to Web sites you visit? Do you "draw the line" against ads in all of these places? Some? None? Be prepared to defend your position on venues appropriate—or inappropriate—for advertising.

BANNON CALLED THE MEDIA THE "OPPOSITION." HE'S RIGHT, AND IT'S A GOOD THING. | SANFORD J. UNGAR

Educated at Harvard and the London School of Economics, Sanford Ungar was president of Goucher College from 2001 to 2014. He is now a distinguished scholar in residence at Georgetown University and a Lumina Foundation fellow. His essay here appeared February 8, 2017, in *The Washington Post*.

PREREADING QUESTIONS In his title, Ungar seems to be agreeing with President Trump's White House former strategist Stephen Bannon. What in the title suggests that Ungar may in fact not agree with Bannon's concept? What type of argument might be suggested by this catchy title?

Stephen K. Bannon, the former White House strategist, roving provocateur and now foreign policy guru for President Trump, stirred up a hornet's nest recently "[in 2017]" when he called the national media "the opposition party." 1

Mainstream media organizations howled in protest at Bannon's mischaracterization of their role and pledged anew their dedication to fairness, truth and accuracy. As they should. 2

But I suggest they also take a deep breath—and eagerly embrace Bannon's (and subsequently Trump's) description of the media's mandate in these deeply troubled times for American democracy. Not the "party" part, of course. But being an independent "opposition"—an outside check on abuses of power by government and by other public and private institutions—is exactly what the Founding Fathers had in mind for the feisty, boisterous scribes and pamphleteers of their time. It's just what the media should do, and what the country needs, today. 3

Surely Bannon is aware of the rich history behind the concept of the media as opposition: Journalist Benjamin Franklin Bache, grandson of the great philosopher of the American Revolution, was such a vociferous critic of figures including George Washington that he was jailed under the Alien and Sedition Acts. Abraham Lincoln was denounced as a "tyrant" by the media of his time for the way he centralized power and suspended habeas corpus during the Civil War. 4

5   For an extended period in the mid-20th century, some theorists extolled the potential of the press to serve as a "fourth branch of government," albeit an unofficial one, working in concert with the legislative, executive and judicial branches to advance a post-World War II agenda around which there seemed to be a national consensus. One consequence was to ignore or help cover up questionable practices of presidents and other high officials.

6   But even then, the U.S. Information Agency was sending American journalists and scholars around the world to help developing countries learn how to nurture and protect independent and, yes, opposition media.

7   Perhaps that overseas experience helped debunk the dewy-eyed patriotic notion that we were all one big happy family working together in concert. Indeed, in some of the most memorable crises of recent times, the media moved into the vanguard of reform. During the civil rights movement, for example, it was courageous editors, reporters and photographers, particularly in the South, not mainstream elected officials of either major party, who perceived the growing unrest and impelled the revision of unjust laws and social practices.

8   Likewise, in the case of the long, withering war in Vietnam, America's formal political institutions failed miserably to reflect the degree of dissent over a dramatically unsuccessful policy. Even the few members of Congress who began to speak out against the war generally voted for massive appropriations to keep it going.

9   Famously, President John F. Kennedy asked *The New York Times* to withdraw David Halberstam from Saigon, where Halberstam and other independent-minded war correspondents were raising difficult questions about the quagmire. Ultimately, it was the people of all ages protesting in the streets of U.S. cities (counted more accurately by the media than by the government) and hard-driving journalists, not politicians, who brought about a shift in policy.

10   The unauthorized publication of the Pentagon Papers in 1971 did not end the war, as Daniel Ellsberg, who leaked the documents, thought it might, but finally made it more respectable for reluctant critics to go public with their misgivings. Solidarity among various journalistic organizations outweighed competitive instincts, making it feasible to beat back the government's efforts to persuade the Supreme Court to suspend the revelations.

11   Certainly there were moments when the Nixon administration treated journalists as the true opposition, and realistically so. When *Times* reporter Earl Caldwell managed to report from the inside about the activities of the Black Panther Party, Nixon's Justice Department sought to compel him to testify before a federal grand jury and reveal his sources; he was willing to face jail time rather than do so.

12   It took intrepid young reporters from *The Post* to convince the public, not to mention Democratic members of Congress, that the break-in at the Democratic National Committee headquarters in the Watergate complex in 1972 was more than a "third-rate burglary." The rest is history.

13   And so it goes. Awkward as it may be, at the moment, for the media to accept the mantle of "the opposition" that Bannon has conferred upon them, that is surely how events will play out. Having helped Trump climb to power by paying

so much attention to him in the early days of his candidacy, they will by no means now be intimidated and keep their mouths shut, as Bannon has suggested.

Perceiving American journalists—the real ones, that is, who reject "alternative 14 facts" and tell the carefully researched truth in the face of power—as the only genuine protection against autocracy and tyranny is exactly right. Long live the real opposition.

Sanford J. Ungar, "Bannon Called the Media the 'Opposition.' He's Right, and It's a Good Thing," *The Washington Post,* 7 Feb. 2017. Used with permission of the author. Sanford J. Ungar, a veteran journalist and president emeritus of Goucher College, is distinguished scholar in residence at Georgetown University and a Lumina Foundation fellow. He teaches seminars on free speech at Harvard University and Georgetown.

QUESTIONS FOR READING

1. How did mainstream news organizations react to Bannon's assertion that the national media comprise the "opposition party"?
2. How does Ungar think they ought to respond?
3. What does the history of journalism tell us about the role of the press in covering government officials?
4. What led to a change of policy in the Vietnam War? What role did reporters play in exposing Watergate?
5. Who are the "real" American journalists in Ungar's view?

QUESTIONS FOR REASONING AND ANALYSIS

6. What is Ungar's claim? Add a "because clause" to the claim to clarify the author's central argument.
7. What *type* of support does the author provide?
8. Ungar puts the term "alternative facts" in quotation marks. Why? What does he communicate by this strategy?

QUESTIONS FOR REFLECTION AND WRITING

9. Do you know who the "intrepid young reporters" at *The Washington Post* were? (If not, you might want to find out; their investigative reporting is famous—and led to Nixon's resignation.) Ungar applauds their work; do you agree? If so, how would you defend their work? If you disagree, why?
10. Our second president, John Adams, once noted: "Facts are stubborn things; and whatever may be our wishes, our inclinations, or the dictates of our passions, they cannot alter the state of facts and evidence." What would Adams think of "alternative facts"? What is your reaction to this term first used by White House senior advisor Kellyanne Conway?
11. All humans can—and usually do—make mistakes, but journalists who want to work for the respected news organizations do seek the facts and embrace in-depth research— Ungar's "real" journalists. Can you make the case that a democracy depends upon facts? If so, how? If you disagree, how would you refute this idea?

"I'M PREJUDICED," HE SAID. AND THEN WE KEPT TALKING.

HEATHER C. MCGHEE

Heather McGhee is president of Demos, a public-policy organization working for equal opportunity. She is a member of the World Economic Forum's Global Agenda Council on Civic Participation and also sits on several boards. Holding a law degree from the University of California at Berkeley, McGhee writes for newspapers and magazines and also appears frequently on television talk shows such as *Meet the Press*. The essay here was first published in *The New York Times*.

PREREADING QUESTIONS What is your reaction to the author's title? Did she get your attention?

1   One morning in August, when I was a guest on C-Span, I got a phone call that took my breath away.

2   "I'm a white male," said the caller, who identified himself as Garry from North Carolina. "And I'm prejudiced."

3   As a black leader often in the media, I have withstood my share of racist rants, so I braced myself. But what I heard was fear—of black people and the crime he sees on the news—not anger.

4   "What can I do to change?" he asked. "To be a better American?"

5   I thanked him for admitting his prejudice, and gave him some ideas—get to know black families, recognize the bias in news coverage of crime, join an interracial church, read black history. In a professional capacity, I typically speak about race in terms of law and policy. But with this man on the phone it felt right to speak to the basic human need I heard in his voice: to connect.

Good advice from McGhee: Find a church with a mixed-race choir.

The video of us went viral, surpassing eight million views. After a racially 6
charged summer, a lot of people saw something they hungered for in our
exchange. To white viewers, here was a black woman who was morally clear but
not angry. To people of color, here was a white man admitting his racism—finally.

Garry found me on Twitter after our televised call, and shortly before the [2016] 7
election, I visited him near his hometown in the Appalachian foothills of North Carolina. We met on a patio amid the changing fall colors as his dog kept a watchful
eye nearby. There we were: two products of this country who couldn't be more
different, having the oft-invoked but seldom practiced "conversation about race."

I was surprised when he said that he had followed my suggestions and was 8
dedicated to "getting right about this before I die." He talked about the fear he
carried toward people of color, and how it had become a physical weight. "It's
killing me on the inside," he said. "If I don't change things, I could have a stroke."

Although Garry didn't vote for Donald J. Trump, he is the media's image of a 9
Trump voter: a rural, middle-aged white male from a working-class background.
"We're a troubled group right now," he said to me when we met. "We're not a
growing part of the population, we're diminishing. I think our culture is mixing
real fast. Instead of the usual 20 years it takes to change society, it's happening
in five years. It feels like an overwhelming wave is rushing over us."

Research shows that when white people become attuned to demographic 10
change, they become more conservative. The right-wing narrative is that such change
is the unmaking of America. I told Garry I believed it was the fulfillment of our country.

We talked about what it would mean to be the "better American" he invoked 11
on our call. I said that person would be able to find common cause with people
of all backgrounds. Garry's eyes brightened, but he said that it would take time.

"I speak for a lot of unspoken people," he told me. "Maybe millions of white 12
people who are afraid to admit" their racial fears and prejudices. "They're not
bad people. They just don't know how to behave and how to interact" with
people of different races.

Garry had some advice for me, too. "Talk to white people," he said. "We need 13
a little bit of guidance. We're not really getting it from our politicians. They want
to play one side against the other for votes."

We steered clear of politics in our first few conversations, but after the 14
election, he was eager to talk. Garry saw Mr. Trump as the peddler of all the toxic
ideas about people of color that he now avoids on television. (He said "watching
too much TV" is something he has in common with both Mr. Trump and his voters;
we did meet, after all, through a C-Span call.) He thinks many Trump voters could
benefit from the journey he's taken.

With Mr. Trump headed to the White House, my now-friendship with the 15
"racist caller" on C-Span seems like a glimpse of a path not taken. Garry makes
me believe that even though a man endorsed by the Ku Klux Klan won the
majority of white support, people can change. He told me he now notices his
own stereotypes and is eager to replace them with something more generous
and true about his fellow Americans.

We need conversations like mine and Garry's to happen across the country, 16
outside of politics. Societies that have been through traumas have embarked on
racial reconciliation processes; South Africa's is the most famous, but there are
dozens more. There's no reason we can't do that here.

17   Demos, the think tank I run, is working with a variety of other groups on such an effort in 10 communities next year. I spent the past week meeting with hundreds of people—librarians and teachers, community organizers and police officers—who are preparing for conversations in their communities.

18   "What can I do to change?" Garry asked when he called in this summer.

19   I was able to answer him because he had first acknowledged what so many people deny: the persistence of prejudice. That's the first step for all of us to become better Americans.

Heather C. McGhee., "'I'm Prejudiced,' He Said. Then We Kept Talking," *The New York Times*. 12 Dec. 2016 Used with permission of the author.

QUESTIONS FOR READING

1. What is the situation McGhee introduces as her subject?
2. What was McGhee's response to her caller? What did Garry and McGhee do later?
3. What did Garry observe about watching TV?
4. Why does the author think that Americans can change?

QUESTIONS FOR REASONING AND ANALYSIS

5. Analyze McGhee's essay. What are its marks of a personal essay?
6. What makes this essay also an argument? What is the author's claim?
7. McGhee supports her claim with, essentially, an extended example. What does Garry reveal about the causes of prejudice? What solution does the author recommend?

QUESTIONS FOR REFLECTION AND WRITING

8. Psychologists tell us that it is difficult to change until we acknowledge a problem. Does this make sense to you? Is Garry on the right track, then?
9. If prejudice stems from a lack of knowledge, then the suggestion that Garry find ways to interact with African Americans seems good advice. But what about Garry's fears? Is fear also caused by a lack of knowledge, or are there other causes that should be considered? What does Garry suggest as possible causes of his anxiety? Reflect on these questions.
10. Is the medium of television part of the problem? Wouldn't the answer depend on what TV is watched? For example, if one watched reliable news and then a lot of sports—especially football and basketball—would this TV experience lead to prejudice against blacks? Are there other viewing habits that might reinforce prejudice? Be prepared to discuss the role of TV in encouraging vs. debunking racial and/or ethnic stereotypes.

CHAPTER 16

The Web and Social Media: Their Impact on Our Lives

READ: Where is Rat? Why is he there?

REASON: What are the differences in Rat's poses as he reacts to the screen?

REFLECT/WRITE: What is the point of the story that the cartoon tells?

The influence of computers today—especially as a source of information and social interaction—is so great, and so complex, that it warrants its own chapter. Virtually no one under forty today turns first to a reference book. Meanwhile people of all ages, although most typically young people, spend many hours emailing, texting, tweeting, and posting on Facebook, Instagram, or Snapchat. The time that we devote to these activities demands that we pause and think about the effects of this dramatic change in today's world. We can all cite the advantages of the Web, including the ways in which it shrinks the world—or captures events that might not otherwise have been covered by news organizations. But what about the personal details or revealing images that may unfairly hurt individuals? Consider this question and the following ones as you read and study the essays in this chapter.

PREREADING QUESTIONS

1. Has emailing made us more—or less—productive?
2. Is Twitter a useful form of communication—or a waste of time? What about Snapchat? Instagam?
3. Is the Web making us smarter—or interfering with the development of knowledge?
4. What is the difference between having knowledge and having access to knowledge? Can the difference affect critical thinking?
5. What kinds of problems may people face who do not have regular access to technology?
6. What restrictions—if any—should be placed on sites that seek to spread misinformation?

MIND OVER MASS MEDIA | STEVEN PINKER

Professor of psychology at Harvard University, Steven Pinker is the author of significant articles and books on visual cognition and the psychology of language—his areas of research. His books include *The Better Angels of Our Nature* (2011) and *How the Mind Works* (2009). *Time* magazine has listed Pinker as one of the "100 most influential people in the world." His contribution to the ongoing debate over the impact of the Web and social media was published on June 12, 2010.

PREREADING QUESTIONS Given Pinker's title and the headnote information, what do you expect him to write about? Can you anticipate his position—or will you have to read to discover it?

1   New forms of media have always caused moral panics: the printing press, newspapers, paperbacks and television were all once denounced as threats to their consumers' brainpower and moral fiber.

2   So too with electronic technologies. PowerPoint, we're told, is reducing discourse to bullet points. Search engines lower our intelligence, encouraging us to skim on the surface of knowledge rather than dive to its depths. Twitter is shrinking our attention spans.

3   But such panics often fail basic reality checks. When comic books were accused of turning juveniles into delinquents in the 1950s, crime was falling to

record lows, just as the denunciations of video games in the 1990s coincided with the great American crime decline. The decades of television, transistor radios and rock videos were also decades in which I.Q. scores rose continuously.

For a reality check today, take the state of science, which demands high levels of brainwork and is measured by clear benchmarks of discovery. These days scientists are never far from their email, rarely touch paper and cannot lecture without PowerPoint. If electronic media were hazardous to intelligence, the quality of science would be plummeting. Yet discoveries are multiplying like fruit flies, and progress is dizzying. Other activities in the life of the mind, like philosophy, history and cultural criticism, are likewise flourishing, as anyone who has lost a morning of work to the website *Arts & Letters Daily* can attest.

©Rick Gayle/Corbis/Getty Images RF

4

Multitasking looks like fun, but it doesn't work well, as Pinker reveals.

Critics of new media sometimes use science itself to press their case, citing   5
research that shows how "experience can change the brain." But cognitive neuroscientists roll their eyes at such talk. Yes, every time we learn a fact or skill the wiring of the brain changes; it's not as if the information is stored in the pancreas. But the existence of neural plasticity does not mean the brain is a blob of clay pounded into shape by experience.

Experience does not revamp the basic information-processing capacities of   6
the brain. Speed-reading programs have long claimed to do just that, but the verdict was rendered by Woody Allen after he read *War and Peace* in one sitting: "It was about Russia." Genuine multitasking, too, has been exposed as a myth, not just by laboratory studies but by the familiar sight of an S.U.V. undulating between lanes as the driver cuts a deal on his cellphone.

Moreover, as the psychologists Christopher Chabris and Daniel Simons   7
show in their new book *The Invisible Gorilla: And Other Ways Our Intuitions Deceive Us,* the effects of experience are highly specific to the experiences themselves. If you train people to do one thing (recognize shapes, solve math puzzles, find hidden words), they get better at doing that thing, but almost nothing else. Music doesn't make you better at math, conjugating Latin doesn't make you more logical, brain-training games don't make you smarter. Accomplished people don't bulk up their brains with intellectual calisthenics; they immerse themselves in their fields. Novelists read lots of novels, scientists read lots of science.

The effects of consuming electronic media are also likely to be far more   8
limited than the panic implies. Media critics write as if the brain takes on the qualities of whatever it consumes, the informational equivalent of "you are what

you eat." As with primitive peoples who believe that eating fierce animals will make them fierce, they assume that watching quick cuts in rock videos turns your mental life into quick cuts or that reading bullet points and Twitter turns your thoughts into bullet points and Twitter postings.

9   Yes, the constant arrival of information packets can be distracting or addictive, especially to people with attention deficit disorder. But distraction is not a new phenomenon. The solution is not to bemoan technology but to develop strategies of self-control, as we do with every other temptation in life. Turn off email or Twitter when you work, put away your BlackBerry at dinner time, ask your spouse to call you to bed at a designated hour.

10   And to encourage intellectual depth, don't rail at PowerPoint or Google. It's not as if habits of deep reflection, thorough research and rigorous reasoning ever came naturally to people. They must be acquired in special institutions, which we call universities, and maintained with constant upkeep, which we call analysis, criticism and debate. They are not granted by propping a heavy ency- clopedia on your lap, nor are they taken away by efficient access to information on the Internet.

11   The new media have caught on for a reason. Knowledge is increasing exponentially; human brainpower and waking hours are not. Fortunately, the Internet and information technologies are helping us manage, search and retrieve our collective intellectual output at different scales, from Twitter and previews to e-books and online encyclopedias. Far from making us stupid, these technologies are the only things that will keep us smart.

Steven Pinker, "Mind Over Mass Media," *The New York Times/International Herald Tribune*, 12 Jun. 2010. A31. Reprinted by permission of the author.

QUESTIONS FOR READING

1. What is Pinker's subject? (Be precise.)
2. What happened to the crime rate during the 1990s?
3. What happened during the years of heavy TV use and the broadcast of rock videos?
4. What changes occur in the brain when we learn new information? What does not change?
5. What do people do to be successful in their fields?

QUESTIONS FOR REASONING AND ANALYSIS

6. What is Pinker's response to those who complain about the new electronic technolo- gies? What is his claim?
7. What kinds of evidence does Pinker provide?
8. Pinker's writing is clear, even amusing. Find several metaphors and examples and analyze them to show how they contribute to his writing.

QUESTIONS FOR REFLECTION AND WRITING

9. Pinker asserts that speed reading and multitasking have been shown to be myths. Is this idea new to you? Are you surprised? Do you believe that you can multitask successfully? If so, how would you seek to refute Pinker?

10. Is the author convincing in his refutation of those who argue that electronic technologies will make us stupid? If so, why? If not, why not?

THE NEW DIGITAL DIVIDE | SUSAN P. CRAWFORD

A specialist in communications law and privacy issues, Susan Crawford is a professor at Harvard University. She holds her undergraduate and law degrees from Yale. During a part of Obama's presidency, Crawford was special assistant to the president for science, technology, and innovation policy. She is the author, with Stephen Goldsmith, of *The Responsive City: Engaging Communities through Data-Smart Governance* (2014). Her article on the digital divide appeared December 4, 2011.

PREREADING QUESTIONS To what kind of "digital divide" might the title refer? Do you think this might be a problem, at least in the author's view?

For the second year in a row, the Monday after Thanksgiving—so-called Cyber   1
Monday, when online retailers offer discounts to lure holiday shoppers—was the biggest sales day of the year, totaling some $1.25 billion and overwhelming the sales figures racked up by brick-and-mortar stores three days before, on Black Friday, the former perennial record-holder.

Such numbers may seem proof that America is, indeed, online. But they mask   2
an emerging division, one that has worrisome implications for our economy and society. Increasingly, we are a country in which only the urban and suburban well-off have truly high-speed Internet access, while the rest—the poor and the working class—either cannot afford access or use restricted wireless access as their only connection to the Internet. As our jobs, entertainment, politics and even health care move online, millions are at risk of being left behind.

Telecommunications, which in theory should bind us together, has often   3
divided us in practice. Until the late 20th century, the divide split those with phone access and those without it. Then it was the Web: in 1995 the Commerce Department published its first look at the "digital divide," finding stark racial, economic and geographic gaps between those who could get online and those who could not.

"While a standard telephone line can be an individual's pathway to the riches   4
of the Information Age," the report said, "a personal computer and modem are rapidly becoming the keys to the vault." If you were white, middle-class and urban, the Internet was opening untold doors of information and opportunity. If you were poor, rural or a member of a minority group, you were fast being left behind.

Over the last decade, cheap Web access over phone lines brought millions   5
to the Internet. But in recent years the emergence of services like video-on-demand, online medicine and Internet classrooms have redefined the state of the art: they require reliable, truly high-speed connections, the kind available

almost exclusively from the nation's small number of very powerful cable companies. Such access means expensive contracts, which many Americans simply cannot afford.

6   While we still talk about "the" Internet, we increasingly have two separate access marketplaces: high-speed wired and second-class wireless. High-speed access is a superhighway for those who can afford it, while racial minorities and poorer and rural Americans must make do with a bike path.

7   Just over 200 million Americans have high-speed, wired Internet access at home, and almost two-thirds of them get it through their local cable company. The connections are truly high-speed: based on a technological standard called Docsis 2.0 or 3.0, they can reach up to 105 megabits per second, fast enough to download a music album in three seconds.

8   These customers are the targets for the next generation of Internet services, technology that will greatly enhance their careers, education and quality of life. Within a decade, patients at home will be able to speak with their doctors online and thus get access to lower-cost, higher-quality care. High-speed connections will also allow for distance education through real-time videoconferencing; already, thousands of high school students are earning diplomas via virtual classrooms.

9   Households will soon be able to monitor their energy use via smart-grid technology to keep costs and carbon dioxide emissions down. Even the way that wired America works will change: many job applications are already possible only online; soon, job interviews will be held by way of videoconference, saving cost and time.

10   But the rest of America will most likely be left out of all this. Millions are still offline completely, while others can afford only connections over their phone lines or via wireless smartphones. They can thus expect even lower-quality health services, career opportunities, education and entertainment options than they already receive. True, Americans of all stripes are adopting smartphones at breakneck speeds; in just over four years the number has jumped from about 10 percent to about 35 percent; among Hispanics and African-Americans, it's roughly 44 percent. Most of the time, smartphone owners also have wired access at home: the Pew Internet and American Life Project recently reported that 59 percent of American adults with incomes above $75,000 had a smartphone, and a 2010 study by the Federal Communications Commission found that more than 90 percent of people at that income level had wired high-speed Internet access at home.

11   But that is not true for lower-income and minority Americans. According to numbers released last month by the Department of Commerce, a mere 4 out of every 10 households with annual household incomes below $25,000 in 2010 reported having wired Internet access at home, compared with the vast majority—93 percent—of households with incomes exceeding $100,000. Only slightly more than half of all African-American and Hispanic households (55 percent and 57 percent, respectively) have wired Internet access at home, compared with 72 percent of whites.

12   These numbers are likely to grow even starker as the 30 percent of Americans without any kind of Internet access come online. When they do, particularly if the next several years deliver subpar growth in personal income, they will probably go for the only option that is at all within their reach: wireless

smartphones. A wired high-speed Internet plan might cost $100 a month; a smartphone plan might cost half that, often with a free or heavily discounted phone thrown in.

The problem is that smartphone access is not a substitute for wired. The vast 13 majority of jobs require online applications, but it is hard to type up a résumé on a hand-held device; it is hard to get a college degree from a remote location using wireless. Few people would start a business using only a wireless connection.

It is not just inconvenient—many of these activities are physically impossible 14 via a wireless connection. By their nature, the airwaves suffer from severe capacity limitations: the same five gigabytes of data that might take nine minutes to download over a high-speed cable connection would take an hour and 15 minutes to travel over a wireless connection.

Even if a smartphone had the technical potential to compete with wired, 15 users would still be hampered by the monthly data caps put in place by AT&T and Verizon, by far the largest wireless carriers in America. For example, well before finishing the download of a single two-hour, high-definition movie from iTunes over a 4G wireless network, a typical subscriber would hit his or her monthly cap and start incurring $10 per gigabyte in overage charges. If you think this is a frivolous concern, for "movie" insert an equally large data stream, like "business meeting."

Public libraries are taking up the slack and buckling under the strain. Nearly 16 half of librarians say that their connections are insufficient to meet patrons' needs. And it is hard to imagine conducting a job interview in a library.

In the past, the cost of new technologies has dropped over time, and 17 eventually many Americans could afford a computer and a modem to access a standard phone line. Phone service—something 96 percent of Americans have—was sold at regulated rates and the phone companies were forced to allow competing Internet access providers to share their lines.

But there is reason to believe this time is different. Today, the problem is 18 about affording unregulated high-speed Internet service—provided, in the case of cable, by a few for-profit companies with very little local competition and almost no check on their prices. They have to bear all the cost of infrastructure and so have no incentive to expand into rural areas, where potential customers are relatively few and far between. (The Federal Communications Commission recently announced a plan to convert subsidies that once supported basic rural telephone services into subsidies for basic Internet access.)

The bigger problem is the lack of competition in cable markets. Though 19 there are several large cable companies nationwide, each dominates its own fragmented kingdom of local markets: Comcast is the only game in Philadelphia, while Time Warner dominates Cleveland. That is partly because it is so expensive to lay down the physical cables, and companies, having paid for those networks, guard them jealously, clustering their operations and spending tens of millions of dollars to lobby against laws that might oblige them to share their infrastructure.

Cable's only real competition comes from Verizon's FiOS fiber-optic service, 20 which can provide speeds up to 150 megabits per second. But FiOS is available to only about 10 percent of households. AT&T's U-verse, which has about 4 percent of the market, cannot provide comparable speeds because, while it uses fiber-op-tic cable to reach neighborhoods, the signal switches to slower copper lines to connect to houses. And don't even think about DSL, which carries just a fraction of the data needed to handle the services that cable users take for granted.

21   Lacking competition from other cable companies or alternate delivery technologies, each of the country's large cable distributors has the ability to raise prices in its region for high-speed Internet services. Those who can still afford it are paying higher and higher rates for the same quality of service, while those who cannot are turning to wireless.

22   It doesn't have to be this way, as a growing number of countries demonstrate. The Organization for Economic Cooperation and Development ranks America 12th among developed nations for wired Internet access, and it is safe to assume that high prices have played a role in lowering our standing. So America, the country that invented the Internet and still leads the world in telecommunications innovation, is lagging far behind in actual use of that technology.

23   The answer to this puzzle is regulatory policy. Over the last 10 years, we have deregulated high-speed Internet access in the hope that competition among providers would protect consumers. The result? We now have neither a functioning competitive market for high-speed wired Internet access nor government oversight.

24   By contrast, governments that have intervened in high-speed Internet markets have seen higher numbers of people adopting the technology, doing so earlier and at lower subscription charges. Many of these countries have required telecommunications providers to sell access to parts of their networks to competitors at regulated rates, so that competition can lower prices.

25   Meanwhile, they are working toward, or already have, fiber-optic networks that will be inexpensive, standardized, ubiquitous and equally fast for uploading and downloading. Many of those countries, not only advanced ones like Sweden and Japan but also less-developed ones like Portugal and Russia, are already well on their way to wholly replacing their standard telephone connections with state-of-the-art fiber-optic connections that will even further reduce the cost to users, while significantly improving access speeds.

26   The only thing close is FiOS. But, according to Diffraction Analysis, a research firm, it costs six times as much as comparable service in Hong Kong, five times as much as in Paris and two and a half times as much as in Amsterdam. When it comes to the retail cost of fiber access in America, we do about as well as Istanbul.

27   The new digital divide raises important questions about social equity in an information-driven world. But it is also a matter of protecting our economic future. Thirty years from now, African-Americans and Latinos, who are at the greatest risk of being left behind in the Internet revolution, will be more than half of our work force. If we want to be competitive in the global economy, we need to make sure every American has truly high-speed wired access to the Internet for a reasonable cost.

Susan P. Crawford, "The New Digital Divide," *The New York Times,* 4 Dec. 2011. SR1. Reprinted by permission of the author.

QUESTIONS FOR READING

1. How has online access created a divide in our society?

2. Who are those with access? What groups are, in general, left out?

3. To what do those with wired high-speed connections have access?

4. What percentage of Americans have smartphones? What group of Americans have wired high-speed Web access at home? What percentage have no Web access?

5. What are the limitations of smartphones?

QUESTIONS FOR REASONING AND ANALYSIS

6. Explain how and where wired (cable) access is provided; why is this a problem?

7. How do our costs and availability compare to that in other countries? Why should this comparison bother us?

8. What is Crawford's claim? Where does she state it? What does she gain with her choice of placement?

QUESTIONS FOR REFLECTION AND WRITING

9. Has the author convinced you that the digital divide is a problem? Why or why not?

10. Some studies become outdated rather quickly; probably the specifics given by Crawford are no exception. However, in your experience, does the general problem continue to exist—that the rural, the poor, and minorities continue to have fast Web access less than other Americans?

11. Do you agree with her solution? If so, why? If not, how would you refute Crawford's proposal?

BILE, VENOM, AND LIES: HOW I WAS TROLLED ON THE INTERNET | FAREED ZAKARIA

Holding degrees from Yale and Harvard, Indian American Fareed Zakaria is the host of CNN's international affairs program *GPS*, which is aired worldwide. Zakaria is also a columnist for *The Washington Post* and the author of several books, including *The Post-American World* (2008) and *In Defense of a Liberal Education* (2015). The following column on his trolling experience appeared in *The Washington Post* on January 14, 2016.

PREREADING QUESTIONS What does trolling mean? How do you think it makes a person feel to have this experience?

Thomas Jefferson often argued that an educated public was crucial for the sur- 1 vival of self-government. But cognitive neuroscientists roll their eyes at such talk. Social networks—Facebook, Twitter, Instagram, etc.—are the main mechanisms by which people receive and share facts, ideas and opinions. But what if they encourage misinformation, rumors and lies?

In a comprehensive new study of Facebook that analyzed posts made 2 between 2010 and 2014, a group of scholars found that people mainly shared

A troll doing his mean thing.

©RichVintage/Getty Images RF

information that confirmed their prejudices, paying little attention to facts and veracity. (Hat tip to Cass Sunstein, the leading expert on this topic.) The result, the report says, is the "proliferation of biased narratives fomented by unsubstantiated rumors, mistrust and paranoia." The authors specifically studied trolling—the creation of highly provocative, often false information, with the hope of spreading it widely. The report says that "many mechanisms cause false information to gain acceptance, which in turn generate false beliefs that, once adopted by an individual, are highly resistant to correction."

3   As it happens, in recent weeks I was the target of a trolling campaign and saw exactly how it works. It started when an obscure website published a post titled "CNN host Fareed Zakaria calls for jihad rape of white women." The story claimed that in my "private blog" I had urged the use of American women as "sex slaves" to depopulate the white race. The post further claimed that on my Twitter account, I had written the following line: "Every death of a white person brings tears of joy to my eyes."

4   Disgusting. So much so that the item would collapse from its own weight-lessness, right? Wrong. Here is what happened next: Hundreds of people began linking to it, tweeting and retweeting it, and adding their comments, which are too vulgar or racist to repeat. A few ultra-right-wing websites reprinted the story as fact. With each new cycle, the levels of hysteria rose, and people started demanding that I be fired, deported or killed. For a few days, the digital intimidation veered out into the real world. Some people called my house late one night and woke up and threatened my daughters, who are 7 and 12.

5   It would have taken a minute to click on the link and see that the original post was on a fake news site, one that claims to be satirical (though not very prominently). It would have taken simple common sense to realize the absurdity of the charge. But none of this mattered. The people spreading this story were not interested in the facts; they were interested in feeding prejudice. The original story was cleverly written to provide conspiracy theorists with enough ammuni-tion to ignore evidence. It claimed that I had taken down the post after a few hours when I realized it "receive[d] negative attention." So, when the occasional debunker would point out that there was no evidence of the post anywhere, it made little difference. When confronted with evidence that the story was utterly false, it only convinced many that there was a conspiracy and coverup.

6   In my own experience, conversations on Facebook are somewhat more civil, because people generally have to reveal their identities. But on Twitter and in other places—the online comments section of *The Post*, for example—people

can be anonymous or have pseudonyms. And that is where bile and venom flow freely. The *Post*'s Dana Milbank recently quoted a tweet about a column of his that said, "Let's not mince words: Milbank is an anti-white parasite and a bigoted kike supremacist." The comments about me were often nastier.

Elizabeth Kolbert, writing in the *The New Yorker*, recalled an experiment performed by two psychologists in 1970. They divided students into two groups based on their answers to a questionnaire: high prejudice and low prejudice. Each group was told to discuss controversial issues such as school busing and integrated housing. Then the questions were asked again. "The surveys revealed a striking pattern," Kolbert noted. "Simply by talking to one another, the bigoted students had become more bigoted and the tolerant more tolerant." This "group polarization" is now taking place at hyper speed, around the world. It is how radicalization happens and extremism spreads. 7

I love social media. But somehow we have to help create better mechanisms in it to distinguish between fact and falsehood. No matter how passionate people are, no matter how cleverly they can blog or tweet or troll, no matter how viral things get, lies are still lies. 8

QUESTIONS FOR READING AND ANYSIS

1. What have we learned about the information shared on Facebook?
2. What happens when people accept false information obtained through this medium?
3. How was Zakaria trolled? What were some of the extreme responses?
4. Where can we find bile and venom flowing freely?
5. What tends to happen when bigoted people converse with one another?
6. What is meant by "group polarization"? Where is this happening?

QUESTIONS FOR REASONING AND ANALYSIS

7. Why does Zakaria believe that trolling is a serious issue? What is his claim?
8. In his last paragraph, Zakaria asserts that he loves social media. Why does he include that statement?

QUESTIONS FOR REFLECTION AND WRITING

9. If you had read the statements about Zakaria, would you have been likely to accept them as truthful? If so, why? If not, why not?
10. Much has now been written about the spread of lies on social media, and most writers consider this a major problem. Do you agree? If so, why? If not, why not?
11. Have you been trolled or bullied online? If so, how did you handle it? Do you have suggestions for others? Do you have suggestions for dealing with the problem overall?

THE RIGHT TO BURY THE (ONLINE) PAST | LIZA TUCKER

Liza Tucker is a journalist, consultant, and translator. She is currently a consumer advocate for the website *Consumer Watchdog*. She also spent ten years as a journalist on a public radio station, has traveled extensively, and has translated letters and memoirs from Russian for publication in English. Tucker wrote the following column as the response from *Consumer Watchdog* to the issue of removing cruel and irrelevant personal material from online access; the column appeared September 14, 2015.

PREREADING QUESTIONS Do you know what Google shows first to anyone searching your name? Are there any early photos you posted that you would now like to remove? What other information appears about you in a Google search?

1   Imagine your 18-year-old daughter is decapitated in a car accident. Gruesome police photographs of her body are leaked onto the Internet. Every time someone searches your family's name, the photos pop up at the top of the page. That's what happened to Christos and Lesli Catsouras because in the United States, unlike in Europe, search engines are not required to act on requests by individuals to remove such links.

2   That's why our nonprofit consumer group has petitioned the Federal Trade Commission to grant every American "the right to be forgotten," a position *The Post* criticized in an Aug. 28 editorial, "Stifling the Internet," for potentially opening the door to the purging of "unflattering" links upon request. We believe that families such as the Catsourases should have the right to ask the Internet's corporate gatekeepers to stop elevating deeply disturbing, unauthorized, irrelevant, excessive or distorted personal information to the top of search results associated with their names.

3   Extending the right to be forgotten to Americans would not mean that government would limit freedom of expression, as *The Post* suggested. True suppression of speech happens when a government reviews all media and suppresses those parts it deems objectionable on moral, political, military or other grounds. With a right to be forgotten, Google, Yahoo and other corporations—not the government—would decide what material should not be provided in response to search requests, while the material would still remain on any Web sites that posted it.

4   Google may be battling this right in the United States, but in Europe it has shown that it is perfectly capable of separating the wheat from the chaff. Google reports that it has evaluated more than 310,000 requests to remove more than 1.1 million URLs. It has removed about 42 percent and left 58 percent alone.

5   The sorts of requests that Google had denied involve people who want embarrassing, but still relevant, information excised from the Web. For example, Google did not remove links to recent articles reporting on the arrest and conviction of a Swiss financial professional for financial crimes. He's still in that business, so those who might deal with him should know. Google denied a request from a man in Britain to remove references to his dismissal for sexual crimes committed on the job. Such information is relevant to his next employer.

Requests that Google has honored also make sense. A rape victim in Ger- 6 many asked it to remove a link to a newspaper article about the crime. A woman in Italy asked for the removal of links to a decades-old article about the murder of her husband in which her name was used. Google rightly complied as the widely accessible information victimized individuals all over again.

Such readily accessible material can be devastating, unjustly foreclosing 7 economic and social opportunities. The more prominent the result, the more credible, accurate and relevant it can seem, even if the opposite is true.

For example, a Florida doctor locked herself into a bedroom to avoid a 8 violent boyfriend. After he jimmied the lock with a knife, she scratched his chest with her fingernails. He told police she had used the knife on him. Police arrested them both and charged her with aggravated assault with a deadly weapon. The charges against her were soon dropped, but she had to pay thousands to Web sites to remove her mug shot.

A middle-aged school guidance counselor disclosed the fact that she 9 modeled lingerie in her late teens when she was hired, but she still was fired after the photos surfaced on the Web. It made no difference that the photos were irrelevant to her job.

U.S. law already recognizes that certain information should become irrele- 10 vant after the passage of the time has demonstrated that an individual is not likely to repeat a mistake. The Fair Credit Reporting Act, which is enforced by the FTC, dictates that debt collections, civil lawsuits, tax liens and even arrests for criminal offenses in most cases be considered obsolete after seven years and so excluded from credit reports.

This concept is not lost on Google. When a teacher in Germany who was 11 convicted for a minor crime over 10 years ago contacted the company, it removed links to an article about the conviction from search results for the individual's name. But public figures are a different matter. When a high-ranking public official asked to remove recent articles discussing a decades-old criminal conviction, Google declined.

Google touts its privacy principles, claiming that it strives to offer its diverse 12 users "meaningful and fine-grained choices over the use of their personal information." It's deceptive and unfair for Google to make this claim but not to honor the privacy it purports to protect.

Google makes money off online searches. It has an obligation not to exploit 13 or appropriate the salacious details of peoples' lives in the pursuit of clicks and money without considering petitions to have such details removed.

The Catsouras family and others have the right not to be traumatized forever 14 by images or information that never belonged in the public domain. They deserve the right to bury the past and move on. Google's refusal to answer the family's pleas without a law in place compelling it to do so shows exactly why the FTC needs to act.

Liza Tucker, "The Right to Bury the (Online) Past," *The Washington Post,* 14 Sept. 2015. Used with permission of Liza Tucker, Consumer Watchdog, www.consumerwatchdog.org.

QUESTIONS FOR READING

1. What has *Consumer Watchdog* petitioned the FTC to do? Why is such a petition required in the United States?

2. Why is the right to request search engines to remove some personal information not considered a suppression of speech, according to the author?

3. What has been Google's experience with this issue in Europe?

4. How does U.S. law already allow for similar kinds of removal?

QUESTIONS FOR REASONING AND ANALYSIS

5. What type of argument is Tucker's? State her claim to indicate the argument type.

6. What kind of evidence does Tucker provide to support her claim? What is important to note about Google's response to requests in Europe?

7. What is effective about the author's opening and closing paragraphs?

QUESTIONS FOR REFLECTION AND WRITING

8. Should Google be required to consider requests for removing personal information in the United States? Why or why not?

9. If you oppose a law requiring search engines to consider requests, is it because you do not trust the search engines? Or do you oppose, in general, any controls on the Web? If the former, what evidence do you have that the search engines are not competent to make these decisions? If the latter, how would you defend such a position? Would you, for example, oppose Google's removal of obviously false information?

CLEVER IS FOREVER | CAITLIN GIBSON

A freelance writer for newspapers and magazines since 2005, Caitlin Gibson is now a staff writer for *The Washington Post*. Gibson, a native Washingtonian and graduate of the University of Maryland, writes news stories, feature articles, and essays. She was a 2016 finalist for the Livingston Awards for Young Journalists and, also in 2016, Best in Show for Feature Writing, an award from the MDDC Press Association. The following article appeared in *The Post*.

PREREADING QUESTIONS After reading the title, can you determine the essay's subject? What does the author count on you to notice to solve the problem?

1 There have been speeches, chants and protest anthems, both soulful and scathing—but as the masses have rallied and marched against President Trump's policies over the past two weeks, it is the signs they carried that are being stamped into memory.

2 Protesters turned Trump's own words against him, with their "Nasty Woman" banners and flaunting signs that declared "This p—grabs back." They scorned his seemingly cozy relationship with Russia: "Tinkle tinkle little czar, Putin made you what you are." They mocked his appearance: "We Shall Overcomb" and "Hands too small to build a wall." They found many different ways to reject his authority:

Not my President
Not my Führer
Not my Comrade
Not my Cheeto

With a pithy mix of humor and combativeness, this is protest art for the social-media era. While many kept their messages serious and straightforward—"Refugees Welcome," "Keep Abortion Safe and Legal"—it was the new breed of signage that went viral long after the

Demonstrations—and their clever signs—can make a difference in our ongoing political dialogue.

crowds dispersed. Gaining wide circulation on Twitter, Facebook, Instagram or various "best protest signs" listicles, they reached a vast audience that never went near a march or rally.

Protest signs have been around since the American Revolution, says Ralph 5 Young, a Temple University history professor and the author of "Dissent: History of an American Idea." But now that signs can have a long digital afterlife, the pressure is on to create ever-more memorable and creative messages.

"It became far more prevalent after photography was invented, and then 6 even more so because of television," Young says. "And now, even *more* so because of social media."

The Twitter generation is well versed at crafting sharp, short messages, 7 seeking the biggest impact with a limited amount of space.

There were plenty of clever signs on display during the civil rights and 8 anti-Vietnam protests, Young says, and a smattering of pop-culture references too. But today's protest signs are a veritable celebration of favorite characters from movies, TV and literature.

Princess Leia, Xena the Warrior Princess, the Cat in the Hat and sitcom 9 heroines from *Arrested Development* and *Parks and Recreation* were all poster-boarded for the various women's marches. Marchers also made reference to *Harry Potter* ("Even Slytherins find Trump Too Evil") and *Game of Thrones* ("Even the Lannisters Pay Their Debts"). There were Beyoncé quotes ("Okay, ladies, now let's get in formation"), '80s music puns ("Girls just wanna have fundamental human rights") and music-snob disses ("Trump Likes 3 Doors Down").

"Politics and pop culture have converged more" since the 1960s, says 10 Randall Lake, an associate professor of communications at the University of Southern California. "Especially as politics becomes more like entertainment, I think the crossover is easier."

But many signs have gone viral without pop-culture cred or incisive wit— 11 even if the message was more meta than pointed...

. . . or didn't display actual words . . . 12

Many of the boldest signs aren't printable in a family newspaper—and 13 some activists have fretted that raunchy jokes and offensive language could undermine the gravity of the cause or the protesters' moral ground. But those qualities aren't new to protest, Young says—consider the famous image of an anti-Vietnam protester raising a sign that says: "Bombing for Peace is like F— for Virginity." And many veteran protesters embraced blunt messages. Flocks of "Nasty Grandmas" and middle-aged women holding signs declaring "I can't believe I still have to protest this s—" have been spotted at demonstrations across the country.

14   Plus, as many protesters would point out, protest is *supposed* to make people uncomfortable.

15   "The norms of appropriateness have kind of loosened up, but there are still norms, and they're still constraining," Lake says. "And almost by definition, protesters have to push the boundary in order to challenge the norm."

16   There is a long tradition of humor in dissent, adds Young, from medieval court jesters to the 20th-century satire of H.L. Mencken to modern-day stars such as Jon Stewart and John Oliver.

17   But: "You don't want people to get a good laugh, and then go home and forget about it," Young notes. "You want to stir people to action. As with all things, you've got to think through how you're giving out your message, and you want to do it in an effective way."

18   This election has "made dissent and protest a lot more popular," he says. "And that's really good to see, people taking democracy seriously, no longer taking it for granted."

19   Or, in the words of one sign recently spotted outside the Trump hotel in the District: PROTEST IS THE NEW BRUNCH.

QUESTIONS FOR READING

1. What from the protests immediately after Trump's inauguration will be most remembered?

2. How have those who did not participate learned about the protests?

3. What is new about the protest signs?

4. What are some of the sources used by the sign-makers?

5. How do protesters justify the language used on some signs?

QUESTIONS FOR REASONING AND ANALYSIS

6. Gibson makes a number of points about the protest signs. Combine them in your mind to create a claim statement for the essay.

7. How does the author use her expert source Professor Ralph Young to provide a way to organize her examples?

8. What issues about the signs does Gibson explore with help from Professor Randall Lake's comments? What is Lake's position on this issue? Do you agree with him? Why or why not?

QUESTIONS FOR REFLECTION AND WRITING

9. The protest signs may be forever, but will they lead to more people staying politically involved? From your perspective some time after the protests early in 2017, how would you answer this question? What makes this point an effective conclusion for the author?

10. Many young people today are not politically engaged. They don't follow current events; they don't have a party affiliation; they don't vote. Does this description fit you? If so, have the election of President Trump and the subsequent protests with their clever signs influenced you in any way? If so, why? If not, why not?

11. The norms of political discourse have certainly been loosened in recent years. Are you comfortable with the language used in the 2016 election? With the language (and drawings!) of some of the protest signs? What happens when language becomes more coarse or vulgar? Reflect on this issue remembering that words do matter.

I AM A DANGEROUS PROFESSOR | GEORGE YANCY

George Yancy is a philosophy professor at Emory University with research interests in the philosophy of race. He is the author, coauthor, or editor of many books and articles. He is author of *Black Bodies, White Gazes: The Continuing Significance of Race in America* (2016) and editor of the Philosophy of Race book series for Lexington Books. The following essay appeared in *The New York Times* November 2016.

PREREADING QUESTIONS What is your reaction to Yancy's title? To a reference to *1984* in the opening sentence?

Those familiar with George Orwell's *1984* will recall that "Newspeak was de- 1 signed not to extend but to *diminish* the range of thought." I recently felt the weight of this Orwellian ethos when many of my students sent emails to inform me, and perhaps warn me, that my name appears on the Professor Watchlist, a new website created by a conservative youth group known as Turning Point USA.

I could sense the gravity in those email messages, a sense of relaying what 2 is to come. The Professor Watchlist's mission, among other things, is to sound an alarm about those of us within academia who "advance leftist propaganda in the classroom." It names and includes photographs of some 200 professors.

The Watchlist appears to be consistent with a nostalgic desire "to make 3 America great again" and to expose and oppose those voices in academia that are anti-Republican or express anti-Republican values. For many black people, making America "great again" is especially threatening, as it signals a return to a more explicit and unapologetic racial dystopia. For us, dreaming of yesterday is not a privilege, not a desire, but a nightmare.

The new "watchlist" is essentially a new species of McCarthyism, especially in 4 terms of its overtones of "disloyalty" to the American republic. And it is reminiscent of Cointelpro, the secret F.B.I. program that spied on, infiltrated and discredited American political organizations in the '50s and '60s. Its goal of "outing" professors for their views helps to create the appearance of something secretly subversive. It is a form of exposure designed to mark, shame and silence.

5   So when I first confirmed my students' concerns, I was engulfed by a feeling of righteous indignation, even anger. The list maker would rather that we run in shame after having been called out. Yet I was reminded of the novel *The Bluest Eye* in which Toni Morrison wrote that anger was better than shame: "There is a sense of being in anger. A reality and presence. An awareness of worth." The anger I experienced was also—in the words the poet and theorist Audre Lorde used to describe the erotic—"a reminder of my capacity for feeling." It is that feeling that is disruptive of the Orwellian gestures embedded in the Professor Watchlist. Its devotees would rather I become numb, afraid and silent. However, it is the anger that I feel that functions as a saving grace, a place of being.

6   If we are not careful, a watchlist like this can have the impact of the philosopher Jeremy Bentham's Panopticon—a theoretical prison designed to create a form of self-censorship among those imprisoned. The list is not simply designed to get others to spy on us, to out us, but to install forms of psychological self-policing to eliminate thoughts, pedagogical approaches and theoretical orientations that it defines as subversive.

7   Honestly, being a black man, I had thought that I had been marked enough—as bestial, as criminal, as inferior. I have always known of the existence of that racialized scarlet letter. It marks me as I enter stores; the white security guard never fails to see it. It follows me around at predominantly white philosophy conferences; I am marked as "different" within that space not because I *am* different, but because the conference space is filled with whiteness. It follows me as white police officers pull me over for no other reason than because I'm black. As Frantz Fanon writes, "I am overdetermined from without."

8   But now I feel the multiple markings; I am now "un-American" because of my ideas, my desires and passion to undo injustice where I see it, my engagement in a form of pedagogy that can cause my students to become angry or resistant in their newfound awareness of the magnitude of suffering that exists in the world. Yet I reject this marking. I refuse to be philosophically and pedagogically adjusted.

9   To be "philosophically adjusted" is to belie what I see as one major aim of philosophy—to speak to the multiple ways in which we suffer, to be a voice through which suffering might speak and be heard, and to offer a gift to my students that will leave them maladjusted and profoundly unhappy with the world as it is. Bringing them to that state is what I call doing "high stakes philosophy." It is a form of practicing philosophy that refuses to ignore the horrible realities of people who suffer and that rejects ideal theory, which functions to obfuscate such realities. It is a form of philosophizing that refuses to be seduced by what Friedrich Nietzsche called "conceptual mummies." Nietzsche notes that for many philosophers, "nothing actual has escaped from their hands alive."

10   In my courses, which the watchlist would like to flag as "un-American" and as "leftist propaganda," I refuse to entertain my students with mummified ideas and abstract forms of philosophical self-stimulation. What leaves their hands is always philosophically alive, vibrant and filled with urgency. I want them to engage in the process of freeing ideas, freeing their philosophical imaginations. I want them to lose sleep over the pain and suffering of so many lives that many of us deem

The Death of Socrates, painting by Jacques-Louis David.

disposable. I want them to become conceptually unhinged, to leave my classes discontented and maladjusted.

Bear in mind that it was in 1963 that the Rev. Dr. Martin Luther King, Jr., raised 11 his voice and said: "I say very honestly that I never intend to become adjusted to segregation and discrimination. I never intend to become adjusted to religious bigotry. I never intend to adjust myself to economic conditions that will take necessities from the many to give luxuries to the few. I never intend to adjust myself to the madness of militarism, to self-defeating effects of physical violence."

I also recall the words Plato attributed to Socrates during his trial: "As long as 12 I draw breath and am able, I shall not cease to practice philosophy." By that Socrates meant that he would not cease to exhort Athenians to care more for justice than they did for wealth or reputation.

So, in my classrooms, I refuse to remain silent in the face of racism, its subtle 13 and systemic structure. I refuse to remain silent in the face of patriarchal and sexist hegemony and the denigration of women's bodies, or about the ways in which women have internalized male assumptions of how they should look and what they should feel and desire.

I refuse to be silent about forms of militarism in which innocent civilians are 14 murdered in the name of "democracy." I refuse to remain silent when it comes to acknowledging the existential and psychic dread and chaos experienced by those who are targets of xenophobia and homophobia.

I refuse to remain silent when it comes to transgender women and men who 15 are beaten to death by those who refuse to create conditions of hospitality.

16   I refuse to remain silent in a world where children become targets of sexual violence, and where unarmed black bodies are shot dead by the state and its proxies, where those with disabilities are mocked and still rendered "monstrous," and where the earth suffers because some of us refuse to hear its suffering, where my ideas are marked as "un-American," and apparently "dangerous."

17   Well, if it is dangerous to teach my students to love their neighbors, to think and rethink constructively and ethically about who their neighbors are, and how they have been taught to see themselves as disconnected and neoliberal subjects, then, yes, I am dangerous, and what I teach is dangerous.

George Yancy, "I Am a Dangerous Professor," *The New York Times*, 30 Nov. 2016. Used with permission of the author.

QUESTIONS FOR READING

1. What is the Professor Watchlist? What seems to be its purpose?
2. What is the reaction of many black people to the nostalgic "make America great again" idea?
3. Why is the reaction of anger better than a reaction of shame?
4. How does Yancy want to influence his students?

QUESTIONS FOR REASONING AND ANALYSIS

5. You know the occasion for Yancy's essay; what is his claim?
6. How does Yancy develop and support his position? Is his support effective for his subject and claim?
7. Examine the author's use of a rhetorical strategy in the latter part of his essay. What makes this strategy effective?
8. What are the essay's earmarks of a personal essay? Explain why the essay is still an argument.

QUESTIONS FOR REFLECTION AND WRITING

9. Yancy uses a number of quotations. Which one(s) would you choose as most effective? Why?
10. Would you choose to take a class from a professor on the watchlist? If so, why? If not, why not?
11. How do you think Yancy's article is related to *The Death of Socrates* painting included in this text? Do you think it is an appropriate reference? If yes, why? If not, why?

CHAPTER 17

Marriage and Gender Issues: The Debates Continue

READ: The picture above shows a large marriage ceremony in Seattle, Washington. Look closely—what do you notice about the people getting married that is different from traditional marriages?

REASON: Why do you think these types of marriage ceremonies drew media and public attention? What political, religious, and cultural issues does this picture raise?

REFLECT/WRITE: What is your position on who you think should be able to marry?

Five writers provide much for readers to debate and reflect upon in this chapter on marriage and gender issues. The writers examine the incredible—and in some cases still controversial—changes to the institution of marriage and—by extension—to the family. And that extension immediately takes us to gender issues, to debates over "who's up and who's down," men or women, and to changing views—and laws—regarding LGBTQ+ marriage and LGBTQ+ families. (About one-third of LGBTQ+ partnerships have one or more children, an important statistic in these discussions.)

Here are a few more interesting statistics relevant to the debates in this chapter: In 2010, according to a Gallup poll, for the first time more than 50 percent of Americans supported gay and lesbian relationships. And for the first time, more men than women supported gay partnerships, with the greatest shifts in support coming from both young adult men and older men.

Some of the writers in this chapter approach the changes in marriage and gender views—and their effects on our politics, our culture, and our personal lives—from a social science perspective; others take a more jocular or satiric approach. Some write from the perspective of research data; others develop arguments from emotion or from a legal perspective. Some express strongly held views; others seek common ground. But whatever the writer's specific topic, or the basis for the argument, or the values expressed, all would agree that the changes of the past thirty years have had a profound effect on our lives. All would probably also agree that while some issues will continue to benefit from both research and reflection, the reality is that the United States has accepted LGBTQ+ partnerships.

PREREADING QUESTIONS

1. Do you expect to have a career? To have a spouse and children? Should society support both men and women having these choices? If so, how?

2. What role, if any, should government and the courts have in defining marriage?

3. What has been meant by the "traditional family"? In what ways has the "family" been reshaped in the twenty-first century?

4. Do you have a position on LGBTQ+ marriage? On partnership recognition and rights? If you have a position, what is it, and what is its source?

5. Do you expect to live with someone prior to marriage? Do you think such arrangements will benefit the marriage that you assume will follow? Would it be a good idea to learn more about cohabiting?

6. Much has been written recently about women getting ahead at the expense of men; do you think this is the case? Would it be useful to look at some of the facts?

THE DOWNSIDE OF LIVING TOGETHER | MEG JAY

A clinical psychologist, Meg Jay is an assistant clinical professor at the University of Virginia who also has a private practice in Charlottesville. She specializes in "twentysomethings." She is the author of *The Defining Decade: Why Your Twenties Matter—and How to Make the Most of Them* (2012).

PREREADING QUESTIONS Are you cohabiting or do you picture yourself cohabiting in the future? If so, do you see this lifestyle as "convenient" or as "a logical step to marriage"?

At 32, one of my clients (I'll call her Jennifer) had a lavish wine-country   1
wedding. By then, Jennifer and her boyfriend had lived together for more than four years. The event was attended by the couple's friends, families and two dogs.

When Jennifer started therapy with me less than a year later, she was looking   2
for a divorce lawyer. "I spent more time planning my wedding than I spent happily married," she sobbed. Most disheartening to Jennifer was that she'd tried to do everything right. "My parents got married young so, of course, they got divorced. We lived together! How did this happen?"

Cohabitation in the United States has increased by more than 1,500 percent   3
in the past half century. In 1960, about 450,000 unmarried couples lived together. Now the number is more than 7.5 million. The majority of young adults in their 20s will live with a romantic partner at least once, and more than half of all marriages will be preceded by cohabitation. This shift has been attributed to the sexual revolution and the availability of birth control, and in our current economy, sharing the bills makes cohabiting appealing. But when you talk to people in their 20s, you also hear about something else: cohabitation as prophylaxis.

In a nationwide survey conducted in 2001 by the National Marriage Project,   4
then at Rutgers and now at the University of Virginia, nearly half of 20-somethings agreed with the statement, "You would only marry someone if he or she agreed to live together with you first, so that you could find out whether you really get along." About two-thirds said they believed that moving in together before marriage was a good way to avoid divorce.

But that belief is contradicted by experience. Couples who cohabit before   5
marriage (and especially before an engagement or an otherwise clear commitment) tend to be less satisfied with their marriages—and more likely to divorce—than couples who do not. These negative outcomes are called the cohabitation effect.

Researchers originally attributed the cohabitation effect to selection, or the idea   6
that cohabitors were less conventional about marriage and thus more open to divorce. As cohabitation has become a norm, however, studies have shown that the effect is not entirely explained by individual characteristics like religion, education or politics. Research suggests that at least some of the risks may lie in cohabitation itself.

As Jennifer and I worked to answer her question, "How did this happen?" we   7
talked about how she and her boyfriend went from dating to cohabiting. Her response was consistent with studies reporting that most couples say it "just happened."

"We were sleeping over at each other's places all the time," she said. "We   8
liked to be together, so it was cheaper and more convenient. It was a quick decision but if it didn't work out there was a quick exit."

9   She was talking about what researchers call "sliding, not deciding." Moving from dating to sleeping over to sleeping over a lot to cohabitation can be a gradual slope, one not marked by rings or ceremonies or sometimes even a conversation. Couples bypass talking about why they want to live together and what it will mean.

10   When researchers ask cohabitors these questions, partners often have different, unspoken—even unconscious—agendas. Women are more likely to view cohabitation as a step toward marriage, while men are more likely to see it as a way to test a relationship or postpone commitment, and this gender asymmetry is associated with negative interactions and lower levels of commitment even after the relationship progresses to marriage. One thing men and women do agree on, however, is that their standards for a live-in partner are lower than they are for a spouse.

11   Sliding into cohabitation wouldn't be a problem if sliding out were as easy. But it isn't. Too often, young adults enter into what they imagine will be low-cost, low-risk living situations only to find themselves unable to get out months, even years, later. It's like signing up for a credit card with 0 percent interest. At the end of 12 months when the interest goes up to 23 percent you feel stuck because your balance is too high to pay off. In fact, cohabitation can be exactly like that. In behavioral economics, it's called consumer lock-in.

12   Lock-in is the decreased likelihood to search for, or change to, another option once an investment in something has been made. The greater the setup costs, the less likely we are to move to another, even better, situation, especially when faced with switching costs, or the time, money and effort it requires to make a change.

13   Cohabitation is loaded with setup and switching costs. Living together can be fun and economical, and the setup costs are subtly woven in. After years of living among roommates' junky old stuff, couples happily split the rent on a nice one-bedroom apartment. They share wireless and pets and enjoy shopping for new furniture together. Later, these setup and switching costs have an impact on how likely they are to leave.

14   Jennifer said she never really felt that her boyfriend was committed to her. "I felt like I was on this multiyear, never-ending audition to be his wife," she said. "We had all this furniture. We had our dogs and all the same friends. It just made it really, really difficult to break up. Then it was like we got married because we were living together once we got into our 30s."

15   I've had other clients who also wish they hadn't sunk years of their 20s into relationships that would have lasted only months had they not been living together. Others want to feel committed to their partners, yet they are confused about whether they have consciously chosen their mates. Founding relationships on convenience or ambiguity can interfere with the process of claiming the people we love. A life built on top of "maybe you'll do" simply may not feel as dedicated as a life built on top of the "we do" of commitment or marriage.

16   The unfavorable connection between cohabitation and divorce does seem to be lessening, however, according to a report released last month by the Department of Health and Human Services. More good news is that a 2010 survey by the Pew Research Center found that nearly two-thirds of Americans saw cohabitation as a step toward marriage.

This shared and serious view of cohabitation may go a long way toward 17 further attenuating the cohabitation effect because the most recent research suggests that serial cohabitators, couples with differing levels of commitment and those who use cohabitation as a test are most at risk for poor relationship quality and eventual relationship dissolution.

Cohabitation is here to stay, and there are things young adults can do to 18 protect their relationships from the cohabitation effect. It's important to discuss each person's motivation and commitment level beforehand and, even better, to view cohabitation as an intentional step toward, rather than a convenient test for, marriage or partnership.

It also makes sense to anticipate and regularly evaluate constraints that may 19 keep you from leaving.

I am not for or against living together, but I am for young adults knowing that, far 20 from safeguarding against divorce and unhappiness, moving in with someone can increase your chances of making a mistake—or of spending too much time on a mistake. A mentor of mine used to say, "The best time to work on someone's marriage is before he or she has one," and in our era, that may mean before cohabitation.

Excerpted from Meg Jay, *The Defining Decade: Why Your Twenties Matter—and How to Make the Most of Them Now*. Twelve, an imprint of Grand Central Publishing, 2012. Reprinted by permission of the author.

QUESTIONS FOR READING

1. How popular has cohabiting become? What percentage of marriages will be preceded by cohabiting?

2. In the opinion of two-thirds of twentysomethings, what impact will cohabiting have on marriage or divorce?

3. How can cohabiting result in "lock-in"?

4. How has the connection between cohabitation and divorce recently changed?

QUESTIONS FOR REASONING AND ANALYSIS

5. What is Jay's claim? Where does she state it?

6. What does the author gain by starting with a specific example of a client and holding her claim until later?

7. What is the author's advice for protecting oneself from the "cohabitation effect"? Is this good advice for all couples at any stage in a relationship? Explain.

QUESTIONS FOR REFLECTION AND WRITING

8. Are you surprised by the "cohabitation effect"? Why or why not?

9. What is the most important idea in this article that you want to share with friends? Why?

10. Many young people today do more hooking up than long-term dating of one person. Could this new form of "dating" with so little commitment have the effect of leading to cohabitation with little commitment? Reflect on and be prepared to discuss these relationship patterns.

WANT A HAPPIER MARRIAGE, DADS? THEN TAKE PATERNITY LEAVE.

STEPHANIE COONTZ

Stephanie Coontz teaches history and family studies at Evergreen State College and is the author of several books, including *A Strange Stirring: The Feminine Mystique and American Women at the Dawn of the 1960s* (2012). Coontz also serves as co-chair and director of public education at the Council on Contemporary Families; she publishes in the popular press and appears frequently on radio and TV talk shows. The following article originally appeared in *The Guardian* in 2015.

PREREADING QUESTIONS How might paternity leave enrich families?

1   Next week a new parental leave policy goes into effect in the UK, extending the length of leave for up to 50 weeks after the birth or adoption of a baby, with 39 of the 50 weeks subsidised. After the first two weeks, a mother in a two-earner family can transfer all or some of the remaining weeks to the father, allowing her to go back to work earlier and him to stay home longer than in the past.

2   As someone living in the U.S., where there is no guaranteed paid leave for mothers, let alone fathers, it's tempting to look at the UK policies and say "count your blessings". But as a researcher who has studied how men's secondary role at home and women's second-class role at work are mutually reinforcing, I believe there is good reason to ask for more than is currently on offer.

3   For one thing, fathers are only eligible for leave if their wives are also employed outside the home. The pay rates for male leave-takers are also pegged too low, making the financial penalty for paternal leave-taking prohibitively high for many families. And as long as the leave is transferable, the experience of other countries suggests that in most families the mother will still use the bulk of it. Only when countries combine generous pay replacement with a use-it-or-lose-it quota for men does fathers' participation rise significantly.

Everyone in the family is happy when dads participate in child care.

©Inti St Clair/Blend Image LLC RF

Some might say that if a couple really want the mother to take the 4
entire leave, we should respect that choice. But when women first won the right
to apply for jobs and promotions that were formerly reserved for men, many
hesitated to take full advantage of the new opportunities. Only with active
encouragement and recruitment, including the establishment of quotas, did
women gain the confidence and experience to take on new challenges at work.

Men are in a similar position today when it comes to exercising their rights 5
and obligations in the family. Many of them hesitate to claim family responsibilities
traditionally associated with women, fearing they'll be penalised if they deviate
from traditionally masculine roles. In this regard they are right. Studies show that
men who take family leave are more likely to be harassed at work, face a greater
risk of being demoted, and earn significantly less than other male employees
over the long run. No wonder so few men take family leave in countries that fail
to make care-giving a social norm for fathers as well as mothers.

But recent research also suggests that once some fathers are induced to 6
take paternity leave, others will follow suit. In Norway, for example, researchers
found that having just one person in a workplace or family take leave increased
the chance that a co-worker would also do so by 11% and that a brother would do
so by 15%.

Furthermore, the experience of taking leave changes men's behaviour even 7
after they return to work, altering the division of labour at home and at work for
years to come. Sociologist Ankita Patnaik found that after Quebec increased
parental leave benefits and established a use it or lose it five-week quota for
fathers in 2006, men's take-up rates increased by 250%. By 2010, 80% of eligible
men were using the leave, and the duration of their leaves had increased by
150%. Even after exhausting their leave, these fathers kept doing more cooking
and shopping, while their partners increased their paid labour. A study of the
impact of one "daddy quota" reform in Norway found that couples who bore
their last child just after the reform were 50% more likely to share laundry duties
than those who had their last child just before the reform. Not surprisingly, they
also reported fewer conflicts over housework.

The longer the leave, the greater its impact. In Sweden, fathers who take 8
longer leaves than average remain more involved in childcare and household
work than fathers who take shorter leaves.

Just as every generation of working women has passed on more egalitarian 9
values to their children, each generation of involved fathers will do the same.
Young men were much more likely to share housework and childcare with their
partner if they saw their fathers doing so when they were children. And daughters
of hands-on fathers are less likely to be channelled into traditional gender roles
at home. In Norway, girls born after the paternity leave reform were assigned
fewer household chores as teenagers—many years after their fathers had
returned to work—than their counterparts born just before it.

There is already ample research showing that workplaces function better 10
when women are integrated into positions of responsibility, but it also appears
that families run more smoothly when men are integrated into household

responsibilities. In the UK, Sweden, and the Netherlands, couples in which fathers are more involved in childcare have a lower rate of divorce than couples where the man is less involved. Throughout the Nordic countries, men who take parental leave are less likely to dissolve their unions. In the United States, where low-income cohabiting couples with children tend to have very unstable relationships, a father's involvement in childcare lowers the risk of dissolution and slightly increases the chance that a couple will marry at some point.

11   There is even evidence to suggest that recent upturns in fertility in several European countries are associated with increases in the contribution of fathers to childcare and core domestic chores. Working women who see their partner spend time in primary childcare after the birth of a child are more likely to consider having a second child.

12   The first stage of the gender revolution, which involved integrating women more fully into the public sphere, destabilised traditional male-female relationships. But, as Brown University demographer Frances Goldscheider argues, the next stage, which involves integrating men more fully into the private sphere, may actually strengthen family relationships.

13   As for those diehards who think that the erosion of traditional gender roles is emasculating men and creating women who put their work life above their love life, a new U.S. study shows just the opposite. In marriages formed since the 1990s, couples who share household work more equally tend to have more sex and to rate their sex lives and marital happiness higher than couples who cling to a more rigid division of labour. If that doesn't motivate a man to take paid leave when it's offered, well maybe he just isn't "man enough" to handle a modern family.

Stephanie Coontz, "Want better sex, dads? Then take paternity leave," *The Guardian,* 2 Apr. 2015. Used with permission of the author.

QUESTIONS FOR READING

1. What new parental policy went into effect in England in 2015?

2. What weakness does Coontz see in this new policy?

3. How eager are many fathers to take paternal leave? What tends to happen in the work-place to those who do use the program?

4. By contrast, what has happened in Norway? What has resulted from the use of paternal leave in Quebec and Sweden?

5. What does a U.S. study show about couples who share household chores more equally?

QUESTIONS FOR REASONING AND ANALYSIS

6. Coontz refers to a number of studies from a variety of countries. What general subject do they have in common?

7. What, then, is the author's subject? What is her claim?

8. The author sees paternal leave and its consequences as part of an ongoing process; explain this process and its effects on society.

9. What does the author accomplish with her final paragraph?

QUESTIONS FOR REFLECTION AND WRITING

10. Have you reflected on the social changes Coontz chronicles in family life? Does it make sense that when we experience changes in the workplace and in the home, we find our attitudes change as well? Reflect and respond.

11. Which study interested or surprised you the most? Why?

WOMEN WILL MAKE UNITS STRONGER | LISA JASTER

One of only three women to complete the U.S. Army Ranger School, Major Lisa Jaster, now in the Army Reserve, is an engineer with Shell Oil. Jaster completed the elite training program as a wife and mother aged thirty-seven, an amazing feat. Her article below was initially published in 2015.

PREREADING QUESTIONS From Jaster's biography, what "units" do you think she will be writing about? If women are the "weaker sex," how might women make units stronger?

Last week, Defense Secretary Ashton B. Carter directed that all jobs in the   1
U.S. military be opened to women. The announcement provoked strong reactions, but all sides concurred that we cannot let our standards fall or force quotas on our combat units. As an Army officer, a combat veteran and one of the first three women to graduate from U.S. Army Ranger School, I strongly agree.

©Jessica McGowan/Getty Images

The Army's first two females graduate from the Army Ranger Program.

2   The critics worry about strength and stamina, often comparing infantry units to professional sports teams. But just as a successful football team needs a smart quarterback, fast receivers, strong linemen and talented special teams, our war fighters must dominate all aspects of the battle space. At Ranger School, individuals are referred to as either Strong Rangers or Smart Rangers. Some exceptional soldiers are both, but most fit predominantly into one category or the other. I wasn't the strongest Ranger, but I spent almost every morning in the center of the patrol base helping plan the day's mission. Did my intellect make me an asset to the team? I know a few guys who would say it did. As with every team, some members need to be smarter while others need to be stronger. But no one can be a physical liability.

3   I keep hearing that the change means politicians will force military training schools to graduate women. Some think that if allowances are not made, no women will successfully graduate from some schools or be able to join certain units. But that's okay—no one wants those allowances. Secretary Carter said there would be no quotas, and there shouldn't be. Elite training courses such as Basic Underwater Demolition ensure that only individuals with extremely high levels of mental and physical prowess can serve in these niche capacities. That should not change.

4   Just as the military gets tested on tactical tasks, everyone in the ranks should get tested on job-specific physical requirements. For example, if you want to be in an armor or field artillery unit, you must prove that you are capable of lifting and moving the heaviest round in the arsenal. Consideration should be given to the addition of job-specific physical testing, which could solve a problem in many of our combat units and may quell concerns around the integration of women.

5   Many comments I have seen about this topic allude to "female issues." Look, women have been running around the woods for hundreds of years without anyone having to tell them how to deal with bodily functions. Trust me, we got this.

6   Countless people also question how units will maintain the mystical alchemy of the bro-bond once women join the ranks, but unit cohesion doesn't develop because men act like teenagers in a locker room. Overcoming adversity builds that bond. Ask a cop after a shootout or a firefighter who ran into a burning building. The man or woman to his left or right becomes his "brother" regardless of gender, religion or politics.

7   None of these arguments is new. And all of them ignore the fundamental fact that brute strength is not the only, or even the most important, factor in a successful combat mission. Courage, ingenuity, strategic thinking, levelheadedness, marksmanship and an ability to read people all factor into whether a unit succeeds or a mission goes south. Yes, we will maintain physical standards, and some women will fail, but the ones who succeed will bring new strengths as well, making their units stronger and more agile.

8   Finally, a word to those women interested in joining combat arms: Carry your load. Meet or exceed the same standard as a man your size, and be prepared for

the possibility of failure. Above all, strive to be an asset to our forces daily. Understand that your behavior will affect generations to come. Women don't have to prove we are worthy of this opportunity, but we have to make sure that we don't prove the naysayers right.

Lisa Jaster, "Women Will Make Units Stronger," *The Washington Post,* 12 Dec. 2015. Used with permission of the author.

QUESTIONS FOR READING

1. What announcement has led to Jaster's essay?
2. What responses to the announcement does Jaster agree with? How do these agreements reinforce Jaster's argument?
3. How should physical requirements and standards be maintained?
4. How do military units form a "brotherhood"?
5. What qualities are important to a successful mission?

QUESTIONS FOR READING AND ANALYSIS

6. Around what points does Jaster organize her essay? Then, what *type* of argument is this? State her claim to reveal her approach.
7. If Jaster argues to maintain standards and opposes any use of quotas, how does she support her position that women will make units "stronger"?
8. Find a metaphor and explain how the author uses it to support her position.

QUESTIONS FOR REFLECTION AND WRITING

9. Has Jaster convinced you that women can strengthen army units? If so, why? If not, why not?
10. Is it time to stop defining—and limiting—individuals by their gender and instead evaluate each person on his or her particular skills and abilities? This is a key question for our times, worthy of serious reflection.

HERE'S HOW 9 PREDICTIONS ABOUT GAY MARRIAGE TURNED OUT | JONATHAN RAUCH

A senior fellow at the Brookings Institution, Jonathan Rauch is the author of numerous columns in newspapers and magazines. He is also the author of six books, including his 2015 e-book *Political Realism.* His primary focus has been on public policy, but he also writes on cultural issues, especially gay marriage. In 2014, he published *Gay Marriage: Why It Is Good for Gays, Good for Straights, and Good for America.* In 2013, he published *Denial: My 25 Years without a Soul,* a memoir of his experience with his sexuality. Rauch summed up his years of writing on same-sex marriage in the following essay.

PREREADING QUESTIONS How effective do you expect Rauch to have been in his predictions? If you had anticipated the issue of same-sex marriage going to the Supreme Court in 2015, how would you have predicted the outcome?

1   Not often—in fact, pretty much never—have I been lost for words in the gay-marriage debate. But the Supreme Court's national legalization of marriage equality leaves me gaping and gawping like a guppy. For a homosexual man of my generation, born in 1960 and deeply etched with wounds of self-loathing, discrimination, and bigotry, events in America now feel like the end of a Hollywood movie. Or, perhaps, the beginning a classic rock song, by Queen. Is this the real life? Is this just fantasy?

©Greg Hinsdale/Corbis/VCG/Getty Images

2   Although most people correctly predicted how the Supreme Court would rule in Obergefell v. Hodges, my overriding feeling is still, in a word: surprise. How—how in the world—did we get here? I've written hundreds of thousands of words about same-sex marriage over a period of two decades, including many predictions. Perhaps there is insight to be had by looking back on nine of them.

3   How did I do? A mixed bag. Three of my predictions have been wrong, indeed spectacularly (and revealingly) so. Three have been borne out (also revealingly). The jury remains out on three more. Let's start with those.

4 1) "A Supreme Court decision imposing gay marriage will spark a fierce backlash."

For years, I said the federal courts should butt out of the gay marriage debate and leave it to states, where consensus could be gradually and organically developed. I feared that involving the U.S. Constitution too soon would short-circuit a vital process of social persuasion and deprive us of the deeper kind of civil rights victory that comes only from broad public consensus, not from courts.

5   It's too early to know how Obergefell will go down. Republican presidential candidates are mostly hostile. But I believe my prediction, although sensible at the time, has passed its sell-by date. A solid national majority now supports same-sex marriage, and holdout states are moving in that direction. When I asked a couple of well-connected social conservatives whether they or others in their world were likely to go to the barricades in a multi-decade campaign of resistance

like the one over abortion, both said no. One of them told me, "We could all see that the battle over same-sex marriage was over, and that was true regardless of how the court ruled in this case."

Here is my guess: Supreme Court Justice Anthony Kennedy, the author of   6
the court's five-member-majority decision, is the most astute politician in America (counting Bill Clinton as retired). He has shown a flawless knack for knowing how far he can bend public opinion without breaking it, and I believe he has correctly judged that the country is ready to accept his decision.

2) "Gay marriage won't lead to polygamous marriage."   7

Predictably, the Court's decision led to another of countless rounds of forecasts that the marriage-rights movement will now expand to multiples. (Like this.) Again, we'll see, but I'm willing to stand by what I've long said: the case for gay marriage is the case against polygamy, and the public will be smart enough to understand the difference.

Gay marriage is about extending the opportunity to marry to people who   8
lack it; polygamy, in practice, is about exactly the opposite: withdrawing marriage opportunity from people who now have it. Gay marriage succeeded because no one could identify any plausible channels through which it might damage hetero-sexual marriage; with polygamy, the worries are many, the history clear, and the channels well understood.

I won't repeat the reasons; you can read some of them in this article by me   9
or this new book by Stephen Macedo, among many other places. Predicting politics is hard, but I believe polygamy, if it even gets traction as a matter of public debate, will be decided as a policy question, not a civil-rights question—and the answer, correctly, will be no.

3) "Same-sex marriage will be part of a broader renewal of the culture of marriage."   10

I've always believed that cultural conservatives misunderstood the gay-marriage movement: far from being an attack on the culture of marriage, it represented a shift back toward family values by a group that had learned the hard way, through eviction by their own parents and suffering in the AIDS crisis, how important marriage and commitment and family really are.

Perhaps same-sex marriage will not have cultural coattails. I hope and   11
believe, however, that gay America's embrace of marriage has sparked re-newed interest and appreciation among straight Americans. And the mar-riage-equality movement has warmed many on the social left to a pro-family agenda. It's possible now, as never before, to be pro-marriage without being anti-gay. And the big message of gay marriage—"Pro-marriage is pro-equal-ity"—resonates across the spectrum. More than 100 prominent Americans, of varied political and partisan stripe, have already signed a statement calling for a new Marriage Opportunity movement building on the cultural momentum of gay marriage. This is only a beginning, but it is a breeze in the right direction.

So those are predictions where the jury remains out. Now for three I was   12
right about.

13 **4) "Marriage will transform gay culture."**

I supported same-sex marriage for many reasons: its message of legal and civic equality; its promise of support and stability for gay couples and their kids; its potential to broaden and universalize the culture of marriage; and more. Right up there was my belief that the gay culture I grew up in was toxic and that marriage could change it.

14   In the 1970s, when I came of age, being gay seemed to mean leading life in a Mephistophelean subculture that was obsessed with sex and alienated from love. In that world, gay people could have casual sex with multiple strangers, but publicly holding hands and exchanging vows were unthinkable. Gay culture internalized the legal and social repression of committed relationships in ways that twisted our psyches, distorted our communities, and ultimately fed the tragedy of AIDS.

15   Today's national debate about a culture of promiscuity and dangerous sexual behavior revolves around drunken straight frat parties, not gay bathhouses. This is partly because of AIDS, which shut down the baths. But it is also largely because of something I was right about: by tying sex, love, and commitment together into a coherent whole, marriage could heal a broken gay culture. The sexual underworld was not an inherent feature of homosexuality, as our critics charged; it was an artifact of life without marriage, and therefore without a destination for love.

16   Though casual sex and dangerous promiscuity aren't dead (and never will be, among gays or straights), they no longer define gay culture—and never will again. Gay marriage represents our time's greatest triumph of social conservatism, as today everyone except social conservatives can see.

17 **5) "Marriage will heal gay kids like Jon."**

My biggest interest in marriage, though, was very personal. I understood as a young boy, long before I had any inkling about homosexuality or sex, that marriage was not for me. And this knowledge was devastating. Every step I took toward sexual love was a step away from marriage and all the social approval and personal stability that went with it. I had seen my own parents' marriage fail painfully and harmfully (not least to me), and I yearned for the kind of stability and contentment that I saw marriage bring to my friends' parents. Desperate to keep that option open, I spent 25 years twisting myself into neurotic knots in an effort not to be gay.

18   When the idea of same-sex marriage came on the scene, I immediately saw it as a form of vaccine against homosexual self-hatred. I imagined how much different, and better, my life would have been had I assumed as a young child that the path to marriage was open to me: that I could love, and be loved, within adult life's most sustaining and engulfing institution.

19   Today, young gay children know from the first whispers of sexual awakening that they can progress from their first crush to dating, committed relationships, and a destination in marriage. And for the most part that's what they are doing. Marriage has been a miracle cure for gay self-hate. Of course being young and gay will always be difficult and confusing for many people. But now it can also be something it never could be before: normal.

6) "Gays will actually get married."   20

Actually, I didn't quite have the nerve to predict this. In fact, I worried about it. In 1996, when I published a big article on gay marriage in *The New Republic*, I ended it this way: "The biggest worry about gay marriage, I think, is that homosexuals might get it but then mostly not use it. . . . It is not enough, I think, for gay people to say we want the right to marry. If we do not use it, shame on us." Twenty years ago, after all, many in the gay-rights movement saw themselves as sexual liberators, rejecting "heteronormative" straitjackets like marriage.

I'm going to put this in the win column, because in my heart I always   21 believed that gay America would embrace marriage. Before long, I saw I was right. A turning point came on that day in San Francisco in 2004, when same-sex marriage was briefly legalized and the world saw gay couples lining up outside the courthouse and around the block. Massachusetts, legalizing gay marriage a few months later, saw a similar rush to the altar—a rush that has never stopped.

Irving Kristol, the late conservative editor and commentator, used to joke   22 about gays and marriage: "Let them have it, they won't like it." Boy, was he wrong. Gay couples have reminded the straight world how much marriage really matters.

And, finally: what was I wrong about? Here are the biggest three surprises: 23

7) "Gay marriage will take decades, if it ever happens at all."   24

When I published my first words advocating same-sex marriage (for a memorable *Economist* cover and editorial in January of 1996), I thought I was writing for some future generation. Almost nobody supported the idea or even took it seriously. Getting a gay-marriage bill introduced in even a single house of a single state legislature was unthinkable. The courts were rudely dismissive, except in Hawaii, where their openness to the idea sparked a state and national backlash—led by Democrats, notably President Bill Clinton. This was not an uphill battle. It was no battle at all. It was a flea annoying an elephant.

I was astonished when Massachusetts' supreme court legalized gay   25 marriage there in 2004, only eight years after the notorious Defense of Marriage Act swept through Congress: and I've been astonished ever since. I was not only wrong about the pace of change, I was wrong by an order of magnitude. I forever nagged gay-rights advocates to be patient and go slow. They retorted that I was underestimating the country's movability. It took a few more years, but starting in 2012, when the tide turned, they proved right. I have never been so happy to be wrong.

In my defense, there is no precedent in American history for so rapid a   26 fundamental social change. Everything I knew about social change foretold a long, slow battle. Why change came so quickly and dramatically will be debated for generations. It could only happen, I think, because a lot of vectors converged. I've tried to explain some of them in a 2013 article. Whatever the reasons eventually prove to be, I stand by what I concluded in that piece:

"At the end of the day, however, to me an element of mystery remains.   27 America's change of heart toward its gay citizens is the greatest awakening of mass conscience in the United States since the civil rights movement of the

1960s, but it was achieved with far less bloodshed and bitterness. It is born of persuasion and love, not violence and hate."

28   "Witnessing this awakening has been the most exhilarating and humbling experience of my life. Explaining it completely is, perhaps, impossible. Or perhaps I just want completely explaining it to be impossible. It feels, after all, like a miracle."

29   **8) "Marriage will retire the gay civil-rights agenda."**

Marriage, it always seemed to me, was the big kahuna for gay equality: so powerful in its symbolism and social reach as to come about only when there was little or nothing else left to be done. I assumed that traditional civil rights protections forbidding anti-gay discrimination by employers, landlords, and commercial businesses would be much less controversial than marriage and would be settled much earlier.

30   Oddly, I was wrong. Marriage was indeed much more controversial; today most Americans believe, incorrectly, that discrimination based on sexual orientation is already generally illegal. Yet marriage is now legal nationwide, but a majority of states and the federal government still lack antidiscrimination laws!

31   Indeed, antidiscrimination laws appear to be growing more controversial, because religious organizations see them as coercing participation in gay marriage. Conservative states are lining up to pass laws that shelter religious organizations, people, and businesses from antidiscrimination provisions. Like it or not, marriage or no, the battle over gay civil rights rages on.

32   **9) "Writing about gay marriage will wreck my career."**

This was my father's prediction, not my own. In 1995, he begged me to reconsider my leap into advocacy for same-sex marriage because, he said, the whole idea was so nutty that by favoring it I would give up my standing as a serious journalist. Twenty years ago, his qualms seemed perfectly reasonable.

33   I leapt anyway. And opprobrium never came. Instead I found astonishing receptivity. Never, to my knowledge, have I been punished or marginalized for saying my piece about marriage; time and again, my case has been welcomed in America's most prominent journals—including some leading conservative ones, such as *The National Review* and *The Wall Street Journal*, whose editorial positions were very different from my own.

34   In the wake of Obergefell, I received tweets and emails lauding my heroism. The truth is more like the opposite: after taking some risk initially, I never suffered or sacrificed at all. The real heroism was displayed by the culture and country, which opened its ears and ultimately its mind. For all the talk (some of it justified) of political correctness on the left and epistemic closure on the right and shrillness and polarization everywhere, I have learned that America, today as much as ever, or maybe more than ever, is a place where people can be brought to listen, consciences can be pricked, ideas can matter, and small, marginal voices can make themselves heard. That, to me, is a greater miracle even than gay marriage.

Jonathan Rauch, "Here's How 9 Predictions About Gay Marriage Turned Out," *Time*, 27 June 2015. Used with permission of the author.

QUESTIONS FOR READING

1. What was Rauch's response to the Supreme Court's ruling on same-sex marriage?

2. What are the three predictions not yet assured according to Rauch?

3. How has marriage transformed gay culture? How has it changed the lives of gay children?

4. How does the author defend his conviction that gay marriage would not come for decades?

5. What, for Rauch, is an even greater miracle than same-sex marriage?

QUESTIONS FOR REASONING AND ANALYSIS

6. Organizing by the success or failure of nine predictions provides an interesting approach for Rauch—but can obscure his central point. What is the author's main idea?

7. From the perspective of several years past 2015, examine the first three predictions. Rauch thought, in 2015, that these three predictions were still uncertain. Do you still agree, or do you think that one or more of the predictions can now be moved to the "correct" column?

8. Do you accept that Rauch was correct with predictions four through six? If not, what evidence would you use to challenge one or more of these predictions?

9. Do you agree with the author's explanation for the speed in which same-sex marriage has become the law? Are there additional reasons that can be added to his explanation? Or is it best viewed as a miracle?

QUESTIONS FOR REFLECTION AND WRITING

10. Rauch asserts that gay marriage is "our time's greatest triumph of social conservatism." Why does he see it as a conservative event? Why don't social conservatives agree? How do you view it? Why?

11. Rauch observes that even though same-sex marriage is the law, gays still face discrimination. Who else faces discrimination today? How? Should discrimination be addressed? If so, how? What should be the next advance in human and civil rights? Why?

SUPREMACY CRIMES | GLORIA STEINEM

Editor, writer, and lecturer, Gloria Steinem has been cited in *World Almanac* as one of the twenty-five most influential women in America. She is the cofounder of *Ms.* magazine and of the National Women's Political Caucus and is the author of a number of books and many articles. The following article appeared in *Ms.* in the August/September 1999 issue.

PREREADING QUESTIONS Who are the teens who commit most of the mass shootings at schools? Who are the adults who commit most of the hate crimes and sadistic killings? What generalizations can you make about these groups based on your knowledge from media coverage?

1   You've seen the ocean of television coverage, you've read the headlines: "How to Spot a Troubled Kid," "Twisted Teens," "When Teens Fall Apart."

2   After the slaughter in Colorado that inspired those phrases, dozens of copycat threats were reported in the same generalized way: "Junior high students charged with conspiracy to kill students and teachers" (in Texas); "Five honor students overheard planning a June graduation bombing" (in New York); "More than 100 minor threats reported statewide" (in Pennsylvania). In response, the White House held an emergency strategy session titled "Children, Violence, and Responsibility." Nonetheless, another attack was soon reported: "Youth With 2 Guns Shoots 6 at Georgia School."

3   I don't know about you, but I've been talking back to the television set, waiting for someone to tell us the obvious: it's not "youth," "our children," or "our teens." It's our sons—and "our" can usually be read as "white," "middle class," and "heterosexual."

4   We know that hate crimes, violent and otherwise, are overwhelmingly committed by white men who are apparently straight. The same is true for an even higher percentage of impersonal, resentment-driven, mass killings like those in Colorado; the sort committed for no economic or rational gain except the need to say, "I'm superior because I can kill." Think of Charles Starkweather, who reported feeling powerful and serene after murdering ten women and men in the 1950s; or the shooter who climbed the University of Texas Tower in 1966, raining down death to gain celebrity. Think of the engineering student at the University of Montreal who resented females' ability to study that subject, and so shot to death 14 women students in 1989, while saying, "I'm against feminism." Think of nearly all those who have killed impersonally in the workplace, the post office, McDonald's.

5   White males—usually intelligent, middle class, and heterosexual, or trying desperately to appear so—also account for virtually all the serial, sexually

Aftermath of the mass shooting at a rally for Gabrielle Giffords.

motivated, sadistic killings, those characterized by stalking, imprisoning, torturing, and "owning" victims in death. Think of Edmund Kemper, who began by killing animals, then murdered his grandparents, yet was released to sexually torture and dismember college students and other young women until he himself decided he "didn't want to kill all the coeds in the world." Or David Berkowitz, the Son of Sam, who murdered some women in order to feel in control of all women. Or consider Ted Bundy, the charming, snobbish young would-be lawyer who tortured and murdered as many as 40 women, usually beautiful students who were symbols of the economic class he longed to join. As for John Wayne Gacy, he was obsessed with maintaining the public mask of masculinity, and so hid his homosexuality by killing and burying men and boys with whom he had had sex.

These "senseless" killings begin to seem less mysterious when you consider   6 that they were committed disproportionately by white, non-poor males, the group most likely to become hooked on the drug of superiority. It's a drug pushed by a male-dominant culture that presents dominance as a natural right; a racist hierarchy that falsely elevates whiteness; a materialist society that equates superiority with possessions; and a homophobic one that empowers only one form of sexuality.

As Elliott Leyton reports in *Hunting Humans: The Rise of the Modern Multiple*   7 *Murderer,* these killers see their behavior as "an appropriate—even 'manly'— response to the frustrations and disappointments that are a normal part of life." In other words, it's not their life experiences that are the problem, it's the impossible expectation of dominance to which they've become addicted.

This is not about blame. This is about causation. If anything, ending the   8 massive cultural cover-up of supremacy crimes should make heroes out of boys and men who reject violence, especially those who reject the notion of superiority altogether. Even if one believes in a biogenetic component of male aggression, the very existence of gentle men proves that socialization can override it.

Nor is this about attributing such crimes to a single cause. Addiction to the   9 drug of supremacy is not their only root, just the deepest and most ignored one. Additional reasons why this country has such a high rate of violence include the plentiful guns that make killing seem as unreal as a video game; male violence in the media that desensitized viewers in much the same way that combat killers are desensitized in training; affluence that allows maximum access to violence-as-entertainment; a national history of genocide and slavery; the romanticizing of frontier violence and organized crime; not to mention extremes of wealth and poverty and the illusion that both are deserved.

But it is truly remarkable, given the relative reasons for anger at injustice in   10 this country, that white, non-poor men have a near-monopoly on multiple killings of strangers, whether serial and sadistic or mass and random. How can we ignore this obvious fact? Others may kill to improve their own condition, in self-defense, or for money or drugs; to eliminate enemies; to declare turf in drive-by shootings; even for a jacket or a pair of sneakers—but white males addicted to supremacy kill even when it worsens their condition or ends in suicide.

11   Men of color and females are capable of serial and mass killing, and commit just enough to prove it. Think of Colin Ferguson, the crazed black man on the Long Island Railroad, or Wayne Williams, the young black man in Atlanta who kidnapped and killed black boys, apparently to conceal his homosexuality. Think of Aileen Carol Wuornos, the white prostitute in Florida who killed abusive johns "in self-defense," or Waneta Hoyt, the upstate New York woman who strangled her five infant children between 1965 and 1971, disguising their cause of death as sudden infant death syndrome. Such crimes are rare enough to leave a haunting refrain of disbelief as evoked in Pat Parker's poem "jonestown": "Black folks do not/Black folks do not/Black folks do not commit suicide." And yet they did.

12   Nonetheless, the proportion of serial killings that are not committed by white males is about the same as the proportion of anorexics who are not female. Yet we discuss the gender, race, and class components of anorexia, but not the role of the same factors in producing epidemics among the powerful.

13   The reasons are buried deep in the culture, so invisible that only by reversing our assumptions can we reveal them.

14   Suppose, for instance, that young black males—or any other men of color—had carried out the slaughter in Colorado. Would the media reports be so willing to describe the murderers as "our children"? Would there be so little discussion about the boys' race? Would experts be calling the motive a mystery, or condemning the high school cliques for making those young men feel like "outsiders"? Would there be the same empathy for parents who gave the murderers luxurious homes, expensive cars, even rescued them from brushes with the law? Would there be as much attention to generalized causes, such as the dangers of violent video games and recipes for bombs on the Internet?

15   As for the victims, if racial identities had been reversed, would racism remain so little discussed? In fact, the killers themselves said they were targeting blacks and athletes. They used a racial epithet, shot a black male student in the head, and then laughed over the fact that they could see his brain. What if that had been reversed?

16   What if these two young murderers, who were called "fags" by some of the jocks at Columbine High School, actually had been gay? Would they have got the same sympathy for being gay-baited? What if they had been lovers? Would we hear as little about their sexuality as we now do, even though only their own homophobia could have given the word "fag" such power to humiliate them?

17   Take one more leap of the imagination: suppose these killings had been planned and executed by young women—of any race, sexuality, or class. Would the media still be so disinterested in the role played by gender-conditioning? Would journalists assume that female murderers had suffered from being shut out of access to power in high school, so much so that they were pushed beyond their limits? What if dozens, even hundreds of young women around the country had made imitative threats—as young men have done—expressing admiration for a well-planned massacre and promising to do the same? Would we be discussing their youth more than their gender, as is the case so far with these male killers?

I think we begin to see that our national self-examination is ignoring 18 something fundamental, precisely because it's like the air we breathe: the white male factor, the middle-class and heterosexual one, and the promise of superiority it carries. Yet this denial is self-defeating—to say the least. We will never reduce the number of violent Americans, from bullies to killers, without challenging the assumptions on which masculinity is based: that males are superior to females, that they must find a place in a male hierarchy, and that the ability to dominate someone is so important that even a mere insult can justify lethal revenge. There are plenty of studies to support this view. As Dr. James Gilligan concluded in *Violence: Reflections on a National Epidemic,* "If humanity is to evolve beyond the propensity toward violence . . . then it can only do so by recognizing the extent to which the patriarchal code of honor and shame generates and obligates male violence."

I think the way out can only be found through a deeper reversal: just as we 19 as a society have begun to raise our daughters more like our sons—more like whole people—we must begin to raise our sons more like our daughters—that is, to value empathy as well as hierarchy; to measure success by other people's welfare as well as their own.

But first, we have to admit and name the truth about supremacy crimes.   20

Gloria Steinem, "Supremacy Crimes," *Ms.* magazine, August/September 1999. Reprinted by permission of the author.

QUESTIONS FOR READING

1. What kinds of crimes is Steinem examining? What kinds of crimes is she excluding from her discussion?

2. What messages, according to Steinem, is our culture sending to white, non-poor males?

3. How does Elliott Leyton explain these killers' behavior?

4. What is the primary reason we have not examined serial and random killings correctly, in the author's view? What is keeping us from seeing what we need to see?

5. What do we need to do to reduce "the number of violent Americans, from bullies to killers"?

QUESTIONS FOR REASONING AND ANALYSIS

6. What is Steinem's claim? Where does she state it?

7. What is her primary type of evidence?

8. How does Steinem qualify her claim and thereby anticipate and answer counterarguments? In what paragraphs does she present qualifiers and counterarguments to possible rebuttals?

9. How does the author seek to get her readers to understand that we are not thinking soundly about the mass killings at Columbine High School? Is her strategy an effective one? Why or why not?

10. Steinem concludes by writing that we must first "name the truth" about supremacy violence before we can begin to address the problem. Does this make sense to you? How can this be good advice for coping with most problems? Think of other kinds of problems that this approach might help solve.

11. Do you agree with Steinem's analysis of the causes of serial and random killings? If yes, how would you add to her argument? If no, how would you refute her argument?

Education in America:
Issues and Concerns

To say that the issues in American education are both numerous and serious is certainly an understatement. Bill Clinton wanted to be the "education president." George W. Bush had his No Child Left Behind initiative. Barack Obama had his Race to the Top plan and emphasized the need to give everyone an opportunity to attend college. President Donald J. Trump has plans to use federal funds to support magnet and charter schools. And yet criticism continues amid only a few voices defending U.S. schools. America's best schools and colleges attract students from around the world. However, the variations in funding, facilities, teachers, and test scores from one school to another should be unacceptable to politicians and parents—and the students—who are forced to choose schools that do not best fit their needs.

The differences are noticeable at both the K through 12 and the college levels. States and school districts across the nation struggle with integrating students from different races and socioeconomic backgrounds to give everyone an equal chance at a quality education. Complicating these efforts are teacher shortages in urban and rural schools and in secondary science and math classes. At the college level, educators also struggle with designing curricula that effectively integrate both the humanities and STEM (science, technology, engineering, and math) fields while facing severe budget cuts. On the other side of the situation, students face unprecedented increases in tuition while dealing with overwhelming pressure to succeed.

These are issues in need of contemplation by all involved, including current undergraduates. The chapter begins by looking at how America might use socioeconomic status rather than race to integrate public K through 12 schools and then moves to discussions of public school teacher shortages. Universities strongly support the STEM fields while the humanities have been neglected in recent years. But lessons from history reveal that knowledge of the liberal arts (psychology, history, literature, writing) is just as valuable as STEM training. Authors also examine two campus concerns, rising tuition at public colleges and cheating. These concerns closely tie to the broader debate of what it means to have a college education.

PREREADING QUESTIONS

1. Why do you think placing children from working-class families in middle-class schools increases their math achievement scores?

2. What are the biggest obstacles to filling vacant teaching jobs today?

3. How do you account for the decrease in support for the liberal arts in U.S. schools? Should we, as a nation, be concerned?

4. Why do you think tuition at many community colleges and public universities is increasing every year, and do you think the education students receive at these schools is worth the price? How much control should state and federal governments have over tuition at public universities?

5. What should students get from a college education? Do students, parents, the government, and the business community have differing perceptions on the purpose of college? Should they?

6. Why do good students cheat in college? What are you obligated by your college to do if you know someone has cheated or is cheating? Will you fulfill your responsibility? Why or why not?

TO REALLY INTEGRATE SCHOOLS FOCUS ON WEALTH, NOT RACE | RICHARD D. KAHLENBERG

A senior fellow at the Century Foundation, Richard Kahlenberg is an expert on K through 12 schooling. He is the author of six books, most recently *A Smarter Charter: Finding What Works for Charter Schools and Public Education* (with Halley Potter, 2014), and the editor of ten more. His articles are widely published, and he is a frequent guest on TV talk shows. The following article appeared in *The Washington Post* on July 7, 2016.

PREREADING QUESTIONS In preparation for reading, review the article. What elements of the article give you the impression that the author can be trusted as an expert on the subject matter?

1   School integration is good for kids and for society, but adults have made achieving a diverse school system difficult. A focus on socioeconomic status rather than race could make the latest pro-integration policies more appealing.

2   As a political matter, many leaders have been scared to death of taking steps to racially integrate schools, given the fierce backlash against compulsory busing in the 1970s and 1980s. As a legal matter, the Supreme Court in 2007 made it harder for school districts to use race as a factor when assigning students to schools. Partially as a result of the political and legal impediments, a new report from the Government Accountability Office shows that school segregation has risen sharply in recent years.

©FatCamera/iStock/Getty Images RF

3   The good news, however, is that a small but growing number of school districts—aided by critical leadership from [the former] Education Secretary John B. King Jr.—are beginning to take steps to reimagine integration in the modern era.

New plans focus more on socioeconomic status than race and more on choice and incentives (such as magnet schools) than on compulsory busing. According to a recent Century Foundation report, 91 school districts and charter schools—educating 4 million students—now consider socioeconomic status in student assignment plans.

4   Cambridge, Mass., for example, uses a system of universal public school choice to promote socioeconomic integration. All parents choose from among a variety of magnet schools, and officials honor choices in a way to ensure that all schools have a healthy economic mix of students, as measured by eligibility for free and reduced-price lunch. In Cambridge, 85 percent of low-income students graduated on time in 2014, compared with 65 percent of low-income Boston students and 76 percent of low-income students in Massachusetts as a whole.

5   Building on local efforts—such as those in Cambridge, Dallas and La Crosse, Wis.—King has unleashed a flurry of initiatives aimed at promoting socioeconomic integration: a $120 million "Stronger Together" federal program to support local efforts at economic integration; the creation of a new priority in the administration's Investing in Innovation (known as i3) program for schools and districts that promote diversity; and an increase in magnet school funding with a priority for socioeconomic diversity.

6   In a recent Century Foundation forum, I asked King why new federal efforts are focused primarily on socioeconomic diversity rather than integration by race. He noted that given the overlap between race and class, "places that have smart socioeconomic strategies are able to achieve greater racial diversity," an important outcome for society. But he also suggested that socioeconomic diversity should be pursued for its own sake as well.

7   Researchers have long found that in raising student achievement, the socioeconomic status of one's classmates matters even more than their race. In places like Boston, the integration of working-class white and working-class black students in the 1970s did not raise achievement. By contrast, black students saw large gains when integrated with upper-middle class whites.

8   Research finds that the academic benefits of integration derive not from the pigment of classmates but from being in a middle-class school environment, where peers expect to go on to college, parents are able to be actively involved in school affairs and strong teachers are more often found. Nationwide, low-income fourth-grade students in middle-class schools are as much as two years ahead of low-income fourth-graders in high-poverty schools on the National Assessment of Educational Progress in math.

9   Framing integration primarily in terms of socioeconomic status also has political advantages. One major lesson of the 2016 campaign has been the recognition that working-class whites feel abandoned by conventional political figures, which makes them open to demagogic appeals from the authoritarian right. Socioeconomic integration benefits Hillary Clinton's African American and Latino voters but also Donald Trump's white working-class constituencies. Researchers are in broad agreement that providing children with an economically and racially integrated school environment promotes social mobility in our economy and social cohesion in our democracy.

Socioeconomic integration has become the rallying cry of some of the 10 education reformers who run charter schools. While most charters have traditionally been even more economically and racially segregated than traditional public schools (a difficult thing to be), a new generation of charter leaders is using weighted lotteries and intentional recruiting to create socioeconomically diverse student bodies.

Housing advocates have taken notice as well. In Montgomery County, Md., 11 according to a study by Rand Corp. researcher Heather Schwartz, an "inclusionary zoning" policy that allowed low-income families to live in middle-class neighborhoods and send their children to middle-class schools cut the math achievement gap between low-income and middle-class students in half.

We've been trying for decades to make separate schools equal. The new 12 movement for socioeconomic integration aims higher: to educate students from all walks of life together, as public education was always meant to do.

Richard D. Kahlenberg, "To Really Integrate Schools, Focus on Wealth Not Race," *The Washington Post,* 7 June 2016. Reprinted by permission of the author.

QUESTIONS FOR READING

1. What has happened recently that makes school integration so important?
2. Why is it now more difficult for school districts to use race as a factor when placing students in schools?
3. What factors instead of race are school districts now using to integrate schools?
4. Why is integration good for students and communities?
5. What processes are some school districts using to ensure integration?

QUESTIONS FOR REASONING AND ANALYSIS

6. What is Kahlenberg's purpose in writing? Who is his audience? What is the context of his article? That is, what situation is Kahlenberg responding to in writing this piece? Write a claims statement that reveals Kahlenberg's purpose, audience, and context in writing.
7. What kind of evidence does Kahlenberg provide to support each of his arguments?
8. Is the evidence convincing? Why or why not?

QUESTIONS FOR REFLECTION AND WRITING

9. Are you surprised by any of the information Kahlenberg provides? If so, what information surprised you? If not, why not?
10. To embrace Kahlenberg's argument about integration is to see American society as going in what direction? Presumably we would agree that this direction is not good for our society. So, what should we be doing to correct this problem? What are your suggestions—or the suggestions implied in much of the essay—for making a quality public education more available for all who wish to attend?

THE NATIONAL TEACHER SHORTAGE
IS A MYTH. HERE'S WHAT'S REALLY HAPPENING | KATE WALSH

Kate Walsh has served as the president of the National Council on Teacher Quality since 2003 and has worked on education issues at a number of nonprofit organizations, such as the Abell Foundation and the Core Knowledge Foundation. Previously, she worked in the Baltimore City Public School system and served on the Maryland State School Board. The following article was published in *The Washington Post* on December 2, 2016.

PREREADING QUESTIONS Did the schools that you attended ever have a teacher shortage? If so, what did the school do to address the shortage problem? If not, why do you think that your schools always had enough teachers?

1   Here's something I've been struggling to understand: What makes the prospect of a national teacher shortage such an immediately compelling narrative, capable of spreading with the speed of a brush fire?

2   With almost no real data—because neither states nor the federal government collects the information that would be needed to pronounce the onset of a true teacher shortage—we witness the press, school districts, state school boards and even Congress conclude that we are in the throes of a full-blown national crisis.

3   At the root of this crisis is a *New York Times* news article published two summers ago reporting on six school districts that were having a tough time filling positions (though all but two ultimately started the year just fine). Whoosh! Overnight the teacher shortage became real.

4   That early spark was then steadily fed by news articles reporting that teacher preparation programs were facing unprecedented enrollment drops.

5   Nobody thought it important to consider that teacher preparation programs had for years been graduating twice as many teachers as are needed. According to findings from the American Institutes for Research, over the past 30 years, programs graduated between 175,000 and 300,000 teachers each year, yet consistently school districts have hired only between 60,000 to 140,000 newly minted teachers. Instead, school districts have been far more likely to hire people who already have some teaching experience. Federal data from 1999 to 2012 show that only about 30 percent of districts' new hires were straight out of a teacher prep program.

6   The blaze reached new heights in September with a report from the Learning Policy Institute (LPI) producing a scary chart showing a widening gap between teacher supply and demand over the next five years.

7   But tweaking just one of the assumptions made by LPI leads to results that are altogether different. If we project an average class-size student-to-teacher ratio of 16 to 1 (which it is currently), rather than LPI's estimate of 15.3 to 1, voilà!: The shortage disappears entirely.

8   What I find so frustrating about all of this is that we do actually have a huge, long-standing problem with teacher supply and demand. For 30 years, most districts in the nation have struggled to find enough certified secondary science and math teachers. And rural and urban districts have been unable to tap into a reliable and stable source of new teachers.

9   One answer to the problem is to pay such teachers more than others, but most districts continue to reject that solution because it is untenable with unions.

We also could ramp up the availability of part-time positions for science, technology, engineering and math (STEM) teachers, but—again—few schools and states embrace this option because unions worry that districts will seek to replace full-time employees and their costly benefits with part-timers.

I'm inspired by what can happen when districts work smarter. Take Clark 10 County, Nev., which faced a staggering 1,000 vacancies at the start of the 2015-2016 school year. The next year, district officials began the school year with nearly 700 fewer vacancies. How? They got smart about recruiting and negotiated a higher starting salary for new teachers. They targeted potential applicants from areas with notoriously high costs of living, telling them how they could live better on a teacher's salary in Clark County. State efforts to ease certification requirements and improve certification reciprocity have also helped.

This is an approach that is eminently usable elsewhere. 11

We could also employ supply-side solutions. For decades, school districts 12 have been awash with applicants for elementary teaching positions. That's because teacher prep programs don't see it as their job to tell incoming students they can't all major in elementary education—that more of them need to consider special education, math or teaching English language learners, where there is real need.

Unfortunately, higher ed seems to accept no responsibility for aligning teacher 13 production with district demand. Given that teacher prep programs can't operate without state approval, states could impose limits on production in some areas.

The faux teacher shortage is of tremendous consequence. It routinely results 14 in both states and school districts lowering standards for who is licensed and hired. But more important, it serves to distract us from fixing the chronic and persistent misalignment of teacher supply and demand.

Kate Walsh, "The National Teacher Shortage Is a Myth. Here's What's Really Happening," *The Washington Post*, 2 Dec. 2016. Used with permission of the author.

QUESTIONS FOR READING

1. What caused the perception that there is a national teacher shortage?
2. What information contradicts the perception that there is a national teacher shortage?
3. How many teachers graduate in America each year? How many are hired?
4. Which subjects in school are actually facing a teacher shortage? Which communities are actually facing a teacher shortage?
5. How do states and school districts respond to the perception that there is a national teacher shortage?

QUESTIONS FOR REASONING AND ANALYSIS

6. In some sections of her article, Walsh criticizes political leaders, media outlets, nonprofit organizations, and teacher training programs for contributing to the faux teacher shortage issue. Why does she do this? Why is she so frustrated?
7. What is the real problem Walsh is trying to highlight and address?

8. What are some solutions Walsh presents? How does she go about presenting these solutions?

9. Do you find her solutions to be persuasive? If so, why? If not, why not?

QUESTIONS FOR REFLECTION AND WRITING

10. Walsh offers some insightful solutions to teacher shortage problems in some communities and in some subjects. What are some possible shortcomings and limitations to her solutions?

11. Given the challenges facing educators in America today, do you think that teaching is still a worthy endeavor and a valuable job to pursue? If so, why? If not, why not?

12. Reflect on your education up to this point and the teachers who have influenced your life. What are some of the most memorable experiences you have had? How have they helped form who you are today as a student and a person?

WHY FUTURE OFFICERS SHOULD READ SHAKESPEARE, KNOW HISTORY AND UNDERSTAND PSYCHOLOGY

JOSEPH ZENGERLE

Joseph Zengerle is a lawyer and executive director of the Mason Veterans and Servicemembers Legal Clinic, a branch of the George Mason University School of Law. A West Point graduate and retired U.S. Army veteran, he attended the University of Michigan Law School and was a note and comment editor for the *Michigan Law Review*. The following article was published by *The Washington Post* on October 3, 2016.

PREREADING QUESTIONS Many college students are pressured to major in "practical" subjects like business or engineering as soon as possible. Yet many of America's most successful people studied a field from the humanities, also known as the liberal arts. How do you think courses in the liberal arts may positively impact your studies and your life?

1   The U.S. military understood the importance of STEM long before it became the most coveted acronym in education.

2   Recognizing their critical skills in the conduct of war, George Washington appointed the first engineering officers to the Revolutionary Army on June 16, 1775.

3   Military historian Ian Hope describes how "American military thinking emerged in the young republic solidly committed to . . . the discovery of scientific components of war, with complete faith in the power of reason and with an unprecedented belief in the utility of mathematics as key to all scientific endeavors."

4   That philosophy helped guide the development of the country's military academies. In 1802, President Thomas Jefferson signed legislation establishing West Point as the nation's first engineering school. Its first superintendent, Lt. Col. Jonathan Williams, declared that "we must always have it in view that our officers are to be men of science." Superintendent Sylvanus Thayer, often called the "father" of the military academy, later grounded the school's curriculum firmly in mathematics.

The academy remained true to that mission when I was at West Point in the 5 1960s. We had math every morning, beginning with a slide-rule drill, six days a week for our entire first year. Upon graduation, we could select, according to our place in the order of merit, which of the (then five) branches of combat arms we wanted to join. The quota for the Corps of Engineers always ran out first. (I chose Infantry, which never ran out.) Today, the engineering programs at the service academies are among the best in the country.

There's an understandable premium on scientific expertise at the Pentagon, 6 too. When I was an assistant secretary of the Air Force in the early 1980s, the defense secretary was a physicist. The current secretary also is a physicist. A technical background makes sense for the leader of an institution responsible for so many complex platforms, including nuclear and satellite systems. The threat of terrorism, the operation of drones and the growing challenge of cyberwarfare further illustrate the demand for uniformed leaders to have a sound grasp of technical fields.

But even in an age of highly sophisticated warfare, our military leaders 7 should not be too narrowly focused on STEM. If we want leaders who communicate clearly, solve problems creatively and appreciate cultural differences in theaters where they operate, studying the humanities is just as important as science, technology, engineering and math.

When I attended Ranger and Airborne schools, a mandatory catchphrase 8 was "move, shoot and communicate." Communication was always a critical component of military tactics, and the more complicated combat has become, the more important it is to ensure clarity of thought and expression that relies upon a grounding in softer disciplines.

©*The Washington Post*/Getty Images

West Point students at work in the classroom.

9   Those who lead need to be ready for the moments when they must summon their troops—who may be hurt or drained by fatigue—to rise, to respond, to prevail against the odds. That power doesn't come out of the barrel of a gun or the insignia of rank, much less a math formula. It comes from an understanding of human motivation that can be gained by studying psychology, by analyzing history, by reading great literature. Military leaders should know that the familiar notion of troops as a "band of brothers" originates with the stirring speech Shakespeare's Henry V delivers to his outnumbered forces at the Battle of Agincourt.

10   Military leaders also need to be agile thinkers who can assess an unfamiliar situation and strategize a plan. That might require a cost-benefit analysis, but it also requires an understanding that not everything can be quantified. As a special assistant to Gen. William Westmoreland in 1968, I became familiar with the Hamlet Evaluation System, a monthly report that quantified the level of "pacification" by color-coding each village in South Vietnam. When attacks throughout the country erupted during the Tet Offensive, the HES reports were quickly considered an unreliable gauge. By contrast, the success of the 2007 surge in the Iraq War was under the command of Gen. David Petraeus, who, with a PhD in international relations, employed a counterinsurgency strategy based on the Army manual he co-wrote that emphasized leaders' flexibility and adaptability in dealing with indigenous populations.

11   The utility of non-STEM learning is further reflected in the nature of mission assignments. President Lyndon Johnson said victory in Vietnam would depend on our winning the "hearts and minds" of the Vietnamese, an objective necessitating education in relevant history, language and culture for military personnel assigned to advisory roles. That remains true in many conflicts today.

12   The mission of the military has expanded in ways that make a liberal arts background even more important. When Vice President Biden spoke to the graduating class at West Point in May [2016], he told them: "You're gonna need every tool your predecessors possessed . . . but you're gonna need more." He went on to talk about "next-generation technologies, like unmanned systems and autonomous machines" and the need to "dominate the cyber realm." But he also spoke about "building the capacity of emerging countries" and managing "humanitarian crises posed by climate change, mass migration and the spread of infectious disease." To take on these new challenges, rising military leaders benefit from a familiarity with foreign policy, public health and international development issues.

13   The slide rule my classmates and I struggled to master every day passed out of use a long time ago. But the service academies should be cautious about what they put in its place. If they can expose the minds of officers in training with the right ideas and the right spirit, they will cultivate a cadre of tomorrow's military leaders who will best serve the national interest.

Joseph Zengerle, "Why Future Officers Should Read Shakespeare, Know History and Understand Psychology," *The Washington Post,* 9 Oct. 2016. Used with permission of the author.

QUESTIONS FOR READING

1. What are some of the values of a liberal arts education?

2. Why are the liberal arts more important today than they were in the past?

3. How do the humanities, or "softer disciplines," work with fields like engineering and science?

4. What elements of leadership do the liberal arts foster?

5. How do the liberal arts help prepare future generations of people in the armed services in addressing the complex problems facing our nation and the world?

QUESTIONS FOR REASONING AND ANALYSIS

6. What is Zengerle's main argument, and why is he making this claim?

7. How does the author develop his argument? What are his grounds?

8. Zengerle is careful not to dismiss STEM training while making his argument. What is his strategy for including STEM with other disciplines in undergraduate education for military officers?

9. Zengerle focuses on liberal arts at the service academies. Do you think his reasoning applies for curricula at other institutions of higher education, such as community colleges, state and private schools? If so, why? If not, why not?

QUESTIONS FOR REFLECTION AND WRITING

10. When you think of courses to take, do you think about what knowledge or skills you could acquire from those courses? If not, why not? If so, what sorts of knowledge and skills do you anticipate from the courses you are enrolled in now?

11. As you consider the courses you may take during your time in college, do you think about how they might apply to or help you in your future plans for the workplace or graduate school? If so, how? If not, why not?

12. What has been the most valuable course you have taken so far during your time in college? What has been your favorite? If these two courses aren't the same, how might you combine them in some way to work toward a career you love? If they are the same class, how do you plan to apply the knowledge and skills from this course to your pathway to graduate school or the workplace?

TUITION IS NOW A USELESS CONCEPT IN HIGHER EDUCATION | DANIELLE ALLEN

Holding a PhD in government from Harvard and one in classics from Cambridge, Danielle Allen is the director of the Edmond J. Safra Center for Ethics and professor of government at the Graduate School of Education at Harvard University. She has served as a chair of the Pulitzer Prize Board and chair of the Mellon Foundation. Among her books are *Education and Equality* (2016) and *Why Plato Wrote* (2010). The following article was published in *The Washington Post* on August 19, 2016.

PREREADING QUESTIONS Do you know exactly how much your college education costs? Do you think a college education is worth the cost? If not, why are you in college?

1   If Congress wanted to make an actual difference regarding the rising cost of college, and to give universities and colleges a fighting chance to solve this problem, it would strip from the Higher Education Act the requirement that colleges publish a "tuition" number. The figure is as good as useless now.

2   Colleges should instead publish five numbers: how much they spend each year on educating each student; the range a family is expected to contribute to that expense, from zero to a maximum; how much a family contributes on average; the range of what a college itself will contribute for each student; and how much the college contributes on average to the total expense for each student.

3   Why is the concept of tuition as good as useless? Let me count the ways.

4   1. At Ivy Leagues and top liberal arts colleges, whose tuition announcements get lots of attention, the tuition is only a "sticker price." The majority of families whose children attend these elite schools pay less, as determined by their level of financial need. Increases to tuition matter only for the full-payers. For those on financial aid, changes to aid policies, not to tuition, are what matter. These policies get little public attention or transparency. How often do our major newspapers publish stories on how colleges define need?

5   2. At elite colleges and universities, the actual cost of educating any given student for a year is greater than the "sticker price." For the 2014-2015 school year, Amherst College calculated a cost per student of $95,600. For 2012-2013, Princeton put the number at $92,000. In the Ivies and top liberal arts colleges today, a reasonable estimate would put that number in the territory of $100,000, whereas the "sticker price" clocks in at about $65,000. At research universities, it is especially hard to calculate the annual cost, or investment, per student, because these institutions do so many things in addition to educating undergraduates. But such calculations can be done at liberal arts colleges, and their cost-per-student figures would offer a baseline for a conversation about what we should be investing in students and how we should be paying for it. Such a baseline would be much better than a "tuition" number that provides no useful information other than how much the well-off are asked to pay.

6   3. Tuition decisions made by elite colleges and universities are actually decisions about whom to subsidize. The lower the sticker price, the more the well-to-do are being subsidized for an education that costs well above the sticker price. The higher the sticker price, the more the subsidy is shifted to the less well-off. Over a decade-plus of work in administration in higher education, I've paid attention to how these subsidies have shifted. At one leading liberal arts college, in the early 1980s, all families were being subsidized for about 50 percent of the actual cost of educating their students. That subsidy has increased to 100 percent for the worst off and fallen to about 30 percent for the well-off. The elite colleges and universities are asking full-paying families to increase their contribution so that the colleges and universities can spread their institutional contribution as far as possible. Decisions about how to set "tuition" are having impacts that are the reverse of what our instincts tell us about what a higher or lower number means. A price that goes up is good for the worst off. A price that goes down is bad for them.

7   4. The first three points apply only to the very well-endowed colleges and universities. They top the rankings tables partly because they can invest more

in educating each student they admit. But their tuition sticker prices, which are more redistributive the higher they go, set the terms of the conversation for everyone else. Their high sticker prices give public universities cover, I believe, for raising their own sticker prices. But public universities are not similarly able to discount that price through substantial financial aid packages. In 2014, the University of Virginia, for instance, had to walk away from a much-lauded effort to extend its financial aid offerings. The higher the sticker price rises at the wealthy privates, the more the publics can charge and still appear to be a bargain in comparison. Paradoxically, the redistributive effort at the privates may well have helped erode the public-good commitment to funding public universities.

If you feel confused by now, then you have just experienced a small taste of   8
what conversations about tuition setting are like in higher ed. Which is why, if Congress wants to solve this problem, it should scrap outdated language in the Higher Education Act that is distorting the decision-making at colleges as they try to consider how much to invest in each student annually, how much each family should be asked to contribute to that investment, and how much the college or university should itself commit to contributing, whether from its endowment or, in the case of the publics, public coffers. Those are the concepts, and the parsimonious sets of words, that we should be using to discuss this topic.

Economists talk about the ratio of signals to noise. Efficiency requires that   9
the meaningful signals in a communication far outweigh any accompanying noise. "Tuition" is almost all noise, no signal. Or, we might say, it is sound and fury, signifying next to nothing.

Danielle Allen, "Tuition Is Now a Useless Concept in Higher Education," *The Washington Post,* 21 Aug. 2016. Used with permission of the author.

QUESTIONS FOR READING

1. Why is a college tuition amount, especially at research universities, misleading?
2. What factors actually determine how much a student or her family pays for a college education?
3. What does "subsidize" mean in the context of this article?
4. Who pays more at Ivy League universities and liberal arts colleges when tuition prices go up?
5. As education costs increase at private universities, what is happening at public institutions? How is this outcome detrimental to the taxpayers who support public universities?

QUESTIONS FOR REASONING AND ANALYSIS

6. What problem is Allen addressing in this article? (Think about this.) What, then, is her claim?
7. What are her reasons? (Add a "because" clause to the claim.)

8. Allen presents her argument in a list of numbered paragraphs. Why do you think she does this? Is this organization effective?

9. What kinds of grounds does the author present? How effective are the grounds in support of the claim?

QUESTIONS FOR REFLECTION AND WRITING

10. Do you think that Congress will follow Allen's suggestions? If so, why? If not, why not? Do you think colleges should publish the five numbers Allen mentions even if Congress does not require it? If so, why? If not, why not?

11. How difficult do you think it would be to obtain from your college the five numbers Allen discusses at the beginning of her article?

12. After reading this article, are you reevaluating how much you think your college education is costing and how you might pay for it? If so, why? If not, why not?

PARTISAN POLITICS IS CUTTING THE HEART OUT OF PUBLIC IVIES | CHARLES R. PRUITT

For the past thirteen years, Charles R. Pruitt has served as a member of the University of Wisconsin Board of Regents and is currently a board member and vice chair of the Association of Governing Board of Universities and Colleges. The following article was published by *The Washington Post* on August 26, 2016.

PREREADING QUESTIONS Do you think that states should financially support their institutions of public higher education? If so, how much should states spend? A lot? Not so much?

1   For generations, public universities have been seen as great equalizers in the United States, especially for the middle class. In many states, a high-achieving student could go to a "Public Ivy," a land-grant, flagship university in Michigan, Wisconsin or California, among others, and receive a Harvard- or Yale-caliber education at an affordable price.

2   But this model depends on another that stands in sudden danger of collapse: bipartisan—indeed, nonpartisan—political support. There always have been politicians willing to assail the so-called ivory tower, but elected officials have almost always unified across partisan lines in not merely support of but also pride in their public universities. Increasingly, however, they are retreating behind those lines to attack the schools.

3   This trend, which threatens the fundamental promise of the Public Ivies, is evident in deep and ongoing cuts in state support, renewed political attacks on faculty and the tenure system that protects their freedom, and a growing focus on the economic rather than the humanizing role of education. That those lobbing the attacks are increasingly identifiable by partisan labels is perhaps the most discrete cause for alarm.

4   The Center on Budget and Policy Priorities reports that states have slashed per-student spending at public colleges and universities by 17 percent since the Great Recession, while tuition has shot up by a third.

The University of Michigan's student union.

We've certainly seen it in Wisconsin, where I recently completed 13 years of   5
service on the Board of Regents of the University of Wisconsin system. The
"Wisconsin Idea"—that the university system serves not just students but also the
state as a whole—once bound even intensely divided political leaders in the belief
that the public university was both a point of pride and an anchor of opportunity.

6   Between 2003, when I joined the regents, and 2010, aid declined precipitously while tuition rose by 71 percent. In 2000, almost 10 cents of every tax dollar in Wisconsin went to the university system. Today, it is close to 6 cents. Meanwhile, the same elected officials slashing aid are now forbidding any tuition increases that might compensate for continued cuts.

7   Such policies compromise the historic promise of the Public Ivies: excellence and affordability, made possible by robust state support. Now, having made incompatible promises to slash funding and freeze tuition, politicians have set aside leadership and chosen the course of attack instead. In my state, they say the university is "out of touch," its business model "broken." The idea is to set up a partisan debate between largely Democratic defenders and largely Republican critics of the university.

8   This process of partisan polarization surrounding universities has occurred in other states as well, from Virginia and North Carolina to Colorado and Arizona. In North Carolina, Republican Gov. Pat McCrory said the state should only subsidize university classes that would "get someone a job." Elsewhere, more in-state students are losing their places to "full pay" students from other states or countries as universities desperately search for new revenue to offset budget cuts. A recent "discovery" of "billions" of dollars held in reserve at the University of Virginia stirred legislative criticism even though, as university officials tried to explain, most of these dollars came originally from sources other than state aid or tuition and, in an era of declining state support, a reserve fund is an essential component of sound fiscal management.

9   At a meeting not long ago between state legislative leaders and regents of the University of Wisconsin, for example, the Republican speaker of the Wisconsin Assembly, Robin Vos, told the regents we had a choice: be "cheerleaders for the university or advocates for the taxpayers." The once-unifying "Wisconsin Idea" had held that to be one was to be the other. Meanwhile, in his 2015 budget, Republican Gov. Scott Walker simultaneously proposed slashing a record $350 million from the university while removing tenure protections for faculty.

10   Walker also proposed rewriting the institution's mission statement—which focuses on "the search for truth" and improvement of the human condition, the traditional and noble role of the university—so that it focused on training workers instead.

11   In the face of criticism, Walker called these changes a "drafting error." An error can reveal a great deal about one's underlying values, and this one did. The governor and his allies spoke of "modernizing" the mission statement. But the search for truth and the sifting and winnowing of knowledge in its pursuit are not out of date. They are timeless and, indeed, they have never been more urgently relevant.

12   There are lessons in this for policymakers across the country. The implicit dichotomy between a humanizing education and a lucrative one is false. Employers consistently say they seek graduates who can think independently and analytically. Students learn to do so by means of technical skills, of course— which public universities teach—but also by learning the great and timeless ideas an education at a Public Ivy conveys.

That used to be a unifying idea. But to say the Public Ivies used to unite the ₁₃ parties is to say too little. They used to transcend such divisions. That they are now being used to inflame them bodes ill—not just for the Public Ivies, but for public discourse, too.

Charles R. Pruitt, "Partisan Politics Is Cutting the Heart Out of Public Ivies," *The Washington Post,* 26 Aug. 2016. Used with permission of the author.

QUESTIONS FOR READING

1. What has happened recently that jeopardizes state universities and "Public Ivy" institutions?

2. Specifically, who does Pruitt mention as contributing to the current situation facing public higher education?

3. As college tuition rises and state funding decreases, what is happening to in-state students who try to attend their public universities?

4. What is the "Wisconsin Idea"?

QUESTIONS FOR REASONING AND ANALYSIS

5. What is Pruitt arguing for in this article, and how does he present his claims?

6. What evidence does the author provide to support his claims?

7. What do you think "partisan polarization" means, and why do you think Pruitt uses this term in his argument?

8. Pruitt ends his article by noting that both Public Ivies *and* public discourse are being threatened. What does he mean by "public discourse" and why do you think he ends his piece in this way?

QUESTIONS FOR REFLECTION AND WRITING

9. Since their inception, American state and public universities have focused on searching for truth and improving the human condition. Recently, as Pruitt notes, these ideals have come under attack from politicians who feel that public higher education should be more vocational. Is it possible to do both well—to seek truth and improve the human condition while also preparing people to enter the workforce? If so, why? If not, why not?

10. Were you surprised that Scott Walker, the governor of Wisconsin, slashed spending for his state's public higher education? If so, why? If not, why not?

11. Wisconsin governor Scott Walker attended Marquette University, a private Jesuit university in Milwaukee, Wisconsin. However, he did *not* finish his bachelor's degree. Do you think that his attending a private school and lack of an undergraduate degree in any way influenced his decisions to cut spending for his state's higher education? If so, why? If not, why not?

WHY KIDS CHEAT AT HARVARD | HOWARD GARDNER

Howard Gardner is the John H. and Elisabeth Hobbs Professor of Cognition and Education at the Harvard Graduate School of Education and senior director of the Harvard Zero Project, a project focused on creating performance-based assessments in education. The author of thirty books, he is best known for his theory of multiple intelligences. Among his many books are *Intelligence Reframed: Multiple Intelligences for the 21st Century* (1999) and *The App Generation: How Today's Youth Navigate Identity, Intimacy, and Imagination in a Digital World* (with Katie Davis, 2013). Dr. Gardner has been cited as one of the 100 most influential intellectuals in the world today. The following article appeared in *Newsday* on September 7, 2012.

PREREADING QUESTIONS Why do you think that students at Harvard—or anywhere— cheat on exams and papers? Can we understand the motivation?

1   On August 27 [2012], approximately 1,600 freshmen arrived at Harvard College. Two days later, I had the pleasure of spending 90 minutes with 20 of these students. They impressed me with their intellect but also with their empathy and willingness to listen to and learn from one another. They were excited by the opportunity to be at Harvard; they used such superlatives that I joked to colleagues that in a few years, they would be so critical, if not cynical, they would have a hard time believing their earlier enthusiasm.

2   On August 30 [2012], I and many others learned of the university's largest cheating scandal in living memory. According to news reports, close to half of the 250 undergraduates in "Introduction to Congress" are being investigated for allegedly cheating on a final examination.

3   The fate of individual students is not yet known, but this event will clearly be a stain on Harvard's reputation as large and consequential as that suffered by the service academies in earlier decades.

4   Many wonder how this could have happened at "MGU" (man's greatest university). They will ask whether a large number of the same enthusiastic and loving students I met with last week might well, in a year or two, be part of a cheating scandal themselves. The answer, I fear, is yes.

5   I've been at Harvard for more than half a century—as an undergraduate, a graduate student, a researcher and, for almost three decades, a professor. I know the university well, and in many ways I love it. Yet almost 20 years ago I became concerned about the effect that market ways of thinking have on our society, particularly our young. Colleagues and I undertook a study of "good work." As part of that study, we interviewed 100 of the "best and brightest" students and spoke with them in depth about life and work.

6   The results of that study, reported in *Making Good,* surprised us. Over and over again, students told us that they admired good work and wanted to be good workers. But they also told us they wanted—ardently—to be successful. They feared that their peers were cutting corners and that if they themselves behaved ethically, they would be bested. And so, they told us in effect, "Let us cut corners now and one day, when we have achieved fame and fortune, we'll be good workers and set a good example." A classic case of the ends justify the means.

The beautiful Harvard campus.

We were so concerned by the results that, for the past six years, we have 7 conducted reflection sessions at elite colleges, including Harvard. Again, we have found the students to be articulate, thoughtful, even lovable. Yet over and over again, we have also found hollowness at the core.

Two examples: In discussing the firing of a dean who lied about her academic 8 qualifications, no student supported the firing. The most common responses were "She's doing a good job, what's the problem?" and "Everyone lies on their résumé." In a discussion of the documentary *Enron: the Smartest Guys in the Room,* students were asked what they thought of the company traders who manipulated the price of energy. No student condemned the traders; responses varied from caveat emptor to saying it's the job of the governor or the state assembly to monitor the situation.

One clue to the troubling state of affairs came from a Harvard classmate who 9 asked me: "Howard, don't you realize that Harvard has always been primarily about one thing—success?" The students admitted to Harvard these days have watched their every step, lest they fail in their goal of admission to an elite school. But once admitted, they begin to look for new goals, and being a successful scholar is usually not high on the list. What is admired is success on Wall Street, Silicon Valley, Hollywood—a lavish lifestyle that, among other things, allows you to support your alma mater and get the recognitions that follows.

As for those students who do have the scholarly bent, all too often they see 10 professors cut corners—in their class attendance, their attention to student work, and, most flagrantly, their use of others to do research. Most embarrassingly, when professors are caught—whether in financial misdealings or even plagiarizing others' work—there are frequently no clear punishments. If punishments ensue, they are kept quiet, and no one learns the lessons that need to be learned.

12   Whatever happens to those guilty of cheating, many admirable people are likely to be tarred by their association with Harvard. That's the cost of being a flagship institution. Yet this scandal can have a positive outcome if leaders begin a searching examination of the messages being conveyed to our precious young people and then do whatever it takes to make those messages ones that lead to lives genuinely worthy of admiration.

Howard Gardner, "Why Kids Cheat at Harvard," *The Washington Post*, 7 Sept. 2012. Reprinted by permission of the author.

QUESTIONS FOR READING

1. What is the occasion for Gardner's article?
2. What did the students Gardner interviewed twenty years ago say they admired? Despite their answer, what did they actually want to *be*?
3. What did the students interviewed over the years think they might have to do to be successful?
4. What did Gardner conclude about his students as he continued to interview them?
5. What has Harvard "always been primarily about"?
6. What do the scholarly students often discover about professors?

QUESTIONS FOR REASONING AND ANALYSIS

7. Gardner is not reporting on the cheating incident; he is responding to it. What point does he want to make; that is, what is his claim?
8. How does the author develop and support his claim?
9. What does Gardner gain by telling readers of his long association with Harvard?

QUESTIONS FOR REFLECTION AND WRITING

10. Were you surprised by the students' responses to the fired dean and the Enron traders? Why or why not?
11. What values shape Gardner's definition of good students—or good professors? Do you agree with him? If yes, why? If no, how would you refute him?
12. Can cheating ever be justified—even if others do it? Explain your views on this issue.

The Environment: How Do We Sustain It?

READ: What situation is depicted? Who speaks to whom?

REASON: Who "hasn't noticed yet" and what has he failed to observe? What makes the cartoon clever?

REFLECT/WRITE: Explain the point of the cartoon.

In 2005, psychology professor Glenn Shean published a book titled *Psychology and the Environment*. Dr. Shean argues that we are behaving as if we have no environmental problems to face, and that therefore the biggest first step to solving problems related to environmental degradation is to make people aware of and concerned about the interconnected issues of climate change, the heavy use of fossil fuels, and species extinction. Because we are programmed to make quick decisions based on immediate dangers, we find it difficult to become engaged with dangers that stretch out into an indeterminate future. There is always tomorrow to worry about the polar bears or the increasing levels of CO_2 in the atmosphere, or the rapidly melting ice caps. And besides, who wants to give up a comfortable lifestyle because it might affect future life on this planet?

By 2008, the Bush administration began to give voice to the concerns of environmentalists such as Dr. Shean. During the Obama administration, concerns with the rising sea levels and water pollution and widespread destruction of coral reefs led to the 2016 international Paris Agreement that set goals and guidelines for nations to use to hold temperature increases around the globe. And yet climate change deniers persist, perhaps couching their objections in the context that mandating restrictions and controls is not the business of government.

Why do we resist accepting responsibility for adding to the problem? Because to admit to being a cause means that we have to accept being part of the solution—we have to agree to change some of the things we are doing that are heating up the atmosphere. And here is where sacrifice and cost enter the picture. Do we expect factories to shut down? No, but regulations governing pollutants from their smokestacks will help the atmosphere—at a cost to doing business. Do we expect people to stop enjoying the beach? No, but we could have restrictions on building that destroys the barrier islands and marshlands protecting shorelines from erosion and destruction from storms. Do we expect people to stop driving cars? No, but the government could require manufacturers to build more fuel-efficient cars—at a cost to doing business.

And so, even though the conversation has changed somewhat since 2005, the debate continues over the extent to which human actions make a difference and then what should be done, at what cost, and at whose expense. In five articles and several visuals—including the one that opens this chapter—a variety of voices are heard on this debate.

Professor Alan Townsend of the University of Colorado has expressed an even larger worry—a concern that even though science "sustains us, transports, protects us," our trust in science seems to be eroding. When "science is chewed up in the ugly machinations of partisan politics," Townsend writes, it "threatens society as a whole." Do we want vaccines that save lives to be called into question? Do we want to stop funding the work of protecting endangered species? There is much to consider as you explore the issues raised by the writers in this chapter.

PREREADING QUESTIONS

1. To whom do you listen primarily when you explore scientific questions? Scientists? Politicians? Religious leaders? What is the reasoning behind your choice?

2. How green is your lifestyle? Do you think it matters? Why or why not?

3. Does Dr. Shean describe you when he writes of those who are complacent about environment problems because there does not seem to be an immediate danger? If so, do you think you should reconsider your position? Why or why not?

4. If you accept that we have a problem, what solutions would you support? Reject? Why?

TRASH TALK: REFLECTIONS ON OUR THROWAWAY SOCIETY | GREGORY M. KENNEDY, S.J.

A Canadian, Fr. Kennedy, S.J., holds a PhD in philosophy from the University of Ottawa. He entered the Society of Jesus (known as the Jesuits) in 2006 and earned a master of divinity in 2014, then continued advanced studies at the University of Bogotá. He has spent summers working on organic farms and expects to return from Colombia to the Jesuits' organic farm in Canada.

PREREADING QUESTIONS Knowing that the author is a Jesuit, would you necessarily expect his position on trash to be different from that of any other writer on this topic? How might his education and training influence his approach or writing style?

1   Every morning my colleague's desk captured my passing eye. Nestled beneath the computer screen, between her cup of pens and a stapler, she kept her mid-morning snack. Sometimes it was two chocolates in gold foil, or a pair of sugar biscuits bound together in cellophane, sometimes rose-colored paper enveloping a candy from the Philippines. And always fruit. One day it was an apple, another an orange, a third day a banana. Regardless of the variety, the fruit was invariably as meticulously wrapped as its companion foodstuffs.

2   Now plastic wrap around an apple struck me as redundant. Plastic wrap around a banana or orange still snug in its peel struck me as downright ridiculous. I could not help staring incredulously each morning at these doubly embedded specimens, but never gathered the gumption to query my colleague about her logic.

3   Why, I wondered, would a person spend time, energy, and money to shroud a banana in plastic, which would later require more time, energy and money to get rid of? After all, the good Creator already outfitted the banana with an effective, protective cover. What purpose does that extra layer of petrochemical veneer serve?

4   By no means would my colleague stand alone in the dock before such questions. Nearly every retailer and almost as many customers in this country suspect that no licit commercial transaction has occurred if, in the end, there isn't a bag, or a box, a bottle, or a blister pack to pitch into the garbage pail.

5   In *Gone Tomorrow: The Hidden Life of Garbage,* Heather Rogers estimates that 80% of U.S. products, like plastic wrap, are discarded after a single use. Of course, it takes a special kind of person to use a banana more than once. Food, the quintessential consumer good, has become a Grade-A disposable in the overstocked market. A supersized portion of comestibles in this country does not receive even the fleeting honor of a single use. The average American household wastes a quarter of all the food it presumably worked hard to bring home. Add to that the other waste occurring along the entire length of the production and distribution

Can we do better than this?

line—from the farm to the supermarket deli—and the total percentage of food wasted before tasted approaches a shocking and shaming forty percent.

6   Except in rare instances, for example, pie-throwing contests, food is not intentionally produced in order to be tossed. The same does not hold for food's innumerable, protective accessorizing. Of all municipal solid waste, the single largest share goes to containers and packaging at 30%. Juice boxes, polystyrene clamshells, tin cans, plastic this, that and the other thing—nary a bite comes to our lips that has not recently emerged from an artificial peel.

7   At first glance, it may seem that the plastic cling wrap and the organic banana peel differ only chemically, since they share the same function: packaging. Ever since Aristotle, philosophers have looked to an object's putative purpose in seeking to define its particular essence. This technique often succeeds with manufactured objects, but always stumbles over natural things. Only the consumer conveniently regards the banana peel as packaging. From the standpoint of the banana tree, the peel plays a vital part in procreation. To the soil the peel means future nutrients and increased fertility.

8   Irreducible to a single purpose, natural things exist as waste only temporarily and conditionally. When out one evening picking saskatoon berries, a friend expressed his anxiety to me about the coming nightfall. "If we don't pick these bushes clean, all their berries will go to waste." I conceded a limited truth to this statement. As far as our stomachs were concerned, the berries would not fulfill their function if they never reached our mouths.

9   Had we consulted the bush and berries, however, we might have slowed our hurried harvest. With respect to reproduction, the berries existed as ingeniously designed aerial seed-distribution units. In boyishly biological terms: birds eat the berries, fly a while and poop out the seeds across all the various kinds of soils

one hears about in parables. However, we, the civilized consumers, would, by eating the seeds, destine them to destruction in the sewage treatment plant. So where exactly was the waste, on the bush or in our plumbing?

Plastic wrap does not enjoy this multiplicity of purpose, nor the redemptive 10 ambiguity of "waste." Its design is much less intelligent. Once the wrap fulfills its single function, it is good for nothing. In fact, it is about as good *as* nothing, because it has no more to achieve. If function and essence do go together in manufactured objects, then a consumer item deprived of function will also be devoid of essence. It becomes waste unconditionally and forever, since it no longer serves any possible end.

Since it was originally conceived and produced to lose its function after a 11 single use, the object was in a sense already wasted even before it performed its purpose. So here we have an object that already existed as waste. Planned obsolescence, you could say, renders objects presently obsolete. Such absolute waste, waste considered from all possible angles, waste built right into the conception of an object, I philosophically classify as "trash."

The word "trash" has a modern ring. The reality began littering history only 12 after the Industrial Revolution, when the mass production of goods took off, leaving the ground piled up with discarded, worn out bags. Albert Borgmann, philosopher of technology at the University of Montana, locates the key to modern industry in its division of labor. This is standard history. What moves Borgmann's interpretation well beyond mediocrity is where he draws the most basic lines of division: not between human workers, but within technology itself.

The genius of modern technology, he demonstrates, lies in its unprecedented 13 ability to split the product from its production. Consumers desire commodities, such as tasty food, amusing entertainment, easy transportation. Devices deliver these desirables. Their delivery advances toward perfection the closer they come to providing products in demand without demanding anything in return. Thus the perfect device remains completely hidden behind the convenience of the consumable commodity.

Convenience, the rock on which we have built the consumer world, relies 14 absolutely on the division between commodity and device. Digging your own potatoes is not terribly convenient, especially when compared to dashing into 7-11 for a sealed-fresh bag of salt-and-vinegar chips. A complex, technological and all but invisible industrial food system is the globalized device feeding our hunger for fast-food convenience items. Packaging, of course, is an essential ingredient for making food convenient.

As part of the device, packaging has a sole function: to deliver the commodity 15 of food as safely and conveniently as possible. Its single function necessitates its single use. If the consumer had to fold the plastic wrap and bring it home for tomorrow's snack, or had to wash and dry the take-away cup in preparation for the next injection of java, or had to return the aluminum can to the cola company for refills, then these devices would be delivering their goods inconveniently. But by definition, the device can't make such demands; its whole point is to disappear. As soon as it has accomplished its mission of delivery, the packaging device exhausts the conditions of its existence. It is trash, pure and simple. Into the void of the trash or recycling bin it vanishes.

16   So the banana peel and the plastic wrap differ much more than just chemically. The peel, not limited to a single purpose, exists and functions within an integrated web of relationships. Each relationship lets it be in a unique way. The peel exists as waste only within a limited subset of its total interconnections.

17   The plastic wrap, on the other hand, was expressly designed to deliver just one value: the protection of goods from air, dirt and germs. Once the food is gone then so goes the plastic's *raison d'etre*. The wrap has nothing left to live for; it is curled up and buried. Materially, the object has the same qualities as it had when it first spooled off the roll. But as far as the consumer is concerned, it has instantly become irredeemable waste. How many of us would entrust another sandwich to it? No, it simply must be trashed. It belongs nowhere in our consumer world.

18   We all know that, despite our worst intentions, the disposables we discard do not really disappear. Yet we like to pretend that they do. As consumers we have precious little business with the trash we generate. Our elaborate system of garbage collection, incineration, disposal and recycling is a sophisticated device that delivers to most urban consumers the commodities of sanitation and cleanliness. Undoubtedly, swept streets and clean homes count as real blessings. But hiding our trash within the technological division of commodity and device allows us to consume without concerning ourselves about consequences.

19   And the consequences keep piling up. In spite of all our roused environmental consciousness and the de-materialization of the digital age, our quantity of trash compounds. According to the EPA, Americans generated 2.68 lbs of municipal solid waste per person per day in 1960. By 2010 that total had bloated to 4.43 lbs. The fatter the wedge we drive between the commodity and its device, the more trash we inevitably stuff into the gap.

20   We can and must do otherwise. Some years after WWII, French philosopher Jean-Paul Sartre said: "We were never more free than during German occupation." Sartre had a flair for paradox. Under occupation, every act took on significance; every act, no matter how prosaic, held out the chance for bravery and non-conformity. In a throw-away society, analogous opportunities prevail. Every shopping bag you refuse, every coffee cup you reuse, every piece of plastic you eschew is an act of freedom and conscience against our thoughtless slavery to trash.

Gregory M. Kennedy, "Trash Talk," *America: The National Catholic Weekly,* 7 May 2012. Reprinted by permission of the author.

QUESTIONS FOR READING

1. What percentage of food is wasted?
2. What percentage of solid waste is composed of packaging? How does packaging's purpose differ from food's purpose?
3. How does plastic covering differ from organic covering—such as the banana peel?
4. What do modern consumers want? How does plastic packaging help to deliver this?

QUESTIONS FOR REASONING AND ANALYSIS

5. Explain why plastic packaging is "trash" whereas organic "waste" is not.

6. Our digital age has presumably resulted in less paper, and yet our volume of solid waste continues to increase. What—implies Kennedy—is contributing to the increased tonnage of trash?

7. Review elements of style in Chapter 2 and then analyze Kennedy's writing, focusing on three characteristics that you select to study. How does his style contribute to his argument?

QUESTIONS FOR REFLECTION AND WRITING

8. What specific suggestions for wasting less food and tossing less trash do you have to add to Kennedy's discussion? Explain and defend your suggestions. If you don't think that wasting food along the way or filling solid waste dumps are really that big a problem, prepare your rebuttal of Kennedy's argument.

9. Kennedy concludes his essay by quoting Sartre. Explain Sartre's point and how Kennedy uses it to support his concluding point. Contemplate other ways in which we could use these ideas as guides to living.

THE SIXTH EXTINCTION: IT HAPPENED TO HIM. IT'S HAPPENING TO YOU. | MICHAEL NOVACEK

Paleontologist Michael Novacek is senior vice president and provost of the American Museum of Natural History in New York City. He has been curator of the Division of Paleontology since 1982. Author of more than 200 articles, Novacek's most recent book is *Terra: Our 100-Million-Year-Old Ecosystem—and the Threats That Now Put It at Risk* (2008). "The Sixth Extinction" was published on January 13, 2008, in *The Washington Post.*

PREREADING QUESTIONS Who is the "Him" in Novacek's title? Is it ridiculous to suggest that *we* could be like *him?*

The news of environmental traumas assails us from every side—unseasonal 1 storms, floods, fires, drought, melting ice caps, lost species of river dolphins and giant turtles, rising sea levels potentially displacing inhabitants of Arctic and Pacific islands and hundreds of thousands of people dying every year from air pollution. Last week brought more—new reports that Greenland's glaciers may be melting away at an alarming rate.

What's going on? Are we experiencing one of those major shocks to life on 2 Earth that rocked the planet in the past?

That's just doomsaying, say those who insist that economic growth and 3 human technological ingenuity will eventually solve our problems. But in fact, the scientific take on our current environmental mess is hardly so upbeat.

More than a decade ago, many scientists claimed that humans were 4 demonstrating a capacity to force a major global catastrophe that would lead to a traumatic shift in climate, an intolerable level of destruction of natural habitats, and an extinction event that could eliminate 30 to 50 percent of all living species by the

A T. Rex named Sue, looking sinister even as a skeleton.

©Mark Wilson/Getty Images

middle of the 21st century. Now those predictions are coming true. The evidence shows that species loss today is accelerating. We find ourselves uncomfortably privileged to be witnessing a mass extinction event as it's taking place, in real time.

5   The fossil record reveals some extraordinarily destructive events in the past, when species losses were huge, synchronous and global in scale. Paleontologists recognize at least five of these mass extinction events, the last of which occurred about 65 million years ago and wiped out all those big, charismatic dinosaurs (except their bird descendants) and at least 70 percent of all other species. The primary suspect for this catastrophe is a six-mile-wide asteroid (a mile higher than Mount Everest) whose rear end was still sticking out of the atmosphere as its nose augered into the crust a number of miles off the shore of the present-day Yucatan Peninsula in Mexico. Earth's atmosphere became a hell furnace, with super-broiler temperatures sufficient not only to kill exposed organisms, but also to incinerate virtually every forest on the planet.

6   For several million years, a period 100 times greater than the entire known history of Homo sapiens, the planet's destroyed ecosystems underwent a slow, laborious recovery. The earliest colonizers after the catastrophe were populous species that quickly adapted to degraded environments, the ancient analogues of rats, cockroaches and weeds. But many of the original species that occupied these ecosystems were gone and did not come back. They'll never come back. The extinction of a species, whether in an incinerated 65-million-year-old reef or in a bleached modern-day reef of the Caribbean, is forever.

7   Now we face the possibility of mass extinction event No. 6. No big killer asteroid is in sight. Volcanic eruptions and earthquakes are not of the scale to cause mass extinction. Yet recent studies show that troubling earlier projections about rampant extinction aren't exaggerated.

In 2007, of 41,415 species assessed for the International Union for the 8
Conservation of Nature (IUCN) Red List of Threatened Species, 16,306
(39 percent) were categorized as threatened with extinction: one in three amphibians,
one quarter of the world's pines and other coniferous trees, one in eight birds and
one in four mammals. Another study identified 595 "centers of imminent extinction"
in tropical forests, on islands and in mountainous areas. Disturbingly, only one-third
of the sites surveyed were legally protected, and most were surrounded by areas
densely populated by humans. We may not be able to determine the cause of past
extinction events, but this time we have, indisputably: We are our own asteroids.

Still, the primary concern here is the future welfare of us and our children. 9
Assuming that we survive the current mass extinction event, won't we do okay?
The disappearance of more than a few species is regrettable, but we can't
compromise an ever-expanding population and a global economy whose
collapse would leave billions to starve. This dismissal, however, ignores an
essential fact about all those species: They live together in tightly networked
ecosystems responsible for providing the habitats in which even we humans
thrive. Pollination of flowers by diverse species of wild bees, wasps, butterflies
and other insects, not just managed honeybees, accounts for more than
30 percent of all food production that humans depend upon.

What will the quality of life be like in this transformed new world? Science 10
doesn't paint a pretty picture. The tropics and coral reefs, major sources of the
planet's biological diversity, will be hugely debilitated. The 21st century may mark
the end of the line for the evolution of large mammals and other animals that are
now either on the verge of extinction, such as the Yangtze River dolphin, or, like
the African black rhinoceros, confined to small, inadequately supportive habitats.
And devastated ecosystems will provide warm welcome to all those opportunistic
invader species that have already demonstrated their capacity to wipe out native
plants and animals. We, and certainly our children, will find ourselves largely
embraced by a pest and weed ecology ideal for the flourishing of invasive
species and new, potentially dangerous microbes to which we haven't built up a
biological resistance.

Of course people care about this. Recent surveys show a sharp increase in 11
concern over the environmental changes taking place. But much of this spike in
interest is due to the marked shift in attention to climate change and global
warming away from other environmental problems such as deforestation, water
pollution, overpopulation and biodiversity loss. Global warming is of course a
hugely important issue. But it is the double whammy of climate change combined
with fragmented, degraded natural habitats—not climate change alone—that is
the real threat to many populations, species and ecosystems, including human
populations marginalized and displaced by those combined forces.

Still, human ingenuity, commitment and shared responsibility have great 12
potential to do good. The IUCN Red List now includes a handful of species that
have been revived through conservation efforts, including the European white-
tailed eagle and the Mekong catfish. Narrow corridors of protected habitat now
connect nature preserves in South Africa, and similar corridors link up the coral
reefs of the Bahamas, allowing species in the protected areas to move back and
forth, exchange genes and sustain their populations. Coffee farms planted near

protected forests and benefiting from wild pollinators have increased coffee yields. New York's $1 billion purchase of watersheds in the Catskill Mountains that purify water naturally secured precious natural habitat while eliminating the need for a filtration plant that would have cost $6 to $8 billion, plus annual operating costs of $300 million. Emissions of polluting gases such as dangerous nitrogen oxides have leveled off in North America and even declined in Europe (unfortunately emissions of the same are steeply rising in China). Plans for reflective roofing, green space and increased shade to cool urban "heat islands" are at least under consideration in many cities.

13   These actions may seem puny in light of the enormous problem we face, but their cumulative effect can bring surprising improvements. Yet our recent efforts, however praiseworthy, must become more intensive and global. Any measure of success depends not only on international cooperation but also on the leadership of the most powerful nations and economies.

14   The first step in dealing with the problem is recognizing it for what it is. Ecologists point out that the image of Earth still harboring unspoiled, pristine wild places is a myth. We live in a human-dominated world, they say, and virtually no habitat is untouched by our presence. Yet we are hardly the infallible masters of that universe. Instead, we are rather uneasy regents, a fragile and dysfunctional royal family holding back a revolution.

15   The sixth extinction event is under way. Can humanity muster the leadership and international collaboration necessary to stop eating itself from the inside?

Michael Novacek, "The Sixth Extinction: It Happened to Him. It's Happening to You," *The Washington Post*, 13 Jan. 2008. Reprinted by permission of the author.

QUESTIONS FOR READING

1. What events suggest to scientists that we may be heading for another mass extinction?

2. What is the response of many to this "doomsaying" discussion?

3. How many mass extinctions has the Earth experienced? When was the last one and what happened then?

4. How do scientists describe the consequences of extinction No. 6?

5. What are the specific problems that combine to threaten a disastrous change in our environment?

QUESTIONS FOR REASONING AND ANALYSIS

6. What is the primary cause of a potential extinction No. 6? What, then, needs to be the primary source of the solutions? What, in the author's view, is the necessary first step?

7. In paragraph 12, Novacek describes some actions we have taken to address problems. What does he seek to accomplish by including this paragraph?

8. What is Novacek's claim? State it to reveal a causal argument.

9. Of the various consequences of extinction No. 6, listed in paragraph 10, what seems most frightening or devastating to you? Why?

QUESTIONS FOR REFLECTION AND WRITING

10. Novacek lists numbers and types of endangered species. Do these figures surprise you? Concern you? Why or why not?

11. In your experience, how widespread is the concern for environmental degradation? Do your friends and family discuss this issue? Do most dismiss the seriousness of the issue, as Novacek suggests?

12. Have you made changes to be kinder to the environment? If so, what have you done and what would you recommend that others do?

13. Do you agree with Novacek—or does he overstate the problem? If you agree, how would you contribute to his argument? If you disagree, how would you refute him?

WHY A HALF-DEGREE TEMPERATURE RISE IS A BIG DEAL | BOB SILBERG

Previously a creative writer at Doug Wyles Productions, Bob Silberg has been writing about science and technology for NASA since 2001. In his spare time, he writes songs and musical comedies with his wife Barbara. The following article appeared June 20, 2016, on the NASA Jet Propulsion Lab Climate Change Project website.

PREREADING QUESTIONS How might a half-degree rise in temperature become significant? Can you list some possible effects of such a change?

The Paris Agreement, which delegates from 196 countries hammered out in December 2015, calls for holding the ongoing rise in global average temperature to "well below 2 °C above pre-industrial levels," while "pursuing efforts to limit the temperature increase to 1.5 °C." How much difference could that half-degree of wiggle room (or 0.9 degree on the Fahrenheit scale) possibly make in the real world? Quite a bit, it appears. 1

The European Geosciences Union published a study in April 2016 that examined the impact of a 1.5 degree Celsius vs. a 2.0 C temperature increase by the end of the century, given what we know so far about how climate works. It found that the jump from 1.5 to 2 degrees—a third more of an increase—raises the impact by about that same fraction, very roughly, on most of the phenomena the study covered. Heat waves would last around a third longer, rain storms would be about a third more intense, the increase in sea level would be approximately that much higher and the percentage of tropical coral reefs at risk of severe degradation would be roughly that much greater. 2

But in some cases, that extra increase in temperature makes things much more dire. At 1.5 C, the study found that tropical coral reefs stand a chance of adapting and reversing a portion of their die-off in the last half of the century. But at 2 C, the chance of recovery vanishes. Tropical corals are virtually wiped out by the year 2100. 3

With a 1.5 C rise in temperature, the Mediterranean area is forecast to have about 9 percent less fresh water available. At 2 C, that water deficit nearly doubles. So does the decrease in wheat and maize harvest in the tropics. 4

Jocelyn Augustino/FEMA

Hurricane flooding in Florida.

5   On a global scale, production of wheat and soy is forecast to increase with a 1.5 C temperature rise, partly because warming is favorable for farming in higher latitudes and partly because the added carbon dioxide in the atmosphere, which is largely responsible for the temperature increase, is thought to have a fertilization effect. But at 2 C, that advantage plummets by 700 percent for soy and disappears entirely for wheat.

6   Three climate scientists at NASA's Jet Propulsion Laboratory, who were not involved with this study, shed some light on the study's results, starting with the impact on agriculture.

CORN PLANTS WITH NO CORN

7   Why does a half degree of temperature increase make such a difference to some of the crops that were studied? For one thing, a half degree averaged out over the whole world can mean much more of an increase in some locations and at certain times.

8   "Most of that temperature change may occur during a small fraction of the year, when it actually represents conditions that could be 5 or 10 degrees warmer than pre-industrial temperatures instead of just 1.5 or 2 degrees warmer," said Dave Schimel, who supervises JPL's Carbon Cycle and Ecosystems group.

9   "There are places in the world where, for these important breadbasket crops, they are already close to a thermal limit for that crop species," Schimel said. Adding to the burden, he said, "this analysis (the EGU study) does not take into account the fact that pests and pathogens may spread more rapidly at higher temperatures."

And Schimel pointed out that heat can imperil agriculture even when crops don't 10 die. "If you get really high temperatures or very dry conditions during critical parts of the development of the crop, it produces essentially no grain. For example, above certain temperature thresholds, corn doesn't die but it doesn't grow seed. It doesn't grow a corncob. And other crops are similar to that, where the development of the actual food part of the crop is dramatically inhibited above critical temperatures."

But what about that fertilization effect from carbon dioxide? "It does help a 11 bit, but it doesn't make the underlying problem go away," he said. "And by the way, if the plant was growing really fast when it died, it still died."

Can we avoid the extra half-percent temperature increase? Schimel agrees 12 that we should try hard to do so, but cautions that we don't know how to fine-tune global warming with that much precision. "If we aim for 2 degrees, we might hit 3 degrees," he said. "If we aim for 1.5 degrees, we might still hit 2 degrees."

A MULTI-CENTURY COMMITMENT

Felix Landerer, who studies sea level and ice at JPL, said timescale is critical 13 to forecasting how high the ocean will rise.

"This paper looks at this century," he said. "So the effects appear to be fairly 14 linear." That is, a third more increase in temperature produces about a third more increase in sea level.

"But," he said, "I would frame the discussion in the context that in recent 15 studies—in particular of ocean-ice interactions—there is growing concern that the ice sheets are very sensitive to the surrounding ocean warming." These studies show that giant glaciers in Greenland and Antarctica melt not only from the top down, but also from the bottom up as relatively warm ocean water makes its way to their undersides.

"At two degrees (of temperature increase)," he said, "you might have crossed 16 a threshold for significantly more sea-level rise than indicated here." In other words, even if we are able to limit the rise in global air temperature to 2 degrees Celsius by the end of the century and stop the increase at that point, the ocean holds so much heat that it can continue melting ice sheets and thus raising sea level far beyond that point in time.

"The air temperatures level off, you (hypothetically) stabilize them, but you 17 have committed to sea-level rise over multiple centuries," Landerer said. "So it's good to stay away from two degrees. That's an experiment you don't want to run. Because that experiment would potentially wipe Florida off the map."

GENERATIONS DOWN THE ROAD

The EGU study found that the difference between 1.5 and 2 degrees Celsius 18 of warming "is likely to be decisive for the future of tropical coral reefs." JPL's Michelle Gierach was not surprised.

"Reef-building corals are extremely vulnerable to warming," she said. 19 "Prolonged warming harms warm-water corals not only through bleaching (a phenomenon in which corals under stress, such as from water that is too warm, expel the algae they need to survive), but also through making them more susceptible to disease."

20   Gierach attended the international conference that produced the Paris Agreement and she was happy to see the ocean and climate getting their due attention. But she acknowledges the difficulty in turning that attention into action over a long period of time.

21   "It's very against how our society is now," she said. "We want to see instant results. That's not something that's going to happen with climate change. You need to just keep pursuing it and know that generations down the road will reap the benefits."

22   The Paris Agreement goes into effect when 55 nations, accounting for at least 55 percent of total global greenhouse-gas emissions, ratify it. The status so far: 19 nations, accounting for 0.18 percent of total greenhouse-gas emissions, have ratified the agreement as of June 30, 2016. Updates are available from the U.N. Framework Convention on Climate Change.*

---

*The Paris Climate Accord was ratified, but then on June 1, 2017, President Trump announced that the United States was withdrawing.—Ed.

Bob Silberg, "Why a Half-degree Temperature Rise Is a Big Deal," *NASA's Global Climate Change: Vital Signs of the Planet*, Used with permission of the author.

QUESTIONS FOR READING

1. What seems to be the general impact of a 2-degree rise in temperature rather than a 1.5 degree rise?

2. In what ways does the extra increase do more significant damage by the end of the century?

3. What can happen to corn with the greater temperature increase?

4. Why are increased temperatures likely to lead to greater glacier melting than might be predicted in the basically linear studies?

5. Why are coral reefs at a much greater threat with 2 degrees of warming?

QUESTIONS FOR REASONING AND ANALYSIS

6. What type of argument is this? (What word in the title is key to recognizing the type of argument?)

7. What is Silberg's claim? State it so that the type of argument is clear.

8. Silberg is explaining the results of complex studies by specialists. List the ways that the author continues to remind readers of his "backing" (Toulmin's term). How does this providing of backing affect his discussion?

QUESTIONS FOR REFLECTION AND WRITING

9. Do you find Silberg's analysis clear and detailed? Convincing? If you are not convinced that we should try to hold temperature increases to 1.5 degrees, how would you refute Silberg?

10. Are you worried about the impact of climate change? If so, why? What specific recent events would you use to convince a skeptic? If you are not worried, why not? How would you argue that current conditions do not suggest that Florida could be lost by the end of this century?

ON CLIMATE CHANGE, GOVERNMENT IS NOT THE ANSWER | ART CARDEN

Holding a PhD in economics from Washington University in St. Louis, Art Carden is assistant professor of economics at Samford University. He is also a senior research fellow with the Institute of Faith, Work, and Economics and a senior fellow with the Beacon Center of Tennessee. He has published in economics journals and magazines and is a regular contributor to *Forbes.com*. The following article on climate change appeared in the *Washington Examiner* on November 7, 2012.

PREREADING QUESTIONS What answers to the problems of climate change do you expect the author to suggest? Do you have answers to the problems of climate change?

1   Climate change is a textbook example of the economic case for government intervention. In the language of an economics textbook, it involves a pretty clear market failure created by the fact that my actions (emitting carbon dioxide) spill over onto non-consenting third parties.

2   Consider: I burn fossil fuels, to my own benefit. The climate changes. You might also benefit if you own land in northern Canada, but you might be worse off if you live in Miami or Bangladesh. How can you be compensated for the harm I cause to benefit myself? On the face of it, there's a plausible case for government involvement.

3   But in light of political responses to natural disasters and political outcomes more generally, I'm inclined to think that political "solutions" are not solutions at all. Consider how governments respond to natural disasters like Hurricane Sandy. They openly defy the laws of the marketplace and impose laws against price gouging. These laws in turn create shortages, which in turn create unnecessary suffering.

4   Consider also the China-bashing that was on display in the recent presidential election and the more general foreigner-bashing that is part and parcel of the political scene. Such rhetoric and the policies based on it are at odds with what economists left, right and center have known about trade for centuries. Trade creates wealth, and free trade among nations is a rising tide that lifts all boats. In spite of this, few things are as unpopular as free trade (on the Left) and open immigration (on the Right).

5   The rhetorical, cultural and political environment in which climate change policy is made will never be one characterized by wise and benevolent leaders seeking only the good of a populace consisting of recently enlightened New Environmentalist Men and Women. People have all sorts of biases that warp their political judgment, as Bryan Caplan has discussed in his book *The Myth of the Rational Voter.*

6   With systematically biased voters, tangled webs of interest groups and politicians who are all eager to cater to these biases and these interest groups, the policies we get in the real world are likely to differ from the optimal policies that get discussed in the "externalities and public goods" lectures in introductory economics classes by a pretty wide margin.

7   The lesson for climate change policy is dismal. Even if we agree that climate change is a problem, and even if we agree that climate change could have very, very bad effects, ongoing research in "robust political economy" is showing us that passing seemingly plausible ideas through the filters of political bias will give us something very different from the "solutions" we would like to see.

8   How, then, should we address climate change? Adaptation is probably a better strategy than prevention. Large-scale, top-down solutions are unlikely to work, so the best way to proceed might be to recognize some of the key insights of 2009 Nobel laureate Elinor Ostrom. Her work focused on how "bottom-up" solutions to resource management problems evolve. To translate it into the language of a bumper sticker you might have seen, "Think globally, act locally." Let's look for ways to devolve authority and to develop markets for goods and for risks that are not currently priced. Let's trust the initiative of innovative economic, social and cultural entrepreneurs rather than politicians.

Art Carden, "On Climate Change, Government Is Not the Answer," *Washington Examiner,* 7 Nov. 2012. Reprinted with permission from the author.

QUESTIONS FOR READING

1. Why does it seem that government should seek solutions to climate change?
2. Why are political solutions not likely to be good ones? What are Carden's views of politicians and voters?
3. Does the author seem convinced that climate change is a serious problem?

QUESTIONS FOR REASONING AND ANALYSIS

4. What, exactly, is Carden refuting? What is his claim?
5. What alternative approach does he present?
6. What are the grounds for his rejection of government seeking solutions to climate change? Is his argument against a government approach convincing? (Does he ever explain which governments—or should we assume that he means both federal and state governments?)
7. Does Carden demonstrate that the only two choices are government prevention or local adaptation? (Scientists have described the Arctic ice melt as faster than they had predicted years ago. Is "prevention" really an option?)

QUESTIONS FOR REFLECTION AND WRITING

8. Do you think that state and federal governments cope reasonably well with natural disasters such as hurricanes—keeping in mind what the word *disaster* means? Can communities and individuals cope better? (If you lost your home in a flood, would you be able to pay for a hotel room and, in a short time, find another home in which to live? Do most people have the resources to cope with disasters without government assistance?)
9. What suggestions do you have for managing our lives, individually and collectively, in a time of climate change that includes rising temperatures, rising sea levels, and more violent and unusual weather?

THE CLEVEREST COUNTRIES ON CLIMATE CHANGE—AND WHAT WE CAN LEARN FROM THEM | ALEXANDER STARRITT

Educated at Edinburgh and Oxford, Alexander Starritt is a writer, translator, and journalist living in London. He is currently editor of *Apolitical*. Starritt has published translations from German as well as short fiction. His first novel, *The Beast*, appeared in 2017. The following article was published on the *World Economic Forum* on November 15, 2016.

PREREADING QUESTIONS Do you know countries that have found strategies for delivering clean energy? What strategies for producing clean energy can you list?

1   Virtually every clean energy record in the world has been broken in the past year. The most investment in clean energy ($329 billion in 2015), the most new renewable capacity (a third more than in 2014), the cheapest ever solar power (in Chile, where it's half the cost of coal), the longest a country has been run entirely on renewable electricity—113 days over this summer in Costa Rica.

2   The pace of the shift to a clean economy is astonishing. This year, half a million solar panels have been installed every day, while China has erected two wind turbines an hour. Wind farms off Denmark, solar farms in Morocco, wave farms off Scotland—everywhere you look, an unparalleled global effort is taking place, one that dwarfs the achievements of the space race.

3   Nevertheless, the scale of the problem is immense. Even as Barack Obama was announcing the ratification of the historic Paris Agreement* on climate change, which aims to hold global temperatures to no more than two degrees above pre-industrial levels, he had to concede, 'Even if we meet every target embodied in the agreement, we'll only get to part of where we need to go.' This is also the first year in which global CO_2 levels crossed the symbolic 400ppm threshold.

4   Never before has our species contemplated a task so vast: to change the composition of the air itself. And when the history of this great green leap comes to be written, it will presumably be told as a story of technologists, of activists, of Elon Musks saving the world from itself. But in fact no greater part is being played than by government, the only kind of institution we have evolved that can co-ordinate an effort of this magnitude, and that is ultimately responsible for doing so.

5   Jigar Shah, founder of the global clean energy company SunEdison and more recently of investment firm Generate Capital, put it like this: 'When you think about the spread of technology like the iPhone, it didn't really replace anything. It wasn't something that people even considered they needed till they got it. It was greenfield. But clean energy is providing the exact same service you've relied on for a hundred years: kilowatt hours. So, how do we get to 100% clean energy? The only answer is government regulation.'

6   Here we've combed through the myriad initiatives, plans, projects and targets to pick out the most groundbreaking innovations from around the world, both to give credit where it's due—and so others can learn from the comparison.

A California wind farm providing energy.

1. THE TEXAS GRID

7   If Texas were a country, it would be the world's sixth largest generator of wind power, right behind Spain. That's partly because of reliable winds, but also because the state built a gigantic transmission system to carry energy from its desolate northwest to the metropolises of the south and east. The power lines were agreed in 2007, costing nearly $7 billion dollars, and their construction means there are three primary grids in the U.S.: the Eastern Interconnection, the Western Interconnection and the Texas. Spurred on by federal wind subsidies, private companies have proliferated across the lone star state, such that on a windy winter's day, more than 40% of its electricity comes from turbines.

8   But even the Texas grid is now approaching capacity, bringing the same problem that has arisen in Germany, one of the pioneers of large-scale renewable energy. Earlier this year, the German government had to announce moves to slow the pace at which renewables, especially offshore wind turbines, are built because the industry's rapid growth has outpaced the construction of cables to carry energy from the north coast to the cities of the south. Meanwhile, China has proposed a global long-range super-grid tapping everything from Arctic wind to equatorial sunlight, costing an estimated $50 trillion and taking until at least 2050 to construct.

2. SIMPLY BANNING FOSSIL FUELS

9   Nobody likes coal any more. Once the driving force of the industrial revolution and the purpose of whole coal-mining communities from the Appalachians to Wales, the Saarland to South Australia, it is now the obvious enemy: dirty, replaceable and lacking obvious defenders. Countries like the UK and Holland have announced plans to shut their coal fleets early, and in May this year the UK

was powered without recourse to coal for the first time since its first steam-driven power station opened in 1882. In the U.S., too, regulations are pushing the coal industry towards extinction: 94 coal-fired plants closed in 2015 and another 41 are due to have closed by the end of this year, together equivalent to all the coal plants in Kentucky and Colorado. Only three are scheduled to open by 2021.

There have also been tentative moves towards banning petrol. Norway, [10] Denmark and the Netherlands have all considered proposals to ban internal combustion vehicles by 2025. And a few weeks ago, the council of federal states in Germany—lest we forget, the country of BMW, Porsche, Volkswagen, Mercedes and Audi—voted to ban petrol and diesel cars by 2030. The vote is non-binding, but hugely significant of the direction things are heading.

That said, the International Energy Agency estimated global subsidies for [11] fossil fuels at $493 billion in 2014. And the IMF calculates that if you factor in the costs borne by governments because of pollution causing ill health and climate change, the subsidies total £5.3 trillion annually, or $10 million per minute. In 2009, the G20 pledged to phase them out, and didn't. This year, the G7 pledged to do it, and haven't.

3. THE TECHNOLOGY OF TOMORROW

At the Paris climate talks, Presidents Obama, Modi and Hollande, together [12] with Bill Gates, announced that 20 countries would be doubling their budgets for research into clean energy over the five years to 2020. Including the world's five most populous countries—China, India, the U.S., Indonesia and Brazil—the Mission Innovation cohort in June declared that this would make more than $30 billion available for research into the new technologies that will make an energy transition possible.

Cameron Hepburn, Professor of Environmental Economics at Oxford [16] University, told Apolitical, "This is a long-run game. It's about starting to shift the tanker immediately, but the technologies we'll be deploying in twenty years' time will be ones that we're developing now. One area that's super important is technologies to integrate renewable energy into the grid, whether it's the rapidly falling cost of batteries and new sorts of batteries, or chemical storage or use of industrial gas and hydrogen systems. Doubling that spend is hugely significant."

Bill Gates was on the stage because he and a group of other billionaires, [17] including the head of Amazon Jeff Bezos and the financier George Soros, have formed the Breakthrough Energy Coalition, pooling $20 billion to invest in high-risk clean energy companies that traditional investors might shy away from, and make them commercially viable.

4. ELECTRIC FILLING STATIONS

Around a fifth of global greenhouse gas emissions come from road [18] vehicles and the most feasible solution is to replace them with electric vehicles (powered by a clean energy source). But if you buy an electric car, where do you charge it?

To make the switch to a transport infrastructure built for electric cars, Russia [19] last year made it mandatory for every petrol station to include an electric charging port, and the EU has announced plans to make it mandatory for every new house to include one. The Obama administration is investing $4.5 billion to create a coast-to-coast network to reduce "range anxiety" and encourage consumers to go electric.

20   A survey by Nissan found that Japan already has more electric car charge ports than petrol stations, and several reports have predicted that electric cars will dominate by 2030. It's also worth noting that the UK and South Korea are testing "electric motorways" that recharge cars as they drive over them.

5. BORING BUT IMPORTANT

21   In 2014, better insulation, more efficient appliances and greater fuel economy saved the European Union as much energy as is used by the whole of Finland. And Finland is a cold country. Energy efficiency is obviously far less fun than a shiny new solar plant or a Tesla sports car, but the potential gains are enormous.

22   Professor Martin Beniston, Director of the Institute for Environmental Sciences at the University of Geneva, told Apolitical, "When we think about energy, we always think about generating power. But some estimates are that European cities could actually save 60% of their energy bill by retrofitting offices, houses, and apartment blocks. If you could get some large fraction of that, you wouldn't need additional sources of energy to supply households and offices and so on."

6. CLEVER KETTLES

23   Last month, the UK became the first country to successfully transmit data across the national grid. If that continues to work, it will mean that the grid can balance out the fluctuations in supply and demand that bedevil renewable energy. The way it works is that information and power are sent over the same cable—as in a USB lead—meaning that electricity could be priced differently at different points on the grid. So if there's a drop in supply because, say, a bank of cloud has covered the nation's solar panels, the price would go up. And you could set your smart kettle or computer or any other appliance so that, if the price rises above a certain point, it will switch to battery or power-saving mode. In that way, demand would drop, easing strain on the grid.

24   Jigar Shah said, "It wasn't until 1970 that the electric utility industry thought that it knew how to provide reliable electricity without power outages and blackouts. And now what happens if every single person on your block gets a Tesla? That's 20kw worth of power draw per car. So instead of each home drawing 7kw, it draws 27kw, and you can imagine that the electrical infrastructure on your street is not equipped for that. So the question becomes, do you let the utility company spend a million pounds upgrading it or, for eighty thousand pounds, have everyone put in some next generation software that regulates how many cars can be charging at any one time?"

7. A PRICE ON CARBON DIOXIDE—OR EVEN A TAX

25   For the past couple of years, China has been running seven separate pilot schemes for carbon trading, and seemingly plans to launch a nationwide emissions trading scheme in 2017, while the EU has an emissions trading scheme covering 11,000 factories, power plants and other big installations.

One of the most forward-thinking developments, however, has found its 26 latest incarnation in Canada, which has unveiled plans to levy a tax of ten Canadian dollars (around $7.50) per tonne of carbon emitted by 2018. That would rise to around $37.50 by 2022. Several other countries, including Sweden, already levy a carbon tax.

The point of all this is to integrate the social costs of carbon into the 27 economy, so that it influences the decisions of people who are not primarily interested in climate change.

Kate Gordon, Vice Chair of Climate at the Paulson Institute, which 28 specialises in sustainable economics, told Apolitical, "I don't think most businesses can or should be thinking about the global health impacts of climate change in their pricing, right? But governments can and should, because that's the kind of problem that governments are for. The crucial economic measure is somehow internalising the risks of carbon, and how you do that comes down to a political question in each country, whether it's taxes or carbon trading or whatever, so that people act with the short and long-term impacts in mind."

---

*On June 1, 2017, President Trump announced that the United States was withdrawing from the Paris Climate Accord.

Alex Starritt, "The Cleverest Countries on Climate Change—and What We Can Learn from Them," *Apolitical*, 3 Nov. 2016. Copyright ©2016 apolitical.com. Used with permission of Alex Starritt, Media Director at Apolitical, the international platform for innovators in public service.

QUESTIONS FOR READING

1. How big is the job to combat the impact of climate change? What institution is best equipped to manage the effort?

2. On a windy day, how much of Texas's energy can come from turbines? How does this energy source get disbursed in the state?

3. What is the general attitude toward coal use? How successful have countries been in getting rid of fossil fuels?

4. To get more drivers to purchase electric cars, what is needed?

5. What is one way to save energy without using fancy new technologies?

6. With regard to carbon emissions, what is seen as the most "forward-thinking development"?

QUESTIONS FOR REASONING AND ANALYSIS

7. It might be easy to see this article as just providing information, an update on what some countries are doing, not an argument. How would you explain to readers that they are, indeed, reading an argument?

8. What, then, is Starritt's claim? How does his information serve as evidence supporting his claim?

9. Starritt presents many details here; how does he help readers to take in the material?

QUESTIONS FOR REFLECTION AND WRITING

10. Do Starritt's details—and his numbers—provide good support for his claim? Are governments best equipped to support clean energy efforts? Why or why not?

11. Which of the various initiatives discussed here strike you as the best possible approaches for the United States? Why? Which would you oppose? Why?

We Can Solve It advertisement courtesy of The Climate Reality Project.

QUESTIONS FOR READING

1. What does the visual on this page represent?
2. What do the words in the visual communicate?

QUESTIONS FOR REASONING AND ANALYSIS

3. What is the ad's claim?
4. Does the ad's visual effectively support the claim? Why or why not?

QUESTIONS FOR REFLECTION AND WRITING

5. Who has to work together to solve the climate crisis? (Think about this and also draw from your reading in this chapter.) Are all of the significant players likely to work together? Why or why not?
6. Does this ad catch your attention sufficiently for you to check out the organization's website? For you to think about ways that you can help solve the climate problem? Why or why not?

ELEPHANT LOSS TIED TO IVORY TRADE | RACHEL NUWER

Rachel Nuwer is a freelance journalist writing about science, travel, and adventure in publications such as *National Geographic* and *The New York Times*. She holds a master's degree in ecology from the University of East Anglia. Her book on the illegal wildlife trade was published in 2017. The following essay appeared in *Smithsonian.com* in 2016.

PREREADING QUESTIONS Why should we care about species loss? Do you know which of the large mammals is closest to extinction?

When notorious ivory trader Edouodji Emile N'Bouke was brought to court in 2014, he plead not guilty. This seemed unlikely, as authorities had just seized 1,540-pounds of ivory from his shop and home in Togo. But N'Bouke claimed the ivory was all old stuff, acquired well before 1990 when the international ivory ban took effect. Was he lying?

Normally, authorities would have no way of knowing. But in this case, samples from N'Bouke's stash had undergone a cutting-edge forensics analysis, revealing that some of the ivory came from elephants killed just four years earlier. N'Bouke was found guilty and sentenced to 15 months in jail.

Now, the same powerful tool has been applied not just to a single case, but to hundreds of samples of ivory from around the world. The analysis has revealed that most of the ivory entering into the illegal trade today comes from elephants killed less than three years ago, researchers report in *Proceedings of the National Academy of Sciences*. This finding suggests that the recent surge in elephant deaths—savannah-dwelling populations have declined by 30 percent in the last seven years, while elephants living in forests dropped 62 percent from 2002 to 2013—are intimately linked with the illegal global trade in ivory.

A typical elephant family—females, teens, and babies.

Villiers Steyn/Shutterstock.com RF

4   "There's been controversy for some time as to how to determine the killing rate of elephants," says lead author Thure Cerling, a distinguished professor of geology, geophysics and biology at the University of Utah. "This shows that everything that has been seized comes from animals that died very, very recently."

5   Ivory's age has been the subject of an ongoing debate among conservationists. Some have suspected that older material is leaking out of government storage facilities, or that traders hoard tusks for many years before sneaking them onto the black market. If true, this would mean that the poaching crisis isn't as acute as it might seem, since much of the ivory entering into the market today comes from elephants long dead. Others insist that the ivory currently flooding markets in Asia must be from recently killed animals, given the rate at which elephants across Africa are being slaughtered.

6   To settle this debate, Cerling and his colleagues used carbon-14 dating, a well-established method that relies on radiocarbon produced by nuclear tests carried out in the 1950s and 1960s. In that time period, the U.S. and Soviet Union detonated so many bombs that they changed the concentration of carbon-14 in the atmosphere by a factor of two. The isotope has been slowly changing since then, and scientists refer to compiled measurements of its concentration over time as the bomb curve.

7   Additionally, every living thing on the planet contains carbon-14, acquired either through the atmosphere (if you're a plant) or by eating plant-based food (if you're an animal). Measuring the amount of carbon-14 in a biological sample and then matching it to corresponding values in the bomb curve tells scientists when the tissue formed, plus or minus six months. This method has been used in

forensics to date mummified corpses found in the desert, for example, or to determine how long it takes for cocaine to travel from forest to urban consumer.

Until now, however, no one had applied the method to the ivory trade— mostly because of its expense and the fact that only about a dozen labs around the world are able to perform these tests. Cerling and his colleagues analyzed 231 ivory specimens collected from 14 large seizures made between 2002 and 2014 in Africa and Asia. The researchers found that 90 percent of the samples came from elephants that died less than three years before their ivory was confiscated. The oldest piece was from an elephant killed 19 years before its ivory was seized; the youngest, just a few months. [8]

The dates also shed light on global patterns of the ivory trade: researchers found that ivory from East Africa tends to enter into the trade faster than ivory from the Tridom region of Cameroon, Gabon and Congo, where forest elephants live. That difference might reflect dwindling elephant populations in the Tridom, Cerling says, making it more difficult to collect enough ivory to form a worthwhile shipment. Alternatively, it could be that East Africa has more established illegal networks for moving contraband goods, or that savannah elephants are simply easier to find and kill. [9]

The paper provides a convincing link between recent poaching and illegal trade of ivory. It also presents a practical way to keep ivory thieves more accountable in the future, says Edouard Bard, chair of climate change and ocean sciences at the College de France in Paris, who was not involved in the research. "One can no longer hide and pretend ignorance, in the hope that illegal objects such as ivory will remain untested," he says. [10]

For instance, while China, Japan and the European Union still have legal domestic trade of antique ivory, much of what is legally for sale today could be from recently poached animals that traders have laundered into the market, says Cerling. "With this method, you can tell exactly when the animal died and see if the ivory is actually as old as the person who is selling it claims it to be," he says. However, N'Bouke's groundbreaking case notwithstanding, this method is less likely to be applied in Africa, where many seizures are being made but funds and technical expertise are lacking. [11]

While (relatively) new technology can help researchers understand how the trade works, it certainly won't end the practice on its own, points out Elizabeth Bennett, vice president of species conservation at the Wildlife Conservation Society, who was not involved in the research. Instead, Bennett says, countries should focus on shutting down ivory trade within their borders. "If all domestic markets globally were illegal, it would be much more difficult to sell the newly poached ivory," she says. "And without a ready market, the incentives to poach and traffic are reduced or removed." [12]

QUESTIONS FOR READING

1. What have scientists learned about the ivory flooding the market? How did they learn about the age of this ivory?

2. How much has the elephant population declined?

3. What are the limits in dating the ivory as a way to end the killing of elephants? What is a better way to save elephants?

QUESTIONS FOR REASONING AND ANALYSIS

4. In some arguments a claim is clearly stated; in others it is more implied. We could say that Nuwer's subject is the use of carbon dating to reveal that much of the ivory for sale has come from recently killed elephants. What, though, is her larger issue—which will lead us to the claim of her argument?

5. What details come together to support her larger issue?

6. Nuwer does not write about one specific ivory dealer; why does she begin with N'Bouke's guilty sentence?

7. What does the author accomplish by concluding with the words of Elizabeth Bennett?

QUESTIONS FOR REFLECTION AND WRITING

8. The ivory trade is illegal in the United States but quite extensive in Asia. What country announced that it would close down all ivory trade by the end of 2017? Will this move alone save the elephants? Why or why not?

9. In what other ways is human activity endangering the large mammals? How can we solve this problem?

CHAPTER 20

Laws and Rights: Gun Control and Immigration Debates

READ: What is the situation? Where are we?

REASON: Who speaks the lines? What is the speaker doing?

REFLECT/WRITE: What is amusing about the cartoon? What more serious point does Morin make?

The visuals and articles in this chapter explore and debate two current issues: firearm regulation and immigration. In the spring of 2008, the Supreme Court, in a close decision, struck down the District of Columbia's ban on handguns. Some saw the landmark decision as affirming the Second Amendment's guarantee of gun ownership to individuals. The Court, however, did not rule out all restrictions. Several mass shootings and the 2016 presidential race following the Court's ruling have led to a renewed interest in firearm laws. For instance, during his campaign, President Donald J. Trump promised a more permissive approach to firearm regulation, while former Secretary of State Hillary Clinton ran on a "commonsense" platform to reduce gun violence.

In addition to firearm regulation, immigration proved an important but divisive issue during the 2016 Presidential election. Secretary Hillary Clinton ran on a platform of comprehensive immigration reform and a pathway to citizenship. On the other hand, President Trump promised to deport undocumented people and build an "impenetrable wall" between the United States and Mexico. Are such measures realistic and humane ways to deal with the challenges of immigration? What does increasing diversity—including different languages, cultures, and religions—do to our national identity? And is a rigid national identity even necessary (or possible) in a global economy? This chapter raises these and other tough questions. Reflect on the following questions as a guide to your study of the current debates on firearm regulation and immigration.

PREREADING QUESTIONS

1. What kinds of restrictions—if any—on guns will be consistent with the Supreme Court's 2008 ruling and the Second Amendment?

2. Is there any reason for citizens to own semiautomatic assault-type weapons (AR-15s, etc.) and/or high-capacity magazines that hold more than ten bullets?

3. Should people be allowed to carry firearms everywhere in the United States, even on college campuses, where teenage students are most at risk for mental illness, as well as drug and alcohol use?

4. Is there any reason why young adults brought here illegally as children should be deprived of a college education or U.S. citizenship?

5. If you wanted to change any of the current laws on these issues to have them reflect your views, how would you go about trying to get your legislation passed?

ALLOWING GUNS ON CAMPUS WILL INVITE TRAGEDIES, NOT END THEM | DANIEL WEBSTER AND RONALD DANIELS

Dr. Daniel W. Webster is professor of health policy and management at the Johns Hopkins Bloomberg School of Public Health and director of the Johns Hopkins Center for Gun Policy and Research. He coedited and contributed to *Reducing Gun Violence in America: Informing Policy with Evidence* (with Jon S. Vernick, 2013), and he publishes widely in other venues on firearm policy and preventing gun violence.

With law degrees from Yale University and the University of Toronto, Dr. Ronald Daniels is president of Johns Hopkins University and a professor in the department of political science at Johns Hopkins University. As president of Johns Hopkins, Dr. Daniels has led efforts to support Baltimore City through community engagement programs. As author and coauthor of seven books and numerous journal publications, Dr. Daniels studies and writes about public policy, economics, and community development. The following article was published in *The Washington Post* on October 21, 2016.

PREREADING QUESTIONS From the title it is clear the authors are discussing guns in college settings. Based on your experiences in college so far, would you feel more or less safe if firearms were permitted at your institution? If guns are already allowed on your campus, how do you feel about it? Why do you feel this way?

Children led from Sandy Hook school after mass shooting.

©Shannon Hicks/Newtown Bee/Polaris/Newscom

Texas this year became the eighth state to require state colleges and   1
universities to allow civilians with permits to carry concealed guns in public places. As a result, the University of Texas at Austin—a school that 50 years ago suffered the trauma of the nation's first campus mass killing—must allow guns to be brought onto campus.

To those behind the campus-carry movement making such inroads in Austin   2
and other state capitals, that's a good thing. This effort is based on the belief that allowing more guns in public places will lead to less violence. But does the evidence support this premise? A new report released by Johns Hopkins University, with co-authors from Stanford University and the University of Massachusetts at Boston, surveys the best available research and says no.

3   Proponents of expanding civilian gun-carrying argue that many mass shootings occur because perpetrators know victims will be unarmed and defenseless due to legal restrictions on carrying in public places. They also contend that citizens, if armed with firearms, can effectively end the carnage of active shootings.

4   But the latest research on mass shootings, much of it detailed in a new book by report co-author Louis Klarevas, tells a different story. First, the overwhelming majority of fatal mass shootings occur in places where guns are allowed. Second, when rampage shootings do occur, gun-wielding civilians rarely are able to stop them. Effective and responsible use of a firearm under the conditions of an active shooter requires significant training and the ability to make good decisions and shoot accurately under the most challenging circumstances. Even some trained law-enforcement officers perform poorly under such circumstances. These facts explain why the best research shows that right-to-carry gun laws do not decrease mass shootings or the number of people shot in those incidents.

5   Campus-carry proponents have turned to another equally specious argument: If guns were permitted at colleges and universities, victims of sexual assault could use them to fend off their attackers. This argument, too, is starkly at odds with the best evidence. If carrying a gun were effective in warding off would-be rapists in a nation where civilian gun-carrying is not uncommon, you would expect many to report using a gun in this manner. Yet a study by Harvard's David Hemenway using data from the National Crime Victimization Survey from 2007 to 2011 showed that out of the 62 cases in which a respondent reported being a victim of a violent crime and using a gun in self-defense, not one involved a sexual assault. In fact, once a crime is in progress, the use of a gun by a victim in self-defense did not affect his or her risk of being injured one way or the other.

6   The fact is that the evidence for guns as a deterrent to campus crime is weak or nonexistent. And profound evidence shows that the college environment is particularly ill-suited to gun possession.

7   The risks and interconnectedness of violence, alcohol abuse and reckless behavior are elevated among college-age youths. The frequency of binge drinking among college students is a deep and enduring problem, and the evidence from studies of criminal assaults both outside and inside the home and comparisons of victims who are treated at hospitals for nonlethal assault-related injuries with homicides shows that the presence of firearms dramatically increases the risk of death and injury during altercations. Freely inserting firearms into this environment is a recipe for tragedy.

8   Similarly, a recent study of campus shootings conducted by Everytown for Gun Safety (founded by former New York mayor Michael Bloomberg, who also is a major donor to Johns Hopkins University) shows that the vast majority are neither mass shootings nor active-shooter incidents but instead involve situations where the presence of guns is shown to be far more lethal—interpersonal disputes, targeted attacks, accidents and suicide.

9   Suicide attempts that lead to hospital treatment or death rise dramatically and peak during the college years, and they have been increasing in recent years. A large body of research ranging from comparative studies of households

where suicides have occurred and ones where they have not, studies examining the association between states' suicide rates and gun ownership, and evaluations of laws designed to restrict firearms access of high-risk individuals clearly shows that access increases the risk of suicide. Should this not be a serious consideration for those advocating for guns on campus?

A university should be a place where ideas are celebrated and contentious 10 views are faithfully explored. Here, we seek evidence that can shine light on our darkest challenges.

As the president of Johns Hopkins University and a gun violence researcher 11 at the university's Bloomberg School of Public Health, we work with city leaders and partners in the community to find solutions that can improve lives—and save them, in Baltimore and beyond. We oppose guns on campus not in the hackneyed stereotype of liberals scolding from the ivory tower but as a result of a searching examination of relevant research, as well as a common-sense assessment of reality. What the evidence to date shows—and what we hope state legislators across the nation who are pondering such measures will consider—is that campus-carry laws will invite tragedies on college campuses, not end them.

Daniel Webster and Ronald Daniels, "Allowing Guns on Campus Will Invite Tragedies, Not End Them," *The Washington Post*, 21 Oct. 2016. Used with permission of the authors.

QUESTIONS FOR READING

1. What events have led Webster and Daniels to write their article?
2. According to research cited by the authors, do right-to-carry gun laws decrease mass shootings or the number of people shot during mass shootings?
3. At what age do risks of violence, alcohol abuse, and reckless behavior increase?
4. Are high-risk people more or less likely to commit suicide if they have access to firearms?

QUESTIONS FOR REASONING AND ANALYSIS

5. What are Webster and Daniels arguing? Can you find their thesis statement?
6. How do they organize their argument, and what sources do they use?
7. How would you describe their tone? What elements of style help create that tone?
8. Who is the audience for this article? To what extent does this audience influence the approach and style Webster and Daniels use?

QUESTIONS FOR REFLECTION AND WRITING

9. How do you feel about campus carry laws? Do you agree with Webster and Daniels? If so, why? If not, why not?
10. Have any mass killings taken place since this essay was published? If so, has the gun debate been affected? Does it bother you that mass shootings occur? How do you respond? How do others you know respond? Explain.

GUN CONTROL PROPOSALS IN THE WAKE OF ORLANDO COULD ENDANGER CONSTITUTIONAL RIGHTS

DAVID B. RIVKIN JR AND ANDREW M. GROSSMAN

A former White House counsel and member of the Justice Department under Presidents Ronald Reagan and George H. W. Bush, David B. Rivkin Jr. currently works as a Washington, D.C., attorney. He is a nationally recognized political commentator and an award-winning legal writer on issues involving the U.S. Constitution and international affairs. He holds advanced degrees from both Georgetown and Columbia Universities.

Andrew M. Grossman is an adjunct scholar at the Cato Institute and a Washington, D.C., attorney who litigates cases involving constitutional law and legal policy. He has argued cases before the U.S. Supreme Court and the federal courts of appeal and has published widely on legal matters. He has also appeared on national cable networks as a legal policy analyst. Grossman holds a JD from the George Mason School of Law. This article appeared in 2016.

PREREADING QUESTIONS After reading about the two authors, are you surprised that they are coauthoring an article on gun control issues? Are you even more interested in what they have to say together on this issue?

1   In the aftermath of horrific terrorist massacres such as the Orlando nightclub shooting, the natural impulse of the American people is to ask what the government can do to prevent such tragedies. Securing public safety is indeed the government's most important job; keeping guns away from terrorists has obvious value. But this must be done in a way that complies with the Constitution.

2   This admonition has animated much of the recent debate about the rules governing National Security Agency surveillance of suspected terrorists. Regrettably, it has not been embraced in the gun control debate unfolding in the aftermath of Orlando.

3   Yet the Constitution's due-process protections are the vital safeguard of individual liberty and mitigate against arbitrary government action by setting the procedures the government must observe when it seeks to deprive an individual of a given substantive right.

4   Constitutionally "appropriate" procedure varies based on the importance of the right at issue and the risk of an erroneous deprivation of that right, and the government's interest. For example, while government officials may commit a person who is dangerous to himself or others on an emergency basis, a judicial determination of the validity of the commitment must follow. Law enforcement officers may arrest a person they believe to be guilty of a crime, but the person who has been arrested is entitled to appear before a judge.

5   Our legal traditions spell out the process that is due for the categories of people currently denied the right to keep and bear arms. Those include felons and those charged with felonies, people adjudged "mentally defective" and those dishonorably discharged from the military. The unifying factor is that people subject to these bars have all received their day in court.

But that's not the case with the new gun control proposals. One proposal is 6 to block gun sales to those named on the terrorist watch list maintained by the FBI's Terrorist Screening Center. The list, however, is entirely unsuited to that task.

According to National Counterterrorism Center guidance, agencies can add 7 someone to the list based on a "reasonable suspicion" or "articulable evidence" that the person is a "known or suspected terrorist." Listings can be based on anything from civilian tips and social-media postings to actual government investigations. The guidance makes clear that "irrefutable evidence or concrete facts are not necessary."

The predictable result is a very long list, with entries of varying quality. As of 8 July 2014, the main list contained about 800,000 names. More than 40 percent are designated as having "no recognized terrorist group affiliation." This kind of list may be valuable for prioritizing counterterrorism activities, supporting investigations and determining where additional scrutiny may be warranted, such as with visa applications.

However, the watch list was never intended to be used to punish listed 9 individuals by depriving them of their constitutionally protected rights. And, legally, it is unsuitable for that task. While there is an administrative redress process to remove a name from the list, there is no judicial review, no hearing and not even notification of whether a request was granted or denied, much less the grounds of the decision.

The no-fly list, which contained about 47,000 names in 2013, is subject to the 10 same shortcomings. Individuals are never informed why they've been listed and have no opportunity for a hearing before a neutral judge to clear their names. In court filings, the government has explained that the list represents officials' "predictive judgments" about who may pose a threat. Whatever the merits of that approach as applied to the eligibility for air travel, it falls far short of the kind of concrete proof and procedure necessary to deprive a person of a constitutionally protected right.

Even narrower approaches being bandied about raise similar concerns. For 11 example, an amendment by Sen. Dianne Feinstein (D-Calif.) would authorize the attorney general to block a firearms sale if the attorney general determined that the buyer was engaged in conduct relating to terrorism. The amendment does provide that a frustrated buyer may bring a lawsuit in federal court to challenge a denial. But its text suggests that this is just window dressing: The attorney general may withhold the evidence underlying the denial from the plaintiff, placing the burden on the plaintiff to prove his innocence by rebutting evidence that he's never seen.

Those agitating for firearms restrictions now should understand that the 12 precedent they set is a dangerous one that extends far beyond the realm of the Second Amendment. If the government's say-so is sufficient to block a gun sale—thereby abridging a right enumerated in the Constitution, with little or no ability for redress—what right wouldn't be at risk of arbitrary deprivation, particularly among the powerless?

Daniel B. Rivkin Jr. and Andrew M. Grossman, "Gun Control in the Wake of Orlando Could Endanger Constitutional Rights," *The Washington Post*, 21 June 2016. Used with permission of the authors.

QUESTIONS FOR READING

1. What happened that led Rivkin and Grossman to write this article?
2. What are some limitations to the terrorist watch list and the no-fly list that the authors point out?
3. Who is currently denied the right to keep and bear arms? Why are they denied this constitutionally protected right?
4. Who proposed a constitutional amendment that would allow the U.S. Attorney General to block a firearms sale if the buyer were engaged in terrorist activity?

QUESTIONS FOR REASONING AND ANALYSIS

5. What is the authors' claim? Where do they state it?
6. How do the authors build their argument? Explain.
7. Rather than arguing against the existence of the terrorist watch list and the no-fly list, what do the authors do? Do you agree? If so, why? If not, why not?
8. How do Rivkin and Grossman end their article? What impact does this have on their overall argument?
9. Analyze the authors' style and tone. What strategies shape their style and create their tone?

QUESTIONS FOR REFLECTION AND WRITING

10. In the wake of the Pulse nightclub massacre in Orlando, Florida, where the shooter used a semiautomatic assault-type weapon and a 9mm pistol, both with high-capacity magazines, how do you feel about people's access to these sorts of firearms in the United States?
11. If you strongly support the Second Amendment and feel that no restrictions should be placed on law-abiding Americans' access to firearms, how do you propose addressing the problem of mass shootings like the one in Orlando? If you believe the U.S. government should enact strong gun control laws, how might this happen without infringing on the Second Amendment? Be prepared to discuss these issues in class and write about them in a paper.

IT'S TIME FOR POLICE OFFICERS TO START DEMANDING GUN LAWS THAT COULD END UP SAVING THEIR OWN LIVES | ROBERT WILSON

With an undergraduate degree from Washington and Lee University and a master's degree from the University of Virginia, Robert Wilson has worked at *The Washington Post* and *USA Today*, as well as served as an editor at the magazines *Civilization* and *Preservation*. He has published three books: *A Certain Somewhere: Writers on the Places They Remember* (2002); *The Explorer King: Adventure, Science, and the Great Diamond Hoax; Clarence King in the Old West* (2006); and *Mathew Brady: Portraits of a Nation* (2013). Wilson is currently the editor of *The American Scholar*. This article was published in *The American Scholar* on February 29, 2016.

PREREADING QUESTIONS What does the title of this article tell you about the content and direction of the argument? Does the title hint at a typical firearm regulation editorial, or might this piece take a different approach to this topic?

When we send our soldiers, spies, and mercenaries into dangerous   1
situations, we have and should have high expectations for how they will behave. Murder, rape, and pillage—the dark acts of soldiery in wartime—are heinous crimes even when our own soldiers commit them, and lesser acts of cruelty and destruction are also intolerable. Although it would be naïve to think that we prosecute more than a fraction of such crimes, that we prosecute them at all speaks to our values and to the standards we have for the behavior of our soldiers. Still, if we are honest about what war is and what can reasonably be expected of those we expose to the boredom, tension, and danger of combat, then we know that criminal acts are inevitable, and that when we send people to kill our enemies, innocent people will also die or be exposed to horrible injury or loss. Those who commit the felonies and misdemeanors of war are of course responsible for them, and deserve to be condemned and punished. But the rest of us who are not exposed to danger can't wash our hands of the consequences or profess to be shocked when shocking crimes are committed under the pressures of soldiering.

In the past two or three decades, we have increasingly exposed the civilians   2
we pay to police and protect us to conditions approaching those into which we interject our soldiers in wartime. Partly this is due to our national security fixation since 9/11, resulting in big-city police departments with antiterrorism units that rival those of entire countries, and in the militarization of police departments large and small, with the special uniforms, weapons, and materiel we might formerly have associated with National Guard units. The relentless emphasis on security, the evidence that the next mass shooting can happen anywhere, the hot focus of the media on each outburst of violence, and the political necessity of making people feel safer than they are—all of these factors create for civilian law enforcers expectations similar to those that soldiers and their commanders experience. The stress produced by these expectations is one thing the police must live with, but the danger they face as they do their jobs in a militarized environment is even more consequential.

Beginning well before 9/11, Second Amendment absolutism began to make   3
the accessibility, variety, and sheer number of powerful weapons pervasive throughout our society. Back in the late 1960s, it was possible to conclude that gun violence was essentially a black, inner-city problem, and the Gun Control Act of 1968 was intended to block the flow of cheap handguns known in racially tinged jargon as Saturday night specials. A quarter-century later, the 1994 federal assault weapons ban recognized the increasing prevalence and danger to society of military-style weapons and ammunition. It prevented the manufacture of semiautomatic assault weapons and high-capacity ammunition magazines. Former presidents Gerald Ford, Jimmy Carter, and Ronald Reagan all publicly supported the bill, which Bill Clinton signed into law. The ban lasted 10 years and expired. An attempt by President Obama to pass a new ban on assault weapons

after the Sandy Hook massacre failed a Senate vote in 2013. A year ago, the U.S. Bureau of Alcohol, Tobacco, Firearms and Explosives proposed a ban on a certain type of armor-piercing bullet that has been legal to use in semiautomatic rifles. When President Reagan signed a bill banning similar sorts of bullets in 1986, he referred to these munitions as "so-called cop-killer bullets, which pose an unreasonable threat to law enforcement officers who use soft body armor." The ATF proposed to add the currently legal bullet to the ban because it can now be used in a concealable semiautomatic pistol, making it more dangerous to the police. But the ATF reversed itself even before a month-long comment period was up because the National Rifle Association mustered so many negative responses: of a total of 80,000, "the vast majority" were critical, according to the ATF. More than half the members of the House and of the Senate also spoke in opposition to the proposal.

4   Is there a connection between a citizenry armed with military-style weapons and the appalling acts of violence committed by some cops that have been widely publicized and rightly criticized? Every law enforcement officer working today knows that any routine traffic stop, delivery of a warrant or court order, or response to a domestic disturbance anywhere in the country involving people of any race or age can put them face to face with a weapon. Guns are everywhere, not just in the inner city. A 2014 Pew Research Center survey showed that half as many black households as white own guns, half as many urbanites own guns as do rural people, and those under 30 are far less likely to own a gun than those over 50. As the Black Lives Matter movement makes clear, it is impossible to take race out of a discussion of police violence, but it is also true that if a cop or deputy leaves the station house or sheriff's office anywhere in this country, whatever the racial or economic composition of the place where he or she works, the fear of being harmed and the tension this causes are always present.

5   Most police officers handle this daily threat as we expect them to, acting calmly and rationally, just as they are trained to behave in tense situations. But fear brings out the irrational, and racism is one of the irrationalities quickest to rise to the surface. Although we have a right to expect our law enforcers to be better than we are, to be more cool-headed and evenhanded, to check their prejudices at the door as they go out on their shift, we must recognize, given the stress and potential danger to which they are constantly exposed, that like the soldiers who fight in our name, the cops we pay to protect us are not all going to behave honorably. How much greater is our share of the blame when we allow our streets, residences, businesses, and in some places even our schools and churches to bristle with dangerous weapons—when we choose not to do everything we can to keep police officers as safe as possible as they go about their jobs?

One weapon that has lost much of its power in this country is the force of   6
argument. Those who believe that the Second Amendment does not apply to
individuals are not going to change the minds of, or have their minds changed
by, those who believe that the Second Amendment means the government has
little authority to restrict a citizen's right to bear arms. So perhaps it is also naïve
to think that a plea to make cops safer is going to change passionately held
positions, even when the issue at hand is a sensible measure like restricting gun
show loopholes on background checks.

Can anything clear away the impasse? Does any person or group of people   7
have the power, the respect, or the moral standing to make things even a little
saner? To me, saner would mean closing the background check loopholes for
those who buy weapons at gun shows or on the Internet, making it harder for
people with mental illness to buy guns, restoring the ban on semiautomatic
weapons and large-capacity magazines, encouraging the development of smart
guns that can be fired only by the owner (which would protect cops whose guns
are taken from them, a major cause of police deaths), and funding the U.S.
Centers for Disease Control and Prevention to study gun violence as a public
health matter (something that Congress stopped the agency from doing in 1996
after the NRA suggested it was pushing for gun control). But that's just my list.

Who could advocate successfully for these modest measures, or for any   8
measures whatsoever, especially those specifically designed to make the police,
and by extension the rest of us, safer? Not President Obama or other political
leaders, clearly; not Michael Bloomberg with his billions; not the families of the
many victims of gun violence; not an electorate that polls show vastly favors
certain measures; and not even the police chiefs of major cities, who met in

Washington, D.C., last summer and called for, according to *The Washington Post,* "more stringent gun laws, including harsher penalties for gun crimes and the use of high-capacity magazines."

9   But this last group strikes me as having the best chance to make something happen. Not just chiefs of big-city departments but those involved in law enforcement from top to bottom. Police officers have the most to gain from sensible attempts to restrict access to dangerous weapons and munitions, and to reduce their numbers. Because they put themselves at risk each day, they have the moral authority to advocate for what will make them safer. Many of us who would like to see smarter gun laws are among the growing majority of Americans who do not own guns for hunting or sport shooting or self-defense and thus have less connection to the culture of gun ownership than previous generations did. But cops know guns and gun culture. In fact, there are police officers who oppose gun control, and some sheriffs (who are of course elected, not appointed) have said they would refuse to enforce certain new gun measures—although the term *gun control* means different things to different people, and polls suggest that most cops support at least some items from my wish list. And if all of those we pay to enforce our laws created, en masse, a wish list of their own, it would be hard for critics to make the slippery slope argument— the assertion that these modest steps would only be first steps because the police want to take away our weapons and repeal the Second Amendment. Nobody this side of the NRA leadership could really believe that to be true.

10   We need a national convention of law enforcement officials and officers, including police chiefs, police union heads, sheriffs, and deputies; the dozens of federal agencies with police powers ranging from the FBI, ATF, Drug Enforcement Administration, and Customs and Border Protection to the National Park Service and Bureau of Prisons; state police and the National Guard—everyone who carries a weapon to protect us and is at risk from weapons legally or illegally possessed. Groups representing other types of first responders, such as fire and rescue, might also participate, since they are often put at risk. The purpose of the convention would be to see what measures these groups could agree upon and to convince the rest of us that the present situation can be improved. A convention of sufficient size and scope could get the message across, and it could give political cover to elected officials and potential candidates who are willing to buck NRA intransigence for changes that large majorities of Americans would like to see. A state senator running for reelection who has been targeted by the NRA could tell voters that she values the collective wisdom of our cops over the wishes of gun lobbyists. If this possibility gave courage to even a few politicians in the middle who would like to vote with their conscience and their constituencies but are afraid of NRA backlash, many narrow votes in state legislatures and Congress could be turned around.

11   The sorts of changes that cops are likely to support won't in themselves stop mass murders or terrorist plots, won't keep guns out of the possession of all mentally ill people, criminals, or those who deal weapons to them. Still, these measures are bound to save the lives of some policemen. And if they make cops feel safer when they do their jobs and if that makes the small percentage of

police officers who have the capacity to behave irrationally comfortable enough to keep control of their emotions more often, wouldn't this improve the lives of those protecting us, improve the lives of their families, improve the lives, black and otherwise, of those who come into contact with the police? And ultimately, wouldn't it make us all safer?

QUESTIONS FOR READING

1. What event seems to have led Wilson to write this editorial?

2. What has caused the increase in the perceived need for more security in the United States?

3. What weapon has lost power in the United States, according to Wilson? Why do you think he would add this point to his article?

4. What items make up Wilson's wish list?

QUESTIONS FOR REASONING AND ANALYSIS

5. Wilson's article is a little more complex than other articles included in this book; while he makes one overarching argument, he also makes other points, weaving these into his editorial. What is Wilson's primary argument, and what are some of his secondary arguments?

6. *The American Scholar* is the magazine of Phi Beta Kappa, the oldest and most prestigious honor society in America. Do you think this article's audience influenced Wilson's argumentative strategy? If so, how? If not, why not?

7. Wilson begins his article by discussing war crimes and how our country responds to them when they are perpetrated by our soldiers. Why do you think he starts out this way? What do you think he hopes to accomplish?

8. What does Wilson propose as a solution to address gun violence against the police and against civilians in the United States? Do you think this will work? If so, why? If not, why not? Be prepared to discuss and defend your position.

QUESTIONS FOR REFLECTION AND WRITING

9. Imagine that you have a family member who is a police officer (if you have a relative who is in law enforcement, you won't have to pretend). How do you feel about your loved one serving as a police officer with so many readily available firearms? Would you want more or fewer guns available in the United States? If more, why? If fewer, why?

10. Why is it so difficult for people who disagree about firearm regulations to discuss this topic? What do you think we can do to improve discourse between these differing camps? If it's difficult for you to imagine a solution that would impact our entire country, try to think of what *you* might do to improve discourse with someone who doesn't agree with your point of view on guns. Does your method involve careful listening? If it doesn't, should it?

IMMIGRATE, ASSIMILATE | AMY CHUA

A professor at Yale Law School since 2001, Amy Chua specializes in international business transactions, ethnic conflict, and globalization and the law. She is the author of *Battle Hymn of the Tiger Mother* (2011). She cowrote *The Triple Package: How Three Unlikely Traits Explain the Rise and Fall of Cultural Groups* with her husband, Jed Rubenfeld, in 2014. Her essay on immigration, published February 3, 2008, was a special to *The Washington Post*.

PREREADING QUESTIONS Given the title, where do you expect to find Chua on the immigration debate? Given her education and expertise, how do you expect her to support her argument?

1   If you don't speak Spanish, Miami really can feel like a foreign country. In any restaurant, the conversation at the next table is more likely to be in Spanish than English. And Miami's population is only 65 percent Hispanic. El Paso is 76 percent Latino. Flushing, N.Y., is 60 percent immigrant, mainly Chinese.

2   Chinatowns and Little Italys have long been part of America's urban landscape, but would it be all right to have entire U.S. cities where most people spoke and did business in Chinese, Spanish or even Arabic? Are too many Third World, non-English-speaking immigrants destroying our national identity?

3   For some Americans, even asking such questions is racist. At the other end of the spectrum, conservative talk-show host Bill O'Reilly* fulminates against floods of immigrants who threaten to change America's "complexion" and replace what he calls the "white Christian male power structure."

4   But for the large majority in between, Democrats and Republicans alike, these questions are painful, and there are no easy answers. At some level, most of us cherish our legacy as a nation of immigrants. But are all immigrants really equally likely to make good Americans? Are we, as Samuel Huntington warns, in danger of losing our core values and devolving "into a loose confederation of ethnic, racial, cultural and political groups, with little or nothing in common apart from their location in the territory of what had been the United States of America"?

5   My parents arrived in the United States in 1961, so poor that they couldn't afford heat their first winter. I grew up speaking only Chinese at home (for every English word accidentally uttered, my sister and I got one whack of the chopsticks). Today, my father is a professor at Berkeley, and I'm a professor at Yale Law School. As the daughter of immigrants, a grateful beneficiary of America's tolerance and opportunity, I could not be more pro-immigrant.

6   Nevertheless, I think Huntington has a point.

7   Around the world today, nations face violence and instability as a result of their increasing pluralism and diversity. Across Europe, immigration has resulted in unassimilated, largely Muslim enclaves that are hotbeds of unrest and even terrorism. The riots in France late last year were just the latest manifestation. With Muslims poised to become a majority in Amsterdam and elsewhere within a

---

* O'Reilly was fired by Fox News in 2017. — Ed.

decade, major West European cities could undergo a profound transformation. Not surprisingly, virulent anti-immigration parties are on the rise.

Not long ago, Czechoslovakia, Yugoslavia and the Soviet Union disintegrated 8
when their national identities proved too weak to bind together diverse peoples. Iraq is the latest example of how crucial national identity is. So far, it has found no overarching identity strong enough to unite its Kurds, Shiites and Sunnis.

The United States is in no danger of imminent disintegration. But this is 9
because it has been so successful, at least since the Civil War, in forging a national identity strong enough to hold together its widely divergent communities. We should not take this unifying identity for granted.

The greatest empire in history, ancient Rome, collapsed when its cultural and 10
political glue dissolved, and peoples who had long thought of themselves as Romans turned against the empire. In part, this fragmentation occurred because of a massive influx of immigrants from a very different culture. The "barbarians" who sacked Rome were Germanic immigrants who never fully assimilated.

Does this mean that it's time for the United States to shut its borders and 11
reassert its "white, Christian" identity and what Huntington calls its Anglo-Saxon, Protestant "core values"?

ANTI-IMMIGRANT MISTAKES

No. The anti-immigration camp makes at least two critical mistakes.   12

First, it neglects the indispensable role that immigrants have played in 13
building American wealth and power. In the 19th century, the United States would never have become an industrial and agricultural powerhouse without the millions of poor Irish, Polish, Italian and other newcomers who mined coal, laid rail and milled steel. European immigrants led to the United States' winning the race for the atomic bomb.

Today, American leadership in the Digital Revolution—so central to our 14
military and economic preeminence—owes an enormous debt to immigrant contributions. Andrew Grove (co-founder of Intel), Vinod Khosla (Sun Microsystems) and Sergey Brin (Google) are immigrants. Between 1995 and 2005, 52.4 percent of Silicon Valley startups had one key immigrant founder. And Vikram S. Pundit's recent appointment to the helm of Citigroup means that 14 CEOs of Fortune 100 companies are foreign-born.

The United States is in a fierce global competition to attract the world's best 15
high-tech scientists and engineers—most of whom are not white Christians. Just this past summer, Microsoft opened a large new software-development center in Canada, in part because of the difficulty of obtaining U.S. visas for foreign engineers.

Second, anti-immigration talking heads forget that their own scapegoating 16
vitriol will, if anything, drive immigrants further from the U.S. mainstream. One reason we don't have Europe's enclaves is our unique success in forging an ethnically and religiously neutral national identity, uniting individuals of all

backgrounds. This is America's glue, and people like Huntington and O'Reilly unwittingly imperil it.

17   Nevertheless, immigration naysayers also have a point.

18   America's glue can be subverted by too much tolerance. Immigration advocates are too often guilty of an uncritical political correctness that avoids hard questions about national identity and imposes no obligations on immigrants. For these well-meaning idealists, there is no such thing as too much diversity.

MAINTAINING OUR HERITAGE

19   The right thing for the United States to do—and the best way to keep Americans in favor of immigration—is to take national identity seriously while maintaining our heritage as a land of opportunity. U.S. immigration policy should be tolerant but also tough. Here are five suggestions:

- **Overhaul Admission Priorities.**

20   Since 1965, the chief admission criterion has been family reunification. This was a welcome replacement for the ethnically discriminatory quota system that preceded it. But once the brothers and sisters of a current U.S. resident get in, they can sponsor their own extended families. In 2006, more than 800,000 immigrants were admitted on this basis. By contrast, only about 70,000 immigrants were admitted on the basis of employment skills, with an additional 65,000 temporary visas granted to highly skilled workers.

21   This is backward. Apart from nuclear families (spouse, minor children, possibly parents), the special preference for family members should be drastically reduced. As soon as my father got citizenship, his relatives in the Philippines asked him to sponsor them. Soon, his mother, brother, sister and sister-in-law were also U.S. citizens or permanent residents. This was nice for my family, but frankly there is nothing especially fair about it.

22   Instead, the immigration system should reward ability and be keyed to the country's labor needs, skilled or unskilled, technological or agricultural. In particular, we should significantly increase the number of visas for highly skilled workers, putting them on a fast track for citizenship.

- **Make English the Official National Language.**

23   A common language is critical to cohesion and national identity in an ethnically diverse society. Americans of all backgrounds should be encouraged to speak more languages—I've forced my own daughters to learn Mandarin (minus the threat of chopsticks)—but offering Spanish-language public education to Spanish-speaking children is the wrong kind of indulgence. Native-language education should be overhauled, and more stringent English proficiency requirements for citizenship should be set up.

A Hispanic American shows his dual loyalties in a march on Washington.

©REUTERS/Alamy Stock Photo

• Immigrants Must Embrace the Nation's Civic Virtues.

It took my parents years to see the importance of participating in the larger 24 community. When I was in third grade, my mother signed me up for Girl Scouts. I think she liked the uniforms and merit badges, but when I told her that I was picking up trash and visiting soup kitchens, she was horrified.

For many immigrants, only family matters. Even when immigrants get 25 involved in politics, they often focus on protecting their own and protesting discrimination. That they can do so is one of the great virtues of U.S. democracy. But a mind-set based solely on taking care of your own factionalizes our society.

Like all Americans, immigrants have a responsibility to contribute to the 26 social fabric. It's up to each immigrant community to fight off an "enclave" mentality and give back to their new country. It's not healthy for Chinese to hire only Chinese, or Koreans only Koreans. By contrast, the free health clinic set up by Muslim Americans in Los Angeles—serving the entire poor community—is a model to emulate. Immigrants are integrated at the moment they realize that their success is intertwined with everyone else's.

• Enforce the Law.

Illegal immigration, along with terrorism, is the chief cause of today's anti- 27 immigration backlash. It is also inconsistent with the rule of law, which, as any immigrant from a developing country will tell you, is a critical aspect of U.S. identity. But if we're serious about this problem, we need to enforce the law against not only illegal aliens, but also against those who hire them.

28   It's the worst of all worlds to allow U.S. employers who hire illegal aliens—thus keeping the flow of illegal workers coming—to break the law while demonizing the aliens as lawbreakers. An Arizona law that took effect Jan. 1 tightens the screws on employers who hire undocumented workers, but this issue can't be left up to a single state.

- **Make the United States an Equal-Opportunity Immigration Magnet.**

29   That the 11 million to 20 million illegal Immigrants are 80 percent Mexican and Central American is itself a problem. This is emphatically not for the reason Huntington gives—that Hispanics supposedly don't share America's core values. But if the U.S. immigration system is to reflect and further our ethnically neutral identity, it must itself be ethnically neutral, offering equal opportunity to Sudanese, Estonians, Burmese and so on. The starkly disproportionate ratio of Latinos—reflecting geographical fortuity and a large measure of lawbreaking—is inconsistent with this principle.

30   Immigrants who turn their backs on American values don't deserve to be here. But those of us who turn our backs on immigrants misunderstand the secret of America's success and what it means to be American.

Amy Chua, "Immigrate, Assimilate." *The Washington Post*, February 3, 2008. Reprinted by permission of the author.

QUESTIONS FOR READING

1. What is Huntington's concern for America?
2. What has happened in some European cities? To several European countries? What causes internal conflict in Iraq?
3. What are the two mistakes of those who oppose immigration, in the author's view?
4. What are the author's suggestions for a tough immigration policy? State her five proposals in your own words.

QUESTIONS FOR REASONING AND ANALYSIS

5. Why does Chua provide her immigrant experience and family success story? As a part of her argument, what purpose does it serve?
6. What is clever about her concluding paragraph? How does it mirror the approach of her argument?
7. What is Chua's claim? Express her position as a problem/solution argument.
8. Look at Chua's five proposals. What kinds of grounds does she provide in support?
9. Is the author convincing? If so, what makes her argument effective? If not, why not?

QUESTIONS FOR REFLECTION AND WRITING

10. Chua asserts that the chief cause of anti-immigration attitudes is a combination of terrorism and illegal aliens. Do you agree with this assessment? If not, why not?

11. Where do you stand on immigration? In opposition? Embracing diversity? Or some-where in the middle? Has Chua established a good argument for the middle ground? Why or why not?

12. Is there any specific proposal with which you disagree? If so, why? How would you refute Chua's defense of that proposal?

LEGAL, ILLEGAL | ROBERTO SURO

Roberto Suro directs the Tomás Rivera Policy Institute and holds a joint appointment as a professor in the School of Policy, Planning and Development and the Annenberg School for Communication and Journalism at the University of Southern California. Suro is the author or editor of several books on immigration, including *Writing Immigration: Scholars and Journalists in Dialogue* (2011). He is also active in the community, serving on the board of directors of an association of charities and as a trustee of a foundation supporting social science research. The following was published in *The Washington Post* on July 13, 2012.

PREREADING QUESTIONS Can you find any clues to Suro's essay from his title? What do you expect to discover?

A century ago, the immigrants from across the Atlantic included settlers and sojourners. Along with the many folks looking to make a permanent home in the United States came those who had no intention to stay, and who would make some money and then go home. Between 1908 and 1915, about 7 million people arrived while about 2 million departed. About a quarter of all Italian immigrants, for example, eventually returned to Italy for good. They even had an affectionate nickname, "uccelli di passaggio," birds of passage.

Today, we are much more rigid about immigrants. We divide newcomers into two categories: legal or illegal, good or bad. We hail them as Americans in the making, or brand them as aliens fit for deportation. That framework has contributed mightily to our broken immigration system and the long political paralysis over how to fix it. We don't need more categories, but we need to change the way we think about categories. We need to look beyond strict definitions of legal and illegal. To start, we can recognize the new birds of passage, those living and thriving in the gray areas. We might then begin to solve our immigration challenges.

Crop pickers, violinists, construction workers, entrepreneurs, engineers, home health-care aides and particle physicists are among today's birds of passage. They are energetic participants in a global economy driven by the flow of work, money and ideas. They prefer to come and go as opportunity calls them. They can manage to have a job in one place and a family in another.

With or without permission, they straddle laws, jurisdictions and identities with ease. We need them to imagine the United States as a place where they can be productive for a while without committing themselves to staying forever. We need them to feel that home can be both here and there and that they can belong to two nations honorably.

©John Moore/Getty Images

A civilian paramilitary man patrols the U.S.–Mexican border.

5   Imagine life with a radically different immigration policy: The Jamaican woman who came as a visitor and was looking after your aunt until she died could try living in Canada for a while. You could eventually ask her to come back to care for your mother. The Indian software developer could take some of his Silicon Valley earnings home to join friends in a little start-up, knowing that he could always work in California again. Or the Mexican laborer who busts his back on a Wisconsin dairy farm for wages that keep milk cheap would come and go as needed because he could decide which dairy to work for and a bi-national bank program was helping him save money to build a better life for his kids in Mexico.

6   Accommodating this new world of people in motion will require new attitudes on both sides of the immigration battle. Looking beyond the culture war logic of right or wrong means opening up the middle ground and understanding that managing immigration today requires multiple paths and multiple outcomes, including some that are not easy to accomplish legally in the existing system.

7   A new system that encourages both sojourners and settlers would not only help ensure that our society receives the human resources it will need in the future, it also could have an added benefit: Changing the rigid framework might help us resolve the status of the estimated 11 million unauthorized migrants who are our shared legacy of policy failures.

8   Currently, we do not do gray zones well. Hundreds of thousands of people slosh around in indeterminate status because they're caught in bureaucratic limbo or because they have been granted temporary stays that are repeatedly extended. President Obama created a paler shade of gray this summer by

exercising prosecutorial discretion not to deport some young people who were brought to this country illegally as children. But these are exceptions, not rules.

The basic mechanism for legal immigration today, apart from the special 9 category of refugee, is the legal permanent resident visa, or green card. Most recipients are people sponsored by close relatives who live in the United States. As the name implies, this mechanism is designed for immigrants who are settling down. The visa can be revoked if the holder does not show "intent to remain" by not maintaining a U.S. address, going abroad to work full time or just traveling indefinitely. Legal residents are assumed to be on their way to becoming Americans, physically, culturally and legally. After five years of living here, they become eligible for citizenship and a chance to gain voting rights and full access to the social safety net.

This is a fine way to deal with people who arrive with deep connections to 10 the country and who resolve to stay. That can and should be most immigrants. But this mechanism has two problems: The nation is not prepared to offer citizenship to every migrant who is offered a job. And not everyone who comes here wants to stay forever.

It may have once made sense to think of immigrants as sodbusters who 11 were coming to settle empty spaces. But that antique reasoning does not apply when the country is looking at a long, steep race to remain competitive in the world economy, particularly not when innovation and entrepreneurship are supposed to be our comparative advantage. To succeed, we need modern birds of passage.

The challenges differ depending on whether you are looking at the high end 12 of the skills spectrum, the information workers or at low-skilled laborers.

A frequent proposal for highly skilled workers comes with the slogan, "Staple 13 a green card to the diploma." That is supposed to ensure that a greater share of brainy international students remain in the United States after earning degrees in science and technology. But what if they are not ready for a long-term commitment? No one would suggest that investment capital or design processes need to reside permanently in one nation. Talent today yearns to be equally mobile. Rather than try to oblige smart young people from abroad to stay here, we should allow them to think of the United States as a place where they can always return, a place where they will spend part, not all, of their lives, one of several places where they can live and work and invest.

Temporary-worker programs are a conventional approach to meeting low- 14 skilled labor needs without illegal immigration. That's what President George W. Bush proposed in 2004, saying the government should "match willing foreign workers with willing American employers." An immigrant comes to do a particular job for a limited period of time and then goes home. But such programs risk replacing one kind of rigidity with another. The relatively small programs currently in place don't manage the matchmaking very well. Competing domestic workers need to be protected, as do the migrant workers, and the process must be nimble enough to meet labor market demand. Nobody really has pulled that off, and there is no reason to believe it can be done on a grand scale. Rather than trying to link specific migrants to specific jobs, different types of temporary work visas could be pegged to industries, to places or to time periods. You could get an engineering visa, not only a visa to work at Intel.

15   Both short-term visas and permanent residence need to be part of the mix, but they are not the whole answer. Another valuable tool is the provisional visa, which Australia uses as a kind of intermediary stage in which temporary immigrants spend several years before becoming eligible for permanent residency. The U.S. system practically obliges visitors to spend time here without authorization when they've married a citizen, gotten a job or done something else that qualifies them to stay legally.

16   We also could borrow from Europe and create long-term permission to reside for certain migrants that is contingent on simply being employed, not on having a specific job. And, legislation could loosen the definitions of permanent residency so that migrants could gain a lifetime right to live and work in the United States without having to be here (and pay taxes here) more or less continuously.

17   The idea that newcomers are either saints or sinners is not written indelibly either in our hearts or in our laws. As the size of the unauthorized population has grown over the past 20 years or so, the political response has dictated seeing immigration policy through the stark lens of law enforcement: Whom do we lock up, kick out, fence off? Prominent politicians of both parties, including both presidential candidates, have engaged in macho one-upmanship when it comes to immigration. So, President Obama broke records for deportations. Mitt Romney, meanwhile, vows to break records for border security.

18   Breaking out of the either/or mentality opens up many avenues for managing future immigration. It could also help break the stalemate over the current population of unauthorized migrants. No election result will produce a Congress that offers a path to citizenship for everybody, but there is no support for total deportation, either.

19   If we accept that there are spaces between legal and illegal, then options multiply.

20   Citizenship could be an eventual outcome for most, not all, people here illegally, but everyone would get some kind of papers, and we can engineer a way for people to work their way from one status to another. The newly arrived and least attached could be granted status for a limited time and receive help with returning to their home countries. Others might be offered life-long privileges to live and work here, but not citizenship. We'd give the fullest welcome to those with homes, children or long time jobs.

21   By insisting that immigrants are either Americans or aliens, we make it harder for some good folks to come and we oblige others to stay for the wrong reasons. Worse, we ensure that there will always be people living among us who are outside the law and that is not good for them or us.

Robert Suro, "Legal, Illegal," *The Washington Post*, 13 July 2012. Reprinted by permission of the author.

QUESTIONS FOR READING

1. What, for Suro, was—and still is—a bird of passage?
2. How do we view these sojourners today?
3. How do immigrants typically come to the United States today? What are they expected to do?
4. What are the problems with this approach?
5. What are the two primary groups of sojourners? How does each group need to be accommodated?

QUESTIONS FOR REASONING AND ANALYSIS

6. What kind (genre) of argument is this? State Suro's claim to reveal the essay's argument type.
7. What approach to immigration issues is not the solution, in Suro's view? Why not? What are the problems with the current approach?
8. List the specific strategies Suro presents for handling various kinds of immigrants. Which ones will require new legislation?
9. What other problem will be easier to address once we agree to Suro's recommendations?
10. Analyze Suro's style and tone; how do they help his argument?

QUESTIONS FOR REFLECTION AND WRITING

11. Do you, in general, agree with Suro that seeing only two categories of immigrants is not the way to approach this issue? If yes, why? If no, why not?
12. Which of the author's specific proposals makes sense to you? Why?
13. Suro concludes that illegal immigrants are not good for either them or us. Why are illegals not good for us—we who are legal? Do you agree? If so, why? If not, why not? Reflect on this question.

THE TRUTH ABOUT YOUNG IMMIGRANTS AND DACA | JANET NAPOLITANO

A former U.S. Secretary of Homeland Security, Janet Napolitano now serves as the president of the University of California system. From 2003 to 2009, she served as the governor of the state of Arizona, and before that, she served as the U.S. Attorney for the District of Arizona, appointed to that position by President Bill Clinton. She holds an undergraduate degree from Santa Clara University and a JD from the University of Virginia School of Law. The following article was published in *The New York Times* on November 30, 2016.

PREREADING QUESTIONS What information in the author's biographical paragraph indicates that she is an expert on the subject matter of her article?

OAKLAND, Calif.—Maybe you've heard this story line before. With the blithe   1
stroke of a pen and without congressional approval, President Obama gave legal

status to a vast population of immigrants who entered the country unlawfully—because he wanted to, and because he found a way.

2   I'm referring to the Deferred Action for Childhood Arrivals program. That program is called DACA, which until the recent presidential campaign was an acronym known by few beyond the nation's immigrant communities or the Washington beltway. Now DACA is trending news, and not in a good way.

3   This narrative about an initiative that has given temporary haven and work authorization to more than 700,000 undocumented minors, the so-called Dreamers, still has critics howling about presidential overreach, about brazen nose-thumbing at the rule of law and about encouraging others to breach the borders of the United States.

4   But there's a problem with this take on the program. It is dead wrong. While much has been made about our incoming president possibly eliminating DACA with his own swift pen stroke, there has been scant attention paid to the careful, rational and lawful reasons for creating the program, which, especially now that its future is in doubt, merit a closer look.

5   As secretary of the Department of Homeland Security, I signed the June 15, 2012, directive that began, "I am setting forth how, in the exercise of our prosecutorial discretion, the Department of Homeland Security (D.H.S.) should enforce the nation's immigration laws against certain young people who were brought to this country as children and know only this country as home." On the same day, President Obama announced DACA from the Rose Garden in a message heavy on common-sense law enforcement—and hope.

6   I arrived in the department as a former United States attorney, attorney general and governor of a border state, and I already knew that many of our immigration policies made little, if any, sense because they did not prioritize the use of enforcement resources.

7   As secretary, I changed enforcement policies to focus on those immigrants who posed a national security or public safety threat, such as gang members and violent felons, and not on veterans, nursing mothers and those with longstanding ties to their communities.

8   Prioritizing the use of resources in law enforcement is nothing new. It is known as "prosecutorial discretion," and we can see it all around us—from local police departments deciding whom to pull over instead of stopping every speeding car to federal prosecutors focusing on larger financial fraud instead of going after every bad check.

9   Indeed, the authority of the federal government to exercise prosecutorial discretion has been repeatedly recognized by the Supreme Court, including in a seminal opinion by Justice Antonin Scalia.

10   Our efforts to use immigration enforcement resources wisely made a real difference. But when it became clear that Congress was not going to take action on comprehensive immigration reform, I realized that more needed to be done with respect to one special population—Dreamers.

11   Dreamers, among other requirements, came to the United States as children, developed deep roots in the country and have become valuable contributors to

their community. They must be in high school or have a diploma, or be a veteran, and they cannot have been convicted of a felony or major misdemeanor.

For this population, we developed DACA. Under this program, qualifying 12 individuals apply for what is known as "deferred action," which provides recipients security against removal and the ability to work lawfully for two years, subject to renewal.

Contrary to the sometimes overheated political rhetoric, the program is not 13 the same as amnesty. Each case is assessed on its own merits to ensure the applicant meets the criteria and poses no security threat. This is similar, but not identical, to how a prosecutor decides to charge a case. The program does not grant categorical relief to an entire group.

Today, there are nearly three-quarters of a million Dreamers who no longer 14 have to constantly fear an encounter with an immigration enforcement agent. Instead, they can live, study and work freely. Many are now studying at the system I lead, the University of California.

Students collaborating on campus.

They are the Berkeley graduate who emigrated to San Francisco at the age 15 of 9 and is now in the system's medical school there. They are the U.C.L.A. student who, at the age of 12, worked in construction to help support his family, an experience that led him to study urban planning and community development.

Some of the debate about the future of DACA suggests that it provides 16 Dreamers an official immigration status or a pathway to citizenship. As the memorandum establishing the program made clear, this is not the case. Only Congress has the power to confer those rights.

17   Rather, the program reflects the executive branch doing what it properly does every day—making decisions about how to best use resources within the framework of existing law. There is no reason to abandon these sensible priorities now.

Janet Napolitano, "The Truth About Young Immigrants and DACA," *The New York Times*, 30 Nov. 2016. Reprinted by permission of the author.

QUESTIONS FOR READING

1. What is DACA and how did it come about?
2. What is prosecutorial discretion and why is it important to the issues discussed in the article?
3. Who are the Dreamers and how does DACA affect them?
4. What may happen to the Dreamers if DACA is repealed?

QUESTIONS FOR REASONING AND ANALYSIS

5. What is Napolitano's primary claim?
6. What evidence does she provide to support her primary claim? How does she organize her argument?
7. How does the author use induction and deduction? Can you find any enthymemes? Can you find any logical fallacies?
8. Do you agree with Napolitano's claim? If so, why? If not, why not?

QUESTIONS FOR REFLECTION AND WRITING

9. Should the President of the United States be able to use her or his executive powers to create programs like the one described in the article? If so, why? If not, why not?
10. How would feel if friends of yours enrolled at your college were deported because they were undocumented? Is this a fair and humane approach to America's immigration challenges? If so, why? If not, why not?
11. Since we are a nation of immigrants, what do you think we should do to ensure rule of law in the United States but also live up to the message by poet Emma Lazarus on the Statue of Liberty: *"Give me your tired, your poor, / Your huddled masses yearning to breathe free, / The wretched refuse of your teeming shore. / Send these, the homeless, tempest-tossed to me, / I lift my lamp beside the golden door!"*?

CHAPTER 21

America: Past, Present, Future

Official White House Photo by Pete Souza

READ: Where are we? What are the people in the photo doing? Who in the photo do you recognize?

REASON: What can you conclude about this gathering? (Think about critical events in the 21st century.)

REFLECT/WRITE: What feelings are captured in the photo? What makes the image arresting?

Eighteen years into the 21st century, we might be forgiven for harboring some uncertainties about the country's future. Although some have written of America's decline, we seem to have survived the last recession better than many other countries, and we are still the land of entrepreneurs, the country driving technological innovation. The number of people living in poverty continues to drop worldwide, and at home we continue to hold elections followed by the peaceful transfer of power.

That's the good news. Unfortunately, it does not tell the whole story. We continue a presence in both Iraq and Afghanistan and struggle with other nations to combat ISIS. We must surely wonder if our efforts will ever bring about a sustainable peace and better society in the Middle East. At home, Republicans and Democrats have wasted time, refusing to work together to solve the country's problems. Budget cuts are hurting education at all levels, and far too many schools are failing to educate the next generation of workers and leaders. All too often we find hatred and bigotry here at home, not just in trouble spots far away. How will the future judge us? How do we find ways to embrace what is good for the individual with what is good for all citizens?

Some other good news. Younger Americans are more concerned about the environment and far more accepting of diversity than older Americans. If the country's youth will commit to becoming and staying informed and to participating in elections (older Americans vote in far greater numbers than younger Americans) based on a knowledgeable consideration of the candidates and the country's needs, there is hope that we can make ourselves anew and journey forward together, as so eloquently put by both Abraham Lincoln and Barack Obama.

You can begin by seeking out the authors in this text who have impressed you with their knowledge, wisdom, and perhaps calm approach to examining problems and offering solutions. Learn, and reflect on what you learn. Think about the kind of world you want to have for yourself and for generations to come. You might also ask yourself: What can I do to make a difference?

SECOND INAUGURAL ADDRESS | ABRAHAM LINCOLN

A mostly self-educated country lawyer on the western frontier, Abraham Lincoln (1809–1865) rose to become the sixteenth president of the United States. He first served in the Illinois State Legislature and one term in the U.S. House of Representatives before securing the Republican Party's nomination for president. He won the 1860 election by sweeping the North, his opposition to the spread of slavery resulting in few votes in the southern states. His moving appeals to the electorate won him reelection in spite of less moderate Republicans unhappy with him and those committed to secession wishing him dead. Six days after Robert E. Lee surrendered to General Grant, ending the Civil War, Lincoln was assassinated at Ford's Theater in Washington, D.C. by Confederate supporter John Wilkes Booth. Scholars rank Lincoln as one of the top three greatest presidents, along with George Washington and Franklin D. Roosevelt. Lincoln delivered his brief but powerful address below at the swearing-in for his second term as president.

PREREADING QUESTIONS With the country still torn by war, Lincoln chose to speak only briefly; does this seem a wise and sensitive decision, or would you have wished for a longer discussion of the issues surrounding the war?

At this second appearing to take the oath of the presidential office, there is 1
less occasion for an extended address than there was at the first. Then a
statement, somewhat in detail, of a course to be pursued, seemed fitting and
proper. Now, at the expiration of four years, during which public declarations
have been constantly called forth on every point and phase of the great contest
which still absorbs the attention, and engrosses the enerergies [sic] of the nation,
little that is new could be presented. The progress of our arms, upon which all
else chiefly depends, is as well known to the public as to myself; and it is, I trust,
reasonably satisfactory and encouraging to all. With high hope for the future, no
prediction in regard to it is ventured.

©Image Source RF

On the occasion corresponding to this four 2
years ago, all thoughts were anxiously directed to
an impending civil-war. All dreaded it—all sought
to avert it. While the inaugural address was being
delivered from this place, devoted altogether to
saving the Union without war insurgent agents
were in the city seeking to *destroy* it without war—
seeking to dissol[v]e the Union, and divide effects,
by negotiation. Both parties deprecated war; but
one of them would *make* war rather than let the
nation survive; and the other would *accept* war
rather than let it perish. And the war came.

One eighth of the whole population were 3
colored slaves, not distributed generally over the
Union, but localized in the Southern part of it.
These slaves constituted a peculiar and powerful
interest. All knew that this interest was, somehow,
the cause of the war. To strengthen, perpetuate,
and extend this interest was the object for which the insurgents would rend the
Union, even by war; while the government claimed no right to do more than to
restrict the territorial enlargement of it. Neither party expected for the war, the
magnitude of the duration, which it has already attained. Neither anticipated that
the *cause* of the conflict might cease with, or even before, the conflict itself should
cease. Each looked for an easier triumph, and a result less fundamental and
astounding. Both read the same Bible, and pray to the same God; and each
invokes His aid against the other. It may seem strange that any men should dare to
ask a just God's assistance in wringing their bread from the sweat of other men's
faces; but let us judge not that we be not judged. The prayers of both could not be
answered; that of neither has been answered fully. The Almighty has His own purposes. "Woe unto the world because of offences! For it must needs be that
offences comes; but woe to that man by whom the offence cometh!" If we shall
suppose that American Slavery is one of those offences which, in the providence
of God, must needs come, but which, having continued through His appointed
time, He now wills to remove, and that He gives to both North and South, this terrible war, as the woe due to those by whom the offence came, shall we discern

therein any departure from those divine attributes which the believers in a Living God always ascribe to Him? Fondly do we hope—fervently do we pray—that this mighty scourge of war may speedily pass away. Yet, if God wills that it continue, until all the wealth piled by the bond-man's two hundred and fifty years of unrequited toil shall be sunk, and until every drop of blood drawn with the lash, shall be paid by another drawn with the sword, as was said three thousand years ago, so still it must be said, "the judgments of the Lord, are true and righteous altogether."

4   With malice toward none; with charity for all; with firmness in the right, as God gives us to see the right, let us strive on to finish the work we are in; to bind up the nation's wounds; to care for him who shall have borne the battle, and for his widow, and his orphan—to do all which may achieve and cherish a just, and a lasting peace, among ourselves, and with all nations.

QUESTIONS FOR READING

1. What is the great contest to which Lincoln refers?
2. Who chose to "make war"?
3. What cause does Lincoln give for the war?
4. How has the cause ceased while the war continues?
5. What guidelines for responding to the war's end does Lincoln establish?

QUESTIONS FOR REASONING AND ANALYSIS

6. In the long third paragraph, how does Lincoln explain why both sides in the war are suffering?
7. Analyze Lincoln's final paragraph—one long sentence: What elements of style do you find? What makes his oratory so powerful?

QUESTIONS FOR REFLECTION AND WRTING

8. Although this address is admired perhaps second only to "The Gettysburg Address," too few have read it. What surprised you most in his "Second Inaugural"? Why?
9. What can today's leaders learn from Lincoln's speech? Explain.

THE FORMULA FOR A RICHER WORLD? EQUALITY, LIBERTY, JUSTICE AND WEALTH | DEIDRE N. McCLOSKEY

Professor emerita of economics, history, and English at the University of Illinois at Chicago, Deidre McCloskey is the author of a number of books. Her latest is *Bourgeois Equality: How Ideas, Not Capital or Institutions, Enriched the World* (2016). Her essay below first appeared in *The New York Times* on September 4, 2016.

PREREADING QUESTIONS Which of the terms in the title seems out of place to you? What does that suggest to you about the author's possible subject?

The world is rich and will become still richer. Quit worrying. [1]

Not all of us are rich yet, of course. A billion or so people on the planet drag along on the equivalent of $3 a day or less. But as recently as 1800, almost everybody did. [2]

The Great Enrichment began in 17th-century Holland. By the 18th century, it had moved to England, Scotland and the American colonies, and now it has spread to much of the rest of the world. [3]

Economists and historians agree on its startling magnitude: By 2010, the average daily income in a wide range of countries, including Japan, the United States, Botswana and Brazil, had soared 1,000 to 3,000 percent over the levels of 1800. People moved from tents and mud huts to split-levels and city condominiums, from waterborne diseases to 80-year life spans, from ignorance to literacy. [4]

You might think the rich have become richer and the poor even poorer. But by the standard of basic comfort in essentials, the poorest people on the planet have gained the most. In places like Ireland, Singapore, Finland and Italy, even people who are relatively poor have adequate food, education, lodging and medical care—none of which their ancestors had. Not remotely. [5]

Inequality of financial wealth goes up and down, but over the long term it has been reduced. Financial inequality was greater in 1800 and 1900 than it is now, as even the French economist Thomas Piketty has acknowledged. By the more important standard of basic comfort in consumption, inequality within and between countries has fallen nearly continuously. [6]

In any case, the problem is poverty, not inequality as such—not how many yachts the L'Oréal heiress Liliane Bettencourt has, but whether the average Frenchwoman has enough to eat. At the time of *Les Misérables*, she didn't. In the last 40 years, the World Bank estimates, the proportion of the population living on an appalling $1 or $2 a day has halved. Paul Collier, an Oxford economist, urges us to help the "bottom billion" of the more than seven billion people on earth. Of course. It is our duty. But he notes that 50 years ago, four billion out of five billion people lived in such miserable conditions. In 1800, it was 95 percent of one billion. [7]

We can improve the conditions of the working class. Raising low productivity by enabling human creativity is what has mainly worked. By contrast, taking from the rich and giving to the poor helps only a little—and anyway expropriation is a one-time trick. Enrichment from market-tested betterment will go on and on and, over the next century or so, will bring comfort in essentials to virtually everyone on the planet, and more to an expanding middle class. [8]

Look at the astonishing improvements in China since 1978 and in India since 1991. Between them, the countries are home to about four out of every 10 humans. Even in the United States, real wages have continued to grow—if [9]

McCloskey notes that business success comes from countries embracing the values of equality, liberty, and justice for all.

slowly—in recent decades, contrary to what you might have heard. Donald Boudreaux, an economist at George Mason University, and others who have looked beyond the superficial have shown that real wages are continuing to rise, thanks largely to major improvements in the quality of goods and services, and to nonwage benefits. Real purchasing power is double what it was in the fondly remembered 1950s—when many American children went to bed hungry.

10   What, then, caused this Great Enrichment?

11   Not exploitation of the poor, not investment, not existing institutions, but a mere idea, which the philosopher and economist Adam Smith called "the liberal plan of equality, liberty and justice." In a word, it was liberalism, in the free-market European sense. Give masses of ordinary people equality before the law and equality of social dignity, and leave them alone, and it turns out that they become extraordinarily creative and energetic.

12   The liberal idea was spawned by some happy accidents in northwestern Europe from 1517 to 1789—namely, the four R's: the Reformation, the Dutch Revolt, the revolutions of England and France, and the proliferation of reading. The four R's liberated ordinary people, among them the venturing bourgeoisie. The Bourgeois Deal is, briefly, this: In the first act, let me try this or that improvement. I'll keep the profit, thank you very much, though in the second act those pesky competitors will erode it by entering and disrupting (as Uber has done to the taxi industry). By the third act, after my betterments have spread, they will make you rich.

And they did.   13

You may object that ideas are a dime a dozen and that to make them fruitful 14 we must start with adequate physical and human capital and good institutions. It's a popular idea at the World Bank, but a mistaken one. True, we eventually need capital and institutions to embody the ideas, such as a marble building with central heating and cooling to house the Supreme Court. But the intermediate and dependent causes like capital and institutions have not been the root cause.

The root cause of enrichment was and is the liberal idea, spawning the 15 university, the railway, the high-rise, the internet and, most important, our liberties. What original accumulation of capital inflamed the minds of William Lloyd Garrison and Sojourner Truth? What institutions, except the recent liberal ones of university education and uncensored book publishing, caused feminism or the antiwar movement? Since Karl Marx, we have made a habit of seeking material causes for human progress. But the modern world came from treating more and more people with respect.

Ideas are not all sweet, of course. Fascism, racism, eugenics and nationalism 16 are ideas with alarming recent popularity. But sweet practical ideas for profitable technologies and institutions, and the liberal idea that allowed ordinary people for the first time to have a go, caused the Great Enrichment. We need to inspirit masses of people, not the elite, who are plenty inspirited already. Equality before the law and equality of social dignity are still the root of economic, as well as spiritual, flourishing—whatever tyrants may think to the contrary.

Deirdre Nansen McCloskey, "Equality, Liberty, Justice and Wealth," *The New York Times*, 4 Sept. 2016. Used with permission of the author.

QUESTIONS FOR READING

1. When did the world's "enrichment" begin? What happened in the 18th century?
2. What is the best way to improve working-class conditions? Why is taking from the rich not the best strategy?
3. What has caused the continual rise of wages and improved lifestyles?
4. What are McCloskey's "four R's"?

QUESTIONS FOR REASONING AND ANALYSIS

5. What is the author's subject? What *type* of argument is this? Write a claim statement that makes the type of argument clear.
6. What is the difference between poverty and inequality? Why, according to the author, is poverty the more important problem to worry about?
7. How does McCloskey qualify her claim? Note especially paragraph 14 and the last paragraph.
8. Has McCloskey made her case? If yes, why? If you disagree, how would you refute her argument?

QUESTIONS FOR REFLECTION AND WRITING

9. Select one of the ideas listed in the final paragraph that the author does not consider "sweet" and explain why it should be rejected. If you disagree that all four ideas listed are bad ones, explain your defense of this position.

10. How, in practical, money-making terms, can providing equality and social dignity to individuals empower them? Explain this concept in specifics to someone facing this idea for the first time.

REMARKS BY THE PRESIDENT AT THE 50TH ANNIVERSARY OF THE SELMA TO MONTGOMERY MARCHES | BARACK H. OBAMA

The forty-fourth president of the United States was born in Hawaii on August 4, 1961, to a white American mother and a black Kenyan father while both were in college. After Obama attended Columbia College and Harvard Law School—where he became the first African American editor of the *Harvard Law Review*—Obama returned to Chicago to teach at the University of Chicago Law School and to practice civil rights law. Elected first to the Illinois State Senate, he was then, in 2004, elected to the U.S. Senate. In 2008, Obama became the first African American president of the United States. He was reelected in 2012 to a second term as president. Obama delivered the following address to commemorate the 50th anniversary of the Selma to Montgomery civil rights marches led by Dr. Martin Luther King Jr.

PREREADING QUESTIONS You may already know about the Selma to Montgomery civil rights marches, but perhaps you do not. How does Obama help people who do not know about the original marches understand the history and significance of the commemoration so that he reaches the broadest possible audience?

Edmund Pettus Bridge
Selma, Alabama
2:17 P.M. CST

1   AUDIENCE MEMBER: We love you, President Obama!

2   THE PRESIDENT: Well, you know I love you back. (Applause.)

3   It is a rare honor in this life to follow one of your heroes. And John Lewis is one of my heroes.

4   Now, I have to imagine that when a younger John Lewis woke up that morning 50 years ago and made his way to Brown Chapel, heroics were not on his mind. A day like this was not on his mind. Young folks with bedrolls and backpacks were milling about. Veterans of the movement trained newcomers in the tactics of non-violence; the right way to protect yourself when attacked. A doctor described what tear gas does to the body, while marchers scribbled down instructions for contacting their loved ones. The air was thick with doubt, anticipation and fear. And they comforted themselves with the final verse of the final hymn they sung:

"No matter what may be the test, God will take care of you; Lean, weary one, 5 upon His breast, God will take care of you."

And then, his knapsack stocked with an apple, a toothbrush, and a book on 6 government—all you need for a night behind bars—John Lewis led them out of the church on a mission to change America.

President and Mrs. Bush, Governor Bentley, Mayor Evans, Sewell, Reverend 7 Strong, members of Congress, elected officials, foot soldiers, friends, fellow Americans:

As John noted, there are places and moments in America where this nation's 8 destiny has been decided. Many are sites of war—Concord and Lexington, Appomattox, Gettysburg. Others are sites that symbolize the daring of America's character—Independence Hall and Seneca Falls, Kitty Hawk and Cape Canaveral.

Selma is such a place. In one afternoon 50 years ago, so much of our 9 turbulent history—the stain of slavery and anguish of civil war; the yoke of segregation and tyranny of Jim Crow; the death of four little girls in Birmingham; and the dream of a Baptist preacher—all that history met on this bridge.

It was not a clash of armies, but a clash of wills; a contest to determine the 10 true meaning of America. And because of men and women like John Lewis, Joseph Lowery, Hosea Williams, Amelia Boynton, Diane Nash, Ralph Abernathy, C.T. Vivian, Andrew Young, Fred Shuttlesworth, Dr. Martin Luther King, Jr., and so many others, the idea of a just America and a fair America, an inclusive America, and a generous America—that idea ultimately triumphed.

As is true across the landscape of American history, we cannot examine this 11 moment in isolation. The march on Selma was part of a broader campaign that spanned generations; the leaders that day part of a long line of heroes.

©White House Photo/Alamy Stock Photo

In 2015, President and Mrs. Obama lead a march into Selma, Alabama, commemorating the Bloody Sunday march during the civil rights movement.

12   We gather here to celebrate them. We gather here to honor the courage of ordinary Americans willing to endure billy clubs and the chastening rod; tear gas and the trampling hoof; men and women who despite the gush of blood and splintered bone would stay true to their North Star and keep marching towards justice.

13   They did as Scripture instructed: "Rejoice in hope, be patient in tribulation, be constant in prayer." And in the days to come, they went back again and again. When the trumpet call sounded for more to join, the people came—black and white, young and old, Christian and Jew, waving the American flag and singing the same anthems full of faith and hope. A white newsman, Bill Plante, who covered the marches then and who is with us here today, quipped that the growing number of white people lowered the quality of the singing. (Laughter.) To those who marched, though, those old gospel songs must have never sounded so sweet.

14   In time, their chorus would well up and reach President Johnson. And he would send them protection, and speak to the nation, echoing their call for America and the world to hear: "We shall overcome." (Applause.) What enormous faith these men and women had. Faith in God, but also faith in America.

15   The Americans who crossed this bridge, they were not physically imposing. But they gave courage to millions. They held no elected office. But they led a nation. They marched as Americans who had endured hundreds of years of brutal violence, countless daily indignities—but they didn't seek special treatment, just the equal treatment promised to them almost a century before. (Applause.)

16   What they did here will reverberate through the ages. Not because the change they won was preordained; not because their victory was complete; but because they proved that nonviolent change is possible, that love and hope can conquer hate.

17   As we commemorate their achievement, we are well-served to remember that at the time of the marches, many in power condemned rather than praised them. Back then, they were called Communists, or half-breeds, or outside agitators, sexual and moral degenerates, and worse—they were called everything but the name their parents gave them. Their faith was questioned. Their lives were threatened. Their patriotism challenged.

18   And yet, what could be more American than what happened in this place? (Applause.) What could more profoundly vindicate the idea of America than plain and humble people—unsung, the downtrodden, the dreamers not of high station, not born to wealth or privilege, not of one religious tradition but many, coming together to shape their country's course?

19   What greater expression of faith in the American experiment than this, what greater form of patriotism is there than the belief that America is not yet finished, that we are strong enough to be self-critical, that each successive generation can look upon our imperfections and decide that it is in our power to remake this nation to more closely align with our highest ideals? (Applause.)

20   That's why Selma is not some outlier in the American experience. That's why it's not a museum or a static monument to behold from a distance. It is instead the manifestation of a creed written into our founding documents: "We the People . . . in order to form a more perfect union." "We hold these truths to be self-evident, that all men are created equal." (Applause.)

These are not just words. They're a living thing, a call to action, a roadmap 21 for citizenship and an insistence in the capacity of free men and women to shape our own destiny. For founders like Franklin and Jefferson, for leaders like Lincoln and FDR, the success of our experiment in self-government rested on engaging all of our citizens in this work. And that's what we celebrate here in Selma. That's what this movement was all about, one leg in our long journey toward freedom. (Applause.)

The American instinct that led these young men and women to pick up the 22 torch and cross this bridge, that's the same instinct that moved patriots to choose revolution over tyranny. It's the same instinct that drew immigrants from across oceans and the Rio Grande; the same instinct that led women to reach for the ballot, workers to organize against an unjust status quo; the same instinct that led us to plant a flag at Iwo Jima and on the surface of the Moon. (Applause.)

It's the idea held by generations of citizens who believed that America is a 23 constant work in progress; who believed that loving this country requires more than singing its praises or avoiding uncomfortable truths. It requires the occasional disruption, the willingness to speak out for what is right, to shake up the status quo. That's America. (Applause.)

That's what makes us unique. That's what cements our reputation as a bea- 24 con of opportunity. Young people behind the Iron Curtain would see Selma and eventually tear down that wall. Young people in Soweto would hear Bobby Kennedy talk about ripples of hope and eventually banish the scourge of apartheid. Young people in Burma went to prison rather than submit to military rule. They saw what John Lewis had done. From the streets of Tunis to the Maidan in Ukraine, this generation of young people can draw strength from this place, where the powerless could change the world's greatest power and push their leaders to expand the boundaries of freedom.

They saw that idea made real right here in Selma, Alabama. They saw that 25 idea manifest itself here in America.

Because of campaigns like this, a Voting Rights Act was passed. Political and 26 economic and social barriers came down. And the change these men and women wrought is visible here today in the presence of African Americans who run boardrooms, who sit on the bench, who serve in elected office from small towns to big cities; from the Congressional Black Caucus all the way to the Oval Office. (Applause.)

Because of what they did, the doors of opportunity swung open not just for black 27 folks, but for every American. Women marched through those doors. Latinos marched through those doors. Asian Americans, gay Americans, Americans with disabilities— they all came through those doors. (Applause.) Their endeavors gave the entire South the chance to rise again, not by reasserting the past, but by transcending the past.

What a glorious thing, Dr. King might say. And what a solemn debt we owe. 28 Which leads us to ask, just how might we repay that debt?

First and foremost, we have to recognize that one day's commemoration, no 29 matter how special, is not enough. If Selma taught us anything, it's that our work is never done. (Applause.) The American experiment in self-government gives work and purpose to each generation.

30   Selma teaches us, as well, that action requires that we shed our cynicism. For when it comes to the pursuit of justice, we can afford neither complacency nor despair.

31   Just this week, I was asked whether I thought the Department of Justice's Ferguson report shows that, with respect to race, little has changed in this country. And I understood the question; the report's narrative was sadly familiar. It evoked the kind of abuse and disregard for citizens that spawned the Civil Rights Movement. But I rejected the notion that nothing's changed. What happened in Ferguson may not be unique, but it's no longer endemic. It's no longer sanctioned by law or by custom. And before the Civil Rights Movement, it most surely was. (Applause.)

32   We do a disservice to the cause of justice by intimating that bias and discrimination are immutable, that racial division is inherent to America. If you think nothing's changed in the past 50 years, ask somebody who lived through the Selma or Chicago or Los Angeles of the 1950s. Ask the female CEO who once might have been assigned to the secretarial pool if nothing's changed. Ask your gay friend if it's easier to be out and proud in America now than it was thirty years ago. To deny this progress, this hard-won progress—our progress—would be to rob us of our own agency, our own capacity, our responsibility to do what we can to make America better.

33   Of course, a more common mistake is to suggest that Ferguson is an isolated incident; that racism is banished; that the work that drew men and women to Selma is now complete, and that whatever racial tensions remain are a consequence of those seeking to play the "race card" for their own purposes. We don't need the Ferguson report to know that's not true. We just need to open our eyes, and our ears, and our hearts to know that this nation's racial history still casts its long shadow upon us.

34   We know the march is not yet over. We know the race is not yet won. We know that reaching that blessed destination where we are judged, all of us, by the content of our character requires admitting as much, facing up to the truth. "We are capable of bearing a great burden," James Baldwin once wrote, "once we discover that the burden is reality and arrive where reality is."

35   There's nothing America can't handle if we actually look squarely at the problem. And this is work for all Americans, not just some. Not just whites. Not just blacks. If we want to honor the courage of those who marched that day, then all of us are called to possess their moral imagination. All of us will need to feel as they did the fierce urgency of now. All of us need to recognize as they did that change depends on our actions, on our attitudes, the things we teach our children. And if we make such an effort, no matter how hard it may sometimes seem, laws can be passed, and consciences can be stirred, and consensus can be built. (Applause.)

36   With such an effort, we can make sure our criminal justice system serves all and not just some. Together, we can raise the level of mutual trust that policing is built on—the idea that police officers are members of the community they risk their lives to protect, and citizens in Ferguson and New York and Cleveland,

they just want the same thing young people here marched for 50 years ago—the protection of the law. (Applause.) Together, we can address unfair sentencing and overcrowded prisons, and the stunted circumstances that rob too many boys of the chance to become men, and rob the nation of too many men who could be good dads, and good workers, and good neighbors. (Applause.)

With effort, we can roll back poverty and the roadblocks to opportunity. 37 Americans don't accept a free ride for anybody, nor do we believe in equality of outcomes. But we do expect equal opportunity. And if we really mean it, if we're not just giving lip service to it, but if we really mean it and are willing to sacrifice for it, then, yes, we can make sure every child gets an education suitable to this new century, one that expands imaginations and lifts sights and gives those children the skills they need. We can make sure every person willing to work has the dignity of a job, and a fair wage, and a real voice, and sturdier rungs on that ladder into the middle class.

And with effort, we can protect the foundation stone of our democracy for 38 which so many marched across this bridge—and that is the right to vote. (Applause.) Right now, in 2015, 50 years after Selma, there are laws across this country designed to make it harder for people to vote. As we speak, more of such laws are being proposed. Meanwhile, the Voting Rights Act, the culmination of so much blood, so much sweat and tears, the product of so much sacrifice in the face of wanton violence, the Voting Rights Act stands weakened, its future subject to political rancor.

How can that be? The Voting Rights Act was one of the crowning 39 achievements of our democracy, the result of Republican and Democratic efforts. (Applause.) President Reagan signed its renewal when he was in office. President George W. Bush signed its renewal when he was in office. (Applause.) One hundred members of Congress have come here today to honor people who were willing to die for the right to protect it. If we want to honor this day, let that hundred go back to Washington and gather four hundred more, and together, pledge to make it their mission to restore that law this year. That's how we honor those on this bridge. (Applause.)

Of course, our democracy is not the task of Congress alone, or the courts 40 alone, or even the President alone. If every new voter-suppression law was struck down today, we would still have, here in America, one of the lowest voting rates among free peoples. Fifty years ago, registering to vote here in Selma and much of the South meant guessing the number of jellybeans in a jar, the number of bubbles on a bar of soap. It meant risking your dignity, and sometimes, your life.

What's our excuse today for not voting? How do we so casually discard the 41 right for which so many fought? (Applause.) How do we so fully give away our power, our voice, in shaping America's future? Why are we pointing to somebody else when we could take the time just to go to the polling places? (Applause.) We give away our power.

42   Fellow marchers, so much has changed in 50 years. We have endured war and we've fashioned peace. We've seen technological wonders that touch every aspect of our lives. We take for granted conveniences that our parents could have scarcely imagined. But what has not changed is the imperative of citizenship; that willingness of a 26-year-old deacon, or a Unitarian minister, or a young mother of five to decide they loved this country so much that they'd risk everything to realize its promise.

43   That's what it means to love America. That's what it means to believe in America. That's what it means when we say America is exceptional.

44   For we were born of change. We broke the old aristocracies, declaring ourselves entitled not by bloodline, but endowed by our Creator with certain inalienable rights. We secure our rights and responsibilities through a system of self-government, of and by and for the people. That's why we argue and fight with so much passion and conviction—because we know our efforts matter. We know America is what we make of it.

45   Look at our history. We are Lewis and Clark and Sacajawea, pioneers who braved the unfamiliar, followed by a stampede of farmers and miners, and entrepreneurs and hucksters. That's our spirit. That's who we are.

46   We are Sojourner Truth and Fannie Lou Hamer, women who could do as much as any man and then some. And we're Susan B. Anthony, who shook the system until the law reflected that truth. That is our character.

47   We're the immigrants who stowed away on ships to reach these shores, the huddled masses yearning to breathe free—Holocaust survivors, Soviet defectors, the Lost Boys of Sudan. We're the hopeful strivers who cross the Rio Grande because we want our kids to know a better life. That's how we came to be. (Applause.)

48   We're the slaves who built the White House and the economy of the South. (Applause.) We're the ranch hands and cowboys who opened up the West, and countless laborers who laid rail, and raised skyscrapers, and organized for workers' rights.

49   We're the fresh-faced GIs who fought to liberate a continent. And we're the Tuskeegee Airmen, and the Navajo code-talkers, and the Japanese Americans who fought for this country even as their own liberty had been denied.

50   We're the firefighters who rushed into those buildings on 9/11, the volunteers who signed up to fight in Afghanistan and Iraq. We're the gay Americans whose blood ran in the streets of San Francisco and New York, just as blood ran down this bridge. (Applause.)

51   We are storytellers, writers, poets, artists who abhor unfairness, and despise hypocrisy, and give voice to the voiceless, and tell truths that need to be told.

52   We're the inventors of gospel and jazz and blues, bluegrass and country, and hip-hop and rock and roll, and our very own sound with all the sweet sorrow and reckless joy of freedom.

53   We are Jackie Robinson, enduring scorn and spiked cleats and pitches coming straight to his head, and stealing home in the World Series anyway. (Applause.)

We are the people Langston Hughes wrote of who "build our temples for 54 tomorrow, strong as we know how." We are the people Emerson wrote of, "who for truth and honor's sake stand fast and suffer long;" who are "never tired, so long as we can see far enough."

That's what America is. Not stock photos or airbrushed history, or feeble 55 attempts to define some of us as more American than others. (Applause.) We respect the past, but we don't pine for the past. We don't fear the future; we grab for it. America is not some fragile thing. We are large, in the words of Whitman, containing multitudes. We are boisterous and diverse and full of energy, perpetually young in spirit. That's why someone like John Lewis at the ripe old age of 25 could lead a mighty march.

And that's what the young people here today and listening all across the 56 country must take away from this day. You are America. Unconstrained by habit and convention. Unencumbered by what is, because you're ready to seize what ought to be.

For everywhere in this country, there are first steps to be taken, there's new 57 ground to cover, there are more bridges to be crossed. And it is you, the young and fearless at heart, the most diverse and educated generation in our history, who the nation is waiting to follow.

Because Selma shows us that America is not the project of any one person. 58 Because the single-most powerful word in our democracy is the word "We." "We The People." "We Shall Overcome." "Yes We Can." (Applause.) That word is owned by no one. It belongs to everyone. Oh, what a glorious task we are given, to continually try to improve this great nation of ours.

Fifty years from Bloody Sunday, our march is not yet finished, but we're 59 getting closer. Two hundred and thirty-nine years after this nation's founding our union is not yet perfect, but we are getting closer. Our job's easier because somebody already got us through that first mile. Somebody already got us over that bridge. When it feels the road is too hard, when the torch we've been passed feels too heavy, we will remember these early travelers, and draw strength from their example, and hold firmly the words of the prophet Isaiah: "Those who hope in the Lord will renew their strength. They will soar on [the] wings like eagles. They will run and not grow weary. They will walk and not be faint." (Applause.)

We honor those who walked so we could run. We must run so our children 60 soar. And we will not grow weary. For we believe in the power of an awesome God, and we believe in this country's sacred promise.

May He bless those warriors of justice no longer with us, and bless the 61 United States of America. Thank you, everybody. (Applause.)

END
2:50 P.M. CST

Barack Obama, Remarks by the President at the 50th Anniversary of the Selma to Montgomery Marches, 7 Mar. 2015.

QUESTIONS FOR READING

1. Why is it especially poignant that Obama delivered this address?

2. Why were the original protestors marching in Selma, Alabama? Be more specific than "they were marching for civil or equal rights."

3. What idea from the Declaration of Independence does Obama use in his speech?

4. What events does Obama reference as reminders that racism still exists in America? How does he tie these events to the continuing struggle for equal rights for all Americans?

5. What does Obama want attendees of this event and readers of this speech to do to honor those who protested and died during the Selma to Montgomery marches?

QUESTIONS FOR REASONING AND ANALYSIS

6. Normally, U.S. presidents begin speeches by acknowledging other elected officials. How does Obama do this? Why do you think he begins his speech in this way?

7. What is Obama's primary claim, and how does he support it?

8. Obama's speech is meant to be part history lesson, part tribute, and part call to action. How does he interweave these elements throughout his address?

9. Political scientists and experts in speech communication have noted that Obama is one of the most gifted public orators of our time. Do you agree? If so, why? If not, why not?

QUESTIONS FOR REFLECTION AND WRITING

10. The civil rights movement in America did not begin in the 1960s; rather, it has been a part of our history from the beginning—original signers of the Declaration of Independence wrangled over slavery, an issue that eventually led to the Civil War. What are your thoughts and concerns about race relations and civil rights in America today?

11. Are you registered to vote? If so, do you participate in local and national elections? If not, why not? Are you involved in political civil activities and why? If so, what do you do? If not, what would it take for you to be more civically engaged?

HOW THE FUTURE WILL JUDGE US | KWAME ANTHONY APPIAH

The son of a Ghanian lawyer and politician and British novelist, Appiah was educated in both Ghana and England. He holds a PhD in philosophy from Cambridge University, and, since 2002, he has held appointments in both the philosophy department at Princeton University and is now at New York University. Appiah is the author of many books, including *The Ethics of Identity* (2003) and *The Honor Code: How Moral Revolutions Happen* (2010). He is recognized as one of the world's most significant contemporary thinkers.

PREREADING QUESTIONS Given Appiah's areas of study and interest, what kinds of current problems do you think he will select for future judgment? What have we repudiated from our country's past?

1   Once, pretty much everywhere, beating your wife and children was regarded as a father's duty, homosexuality was a hanging offense, and waterboarding was approved—in fact, invented—by the Catholic Church. Through the middle of the 19th century, the United States and other nations in the Americas condoned plantation slavery. Many of our grandparents were born in states where women were forbidden to vote. And well into the 20th century, lynch mobs in this country stripped, tortured, hanged and burned human beings at picnics.

2   Looking back at such horrors, it is easy to ask: What were people thinking?

3   Yet, the chances are that our own descendants will ask the same question, with the same incomprehension, about some of our practices today.

4   Is there a way to guess which ones? After all, not every disputed institution or practice is destined to be discredited. And it can be hard to distinguish in real time between movements, such as abolition, that will come to represent moral common sense and those, such as prohibition, that will come to seem quaint or misguided. Recall the book-burners of Boston's old Watch and Ward Society or the organizations for the suppression of vice, with their crusades against claret, contraceptives and sexually candid novels.

5   Still, a look at the past suggests three signs that a particular practice is destined for future condemnation.

6   First, people have already heard the arguments against the practice. The case against slavery didn't emerge in a blinding moment of moral clarity, for instance; it had been around for centuries.

7   Second, defenders of the custom tend not to offer moral counterarguments but instead invoke tradition, human nature or necessity. (As in, "We've always had slaves, and how could we grow cotton without them?")

8   And third, supporters engage in what one might call strategic ignorance, avoiding truths that might force them to face the evils in which they're complicit. Those who ate the sugar or wore the cotton that the slaves grew simply didn't think about what made those goods possible. That's why abolitionists sought to direct attention toward the conditions of the Middle Passage, through detailed illustrations of slave ships and horrifying stories of the suffering below decks.

9   With these signs in mind, here are four contenders for future moral condemnation.

OUR PRISON SYSTEM

10   We already know that the massive waste of life in our prisons is morally troubling; those who defend the conditions of incarceration usually do so in non-moral terms (citing costs or the administrative difficulty of reforms); and we're inclined to avert our eyes from the details. Check, check and check.

11   Roughly 1 percent of adults in this country are incarcerated. We have 4 percent of the world's population but 25 percent of its prisoners. No other nation has as large a proportion of its population in prison; even China's rate is less than half of ours. What's more, the majority of our prisoners are non-violent offenders, many of them detained on drug charges. (Whether a country that was truly free would criminalize recreational drug use is a related question worth pondering.)

12   And the full extent of the punishment prisoners face isn't detailed in any judge's sentence. More than 100,000 inmates suffer sexual abuse, including rape, each year; some contract HIV as a result. Our country holds at least 25,000 prisoners in isolation in so-called supermax facilities, under conditions that many psychologists say amount to torture.

INDUSTRIAL MEAT PRODUCTION

13   The arguments against the cruelty of factory farming have certainly been around a long time; it was Jeremy Bentham, in the 18th century, who observed that, when it comes to the treatment of animals, the key question is not whether animals can reason but whether they can suffer. People who eat factory-farmed bacon or chicken rarely offer a moral justification for what they're doing. Instead, they try not to think about it too much, shying away from stomach-turning stories about what goes on in our industrial abattoirs.

14   Of the more than 90 million cattle in our country, at least 10 million at any time are packed into feedlots, saved from the inevitable diseases of overcrowding only by regular doses of antibiotics, surrounded by piles of their own feces, their nostrils filled with the smell of their own urine. Picture it—and then imagine your grandchildren seeing that picture. In the European Union, many of the most inhumane conditions we allow are already illegal or—like the sow stalls into which pregnant pigs are often crammed in the United States—will be illegal soon.

THE INSTITUTIONALIZED AND ISOLATED ELDERLY

15   Nearly 2 million of America's elderly are warehoused in nursing homes, out of sight and, to some extent, out of mind. Some 10,000 for-profit facilities have arisen across the country in recent decades to hold them. Other elderly Americans may live independently, but often they are isolated and cut off from their families. (The United States is not alone among advanced democracies in

this. Consider the heat wave that hit France in 2003: While many families were enjoying their summer vacations, some 14,000 elderly parents and grandparents were left to perish in the stifling temperatures.) Is this what Western modernity amounts to—societies that feel no filial obligations to their inconvenient elders?

Sometimes we can learn from societies much poorer than ours. My English 16 mother spent the last 50 years of her life in Ghana, where I grew up. In her final years, it was her good fortune not only to have the resources to stay at home, but also to live in a country where doing so was customary. She had family next door who visited her every day, and she was cared for by doctors and nurses who were willing to come to her when she was too ill to come to them. In short, she had the advantages of a society in which older people are treated with respect and concern.

Keeping aging parents and their children closer is a challenge, particularly in 17 a society where almost everybody has a job outside the home (if not across the country). Yet the three signs apply here as well: When we see old people who, despite many living relatives, suffer growing isolation, we know something is wrong. We scarcely try to defend the situation; when we can, we put it out of our minds. Self-interest, if nothing else, should make us hope that our descendants will have worked out a better way.

THE ENVIRONMENT

Of course, most transgenerational obligations run the other way—from 18 parents to children—and of these the most obvious candidate for opprobrium is our wasteful attitude toward the planet's natural resources and ecology. Look at a satellite picture of Russia, and you'll see a vast expanse of parched wasteland where decades earlier was a lush and verdant landscape. That's the Republic of Kalmykia, home to what was recognized in the 1990s as Europe's first man-made desert. Desertification, which is primarily the result of destructive land-management practices, threatens a third of the Earth's surface; tens of thousands of Chinese villages have been overrun by sand drifts in the past few decades.

It's not as though we're unaware of what we're doing to the planet: We know 19 the harm done by deforestation, wetland destruction, pollution, overfishing, greenhouse gas emissions—the whole litany. Our descendants, who will inherit this devastated Earth, are unlikely to have the luxury of such recklessness. Chances are, they won't be able to avert their eyes, even if they want to.

Let's not stop there, though. We will all have our own suspicions about which 20 practices will someday prompt people to ask, in dismay: What were they thinking?

Even when we don't have a good answer, we'll be better off for anticipating 21 the question.

Kwame Anthony Appiah, "How the Future Will Judge Us," *The Washington Post,* 26 Sept. 2010. Reprinted by permission of the author.

QUESTIONS FOR READING

1. On what basis are current practices likely to be repudiated by future Americans? What three signs mark a practice for future condemnation?

2. How do the three signs suggest that our prison system is likely to be condemned?

3. What are the problems with our industrial meat production?

4. What in our work situations contributes to the isolation of the elderly? What happened to many older people in France in 2003?

5. How will the next generation have to react to the environment?

QUESTIONS FOR REASONING AND ANALYSIS

6. What is Appiah's claim? (You will need a complex statement that combines both a general idea and specific practices.)

7. How do Appiah's four practices illustrate his idea of the three warning signs?

8. What else does the author provide to defend his choice of the specific four practices?

9. Appiah is making some devastating judgments of people past and present. How would you describe his tone? How does his tone help him keep readers from feeling attacked or judged?

QUESTIONS FOR REFLECTION AND WRITING

10. Has Appiah convinced you that the future will judge the four practices he discusses? Why or why not?

11. Did any of the four practices chosen by the author surprise you? If so, which one(s)? Why?

12. If you had been asked to select four current practices for condemnation, would you have included any of Appiah's? Why or why not? What other(s) would have been on your list? Why?

TRUMP'S DARK PROMISE TO RETURN TO A MYTHICAL PAST | ANNE APPLEBAUM

Pulitzer Prize-winning journalist Anne Applebaum is an American who holds dual citizenship with Poland. A graduate of Yale University, Applebaum focuses on foreign affairs in her *Washington Post* columns. Her book *Gulag: A History* won the Pulitzer for nonfiction in 2004. Her most recent book, *Iron Curtain: The Crushing of Eastern Europe, 1944–1956*, won the Cundill Prize for Historical Literature in 2016. Her column reprinted below explores the Trump presidency in a global context. This article appeared on January 20, 2017.

PREREADING QUESTIONS What is your initial reaction to the essay's title? Are you intrigued enough to read on?

A green lawn, a white picket fence, a shining sun. Small children walk home   1
from school; their mother, clad in an apron, waves to greet them. Father comes
home in the evening from his well-paid job, the same one he has had all of his
life. He greets the neighbors cheerfully—they are all men and women who look
and talk like he does—and sits down to watch the 6 o'clock news while his wife
makes dinner. The sun sets. Everyone sleeps well, knowing that the next day will
bring no surprises.

In the back of their minds, all Americans know this picture. We've seen this   2
halcyon vision in movies, we've heard it evoked in speeches and songs. We also
know, at some level, what it conceals. There are no black people in the picture—
they didn't live in those kinds of neighborhoods in the 1940s or 1950s—and the
Mexican migrants who picked the tomatoes for the family dinner are invisible,
too. We don't see the wife popping Valium in the powder room. We don't see the
postwar devastation in Europe and Asia that made U.S. industry so dominant,
and U.S. power so central. We don't see half the world is dominated by totalitarian
regimes. We don't see the technological changes that are about to arrive and
transform the picture.

We also know, at some level, that this vision of a simpler America—before   3
civil rights, feminism, the rise of other nations, the Internet, globalization, free
trade—can never be recovered, not least because it never really existed. But
even if we know this, that doesn't mean that the vision has no power.

We live in a culture that celebrates disruption, innovation, entrepreneurship,   4
risk, diversity and change. Yet many people dream of stability, security and
homogeneity, even racial purity, as well as a world in which the United States is
always and forever unchallenged. Indeed, the desire to turn the clock back is so
powerful, so persuasive and so appealing to the "real Americans" who support it,
the "forgotten men and women" of the inaugural address, that it has brought us
the presidency of Donald Trump.

Over the past few days, multiple polls have shown that Trump is the least   5
popular new president in recent memory. He received 3 million fewer votes than
his opponent. He won with the aid of a massive Russian intelligence operation,
and by propagating lies about Barack Obama and Hillary Clinton. But don't let
any of this fool you: Do not underestimate the appeal of his nostalgic vision. His
call for America to "start winning again," his denunciation of the "crime and
gangs and drugs" of the present, these are so powerful that he has triumphed
despite his dishonesty, his vulgarity, his addiction to social media, his lack of
religious faith, his many wives, all of the elements of his character and personal
history that seemed to disqualify him. Surrounded by the trappings of the White
House, its appeal may well increase.

On the contrary, this appeal to the so-called real America, a tribe that exists   6
within the United States of America, deliberately excludes anyone black or
brown, anyone who does not live in a nuclear family and anyone who cannot or
will not aspire to a house with a white picket fence. Nor can it succeed: The
"jobs" and the "borders" that Trump promised to "bring back" do not exist
anymore, in a world of air travel and artificial intelligence and automation. But

Trump is not the first demagogue to succeed by offering an impossible, idealized national vision. Anybody who reads history knows that people have argued with one another, competed with one another and even murdered one another in the name of countless national and tribal utopias, religious and secular, right wing and left wing, over many centuries.

7   Nor is it unique. Trump's America has parallels in contemporary Europe, in the nationalist rhetoric of politicians who also seek to drag France, Britain or Germany violently backward into an allegedly simpler, safer, whiter and purer time. Now that he is in office, many others with radical, even bloody visions of change will seek to align with him, too.

8   Still others will reject his utopian American nationalism, his "America First" rhetoric and his brutal calls for protectionism and selfish tribalism. Indeed, it is likely the Trump administration will be remembered around the world as the tipping point, the moment when U.S. influence, which always had a base in ideas and morality as well as economic and military power, finally went into steep and irreversible decline. But the people who believe in Trump's vision will not see that decline, they will not understand it and they will not have their hearts changed by it. The promise of the mythical past, now to be recovered, is far, far too strong.

Anne Applebaum, "Trump's Dark Utopian Nationalism," *The Washington Post*, 20 Jan. 2017. Reprinted by permission of the author.

QUESTIONS FOR READING

1. What is missing from the 1950s vision of America that so many people recognize?

2. Why is it impossible to go back to this simpler world, assuming it actually existed as imagined?

3. If a simpler, all-powerful America cannot be brought back, why are people moved by someone's promise to do the impossible?

4. What possible outcome of the Trump presidency does the author forecast?

QUESTIONS FOR REASONING AND ANALYSIS

5. Applebaum announces her subject in her title. What is her claim? (You will need a complex sentence to capture the key points of her argument.)

6. The author labels Trump a demagogue. Is this an accurate label? (Be sure you know what the word means.) If you disagree with this label, how would you challenge the author?

7. How does Applebaum account for those who share Trump's vision? What motivates their need to embrace a vision that cannot be made real? Does the motivation make sense to you—whether or not you agree with the vision?

8. Analyze Applebaum's style. What tone does she create? What makes this an effective way to reinforce her claim?

QUESTIONS FOR REFLECTION AND WRITING

9. Is the author's view of America's future reasonable? Too negative? Entirely wrong? Explain and defend your response to her position.

10. Trump's presidency began with numerous marches and protests. Has this controversial administration engaged you politically? If so, why? If not, why not?

11. We hear so often of our human and civil rights as Americans. Do Americans old enough to vote also have a civic duty to do so as a knowledgeable citizen? Explain and defend your position.

A COSMIC PERSPECTIVE | NEIL DEGRASSE TYSON

An astrophysicist whose research interests include star formation and the structure of the Milky Way, Neil deGrasse Tyson is director of the Hayden Planetarium in New York City and the author of ten books. He is also one of today's most important figures in bringing science to the nonspecialist. He was host of the PBS show *NOVA ScienceNOW* for its five seasons and was on-camera host and narrator of *Cosmos: A Space Odyssey* for thirteen episodes. He wrote 100 monthly essays for the *Natural History Magazine*, concluding with the following essay in April 2007.

PREREADING QUESTIONS What does the phrase "cosmic perspective" mean to you? What do you expect Tyson to explore in this essay?

Neil deGrasse Tyson.
©Sean Zanni/Patrick McMullan/Getty Images

Of all the sciences cultivated by mankind, Astronomy is acknowledged to be, and undoubtedly is, the most sublime, the most interesting, and the most useful. For, by knowledge derived from this science, not only the bulk of the Earth is discovered . . . ; but our very faculties are enlarged with the grandeur of the ideas it conveys, our minds exalted above [their] low contracted prejudices.

—James Ferguson, *Astronomy Explained upon Sir Isaac Newton's Principles, and Made Easy to Those Who Have Not Studied Mathematics* (1757)

Long before anyone knew that the universe had a beginning, before we knew that the nearest large galaxy lies two and a half million light-years from Earth, before we knew how stars work or whether atoms exist, James Ferguson's enthusiastic introduction to his favorite science rang true.

Yet his words, apart from their eighteenth-century flourish, could have been written yesterday.

3   But who gets to think that way? Who gets to celebrate this cosmic view of life? Not the migrant farmworker. Not the sweatshop worker. Certainly not the homeless person rummaging through the trash for food. You need the luxury of time not spent on mere survival. You need to live in a nation whose government values the search to understand humanity's place in the universe. You need a society in which intellectual pursuit can take you to the frontiers of discovery, and in which news of your discoveries can be routinely disseminated. By those measures, most citizens of industrialized nations do quite well.

4   Yet the cosmic view comes with a hidden cost. When I travel thousands of miles to spend a few moments in the fast-moving shadow of the Moon during a total solar eclipse, sometimes I lose sight of Earth.

5   When I pause and reflect on our expanding universe, with its galaxies hurtling away from one another, embedded within the ever-stretching, four-dimensional fabric of space and time, sometimes I forget that uncounted people walk this Earth without food or shelter, and that children are disproportionately represented among them.

6   When I pore over the data that establish the mysterious presence of dark matter and dark energy throughout the universe, sometimes I forget that every day—every twenty-four-hour rotation of Earth—people kill and get killed in the name of someone else's conception of God, and that some people who do not kill in the name of God kill in the name of their nation's needs or wants.

7   When I track the orbits of asteroids, comets, and planets, each one a pirouetting dancer in a cosmic ballet choreographed by the forces of gravity, sometimes I forget that too many people act in wanton disregard for the delicate interplay of Earth's atmosphere, oceans, and land, with consequences that our children and our children's children will witness and pay for with their health and well-being.

8   And sometimes I forget that powerful people rarely do all they can to help those who cannot help themselves.

9   I occasionally forget those things because, however big the world is—in our hearts, our minds, and our outsize atlases—the universe is even bigger. A depressing thought to some, but a liberating thought to me.

10   Consider an adult who tends to the traumas of a child: a broken toy, a scraped knee, a schoolyard bully. Adults know that kids have no clue what constitutes a genuine problem, because inexperience greatly limits their childhood perspective.

11   As grown-ups, dare we admit to ourselves that we, too, have a collective immaturity of view? Dare we admit that our thoughts and behaviors spring from a belief that the world revolves around us? Apparently not. And the evidence abounds. Part the curtains of society's racial, ethnic, religious, national, and cultural conflicts, and you find the human ego turning the knobs and pulling the levers.

Now imagine a world in which everyone, but especially people with power 12 and influence, holds an expanded view of our place in the cosmos. With that perspective, our problems would shrink—or never arise at all—and we could celebrate our earthly differences while shunning the behavior of our predecessors who slaughtered each other because of them.

Back in February 2000, the newly rebuilt Hayden Planetarium featured a 13 space show called "Passport to the Universe," which took visitors on a virtual zoom from New York City to the edge of the cosmos. En route the audience saw Earth, then the solar system, then the 100 billion stars of the Milky Way galaxy shrink to barely visible dots on the planetarium dome.

Within a month of opening day, I received a letter from an Ivy League 14 professor of psychology whose expertise was things that make people feel insignificant. I never knew one could specialize in such a field. The guy wanted to administer a before-and-after questionnaire to visitors, assessing the depth of their depression after viewing the show. "Passport to the Universe," he wrote, elicited the most dramatic feelings of smallness he had ever experienced.

How could that be? Every time I see the space show (and others we've 15 produced), I feel alive and spirited and connected. I also feel large, knowing that the goings-on within the three-pound human brain are what enabled us to figure out our place in the universe.

Allow me to suggest that it's the professor, not I, who has misread nature. His 16 ego was too big to begin with, inflated by delusions of significance and fed by cultural assumptions that human beings are more important than everything else in the universe.

In all fairness to the fellow, powerful forces in society leave most of us 17 susceptible. As was I . . . until the day I learned in biology class that more bacteria

©Stocktrek Images/Luis Argerich/Getty Images RF

The night sky.

live and work in one centimeter of my colon than the number of people who have ever existed in the world. That kind of information makes you think twice about who—or what—is actually in charge.

18   From that day on, I began to think of people not as the masters of space and time but as participants in a great cosmic chain of being, with a direct genetic link across species both living and extinct, extending back nearly 4 billion years to the earliest single-celled organisms on Earth.

19   I know what you're thinking: we're smarter than bacteria.

20   No doubt about it, we're smarter than every other living creature that ever walked, crawled, or slithered on Earth. But how smart is that? We cook our food. We compose poetry and music. We do art and science. We're good at math. Even if you're bad at math, you're probably much better at it than the smartest chimpanzee, whose genetic identity varies in only trifling ways from ours. Try as they might, primatologists will never get a chimpanzee to learn the multiplication table or do long division.

21   If small genetic differences between us and our fellow apes account for our vast difference in intelligence, maybe that difference in intelligence is not so vast after all.

22   Imagine a life-form whose brainpower is to ours as ours is to a chimpanzee's. To such a species our highest mental achievements would be trivial. Their toddlers, instead of learning their ABCs on Sesame Street, would learn multivariable calculus on Boolean Boulevard. Our most complex theorems, our deepest philosophies, the cherished works of our most creative artists, would be projects their schoolkids bring home for Mom and Dad to display on the refrigerator door. These creatures would study Stephen Hawking (who occupies the same endowed professorship once held by Newton at the University of Cambridge) because he's slightly more clever than other humans, owing to his ability to do theoretical astrophysics and other rudimentary calculations in his head.

23   If a huge genetic gap separated us from our closest relative in the animal kingdom, we could justifiably celebrate our brilliance. We might be entitled to walk around thinking we're distant and distinct from our fellow creatures. But no such gap exists. Instead, we are one with the rest of nature, fitting neither above nor below, but within.

24   Need more ego softeners? Simple comparisons of quantity, size, and scale do the job well.

25   Take water. It's simple, common, and vital. There are more molecules of water in an eight-ounce cup of the stuff than there are cups of water in all the world's oceans. Every cup that passes through a single person and eventually rejoins the world's water supply holds enough molecules to mix 1,500 of them into every other cup of water in the world. No way around it: some of the water you just drank passed through the kidneys of Socrates, Genghis Khan, and Joan of Arc.

26   How about air? Also vital. A single breathful draws in more air molecules than there are breathfuls of air in Earth's entire atmosphere. That means some of the air you just breathed passed through the lungs of Napoleon, Beethoven, Lincoln, and Billy the Kid.

Time to get cosmic. There are more stars in the universe than grains of sand 27
on any beach, more stars than seconds have passed since Earth formed, more
stars than words and sounds ever uttered by all the humans who ever lived.

Want a sweeping view of the past? Our unfolding cosmic perspective takes 28
you there. Light takes time to reach Earth's observatories from the depths of
space, and so you see objects and phenomena not as they are but as they once
were. That means the universe acts like a giant time machine: the farther away
you look, the further back in time you see—back almost to the beginning of time
itself. Within that horizon of reckoning, cosmic evolution unfolds continuously, in
full view.

Want to know what we're made of? Again, the cosmic perspective offers a 29
bigger answer than you might expect. The chemical elements of the universe
are forged in the fires of high-mass stars that end their lives in stupendous
explosions, enriching their host galaxies with the chemical arsenal of life as we
know it. The result? The four most common chemically active elements in the
universe—hydrogen, oxygen, carbon, and nitrogen—are the four most common
elements of life on Earth. We are not simply in the universe. The universe is in us.

Yes, we are stardust. But we may not be of this Earth. Several separate lines 30
of research, when considered together, have forced investigators to reassess
who we think we are and where we think we came from.

First, computer simulations show that when a large asteroid strikes a planet, 31
the surrounding areas can recoil from the impact energy, catapulting rocks into
space. From there, they can travel to—and land on—other planetary surfaces.
Second, microorganisms can be hardy. Some survive the extremes of temperature,
pressure, and radiation inherent in space travel. If the rocky flotsam from an
impact hails from a planet with life, microscopic fauna could have stowed away in
the rocks' nooks and crannies. Third, recent evidence suggests that shortly after
the formation of our solar system, Mars was wet, and perhaps fertile, even before
Earth was.

Those findings mean it's conceivable that life began on Mars and later 32
seeded life on Earth, a process known as panspermia. So all earthlings might—
just might—be descendants of Martians.

Again and again across the centuries, cosmic discoveries have demoted our 33
self-image. Earth was once assumed to be astronomically unique, until
astronomers learned that Earth is just another planet orbiting the Sun. Then we
presumed the Sun was unique, until we learned that the countless stars of the
night sky are suns themselves. Then we presumed our galaxy, the Milky Way,
was the entire known universe, until we established that the countless fuzzy
things in the sky are other galaxies, dotting the landscape of our known universe.

Today, how easy it is to presume that one universe is all there is. Yet 34
emerging theories of modern cosmology, as well as the continually reaffirmed
improbability that anything is unique, require that we remain open to the latest
assault on our plea for distinctiveness: multiple universes, otherwise known as
the "multiverse," in which ours is just one of countless bubbles bursting forth
from the fabric of the cosmos.

35   The cosmic perspective flows from fundamental knowledge. But it's more than just what you know. It's also about having the wisdom and insight to apply that knowledge to assessing our place in the universe. And its attributes are clear:

36   The cosmic perspective comes from the frontiers of science, yet it's not solely the province of the scientist. The cosmic perspective belongs to everyone.

37   The cosmic perspective is humble.

38   The cosmic perspective is spiritual—even redemptive—but not religious.

39   The cosmic perspective enables us to grasp, in the same thought, the large and the small.

40   The cosmic perspective opens our minds to extraordinary ideas but does not leave them so open that our brains spill out, making us susceptible to believing anything we're told.

41   The cosmic perspective opens our eyes to the universe, not as a benevolent cradle designed to nurture life but as a cold, lonely, hazardous place.

42   The cosmic perspective shows Earth to be a mote, but a precious mote and, for the moment, the only home we have.

43   The cosmic perspective finds beauty in the images of planets, moons, stars, and nebulae but also celebrates the laws of physics that shape them.

44   The cosmic perspective enables us to see beyond our circumstances, allowing us to transcend the primal search for food, shelter, and sex.

45   The cosmic perspective reminds us that in space, where there is no air, a flag will not wave—an indication that perhaps flag waving and space exploration do not mix.

46   The cosmic perspective not only embraces our genetic kinship with all life on Earth but also values our chemical kinship with any yet-to-be discovered life in the universe, as well as our atomic kinship with the universe itself.

47   At least once a week, if not once a day, we might each ponder what cosmic truths lie undiscovered before us, perhaps awaiting the arrival of a clever thinker, an ingenious experiment, or an innovative space mission to reveal them. We might further ponder how those discoveries may one day transform life on Earth.

48   Absent such curiosity, we are no different from the provincial farmer who expresses no need to venture beyond the county line, because his forty acres meet all his needs. Yet if all our predecessors had felt that way, the farmer would instead be a cave dweller, chasing down his dinner with a stick and a rock.

49   During our brief stay on planet Earth, we owe ourselves and our descendants the opportunity to explore—in part because it's fun to do. But there's a far nobler reason. The day our knowledge of the cosmos ceases to expand, we risk regressing to the childish view that the universe figuratively and literally revolves around us. In that bleak world, arms-bearing, resource-hungry people and nations would be prone to act on their "low contracted prejudices." And that would be the last gasp of human enlightenment—until the rise of a visionary new culture that could once again embrace the cosmic perspective.

Neil deGrasse Tyson, "Cosmic Perspective," *Natural History Magazine*, Apr. 2007. Used with permission of Natural History Magazine, Inc.

QUESTIONS FOR READING

1. Who gets to celebrate a cosmic view of life? Who does not usually have that chance?
2. What might astrophysicists forget about when they are busy studying the universe far away from what humans are experiencing here and now?
3. How can a cosmic perspective alter the way we perceive daily problems?
4. Although a cosmic perspective can make us feel small, it can also make us feel "alive" and "connected." Why?
5. How is the universe "in us"?
6. How is it possible that we could be descendants of Martians?
7. Why is continued exploration so important?

QUESTIONS FOR REASONING AND ANALYSIS

8. In general, what does Tyson mean by a cosmic perspective? Why does he think it is so important? What, then, is his claim?
9. What does the author accomplish with his opening quotation?
10. How does Tyson use his example of the psychology professor to develop and support his claim? How do his examples of quantity, size, and scale advance his argument?
11. Study Tyson's twelve advantages of the cosmic perspective both as a rhetorical strategy and as support for his claim. What makes his list an effective strategy?

QUESTIONS FOR REFLECTION AND WRITING

12. Which of the twelve items in the cosmic perspective list do you find most moving? Most surprising? Most worthy of sharing with others? Select at least one for each of the three questions and support your choice. If none strike you as memorable, explain why.
13. Tyson asserts at the end that exploration is essential to human enlightenment. Do you agree? If so, why? If not, why not?
14. Are you fascinated and in awe of the universe, or does it bother or depress you? Explain your reaction and reflect on it.

Understanding Literature

The same process of reading nonfiction can be used to understand literature—fiction, poetry, and drama. You still need to read what is on the page, looking up unfamiliar words and tracking down references you don't understand. You still need to examine the context, to think about who is writing to whom, under what circumstances, and in what literary format. And, to respond fully to the words, you need to analyze the writer's techniques for developing ideas and expressing attitudes.

Although it seems logical that the reading process should be much the same regardless of the work, not all readers of literature are willing to accept that logic. Some readers want a work of literature to mean whatever they think it means. But what happened to the writer's desire to communicate? If you decide that a Robert Frost poem, for example, should mean whatever you are feeling when you read it, you might as well skip the reading of Frost and just commune with your feelings. Presumably you read Frost to gain some new insight from him, to get beyond just your vision and see something of human experience and emotion from a new vantage point.

Other readers of literature hesitate over the concept of *literary analysis,* or at least over the word *analysis.* These readers complain that analysis will "tear the work apart" and "ruin it." If you are inclined to share this attitude, stop for a minute and think about the last sports event you watched. Perhaps a friend explained: "North Carolina is so good at stalling to use up the clock; Duke will have to foul to get the ball and have a chance to tie the game." The game is being analyzed! And that analysis makes the event more fully experienced by those who understand at least some of the elements of basketball.

The analogy is clear. You, too, can be a fan of literature. You can enjoy reading and discussing your reading once you learn to use your active reading and analytic skills to open up a poem or story, and once you sharpen your knowledge of literary terms and concepts so that you can "speak the language" of literary criticism with the same confidence with which you discuss the merits of a full-court press.

GETTING THE FACTS: ACTIVE READING, SUMMARY, AND PARAPHRASE

Let's begin with the following poem by Paul Dunbar. As you read, make marginal notes, circling a phrase you fancy, putting a question mark next to a difficult line, underscoring words you need to look up. Note, too, your emotional reactions as you read.

PROMISE | PAUL LAWRENCE DUNBAR

Born of former slave parents, Dunbar (1872–1906) was educated in Dayton, Ohio. After a first booklet of poems, *Oak and Ivy*, was printed in 1893, several friends helped Dunbar get a second collection, *Majors and Minors*, published in 1895. A copy was given to author and editor William Dean Howells, who reviewed the book favorably, increasing sales and Dunbar's reputation. This led to a national publisher issuing *Lyrics of Lowly Life* in 1896, the collection that secured Dunbar's fame.

I grew a rose within a garden fair,
And, tending it with more than loving care,
I thought how, with the glory of its bloom,
I should the darkness of my life illume;
And, watching, ever smiled to see the lusty bud   5
Drink freely in the summer sun to tinct its blood.

My rose began to open, and its hue
Was sweet to me as to it sun and dew;
I watched it taking on its ruddy flame
Until the day of perfect blooming came,   10
Then hasted I with smiles to find it blushing red—
Too late! Some thoughtless child had plucked my rose and fled!

Paul Laurence Dunbar, "Promise," *Lyrics of Lowly Life* (1913).

"Promise" should not have been especially difficult to read, although you may have paused a moment over "illume" before connecting it to "illuminate," and you may have to check the dictionary for a definition of "tinct." Test your knowledge of content by listing all the facts of the poem. Pay attention to the poem's basic situation. Who is speaking? What is happening, or what thoughts is the speaker sharing? In this poem, the "I" is not further identified, so you will have to refer to him or her as the "speaker." You should not call the speaker "Dunbar," however, because you do not know if Dunbar ever grew a rose.

In "Promise" the speaker is describing an event that has taken place. The speaker grew a rose, tended to it with care, and watched it begin to bloom. Then, when the rose was in full bloom, some child picked the rose and took it away. The situation is fairly simple, isn't it? Too simple, unfortunately, for some readers who decide that the speaker never grew a rose at all. But when anyone writes, "I grew a rose within a garden fair," it is wise to assume that the writer means just that. People do grow roses, most often in gardens, and then the gardens are made "fair" or beautiful by the flowers growing there. Read first for the facts; try not to jump too quickly to broad generalizations.

As with nonfiction, one of the best ways to make certain you have understood a literary work is to write a summary or paraphrase. Since a summary condenses, you are most likely to write a summary of a story, novel, or play, whereas a paraphrase is usually reserved for poems or complex short passages. When you paraphrase a difficult poem, you are likely to end up with more words than in the original because your purpose is to turn cryptic lines into more ordinary sentences. For example, Dunbar's "Then hasted I with smiles" can be paraphrased to read: "Then, full of smiles, I hurried."

When summarizing a literary work, remember to use your own words, draw no conclusions, giving only the facts, but focus your summary on the key events in the story. (Of course, the selecting you do to write a summary represents preliminary analysis; you are making some choices about what is important in the work.) Read the following short story by Kate Chopin and then write your own summary. Finally, compare yours to the summary that follows the story.

THE STORY OF AN HOUR | KATE CHOPIN

Now recognized as an important voice from 19th-century America, Kate Chopin (1851–1904) enjoyed popularity for her short stories from 1890 to 1900 and then condemnation and neglect for sixty years. She saw two collections of stories published—*Bayou Folk* in 1894 and *A Night in Acadie* in 1897—before losing popularity and critical acclaim with the publication of her short novel *The Awakening* in 1899, the story of a woman struggling to free herself from years of repression and subservience.

1   Knowing that Mrs. Mallard was afflicted with a heart trouble, great care was taken to break to her as gently as possible the news of her husband's death.

2   It was her sister Josephine who told her, in broken sentences; veiled hints that revealed in half concealing. Her husband's friend Richards was there, too, near her. It was he who had been in the newspaper office when intelligence of the railroad disaster was received, with Brently Mallard's name leading the list of "killed." He had only taken the time to assure himself of its truth by a second telegram, and had hastened to forestall any less careful, less tender friend in bearing the sad message.

3   She did not hear the story as many women have heard the same, with a paralyzed inability to accept its significance. She wept at once, with sudden, wild abandonment, in her sister's arms. When the storm of grief had spent itself she went away to her room alone. She would have no one follow her.

4   There stood, facing the open window, a comfortable, roomy armchair. Into this she sank, pressed down by a physical exhaustion that haunted her body and seemed to reach into her soul.

5   She could see in the open square before her house the tops of trees that were all aquiver with the new spring life. The delicious breath of rain was in the air. In the street below a peddler was crying his wares. The notes of a distant song which some one was singing reached her faintly, and countless sparrows were twittering in the eaves.

6   There were patches of blue sky showing here and there through the clouds that had met and piled one above the other in the west facing her window.

She sat with her head thrown back upon the cushion of the chair, quite 7 motionless, except when a sob came up into her throat and shook her, as a child who has cried itself to sleep continues to sob in its dreams.

She was young, with a fair, calm face, whose lines bespoke repression and 8 even a certain strength. But now there was a dull stare in her eyes, whose gaze was fixed away off yonder on one of those patches of blue sky. It was not a glance of reflection, but rather indicated a suspension of intelligent thought.

There was something coming to her and she was waiting for it, fearfully. 9 What was it? She did not know; it was too subtle and elusive to name. But she felt it, creeping out of the sky, reaching toward her through the sounds, the scents, the color that filled the air.

Now her bosom rose and fell tumultuously. She was beginning to recognize 10 this thing that was approaching to possess her, and she was striving to beat it back with her will—as powerless as her two white slender hands would have been.

When she abandoned herself a little whispered word escaped her slightly 11 parted lips. She said it over and over under her breath: "free, free, free!" The vacant stare and the look of terror that had followed it went from her eyes. They stayed keen and bright. Her pulses beat fast, and the coursing blood warmed and relaxed every inch of her body.

She did not stop to ask if it were or were not a monstrous joy that held her. 12 A clear and exalted perception enabled her to dismiss the suggestion as trivial.

She knew that she would weep again when she saw the kind, tender hands 13 folded in death; the face that had never looked save with love upon her, fixed and gray and dead. But she saw beyond that bitter moment a long procession of years to come that would belong to her absolutely. And she opened and spread her arms out to them in welcome.

There would be no one to live for her during those coming years; she would 14 live for herself. There would be no powerful will bending hers in that blind persistence with which men and women believe they have a right to impose a private will upon a fellow-creature. A kind intention or a cruel intention made the act seem no less a crime as she looked upon it in that brief moment of illumination.

And yet she had loved him—sometimes. Often she had not. What did it matter! 15 What could love, the unsolved mystery, count for in face of this possession of self-assertion which she suddenly recognized as the strongest impulse of her being!

"Free! Body and soul free!" she kept whispering. 16

Josephine was kneeling before the closed door with her lips to the keyhole, 17 imploring for admission. "Louise, open the door! I beg; open the door—you will make yourself ill. What are you doing, Louise? For heaven's sake open the door."

"Go away. I am not making myself ill." No; she was drinking in a very elixir of 18 life through that open window.

Her fancy was running riot along those days ahead of her. Spring days, and 19 summer days, and all sorts of days that would be her own. She breathed a quick prayer that life might be long. It was only yesterday she had thought with a shudder that life might be long.

She arose at length and opened the door to her sister's importunities. There 20 was a feverish triumph in her eyes, and she carried herself unwittingly like a goddess of Victory. She clasped her sister's waist, and together they descended the stairs. Richards stood waiting for them at the bottom.

21   Someone was opening the front door with a latchkey. It was Brently Mallard who entered, a little travel-stained, composedly carrying his grip-sack and umbrella. He had been far from the scene of accident, and did not even know there had been one. He stood amazed at Josephine's piercing cry; at Richards' quick motion to screen him from the view of his wife.

22   But Richards was too late.

23   When the doctors came they said she had died of heart disease—of joy that kills.

Kate Chopin, "The Story of an Hour," (1894).

Summary of "The Story of an Hour"

Mrs. Mallard's sister Josephine and her husband's friend Richards come to tell her that her husband has been listed as killed in a train accident. They try to be gentle because Mrs. Mallard has a heart condition. She cries and then goes to her bedroom alone. She sits in an armchair and gazes out the open window. Her dull stare gives way to some new thought that she cannot push away. She whispers the word "free" and thinks about a future directed by herself. Responding to Josephine's pleas, she leaves the bedroom and sees Richards below—and then Mr. Mallard letting himself in the front door. Mrs. Mallard dies, and the doctors who attend her say she died of heart disease—of "joy that kills."

Note that the summary is written in the present tense. Brevity is achieved by leaving out dialogue and the details of what Mrs. Mallard sees outside her window and the future life she imagines. Observe that the summary is not the same as the original story. The drama and emotion are missing, details that help us to understand the story's ending.

Now for a paraphrase. Read the following sonnet by Shakespeare, looking up unfamiliar words and making notes. Remember to read to the end of a unit of thought, not just to the end of a line. Some sentences continue through several lines; if you pause before you reach punctuation, you will be confused. Write your own paraphrase, not looking ahead in the text, and then compare yours with the one that follows the poem.

SONNET 116 | WILLIAM SHAKESPEARE

Surely the best-known name in literature, William Shakespeare (1564–1616) is famous as both a dramatist and a poet. Rural Warwickshire and the market town of Stratford -upon-Avon, where he grew up, showed him many of the character types who were to enliven his plays, as did the bustling life of a young actor in London. Apparently his sonnets were intended to be circulated only among his friends, but they were published nonetheless in 1609. His thirty-seven plays were first published together in 1623. Shakespeare's 154 sonnets vary, some focusing on separation and world-weariness, others on the endurance of love.

> Let me not to the marriage of true minds
> Admit impediments. Love is not love
> Which alters when it alteration finds,
> Or bends with the remover to remove.
5   O, no! it is an ever-fixed mark

That looks on tempests and is never shaken;
It is the star to every wand'ring bark,
Whose worth's unknown, although his height be taken.
Love's not Time's fool, though rosy lips and cheeks
Within his bending sickle's compass come;   10
Love alters not with his brief hours and weeks,
But bears it out even to the edge of doom.
     If this be error and upon me proved,
     I never writ, nor no man ever loved.

William Shakespeare, "Sonnet 116," (1609).

Paraphrase of "Sonnet 116"

I cannot accept barriers to the union of steadfast spirits. We cannot call love love if
it changes because it discovers change or if it disappears during absence. On the
contrary, love is a steady guide that, in spite of difficulties, remains unwavering.
Love can define the inherent value in all who lack self-knowledge, though
superficially they know who they are. Love does not lessen with time, though signs
of physical beauty may fade. Love endures, changeless, eternally. If anyone can show
me to be wrong in this position, I am no writer and no man can be said to have loved.

We have examined the facts of a literary work, what we can call the internal situation.
But, as we noted in Chapter 2, there is also the external situation or context of any piece
of writing. For many literary works, the context is not as essential to understanding as it
is with nonfiction. You can read "The Story of an Hour," for instance, without knowing
much about Kate Chopin, or the circumstances in which she wrote the story, although
such information would enrich your reading experience. There is a body of information,
however, that is important: the external literary situation. Readers should take note of
these details before they begin to read:

- First, don't make the mistake of calling every work a "story." Make clear distinctions among stories, novels, plays, and poems.
- Poems can be further divided into narrative, dramatic, and lyric poems.
- A *narrative poem,* such as Homer's *The Iliad,* tells a story in verse. A *dramatic poem* records the speech of at least one character.
- A poem in which only one figure speaks—but clearly addresses words to someone who is present in a particular situation—is called a *dramatic monologue.*
- *Lyric poems,* Dunbar's "Promise" for example, may place the speaker in a situation or may express a thought or feeling with few, if any, situational details, but lyric poems have in common the convention that we as readers are listening in on someone's thoughts, not listening to words directed to a second, created figure. These distinctions make us aware of how the words of the poem are coming to us. Are we hearing a storyteller or someone speaking? Or are we overhearing someone's thoughts?

> **REMEMBER:** Active reading includes looking over a work first and predicting what will come next. Do not just start reading words without first understanding what kind of work you are about to read.

Lyric poems can be further divided into many subcategories or types. Most instructors will expect you to be able to recognize some of these types. You should be able to distinguish between a poem in *free verse* (no prevailing metrical pattern) and one in *blank verse* (continuous unrhymed lines of iambic pentameter). (*Note:* A metrical line will contain a particular number—pentameter is five—of one kind of metrical "foot." The iambic foot consists of one unstressed syllable followed by one stressed syllable.) You should also be able to tell if a poem is written in some type of *stanza* form (repeated units with the same number of lines, same metrical pattern, and same rhyme scheme), or if it is a *sonnet* (always fourteen lines of iambic pentameter with one of two complex rhyme schemes labeled either "English" or "Italian"). You want to make it a habit to observe these external elements before you read. To sharpen your observation, complete the following exercise.

EXERCISE: Observing Literary Types and Using Literary Terms

1. After surveying this appendix, make a list of all the works of literature by primary type: short story, poem, play.
2. For each work on your list, add two more pieces of information: whether the author is American or British, and in what century the work was written. Why should you be aware of the writer's dates and nationality as you read?
3. Further divide the poems into narrative, dramatic, or lyric.
4. List as many of the details of type or form as you can for each poem. For example, if the poem is written in stanzas, describe the stanza form used: the number of lines, the meter, the rhyme scheme. If the poem is a sonnet, determine the rhyme scheme. (*Note:* Rhyme scheme is indicated by using letters, assigning *a* to the first sound and using a new letter for each new sound. Thus, if two consecutive lines rhyme, the scheme is *aa, bb, cc, dd,* and so on.)

SEEING CONNECTIONS: ANALYSIS

Although we read first for the facts and an initial emotional response, we do not stop there, because as humans we seek meaning. Surely there is more to "The Story of an Hour" than the summary suggests; emotionally we know this to be true. As with nonfiction, one of the best places to start analysis is with a work's organization or structure. Lyric poems will be shaped by many of the same structures found in essays: chronological, spatial, general to particular, particular to general, a list of particulars with an unstated general point, and so forth. In "Promise," Dunbar gives one illustration, recounted chronologically, to make a point that is left unstated. "Sonnet 116" contains a list of characteristics of love underscored in the conclusion by the speaker's conviction that he is right.

Analysis of Narrative Structure

In stories (and plays and narrative poems) we are given a series of events, in time sequence, involving one or more characters. In some stories, episodes are only loosely connected but are unified around a central character (Mark Twain's *Adventures of Huckleberry Finn,* for example). Most stories present events that are at least to some extent related causally; that is, action A by the main character leads to event B, which requires action C by the main character. This kind of plot structure can be diagrammed, as in Figure 1.

Figure 1 introduces some terms and concepts useful in analyzing and discussing narratives. The story's *exposition* refers to the background details needed to get the story started, including the time and place of the story and relationships of the characters. In "The Story of an Hour," a key detail of exposition is the fact that Mrs. Mallard has a heart condition. The *complication* refers to an event: Something happens to produce tension or *conflict.* In Chopin's story, the announcement of Mr. Mallard's death seems to be an immediate complication. But, after her initial tears, we do not see Mrs. Mallard dealing with this complication in the "typical" way. Instead, when she sits in her bedroom, she experiences a *conflict.* She struggles within herself. Why does she struggle? Why not just embrace the new idea that comes to her?

Although some stories present one major complication leading to a *climax* of decision or insight for the main character, many actually repeat the pattern, presenting several complications—each with an attempted resolution that causes yet another complication—until we reach the high point of tension, the *climax.* The action—or inaction—of the climactic moment leads to the story's *resolution* and ending.

These terms are helpful in analysis, even though some stories end abruptly, with little apparent resolution. A stark "resolution" is part of the modern writer's view of reality, that life goes on, with problems often remaining unresolved. A character in an unpleasant marriage continues in that marriage, perhaps ruefully, perhaps a bit wiser but no happier and unable to act to change the situation. What is the climactic moment in "The Story of an Hour"? How is the story resolved? What is significant about the doctors' explanation at the end? Are they correct?

Analysis of Character

An analysis of plot structure suggests to us that Mrs. Mallard is not in conflict over her husband's death. She is in conflict, initially, over her reaction to that death, but she resolves her conflict, only to have Mr. Mallard open the front door. Note the close

FIGURE 1 Plot Structure

connection between complication (event) and conflict (what the characters are feeling). Fiction requires both plot and character, events and players in those events. In serious literature the greater emphasis is usually on character, on what we learn about human life through the interplay of character and incident.

As we shift from plot to character, we can enhance our analysis by considering how writers present character. Writers will usually employ several techniques from the following list:

- Descriptive details. (Mrs. Mallard's heart condition. Josephine and Richards worry about her health.)
- Dramatic scenes. (Instead of telling, they show us. Much of "The Story of an Hour" is dialogue. When Mrs. Mallard is in her bedroom alone, we overhear her internal dialogue.)
- Contrast among characters. (Josephine assumes that Mrs. Mallard continues to be the distraught, bereft widow, whereas she is actually embracing a future on her own. Note the contrast between the gentle, kind control of Mr. Mallard in their marriage and the way the control actually feels in his wife's experience of it.)
- Other elements in the work. (Names can be significant, or characters can become associated with significant objects, or details of setting can become symbolic. Note all of the specific details of events outside Mrs. Mallard's window. What, altogether, do they represent?)

Understanding character can be a challenge because we must infer from a few words, gestures, and actions. Looking at all of a writer's options for presenting character will keep us from overlooking important details.

Analysis of Elements of Style and Tone

All the elements, discussed in Chapter 2, that shape a writer's style and create tone can be found in literary works as well and need to be considered as part of your analysis. We can begin with Chopin's title. How much can happen in one hour? Well, the person we thought was dead is alive, and the "widow" ends up dead, quite a reversal of fortunes in such a short time. This situation is filled with irony. The doctors' misunderstanding of the cause of Mrs. Mallard's shock at the sight of her husband also adds irony to the story. The doctors express society's conventional thinking: Dear Mrs. Mallard is so happy that her husband is really alive that her heart cannot stand it. But is that really what shocks her into an early death?

Shakespeare's "Sonnet 116" develops the speaker's ideas about love through a series of metaphors. The rose in Dunbar's "Promise" is not a metaphor, though, because it is not part of a comparison. Yet, as we read the poem we sense that it is about something more serious than the nurturing and then stealing of one flower, no matter how beautiful. The poem's title gives us a clue that the rose stands for something more than itself; it is a symbol. Traditionally the red rose is a symbol of love. To tie the poem together, we will have to see how the title, the usual symbolic value of the rose, and specifics of the poem connect.

DRAWING CONCLUSIONS: INTERPRETATION

We have studied the facts of several works and analyzed their structures and other key elements. To reach some conclusions and shape our thinking into a coherent whole is to offer an interpretation of the work. At this point, readers can be expected to disagree somewhat, but if we have all read carefully and applied our knowledge of literature, differences should, most of the time, be ones of focus and emphasis. Presumably no one is prepared to argue that "Promise" is about pink elephants or "The Story of an Hour" about the Queen of England. Neither work contains any facts to support those conclusions.

What conclusions can we reach about "Promise"? A beautiful flower has been nurtured into bloom by a speaker who expects it to brighten his or her life. The title lets us know that the rose represents great promise. Has a rival stolen the speaker's loved one, represented symbolically by the rose? A thoughtless child would not be an appropriate rival for an adult speaker. In the context of this poem, the rose represents, more generally, something that the speaker cherishes in anticipation of the pleasure it will bring, only to lose that something.

What conclusions have you reached about "The Story of an Hour"? What is the real irony of the story? When Mr. Mallard, very much alive, opens the door to his home, what door does he shut for Mrs. Mallard?

WRITING ABOUT LITERATURE

When you are assigned a literary essay, you will usually be asked to write either an explication or an analysis. An *explication* presents a reading of a complex poem. It will combine paraphrase and explanation to clarify the poem's meaning. A *literary analysis* can take many forms. You may be asked to analyze one element in a work: character conflict, the use of setting, the tone of a poem. Or you could be asked to contrast two works. Usually an analytic assignment requires you to connect analysis to interpretation, for we analyze the parts to better understand the whole. If you are asked to examine the metaphors in a Shakespeare sonnet, for example, you will want to show how understanding the metaphors contributes to an understanding of the entire poem. In short, literary analysis is much the same as a style analysis of an essay. Thus the guidelines for writing about style discussed in Chapter 2 apply here as well.[*] Successful analyses are based on accurate reading, reflection on the work's emotional impact, and the use of details from the work to support conclusions.

Literary analyses can also incorporate material beyond the particular work. We can analyze a work in the light of biographical information or from a particular political ideology. Or we can study the social-cultural context of the work, or relate it to a literary tradition. These are only a few of the many approaches to the study of literature, and they depend on the application of knowledge outside the work itself. For undergraduates, topics based on these approaches usually require research. The student research essay at the end of the appendix is a literary analysis. Alan examines Faulkner's *Intruder in the Dust* as an initiation novel. He connects his analysis to works by Hawthorne and Arthur Miller. What is taken from his research is documented and helps develop and support his own conclusions about the story.

To practice close reading, analysis, and interpretation of literature, read the following works. Use the questions after each work to aid your response.

TO HIS COY MISTRESS | ANDREW MARVELL

One of the last poets of the English Renaissance, Andrew Marvell (1621–1678) graduated from Cambridge University, spent much of his young life as a tutor, and was elected to Parliament in 1659. He continued in public service until his death. Most of his best-loved lyric poems come from his years as a tutor. "To His Coy Mistress" was published in 1681.

Had we but world enough, and time,
This coyness, lady, were no crime.
We would sit down, and think which way
To walk, and pass our long love's day.
5   Thou by the Indian Ganges' side
Shouldst rubies find; I by the tide
Of Humber would complain. I would
Love you ten years before the Flood,
And you should, if you please, refuse
10   Till the conversion of the Jews.
My vegetable° love should grow   *slowly vegetative*
Vaster than empires, and more slow;
An hundred years should go to praise
Thine eyes, and on thy forehead gaze;
15   Two hundred to adore each breast,
But thirty thousand to the rest;
An age at least to every part,
And the last age should show your heart.
For, lady, you deserve this state,
20   Nor would I love at lower rate.
     But at my back I always hear
Time's wingèd chariot hurrying near;
And yonder all before us lie
Deserts of vast eternity.
25   Thy beauty shall no more be found,
Nor in thy marble vault shall sound
My echoing song; then worms shall try
That long preserved virginity,
And your quaint honor turn to dust,
30   And into ashes all my lust.
The grave's a fine and private place,
But none, I think, do there embrace.
    Now therefore, while the youthful hue
Sits on thy skin like morning dew,
35   And while thy willing soul transpires
At every pore with instant fires,
Now let us sport us while we may,

And now, like amorous birds of prey,
Rather at once our time devour
Than languish in his slow-chapped power.   40
Let us roll all our strength and all
Our sweetness up into one ball,
And tear our pleasures with rough strife
Thorough° the iron gates of life.   *through*   45
Thus, though we cannot make our sun
Stand still, yet we will make him run.

Andrew Marvell, "To His Coy Mistress," (1660).

QUESTIONS FOR READING, REASONING, AND REFLECTION

1. Describe the poem's external form.
2. How are the words coming to us? That is, is this a narrative, dramatic, or lyric poem?
3. Summarize the speaker's argument, using the structures *if*, *but*, and *therefore*.
4. What figure of speech do we find throughout the first verse paragraph? What is its effect on the speaker's tone?
5. Find examples of irony and understatement in the second verse paragraph.
6. How does the tone shift in the second section?
7. Explain the personification in line 22.
8. Explain the metaphors in lines 30 and 45.
9. What is the paradox of the last two lines? How can it be explained?
10. What is the idea of this poem? What does the writer want us to reflect on?

THE PASSIONATE SHEPHERD TO HIS LOVE | CHRISTOPHER MARLOWE

Cambridge graduate, Renaissance dramatist second only to Shakespeare, Christopher Marlowe (1564–1593) may be best known for this lyric poem. Not only is it widely anthologized, it has also spawned a number of responses by such significant writers as the 17th-century poet John Donne and the 20th-century humorous poet Ogden Nash. For the Renaissance period, the shepherd was a standard figure of the lover.

Come live with me and be my love,
And we will all the pleasures prove
That valleys, groves, hills, and fields,
Woods, or steepy mountain yields.

And we will sit upon the rocks,   5
Seeing the shepherds feed their flocks,
By shallow rivers to whose falls
Melodious birds sing madrigals.

And I will make thee beds of roses
And a thousand fragrant posies,   10

A cap of flowers, and a kirtle
Embroidered all with leaves of myrtle;

A gown made of the finest wool
15   Which from our pretty lambs we pull;
Fair lined slippers for the cold,
With buckles of the purest gold;

A belt of straw and ivy buds,
With coral clasps and amber studs:
20   And if these pleasures may thee move,
Come live with me, and be my love.

The shepherds' swains shall dance and sing
For thy delight each May morning:
If these delights thy mind may move,
Then live with me and be my love.

Christopher Marlowe, "The Passionate Shepherd to His Love," (1599).

QUESTIONS FOR READING, REASONING, AND REFLECTION

1. Describe the poem's external structure.
2. What is the speaker's subject? What does he want to accomplish?
3. Summarize his "argument." How does he seek to convince his love?
4. What do the details of his argument have in common—that is, what kind of world or life does the speaker describe? Is there anything missing from the shepherd's world?
5. Would you like to be courted in this way? Would you say yes to the shepherd? If not, why?

THE NYMPH'S REPLY TO THE SHEPHERD | SIR WALTER RALEIGH

The renowned Elizabethan courtier Sir Walter Raleigh (1552–1618) led a varied life as both a favorite of Queen Elizabeth and out of favor at court, as a colonizer and writer, and as one of many to be imprisoned in the Tower of London. In the following poem, Raleigh offers a response to Marlowe, using the nymph as the voice of the female lover.

If all the world and love were young,
And truth in every shepherd's tongue,
These pretty pleasures might me move
To live with thee and be thy love.

5   Time drives the flocks from field to fold
When rivers rage and rocks grow cold,
And Philomel becometh dumb;
The rest complains of cares to come.

The flowers do fade, and wanton fields
10   To wayward winter reckoning yields;

A honey tongue, a heart of gall,
Is fancy's spring, but sorrow's fall.

Thy gowns, thy shoes, thy beds of roses,
Thy cap, thy kirtle, and thy posies
Soon break, soon wither, soon forgotten,— 15
In folly ripe, in reason rotten.

Thy belt of straw and ivy buds,
Thy coral clasps and amber studs,
All these in me no means can move
To come to thee and be thy love. 20

But could youth last and love still breed,
Had joys no date nor age no need,
Then these delights my mind might move
To live with thee and be thy love.

Sir Walter Raleigh, "The Nymph's Reply to the Shepherd," (1600).

QUESTIONS FOR READING, REASONING, AND REFLECTION

1. Describe the poem's external structure.
2. What is the context of the poem, the reason the speaker offers her words?
3. Analyze the speaker's argument, using *if* and *but* as your basic structure—and then the concluding, qualifying *but*.
4. What evidence does the speaker provide to support her argument?
5. Who has the more convincing argument: Marlowe's shepherd or Raleigh's nymph? Why?

IS MY TEAM PLOUGHING | A. E. HOUSMAN

British poet A. E. Housman (1859–1936) was a classicist, first a professor of Latin at University College, London, and then at the University of Cambridge. He spent the rest of his life at Trinity College, Cambridge. He is best known for his first volume of poetry, *A Shropshire Lad* (1896), a collection of crystal-clear and deceptively simple verses that give expression to a world that has been lost—perhaps the innocence of youth.

"Is my team ploughing,
    That I was used to drive
And hear the harness jingle
    When I was man alive?"

Ay, the horses trample, 5
    The harness jingles now:
No change though you lie under
    The land you used to plough.

"Is football playing
   Along the river shore,
With lads to chase the leather,
   Now I stand up no more?"

Ay, the ball is flying,
   The lads play heart and soul;
The goal stands up, the keeper
   Stands up to keep the goal.

"Is my girl happy,
   That I thought hard to leave,
And has she tired of weeping
   As she lies down at eve?"

Ay, she lies down lightly,
   She lies not down to weep:
Your girl is well contented.
   Be still, my lad, and sleep.

"Is my friend hearty,
   Now I am thin and pine,
And has he found to sleep in
   A better bed than mine?"

Yes, lad, I lie easy,
   I lie as lads would choose;
I cheer a dead man's sweetheart,
   Never ask me whose.

A.E. Houseman, "Is My Team Ploughing," (1896).

QUESTIONS FOR READING, REASONING, AND REFLECTION

1. Classify the poem according to its external structure.
2. Is this a narrative, dramatic, or lyric poem? How are we to read the words coming to us?
3. What is the relationship between the two speakers? What has happened to the first speaker? What has changed in the life of the second speaker?
4. What ideas are suggested by the poem? What does Housman want us to take from his poem?

TAXI | AMY LOWELL

Educated at private schools and widely traveled, American Amy Lowell (1874–1925) was both a poet and a critic. Lowell frequently read her poetry and lectured on poetic techniques, defending her verse and that of other modern poets.

When I go away from you
The world beats dead
Like a slackened drum.
I call out for you against the jutted stars
And shout into the ridges of the wind.   5
Streets coming fast,
One after the other,
Wedge you away from me,
And the lamps of the city prick my eyes
So that I can no longer see your face.   10
Why should I leave you,
To wound myself upon the sharp edges of the night?

Amy Lowell, "Taxi," from *Sword Blades and Poppy Seed* (1914).

QUESTIONS FOR READING, REASONING, AND REFLECTION

1. Classify the poem according to its external structure.
2. Is this a narrative, dramatic, or lyric poem?
3. Explain the simile in the opening three lines and the metaphor in the last line of the poem.
4. What is the poem's subject? What seems to be the situation in which we find the speaker?
5. How would you describe the tone of the poem? How do the details and the emotional impact of the metaphors help to create tone?
6. What is the poem's meaning or theme? In other words, what does the poet want us to understand from reading her poem?

THE LAST CIVILIZED ACT | JANET TALIAFERRO

Janet Taliaferro is a resident of northern Virginia in winter and northern Wisconsin in summer. She holds a BA from Southern Methodist University of Central Oklahoma in comparative literature and an MA in creative studies from the University of Central Oklahoma, where she received the Geoffrey Bocca Memorial Award for Graduate Studies. Her short stories and poetry have appeared in many small magazines and anthologies. Her novel, *A Sky for Aradia,* was a finalist in the Oklahoma Center for the Book Award. The following story was first published in the spring 2007 issue of *The Northern Virginia Review.*

Lunch in Washington and dinner in New York—all in one day—would be perfect, 1 Constance Steele thought, if you just didn't have to go through New Jersey.

She stared out the window of the Amtrak coach thinking how much she 2 hated the disorder of the right-of-way. Even nature conspired to create a mess, bunching piles of fall leaves in gullies and around trees. Scattered among them were the discards of habitation: a refrigerator, a sofa of indeterminate color, a stove, its oven door ajar like the slack jaw of a skull.

This trip is a paradigm, she thought—one end of her life anchored in the 3 legal career that had taken her to Washington for the day, and the other firmly attached to her husband, Graham, in New York. Gentle Graham, whose only passions were for her and for his books. Somewhere between the law and Graham was the truth. Truth was in her own body. The truth was that she was dying.

4   It also was her birthday and Graham would be waiting to take her to dinner. Nausea tugged at her stomach, but she would not plead illness and deprive him of the pleasure of celebration.

5   The tunnel under the Hudson cut out what was left of a gray autumn sunset and made a mirror of the dark window. Constance examined her reflection as she stood to retrieve her worn briefcase from the overhead rack. The Chanel jacket, piped in black, disguised the fact that she was wearing the latest in medical paraphernalia, a miniature pump strapped to her waist that dripped poison into her liver upon the command of a silicon chip.

6   "The device," she called it, and proudly explained its workings to the few close friends and family who inquired about the experimental treatment. To herself she called it "the vise"; she hated the feeling of being at the mercy of modern technology and ignored the fact that it represented a last, desperate effort to stem the ravages of cells gone mad. At least it did not show. A judicious choice of clothing kept her silhouette unremarkable. Her hand smoothed the waist of the reflection. She did not look at her face. The train moved into the station and the image disappeared, erased by dirty yellow lights.

7   Graham stood in their glare, a small man in a dark suit, dark hat, British all-weather coat in the crook of his left arm, and hands folded over the grip of a collapsible black umbrella. There must be only ten men in Manhattan who still wear a homburg, she thought, smiling at the ridiculous hat on his head. He reminded her of a Magritte painting. His clear gray eyes often allowed his thoughts to be seen as easily as a bird flitting about an open cage. Lately, the cage seemed to be draped.

8   He came toward her as she reached the door of the car, ready to offer assistance. She wasn't too proud to take his arm and hand him the heavy briefcase. As they made their way into the terminal, she slipped her arms into a mauve silk raincoat.

9   "How was your day?" he asked. Concern pulled his eyebrows toward the bridge of his nose.

10   "Spectacular. I think we're going to win before the S.E.C.," she said.

11   His expression did not change during her short recitation of the day's events. "But, how do you feel?" he asked when she had finished.

12   "Oh, all right. Look, let's not talk about it. Okay?"

13   Graham didn't answer, but turned his attention to hailing a taxi. They used to walk everywhere from their apartment just east of Central Park: to the grocery and meat market, the cleaners, drug store, and shopping. One lazy Sunday, they walked all the way to the Battery, just for exercise, but now he insisted they ride in cabs for even short distances.

14   He directed the cab to a restaurant, a half-block off Washington Square. It was their favorite, an unpretentious Italian restaurant, down a few steps from street level.

The sight of snowy linen and clean crystal, dark wood, and a minimum of red 15 wallpaper pleased Constance. Ordinarily she also anticipated the well-blended odor of tomatoes, garlic, and olive oil. Tonight, she fought a battle with her gorge instead.

Graham ordered carbonara, she a plainly-dressed angel hair, half of which 16 she ate, along with a crusty roll. The wine was sour on her tongue.

Conversation ranged from news to sports, to weather, to inane, and 17 culminated in a near fight over whether their tickets to a performance at the Vivian Beaumont Theatre were for Friday or Saturday evening of the following week.

"Okay, Graham, okay," Constance said, "I give up. I was wrong."   18

He looked at her, uncertain.   19

"Not about the damned tickets, about it—me. We're acting like the prover- 20 bial elephant is in the room, which everyone ignores. The elephant's real and I can't ignore it another second. It's my birthday and we both know it's probably the last one." The word "probably" echoed in her ears. Had she inserted that word for herself or for Graham? Short of a miracle, there was no "probably" about it.

"We don't know that. The doctor said. . . ." he began.   21

"Graham, don't." She concentrated on pleating the stiff linen napkin against 22 her thigh.

"But . . ."   23

"Graham! Screw the doctors. I'm dying." The forbidden words were said, and 24 they hung like stale cigarette smoke between them. Constance felt a rush of relief followed by pangs of doubt. She stole a look at her husband.

His face sagged like the hem of an old gray sweater.   25

"Oh, darling," she said, "it's bad enough for me, but I *hate* it for you. God—to 26 have to go through it all over again. It just kills me." She winced at the inappropri-ate cliché.

Graham seemed to rally. "That was different," he said.   27

"How? Hers was breast and mine's liver. What's the difference?"   28

"Well," he hesitated, "Mother was sick so long."   29

"What makes you think I won't be?"   30

"There's no reason to discuss what we can't possibly know, Constance." His 31 tone was dismissive, but his pale eyes slid away as if in fear.

The waiter brought coffee and cannoli, one with a single birthday candle, the 32 dessert Graham had arranged in lieu of a cake.

Constance dutifully made a wish and blew out the candle.   33

"Did you make a wish?" Graham asked.   34

She nodded. She could see the curiosity in his eyes, but he probably had 35 guessed what the wish was. "God, please make it quick and I don't want to hurt . . . at least for very long."

After a bite of the cannoli, she said, "Promise me something, Graham"   36

He waited, wary.   37

"No extreme measures . . . and lots of drugs. If it can't be quick, have them 38 make it painless, and if it can't be painless, for God's sake make it quick. For both our sakes."

39   "I doubt if there is often much of a choice in that respect," he said. He looked helpless.

40   "But there might be. So promise."

41   "What are you asking me?"

42   She stared at him and he returned her gaze without wavering.

43   "Constance, in all my life I have tried never to do an uncivilized act. Please don't ask it of me at this point."

44   "Not uncivilized, Graham; just be kind." She hesitated and added, "I'm afraid."

45   For a moment, he did not respond. His fingers absently stacked and restacked the teaspoons, which lay unused by his plate. Constance could see the same faraway look in his gray eyes that shut her out when he was engrossed with his books.

46   "You are asking me to be your *kaishaku*," he said.

47   "My what?"

48   "In Japan, according to Shinto tradition, when someone commits suicide, ritual hara-kiri, there is always a second, the *kaishaku*, a nobleman who stands by with a sword, ready to cut off the head of the victim and end the pain. You're asking me to do that."

49   She felt a tiny prick of guilt. "I don't know. I guess so," she faltered.

50   "The problem is," Graham continued, "it sounds like a good idea now, sitting here at the table. I almost feel noble about being asked. About your confidence. But what happens when I have to act?"

51   "I don't know," she said, her voice hollow and forlorn. A moment ago, in the urgency of trying to make him understand her feelings, she had felt sure.

52   He looked away and signaled for the check. She stirred her cold coffee to hide the tears.

53   "Connie," he said and gently pulled her chin up so that she had to look at him, "I don't want to talk about any of this because I'm scared. I don't know if I can take it. Not just the end, but everything in between. I know it's selfish, but it's me I'm worried about. It was so long with Mother, and I guess I'm afraid I don't have what it takes to stand up to what's coming. You'll be fine. You'll bear up. But, I feel . . . out of gas."

54   As the waiter approached with the bill, Connie excused herself and made her way casually between the tables to the ladies room. Her lack of haste was a deception, for the benefit of those around her and for herself. The moment she was in the bathroom, she went to one of the stalls and vomited everything she had eaten. She leaned with her hands against the wall until she felt settled enough to flush the toilet and turn to the lavatory. The girl from the coat check counter came in.

55   "You okay, Mrs. Steele?" she asked, a look of concern on her pretty face.

56   Connie nodded, "I'm fine."

57   "Okay," the girl said. "Just thought I'd check. I saw you come in and you looked a little pale."

58   "Thanks," Connie said, "I appreciate your trouble."

59   The warm feeling of being cared for eased away some of the lingering nausea. When the girl had gone, Connie filled her palm twice with cold water

and rinsed her mouth. Then she filled it twice again to get enough water to wash down two Dilaudid capsules. She had eaten them like candy all day. Smoothing her jacket, she could feel the plastic pack at her waist.

Graham looked at her suspiciously when she rejoined him. 60

She raised her eyebrows in dismissal and shrugged into her coat. 61

They left the restaurant and began to quarrel over transportation. 62

"Come on," she said, "the Fourth Street Station is right here and we can 63 catch the F . . ."

"No, let me get a cab." 64

"Please, I want to walk. I love New York in the rain." 65

"But those gangs, or punks, or students, or whatever the stupid people are 66 called sometimes ride the F. And there's all that business of transferring at Fifty-third and the walk home."

"Gra-ham," she pleaded. 67

"Oh, all right. What the hell do I care if we get mugged or . . ." The words 68 came in a rush of anger and then stopped abruptly, leaving him panting. His breath smeared almost invisible traces on the damp air.

"Killed?" 69

He didn't answer. 70

Constance put her arms around his waist. She could feel the smooth twill of 71 the coat beneath her palms. The muscles of his back were tense columns flanking his spine.

"Oh, God, I'm sorry," she said. 72

He put his free arm hard against her shoulders, pulling her against him. He 73 spoke the words into her damp hair.

"Connie, a man is bound by the marriage oath to protect his wife. Right now, 74 I just don't know how."

She looked up and smiled a radiant smile. Graham's reference once again to 75 duty, honor, and contracts warmed her with the first real amusement she had felt all day.

He smiled in return, shook his head and kissed her. Then he turned away 76 from her embrace and guided her firmly toward the subway station. Their heels on the pavement tapped a companionable duet. He carried her briefcase in his left hand and held the umbrella open above her against the first real drops of rain.

The subway platform was neither crowded nor deserted. Constance stood 77 close to Graham, his right hand protective against the small of her back. The lightly furled umbrella hung from his wrist and she sometimes felt it tap against her buttocks.

Like a herd of gazelles, the knots of silent, waiting people raised heads 78 in unison as a rush of teenage boys with the faces of men poured through the turnstiles onto the platform. Their voices were loud, shouting in the intimate assurance of a private patois.

Graham's worst fears, thought Constance. But the gang seemed more rest- 79 less than threatening. Heedless, they roiled across the concrete, jostling the people on the platform, pushing them toward the tracks. Graham's hand pressed against Constance's back, making little grasping motions against the silk of her raincoat, as though to keep her from falling into the pit. They were pushed to the steel edge of the platform. Still the crowd pressed forward. Someone bumped roughly against her elbow, her shoulder. She heard the thud of the briefcase as Graham dropped it and clutched at her with both hands. Other, younger hands grasped at her body, arms, hair, thighs. She felt the slick fabric that encased her slip away from the pressure of fingers. She was falling; damp gravel and bits of waste paper, steel rails, and torn Styrofoam rushed at her. Excruciating pain in her hip pierced the shield of Dilaudid. She moaned, her mouth wide open. She tried to rise, to move away from the rail. Pain and the rasp of grinding bone prevented her from doing more than moving her right arm and her head. Then, the pain seemed to drain away into a great lethargy. Only her arm and her mind had energy or volition.

80   A sea of white eyes, round with surprise, looked down at her. A young man paused in the act of climbing down from the platform, one long leg over the steel edge, a white sneaker almost touching the dirty gravel. He stared as she stretched her hand toward the third rail, her fingers barely missing the lethal electrified metal.

81   Graham saw the movement, too, his sad face a pale, almost featureless oval below the somber hat.

82   Constance tried to speak but no sound came. "Help me." She mouthed the words to Graham. With a barely perceptible movement, he flicked the half-open umbrella from his wrist. It made a graceful arc and fell just within her reach.

Janet Taliaferro, "The Last Civilized Act," from *CityScapes: Short Stories Inspired by Urban Living* by Janet Taliaferro. Reprinted by permission of the author.

QUESTIONS FOR READING, REASONING, AND REFLECTION

1. Note the story's key facts of exposition, established in the opening paragraphs: Who is the central character? Where are we? What do we learn about Constance and Graham?

2. How does Taliaferro use details of the setting to create tone? How do they connect to the key details about Constance?

3. Over dinner, what does Constance ask Graham? What is his response? Why does he feel "out of gas"?

4. How does the author prepare readers for Constance's fall and the characters' final actions, made or implied?

5. What, finally, is the story about? How would you characterize Graham's actions? Constance's? Could this be described as a love story? If so, why? If not, why not?

TRIFLES | SUSAN GLASPELL

Born in Iowa, Susan Glaspell (1876–1948) attended Drake University and then began her writing career as a reporter with the *Des Moines Daily News.* She also started writing and selling short stories; her first collection, *Lifted Masks,* was published in 1912. She completed several novels before moving to Provincetown with her husband, who started the Provincetown Players in 1915. Glaspell wrote seven short plays and four long plays for this group, including *Trifles* (1916). The well-known "Jury of Her Peers" (1917) is a short-story version of the play *Trifles*. Glaspell must have recognized that the plot of *Trifles* was a gem worth working with in more than one literary form.

Characters

> George Henderson, County Attorney
> Henry Peters, Sheriff
> Lewis Hale, A Neighboring Farmer
> Mrs. Peters
> Mrs. Hale

SCENE: *The kitchen in the now abandoned farmhouse of* JOHN WRIGHT, *a gloomy kitchen, and left without having been put in order—unwashed pans under the sink, a loaf of bread outside the bread-box, a dish-towel on the table—other signs of incompleted work. At the rear, the outer door opens and the* SHERIFF *comes in followed by the* COUNTY ATTORNEY *and* HALE. *The* SHERIFF *and* HALE *are men in middle life; the* COUNTY ATTORNEY *is a young man; all are much bundled up and go at once to the stove. They are followed by the two women—the* SHERIFF'S *wife first; she is a slight wiry woman, a thin nervous face.* MRS. HALE *is larger and would ordinarily be called more comfortable looking, but she is disturbed now and looks fearfully about as she enters. The women have come in slowly, and stand close together near the door.*

COUNTY ATTORNEY

[*Rubbing his hands.*] This feels good. Come up to the fire, ladies.

MRS. PETERS

[*After taking a step forward.*] I'm not—cold.

SHERIFF

[*Unbuttoning his overcoat and stepping away from the stove as if to mark the beginning of official business.*] Now, Mr. Hale, before we move things about, you explain to Mr. Henderson just what you saw when you came here yesterday morning.

COUNTY ATTORNEY

By the way, has anything been moved? Are things just as you left them yesterday?

SHERIFF

[*Looking about.*] It's just the same. When it dropped below zero last night I thought I'd better send Frank out this morning to make a fire for us—no use getting pneumonia with a big case on, but I told him not to touch anything except the stove—and you know Frank.

COUNTY ATTORNEY
Somebody should have been left here yesterday.

SHERIFF
Oh—yesterday. When I had to send Frank to Morris Center for that man who went crazy—I want you to know I had my hands full yesterday. I knew you could get back from Omaha by today and as long as I went over everything here myself—

COUNTY ATTORNEY
Well, Mr. Hale, tell just what happened when you came here yesterday morning.

HALE
Harry and I had started to town with a load of potatoes. We came along the road from my place and as I got here I said, "I'm going to see if I can't get John Wright to go in with me on a party telephone." I spoke to Wright about it once before and he put me off, saying folks talked too much anyway, and all he asked was peace and quiet—I guess you know about how much he talked himself; but I thought maybe if I went to the house and talked about it before his wife, though I said to Harry that I didn't know as what his wife wanted made much difference to John—

COUNTY ATTORNEY
Let's talk about that later, Mr. Hale. I do want to talk about that, but tell now just what happened when you got to the house.

HALE
I didn't hear or see anything; I knocked at the door, and still it was all quiet inside. I knew they must be up, it was past eight o'clock. So I knocked again, and I thought I heard somebody say, "Come in." I wasn't sure, I'm not sure yet, but I opened the door—this door [*indicating the door by which the two women are still standing*] and there in that rocker—[*pointing to it*] sat Mrs. Wright.
[*They all look at the rocker.*]

COUNTY ATTORNEY
What—was she doing?

HALE
She was rockin' back and forth. She had her apron in her hand and was kind of—pleating it.

COUNTY ATTORNEY
And how did she—look?

HALE

Well, she looked queer.

COUNTY ATTORNEY

How do you mean—queer?

HALE

Well, as if she didn't know what she was going to do next. And kind of done up.

COUNTY ATTORNEY

How did she seem to feel about your coming?

HALE

Why, I don't think she minded—one way or other. She didn't pay much atten-tion. I said, "How do, Mrs. Wright, it's cold, ain't it?" And she said, "Is it?"—and went on kind of pleating at her apron. Well, I was surprised; she didn't ask me to come up to the stove, or to set down, but just sat there, not even looking at me, so I said, "I want to see John." And then she—laughed. I guess you would call it a laugh. I thought of Harry and the team outside, so I said a little sharp: "Can't I see John?" "No," she says, kind o' dull like. "Ain't he home?" says I. "Yes," says she, "he's home." "Then why can't I see him?" I asked her, out of patience. " 'Cause he's dead," says she. "*Dead?*" says I. She just nodded her head, not getting a bit excited, but rockin' back and forth. "Why—where is he?" says I, not knowing what to say. She just pointed upstairs—like that [*himself pointing to the room above*]. I got up, with the idea of going up there. I walked from there to here—then I says, "Why, what did he die of?" "He died of a rope around his neck," says she, and just went on pleatin' at her apron. Well, I went out and called Harry. I thought I might—need help. We went upstairs and there he was lyin'—

COUNTY ATTORNEY

I think I'd rather have you go into that upstairs, where you can point it all out. Just go on now with the rest of the story.

HALE

Well, my first thought was to get that rope off. It looked . . . [*Stops, his face twitches*] . . . but Harry, he went up to him, and he said, "No, he's dead all right, and we'd better not touch anything." So we went back downstairs. She was still sitting that same way. "Has anybody been notified?" said Harry. He said it business-like—and she stopped pleatin' of her apron. "I don't know," she says. "You don't *know*?" says Harry. "No," says she. "Weren't you sleepin' in the bed with him?" says Harry. "Yes," says she, "but I was on the inside." "Somebody slipped a rope round his neck and strangled him and you didn't wake up?" says Harry. "I didn't wake up," she said after him. We must'a looked as if we didn't see how that could be, for after a minute she said, "I sleep sound." Harry was going to ask her more questions but I said maybe we ought to let her tell her story first to the coroner, or the sheriff, so Harry went fast as he could to Rivers' place, where there's a telephone.

COUNTY ATTORNEY

And what did Mrs. Wright do when she knew that you had gone for the coroner?

HALE

She moved from that chair to this one over here [*Pointing to a small chair in the corner*] and just sat there with her hands held together and looking down. I got a feeling that I ought to make some conversation, so I said I had come in to see if John wanted to put in a telephone, and at that she started to laugh, and then she stopped and looked at me—scared. [*The County Attorney, who has had his notebook out, makes a note.*] I dunno, maybe it wasn't scared. I wouldn't like to say it was. Soon Harry got back, and then Dr. Lloyd came, and you, Mr. Peters, and so I guess that's all I know that you don't.

COUNTY ATTORNEY

[*Looking around.*] I guess we'll go upstairs first—and then out to the barn and around there. [*To the Sheriff.*] You're convinced that there was nothing important here—nothing that would point to any motive.

SHERIFF

Nothing here but kitchen things.
[*The County Attorney, after again looking around the kitchen, opens the door of a cupboard closet. He gets up on a chair and looks on a shelf. Pulls his hand away, sticky.*]

COUNTY ATTORNEY

Here's a nice mess.
[*The women draw nearer.*]

MRS. PETERS

[*To the other woman.*] Oh, her fruit; it did freeze. [*To the Lawyer.*] She worried about that when it turned so cold. She said the fire'd go out and her jars would break.

SHERIFF

Well, can you beat the woman! Held for murder and worryin' about her preserves.

COUNTY ATTORNEY

I guess before we're through she may have something more serious than preserves to worry about.

HALE

Well, women are used to worrying over trifles.
[*The two women move a little closer together.*]

COUNTY ATTORNEY

[*With the gallantry of a young politician.*] And yet, for all their worries, what
would we do without the ladies? [*The women do not unbend. He goes to the
sink, takes a dipperful of water from the pail and pouring it into a basin, washes
his hands. Starts to wipe them on the roller-towel, turns it for a cleaner place.*]
Dirty towels! [*Kicks his foot against the pans under the sink.*] Not much of a
housekeeper, would you say, ladies?

MRS. HALE

[*Stiffly.*] There's a great deal of work to be done on a farm.

COUNTY ATTORNEY

To be sure. And yet [*with a little bow to her*] I know there are some Dickson
County farmhouses which do not have such roller towels.
[*He gives it a pull to expose its full length again.*]

MRS. HALE

Those towels get dirty awful quick. Men's hands aren't always as clean as
they might be.

COUNTY ATTORNEY

Ah, loyal to your sex, I see. But you and Mrs. Wright were neighbors.
I suppose you were friends, too.

MRS. HALE

[*Shaking her head.*] I've not seen much of her of late years. I've not been in
this house—it's more than a year.

COUNTY ATTORNEY

And why was that? You didn't like her?

MRS. HALE

I liked her all well enough. Farmers' wives have their hands full, Mr. Henderson.
And then—

COUNTY ATTORNEY

Yes—?

MRS. HALE

[*Looking about.*] It never seemed a very cheerful place.

COUNTY ATTORNEY

No—it's not cheerful. I shouldn't say she had the homemaking instinct.

MRS. HALE

Well, I don't know as Wright had, either.

COUNTY ATTORNEY

You mean that they didn't get on very well?

MRS. HALE

No, I don't mean anything. But I don't think a place'd be any cheerfuller for John Wright's being in it.

COUNTY ATTORNEY

I'd like to talk more of that a little later. I want to get the lay of things upstairs now.

[*He goes to the left, where three steps lead to a stair door.*]

SHERIFF

I suppose anything Mrs. Peters does'll be all right. She was to take in some clothes for her, you know, and a few little things. We left in such a hurry yesterday.

COUNTY ATTORNEY

Yes, but I would like to see what you take, Mrs. Peters, and keep an eye out for anything that might be of use to us.

MRS. PETERS

Yes, Mr. Henderson.

[*The women listen to the men's steps on the stairs, then look about the kitchen.*]

MRS. HALE

I'd hate to have men coming into my kitchen, snooping around and criticizing.

[*She arranges the pans under the sink which the Lawyer had shoved out of place.*]

MRS. PETERS

Of course it's no more than their duty.

MRS. HALE

Duty's all right, but I guess that deputy sheriff that came out to make the fire might have got a little of this on. [*Gives the roller towel a pull.*] Wish I'd thought of that sooner. Seems mean to talk about her for not having things slicked up when she had to come away in such a hurry.

MRS. PETERS
[*Who has gone to a small table in the left corner of the room, and lifted one end of a towel that covers a pan.*] She had bread set.
[*Stands still.*]

MRS. HALE
[*Eyes fixed on a loaf of bread beside the breadbox, which is on a low shelf at the other side of the room. Moves slowly toward it.*] She was going to put this in there. [*Picks up loaf, then abruptly drops it. In a manner of returning to familiar things.*] It's a shame about her fruit. I wonder if it's all gone. [*Gets up on the chair and looks.*] I think there's some here that's all right, Mrs. Peters. Yes—here; [*holding it toward the window*] this is cherries, too. [*Looking again.*] I declare I believe that's the only one. [*Gets down, bottle in her hand. Goes to the sink and wipes it off on the outside.*] She'll feel awful bad after all her hard work in the hot weather. I remember the afternoon I put up my cherries last summer.
[*She puts the bottle on the big kitchen table, center of the room. With a sigh, is about to sit down in the rocking-chair. Before she is seated realizes what chair it is; with a slow look at it, steps back. The chair which she has touched rocks back and forth.*]

MRS. PETERS
Well, I must get those things from the front room closet. [*She goes to the door at the right, but after looking into the other room, steps back.*] You coming with me, Mrs. Hale? You could help me carry them.
[*They go in the other room; reappear, Mrs. Peters carrying a dress and skirt, Mrs. Hale following with a pair of shoes.*]

MRS. PETERS
My, it's cold in there.
[*She puts the clothes on the big table, and hurries to the stove.*]

MRS. HALE
[*Examining the skirt.*] Wright was close. I think maybe that's why she kept so much to herself. She didn't even belong to the Ladies Aid. I suppose she felt she couldn't do her part, and then you don't enjoy things when you feel shabby. She used to wear pretty clothes and be lively, when she was Minnie Foster, one of the town girls singing in the choir. But that—oh, that was thirty years ago. This all you was to take in?

MRS. PETERS
She said she wanted an apron. Funny thing to want, for there isn't much to get you dirty in jail, goodness knows. But I suppose just to make her feel more natural. She said they was in the top drawer in this cupboard. Yes, here. And then her little shawl that always hung behind the door. [*Opens stair door and looks.*] Yes, here it is.
[*Quickly shuts door leading upstairs.*]

MRS. HALE

[*Abruptly moving toward her.*] Mrs. Peters?

MRS. PETERS

Yes, Mrs. Hale?

MRS. HALE

Do you think she did it?

MRS. PETERS

[*In a frightened voice.*] Oh, I don't know.

MRS. HALE

Well, I don't think she did. Asking for an apron and her little shawl. Worrying about her fruit.

MRS. PETERS

[*Starts to speak, glances up, where footsteps are heard in the room above. In a low voice.*] Mr. Peters says it looks bad for her. Mr. Henderson is awful sarcastic in a speech and he'll make fun of her sayin' she didn't wake up.

MRS. HALE

Well, I guess John Wright didn't wake when they was slipping that rope under his neck.

MRS. PETERS

No, it's strange. It must have been done awful crafty and still. They say it was such a—funny way to kill a man, rigging it all up like that.

MRS. HALE

That's just what Mr. Hale said. There was a gun in the house. He says that's what he can't understand.

MRS. PETERS

Mr. Henderson said coming out that what was needed for the case was a motive; something to show anger, or—sudden feeling.

MRS. HALE

[*Who is standing by the table.*] Well, I don't see any signs of anger around here. [*She puts her hand on the dish towel which lies on the table, stands looking down at table, one half of which is clean, the other half messy.*] It's wiped to here. [*Makes a move as if to finish work, then turns and looks at loaf of bread outside the breadbox. Drops towel. In that voice of coming-back to familiar things.*] Wonder how they are finding things upstairs. I hope she had it a little more red-up up there. You know, it seems kind of sneaking. Locking her up in town and then coming out here and trying to get her own house to turn against her!

MRS. PETERS

But Mrs. Hale, the law is the law.

MRS. HALE

I s'pose 'tis. [*Unbuttoning her coat.*] Better loosen up your things, Mrs. Peters. You won't feel them when you go out.
[*Mrs. Peters takes off her fur tippet, goes to hang it on hook at back of room, stands looking at the under part of the small corner table.*]

MRS. PETERS

She was piecing a quilt.
[*She brings the large sewing basket and they look at the bright pieces.*]

MRS. HALE

It's log cabin pattern. Pretty, isn't it? I wonder if she was goin' to quilt it or just knot it? [*Footsteps have been heard coming down the stairs. The Sheriff enters followed by Hale and the County Attorney.*]

SHERIFF

They wonder if she was going to quilt it or just knot it!
[*The men laugh, the women look abashed.*]

COUNTY ATTORNEY

[*Rubbing his hands over the stove.*] Frank's fire didn't do much up there, did it? Well, let's go out to the barn and get that cleared up.
[*The men go outside.*]

MRS. HALE

[*Resentfully.*] I don't know as there's anything so strange, our takin' up our time with little things while we're waiting for them to get the evidence. [*She sits down at the big table smoothing out a block with decision.*] I don't see as it's anything to laugh about.

MRS. PETERS

[*Apologetically.*] Of course they've got awful important things on their minds. [*Pulls up a chair and joins Mrs. Hale at the table.*]

MRS. HALE

[*Examining another block.*] Mrs. Peters, look at this one. Here, this is the one she was working on, and look at the sewing! All the rest of it has been so nice and even. And look at this! It's all over the place! Why, it looks as if she didn't know what she was about!

[*After she has said this they look at each other, then start to glance back at the door. After an instant Mrs. Hale has pulled at a knot and ripped the sewing.*]

MRS. PETERS

Oh, what are you doing, Mrs. Hale?

MRS. HALE

[*Mildly.*] Just pulling out a stitch or two that's not sewed very good. [*Threading a needle.*] Bad sewing always made me fidgety.

MRS. PETERS

[*Nervously.*] I don't think we ought to touch things.

MRS. HALE

I'll just finish up this end. [*Suddenly stopping and leaning forward.*] Mrs. Peters?

MRS. PETERS

Yes, Mrs. Hale?

MRS. HALE

What do you suppose she was so nervous about?

MRS. PETERS

Oh—I don't know. I don't know as she was nervous. I sometimes sew awful queer when I'm just tired. [*Mrs. Hale starts to say something, looks at Mrs. Peters, then goes on sewing.*] Well I must get these things wrapped up. They may be through sooner than we think. [*Putting apron and other things together.*] I wonder where I can find a piece of paper, and string.

MRS. HALE

In that cupboard, maybe.

MRS. PETERS

[*Looking in cupboard.*] Why, here's a bird-cage. [*Holds it up.*] Did she have a bird, Mrs. Hale?

MRS. HALE

Why, I don't know whether she did or not—I've not been here for so long. There was a man around last year selling canaries cheap, but I don't know as she took one; maybe she did. She used to sing real pretty herself.

MRS. PETERS

[*Glancing around.*] Seems funny to think of a bird here. But she must have had one, or why would she have a cage? I wonder what happened to it.

MRS. HALE

I s'pose maybe the cat got it.

MRS. PETERS

No, she didn't have a cat. She's got that feeling some people have about cats—being afraid of them. My cat got in her room and she was real upset and asked me to take it out.

MRS. HALE

My sister Bessie was like that. Queer, ain't it?

MRS. PETERS

[*Examining the cage.*] Why, look at this door. It's broke. One hinge is pulled apart.

MRS. HALE

[*Looking too.*] Looks as if someone must have been rough with it.

MRS. PETERS

Why, yes.
[*She brings the cage forward and puts it on the table.*]

MRS. HALE

I wish if they're going to find any evidence they'd be about it. I don't like this place.

MRS. PETERS

But I'm awful glad you came with me, Mrs. Hale. It would be lonesome for me sitting here alone.

MRS. HALE

It would, wouldn't it? [*Dropping her sewing.*] But I tell you what I do wish, Mrs. Peters. I wish I had come over sometimes when *she* was here. I—[*looking around the room*]—wish I had.

MRS. PETERS

But of course you were awful busy, Mrs. Hale—your house and your children.

MRS. HALE

I could've come. I stayed away because it weren't cheerful—and that's why I ought to have come. I—I've never liked this place. Maybe because it's down in a hollow and you don't see the road. I dunno what it is, but it's a lonesome place and always was. I wish I had come over to see Minnie Foster sometimes. I can see now—

[*Shakes her head.*]

MRS. PETERS

Well, you mustn't reproach yourself, Mrs. Hale. Somehow we just don't see how it is with other folks until—something comes up.

MRS. HALE

Not having children makes less work—but it makes a quiet house, and Wright out to work all day, and no company when he did come in. Did you know John Wright, Mrs. Peters?

MRS. PETERS

Not to know him; I've seen him in town. They say he was a good man.

MRS. HALE

Yes—good; he didn't drink, and kept his word as well as most, I guess, and paid his debts. But he was a hard man, Mrs. Peters. Just to pass the time of day with him—[*Shivers.*] Like a raw wind that gets to the bone. [*Pauses, her eye falling on the cage.*] I should think she would'a wanted a bird. But what do you suppose went with it?

MRS. PETERS

I don't know, unless it got sick and died.

[*She reaches over and swings the broken door, swings it again, both women watch it.*]

MRS. HALE

You weren't raised round here, were you? [*Mrs. Peters shakes her head.*] You didn't know—her?

MRS. PETERS

Not till they brought her yesterday.

MRS. HALE

She—come to think of it, she was kind of like a bird herself—real sweet and pretty, but kind of timid and—fluttery. How—she—did—change. [*Silence; then as if struck by a happy thought and relieved to get back to everyday things.*] Tell you what, Mrs. Peters, why don't you take the quilt in with you? It might take up her mind.

MRS. PETERS

Why, I think that's a real nice idea, Mrs. Hale. There couldn't possibly be any objection to it, could there? Now, just what would I take? I wonder if her patches are in here—and her things.

[*They look in the sewing basket.*]

MRS. HALE

Here's some red. I expect this has got sewing things in it. [*Brings out a fancy box.*] What a pretty box. Looks like something somebody would give you. Maybe her scissors are in here. [*Opens box. Suddenly puts her hand to her nose.*] Why— [*Mrs. Peters bends nearer, then turns her face away.*] There's something wrapped up in this piece of silk.

MRS. PETERS

Why, this isn't her scissors.

MRS. HALE

[*Lifting the silk.*] Oh, Mrs. Peters—it's—
[*Mrs. Peters bends closer.*]

MRS. PETERS

It's the bird.

MRS. HALE

[*Jumping up.*] But, Mrs. Peters—look at it! Its neck! Look at its neck! It's all— other side *to.*

MRS. PETERS

Somebody—wrung—its—neck.
[*Their eyes meet. A look of growing comprehension, or horror. Steps are heard outside. Mrs. Hale slips box under quilt pieces, and sinks into her chair. Enter Sheriff and County Attorney. Mrs. Peters rises.*]

COUNTY ATTORNEY

[*As one turning from serious things to little pleasantries.*] Well ladies, have you decided whether she was going to quilt it or knot it?

MRS. PETERS

We think she was going to—knot it.

COUNTY ATTORNEY

Well, that's interesting, I'm sure. [*Seeing the bird-cage.*] Has the bird flown?

MRS. HALE

[*Putting more quilt pieces over the box.*] We think the—cat got it.

COUNTY ATTORNEY

[*Preoccupied.*] Is there a cat?
[*Mrs. Hale glances in a quick covert way at Mrs. Peters.*]

MRS. PETERS

Well, not now. They're superstitious, you know. They leave.

COUNTY ATTORNEY

[*To Sheriff Peters, continuing an interrupted conversation.*] No sign at all of anyone having come from the outside. Their own rope. Now let's go up again and go over it piece by piece. [*They start upstairs.*] It would have to have been someone who knew just the—

[*Mrs. Peters sits down. The two women sit there not looking at one another, but as if peering into something and at the same time holding back. When they talk now it is in the manner of feeling their way over strange ground, as if afraid of what they are saying, but as if they can not help saying it.*]

MRS. HALE

She liked the bird. She was going to bury it in that pretty box.

MRS. PETERS

[*In a whisper.*] When I was a girl—my kitten—there was a boy took a hatchet, and before my eyes—and before I could get there—[*Covers her face an instant.*] If they hadn't held me back I would have—[*Catches herself, looks upstairs where steps are heard, falters weakly*]—hurt him.

MRS. HALE

[*With a slow look around her.*] I wonder how it would seem never to have had any children around. [*Pause.*] No, Wright wouldn't like the bird—a thing that sang. She used to sing. He killed that, too.

MRS. PETERS

[*Moving uneasily.*] We don't know who killed the bird.

MRS. HALE

I knew John Wright.

MRS. PETERS

It was an awful thing was done in this house that night, Mrs. Hale. Killing a man while he slept, slipping a rope around his neck that choked the life out of him.

MRS. HALE

His neck. Choked the life out of him.
[*Her hand goes out and rests on the bird-cage.*]

MRS. PETERS

We don't know who killed him. We don't *know.*

MRS. HALE

[*Her own feeling not interrupted.*] If there'd been years and years of nothing, then a bird to sing to you, it would be awful—still, after the bird was still.

MRS. PETERS

[*Something within her speaking.*] I know what stillness is. When we home-steaded in Dakota, and my first baby died—after he was two years old, and me with no other then—

MRS. HALE

[*Moving.*] How soon do you suppose they'll be through, looking for the evidence?

MRS. PETERS

I know what stillness is. [*Pulling herself back.*] The law has got to punish crime, Mrs. Hale.

MRS. HALE

[*Not as if answering that.*] I wish you'd seen Minnie Foster when she wore a white dress with blue ribbons and stood up there in the choir and sang. [*A look around the room.*] Oh, I *wish* I'd come over here once in a while! That was a crime! That was a crime! Who's going to punish that?

MRS. PETERS

[*Looking upstairs.*] We mustn't—take on.

MRS. HALE

I might have known she needed help! I know how things can be—for women. I tell you, it's queer, Mrs. Peters. We live close together and we live far apart. We all go through the same things—it's all just a different kind of the same thing. [*Brushes her eyes, noticing the bottle of fruit, reaches out for it.*] If I was you I wouldn't tell her her fruit was gone. Tell her it *ain't*. Tell her it's all right. Take this in to prove it to her. She—she may never know whether it was broke or not.

MRS. PETERS

[*Takes the bottle, looks about for something to wrap it in; takes petticoat from the clothes brought from the other room, very nervously begins winding this around the bottle. In a false voice.*] My, it's a good thing the men couldn't hear us. Wouldn't they just laugh! Getting all stirred up over a little thing like a— dead canary. As if that could have anything to do with—with—wouldn't they *laugh*!

[*The men are heard coming downstairs.*]

MRS. HALE

[*Under her breath.*] Maybe they would—maybe they wouldn't.

COUNTY ATTORNEY

No, Peters, it's all perfectly clear except a reason for doing it. But you know juries when it comes to women. If there was some definite thing. Something to show—something to make a story about—a thing that would connect up with this strange way of doing it—

[*The women's eyes meet for an instant. Enter Hale from outer door.*]

HALE

Well, I've got the team around. Pretty cold out there.

COUNTY ATTORNEY

I'm going to stay here awhile by myself. [*To the Sheriff.*] You can send Frank out for me, can't you? I want to go over everything. I'm not satisfied that we can't do better.

SHERIFF

Do you want to see what Mrs. Peters is going to take in?

[*The Lawyer goes to the table, picks up the apron, laughs.*]

COUNTY ATTORNEY

Oh, I guess they're not very dangerous things the ladies have picked out. [*Moves a few things about, disturbing the quilt pieces which cover the box. Steps back.*] No, Mrs. Peters doesn't need supervising. For that matter, a sheriff's wife is married to the law. Ever think of it that way, Mrs. Peters?

MRS. PETERS

Not—just that way.

SHERIFF

[*Chuckling.*] Married to the law. [*Moves toward the other room.*] I just want you to come in here a minute, George. We ought to take a look at these windows.

COUNTY ATTORNEY

[*Scoffingly.*] Oh, windows!

SHERIFF

We'll be right out, Mr. Hale.

[*Hale goes outside. The Sheriff follows the County Attorney into the other room. Then Mrs. Hale rises, hands tight together, looking intensely at Mrs. Peters, whose eyes make a slow turn, finally meeting Mrs. Hale's. A moment Mrs. Hale holds her, then her own eyes point the way to where the box is concealed. Suddenly Mrs. Peters throws back quilt pieces and tries to put the box in the bag she is wearing. It is too big. She opens box, starts to take bird out, cannot touch it, goes to pieces, stands there helpless. Sound of a knob turning in the other*] room. *Mrs. Hale snatches the box and puts it in the pocket of her big coat. Enter County Attorney and Sheriff.*]

COUNTY ATTORNEY

[*Facetiously.*] Well, Henry, at least we found out that she was not going to quilt it. She was going to—what is it you call it, ladies?

MRS. HALE

[*Her hand against her pocket.*] We call it—knot it, Mr. Henderson.

Susan Glaspell, "Trifles," (1916).

QUESTIONS FOR READING, REASONING, AND REFLECTION

1. Explain the situation as the play begins.
2. Examine the dialogue of the men. What attitudes about themselves—their work, their abilities, their importance—are revealed? What is their collective opinion of women?
3. When Mrs. Hale and Mrs. Peters discover the dead bird, what do they begin to understand?
4. What other "trifles" in the kitchen provide additional evidence as to what has happened?
5. What trifles can be seen as symbols? What do they reveal about Mrs. Wright's life and character?
6. What is the play about primarily? Is it a murder mystery? Does it speak for feminist values? Is it about not seeing—not really knowing—others? In a few sentences, state what you consider to be the play's dominant theme. Then list the evidence you would use to support your conclusion.
7. Is there any sense in which one could argue that Mrs. Wright had a right to kill her husband? If you were a lawyer, how would you plan her defense? If you were on the jury, what sentence would you recommend?

SAMPLE STUDENT LITERARY ANALYSIS

Peterson 1

Alan Peterson

American Literature 242

May 5, 2010

Appropriate heading when separate title page is not used.

Faulkner's Realistic Initiation Theme

Center the title.

William Faulkner braids a universal theme, the theme of initiation,

into the fiber of his novel *Intruder in the Dust*. From ancient times to the

Double-space throughout.

present, a prominent focus of literature, of life, has been rites of passage, particularly those of childhood to adulthood. Joseph Campbell defines

rites of passage as "distinguished by formal, and usually very severe,

exercises of severance." A "candidate" for initiation into adult society,

Campbell explains, experiences a shearing away of the "attitudes,

attachments and life patterns" of childhood (9). This severe, painful

stripping away of the child and installation of the adult is presented

somewhat differently in several works by American writers.

One technique of handling this theme of initiation is used by

Nathaniel Hawthorne in his story "My Kinsman, Major Molineaux." The

story's main character, Robin, is suddenly awakened to the real world,

the adult world, when he sees Major Molineaux "in tar-and-feathery

dignity" (Hawthorne 528). A terrified and amazed Robin gapes at his

kinsman as the large and colorful crowd laughs at and ridicules the

Major; then an acquiescent Robin joins with the crowd in the mirthful

shouting (Hawthorne 529). This moment is Robin's epiphany, his

sudden realization of reality. Robin goes from unsophisticated rube

to resigned cynical adult in one quick scene. Hawthorne does hold out

hope that Robin will not let this event ruin his life, indeed that he will

perhaps prosper from it.

A similar, but decidedly less optimistic, example of an epiphanic

initiation occurs in Arthur Miller's play *Death of a Salesman*. Miller

develops an initiation theme within a flashback. A teenaged Biff,

shockingly confronted with Willy's infidelity and weakness, has his

boyhood dreams, ambitions—his vision—shattered, leaving his life in

ruins, a truth borne out in scenes in which Biff is an adult during the play

(1083–84, 1101). Biff's discovery of the vices and shortcomings of his

father overwhelms him. His realization of adult life is a revelation made

more piercing when put into the context of his naive and overly hopeful

---

Opening¶ introduces subject, presents thesis, and defines key term—initiation.

Student combines paraphrase and brief quotations in definition.

Summary and analysis combined to explain initiation in Hawthorne's story.

Transition to second example establishes contrast with Hawthorne.

¶ concludes with emphasis on contrast.

Peterson 3

upbringing. A ravaged and defeated Biff has adulthood wantonly thrust upon him. Unlike Hawthorne's Robin, Biff never recovers.

William Faulkner does not follow these examples when dealing with the initiation of his character Chick in *Intruder in the Dust*. In Robin's and Biff's cases, each character's passage into adulthood was brought about by realization of and disillusionment with the failings and weaknesses of a male adult playing an important role in his life. By contrast, Chick's male role models are vital, moral men with integrity. Chick's awakening develops as he begins to comprehend the mechanisms of the adult society in which he would be a member.

Faulkner uses several techniques for illustrating Chick's growth into a man. Early in the novel, at the end of the scene in which Chick tries to pay for his dinner, Lucas warns Chick to "stay out of that creek" (Faulkner 16).[1] The creek is an effective symbol: it is both a physical creek and a metaphor for the boy's tendency to slide into gaffes that perhaps a man could avoid. The creek's symbolic meaning is more evident when, after receiving the molasses, Chick encounters Lucas in town. Lucas again reminds Chick not to "fall in no more creeks this winter" (24). At the end of the novel, Lucas meets Chick in Gavin's office and states: "you ain't fell in no more creeks lately, have you?" (241). Although Lucas phrases this as a question, the answer is obvious to Lucas, as well as to the reader, that indeed Chick has not blundered into his naive boyhood quagmire lately. When Lucas asks his question, Chick's actual falling into a creek does not occur to the reader.

Another image Faulkner employs to show Chick growing into a man is the single-file line. After Chick gets out of the creek, he follows Lucas into the house, the group walking in single file. In the face of Lucas's much stronger adult will, Chick is powerless to get out of the

---

[1] Subsequent references to Faulkner's novel cite page numbers only.

Transition to Faulkner's story by contrast with Hawthorne and Miller.

Footnote first parenthetical reference to inform readers that subsequent citations will exclude the author's name and give only the page number.

Note transition.

line, to go to Edmonds's house (7). Later in the novel, when Miss Habersham, Aleck Sander, and Chick are walking back from digging up the grave, Chick again finds himself in a single-file line with a strong-willed adult in front. Again he protests, then relents, but clearly he feels

Note interpolation in square brackets.

slighted and wonders to himself "what good that [walking single file] would do" (130). The contrast between these two scenes illustrates Chick's growth, although he is not yet a man.

Good use of brief quotations combined with analysis.

Faulkner gives the reader other hints of Chick's passage into manhood. As the novel progresses, Chick is referred to (and refers to himself) as a "boy" (24), a "child" (25), a "young man" (46), "almost a man" (190), a "man" (194), and one of two "gentlemen" (241). Other clues crop up from time to time. Chick wrestles with himself about getting on his horse and riding away, far away, until Lucas's lynching is "all over finished done" (41). But his growing sense of responsibility and outrage quell his boyish desire to escape, to bury his head in the sand. Chick looks in the mirror at himself with amazement at his deeds (125). Chick's mother serves him coffee for the first time, despite the agreement she has with his father to withhold coffee until his eighteenth birthday (127). Chick's father looks at him with pride and envy (128–29).

Characteristics of Chick's gradual and positive initiation explained. Observe coherence techniques.

Perhaps the most important differences between the epiphanic initiations of Robin and Biff and that experienced by Chick are the facts that Chick's epiphany does not come all at once and it does not devastate him. Chick learns about adulthood—and enters adulthood—piecemeal and with support. His first eye-opening experience occurs as he tries to pay Lucas for dinner and is rebuffed (15–16). Chick learns, after trying again to buy a clear conscience, the impropriety and affront of his actions (24). Lucas teaches Chick how he should resolve *his* dilemma by setting him "free" (26–27). Later, Chick feels outrage at the adults crowding into the town, presumably to see a lynching, then

Peterson 5

disgrace and shame as they eventually flee (196–97, 210). As in most lives, Chick's passage into adulthood is a gradual process; he learns a little bit at a time and has support in his growing. Gavin is there for him, to act as a sounding board, to lay a strong intellectual foundation, to confirm his beliefs. Chick's initiation is consistent with Joseph Campbell's explanation: "all rites of passage are intended to touch not only the candidate, but also every member of his circle" (9). Perhaps Gavin is affected the most, but Chick's mother and father, and Lucas as well, are influenced by the change in Chick.

In *Intruder in the Dust*, William Faulkner has much to say about the role of and the actions of adults in society. He depicts racism, ignorance, resignation, violence, fratricide, citizenship, hope, righteousness, lemming-like aggregation, fear, and a host of other emotions and actions. Chick learns not only right and wrong, but that in order to be a part of society, of his community, he cannot completely forsake those with whom he disagrees or whose ideas he challenges. There is much compromise in growing up; Chick learns to compromise on some issues, but not all. Gavin's appeal to Chick to "just don't stop" (210) directs him to conform enough to be a part of the adult world, but not to lose sight of, indeed instead to embrace, his own values and ideals.

Student concludes by explaining the values Chick develops in growing up.

Peterson 6

Works Cited

Campbell, Joseph. *The Hero with a Thousand Faces.* Princeton UP, 1949.

Faulkner, William. *Intruder in the Dust.* Random House, 1948.

Hawthorne, Nathaniel. "My Kinsman, Major Molineaux." 1832.
    The Complete Short Stories of Nathaniel Hawthorne. Doubleday
    Publishers, 1959, pp. 517–30.

Miller, Arthur. *Death of a Salesman.* 1949. *An Introduction to Literature.*
    9th edition. Edited by Sylvan Barnet, et al. Little Brown Publishers,
    1985, pp. 1025–111.

Paging is continuous.

Place Works Cited on separate page.

Double-space throughout.

Use hanging indentation.

SUGGESTIONS FOR DISCUSSION AND WRITING

1. Prepare an explication of either Amy Lowell's "Taxi" or Sir Walter Raleigh's "The Nymph's Reply to the Shepherd." You will need to explain both what the poem says and what it means—or what it accomplishes.

2. Analyze A. E. Housman's attitudes toward life and human relationships in "Is My Team Ploughing."

3. Analyze Mrs. Mallard's conflict, and decision about that conflict, as the basis for your understanding of the dominant theme in "The Story of an Hour."

4. You are Mrs. Wright's attorney (see *Trifles*, pp. 545–61). Write your closing argument in her defense, explaining why only a light sentence is warranted for Mrs. Wright. Select details from the play to support your assertions about Mrs. Wright's character and motivation.

5. What, in your view, are the most important ideas in Taliaferro's "The Last Civilized Act." Support with evidence from the story.

6. John Donne in "The Bait" and Ogden Nash in "Love Under the Republicans (or Democrats)" also have responses to Marlowe's "The Passionate Shepherd to His Love." Select one of these poems, find a copy, read and analyze it, and then evaluate its argument as a response to Marlowe's shepherd.

Index